D1571811

Folklore and Society

Series Editors

Roger Abrahams
Bruce Jackson
Marta Weigle

A list of books in the series appears at the back of the book.

Last Cavalier

Portrait of John A. Lomax by J. Anthony Wills, which hangs in the Lomax Room, Center for American History, University of Texas, Austin. (Courtesy Bess Lomax Hawes and Center for American History, University of Texas, Austin.)

NOLAN PORTERFIELD

Last Cavalier

. . . .

THE LIFE AND TIMES OF John A. Lomax 1867–1948

University of Illinois Press
URBANA AND CHICAGO

Publication of this work was supported by a grant from the Sonneck Society for American Music.

Manufactured in the United States of America
C 5 4 3 2 1

This book is printed on acid-free paper.

Library of Congress Cataloging-in-Publication Data

Porterfield, Nolan.
Last cavalier : the life and times of John A. Lomax, 1867–1948 / Nolan Porterfield.
p. cm. — (Folklore and society)
Includes bibliographical references and index.
ISBN 0-252-02216-5 (acid-free paper)
1. Lomax, John Avery, 1867–1948. 2. Ethnomusicologists—United States—Biography. I. Title. II. Series.
ML423.L635P67 1996
781.62'13'0092—dc20
[B] 95-50212
CIP
MN

For Erika

"My bark of life was tossing down . . ."

Better things, it may be, are coming in to take the place of the cowboys, but to these as the years go by, will be added a glamour that the things that have driven them into the west and down to death can never hold. No furrowed field can ever make a man forget the prairies and the magic of their call when Spring is breaking, no harvest gathering can ever equal the rough assemblage of the round-up, and no man in all the world can ever take the vacant place of "the last cavalier."

—"The Minstrelsy of the Mexican Border" (1898)

We are in the past. I adore
the past. It is so much
more restful than the present
and so much more
reliable than the future.

—The narrator in Max Ophuls's
film, *La Ronde* (1950)

Contents

Last Cavalier

PROLOGUE

• • • • •

Lone Star Trail . . .

Say *Texas* anywhere, and people answer *cowboy.*

—T. R. Fehrenbach, *Lone Star,* 1968

John Lomax was not a native Texan, but he might as well have been. The eyes of Texas were on him early, and the course of the Lone Star fixed his direction for most of his eighty years. He was never a cowboy either, although for years he spoke solemnly of "my father's ranch" (by Texas standards, little more than a homesteader's farm) and as a youth had spent considerable time on the back of a pony, herding milk cows and the occasional family beef. As soon as he could, he hied himself off to the city in earnest pursuit of refined society, books and ideas, the Rotary Club, indoor plumbing. Later he built a national reputation from his interest in the broader fabric of American life, seen through its diverse regional, cultural, and racial minorities. But it was Texas and its cowboy lore that first set him on the path to fame and fulfillment, and the image/mirage of "Texas" in its epic sense—rough and sprawling, dynamic, discordant, and glorious—governed his life and shaped his achievement.

Like Texas, like its cowboys, Lomax had his distinctly cruder qualities. He was in many ways an American primitive, raw, bumptious, xenophobic, yet on the other hand it was his very faith in traditional values, his love of things native and openhearted, that pointed him toward his most important work. In still another paradoxical sense, he was the true pioneer—true American, true Texan—in his eagerness to break new ground, to go where others hadn't and do what they had not. If in later years he became rigidly conservative, throughout his life he had demonstrated much the reverse. He was, in short, like most accomplished human beings, a mass of contradictions. But as in the case of "Texas" and "cowboy," it is the extravagant character and unique mix of opposing elements in "John Avery Lomax" which give his life the force of legend.

• • • • •

The cowboy is not the only symbol of these conflicting impulses, but he is an appropriate one. A figure of considerable romance and spectacle, he was—according to tradition—bold, fearless, and footloose, a hero-adventurer, true descendent of knight and cavalier (in Texas, *caballero*). In the earliest days of the republic, this figure was not "Texan" but "Texian," elevated by the very word into nationality, a separate breed.

The old, romantic view of the cowboy as brave and happy wanderer scarcely needs further debunking. However free and easy the cowboy's life may have seemed, from day to day it was generally narrow, hard, and mean. So was the common run of cowboy. In person and close up, the average ranch hand or trail herder was as much a product of his social order as any middle-class burgher—conformable, conservative, afraid of change, fixed in a role that was tied to the past almost as soon as it was created. Yet it is important to remember that our legends, however extravagant, are rooted in a truth of one kind or another. There were, indeed, cowboys turned from the ideal mold: strong and brave, knightly and gallant, cavalier in many senses of the word: trained in arms and horsemanship, lighthearted, debonair, proud, disdainful—and, to be sure, just as Webster has it, "given to offhand dismissal of important matters."

Perhaps the mind-boggling extremes and anomalies inherent in the concepts of "Texas" and "cowboy" are actually little more than the working out of a sociocultural version of the third law of motion. Seen that way—as merely the action and reaction of opposing forces—it is not remarkable that a society so fundamentally oppressive produces an occasional radical or, from time to time, simply men and women of unusual intelligence, vision, and sensitivity—a J. Frank Dobie, a Bill Moyers, a Barbara Jordan. With the scales so heavily weighted on the side of reaction, what is truly astonishing—and certainly more relevant to an account of the life of John Lomax—is that a tradition of liberalism, however meager and diluted, survives there at all (a Texas liberal, so goes the old joke, is a person who hasn't quite made up his mind about lynching). That prickly sort of liberal tradition, unique to Texas, reaches at least as far back as Sam Houston, the rough-cut old frontiersman, lawyer, and soldier, "a man of his times . . . but something more,"[1] who read Alexander Pope and defended Indian tribes, a man whose vision far transcended the narrow interests of his fellow Texans and who in 1861 retired from public life rather than lead his state out of the Union and defend the dubious principles of the Confederacy.

Politically, socially, temperamentally, John Lomax could scarcely be considered a part of that tradition, yet in much the same way that he absorbed and transmitted the complexities of "cowboy" and "Texas," he was, finally, a synthesis of those greater sympathies and heterogeneous experiences which go to make up the Liberal Imagination, a horned toad produced by some mythical mating of pond frog and turtledove.

PART ONE

• • • • •

Pursuit of the Vision

A boundless vision grows upon us; an untamed continent; vast wastes of forest verdure; mountains silent in primeval sleep; river, lake, and glimmering pool; wilderness oceans mingling with the sky.

—Francis Parkman, *Pioneers of France in the New World* (1865)

CHAPTER ONE

• • • • •

Texian Boys
1867–87

When the Lomax family migrated to Texas from Mississippi in the late fall of 1869, the Lone Star State was, strictly speaking, not even a state. Four troubled years after the Civil War, it was still under military occupation, in chaos and turmoil, its status suspended between that of conquered territory and provisional statehood. A fiercely contested and probably fraudulent election in November of that year gave dictatorial control to carpetbagger Radical Republicans, who won the statehouse by a small majority of some eight hundred votes. With an administration now more or less aligned with the policies of the Reconstruction Congress in Washington, way was finally made for readmission to the Union the following spring. Still, political and economic turbulence continued to boil, even after southern Democrats managed to regain power in the mid-1870s—when the Lomaxes were still settling shakily into their new home. These years constituted, in the words of one historian, "the most disastrous period in Texas history,"[1] worse even than the terrible days of the war itself.

But conditions had been no better for the Lomaxes in Mississippi. Years afterward, John Lomax's father recorded his reasons for leaving "my old home" in Mississippi near Goodman in Holmes County, where he had farmed from time to time and operated a small tanyard. His motive, said James Lomax, was "to get away from the wreck of the war, and take my young family out of a state of society that can only be expressed by the word 'chaos.'"[2] Westward migration was in the air, and James Lomax was caught up in popular notions of wide open spaces and fresh opportunities in Texas. He was anxious, he said, "to give my boys room to expand,"[3] and he was sure that the wholesome Texas climate he'd heard about from zealous land agents would ease the miseries of age and help him recover from the poor health he'd suffered during the war.

He was less open about family problems that weighed on the move to Texas. For some time there had been ill feeling between him and his younger, more prosperous brother, Tillman (who, James felt, owed his wealth and social position mostly to the inheritance of his wife). During the war, Tillman Lomax had been elected captain of a company of Mississippi Home Guard into which James was conscripted as a middle-aged private. When higher authorities relieved James from soldiering and set him to work tanning leather and making shoes for the army, Tillman, out of envy and malice, entered him on the company rolls as a deserter. Years later, young John Lomax and his brother Richard spent much time and money turning up evidence to clear their father's name, but the official record was never corrected.

There was yet another, less presentable reason for leaving Mississippi, also rooted in feelings of prejudice and social inferiority. "I did not want my family raised in contact with the negro either as slave or 'freedman,'" said James Lomax. That was an attitude only to be understood in the context of its time—and highly ironic in light of a son who would one day gain a national reputation from close associations with African-Americans and his efforts to record and popularize their culture.

If James Lomax was something of a bigot by modern standards, he was, however, no ordinary lower-class southern bigot, despite the fact that, many years later, son John would flaunt the term "po' white trash" in describing his family origins. To be sure, John's phrase was "*upper crust* of the po' white trash," but as commonly used by those closest to it, "po' white trash" does not denote an economic level so much as it describes a state of mind and a condition of the spirit. Whatever his financial ups and downs, and despite the racist cast of his social attitudes, James Lomax was a man not without culture, or cultural aspirations. Among his complaints against antebellum Mississippi was that "the ruling classes possessed all the culture and intelligence," clearly indicating that one reason for the move was the hope—poor doomed hope—of finding in Texas those qualities of life which had been denied him in Mississippi. His notions about racial separation must also be considered in light of his declaration that "slavery was a curse to the South," something he had doubtless learned from his own experience as an occasional slave owner on a small and invariably profitless scale; in almost the same breath that he excluded himself and his family from the society of blacks, he spoke against injustices suffered by "ignorant negroes" in the aftermath of the war.[4]

In any event, to associate James Lomax and his family with "po' white trash" requires a considerable distortion of reality—or perhaps merely a bit of errant romanticism. Throughout the course of his long life, John Lomax moved easily from one to the other. As a rising young professional at the turn of the century, long before he could afford to chatter about "po' white trash" in his origins, he preferred the airy assertion that the Lomax family was in fact "Norman-French" and spoke of multiple volumes in "the State Library . . . devoted to our family achievements."[5]

· · · · ·

By and large, the achievements of John Lomax's father were those common to men of his background in the nineteenth century. James Lomax was a native of South Carolina, born in Abbeville County in 1816 to a family rumored to have been prosperous landowners until a land title dispute took their wealth. His grandfather, William Lomax, had emigrated from England three generations earlier and settled in Rockingham County in what was then "the colony of North Carolina."[6] James married in his early twenties and in 1846 migrated to central Mississippi, where he worked as a tanner and farmhand. By 1850 he owned his own small farm in Holmes County and built a tanyard there. His first wife, who bore him five children, died in 1854, when the oldest was only fifteen. Three years later, at the age of forty-one, he married Susan Frances Cooper, twenty years his junior, who lived nearby and had occasionally helped the widower's mother with household chores and tutored his small children. She was a plump, gentle, religious young woman with more schooling than most girls of that time and place, including one year at a "Female Institute." With the same air that he alluded to the "Norman-French" origins of the Lomax family, her young son John would say casually that his mother was of English birth and assert that he himself was a combination of the "vivacity, joyousness, enthusiasm" of the French and the "sober, quiet, religious sentiment of the native Briton."[7]

The marriage between James Avery Lomax and Susan Frances Cooper was typical of many such alliances in those days, as much a matter of convenience as of romance. James valued her strength of character as wife and homemaker; for her part, "I respected him," she said, "and I felt sorry for him."[8] In time they were to become the parents of ten children. Six (two of whom died in infancy) were born in Mississippi prior to the move to Texas. John Avery Lomax was the last of these, born September 23, 1867, and just past his second birthday when the Lomax family arrived in Texas in December 1869.

"Oh, how sorry I was to leave our Mississippi home," said Susan Lomax.[9] Despite the ravages of war and reconstruction, Mississippi was a place familiar to her, settled and civilized. Going to Texas posed numerous hazards, all complicated by the fact that she was several months pregnant (but a circumstance apparently so ordinary that she made no mention of it in the otherwise detailed account of the arduous trip which she wrote later). It was a perilous journey of five hundred miles by mule-drawn wagon, ending somewhere far from relatives and friends in a wild, unknown land. As much as anything else, she dreaded the Indians—and with good reason, in light of reports that bands of hostiles still roamed the frontier region where James planned to homestead. She fretted long and hard over the matter, looking for some alternative short of flatly defying James, but finally rationalized that "my husband had better judgment than I did." There was true grit in her decision to go, but it was also the dutiful submission required of a wife in that time. A woman in her position had few alternatives.

Whatever worries Susan Lomax had about the wild and woolly nature of Texas were well founded. As a popular expression among Texans had it, "the bottom rail was on top"—the entire political, economic, and social order had been overturned by war and the ensuing "reconstruction." Yet civil harmony is a relative matter. While the Lomaxes were hardly immune from the larger turmoil rampant across the state, their daily lives were shaped and ordered by more immediate concerns—finding a home, a roof, food for the table. In fact, one effect of the general upheaval was to create a circumstance that James Lomax found quite favorable: cheap land prices. With cotton depressed to less than twenty cents a pound, rich prairie lands could be bought for as little as fifty cents an acre. But James Lomax was accustomed to water and trees, and he preferred to pay six dollars an acre for a little more than a quarter section of timbered bottom land on the Bosque River ("Bosky," off the Texan tongue) a few miles north of the village of Meridian, in the fertile, rumpled hill lands southwest of Fort Worth. While it lay along the very edge of the frontier, geographically and culturally it was about as close as one could get in those days to deep in the heart of Texas.[10]

Meridian, which John Lomax came to call home, is almost at the exact center of the Bosque Valley and halfway along the river's course. The name, however, comes from the fact that it sits on the 98th meridian—which in 1870 marked the farthest reach of the Texas frontier. The 98th meridian was—and remains—an important dividing line in other respects. Just beyond it lay an unsettled, incredibly harsh land where Comanche and Kiowa raiding bands still roamed, where the annual rainfall was never more than thirty inches and often less, where all life was subject to frequent and violent change: drought, then flood; blazing sun, then high chill winds and blowing snow; feast, then famine.

In the ensuing hundred years, the land beyond the 98th meridian has been settled, in one fashion or another, and the Indians "disappeared." But the weather and the topography remain essentially the same, and they dictate to a large extent the nature of human existence there—not merely the day-to-day life of people, but their ideas and values and attitudes. Historians and sociologists have dealt with the 98th meridian primarily in agricultural terms, as a division between what is "farmable" and "unfarmable"—but farmers speak of "cultivating" the land, and it is the question of "cultivation" in much broader terms that devolves on the homeland of John Lomax as a dividing line between the civilized and the primitive. Growing up in "Bosky" County, Texas, in the 1870s, he absorbed some of both, and a curious mixture of refinement and coarseness shows up in almost everything he did.

· · · · ·

The population of Meridian was about five hundred at the time Lomax was a youngster there. Today it approaches fourteen thousand, but its boundaries and character are much the same. Unlike many small towns in America, it seems a lively and thriving place, no doubt due in part to its climate and location, nestled as it is among rolling cedar hills and high-topped mesas. Although change has come to the Bosque Valley in the past century—not surprisingly, the river itself grows smaller and dirtier—it is not hard to see the land as it was when John Lomax was a boy. In many respects, the vista is that transmitted to the rest of the world—to non-Texans—by the words "Texas" and "cowboy," an almost Ur-western-movie landscape, rivaled in the state only by the Big Bend canyons and Kerrville's Hill Country as a place where one might reasonably expect to see Gene or Roy or Hopalong riding after the bad guys.

Among the first of the old Texians to leave the protection of Stephen Austin's colony on the Brazos and go "outside the line of posts" in the 1840s were those who settled in what is now Bosque County.[11] More concentrated settlement began in the 1850s, and the county was organized in 1854. When the Lomaxes arrived there fifteen years later and settled about eight miles north of Meridian, their neighbors were mostly fellow southerners—Tennesseans, Alabamans, and Missourians (who were southern by culture if not by geography). Some settlers before the war had brought slaves, who as freedmen later remained to work the river bottom cotton lands. In 1865 blacks in Texas numbered about one out of three residents in a population of roughly 600,000, but they were largely concentrated in the east and in plantation areas along the lower Colorado and Brazos rivers.[12] The ratio was considerably smaller in areas along the frontier, as in Bosque County. Still, blacks were there in sufficient number to create a distinctly black subculture—and to serve as a catalyst for bitter, often violent racial prejudice. Among John Lomax's childhood memories—recalled almost obsessively in later years—was the lynching of a Negro accused of raping a white woman.

At another extreme, the cultural pluralism of the region was heightened by the presence of a number of Norwegian families, whose opposition to slavery, secession, and the war had set them apart from the rest of the community. In time still another minority formed as small numbers of Mexican-Americans made their way into the region. The heterogeneous strains of Bosque County blended in various patterns to shape the outlook of young John Lomax; that part of Texas was an ironic settling place for a man like his father, who claimed he wanted to live only among his own kind.

In addition to his wagons and teams and household goods (mostly shipped by rail), James Lomax came to Texas with about $4,000 in gold, largely acquired from the sale of his tanyard and farm in Mississippi. Four thousand dollars was a considerable sum—in terms of buying power, roughly equivalent to $35,000 today—but it was not quite the substantial bankroll it might seem. Texas at the time was essentially a moneyless society. The only cash crop was cotton—fragile, uncertain, labor-intensive—and it was risky in those days, because of severely depressed prices. No matter: in the winter of 1869–70 the Lomaxes were many months away from any crop whatever. Meanwhile, necessities had to be bartered. Money was useful mostly for paying taxes and, as John wrote later, to buy "clothes, sugar, coffee, tobacco, and a gallon jug of whiskey hid behind the kitchen door for morning drams for my father."[13]

The purchase of 183 acres of Bosque river bottom had taken a fourth of James Lomax's capital. Soon after the first of the new year—1870—he finished a small two-room cabin "at the bottom of the second bluff that marked the Bosque river"[14] and set out to clear enough land by spring to plant cotton and corn. He began to raise horses and cattle, and he went after spare cash by putting his older sons to work cutting timber to sell for stove wood. Later, as the boy John grew to it, chopping and hauling firewood to town became one of his major responsibilities. There were other tasks as well, more than enough work for even a large family. By the time he was six, John was laboring alongside his brothers in the field, planting corn, hoeing and picking cotton. He herded the family's work stock, tended the milk cattle, and helped clear new ground, a terrible job that required grubbing the trees out of the ground by their roots with pick and mattock. "Broken to work" is a country phrase used of both horses and boys; by the time he was in his teens, John Lomax was qualified. Soon he would find a way to escape the drudgery of the farm, but a distinguishing mark of his character throughout life was his awesome capacity for labor, an almost compulsive need for it, a seemingly tireless energy that only increased with the passing years.

As a young adult, Lomax reflected that he "forgot to be a boy" and complained that his youth had been closed off by "manual toil and a frontier life."[15] Years later, still obsessed with the hardships of his childhood and recalling them to one of his sons, he wondered if his "barren background" might explain why he was "so angular, twisted mentally, [and] crude . . ."[16] Those early years were no doubt drab and often difficult. Yet life was not without its diversions, and there were times in his old age when Lomax looked more kindly on his childhood. In his autobiography he recounted with considerable feeling the pleasures of roaming the cedar-clad hills and lush valleys of the Bosque tributaries in the days when the river still ran swift and clear, its banks overhung with willows and cottonwoods, elm, sycamore, and hackberry. "The beauty of the region grew in my soul," he wrote, reliving the sensations of galloping his favorite pony, Selim, across the rolling, open pasturelands thick and vivid with native flowers. "I hunted and fished, went in swimming, and lived with my kind," he said.[17] His kind were the common run of country boys, Texas Huck Finns who, left together unattended, romped and wrestled and tumbled like pups, played risky pranks, dodged work whenever they could (which was not often), and generally behaved as boys always have. One or two were town boys—notably Johnny Cochran, who was also an in-law, related to the husband of John's older sister Mary. In his teens young Cochran learned to set type for the weekly *Meridian Blade* and in so doing became for John Lomax one avenue of occasional escape from the harshness and tedium of life in the back country.

Whenever he brought a load of firewood to town, John would stop at the newspaper office to see his friend, and eventually through Cochran he became acquainted with the editor, William Fields, who had served in the Confederate army and was later elected to the Texas legislature. From time to time, Captain Fields (as he was known to John) would give the boy an armful of "exchanges"—newspapers from other towns, sent to the *Blade* in trade for a complimentary subscription. "In those days 'patent sides' [syndicated material] of country newspapers carried columns of general world news," said Lomax. "Reading those papers was the real start of my education—a powerful influence on my mental growth."[18] Headed home in the empty lumber wagon with his lode of newspapers, young John would give the mules, Jack and Fan, full rein to find their own way, while he slipped from the seat and settled himself on the floor of the wagon with his papers, braced his feet against the front corners, and lost himself in boilerplate reports of the outside world. The eight-mile journey often took two or three hours; folks along the way grew accustomed to the sight of an apparently driverless wagon drawn by two plodding mules—and occasionally the top of John Lomax's tousled head, fixed on the newspaper before him, bouncing up momentarily above the sideboards as the procession rolled along over bumps and ruts.

In due course, young John's newspaper reading habits were fed by journals of a larger scope. His father subscribed to several national papers, including the weekly *New York Sun,* with its visions of a faraway, magic metropolis. (In time he would become a casual visitor to its fine hotels and clubs, warmly received, even lionized.) Then there were the *Louisville Courier* and the *Atlanta Constitution,* edited by the formidable Henry W. Grady, a figure of national reputation. Together with the "patent sides" of the county seat weeklies, these papers became, as Lomax said later, "the real start of my education."

By the mid-1870s, when Lomax was old enough to start to school, old-line Democrats had retaken control of the state. Passionately opposed to centralized government (a position the older John Lomax would affirm), they made drastic cuts in state expenditures and essentially wrecked the fledgling state educational system. Supervision was handed over to local committees, tax provisions were weakened, and compulsory attendance was discontinued.[19] While in a broad sense these actions retarded the intellectual climate in Texas, it is unlikely that they seriously altered the course of public education in rural Bosque County, which even under state supervision had been rudimentary. The important thing for John Lomax was that his parents respected education and were determined that their children have as much schooling as possible. Neighboring families, in the face of incessant demands for laboring hands and backs on the farm, were quick to take their children out of school to plant and harvest. Sometimes James Lomax had to do the same—John claimed that he never attended a full school term until after he left home at the age of twenty—but James tried to see that his children, boys and girls alike, attended every school session they could. Although his own education had been brief and spotty, he served as trustee for the Meridian community school and steadfastly asserted the values of "book learning." John Lomax's father was a stolid, straight-ahead man, at times a stern taskmaster, but he was no ordinary frontier yeoman, this James Lomax, who in a stronghold of teetotal Methodism kept a jug of whiskey behind the kitchen door, subscribed to national newspapers at considerable expense, and urged books and education on his children.

In any event, schooling of some sort was a natural part of life for John Lomax from an early age. Even before he was old enough for the first grade, he was frequently taken to visit by his older brothers and sister. The old Bosque cowboy, Ed Nichols, writing his memoirs, remembered seeing the Meridian schoolchildren on their way in the mornings, "two and two, some of them barefooted, laughing, talking, a book satchel over one shoulder, a dinner bucket in one hand." Often Richard Lomax and "his redhaired sister Mollie" (Mary) led the way and "sometimes their little brother Johnny came along to spend the day. . . . He was a pretty, fat little fellow four or five year old, and I can see him now as he ran along by their side, sometimes holding his sister's hand, sometimes holding Richard's. On these days when Johnny came to school, the pupils studied something like half the time and watched him the other half. The little rascal was full of mischief."[20]

The mischief lasted, but it soon took more subtle, subdued forms. By the time he was going to school more or less regularly, on his own, nobody had to "watch" Johnny Lomax. Sobermindedness grew in him like an extra organ. It was probably true, as he later asserted, that in boyhood he was never "discontented or dissatisfied" for very long, but in later years he spoke often of the loneliness and isolation he suffered as a child and felt that he had inherited from his father a nature that was "taciturn, reserved, stubborn, and stern."[21] The picture that emerges is one of an outwardly normal boy, sometimes rowdy yet governable, industrious, always dutiful—but also a child solemn and self-contained, often shy, moody, given to daydreams, filled with the vague but gnawing sense that there was another, better life for him to find. In American culture, it is a familiar, almost legendary image: the sensitive, intelligent youth of the provinces, whose ideas and aspirations find little understanding, even less encouragement, in a crude and hostile environment.

Religion—the "hellfire and damnation of frontier Methodism"—contributed to this temperament, sometimes in paradoxical ways. The Lomaxes were irregular churchgoers (despite Susan Lomax's religiosity and, in large part, because of James's indifference to it), but fundamentalist Christian doctrine was a strong and pervasive influence in their daily lives. Good and evil were strongly delineated, according to the Old Testament. Hard work was a testing ground for the elect; retribution to the fallen was swift and certain. "We were earnest folk," said John, "and we worked hard at our religion."[22] Church might keep or not, but on Sundays the Lomax children were forbidden to play games, go fishing, or swim in the river. In later years a more secular, unbuttoned John Lomax regretted the rigid rules of conduct imposed by his parents, but he also prided himself in having obeyed them—"I cannot remember . . . that I ever felt rebellious," he said with a certain sadness, even regret. "I never flatly disobeyed [my parents] on any important issue."[23]

The rural church of Lomax's time served, on the one hand, to foster this attitude of willing submission, just as it contributed mightily to the drab tedium and painful sameness of life by seeking to impose a single, absolute religious belief, puritanical standards of behavior, and harsh punishments for those who strayed. Ironically, at the heart of such strict fundamentalism was a fiery emotionalism always in danger of erupting—at worst into reactionary rebellion, at best into passionate brotherhood: frontier religion in Texas was as much a force for social cohesion, an occasion for tribal gathering, as it was for the dissemination of theology. Young John Lomax shrank from the dark, terrible doctrines of primitive Methodism, which literally caused him nightmares, but the social aspects of the church—especially its annual camp meetings—appealed to him as welcome relief from the loneliness and dull routine in his life, a source of the fellowship and comradery he always hungered for.

At one such camp meeting, when he was thirteen, he succumbed to "the emotional appeal of Brother Levi Harris' singing" and, to put an end to his mother's humiliating prayers for his conversion, stood to announce that he felt himself "saved." Later he remembered mostly his embarrassment and anxiety at being the center of public attention. His real motives for joining the church, he indicated, were to end his "agony of self-consciousness," to make his mother happy, and to be thereafter spared the vexation of the mourner's bench.[24]

In his mind the mourner's bench was further linked to an innocently amorous but troublesome encounter with a young belle of the congregation, "several years older than I," who had sat down beside him and rubbed her cheek against his. That was hardly sin enough for repentance, he felt, but years later he enjoyed equating it to the "carnal desires of the flesh" which the church required him to renounce. Of the Older Woman's facial nuzzle, he said simply, "I found the sensation pleasant."[25] It was not the only time he would connect some key circumstance in his youth with the romantic or erotic. Remarking on the books he read as a boy, he noted that his family had bought from traveling book agents two popular tracts of the day, *Golden Gems of Thought* and a treatise on phrenology by Dr. O. S. Fowler. The former he found "stupid and dull reading," but "Dr. Fowler's comments and the sexy illustrations appealed powerfully to my imagination. I wanted to get off to myself whenever I read that book."[26]

The rare few books which came his way were at once treasured and consumed. Later he told Lincoln-esque stories of toilsome days in the fields and nights spent reading by a tiny brass lamp in his garret room when the family was asleep. After Fowler, a powerful literary influence in those early years was *Pilgrim's Progress,* "the first book I read completely through." Like many another unlettered country youth, he was largely unaware of its moral and theological allegory and read it simply as "a thrilling adventure." When he was sixteen he fell under the spell of Eugene Sue's grand melodrama, *The Wandering Jew,* a popular sensation of forty years earlier. Again he was immune to the author's weightier intentions. Only later did he learn that *The Wandering Jew* was, among other things, an attack on Catholicism; at the time it was "only a moving drama" which burned in his consciousness with such intensity that for days he went about his chores in a fog. "One more Wandering Jew," said his father derisively, "and you'll be a candidate for the Austin lunatic asylum."[27]

There were other diversions. As an older John Lomax was fond of pointing out, over and over, the family farm was situated "beside a branch of the old Chisholm Trail."[28] In the early years there was a steady procession of covered wagons, trail herds, and riders on horseback. Cowboys and other wayfaring strangers often spent the night in the Lomax home, bringing "the big, outside world [to] our door."[29] These visitors, John felt, first awakened him to the realization that there were important people and ideas beyond the Bosque Valley.

Cowboys were the focus of other compelling events. The rodeo as we know it was yet to be invented, but so-called cowboy tournaments served a similar function. These were riding contests patterned on frontier notions of knights' jousts, as filtered through Sir Walter Scott, Sidney Lanier, and other creaky bastions of "honor" and "chivalry" in the Old South. Mounted and armed with a six-foot lance, each contestant galloped down a two-hundred yard course, aiming his weapon not at another rider but at a series of small rings suspended from posts at regular intervals. The object was to spear as many rings as possible within a given time limit; the winner was the rider who had the most rings after three heats. The contest itself was merely the raison d'être for a panoply of related rituals, displays, and ceremonies. Like similar events in our time—tractor pulls, demolition derbies, road rallies—cowboy tournaments were social as well as competitive occasions, often the centerpiece for county picnics, political debates, and school celebrations. The proceedings were highly ritualized, with a parade before and a dance afterward, featuring a variety of promenades and jigs accompanied by songs and calls in cowboy vernacular.

Young John Lomax was drawn to the music as well as to the derring-do of these events—he credited tournament heroes like Bob Hanna and Ed Nichols with having "deepened my love for cowboy songs," but it is not at all clear just when and how the interest surfaced. In a recollection more than a little tinged with romantic hindsight, he supposedly heard, at the tender age of four, a cowboy somewhere in the night, crooning "Git Along, Little Dogies" to his restless cattle. On other nights, young Lomax would lie awake in bed listening as Hanna and his gang of buckaroos rode by the family farm, singing and shouting on their way home from the saloons in town, "soused to the gills."[30] Many years later, he vividly recalled an incident from his teens that occurred while he was hauling a wagonload of wheat to be milled in an adjoining county. He spent the night at the millyard, sleeping under his wagon, and while sipping coffee by the campfire the next morning, he heard another "camper" across the creek, singing "Cowboy's Gettin'-Up Holler" as he rolled from his bedding. "I carried the tune in my head for some fifty years before writing it down," he said.[31]

• • • • •

Books and camp meetings, cowboys, occasional trips to town—all those brought relief from the daily grind at home. But their pleasures were fleeting, and always at his back Johnny Lomax heard not only Time's winged chariot but the wrenching creak of a Georgia stock and single-row planter. At the same time, recurring bouts of imagination—an ancient affliction of bright farm boys—were rendering him less and less fit for the dull tasks of frontier agriculture. Perversely, as he grew aware of a world beyond Bosque County, his own existence there seemed all the more narrowed and confined, his choices limited, the route of his passage through life already booked and confirmed.

CHAPTER TWO

• • • • •

Hard Times in the Country 1887–95

Boys in John Lomax's circumstances faced a bleak and narrow future. The matter of an occupation—what they would "do" with their lives—was more or less taken for granted: they would till the soil or ride the range. Neither had much appeal for Lomax. Awed as he was by the flamboyant cowboys of trail herd and tournament, he knew deep down that, contrary to the romantic image, punching cattle was a sorry life. Farming was simply hard work with no romance at all.

Increasingly he felt himself tied to the plow, held captive on the Lower Forty. He was almost twenty when he began to see the first faint possibilities of a way out, some glimmering notion of a calling, shaped by events that had taken place in childhood. There are several versions, varying in minor details; according to his earliest written account, he was only eight or nine years old when his father set him to work in the yard one icy winter morning turning the grindstone on which James Lomax was sharpening the axes they would take into the hills to cut firewood. As the boy toiled away, his bare hands clasped to the cold iron handle, there appeared around the corner of the house "a stalwart young negro" from Meridian, looking for work. Given a tryout on the grindstone, he so impressed John's father with his ability and eagerness to work that he was hired on the spot. He was a bond servant named Nat Blythe, who took his last name from his master, Colonel Blythe, a local landowner. Although he was in his late teens, some ten years older than John, they soon formed a friendship so crucial to the younger boy's development that Lomax later said that it "gave my life its bent."[1] Of Nat he would say, "I loved him as I have loved few people."[2]

Coming upon Nat one day struggling over a blue-backed Webster's speller, the boy set about to teach him. The lessons evolved into long summer afternoon sessions in the shade of a mulberry tree. At times the two of them were joined by neighbor children, but Nat was "my first, . . . my star pupil." At the end of their three years together, Nat had gone through the series of readers and was knowledgeable in geography, grammar, history, and arithmetic. He understood basic algebra, and wrote a good hand.[3] Only later would Lomax realize how this experience as Nat's mentor had shaped the course of his own future.

Young John's attention soon turned to other matters—mostly a moldboard plow and the rear end of the mule team that pulled it. But a few years later it was in just such circumstances that memories of his "pupil" filtered back. Sent to plow the big field down by the Bosque, John found himself overtaken by dreams and summer sun. He stopped the team and stretched out under an oak tree on the river bank, gazing at the clouds and reflecting on his past—and his seemingly bleak future. The days when he had been a hero to Nat by teaching him from books seemed far away. But the memory of Nat stood out clearly and distinctly, he wrote years later, and it brought a momentous decision. He resolved to leave the farm, go to college, and train himself for some occupation far from the lonely fields where he toiled like a draft animal. "Nat made me a teacher," he said, and the memories that came to him as he lay beneath the oak tree formed "a vision that I shall follow until I die."[4]

In his favor was a family rule that at the age of twenty each child should go away to school for one year "to complete his twenty-one years of service for the common good of the family."[5] It was a rule sometimes more honored in the breach than in the observance, but encouraged by the example of his next-older brother Jesse, who a year earlier had gone off to a "college" in the adjoining county seat of Granbury, John began to lay his plans. In the spring of 1887, he planted wheat on eleven acres his father had set aside for him, anticipating a crop of some four hundred bushels that would bring ample money for a year at Granbury. But just when the grain was maturing, interminable rains flooded the Bosque, and John's wheat disappeared under ten feet of water (ironically, the rest of Texas was gripped in a record drought that year). The receding waters washed the stalks into the ground. John gathered what he could and had it threshed. The net result, once the thresher had taken his share, was a hundred and sixty bushels, half wheat, half mud.

Showing signs of the financial resourcefulness that he would later develop into an art, he made a deal to trade flour from the "sickly grain" for part of his school expenses. Then, to get the rest of what he needed, he faced a grimmer reality—having to sell his much-loved pony, Selim, to raise the necessary hard cash for tuition and board. The trip to the horse dealer in Dallas was "a ninety-mile funeral journey," and his account of parting with Selim is one of the most touching scenes in his autobiography.[6]

Even with the sixty dollars that Selim brought and his flour-for-board swap, he was still short of the $160 that a year in Granbury would cost. His father offered a small loan, and a larger one came from an older cousin, Alonzo Cooper, John's close friend and supporter, who farmed near the adjoining village of Clifton. There would be modest help from another source, too. The last money anyone ever gave him, he told one of his sons fifty years later, came in small amounts his mother hoarded from her butter and egg sales and sent to him during his year at Granbury.[7]

• • • • •

In the fall of 1887, when Lomax arrived for his year of schooling, Granbury was a flourishing little town of a thousand or more people, roughly twice as big as Meridian. The seat of Hood County, it boasted a fine stone courthouse, erected in 1875, and a busy town square around which were situated twenty or more business establishments common to the time—grocery and dry goods emporiums, drugstores, a livery stable, a furniture and undertaking house, a hotel, a newspaper, and at least two practitioners of the newly invented art-and-science of photography. Conspicuous in their absence were the saloons and "poor men's clubs" of John Lomax's boyhood; during the twenty years of his growing up, the frontier had moved on far to the west, and Granbury, in the tone of civic righteousness rising all over the land, prided itself on being "one of the most healthy, quiet, and moral towns in the state."[8] Throughout Texas, Methodism had been digging in for the long siege against native sin, and its local bastion was Granbury College. As Lomax would wryly note fifty years later, "Today not a stone of the college buildings remains."[9]

A college in little more than name, the institution had presumed to be nothing more than a church-sponsored district high school from its founding in 1873 until 1881, when a new president added the two-year "college" curriculum. By Lomax's time the so-called Collegiate Department offered a full four years of study and a curriculum ranging from English grammar and literature to elocution, physics, "mechanics," "mental philosophy," "moral science," and law.[10] Yet the faculty numbered at most nine people, including the president, and the enrollment was a scant three hundred, the majority in the Primary, Intermediate, and Preparatory Departments (first grade through high school). There cannot have been more than a hundred students in the "college," probably fewer. The student body was nominally coeducational, not so much the result of progressive educational theories as of economic necessity—both pupils and schools were still sparse in that young society and both had to be concentrated wherever they were.

To those in the Collegiate Department who stayed the course and successfully sampled the three-dozen subjects listed in the catalog, the degree of Artium Baccalaureus was awarded at the end of four years. For those students, "especially young ladies," who did not wish to be troubled by foreign languages or mathematics higher than analytical geometry, the school offered a degree of Bachelor of Philosophy—"Ph.B." Finally, there was the one-year Normal Course, chosen by John Lomax (and probably by the majority of those in the Collegiate Department). It covered simply "those branches that are required in order to obtain a first-class [teaching] certificate in any county of the state."[11] (At the time, a graduate of almost any high school in the state could qualify, by examination, for such a certificate; some obtained it with even less schooling.) By any standard, Lomax's education at Granbury cannot have been much; he later claimed that until he went to the University of Texas in 1895, he had never written an essay, "not even a one-page theme."[12]

Official policy of the school stressed "the moral as well as the mental training," as one would expect of an institution directed by the Methodist Episcopal Church, South. Student behavior, in and out of class, was controlled by a long list of rules which, typical of the time and place, were strict and puritanical. Regular attendance at church and Sunday school was taken for granted. Strong emphasis was placed on Work and Duty; students were enjoined to show proper respect for the faculty and were prohibited from "all intoxicating drinks and games of chance" as well as from "balls, parties, shows and all other places of dissipation." Even further, members of the opposite sex were forbidden "any private communication" without permission from the faculty. That regulation, however, fell far down the list; priority was given to prohibitions against "possession of deadly weapons" and wrecking school property—evidence that frontier days were not entirely over. In any event, "Every restraint [was] thrown around the young to keep them in the path of duty," as the school catalog boasted.[13]

Freed from the bleak drudgery of the farm and set down in the presence of books and ideas, Lomax was much too excited by his studies to pay much attention to the strict regimentation of student life. In a year or two he would begin to develop spiritual allergies to the pervasive air of sanctimony, but for the present he felt none of the shortcomings of the disciplinary system, the sparse and poorly trained faculty, the ill-equipped classrooms, the pitiful library. "I was like a fish that had escaped from a shoally stream into a pool of clear, sunshiny water," he wrote later. "I do not think I was ever so happy."[14]

. . . . .

His teachers, despite their deficiencies, were dedicated and full of encouragement, especially with students like Lomax who worked hard and showed promise. The school's president, David S. Switzer, who also taught mathematics and languages, took a particular interest in the young man and was to exert considerable influence on the course of his early career. A stout, affable Mississippian, Switzer, in contrast to the rest of his faculty, was well educated and intellectually suited to his job; he held an M.A. from the University of Mississippi and was largely responsible for what little academic progress had taken place at Granbury College.

Under Switzer, Lomax completed two years of algebra in one and studied geometry, trigonometry, and first-year Latin. Other courses included formal grammar, history, physiology, and calisthenics. He excelled at spelling and won the five-dollar Capt Medal for being the school's best speller. In elocution he memorized and recited the 108 lines of "Lasca," that grand tearjerker which in those days—and for long after—was a staple in rural classrooms all over Texas:

> I gouged out a grave a few feet deep,
> And there in Earth's arms I laid her to sleep;
> And there she is lying, and no one knows,
> And the summer shines and the winter snows;
>
> . . . .
>
> And I wonder why I do not care
> For the things that are like the things that were.
> Does half my heart lie buried there
> In Texas, down by the Rio Grande?

It was, of course, wonderful kitsch, written by Frank Desprez, an English dramatist (born in Bristol in 1853), who had spent a few years on a western ranch, but it was the very sort of thing that was forming the basis of John Lomax's literary notions about the West.

Classroom recitations at Granbury were six days a week, from morning till night, conducted by a handful of teachers who were scarcely more prepared than some of their upperclassmen. All students, from primary through college, sat through the day at their desks in rows, "supervised by a monitor, just as if they were first graders."[15] Dutiful as ever, Lomax willingly, even happily, bent to his tasks and regularly performed at the top of his class, receiving 98s and 100s in every subject on the monthly reports sent home to his parents. He was never absent or tardy and was consistently given 100 in Deportment and Application. There is no record of extracurricular activities or social life, but an early biographer is probably right in assuming that he belonged to the young men's Phaino Literary Society, read the student magazine, *Collegian,* and in what spare time he had gathered with the crowd at one or another of the drugstores on the town square.[16]

On Commencement Day near the end of May 1888, Lomax delivered what he himself later characterized as "a ponderous final oration . . . similar in style and content to one I had heard on 'The Past and the Present and Their Relation to the Future.'"[17] His elocution, unlike his spelling, took no prize, but he felt considerable pride in now possessing the certificate which qualified him to teach "in the schools of the sovereign State of Texas." It was, as he said later, "slender equipment," but with it and the help of his cousin, Alonzo Cooper, he got a teaching job for the coming year in the country school at Clifton, a little village some ten miles southeast of Meridian.

· · · · ·

"Cousin Lon," his wife Mattie, and their large family of boys lived only two miles outside Clifton, and Lomax spent much of his free time with them during his year there in the fall and winter of 1888–89. Lon Cooper was a dozen years older than John, but he had been an important part of the young man's life for some time—"the truest man friend of my life." John's father was distant and aloof, his brothers too numerous and too occupied with their own concerns to form strong emotional bonds. Cousin Lon, described by Lomax as "wise, generous, kindly, loving,"[18] had become a sort of surrogate for both father and brothers. Like John's father (apparently the only quality they shared), Lon Cooper was an avid reader of newspapers and from time to time supplied Lomax with books from his small library. John confided his hopes and aspirations, told Lon his troubles, asked for advice; in turn he was given encouragement, regaled with Lon's whimsical stories, and gently joshed for taking life so seriously. Occasionally the two of them were known to favor, as a third party to their conversations, the little brown jug which Lon kept behind *his* kitchen door.

Cousin Lon's company notwithstanding, Lomax's teaching job soon soured. Exhilarated by his year of "book learning" at Granbury, he was quickly disillusioned by the miserably low pay and the rigors of life in a primitive country school.[19] He boarded on credit and found himself incurring other small debts that would take several years to pay off. Business conditions were bad everywhere, resulting from crop failures and a generally depressed economy. Granbury College, facing bankruptcy, closed its doors and auctioned off the building to meet its indebtedness. David Switzer, his faculty, and what little physical property remained were moved twenty miles north to Weatherford, a thriving town more than twice the size of Granbury. There the Methodist directors merged them with Cleveland College, another erstwhile grammar and high school. The consolidated, reorganized institution was renamed Weatherford College, with Switzer again in the president's chair. It was this position that made it possible for him to reply in the affirmative to his former pupil when John Lomax wrote him in the spring of 1889 asking for a job that would get him away from the drudgery and abuse at Clifton. Switzer hired him as "principal" (and sole faculty member) of the Preparatory Department of Weatherford College at a salary of forty dollars a month.

That move proved to be another mixed blessing. Although the "college" consisted of only a single building, it was huge and imposing, three stories of native stone, set in a grove of stately oaks and surrounded by an immense lawn covering most of two city blocks. The city of Weatherford, county seat of Parker County with a population of some 3,000, was a veritable metropolis compared to Clifton. Located on the divide of the Trinity and Brazos rivers, it offered in those prepollution days a grand view of the Trinity's Clear Fork Valley and the prairies stretching away to Fort Worth, thirty miles to the east. City fathers proclaimed the virtues of climate and altitude—at 1200 feet above sea level the region was free of the malaria which plagued other settled parts of the state; the clean air and salubrious weather were responsible, it was claimed, for the "manly vigor" which made Weatherford a hotbed of "commercial success and progressive ideals."

Despite its scenic splendors and the city's general air of prosperity, Lomax found the cultural atmosphere as narrow and provincial as in Granbury and Clifton. The stern rules of Granbury had been transported intact; "professors" were expected to attend every church service and report all infractions of the rules among students, even such innocent offenses as "any boy noticed walking with his sweetheart up a shady lane."[20] Lomax chose not to see the strolling lovers and in privacy sometimes fired up a forbidden cigar. But he still wore the yoke of his rural, conformist upbringing—and would never be entirely free of it. Much as he resented what he considered the unreasonable discipline of the school, to all outward appearances he was the model young schoolteacher of the time—churchgoing, earnest, obedient, upright, "well-thought-of."

His work in the classroom was more cause for inner turmoil. Although the school's catalog boasted of "laboratories, an observatory, and a library of ten thousand volumes," Lomax found none of it.[21] The poorly trained, mostly ragtag faculty of eight administered to a student body that varied in number from two hundred to four hundred, "from their a-b-c's until they 'finished' fifteen years later."[22] Each teacher was charged with twelve to fifteen classes ("Professor" Switzer may have had fewer) and taught six days a week. Even Lomax, conditioned to the hard physical labor of the farm, found the load difficult. He was further distressed by a growing sense of his own inadequacy, the haunting notion that he was failing in his responsibilities to his students. Fifty years later he wrote in *Adventures of a Ballad Hunter:* "My face flushes with shame as I recall what I did not have to offer those eager boys and girls [at Weatherford]."[23] Still, he was better than he knew; long afterward many students remembered him with great affection and wrote to tell him that he had been a powerful influence in their lives. Said one: "I think that the training you gave your pupils in Weatherford College was of real value, of much more value than you give it in your [autobiography]."[24]

At the outset, Switzer had promised him time for his own studies. It soon became clear that very little such time would materialize. In partial compensation at the end of John's first year, the president found a few dollars to defray Lomax's travel expenses to attend the summer session at Eastman Business College in Poughkeepsie, New York. In retrospect, the sudden notion of going off to the awesome East—locus of money, power, and refinement—surely gave pause to a rough-hewn country boy in John Lomax's situation; it was only a few years earlier that he had read in his father's newspapers of New York and the mystic East, light-years from his Texas dirt farm surroundings.

Now, going there for the first time was clearly a central event in his life, yet he made no personal record of it, then nor later (nor of any of his several trips east for another ten years). The very absence of such an account, from a man who dwelt on himself in countless letters, journals, and jottings, who saved almost every scrap of biographical paper, is in itself illuminating. One can only suppose that his reactions to the cultural distance between rural Texas and the cosmopolitan East were true to character: part awe, part happy enthusiasm, part anger and embarrassment. He was still poor and shabby, and all too conscious of his inadequacies, social and intellectual, for such an experience. But he was also a young man with a vision, who had sold his best pony to buy books and braved surly oafs in country schoolrooms and come all the way to Weatherford, Texas, to be called "professor."

The Eastman Business College in Poughkeepsie was singularly suited to the needs and expectations of John Lomax at that stage of his life. The city itself, in 1891 a modern, thriving place of some 25,000 people, provided the most urban and cosmopolitan environment he had yet known, and the school, which had been established just prior to the Civil War, was then in its prime, with an enrollment of more than a thousand young men very much like Lomax himself—mostly from humble origins but all eager and ambitious, radiating the nineteenth-century confidence that practical education, hard work, a clean collar, and a firm handshake would make them rich. Only a few years earlier, the school's founder, Harvey G. Eastman, had proudly announced that "the Mania for Money-Getting is growing stronger in this country every day" and assured his students they would succeed because "nine out of ten of those who are assuming control of the country come from humbler walks of life, and start without money or friends. . . . [T]o begin life poor is to commence as nearly all great and successful men have."[25] It was just what they wanted to hear.

At Eastman, Lomax enrolled in "Commercial Penmanship and Bookkeeping by Double-entry." In town he shared a room with Edgar Keister, a young businessman from Pennsylvania. Next to them was the parlor, where the landlady's daughter sent forth wheezing melodies from a dilapidated organ. John's ear for music was not especially educated, but he had loved music since childhood and knew pitch—or out-of-pitch—when he heard it. Performances by the landlady's daughter caused him such an "awful expression of pain and disgust" that Keister remembered it thirty years later.[26] By summer's end, Lomax had completed his bookkeeping course with distinction and, ironically, won a diamond-studded gold medal for penmanship (in everyday practice, he wrote one of the worst hands imaginable, and it steadily declined into near-total illegibility over the years).

Back in Texas, Switzer beamed proudly over his former pupil's accomplishments and as a reward created a "Business Department" for John to run—in addition to his duties as head and entire faculty of the Preparatory Department. "Someone once said I ran the Business Department with my left hind foot," Lomax reported later. "Too true, too true."[27]

With this increase in his duties, there was even less time for his own studies or relaxation. In any event, social life in Weatherford was largely limited to church-related activities, and John, by his own admission, was ill prepared for any other sort. There were certain fledgling, inept efforts at boy-girl relationships—much later he could report that "a group of blooming sixteen-year-old girls" had chosen him to be their Sunday school teacher, and that he "loved them all"[28]—but these were little more than casual flirtations. At the time he was much too bound by lack of experience and his own rigid responses to the prevailing moral climate for any serious adventures. Sometime during this period he composed a few lines of doggerel concerning the question "Is Sex Necessary?" which concluded that "Sex is one of nature's tricks / Played on unsuspecting hicks." It was entirely unnecessary, he said, and involved merely "mastering mind over matter." Long afterward he would append the comment: "Written while in my *un*informed twenties" (his emphasis),[29] but meanwhile, despite what was clearly a robust interest in the opposite sex, he would go on "mastering mind over matter" for several years.

Other frustrations continued to mount. His meager salary was gradually being increased—at the end of his six years at Weatherford it had risen from $40 a month to $75—but every spare penny went to pay old debts, assist his family, or underwrite those grim, desperate efforts toward "self-improvement." In 1892 his father died, and he had to contribute substantially, along with his brothers and sisters, to the support of his mother.

Yet on an annual income of less than a thousand dollars he managed to save enough to go "back East" to Chautauqua, New York, for six weeks each summer from 1891 through 1894 to attend the lecture-and-concert series held there on the grounds of a Methodist camp-meeting site ("the most American place in America," said Theodore Roosevelt).[30] In those days before *Reader's Digest* and Dale Carnegie, state chautauquas (of which the western New York version was the eponymous original) catered to the growing quest for "self-improvement" and do-it-yourself education, an outgrowth of the Methodist philosophy of "every man his own college."[31] The program was frequently more entertainment than education, or entertainment disguised as education; lectures on high-minded subjects were given suitably elevated titles but shortened and leavened for easy consumption. Eventually Lomax would come to see the Chautauqua treatises as "stiff, stupid, and insipid,"[32] but at the time they offered the promise of a better, more enlightened life, free of the dullness and drudgery of Weatherford and its "college." The Chautauqua sessions were not entirely a waste of Lomax's time and money. There he improved his mathematics, struggled with Latin, listened to music that stirred him (opera and oratorios, light "classics" of the day), and learned, for the first time, of two poets—Tennyson and Browning—whose work would soon become an integral part of his intellectual equipment.

Despite all this, Lomax continued to fret over what to him was "the lack of any substantial education."[33] More and more he was coming to feel that as a teacher he was failing to meet the needs of his students—among whom, incidentally, were a number of young men who were to have distinguished careers in various fields: Fritz Lanham as journalist and longtime Texas congressman; James G. Wilson as federal judge; Charles S. Potts as professor at Texas A&M, the University of Texas, and Washington University, and ultimately, as renowned dean of law at Southern Methodist University for many years. To these and others Lomax became a sort of older brother, father-confessor, and all-around good companion—a role that grew with the passing years. He was genuinely interested in their personal as well as their academic lives, and to whatever extent he could, he took their side in bouts with oppressive institutional rules, nagging or overprotective parents, unrequited love affairs, and impatient creditors. Despite his generally staid bearing in public—at times bordering, it was said, on the downright regal—up close he could be warm and genial, laughed easily, and even in those early days told stories with the rare verve that would eventually win him a wide reputation as wit and raconteur.

In some respects—notably, with money—he was too generous. For a long time, even when he was living on credit himself, Lomax had been an easy touch for students, friends, family, almost anyone who approached him. In some cases, especially where students were concerned, he made outright gifts, often anonymously, with no thought of repayment. The sums were small and the loans generally repaid, but still it amounted to a considerable sacrifice for someone in his financial condition. One such act of generosity was about to bring him serious grief.

Back when he was still at Clifton, his brother Richard had come to him for what was represented as a modest favor. Nine years older than John, Richard Lomax was an up-and-coming businessman, forever hustling various "deals" and "investments." At the moment (he had told John) things were slow, and he needed a few thousand dollars to protect some surefire venture he had undertaken. A lender was lined up; all he needed was someone to cosign his note as security. At the time John was, to be sure, a poorly paid country school teacher, but everyone knew him to be honest, hardworking, reliable, a man of his word. That alone qualified him to "go the note." Moreover, said Richard, there was practically no risk involved; his business was on solid footing and merely in need of a small cash infusion. With these assurances, John had signed.

Richard Lomax was in fact a genial scamp, an indefatigable optimist and schemer, who through much of his sad, troubled life would blithely distance himself from the distress he caused others. Forever turning up the "perfect deal" that would make him rich, he had sunk everything he owned in a speculative scheme involving undeveloped farm lands southeast of Dallas. But cotton prices had steadily declined, and the long droughts of 1886 and 1887 had wrecked the Texas farm economy.[34] In 1891, when he asked John to sign the note, Richard Lomax was on the verge of financial ruin, and the loan had merely postponed the inevitable. Following the panic of 1893, he declared bankruptcy, found a comfortable sinecure in the state treasury office in Austin, and calmly washed his hands of the whole affair.

For John the issue was not so clear. Richard and other members of the family urged him to do as Richard had done—forget the whole thing—and when he continued to fret, several relatives turned against him, calling him foolish and perhaps even a little crazy. But he had given his word, and signed his name. Feeling betrayed by "a man in whom I had the utmost confidence" (publicly he would never name Richard as the culprit), he nevertheless resolved to pay off the debt, however long it might take. For years he could scarcely afford more than small payments on the interest. At one point (he told a friend several years later) he took out enough life insurance to pay the balance, intending to kill himself "rather than permit a note of mine to go to protest."[35] An early biographer saw in this "something of the Western code of the only men he had heretofore really admired—the cowboys," but as James McNutt rightly pointed out, this overlooks the bitter and also faintly humorous irony of the situation: rather than face dishonor by shirking a debt, he would defraud the insurance company by killing himself.[36]

Tempting as it is to attribute his sense of obligation to that elevated notion of a "Code of the West," there is far more evidence that at this stage of his career the men he admired most were not cowboys but the professors and businessmen who wore white collars and were, as the popular phrase had it, getting ahead in the world. Nor should one overlook in his action a certain degree of native stubbornness, inherited from his father and only stiffened by the ridicule of those who thought he was a fool to worry over the debt. But he was much like his father in yet another sense, a father described by the son himself as "inflexible in his conception of duty and honor."[37] John Lomax had given his word, and he stuck by it, knowing it would cost him years of anxiety and deprivation.

The mess that Richard had gotten him into precipitated a crisis of major proportions. The situation at Weatherford had grown more and more intolerable; he was working long, hard hours with little to show for it, getting nowhere, and increasingly chafed by the rigors of small-town puritanism. Alternately despondent over his inadequacies—real or imagined—and those of his students and colleagues, he dreamed of going to some first-rate university for a degree that would be recognized and respected, a ticket out of Weatherford and into the ranks of true academia. For some time Vanderbilt, "The Athens of the South," with its Methodist connections and wide reputation for excellence, loomed large in these visions. But finally he'd had to admit to himself that he couldn't pass the entrance examinations. And now, once again, there was the problem of money. He'd just about paid off all the old debts lingering from his Granbury and Clifton days when the calamity with Richard struck. That seemed an end to all his hopes.

CHAPTER THREE

The Highly Educated Man
1895–97

By the mid-1890s, with the death of his father in January 1892 and the increasing dereliction of brother Richard, John was by default taking on the role of head of the family. James Lomax's sons and daughters by his first wife had been grown and scattered for years (two were dead, others had children as old as John). Of Susan's flock, the brothers nearest John in age, Jesse and Rob, were struggling along as field hands and part-time country teachers, and the two girls, Sue and Alice, were teenagers still in school. Increasingly, John was being called on to make family decisions and handle business affairs. Even the older boys looked to him for advice and, not infrequently, for financial assistance. Richard's doomed enterprise was merely the most recent and disastrous instance.

All this only heightened the sense of crisis that spring of 1895.

Weatherford, which had once seemed the shining gateway to opportunity, had turned into a dead end. Lomax had come to see its civic boosterism and small-town platitudes for what they were, and the intellectual pretensions of Weatherford College no longer impressed him. Overworked and frustrated, he had begun to cast about, willy-nilly, for escape, but Richard's downfall seemed to close the trap. What's worse, John knew that it was a snare fashioned of his own naivete and self-delusion.

About to fall apart at his psychic seams, Lomax on impulse one weekend took the train down to Clifton to see Cousin Lon and his wife Mattie. After one of Cousin Mattie's big Sunday dinners of fried chicken, mashed potatoes and gravy, country biscuits, five vegetables, and three desserts, the world seemed none so bad. Recovering in the shade of the front gallery, John and Lon fell into their old easy habit of talking, half banter, half serious business. John's situation in Weatherford was not news to Lon, but he'd heard only the vague outlines of Richard's chicanery. As he listened to the details, Lon saw how truly upset John was over the debt he'd assumed, how devastated by his dashed hopes of ever getting a real education at some major university. That night, when Lon took his younger cousin to catch the train back to Weatherford, he said simply, "Go on and make your plans. I'll back you."[1]

Considerably heartened but still uncertain of what move to make, John stopped in Fort Worth to change trains. In Union Station he struck up a conversation with a young hardware salesman from Sherman, Joe Etter, just two years out of the University of Texas. When Lomax mentioned that he might try to qualify for Vanderbilt, Etter said, "The University of Texas is the only place for you."[2] Back in Weatherford, Lomax went at once to Switzer and gave notice that he was leaving.

September was normally the time when new students entered the University, so Switzer assumed that John would teach at Weatherford through the summer term. But when the spring semester ended in early June, Lomax was on the train to Austin. He couldn't wait. "For many years thereafter," he wrote in his autobiography, "the University of Texas was the core of my life."[3] It was in fact the beginning of a love-hate relationship that would last almost to the day of his death—forced out of University-related positions three times in the next thirty years, he would spend a third of that time in exile from the school, and yet in old age bemoan the fact that the University had "never thought me worthy to teach even a Freshman class."[4]

When Lomax went to Austin in the early summer of 1895, the University of Texas was scarcely twelve years old, still rough at the edges and struggling. But it was also energetic and ambitious, asserting for itself a place of prominence among its peers in the region. There weren't many—Vanderbilt and Tulane were the only comparable institutions in the South and Southwest. The University of Missouri, in the distant Midwest, claimed a comparable reputation (and what was perhaps more important to the student body, provided flesh-and-blood rivals for U.T.'s fledgling football team).

In Texas, "The Agricultural and Mechanical College," located in the hinterlands near Bryan, drew small numbers of future farmers, soldiers, and engineers, but as an all-male school which required every student to join its military cadet corps, it earned little academic respect. Newly founded Rice Institute in Houston would in a few years become known as the state's most select and academically rigorous, the mecca for Texas' handful of genuine intellectuals. But standards at the University were sufficient to give it a serious reputation, and it was certainly more fun than the major church schools, Baylor and Texas Christian.

The atmosphere in which the University of Texas hoped to flourish was not always clear and sunny, as Lomax would soon find out. His burning desire for education was not shared by other Texans, especially in rural areas, where the majority of the state's population still lived. Rank and file citizens, notoriously unbookish, found many reasons to oppose higher education, suspicious of anything that lurked about in the guise of "refinement," laid claim to tax dollars, and offered no clear and immediate promise of cash return. Resentment toward the University was fed, ironically, by the state's older institutions of learning, especially Baylor and Texas Christian, which got no tax money and saw the state university as unfair competition. Their opposition was frequently voiced in moral terms, reflecting concern for what many viewed as lax behavior and dangerously liberal thinking ("secular humanism" is the charge these days) on the Austin campus. This was a message more powerful than finances, confirming the worst fears in the minds of the rustic and fundamental, whose numbers were legion.

Even stronger resistance came from Texas A&M, which did have to compete for state funds. Although the "Agricultural and Mechanical College" was, on paper at least, a "branch" of the state university, its existence actually preceded that of the University of Texas by some seven years, and its prerogatives, real or imagined, were jealously guarded by faculty, administration, and a loyal cadre of alumni which included many of the state's prominent farmers, military leaders, and professional men. The University, on the other hand, had not been in business long enough to produce a substantial body of influential graduates and lacked an effective alumni organization—a situation which, in time, John Lomax would play a central role in correcting.

All these problems and conflicts tended to coalesce in the state legislature, which held the purse strings and was prone to act, often irrationally, at times outrageously, as an agent of transmittal for all that was best and worst in the Texas body politic. The University, situated practically at the back door of the Capitol, became a ready target, subject to all sorts of legislative whims and machinations, in the biennial struggle over appropriations. Some lawmakers had noble but wrongheaded intentions, others were merely populist crackpots, a few were genuine friends of the University. The relationship was often that of a nervous protégé and an affluent but quirky benefactor: the University tried to be dutiful but sometimes failed; its moods swung from sycophantic to resentful to openly (if limply) defiant, while the legislature could always be expected to do the unexpected. One result was to instill a certain esprit de corps among students, faculty, and administration, who at times felt themselves drawn together in a unified front—outnumbered and outgunned, not unlike the defenders of the Alamo—against a common enemy.

· · · · ·

To the degree that the University of Texas established itself as an institution of growing promise, such success was due not so much to any truly progressive attitude among the citizens of the state as to a pervasive spirit of enthusiasm for learning that was in the air all across the nation. In the aftermath of the Civil War and Reconstruction had come a renewed faith in the old Jeffersonian ideal of education as inoculation against social and political ills, or at very least, in nineteenth-century thinking, as a prescription for "success in life"—a mighty potion which could induce, as it were, the American Dream.

Texans by and large held a particularly pragmatic view of public education. Their representatives in the state house spoke for the majority in rejecting fuzzy-headed intellectualism and asserting the popular notion that colleges ought to train people for something useful in the rough-and-tumble world of commerce and industry. That attitude was nothing new to John Lomax, and in later years it came to have even greater appeal for him, but his initial elation at finally arriving at what he looked upon as a first-class university was more than a little dampened when, in his second semester there, the governor vetoed funds for the U.T. library, declaring with a straight face that the students would get no new books until they had read the ones they had.

Still, the physical requirements of higher education—buildings, faculties, and curriculum—were in some ways more accessible in Lomax's time than now. A developing state—in this case, Texas—which wished to establish, in the language of the state constitution, "a university of the first class,"[5] could get its Olympian venture underway for a quite modest sum. Texas did it for less than $100,000.

The first requirement was an imposing pseudo-classic edifice with the appropriately pedagogical atmosphere; at the University of Texas it was known as the Main Building, bedecked with Victorian spires, arches, and gables, erected at a cost of $59,000. The second necessity was a small cadre of hirsute professors in stiff collars, necessarily from the East or South and preferably sprinkled with Harvard graduates. When John Lomax arrived at U.T., there were, in fact, more Harvardians (eight) among the faculty of some twenty-two than graduates from any other single school, and the Harvard influence was to have a significant bearing on his future. Nine professors were from southern schools, notably the University of Virginia; the remainder came from Johns Hopkins, Cornell, and Syracuse. Almost half held doctoral degrees, and several were Confederate veterans, including the president, Leslie Waggener, and Proctor James B. "Judge" Clark (both of whom had also attended Harvard). This academic and geographical diversity surely contributed further to the forces at work on John Lomax, reinforcing the cultural complexities begun in Bosque County and extended by his jaunts between Texas and the East.

More than forty years later, Lomax spoke vividly of entering the University of Texas as one of the great adventures of his life, recalling in detail the people he met his first day there and how his heart beat wildly "in a kind of strange gratitude" when anyone noticed him. He was awkward and self-conscious, but happy beyond belief because he was fulfilling a lifelong dream.[6] (He remarked also that he felt then that people who were better dressed and had better manners were somehow superior to him, revealing that deep insecurity which never left him, although he quickly learned to compensate; his outward behavior would soon display a quite opposite notion of just who was superior.)

It did not take him long to survey the campus then taking form on College Hill just north of the state capitol. It amounted to only four buildings scattered across the wide expanse of the famous "Forty Acres" which the state legislature had set aside in 1881 when Austin was chosen as the site for the new state university. Near the center and high on the skyline was the four-story Main Building, still under construction—the tightfisted Texans had begun not with the building proper but with a smaller, cheaper west wing, then later added the central portion and a north wing, and now work was underway on the east wing, to be completed in 1899. Further east was Brackenridge Hall, the newly constructed boys' dormitory, squat, flat-topped, and plain (later, as the famous "B. Hall," it would acquire decorative wings and gingerbread trim). Northwest of the Main Building was the gable-roofed Chemistry Building and to the northeast the Power House and tall smokestack. Although electricity had come to Austin as early as 1889, the University buildings were still lighted by gas and heated by steam. Dust from the cattle trails was still settling, figuratively at least, and everywhere there was lingering evidence of frontier days. When a writer for the student newspaper stopped coming to work, the editor posted a notice, only half-humorously, in language cowboys understood: "A reward is offered for the discovery and return to this staff office of one Robert E. Goree, lost, strayed or stolen. Description: Twenty-three years old, 16 hands high, dun and muckled roan, branded BTP on left vest."[7]

Lomax settled into one of the many boardinghouses near the campus, paid his monthly rent of $15, and, with typical Lomaxian intensity, went straight to work boning up for classes, although the fall semester was still some three months away. He enrolled in the University Preparatory School, a private enterprise operated by the Misses Mignonette and Lillie Carrington and their friend Grace Harrison. Although run independently of the University (or 'Varsity, as nearly everyone called it in those days), the Carrington school had the informal approval of the administration and advertised itself as being "in full affiliation" with the college. Lomax later characterized Mignonette Carrington as "brilliant and fun-loving"; under her tutelage he honed his English grammar, foreign languages (Greek, Latin, French, German), history, and math. Having successfully completed the work, he was admitted conditionally to the sophomore class of the University without taking entrance examinations. With false modesty, he attributed that to some miracle on the part of Miss Carrington, but in fact all students of the school were allowed to enter the University without examination.[8]

His studies were Lomax's initial concern that summer of 1895. Once the work was satisfactorily underway, he allowed himself a few hours here and there to relax and take in the city of Austin, which offered ample diversions. Then as now, it was one of the more interesting, lively, and hospitable of Texas towns—"The City of the Violet Crown," as it was dubbed by one of its famous adopted sons, William Sidney Porter ("O. Henry"), who was publishing his wonderfully eccentric newspaper, the *Rolling Stone*, there in the mid-nineties. (Porter's "violet crown" described the purplish haze which lights the surrounding hills in the late afternoons.)

Like Washington, D.C., which in time would become Lomax's second base of operation, Austin was a city created primarily as a seat of government. Early on, it developed an essential quality which—as compared with Dallas or Houston, for example—has inclined toward the civic and cultural rather than the commercial and hectic. There was the rough and tumble element of Texas politics connected with the capitol, but the city itself had distinctly urbane tendencies. The establishment of the state university there further contributed to a cosmopolitan atmosphere, and the cultural diversity of the population (some 17,000 when John Lomax arrived) is seen in the ethnicity of their celebrations: Texas Independence, Cinco de Mayo, St. Patrick's Day, Friedrich von Schiller's birthday, Diez y Seis, Rosh Hashanah, and Juneteenth.[9]

John Lomax found Austin and its environs immediately congenial. The topography reminded him of Bosque County: wooded, rolling hills, running streams, and distinctive landmarks that appealed to his sense of place. West of the city stood a line of high, tree-covered bluffs and singularly imposing Mt. Bonnell (elev. 785 ft.), where the more athletic and amorous of the college set hiked for romance and a stunning panorama of the countryside. Just southwest of town was McDonald Dam, which spanned the Colorado River to form Lake McDonald, a popular social site for picnics, regattas, and steamboat excursions on the triple-decked sidewheeler *Ben Hur.* In the next few years, as he grew in stature and popularity on the University campus, John Lomax became a familiar figure among the visitors to Mt. Bonnell and the crowds aboard the *Ben Hur.*

The city offered numerous civic attractions, a variety of interesting architectural styles, and the pleasant vista of broad, tree-lined streets. The broadest and busiest was Congress Avenue, stretching north from the river up through the center of town for eleven blocks to the handsome new red granite capitol building that dominated the Austin skyline. But most of the streets, Congress Avenue included, were yet unpaved in 1895, and the town had its seamier, more raucous districts. Along the river west of Congress and south of Fifth Street was an area known as Guy Town, lined with saloons and gambling dens populated by cattlemen, prostitutes, and hustlers of varied stripe. There the spirit of the Old West lived on, and the city as a whole sometimes still suffered from the stigma of its frontier past. About the time John Lomax came to Austin, William Sidney Porter was writing in the *Rolling Stone,* "Austin has one soap factory, one electric light works, one cemetery, one dam, one race track, two beer gardens, one capitol, two city councils, one cocaine factory, and will probably some day have a newspaper."[10]

It was Culture, however, that had drawn John Lomax to Austin. Mignonette Carrington put him in touch with an informal town-and-gown group which was meeting in the evenings that summer to read and discuss Shakespeare. Lomax probably knew some of the plays from his tenure at Weatherford (although he later claimed, disingenuously, that the study group provided his first exposure to the Bard). It was through this society that he became acquainted with one of the University's stalwarts, Professor Leslie Waggener of the English department, who was also serving that year as interim president of the University. Waggener's brief but significant influence on Lomax was perhaps more important than Shakespeare's; in time, Waggener's son, Leslie Jr., then a senior at the University, would play an even larger role in Lomax's destiny.

Dr. Waggener saw the raw talent and burning ambition in John Lomax, praised his contributions to the evening study group, and encouraged him to enroll in his senior Shakespeare class that fall. That was the very thing John had hoped to find. Filled with anxiety over what he felt to be his intellectual shortcomings, he welcomed any opportunity to leap ahead of his lowly freshman status.

That state of mind may also help to explain why he fudged on his date of birth when he registered for the fall semester. Enrollment for the University's 487 students took place on September 23, which, as it happened, was John Lomax's twenty-eighth birthday. Conscious of the disparity between his age and that of the average student, which was just over twenty-one, he began the practice of shortening up the year of his birth, to the extent that by the time he graduated two years later, he was three years younger than when he entered. (He soon settled on 1872, a "year of birth" which prevailed as late as the 1916 edition of *Who's Who.* After that, approaching fifty, he began to revert to the true year, 1867.)

Having signed up in the Academic Department (Arts and Sciences) and paid his $30 "matriculation fee" Lomax waded furiously into the course of study that would take him to the "majestic A. B."—the degree of Artium Baccalaureus. Carrying almost a double load—"twenty-three recitations when the normal number was twelve"[11]—he undertook courses in English, history, math, chemistry, Greek, Latin, and Anglo-Saxon:

> Never was there such a hopeless hodge-podge [he wrote later]. There I was, a Chatauqua-educated country boy who couldn't conjugate an English verb or decline a pronoun, attempting to master three other languages at the same time . . .
>
> But I plunged on through the year, for, since I was older than the average freshman, I must hurry, hurry, hurry. I don't think I ever stopped to think how foolish it all was.[12]

For Dr. Waggener's Shakespeare class he worked all night at a fever pitch on what he claimed was the first essay he'd ever written (an assertion which, like the one about not having read Shakespeare before he came to

Austin, probably ought to be discounted). He turned in the paper reluctantly, fearing he'd disgraced himself forever and would be asked to leave the University. Instead, Waggener praised his work and, on the basis of its merit, awarded him credit for three additional courses in English. With other credits in math, Lomax soon found himself "more than a fifth of the distance to the magical A.B. degree" and was officially classified a sophomore before the end of his first semester.[13]

The hectic pace never slackened, but as he grew more secure in his academic work, Lomax found time for extracurricular activities. He joined the Rusk Literary Society, one of three such campus groups which together published a monthly magazine, the *Texas University,* and he soon became one of its six associate editors. He was also initiated into the oldest (and, in the estimation of its members, most prestigious) fraternity, Phi Delta Theta. Among the current members and later initiates of Phi Delta Theta, he was to meet several men who would become lifelong friends and affect the course of both his personal and professional life.

Among these were the future historian and scholar Eugene C. Barker; Norman Crozier, later longtime superintendent of Dallas schools; and Rhodes Baker, who established a prominent law practice in Dallas. Within three or four years this circle of Phi Delta Theta intimates would be enlarged by the arrival of law students Edward Crane and Edgar E. Witt (later state legislator and lieutenant-governor), the brilliant and ill-fated litterateur, Harry Peyton Steger, and funny, wonderful Roy Bedichek, a man for all seasons. Two of Lomax's instructors, Morgan Callaway and David F. Houston, were Phi Delta Theta "fratres in facultate"; in widely disparate ways, both would have a strong impact on Lomax during this period.

Fraternal activities widened the sphere of his social life, and he found still other relief from the tedium and isolation of burning midnight oil. He was active in the local YMCA, attended more or less regularly the Tenth Street Methodist Church, and joined a campus social organization, the West Texas Club (described by an early biographer as one of several groups "with a serious purpose," but it was in fact an informal fraternity of good-timers who fancied themselves wild and woolly men of the Old Frontier).

In early 1896, Lomax moved into "B. Hall," the men's dormitory, leaving behind the relative isolation of his rooming house and further broadening his circle of acquaintances. By this time he was putting together a monthly *Texas University* magazine column on alumni affairs and occasionally submitting poems and other material.

In January the magazine printed his review essay, "William Lawrence Chittenden—Poet Ranchman," which couples evidence of Lomax's budding literary tastes with an early and instinctive attraction to regional topics. Chittenden, author of "The Cowboy's Christmas Ball" and other occasional pieces published as *Ranch Verses* by G. P. Putnam three years earlier, was an easterner who had inherited a ranch in West Texas and lived there off and on between travels to various parts of the world. Lomax had a personal interest in reviewing Chittenden's book; traveling to Chautauqua in the summer of 1894, he had encountered the author aboard a steamer from Galveston to New York and struck up a friendship—or at least an acquaintance close enough to allow him to refer to Chittenden in print as "Larry."[14]

Lomax's commentary on *Ranch Verses* is most significant for what it reveals of his early interest in topics that were regional and, in particular, Texan. He especially valued "the spirit of the plains" in Chittenden's work and the writer's unique ability, because of his background, to capture the western landscape and atmosphere: "In him is blended and mingled Eastern culture and training and the wild-dash of cowboy life on the plains." Warming to his interest in the odd flow and mix of disjunctive cultures, Lomax approvingly quoted "someone" who had remarked that Chittenden was "a rare combination of Northern force and Southern fire—the Puritan and Cavalier." The statement might have described Lomax himself; if his force was hardly "Northern," it longed to be, intellectually at least, and it was certainly Puritan enough. All his life, John Lomax would look north, not to home, but to approval, power, respectability; and to the degree that these things eluded him—or that he felt they had—the North also would remain a locus of vast ambivalence.

In "William Lawrence Chittenden—Poet Ranchman," the emerging prose style was a product of its time and place—high Victorian as imitated by a bright and ambitious Texas farm boy—but Lomax's ideas were very much his own. Chittenden was not, in fact, a very good poet, and Lomax knew it. "As to the contents of the volume, much might be said and much best be left unsaid," he wrote tactfully, merely suggesting that its "many faults" would be obvious to any careful reader. Ultimately, Chittenden's merit lay in his choice of subject matter; Lomax found it curious and regrettable that "the cowboy has had to wait so long for a poet." Now that Chittenden had appeared, "all Texans should honor him as the faithful painter of a phase of Texas life now being fast supplanted by other industries."[15] Lomax was wrong in thinking that Chittenden's poems would be enduring chronicles of cowboy life, but that notion expresses a major impulse in Lomax's character and work: the urge to preserve the old and valued ways of life he had known, ways which he felt were disappearing forever.

Despite his heavy academic load, in the spring of 1896 Lomax assumed the additional burden of running the *Texas University* magazine when its newly elected editor, Otto Praeger, fell ill and had to leave school. The current issue was already behind schedule and most of the small staff had jumped ship to work on the more glamorous campus yearbook, *Cactus.* Almost singlehandedly Lomax struggled to get out the April magazine, somehow finding time to editorialize on a variety of subjects: the intellectual climate in the South, academic integrity, the merits of the honor system, and the future of higher education. His outlook was invariably that of the unabashed University booster, strong for popular student issues and a high-minded champion of all that bespoke "a noble manhood, a pure womanhood, an unfaltering devotion to the Truth." The only negative note sounded on athletics—or more precisely, on the lamentable emphasis on football at the expense of more noble pursuits.[16] It was an issue that would dog him intermittently for years and eventually involve him in a major crisis at the University.

As his first year at the University of Texas drew to a close, Lomax began to make plans for the summer. His attention was attracted to the University of Chicago, under the vigorous leadership of its new president, William Rainey Harper. Among other innovations, Harper had inaugurated a strong summer school program, which was widely promoted through advertisements in the student publications of other institutions. These included the *Texas University* magazine, where the ads were sponsored by "The Texas Society of the University of Chicago" for the express purpose of recruiting fellow Texans. Few knew of Lomax's plans except Cousin Lon, who again encouraged him and offered to help with expenses. By mid-June he was on his way to the Windy City, where he took lodging in a boardinghouse on Cottage Grove Avenue near the university.

The city excited him, but he had little time for sightseeing or social pleasures. Within a few days he was back at the academic grind, "grubbing away" sixteen hours a day at Latin, Greek, and beginning French. As soon as the session ended, he headed straightaway for Austin, taking off only a few days to visit his mother in Meridian.

· · · · ·

Things were humming along at the University. Lomax returned to find the campus wired for electricity, and work had resumed on the east wing of the Main Building. The regents had approved plans for a gymnasium in the basement, and the much-longed-for University bookstore was about to become a reality. Most important of all, the institution was in the hands of a new president. Leslie Waggener had died in August, only weeks following the appointment of his successor. The new president was George Tayloe Winston, a forty-four-year-old North Carolinian with strong credentials and a reputation as a progressive educator. Following graduate work at Cornell, where he obtained the M.A. and LL.D., he had served some twenty years at the University of North Carolina, first as professor of literature and for the past six years as president. An indefatigable speechmaker and fund-raiser, he had doubled the school's income and almost tripled its enrollment. Now he came to Texas nationally renowned as a champion of higher education and a strong administrator. He was a published scholar as well, and his warm, outgoing manner initially brought him wide support from the diverse constituencies—students, faculty, fellow administrators, townspeople, and legislature—which a state college president must serve. Just such a man was needed to lead the gawky, rough-cut young University of Texas into the twentieth century. Winston seemed—for a time—to be the perfect choice, and like nearly everyone else, John Lomax took to him immediately. "Dr. Winston . . . is manly, courageous, and progressive," he announced in the pages of the campus literary magazine.[17]

By this time, Lomax's opinions were beginning to carry weight among faculty and administrators as well as the student body. After little more than a year's work—severely hard labor, to be sure—he was classified as a senior and due to graduate with the Class of '97—assuming that, as usual, he would plow through another arduous semester, juggling Latin, Greek, French, English, government, history, and philosophy. He was also up to his ears in extracurricular activities: Phi Delta Theta, Rusk Literary Society, YMCA (where he still held the office of corresponding secretary, even as his religious conformity was slipping away),[18] the debate team, recreational tennis, and an increasingly busy social life. Contrary to usual practice, he was reelected editor-in-chief of the *Texas University* (now renamed the *University of Texas Magazine*). And he soon extended his literary interests to the new student newspaper, *Alcalde,* along with staff work on the yearbook.

· · · · ·

The *University of Texas Magazine* continued to struggle for contributions. When Lomax's first issue of the 1896–97 school year finally appeared in November, the *Alcalde,* a persistent critic of the magazine, found it on the whole "not very creditable." Then, in an odd, inexplicable move—perhaps to quell hostilities between the two publications—Lomax got himself named an associate editor of *Alcalde.*

This unusual relationship turned out to be short-lived, but it had some interesting ramifications. *Alcalde* was essentially the private enterprise of a student named L. E. Hill, who also served as manager of the baseball team and general factotum for campus athletics—interests strongly reflected in the pro-sports character of the paper, which contrasted with the *University of Texas Magazine* and its more elevated, literary, Lomaxian tone. (When Hill graduated in 1897, he took *Alcalde* with him and for a time attempted to make it "A Weekly for Texas," based in Austin, but the paper soon foundered. A dozen years later, it was Lomax who revived the name and used it for the ex-students' publication, a role in which it survives today.)[19]

In any event, one immediate consequence of Lomax's brief tenure with *Alcalde* was that in December the paper "re-reviewed" the November issue of the *University of Texas Magazine* and this time found it entirely praiseworthy. John Lomax was discovering an instinctive talent for office politics.

As one of the older and more sober-sided students (one, moreover, with experience as a teacher), Lomax had found favor from the beginning with faculty and administrators, while at the same time his social instincts and natural inclination to play big brother made him a favorite among fellow students. Increasingly, he was drawn into closer association with the University establishment, forming warm relationships with several professors and being called on from time to time to perform small chores related to student affairs, as a sort of informal liaison between the administration and student body. Not infrequently, he and other students thought to be mature and reliable were enlisted to help lobby the legislature, adding still another dimension to his developing political skills.

Outside class hours Lomax was spending considerable time in the office of Judge James B. Clark, who was in effect the University's operating officer—his nominal title was that of proctor, but he also performed the duties of registrar, librarian, secretary to the faculty, and general custodian. Clark, whose white handlebar mustaches and goatee gave him the appearance of a bald Colonel Sanders, was a genial southerner with a droll sense of humor and an unflagging devotion to the University (he had been a member of the original board of regents). Like Leslie Waggener, he was a Harvard man ('55) and an ex-Confederate officer. Throughout his tenure of more than twenty years, Clark was one of the most respected figures on the campus, loved and admired by everyone. More or less under Judge Clark's wing, Lomax was brought into personal contact with President Winston, whose stock John invariably boosted in the *University of Texas Magazine* and the *Alcalde.*

Winston, after taking office with such bright promise, was beginning to need all the support he could get. His aggressive tactics were creating sparks in the legislature and upsetting administrators of other schools, particularly those of religious institutions, who always railed against the state-supported universities and who now saw in Winston a new, double-headed threat: he was mounting a sweeping campaign for more and more tax dollars, and, even worse, the man himself appeared to have no serious religious convictions. Evidence of the latter were acts of omission rather than commission—he attended church only irregularly, belonged to no particular sect, and failed to embellish his public utterances with the familiar old pieties. To fundamentalist Texans that was tantamount to Godless Atheism . . . and no telling what heathenish vileness it would lead to on the campus at Austin, already suspected of lax moral fiber.

Winston's liberal attitudes at first won him strong support with the student body, many of whom, like John Lomax, were less conformable than older generations and eager to slip the bonds of narrow puritanism. But all too soon the president's strong hand began to thrust itself into student affairs. Lomax, trying to work up support for the administration and besieged on all sides by critics, felt himself increasingly alone in his defense of the president. Winston took to visiting classes at random and quizzing students on the spot; he interfered with the seniors' plans for Class Day; and he convened campuswide meetings whenever the notion struck him to make speeches and lecture the student body on a variety of subjects. Worst of all, he made a secret effort to sabotage the school's celebration of Texas Independence Day—and then baldly admitted the crime.

It's debatable, but as holy days go, only Christmas—maybe Easter on the side—is more sacred to true Texans than March 2—the date in 1836 when Texians at Washington-on-the-Brazos declared their independence from Mexico. The flame of patriotism has dimmed a bit in later times, as the noble event fades into the mists of history, but in Lomax's day, loyal sons of Texas, wherever they might be—on native soil or flung 'round the world—raised a glass, fired a gun, and sat down to a celebratory dinner on March 2. Curiously, what the state and its citizens honored as a matter of course, the University of Texas even by 1897 had never formally recognized—at least not by officially suspending classes for the day and otherwise supporting the enthusiasm of patriotic students.

In 1897, correction for that oversight was sought by a delegation of Law School juniors, led by John Lomax's young friend and fraternity brother, Tom Connally, who petitioned President Winston for the day off to hold a campus ceremony.[20] Winston, a foreigner from North Carolina with a broader view of patriotism, replied that he thought the Fourth of July more fitting, and holiday enough. Whereupon the junior Laws marched out to the local arsenal at Camp Mabry, procured an old army cannon, and, on the eve of Texas Independence Day, dragged it to the campus and made ready to fire it off the next morning. Winston, discovering the plot, personally undertook to sneak up in the night and spike the cannon.

The aroused students found the obstruction in time to remove it and fire the cannon on schedule, but such treachery sorely offended them. They were even madder several weeks later when Winston casually confessed that he was the culprit. The *Alcalde*'s editor, L. E. Hill, who had been writing outraged editorials on the matter, referred to Winston as "the wily President" and hinted that had the guilty party been less highly placed, he would have answered to a vigilante band. Winston responded by calling Hill "a stupid ass."[21]

John Lomax was popular with the student faction, many of whom, like Tom Connally and Bates McFarland, had come to rely on him for counsel and leadership. At the same time, he had a long habit of deferring to authority (at times bordering, some felt, on obsequiousness), and his genuine regard for Winston made him a staunch defender of the administration. As battle lines were drawn and the conflict escalated, he found himself in no-man's-land.

All this turmoil, piled on two years of intense mental and physical stress, took its toll. For all his show of strength and outward calm, Lomax was still haunted by feelings of inferiority, sensitive to real or imagined slights, and plagued with periodic spells of depression. Bone weary, he had been subject all along to innumerable minor, undiagnosed illnesses, and still suffered the effects of a bout with the flu back in January. Unable to shake it, he was finally forced a month later to resign the editorship of the *University of Texas Magazine.*[22] This did little to lighten the load; he simply redirected his energies to the college yearbook, the *Cactus,* producing for it a history of the Rusk Literary Society, several incidental poems, and—of greatest consequence—the dedication, a long, adulatory biographical essay on President Winston.

In April, as the yearbook was about to appear and Winston's feud with the *Alcalde* and the student body escalated, the many irritations pressing on Lomax were brought to a head by several unrelated events, producing a mighty, if only momentary, eruption. It began with a flap over who would plan the Final Ball, social event of the year for seniors. Lomax felt he had either been condescended to or slighted—perhaps because of his defense of Winston—and loudly declined to serve on the committee, taking space in the *Alcalde* to announce that use of his name in connection with the affair was "without [my] knowledge or approval." The lingering aftereffects of Winston's calling the *Alcalde* editor a "stupid ass" only exacerbated the situation. Caught in an untenable position between the president and the student body, Lomax abruptly resigned from the *Alcalde* and stalked away in a huff.[23] He may have soon regretted these petty outbursts, but they were the sort of thing that would become a distinguishing mark of his behavior in coming years.

• • • • •

In any event, he had other matters to deal with. His long, wearing struggle to gain a serious education was nearing an end, but the fruits of that labor weren't exactly falling off the tree. Looking back, he regretted the furious pace with which he'd pursued the coveted degree: "I had given myself no time to look around me or plan for the future. I had been blindly rushing somewhere, I didn't know where." Perhaps it was enough that his experience at the University had exposed him to a few true scholars and given him "intellectual independence," as he termed it: "The little I knew, I knew that I knew."[24] Still, there was the matter of earning a livelihood. He'd assumed all along that he'd return to teaching—but no more fifth-rate "academies" and "colleges" like Granbury and Weatherford. Now it was full speed ahead to some fine school—a *real* school—in one of the state's big cities—Galveston or Dallas or even the very largest, San Antonio. With his usual industry and thoroughness, he composed a sober Victorian application in his best copperplate hand and assembled some twenty letters of recommendation from men of eminence in the state, including former governor James Hogg (whose exuberant son Will was Lomax's classmate), the Speaker of the Texas House of Representatives, the state's attorney general, the commissioner of the General Land Office, and a number of prominent bankers across Texas. All praised him highly and without reservation. Said his old mentor at Weatherford, David Switzer: "Mr. Lomax . . . [is] a fine instructor, a good disciplinarian, and an excellent Christian gentleman."[25]

But graduation approached, and nothing happened. He went to San Antonio to interview for a job as a grade school principal, applied for a tutorship in the math department of the University, tried to wrangle an opening at a private school in Austin—all without success. In early June, scarcely two weeks before commencement, the *Alcalde* carried a notice to the effect that Lomax and his classmate Sol Acree would "conduct the summer session of Miss Carrington's University Preparatory School this summer."[26] That didn't happen, either.

CHAPTER FOUR

• • • • •

Come All You Fair and Tender Ladies

1897–99

Two days before his graduation from the University of Texas in June 1897, Lomax was called to the office of President Winston and offered the job of registrar of the University. He saw this as belated but much-deserved recognition of his many talents and his stalwart service as a student leader, just when he was about to despair of any employment at all. But there was both more and less to it than that.

Although he had by this time committed himself to a career in education, his visions of the future were reaching beyond the classroom. He was prepared to teach if he had to, but more and more he had come to feel that his real calling lay in some sort of educational administration—as principal or superintendent or college official, perhaps even (when he dared the greatest dream) a dean or president. He wasn't sure just what a "registrar" did, but it had an imposing ring, and the job seemed likely to point him in the direction he wanted to go.

In reality, "registrar" was just one of many hats which the genial but overworked Judge Clark had been wearing as secretary of the University. The work was essentially clerical; almost anyone could do it, the administration felt, and relieving Clark of such an incidental chore would ease his burden. The whole business may, in fact, have been largely engineered by Clark with the single intention of providing a job for Lomax.

In any event, the work of registrar which the judge had been performing was so thin and ephemeral that when a separate position was created for Lomax, it was immediately necessary to expand the duties of the office. That eventually spelled trouble. In addition to the nominal business of enrolling and maintaining records on each of the University's five hundred or so students, Lomax soon had the responsibility for all official University correspondence, served as the president's personal secretary, and in time was charged with managing the affairs of the men's dormitory, "B. Hall."

That was not all. To get the job, he had to agree to continue being a student and complete the requirements for the M.A. in two years. To Lomax that was another sword which cut in many directions. Once fiercely eager for all the education he could get, he'd now gotten enough of the more formal and sometimes numbing details of "taking courses" and piling up degrees. Moreover, he was worn down physically and mentally; having acquired the coveted "Artium Baccalaureus," he now coveted its rewards, real or imagined: a lucrative salary, professional standing, and the respect that he'd always assumed was due the graduate of a reputable university. It was soon clear that, as registrar-cum-graduate-student, he was little more than a flunky for the administration, a gofer with a modest title. His salary was $75 a month—perhaps $800 in current dollars.[1]

For the time being, however, he needed a job, and here was one. In the face of challenge, he stiffened, as he always had, and plowed soberly into this new task. After all, it was certainly as lofty as anything he could have imagined ten years before, when he'd sold his horse and gone off to school at Granbury.

Approaching the age of thirty that fall of 1897, Lomax had finally reached maturity—rather belatedly in the eyes of some. More important to him, he had tangible evidence of his arrival—"a clawhammer coat and a hand bi'led shirt," as the cowboys back in Bosque County put it, a degree from the state university, and a job in the office of its president. He could be addressed as "professor," and sometimes was (in those days it was often informally applied to any degreed member of the staff; Lomax claimed to disdain the term but made a show of casting it off). Long before, he'd acquired the professorial manner: pictures from the time show him solemn, sometimes stern, gazing coolly straight ahead or magisterially staring off into the distance; in groups he is a marked contrast to the rest of the crowd, who beam, smile, or mug for the camera. Later there developed the image of him as a big round bear of a man, but in fact he was never very large—about 5'10" in height and considered "delicate" in his movements, light on his feet and capable of a distinctly jaunty air. In this period he had yet to gain his distinctive weight and rotundity. The baldness—an equally distinctive feature, of which he was inordinately sensitive—was not yet complete but steadily spreading, a subject of sly humor among his classmates and friends. One of them caught him perfectly in a single telling line; he was, she joked, "a dignified pedagogue with not enough hair to mention."[2] Cousin Lon kidded him about "complaining and doctering" his thinning hair and suggested that "an invalid come [comb] is the propper thing."[3]

Weighty bearing and a balding dome had not impeded his social progress. He worked consciously to overcome his natural shyness and sensitivity. After all, a man on the move did not sit in the corner or hide his light. To his pleasure and some surprise, he had learned that he was not incapable of charm when the occasion required it. He was also an instinctive storyteller, and that had made him popular in a number of circles.

Equally natural was a talent for playing Dutch uncle. Almost from the time he arrived at the University, he'd become a confidant and counselor to the other students, who perceived him as older (few knew just how much older), wiser, and more levelheaded. This included any number of young women. As a member of a social group called "Lover's League," he was known as "J. Amorous Lomax," with the title, "Official Protector of Freshman Girls." His friend Rhodes Baker wrote him news from Dallas of "the young lady who made such a scientific assault on you," and John himself, feigning mild shock, reported that seven girls were simultaneously in love with him.[4]

All this involved a certain amount of flirtation, casual and otherwise, but on the whole he seemed content to play more high-minded roles, in loco parentis—as older brother or father-protector or perhaps, at most, kissing cousin. Many girls treasured him simply as a steadfast good friend and occasional escort: these included his classmate Florence Lewis; Maude Smith, a graduate student; Judge Clark's daughter Edith and her cousin Jessica from Dallas; undergraduates such as Florence Edith Weymouth, Jessie Wood, and the Prather sisters, Grace, Fannie, and Mary Lou (whose father, "Col." William Prather was on the board of regents and later became president of the University). While a few of the younger, more jejune may have thought themselves in love with him, he held them mostly at a distance. Romantic idealist that he was, Lomax was also fastidious and the somewhat spoiled son of a doting mother, a circumstance which, as an early biographer noted, had some bearing on his attitude toward women: "Like the ideal Victorian gentleman, he seemed to consider all women with whom he was more or less intimately connected as designed for both his comfort and his adoration."[5] That was true, and yet a bit harsh; he had not yet found the subject worthy of his undivided attention, and when he did, he could be—or try to be—as selfless as any man in love. In the meantime he was satisfied with Victorian parlor visits, filled with flowers and formality, in the languid Texas Sunday afternoons, along with excursions aboard the *Ben Hur* on Lake McDonald, group outings, and long tramps in the hills west of Austin. Woven through it all was an embroidery of paper, a flurried exchange of invitations, thank-you notes, birthday cards, mannered billets-doux that alternated between sweet blandishments and lofty discourses on literature, religion, ethics, and politics.

One female of Lomax's acquaintance was outside the usual circle of students and in fact did not even live in Austin. She was Shirley Green, a lively, petite, and altogether fetching young woman in the town of Palestine, some 150 miles northeast. The orphaned daughter of a prominent southern family, she had done graduate work in Spanish at Vanderbilt and busied herself with cultural and church-related activities. She was known, according to a contemporary account, as "one of the most accomplished young women in the state and [one who] counted her friends by the score."[6] Making her home with her older brother, Caldwell, a successful real estate developer in Palestine, she traveled about the country, attending literary and art functions as well as those of the Christian Endeavor Societies of Texas, in which she was active. At home she conducted an evening school for students who worked during the day or otherwise wanted to extend their education to prepare for college. Eugene Barker, future Texas historian and by this time one of John Lomax's close friends at the University, had been her pupil as a teenager, in the days when Barker supported his widowed mother by working as a machinist and blacksmith in the shops of the Missouri-Pacific railroad. Shirley Green was a similar force in the lives of other Palestine youths, including Jessie Wood and Norman Crozier, who had gone on to the University and were now prominent in the Lomax circle.

Although she had been enrolled only briefly as a "special student" at the University of Texas, Shirley Green's interest in education made her a strong supporter of the school, and she had taken it upon herself to call on President Winston early in his tenure to voice her confidence and wish him well. Lomax, then in the last semester of his senior year, was introduced to her one day in the course of "helping out" Judge Clark in the president's office. More than a year went by before they met again.

By the spring of '98, it was increasingly clear that George Tayloe Winston's days as president of the University were numbered. His rigorous efforts toward campus reform had alienated the faculty-student population, and the regents were offended by his officious manner and high-handed tactics. Registrar Lomax, seen by many as Winston's toady and an administration spy in the student camp, shared the president's unpopularity. After scarcely six months on the job, he reported himself "the reviled and despised personage of the University."[7] There was open conflict between Lomax and many of the students he had considered his friends. In at least one instance, the principals reverted to the law of the frontier, and fisticuffs ensued.

Engaged in a misunderstanding with the administration, law student Birch Wooldridge, star halfback of the football team, became convinced that Lomax was carrying damaging rumors about him to Winston. Failing to resolve the dispute, Wooldridge withdrew from school in anger and made plans to leave Austin. As he stood at the west entrance, waiting for a hack to carry him to the train station, Lomax strolled by on the way to his office in the Main Building. According to a later account,

> Very little time was spent in preliminaries or discussion. Wooldridge first recalled to Lomax the cause of his grievance and history says that Wooldridge struck the first blow. Wooldridge was not a very large man but was strong as an ox, well trained, active and athletic, while Lomax was a student [i.e., not athletic] and, then as now, was pursuing the divine afflatus of poesy. It is asserted by some that Lomax tried to calm Wooldridge by reading a cow-boy poem to him, but the ire of Wooldridge was not to be soothed by any such homeopathic remedies, and he proceeded to break up the meter of the Registrar, leaving him nothing to do but sail in.[8]

And sail in he did. Seizing an umbrella, Lomax whacked away with such force that the handle broke. Later in the fray, he resorted to a large rock and was about inflict it on Wooldridge's skull when an onlooker stepped in and stopped the contest. Witnesses called it a draw, but all attested to the battle's ferocity: "The walk was torn up from side ditch to side ditch, the abrasions on its surface showing that the fight was not a Sunday school affair by any means."[9]

Harassed and despondent, torn by his loyalty to Winston and his attachment to the University, Lomax pondered some way out. When war with Spain erupted in April, he gave serious thought to joining his young friend Tom Connally, who was trying to enlist in the First Volunteer Cavalry Regiment, led by Col. Teddy Roosevelt. But Connally was turned down, Lomax vacillated, and soon the Rough Riders were landing in Santiago without either of them. Cousin Lon wrote as usual to kid John; he had heard a rumor that his young relative had enlisted but was pleased to know that "you reconsidered the matter and thought that fifty dollars per month at home would beat 13½ and fighting Spaniards in Cuba."[10] When the Splendid Little War ended in August, Lomax was still at the University, fretting through the summer and doing his best to defend the beleaguered Winston. For comfort and diversion there was only the usual dull round of social events, Sunday visits, silly picnics, and boring boat rides. Then things began to brighten.

In late July he had been invited to a gathering at the home of his friend Maude Smith, whose mother boarded prominent female students and saw to it that they were regularly exposed to "culture" beyond the classroom. This occasion was both social and instructional; Lomax was pleased to learn that the guest of honor was Miss Shirley Green of Palestine, the charming young woman he had met in President Winston's office the previous year. She was visiting in Austin for a few days and had been asked to present her views on higher education to the assembled group at Mrs. Smith's. A spirited, experienced speaker, Shirley Green was also an ardent champion of books and ideas. She spoke highly of the progress of liberal education at the local institution, John's alma mater. Here was a kindred spirit, and what's more a very attractive and mature one (she was only a year younger), socially prominent and—unlike the college girls he knew—more nearly elevated to his intellectual level. He was much impressed and praised her "contagious enthusiastic University talk."[11] Very soon, "impressed" turned to "smitten."

There was a lengthy, intense conversation between the two of them after her talk, and the next day they went on an outing to Mt. Bonnell. His first letters reached her the day she returned to Palestine. To "My Dear Friend," Lomax wrote that in their brief time together, she had "aroused the slumbering best in me," but stopped short of saying he was in love with her. He wanted her "dearest friendship" and would persist until he got it. But perhaps she would think him impulsive and prefer that he be more conventional in making his suit. Miss Green replied: "I hope you won't ever be conventional with me, for, to my mind, it tends to shut out many of the 'best things.'" It was a sentence that might have come from a Henry James heroine. Remaining aloof from the main issue, she managed to be coolly proper and at the same time mildly teasing: "You asked for a line, and this is much more. If you hadn't specified, I might have written you a letter. Good'b'ye, Your friend, Shirley R. Green."[12]

The letters continued in a flurry, two and three times a week, well into September. Classes were about to start at the University, and in addition to his duties as registrar and student, Lomax was busy with the affairs of his youngest sister, Alice, whom he had persuaded to come to college at Austin. Alice, then twenty, thought she might prepare to teach school but couldn't make up her mind; she was finally enrolled as an "irregular student," with a full course load but no specific degree plan. Alice seemed mostly interested in having a good time. John wrote Shirley that his sister was leading him into all sorts of dissipation; the previous evening she had taken him to a Negro cake walk on the *Ben Hur,* which he found "ludicrous" but more entertaining than the Negro church services he'd attended.[13]

Within weeks the strain of separation had grown too great. He wrote Shirley that he could visit her in Palestine on the second weekend of the month if she were willing, and she responded politely: "Do come."

He knew that her health was delicate, despite her many activities and busy social schedule. It turned out that she was planning a vacation trip to Mexico, and would depart, via Austin, on the evening of the same day planned for John's visit. Thus it happened that, after a pleasant, formal Sunday afternoon in the Greens' parlor in Palestine, they shared a seat on the night train back to Austin. In the darkened coach, they exchanged confidences and spoke nobly of dreams and hopes for the future. He read to her Browning's "The Last Ride Together" under the flickering light of a wayside station, then gave her his treasured volume of the poet's work. Yet John, still determined not to be impulsive, could not bring himself to declare his love.

A day later that declaration was in the mail, in three separate letters of the same date. He had waited to write, he said, because it did not seem proper to speak of love that night on the train, so early in their acquaintance, although he had known then with certainty that he loved her "beyond the love of a friend." He feared that this headlong rush might overwhelm her (as indeed it did), and should this outpouring diminish him in her eyes, he could only blame "my impetuous, impulsive self."[14] This was followed by a letter almost every day for the next week, fervently asserting his love, apologizing for his "incoherent style," pleading for a response. By this time she was in Mexico and traveling ahead of forwarded mail by several days.

It was more than a week after he first wrote that she received his declaration of love. In the meanwhile, their letters were crossing in the mail; all he got from her were chatty little travelogues posted from San Luis Potosi and Mexico City, stops along her way toward Cuernavaca. Now the outpourings of his soul were being issued daily, sometimes twice a day, scribbled at his office desk whenever he could steal a few minutes from the rush of fall enrollment. By the time he got a response to his first letter, almost two weeks after it was written, he was a wreck, suffering not only immense emotional turmoil but eyestrain and headaches as well. Her letter did not help matters much. Addressed politely to "My Dear Mr. Lomax," it was mostly devoted to another long, breezy account of her travels. Only at the end did she remark merely that she had enjoyed the night on the train and was not offended by what had transpired.[15]

Beside himself but undaunted, Lomax kept up the assault, pleading with her to "write me frankly." After a lapse of several days, she responded only that the reason for her silence on the matter was simply that she didn't know what to say. "Remember, if you will, my tempestuous and emotional temperament, and think what your letters must have been to me since two weeks ago tomorrow." Their friendship must not end, she wrote, but the matter of love must wait until she could face him in person—"or when my heart is quieter."[16] From all accounts, Shirley Green was anything but "tempestuous and emotional," but the situation clearly brought her stress and confusion.

Her letters continued to be filled for the most part with travel news. She reported being "kodaked" by two small boys, and, unlike her traveling companions, tried to avoid being a Tourist. "During the Fiesta I got to be very Mexican," she wrote of a visit to Chapultepec, "rubbing against them in thick crowds, and sitting flat on the pavements and in the Parks among them; the others hired chairs, etc., and seats in the balconies, while I had all the fun."[17] She complained of the Daisy Millers she encountered, young American girls, who "forget that their sisters at home are judged by their conduct abroad. Gaiety is well enough, but pitching bread across the table, though I do it myself sometimes *at home*, is not exactly comprehended by these conservative Mexicans."[18]

In the face of her cool travelogues, Lomax turned formal, reporting enrollment figures (a record 493 by mid-October), news of the football team ("we are weak in the ends and need a full-back"), and other prosaic news from the campus.[19] He further hoped to impress her with long, statesmanlike letters written on the stationery of Phi Delta Theta ("John A. Lomax, President").

When that strategy produced no result, he quickly took matters to the other extreme, telling her that he felt he could continue writing no longer.

Only time ("that grim, relentless, often cruel healer of hurts of the heart") could resolve the question of their relationship. He rebuked her for saying that she enjoyed his letters, remarking that their correspondence was "pitched in too widely differing keys." Yet he could not resist a wry joke at his own expense, telling her he would not be surprised to learn that the discord in their letters as they passed each other on the mail trains awakened the passengers and frightened the train crews.[20] In the meantime another serene missive arrived from Shirley, and he ardently resumed his suit, enclosing fragments of love verse and again proclaiming undying devotion. Fearing that such rapid alterations in his behavior would make her think he was not resolute, he said, "I do not claim to be [resolute] . . . I am only in love."[21]

In this cyclic fashion the affair progressed through the fall—John alternately lofted on the wings of love, then plunged into darkest depression, devastated one minute, on the rebound the next, Shirley all the while sailing calmly along, still addressing him "Dear Mr. Lomax" and signing herself "Your friend, Shirley R. Green."

The brief passages of their letters devoted to intimate matters were surrounded by long, high-minded discourses on Life and Art, complete with reading lists. She recommended *The Rubaiyat* (which her physician pronounced "that horrid book"), *Aucassin and Nicolette, David Harum, Richard Carvel, When Knighthood Was in Flower,* and various issues of the *Atlantic.* He was reading Kant for his philosophy course and Shakespeare's tragedies for the seminar with Prof. Mark Liddell (whose instruction he found "too coldly anatomical to be entirely pleasant to my emotional nature").[22] There was always Browning, of course, and Robert Louis Stevenson and Chesterfield's letters to his son (parts of which John read in French, or said he did). He was much interested in the views of Prominent Men of the day, following Lyman Abbott's series of sermons on "The Seven Stages of Man" in the *Outlook* and quoting David Starr Jordan (the eminent zoologist, then president of Stanford University). Jordan had observed that the best government was not that which administered best, but which made the best men. And great men, said Lomax, were not created by rule or religion but "evolve from within . . . The individual must *become* out of his individuality."[23]

. . . . .

Just what was evolving from within John Lomax was not yet clear. The seeds of his dogged self-reliance and egocentric conservatism are surely contained in that remark, but it reveals almost nothing of the nature of his ambitions at this stage. There is some meager evidence of literary aspirations, but none that indicates that he had either the talent or the intention to pursue a professional career in the world of letters.

In his senior year he'd written a slight piece of doggerel ("Emily to Jack") for the yearbook and during the next year or two continued to publish bits of verse and prose there and in the *University of Texas Magazine*, which by then was under the editorship of his friend, Tom Connally. The subject of his poetry was invariably Romance, the treatment either frivolous or gloomy, the diction stilted (full of phrases like "cliff and scaur," "sore distress," and "desolate sepulchres"), the results adequate but commonplace. There were no poems about cowboys, or Texas, or anything certifiably real in the existence of John Lomax.

Shirley Green may have figured vaguely in the impetus for these efforts, but probably not; the dates are a bit too early and the effect so generalized, so conventional as to suggest nothing more than an uncertain urge to imitate what he'd been reading—Browning, Arnold, and the lesser poets of the time. When his romance with Shirley was in full tilt, he turned to more particularized subjects—"Robert Browning," "On James Thompson," "To a White Violet"—as an outlet for similar feelings, and these on the whole are more successful.[24]

At their best, Lomax's early poems (and there would never be many afterward) are scarcely more than the work of a talented amateur, but they poignantly illustrate not only his lyric sensibilities as a young man but also the attraction which language held for him—especially language shaped and transformed in some way, wrestled out of its everydayness. This natural interest in heightened forms of human communication would reveal itself in due course a few years later, in his growing involvement with the language and songs of ethnic and occupational groups—cowboys, blacks, mountain folk, Hispanics, almost any such element of society whose unique culture might be identified and preserved in the words it spoke and the songs it sang.

Evidence of conscious interest in such material in those early days is scant, and mostly circumstantial. His autobiographical story, first related in 1934, of coming to the University of Texas with a "tightly rolled batch of manuscript of cowboy songs" in his trunk was widely discounted almost as soon as it appeared, and among the scoffers were those who knew Lomax at close range. According to his account, he took the roll of cowboy songs to English professor Morgan Callaway, who pronounced them "tawdry, cheap, and unworthy," whereupon young Lomax, crushed and embarrassed, carried the roll out behind Brackinridge Hall and burned it. The existence of the "tightly rolled batch" of cowboys songs is otherwise unsubstantiated. If his work with such material had its beginnings in this period, no clear proof survives in either his papers or other contemporaneous records.[25] There is, however, one piece of circumstantial evidence to suggest at least a passing interest.

In the January 1898 issue of the *University of Texas Magazine* there appeared an anonymous article entitled "The Minstrelsy of the Mexican Border" (an obvious debt to Scott's *Minstrelsy of the Scottish Border*) which recounts the grandeur of the old days, "the days of the Cattle Kings," when "some uncouth ballad of the ranch and range, or of old fights of the border outlaws, was always on the lips of the cow-boys." The piece is short—only four pages—and the prose sometimes a bit ripe, in the fashion of the time, but it covers much ground and conveys the message cleanly: these songs and singers are dying away, and that is regrettable. The writer's concern is not only for his native area north of the border; attention is also given to "the songs of the Mexicans," which the author finds more numerous than those of the Anglos but having "less right to be called folk-songs" because they are more often changed by those who sing them (clear evidence that, for better or worse, the author lacked a mature sense of folksong scholarship). Fragments of several songs, including "Bury Me Not on the Lone Prairie" and "Sam Bass," are quoted and analyzed. The article closes with a lament for the passing of such songs and the men who sang them: "Better things, it may be, are coming in to take the place of the cowboys, but to these as the years go by, will be added a glamour that the things that have driven them into the west and down to death can never hold. No furrowed field can ever make a man forget the prairies and the magic of their call when Spring is breaking, no harvest gathering can ever equal the rough assemblage of the round-up, and no man in all the world can ever take the vacant place of 'the last cavalier.'"[26]

The coincidences between this piece and Lomax's later work are too great to ignore. Nine years afterward, when he was at Harvard for his M.A., preparing to report to Professor Barrett Wendell on his first formal researches into cowboy songs, the phrase "The Minstrelsy of the Mexican Border" was one he considered, then rejected, as a title for his paper. Only a few pages of that paper survive, so it cannot be compared in detail with the anonymous magazine article of the same title, but the subject and the treatment are the same. "Bury Me Not on the Lone Prairie" and "Sam

Bass" from the earlier essay are presumed to be a part of the report for Wendell; both were later incorporated into Lomax's first published collection. Even more tellingly, a third song mentioned in the magazine piece, "Billy Lamont and Jack Lorell" appears in a class essay which he wrote at Harvard in 1904—and it is found nowhere else (apparently he was never able to collect more than a fragment and so never published it).

Whether Lomax wrote it or not, "The Minstrelsy of the Mexican Border" was ahead of its time; it stands out, alone among all the stilted, hothouse literary vapors wafting through the pages of the *University of Texas Magazine,* as an original, almost radical statement directing attention to the values of an indigenous culture and warning of the necessity to study that culture before it was lost in the passing of time. If Lomax *was* the author, as the evidence strongly indicates, the article is valuable as his first published commentary on matters which would soon become his compelling interest and form the core of his life's work.

· · · · ·

By late 1898, Lomax's affairs were in another serious muddle. He was "not quite morbid," he had written to Shirley, but complained that frequent "attacks of melancholia" had marked him deeply.[27] Overworked and frustrated in love, he was also plagued with health problems, especially eyestrain and headaches. Mental aggravations continued to mount—more repercussions from brother Richard's shoddy business affairs and financial strain from the rest of the family (he was the major source of support for his mother, and others were constantly borrowing from him, or trying to). As usual, he had taken on too much work, trying to juggle three graduate courses in addition to his duties as registrar and aide-de-camp to Winston, whose situation was steadily deteriorating.

By November it had become clear that Shirley did not intend to return to Texas before Christmas. John was disconsolate. He had been counting the days until he could make his suit in person; now it seemed the waiting would go on and on. Then his friend George Halstead, a much-traveled bachelor professor in the mathematics department, announced that he was spending the Christmas holidays in Mexico and invited John to accompany him. Shirley by that time had reached Cuernavaca, a beautiful little resort town some forty miles southwest of Mexico City, long favored by tourists and wealthy *Yanqui* travelers drawn to the region by its zestful climate and historic ambience. Among its attractions were the scenic gardens built by Emperor Maximilian and the majestic villa of his empress,

Carlota. From the Hotel Morelos, a small but popular resort and spa where she was staying, Shirley wrote John a glowing account of the area ("This is the valley, you know, that was granted to Cortes by the Crown"). She made plans for him to visit her there, but fretted politely that he wouldn't come: "See all the Christmas sights in [Mexico] City, and, if you don't come to Cuernavaca, you must tell me about them later."[28]

Wild horses could not have kept him from Cuernavaca. He arrived two days before Christmas, bearing small gifts, copies of *Judge* and *Punch,* and an umbrella she had asked him to retrieve from her hotel in Mexico City. (She also requested strawberries from her favorite stand in Contreras, and he had ordered a monthly supply, but the vendor proved to be a con man, and no strawberries ever arrived.)

Shirley met him in a fashionable red gown with a spray of white violets at the breast, her dark hair draped in a bright serape. That evening on the veranda she played the guitar and sang "La Paloma" and "La Golondrina"—"sensuous love songs in the long, soft, twilight air of this retreat of Montezuman kings and queens," John wrote later. The next day, donning a sombrero and riding habit, she took him on horseback to see the sights. Their outing ended in Maximilian's gardens and a romantic stroll in the twilight. Near a waterfall in a grotto by the lake, among the ruins of fallen statuary, they sat on a weathered pedestal, and John solemnly recounted the story of his life and love which he had been pouring into his letters over the past many weeks. There was a long, poignant silence when neither could speak. Unable to contain himself, he stood and walked away, but she called him back. Another silence. He held her hand to his lips and touched the lace on her sleeve; they rose and went away in the falling light.

Nothing had been openly expressed—except, of course, his love for her, which by now she had heard many times—but there was the tacit understanding between them that matters would proceed apace. She had not said yes, but she had not said no, and John did not want to press his luck. It was enough, for the present. Struck by the languor and romance of the event, he was willing to drift and let fate run its course, insisting, as he wrote later, that now he would "love beauty as I found it," rather than risk tarnishing it by "peering into its secrets."[29] A year later he would still be adrift, still living in the afterglow of Cuernavaca and sadly recalling it to Shirley in yet another desperate plea for her to declare herself.

He had left Cuernavaca determined to believe that she loved him as ardently as he loved her. Now and then one of her letters would betray fleeting evidence of that, but at best they were merely flirtatious. Most were routine accounts of her daily activities. While he was pouring out his heart to "My Dearest Love" and "My Dear Little Sweetheart," she continued to address him as "Mr. Lomax," which drove him wild. He would accuse her of writing merely friendly letters and she would reply earnestly that they were much more, but without saying what she thought they really were—then suddenly she would tell him to stop writing entirely while she thought things out. He almost never heeded these instructions, and indeed, sometimes before he'd even received them, she would have another warm and chatty letter in the mail, perhaps complaining coyly that she hadn't heard from him lately.

But for one reason, all this might be dismissed as little more than the normal convolutions of two emotional, loquacious people very much in love.

Although the announced purpose of Shirley Green's trip had been to "study Mexico," it was widely understood that she was there for her health. For some time she had suffered prolonged colds and coughs, weight loss, and periods of fatigue. Just when the first diagnosis of tuberculosis was made is unknown, but the symptoms were manifest by the time Lomax returned from Mexico. Shirley's brother in Palestine, alarmed by reports he had gotten from her American doctor in Cuernavaca, urged further examination.[30] Shirley cheerfully reported the results to Lomax: "[Dr. LeBaron] did not reverse his decision about the trouble that *had* been, but even his great reserve could not conceal his amazement when he found the air passages, as he expressed it, 'clear as a bell.'"[31] The examination, unsupported by laboratory tests or X ray, was rudimentary by modern standards. But Shirley was determined to view the situation optimistically. Two weeks later, after weighing herself at the Wells Fargo office and finding that she'd dropped to a hundred pounds, "almost two pounds less than three weeks earlier," she dismissed the matter, blaming the station agent who operated the scale. "There is a mistake," she said blithely, "but anyway, one never grows fat in Cuernavaca."[32] Lomax urged beer as a tonic and arranged for a supply to be shipped, but good Methodist that she was, she declined the offer, on the grounds that her doctor forbade it. John was flabbergasted to learn that she had ridden horseback thirty miles one day, and on a man's saddle at that. She needed someone—ostensibly, himself—to look after her, he scolded, "whether or not you will allow it to be done."[33]

In the absence of the miracle drugs and therapy of the twentieth century, tuberculosis was invariably fatal. It is the nature of the disease to progress in cycles—periods of illness followed by apparent recuperation, then eruption again, increasingly severe, a pattern played out over many months, often years. In this progression-regression-progression cycle, the general course is always a downward spiral, yet the patient may be ill one day and seem well the next. By March, Shirley had undergone just such an apparent recovery, and she began to make plans to return to Texas.

There was much to be packed and loaded; she had jokingly warned John that when he saw her he could identify her as the lady with "a Chihuahua dog, a cage of parrots, seven clay pitchers, and three Mexican blankets, not to mention the 'accessories of traveling.'"[34] After several delays because of weather, she was finally on her way. John had implored her to let him meet her en route in San Antonio, but with no explanation she went directly on to Palestine. He took that, and the fact that she did not invite him to visit, as evidence that it was all over. She didn't love him as he had hoped, he wrote, complaining for the hundredth time of her "cold and formal 'Mister Lomax,'" which made him feel that he could never again address her as Shirley. But he couldn't bring himself to that. "Oh, Shirley, Shirley, if only I had won your perfect love!" There his letter ended; he was too overcome—or melodramatic—even to sign it.[35]

Within a few weeks, the crucial invitation to Palestine had been issued, John went to visit, and the affair was on again. She was once more his beloved "Ta" (his pet name for her), although she persisted in calling him "Mr. Lomax." In late May she came to Austin for the University's commencement ceremony, and after an afternoon tryst at the lake, she wrote him that the visit "made my vision much clearer. I am glad . . . that you refused to let me leave unsaid what I had no right to withhold."[36] John's old dreams were renewed, and he plied her again with his visions of their future together.

In August—a year from the beginning of the affair—something cataclysmic happened, so momentous that for the first time Shirley went on the offensive and declared the relationship at an end. Clearly angry and upset, she took him to task for asking "an impossible question" in his last letter and for accusing her of issuing an "ultimatum." "And so I must give it all up—for always, who shall say?" she wrote, "and ask you to withhold that love which has always been so full of charm for me, and which has seemed to me golden—was ever a woman so unhappy in being blest?"[37] The weight of this letter, as well as her anguish in composing it, is borne out by the presence of several drafts among her papers.

Serious and final as it seemed at the time, this contretemps proved not to end the affair, but only to provide it a necessary cathartic. Within a week she had written him using his Christian name for the first time, and she followed that shortly with a letter which was anything but the conventional Dear John: "You must know without my saying it that my life is deepened and beautified through you. You measure up to all the estimates of a man that I read [of] in books, and you have the high and fine integrity, and the clean intellect which do not always go with your rare tenderness. Is this too much for a woman to say except to a man she expects certainly to marry?"[38]

It was another question fraught with Jamesian ambiguity, worthy of the master himself. Regardless of what she thought she meant, or intended to mean, she clearly wanted something from him, but whether it was love or marriage or merely a steadfast friendship (or yet something else, some undefined, still-to-be-invented relationship), she could never be sure for more than a day or two at a time.

Disjunction filled their correspondence. He spoke to her in voluminous detail—about his family, past life, daily routine, reading habits, fears, dreams, ambitions—and he hoped she would respond in like fashion. To his great frustration, she showed little interest in anything he told her, except for events involving the University (and, now and then, his church attendance, which had become increasingly perfunctory). She told him almost nothing personal about herself—it was more than a year before he knew even so minor a detail as her birthday—and despite all the many openings he gave her, she never inquired about his family, or anything else in his life, never confided to him her own emotions or ideas, never revealed any ambitions, never spoke of future plans. The reason seems clear. She knew—consciously or otherwise—that such thoughts and plans were, for her, quite futile. Eventually, they would both come to admit that, although neither would accept its consequences. In the meantime, the cycle continued as usual, over and over. On and on went the letters, "pitched in too widely differing keys."

· · · · ·

Stymied in his relationship with Shirley Green, Lomax's social life thrived on other fronts. As an eligible bachelor and an up-and-coming young man on campus—however besieged by foes of Winston—he was popular with a wide spectrum of people and especially with the wives of his older friends and colleagues, who called on him frequently to act as escort and chaperone at various University functions. He carried on a lively correspondence with Maude Smith, Jessie Foster Wood, and half a dozen other young women who were constantly coming and going. All this was merely a matter of course, with little hint of anything but friendship—although it was at this point that he boasted to Shirley that "a young lady of my acquaintance" had told him at least seven girls were in love with him.[39] At Shirley's insistence, he'd spoken to no one about their relationship, but word had gotten around, without in any way inhibiting his popularity. In addition to the usual round of parties, picnics, and outings on the lake, he played tennis, watched the 'Varsity baseball team beat the "Austin professionals," and went to see *Romeo and Juliet* with his young pal Harry Peyton Steger, a precocious undergraduate from Bonham who would shortly become his assistant in the registrar's office.

The registrar's job was consuming more and more of Lomax's time. In addition to everything else, the state legislature was in session that spring and summer, which meant that the University's budget had to be submitted and defended. Much of that burden fell to Lomax. Lawmakers—in the face of growing animosity toward Winston and general discontent on the campus—had even less reason than usual to act generously toward the school. But largely as a result of much extra work by Lomax, busy "providing our friends in the House with statistics and arguments," he could report at last that the legislators had approved an increased appropriation for the University.[40]

Even that was not enough to save Winston. His resignation was announced in the August *University Record.* Lomax, who owed his job to the man and had embarked upon it with such high zeal, revealed in detail to Shirley just how closely he had been bound up in the tragedies of Winston's tenure at the University. The president's decision to leave had come as a great shock and disappointment, he said, but the failure was not Winston's alone; neither faculty nor students had given him their full support and cooperation. Winston was going away a disappointed man, and he left Lomax "no less disappointed both in myself and in him."[41] Winston, who'd managed to transfer himself to the presidency of North Carolina A.& M., hinted he might find a place there for Lomax. John said that if an offer materialized, he just might consider it, so great was his disgust with the University of Texas.

There was yet another disappointment. Lomax had hoped that Winston's vacated place would be offered to David F. Houston, the brilliant thirty-three-year-old professor of political science who was John's friend, fraternity brother, and former teacher. But Houston's considerable destiny as president of major universities and high cabinet official in national government lay yet some years ahead. To succeed Winston, the University's board of regents named its chairman, Col. William Lambdin Prather, as acting president, and the following year Prather was permanently installed in the post. The choice was reasonable enough (and historically significant—it was Prather's moral earnestness that inspired Lomax's friend John Lang Sinclair to write the famed "Eyes of Texas"), but at the time Lomax saw him mostly as little more than another aging fuddy-duddy who would only add to his woes. He wrote to Shirley of his disappointment that the regents had not elected Houston to the presidency. That would have relieved him of many burdens, he said, for he was being forced to take on "matters outside my province" because he could not bear to see the University suffer.[42] Loyalty to the University of Texas would prevail, but taking on matters outside his province was becoming something of a habit with John Lomax.

CHAPTER FIVE

Trouble, Trouble

1899–1903

Lomax later characterized his six-year tenure as registrar of the University of Texas—from the spring of 1897 to the spring of 1903—as "the worst absolutely soul-repressing, life-killing, truth-crushing situation" he'd experienced to that time.[1] And the major turmoil of Winston's administration simply passed into an endless series of lesser crises under Winston's successor. Colonel Prather, a courtly, aloof figure of some ability, was devoted to the University's best interests, but there was a bureaucratic air about him, and, more seriously in John's view, he lacked Winston's warmth and intelligence.

Further, in defending the former president, Lomax had compromised himself, and the friction between the registrar and others on the campus did not end with Winston's departure. Lomax could pretend to ignore the dissension, but he could not avoid a steadily increasing workload; Prather had a reputation for getting things done, but all too often it was Lomax who had to do them. Under this stress, he began to suffer more eyestrain, severe headaches, and spells of depression—"seasons of the blackest melancholy."[2] Not the least of his afflictions was the lingering, on-again-off-again romance with Shirley Green.

Much of Lomax's difficulty on campus was rooted in a dilemma even he didn't fully understand: his instinctive allegiance to duty was coming into conflict with a growing resistance to any authority but his own. But while his position as a lowly functionary at the University would soon prove untenable, that dismal, difficult time in the registrar's office laid the groundwork for his later prominence across the state. It was here that he gained the experience—and the contacts—that would eventually establish him as a Texas institution.

The job involved a mind-numbing variety of chores. The registrar's office, as he wrote to Shirley Green, constituted only a small part of his duties.[3] Much of what he did related to students' personal lives, work that today is performed by batteries of deans, counselors, advisers, and their staffs. An immense amount of time was spent dealing with prospective students and handling the huge volume of mail that came from poor but ambitious youth across the state ("Can a boy get [a] place down there to work for his bord. And what is the total expense of the school. I am willing to do anything honorable.").[4] Many were letters John Lomax himself might have written only ten years earlier.

Touched by the similarities between their lives and his, Lomax wrote to each one at length, offering encouragement and detailed answers to their questions. Whenever they turned up in Austin, he went out of his way to find them jobs and places to live and often loaned (or gave) them money, in spite of his own meager resources.

These school-hungry, poor-but-honest boys and girls were symptomatic of a rising new order that at first glance seems at odds with the conventional picture of turn-of-the-century Texas as a rough-and-tumble backwash of civilization. It may have been true, as a leading historian has it, that the state "entered the 20th century with its basic society a full two generations, or about sixty years, behind the development of the American mainstream,"[5] but little rivulets of progressivism had begun to bubble up all over: there were any number of Texans who wanted their cultural vistas broadened, their cities modernized, their children sent to college.

Texas would remain predominantly rural for several decades, but it was no longer a frontier state. Its citizens could boast of several beautiful cities (notably San Antonio and Galveston, then first and fourth in population), where modern conveniences such as electricity and the telephone were in common use. Magazines and newspapers were conservative but numerous and widely read. Opera—via touring companies of national reputation—was available in all but the smallest towns (in Austin, pop. 22,258, John Lomax was an avid theater patron). Statewide, a network of railroads and interurban trains took people inexpensively just about anywhere they wanted to go, except, perhaps, in the vast unsettled expanses out west. Lomax, always a ready traveler, had become an almost weekly passenger on a train headed somewhere—to Meridian or Palestine or one of the larger cities. Around the state there was a pervasive sense of "progress," of having outdistanced the raw beginnings of the 1830s and the later calamity of the Civil War and Reconstruction.

The spirit of the times may be detected as early as 1890 in the election of Governor James S. Hogg, who campaigned on a platform promising regulation of big business and espousing a generally altruistic concept of state government. Although any reform of Texas politics is likely to be short-lived, Hogg's influence lasted well into the twentieth century. No little of that influence was due to and sustained by his son, Will, a classmate of John Lomax at the University of Texas. Eventually, as business magnate and philanthropist, Will Hogg applied his father's outlook to financial and civic affairs as well as to art, education, and public health interests. As Lomax's fellow student and sometimes benefactor, he was less successful in spreading the gospel of liberalism, but the two were intimate friends and mutual admirers for years. Lomax called Will Hogg "a typical Texas product," and, for all their philosophical differences, appreciated his virtues as "a civic leader, a renowned cusser, a friend of the underprivileged, a lover of his state and its people, a worthy son of a great father."[6] Had Texas spawned more like Will Hogg, its destiny in the twentieth century might have been far different.

Young Texans who came to Austin in quest of education were propelled by motives similar to those that had driven John Lomax off to Granbury and Weatherford and Eastman and Chautauqua a dozen years earlier. Many were serious in their regard for knowledge as truth-and-beauty, but equally strong was the peculiarly American notion that knowledge was also money, that the surest way to commercial success in the modern world was through the classroom and across the graduation stage. Whatever their motives, increasing numbers were eager to go to college, and the existence of state universities such as the one in Austin made that once-remote dream closer to reality. By the school year of 1901–2, enrollment at the University of Texas had reached 1,240, making it the largest institution of higher learning in the South, just ahead of Vanderbilt. And it was men like John Lomax who, in effect, held the keys to the academy and stood at the gates to anoint the chosen.

The sense of high purpose with which Lomax responded to young seekers after knowledge is one of the more appealing aspects of his character in these early years, before his attitudes were diluted by what one might charitably call a more pragmatic outlook. One can only admire the earnest spirit with which he told Shirley Green that he had almost unlimited opportunities to "help and strengthen young lives, to impart high ideals."[7]

Much as he grumbled about his long hours and low pay, Lomax found the work itself rewarding. The job had one very positive aspect, and he was not unaware of its potential. "The brain and power" that would soon run Texas was being trained at the University, he wrote. "It is great work . . . to control this power."[8] He referred to nothing less than the state's young intellectual and professional elite, rich and poor alike—its future businessmen, mayors, county judges, teachers and school administrators, state commissioners, legal corps, and statehouse politicians (including at least one governor-to-be). These were the people who would run things in the twentieth century; many rose to success performing cultural and technological functions that simply had not existed prior to their generation. They were coming of age at a crucial juncture in the history of the state, poised on the verge of rapid transition from raw frontier to a modern empire of oil and commerce.

Through Lomax's hands filtered the letters of application—indeed, the lives and ambitions and destinies—of those who in a few years would control Texas from courthouse to statehouse, from schoolroom to boardroom. To the extent that he could accommodate them—get them admitted to the University, find them work and housing, lend them money, offer them counsel and comfort—he earned the immediate gratitude of two generations—theirs and their parents'—and invested heavily in the loyalty of still a third, their children yet to be born. It was the beginning of a legendary reputation. John Lomax soon became one of the most visible figures on campus, as well known as President Prather himself.

That was small compensation for all he suffered, but Lomax, steeped in the popular idealism of the nineteenth century, consoled himself with the notion—well founded, as it turned out—that he was making an investment in the future, both his own and that of the young people he served. To Shirley Green he modestly downplayed the importance of his role, but confidently asserted that his influence on students, however slight it might appear, was immediate and would in time prove its worth. When all was said and done, he could honestly assert, "I love the work."[9]

Lomax was saddled from time to time with dozens of other responsibilities. Initially he was the president's secretary (a job later taken over by Roy Bedichek), and he handled virtually all of what would be considered today the University's public relations: advertising for new students, sending out copies of the yearbook and other showcase publications, writing puff pieces for newspapers, corresponding with affluent alumni, and lobbying the legislature. He served on the Alumni Scholarship Committee, oversaw fraternity affairs as president of the southern province of Phi Delta Theta, and from time to time became de facto dean of students and health officer; during a smallpox outbreak in January 1901, the *Texan* reported that "Mr. Lomax is kept busy seeing after the vaccination patients and their friends."[10]

· · · · ·

Another lateral task which Lomax undertook, with more enjoyment and eventually even a bit of profit, was the management of Brackenridge Hall, the men's dormitory, known universally as "B. Hall." Supposedly run on a cooperative plan, the dorm under the previous manager had piled up debts of several hundred dollars. Moreover, students were moving out in large numbers, disgusted by the rowdy behavior of a few and the general lack of control. In January 1901, Lomax was approached with a plan hatched by Lester Bugbee, a popular young history professor. With the encouragement of Professor David Houston, chairman of the dorm's faculty committee, Bugbee, Lomax, and a senior named Frank Lee "volunteered" to run the hall, in return for their room and board and a split of any profits. Unfortunately, after less than a month, Bugbee took sick with what proved to be tuberculosis, left the University, and died within the year. Lomax and Lee toiled on alone. Order was restored and by June the new managers were predicting "extinguishment of the deficit" any day. There was a minor setback when the local bank froze their assets for a time, but Lomax and Bugbee (then trying to recuperate out in El Paso) stood the loss of $150 against back debts, and B. Hall was back in business. By February of the following year, the *Texan* reported that the dorm had a surplus of $300.[11]

For Lomax, the only real monetary profit from his B. Hall venture was realized in the summer of 1901, when the regents in their June meeting "re-elected" him registrar with a raise in salary to $1500 and set aside $600 to hire an assistant to help him run the dormitory.[12] He would continue to grumble that he was underpaid, but it is worth noting that his salary that year precisely matched that of the chief of the Music Division of the Library of Congress, under whom Lomax would serve some three decades later. In current dollars, it was equivalent to about $21,000.[13]

Even with the added burden of B. Hall, Lomax still found pleasure in his work, complaining only of a lack of peace and quiet because his room was too popular with the other residents. For Shirley Green he outlined his daily routine: to bed around midnight and up at 7:30 each morning; after "some gymnastics, a cold bath, and breakfast," he went to his room for a cigar and a few moments to reflect quietly and plan the day. He was at his desk before nine; when the day's work was over, he went for a walk downtown or played tennis.[14] It was not, at least on the face of it, a particularly rigorous schedule for someone who'd once trudged behind a turning plow from dawn to dark in the Bosque County river bottoms. By this time also his workload had been lightened, or at least redistributed, by the appointment of Harry Steger as his student assistant. (The precocious young Steger, described by Lomax as "a nervous, impetuous boy; very bright, very witty," had entered the University at the age of fifteen; he said later that Lomax "stood for several years *in loco parentis* to me.")[15] The only problem with their working arrangement was that both were prone to spells of intense depression; although they formed a fast and enduring friendship, Steger's "violent attacks of gloom" only tended to stir up Lomax's own fits of moodiness. The fact that they were constantly subject to Prather's iron rule and often had to work overtime for weeks at a stretch did not improve the situation.

Still, Lomax found time to socialize, notably as a member of a male campus group known as "The Great and Honorable Order of Gooroos" (he occupied the office of "Sybillene Priest"). He entertained relatives from home—his mother and Cousin Lon were frequent visitors, and his young brother Rob was in and out of town, attending football games, taking summer school classes, and sampling what to him was the rather fashionable life of his bachelor older brother (to whom rural schoolteacher Rob was merely "an unsophisticated country pedagogue").[16] John could afford so cavalier a stance toward his younger brother; he might not be making a lot of money, but he was highly connected at the University, squired pretty girls to the opera, and on a weekday afternoon could report that he was still in his "party clothes"—cutaway coat, white tie, and striped trousers—having just returned from a reception at the governor's mansion.[17] Not bad, as they liked to say, for an old country boy.

Lomax's allegiance to the University of Texas was firm—or so it seemed. In fact, he was reaching another crisis point. Earlier, he had boasted to Shirley Green of all the work he was doing, putting "my heart and life into it," and shortly declared that his "life work and plans" were becoming "strongly entwined with my alma mater."[18] But only a few weeks later, in the summer of 1901, he was considering a move to Texas A&M and that fall wrote to his congressman in Washington about openings in the consular service or "educational work in the Phillipine [*sic*] Islands."[19] When nothing came of those efforts, he talked of moving to Shirley's hometown and starting over at some job better suited to his talents and ambitions but one that would still leave him free to be his own man. Should such an opportunity present itself, he would not hesitate, he said, to abandon his otherwise "promising and permanent work" at the University.[20] Such drastic talk was partly meant to move her at last to "speak the long-sought promise," but it was drastic talk nevertheless.

The crisis had been forming back in the summer. By now the workload in the registrar's office was so heavy that he had virtually suspended his studies for the M.A. Moreover, family matters were again pressing on him. He'd been footing bills for Richard and loaning money to Rob; now his sister Alice was creating problems. After only a year at the University, she'd left to teach school in a small rural community south of San Antonio but grew increasing unhappy there and quit as soon as the first term was over. She seemed entirely at loose ends, disinclined to return to college, get a job, or otherwise conduct herself as the family thought she should. As always they looked to John for help, and he had little choice but to take on Alice's "problem." As if that weren't enough, Cousin Lon had fallen ill with what was later diagnosed as cancer of the throat.

Feeling harassed from all sides, Lomax abruptly laid plans to attend the summer programs at Chautauqua, New York, and take Alice with him, in the hope that the excursion might shake her out of her doldrums. They booked passage on a steamer from Galveston to New York, and at the last minute, brother Rob was added to the party—also at John's expense. The trip was pleasant but largely uneventful, the major exception being an altercation in New York with a pickpocket aboard their streetcar. Catching the thief in the act, Lomax demanded the return of his wallet, containing $250; never one to be careless with a dollar under the best of circumstances, he was not about to let some Yankee street ruffian walk away with a sum of that size. Back at the University, Judge Clark summarized the episode for a friend; Lomax, he said, "attacked the thief then and there, was knocked down by him, 'riz' and went at him again, fought him all the way down the car, women screamed, 'cop' came to the rescue, thief bagged, money restored,—curtain falls on Lomax smiling but a little worse for wear and tear."[21] The story was widely reported in Texas newspapers, and Shirley applauded his bravery.

On their return to Texas, Alice went to Meridian, where their older half brother, James Terrence ("J. T.") Lomax, had opened a general mercantile business with John's childhood friend, Johnny Cochran. John Lomax, a silent partner in the business, suggested that a job might be found for Alice in the store. J. T. agreed but reluctantly; he didn't think Alice would stay—and if she did, there was "a certain man of this place" lurking around and paying her too much attention.[22] The family had had vague suspicions earlier that some star-crossed romance was the cause of Alice's moods, but she earnestly assured John that she was not romantically involved and had no intention of marrying.[23] John believed her, then regretted it when, without a word to him, she suddenly announced her marriage in November. He felt that she had repaid him badly for his efforts to help her. He was much grieved by the affair, but at least, for better or worse, the "Alice problem" was off his hands.

Unfortunately, his own romantic tangle was not so quickly resolved. The Shirley Green affair remained as unsettled and unsettling as it had been from the beginning. John went on issuing periodic declarations of love and proposals of marriage; Shirley warmed from time to time but steadfastly resisted giving him the promise he so avidly sought. On at least a dozen occasions over the next year or so, one or the other—usually John—declared the relationship ended, done, up in smoke, only to have the other breathe it back to life with some gentle, loving gesture and a conciliatory letter.

A serious rift had taken place in the spring of 1901, when John pointed out that more than three years had transpired since Cuernavaca, and a resolution was no nearer than it had been then. A few weeks later he returned her letters and gifts, including "the soiled Cuernavaca handkerchief." Shirley was too despondent to hold a pen, and pleaded for time. By late summer, when he had returned from New York, they were exchanging polite notes, devoted mostly to daily affairs and literary matters.

At one point, however, reflecting over John's old letters and reading Marcus Aurelius in a collection of essays entitled *The Mystery of Life,* she was moved to something deeper. Earlier he had written that he was certain they belong to each other forever: "You are mine now in life or death." Shirley took vigorous exception ("No words have passed our lips, and certainly no thought has been in my heart . . . to justify that conclusion"), but what disturbed her most was the thought that in the event of her passing—all too imminent to her—he might never love again. And with a heavily stressed "*if,*" she managed to be ambivalent even about the "life" part of relationship: "*If* it ever came about that we should belong to each other *in life* wouldn't that be enough—except the poetical thought that beautiful lives together may be held to go on after what we call ('misname') death."[24]

Death was much on her mind; in another letter of this period it was abruptly in the open, stripped of any effort to be stoic or gaily indifferent. Explaining something which he had earlier misunderstood, she wrote:

"Those words meant this: that when I let my nature sound its depths in loving, the knowledge of death and separation would kill me." Just before "death" she started to write "certain," but crossed it out after the first four letters.[25] That was too stark and sudden, even for her. But what had been said, clearly and unequivocally, for the first time, was that she could not marry him because she knew she was dying.

• • • • •

When their letters were not Victorianly romantic (or, increasingly, tragic) they were literary—also according to the manner of the age, in which a part of the courting ritual was to display one's "noble and refined" reading habits. In addition to his constant favorites, Browning and Shakespeare, Lomax reported on Richard Burton, Kipling, Ruskin, Carlyle, Thackeray, J. M. Barrie, John Stuart Mill, and Montaigne. He had struggled manfully with Kant's *Critique of Pure Reason* and pronounced it "an epoch-making conception," but one in which the meaning was "clouded with words—and very hard words at that." (Writing a paper on Kant, he said, was the most difficult thing he'd ever done.)[26]

Although Shirley occasionally dipped into Emerson and Marcus Aurelius, her reading generally followed a lighter vein, with a marked preference for such popular novels of the day as *The Gentleman from Indiana, The Ruling Passion,* and *The Man from Glengarry.* Yet she shrank from anything too modern and forthright, and when she complained of "a certain courseness" [*sic*] in Owen Wister, Lomax defended *The Virginian* on the ground that its author had deliberately set out to write "a novel of realism."[27]

There was more than a little self-interest in that argument, but it affirmed a literary view as well as a personal one. Throughout his life Lomax spoke out against what he considered to be social sham and hypocrisy and leaned heavily on the noble savage argument to justify his own lapses. All of polite society, he said in the same letter, was founded on artifice, and he referred to a German philosopher he had been reading (probably the poet Heine) who said, according to Lomax, that the instinctive love for children and nature was nothing more than a longing for the honest and natural simplicity of ancient Greece.[28]

Curiously, for all the bookish activity in their letters—flurries of titles, lengthy quotations, determined efforts to appear "up" on Literature—the names of major or noteworthy American writers were conspicuously missing. Emerson is one exception; another, more tellingly, is Hawthorne, whom Lomax thought of when he was trying to describe his own bleak state of mind, remarking that it was Hawthorne "who found so much sadness in the . . . isolation of the human soul."[29]

In spite of her determination to keep a happy face, at times even Shirley admitted to feelings of gloom. "*How is* a perfect love to grow out of the exquisite sufferings we undergo?" she wrote him with a rhetorical flourish in September 1901.[30] Their little quarrels and tiffs were taking on an increasingly harder edge, but there were still pleasant interludes. When the Grau Opera Company announced its Texas tour that fall, John and Shirley planned for weeks an excursion to Houston for a performance of *Lohengrin.* At the last minute, her health faltered, and they had to cancel the trip, but a few weeks later she came to Austin and John took her to hear Nordica sing the Brünnhilde of *Die Walküre.*

Wagner was not a favorite of Lomax, who told Shirley that with the exception of an oratorio he had heard at Chautauqua, he preferred small ensembles to mass histrionics: "I like the music without calisthenics, if you please." Violinists or vocal soloists were fine, but he had little use for opera, which he felt was all artifice and "tawdry sham."[31] That was his deep streak of realism speaking, and it would intensify through time. In later years he constantly complained about art music, "citified singers," and choral interpretations of black music by such groups as the Golden Gate Quartet and the Fisk Jubilee Singers, whom he felt were "machine-like and insipid" and produced an artificial music that lacked the feeling of its original sources.[32]

Disagreeing with society's artistic standards and openly criticizing Shirley's tastes was a new tack for John, and more than once the theater was the target of his sniping. When Shirley wrote that she thought Richard Mansfield "fine" in *Monsieur Beaucaire,* he replied bluntly that Mansfield was overestimated. "He mumbles his words; once he roared," and everyone knew Monsieur Beaucaire couldn't roar. Besides, Mansfield was too fat for the role, although he was better as Beaucaire than as Cyrano.[33] Shirley got in her licks as well, roundly trouncing a story, entitled "Shadows," which John had written and published in the 1901 yearbook. "You were your own worst enemy in 'Shadows,'" she said (and she was right; the story is shapeless, pretentious, and unrelievedly sentimental).[34]

Lomax's only other excursion into print during this period—and for some time to come—was a brief document entitled "The Legislature and the University," written for the December 1901 issue of the *University Record* to report the University's recent success in obtaining an appropriation of $380,563, the largest in the school's history. The registrar's office had provided the spadework and adroit public relations which made this victory possible, but except for noting pointedly that he was present throughout the legislative debate, Lomax maintained a properly objective tone, setting forth a balanced, incisive view of the complex issues affecting Texas education. While he obviously needed to sound grateful for the generous appropriation and avoid offending any lawmaker, he used the piece to argue vigorously against privilege for the wealthy and to promote his view of the University as a haven for the poor boys and girls of the state.

Despite his strong interest in student welfare (and quite in contrast to his own activities as a student leader only a few years earlier) he now argued that students should not be allowed to lobby the legislature in behalf of the University. Perhaps it was partly because of his own blighted experiences in that role, but there was a larger reason as well: "Members of the Legislature do not wish instruction from students whom they regard as little more than children." He did not say so, but the implication was clear: it was just possible that students *were* immature, and the registrar ought to distance himself from them. "The men who influence [the legislature's] decision must be tactful and wise; and the clearest manifestation of this tact and wisdom is to wait until information about the University is desired."[35] Yet he continued to insist that students had his sympathy and understanding, writing to a correspondent that he took pride in knowing that he had not forgotten how students felt, nor "how to interpret fairly and justly [their] point of view."[36]

He was remarkably bold in pointing out the University's enemies in the capitol. Some legislators were disinterested or simply too lazy, he said, to make the short walk from the capitol to the campus and see for themselves what grand work the University was doing. Others drew on a narrow interpretation of the state constitution to deny funds, or were simply political hacks and opportunists. Near the top of the list of foes were "men who are out of harmony with the spirit of the founders of the republic"; here Lomax's native sentiment led him to the remarkable assertion that Texas's war for independence from Mexico had been "an educational revolution" to provide proper schooling for its youth—surely news to most of the fierce and rapacious old Texians who fought that war.

Nevertheless, Lomax counted those early patriots first among the University's supporters, along with "men of college training" and "men of broad outlook on all public questions." Thus politically and patriotically he embraced all the critical constituencies. These were the powers arrayed against the forces of evil, and "in the end, the conservatives, the men who think much and talk little, won the battle." Clearly, he was on the side of the conservatives, but to see this as a political statement is to misunderstand the term as it was known to decades of Texans, the great majority of whom liked to think of themselves as "conservative." In lowercase, "conservative" might embrace a spectrum of social and cultural attitudes, none of them particularly consistent. While Lomax would move steadily to the right, his political stance was often subject to some rather baffling mood swings—in "The Legislature and the University," for example, he managed within the space of two sentences to denounce populism at length while attacking the rich and defending the democratic right of poor boys and girls to an education. The seeming inconsistencies were deep in his background and early life, and they would widen and intensify in the coming years.

• • • • •

After "The Legislature and the University," Lomax had little time for writing beyond the routine scribbling required by his job, although his former English professor, Mark Liddell, encouraged him to publish his poetry. He was even too occupied, he told Shirley, for any social life these days, stoically asserting that "My books and thoughts keep me entertained and busy." Yet within weeks his letters were filled with news of tennis games, picnics, and trips to the races with various young ladies. He reported that he was taking Maude Smith to the President's Senior Reception and Edith Weymouth to the Final Ball.[37] Shirley gave him her tacit blessing; for months she had been encouraging him to see others and introducing him to her young female friends, in the hope—unspoken but obvious to them both—that she might, in effect, "hand him off" to someone else.

This was despite the fact that by now she had clearly declared her love for him and, except for her illness, would have given him the promise of marriage that he sought[38]—and thus their relationship took still another unusual turn. It was settled: they loved each other and no one else, but as for going any further, they would simply have to see what the future held. In the meantime, John would go on about his life, having friendly social relationships with any number of young women in Austin, while Shirley remained in Palestine, venturing out whenever her health permitted to attend to her various church and cultural activities. When their paths happened to cross somewhere around the state, they were, however briefly, oddly, and impermanently, "a pair."

One day in June, Lomax was interrupted at his office by a visit from Bess Baumann Brown, one of the young women Shirley had persuaded him to correspond with. Before moving to Dallas from Palestine, Miss Brown had been among the circle of bright young people that Shirley collected about her, a group that also included Eugene Barker, who had overcome severe financial handicaps, earned an M.A. in history at the University, and was beginning to make a name for himself as a publishing scholar.

Miss Brown was down from Dallas, where she had been operating a kindergarten, to visit relatives in Austin and look over the University, with an eye to enrolling there in the fall. The registrar's office was a natural port of call, more especially in view of her previous correspondence with the occupant, and Bess Brown, a pert and outgoing young woman, barged in without an appointment. Busy as he was, Lomax gave her his full attention, delighted to find his correspondent so attractive and charmingly exuberant. They were just working up to a polite Edwardian flirt when old-friend-from-Palestine Eugene Barker appeared. Miss Brown, awed by Barker's new scholarly fame, pronounced him a "celebrity" and, to his lasting embarrassment, gushed on at length. Lomax withdrew.

As it turned out, both Barker and Lomax had been outdistanced by Roy Bedichek, President Prather's student secretary down the hall, who had spotted her in the library the day before and "made an engagement," as Lomax reported it, for the following evening. John had only small favors to be grateful for. Miss Brown had given him such a look of welcome in her "pretty blue eyes," he told Shirley sadly, that he had at least forgotten how weary he was.[39]

All was not lost. A week later, when it was time for Miss Brown to leave Austin on the afternoon train, Lomax called at the home of her aunt and uncle to say good-bye. Whereupon the girl impulsively postponed her departure until the following day, and after conferring with her aunt for the proper approval, she and John went out to dinner. The meal lasted over two hours, he told Shirley: "—the lady has such an astonishing appetite!" Moreover, while they were eating, she had flirtatiously thrown him a kiss ("a real missile," he explained) across the table, then rebuked him for not returning it.

At last he felt that he had met someone who, because she was also an old friend of Shirley's, would understand and sympathize with his situation. When he wrote to Shirley thanking her for finding such a friend for him, she wrote back, "Isn't it delightful to run across a girl like Bess Brown? You won't tire of her either—she gets nicer all the time, and she has an unusual wit upon provocation. There's a girl that you or Eugene should have captured—she is almost nice enough for either of you!"[40]

When Bess finally left on the train Monday morning, John was there to see her off, clearly enchanted. He had taken her to the station and left Harry Steger to deal with the dozen or more people waiting in his office. Miss Brown, he wrote Shirley, was as refreshing "as a glass of old, rare wine."[41] To Bess he apologized for having been "tired and stupid" during their visit and thanked her for letting him talk to her about Shirley. She was a godsend at a time when he needed one desperately, complaining that while he did not want to pose as overworked and unappreciated, he had few friends (his fault entirely, he said) and his time with her had soothed and restored him, enabling him to ignore "the vexing, useless, artificialities that encumber every life."[42]

The purple tone was as instinctive as it was intentional, but the plea genuine: he badly needed a comforting hand and a sympathetic ear, for almost nothing in his life was going well. In April, his mentor and friend David Houston had left the Department of Political Science at the University to take the presidency of the Agricultural and Mechanical College, a job which Lomax wanted and, rather unrealistically, considered himself qualified for.[43] His only consolation was the thought that Houston, once established in office, might rescue him with a job in the English department. Weary of the constant toil of the registrar's office, he considered another trip to Chautauqua when summer school was over in July, but then a special session of the legislature was called for the middle of August. Before that could take place, Lon Cooper began to sink rapidly, and on August 1 he died.

All through the summer Lomax had made hurried trips to Clifton, rushing off on weekends to sit long hours by Lon's bedside. It was an arduous journey by train and wagon out to the farm, and on the morning of Lon's death, just hours before the end, John wrote to Shirley complaining of a sore arm caused by driving a span of mules and cutting firewood (as a result of which his penmanship, which "Miss Brown" had admired, was suffering). Lon's voice was gone, and John reflected sadly on the long talks they once had, in the years when he was teaching in the area and came to visit. Lon always met him at the station, often at night, just so they could talk together alone.[44] The death of the man he knew as his "best friend and foster father" left him grieved and disconsolate for many weeks.

In this mood he told Shirley once more that if she couldn't decide to marry him, he would withdraw completely from her life. Then he backed away again and, even before she could respond, fired off two more letters saying essentially that, whatever ensued, they would "always be friends and companions." When she wrote, Shirley responded more to the flurry of mail than to its content. "Aren't you going to give me a chance to say a word!" she said snappily.[45] And that was all she said.

There matters stood for several weeks, when Shirley announced that in the early fall she would be going East for her health. John first threatened, perhaps jokingly, to run off with her, then wrote that, because of the press of business, he couldn't even come to Galveston to see her off aboard the steamer *Comal.* Instead, he sent his prescription for seasickness, advising her that she'd make a first-rate sailor if she'd only put aside her "teetotaler scruples enough to take a little whiskey and lemon" and stay on deck in the fresh air.[46] She bore the trip well, although by this time her health was so precarious that the slightest relapse sent her to bed for days, and she was never sure which siege might be her last. En route to New York, somewhere off the coast of New Jersey, in a mood of melancholy she copied a stanza of Tennyson's *In Memoriam,* addressed it to John in a watertight package, and slipped it into the sea.

Perhaps trying to rationalize his failure to win her hand, John wrote that he couldn't marry her even if she'd said yes because he was once again in financial straits (later he admitted it was a false alarm). In any case the events of the past year had almost broken him—his doctors told him, he said, that he was "run down from long hours and little recreation"—so he planned to ask for a leave of absence and look for some way out of his situation at the University.[47]

If he expected sympathy from Shirley, it was not forthcoming. She wrote gay little accounts of shopping in New York, playing tennis with "the richest and sportiest" of two young men at her hotel in Bolton-on-Lake George, and gushed over "a charming letter" from Roy Bedichek: "Some of those *boys* there in Austin ought to make a name in letters—if perchance they can do as well by the public." Her health seemed improved, and she even managed to make a fainting spell sound cheerful and unimportant. Her stopping places included the classier spas in the East—at one she noted that another of the guests was "a brother of Henry James [Robertson "Bob" James, apparently]—rather bad mannered—a cousin to Barrie—who teaches Golf." With newlywed relatives she visited Niagara Falls and teasingly told John that the "bride and bridegroom scheme impressed me favorably. . . . I thought of packing my trunk and going straight home to be married." In the next sentence she wrote "Don't run," then crossed it out.[48] Speaking her true heart's dream at last, she had still tried to dismiss it as a joke.

The truth of her deteriorating condition began to show through the cheerful facade. With the first snowfall, she wrote, in an almost Emily

Dickinsonian vision of death, "I love the hints of approaching winter, and someday I think he'll take me in his strong old arms, and tuck me in under his soft snows, and have his winds whistle me to sleep—and the awakening will be better than Spring, and violet and dogwood."[49] She spent Christmas in Syracuse, confined to bed in her hotel room, but on returning to New York felt well enough to attend the opera.

On January 21 she wrote her ultimate "Dear John" letter: "For two weeks I have been trying to get myself together to write this—that I hope it won't bother you much to quit loving me." She had not, she said, found another; "it is only that the heart has died out of me, and I can't feel the proper interest in it."[50] John wrote that he was terribly hurt by her decision, but that he would try to live with it. Earlier he had limply invoked Elizabeth Barrett Browning in his cause, telling Shirley that "Love made a new life for Mrs. Browning," and she lived longer.[51] Now he ventured another halfhearted attempt to change her mind, but there was no further word from Buffalo, where she had gone for medical attention. A month later she was dead.

• • • • •

Accompanied by his loyal friend, Tom Connally, newly elected to the Texas legislature, Lomax attended the funeral in Palestine on February 22. The next day he wrote to Bess Brown that he had seen Shirley laid away beneath a mound of flowers—"my sweet Shirley, the sweetheart of five years of hope and fears."[52] On his desk were the lines Shirley had copied from *In Memoriam* and cast out on the sea, later recovered on the beach by one of a ship's crew at Shore Harbor, New Jersey, and sent to Lomax:

Hence forward wheresoe'er I roam
Thy blessing like a line of light
Is on the waters day and night
And like a beacon guards me home.[53]

PART TWO

• • • • •

Exile and Return

One who never turned his back but marched
 breast forward,
Never doubted clouds would break,
Never dreamed though right were worsted,
 wrong would triumph,
Held we fall to rise, are baffled to fight better,
Sleep to wake.

—Robert Browning, *Asolando* (1889)

CHAPTER SIX

Married Me a Wife

1903–4

When Lomax left the University of Texas early in the summer of 1903, he was gone almost before anyone knew it. The board of regents had renewed his appointment at their June meeting, but by the time their action became official, with the publication of the minutes in the August *University Record,*[1] he was taking afternoon strolls along Lake Michigan and reading Tennyson and Browning in a quiet old manse not far from the University of Chicago.

At the time the regents met back in June to consider hirings and firings for the coming year, Lomax was over at College Station, eighty miles to the east, in the office of David Houston, newly elected president of the Agricultural and Mechanical College of Texas. A few days later, on June 27, Houston confirmed Lomax's appointment as instructor of English at "the A&M," starting in September at a salary of $1,200 for the nine-month term.[2] Lomax cleaned out his desk in the registrar's office, wrote his resignation to President Prather, said a brief but emotional good-bye to Judge Clark, and caught the Morning Flyer northbound to spend the summer in the Windy City before going off to A&M.

The roots of this abrupt defection were deep and varied, but the real crisis had formed in the months following the deaths of Lon Cooper and Shirley Green. The loss within six months of two of the people closest to him—three if Lester Bugbee is counted—crushed whatever spirit he had left from months of hard work, frustration, and disappointment. Time had become a menace; he would soon be thirty-six years old and had little to show for his tenure as registrar but eyestrain and recurring headaches, animosity from students and faculty, the ingratitude of his superiors. If he felt alone and neglected it was not without reason. Family matters were still frayed from the squabbles with Alice and Richard; his coterie of admiring young ladies at the University had graduated; Bedichek was busy finishing his degree; and Steger had gone off to teach school at Bonham. Tom Connally still came occasionally to "stay all night"—an old Texas custom that expressed the closest sort of comradeship—but Connally had the legislature and a law practice in Marlin to occupy his time. That left only John's new friend, Bess Brown, and she was in Dallas, two hundred miles away.

The previous fall, in the wake of Lon's death, Lomax had made vague plans for a year of travel or study—Harvard figured loosely in these plans—but the regents declined to give him leave. After Shirley died in February, he applied again, asking for the summer off, and was again turned down. Only Judge Clark was sympathetic, and his influence was not enough to sway Prather and the regents. Feeling stymied at every turn, Lomax spun on his heel, as it were, and went off to A&M to confer with David Houston and, in due course, to teach English there.

For an erstwhile company man like Lomax, that was a rash act. For a while there were mutterings and rumblings in Austin. But with the campus mostly deserted for the summer, the awkwardness of the affair eventually faded, and wagging tongues consoled themselves with the notion that Lomax had merely jumped from the frying pan into the fire—a thought that had occurred to him as well. But if going to off to A&M turned out to be a comedown, he had at least successfully negotiated what later schools of management would term the First Law of Wingwalking: Don't let go of what you've got a hold on until you've got a hold on something else.

Bess Brown was playing an increasingly larger role in his plans, and it was partly on her account that he had mixed feelings about his hasty decision to resign as registrar. Bess's father had taken a job in Austin as storekeeper and accountant at the State Institution for the Blind and was planning to move his family there from Dallas during the summer. It was now almost certain that Bess would enroll at the University—just as Lomax was leaving.

The relationship between them had taken a decidedly warmer turn following their meeting in Lomax's office the previous summer. That fall, while Shirley Green was touring the East for her health, John and Bess kept up a steady correspondence. In October, with Shirley's blessing, he spent a long weekend in Dallas and escorted Bess to the Texas state fair, two football games, and dinner. Afterward he reported the outing in detail to Shirley; to Bess he wrote that he was "healthier physically, mentally, and spiritually than before."[3]

Shirley's letters had grown more and more impersonal, as she retreated into false gaiety and syntactical mists to hide her true feelings. Bess was a fresh wind—she spoke bluntly, flirted extravagantly but politely, and played on John's considerable ego. To his delight, she wanted to hear all about his life and ambitions. He replied, "How inductively you flatter the innate vanity of one!"[4]

Despite the distance between Austin and Dallas, John and Bess grew steadily closer during the last months of Shirley's life. In one sense, Shirley was the strongest bond between them, in their shared concern for her well-being as well as in their mutual appreciation of her powers of mind and vivacious personality. To them she became, invariably, "the Lady" elevated into capitalized nobility, and they regularly discussed what "the Lady" might think, or did think, of whatever they were doing, reading, or planning. It was a great satisfaction to know that "the Lady" approved of their relationship.

On the day she learned of Shirley's death, Bess wrote John her condolences, adding that now more than ever she needed his friendship. He had nothing to offer her, he responded, "except a broken heart and a lonely and desolated life." Soon he was writing of his plans to go away for a year or so—"not a cowardly running away" but to "grow, to harden the fibers of my resolution."[5] As long ago as the summer of 1901 he had written to Shirley that one of his most cherished ambitions was to spend a year at Harvard or a similar institution where he could study educational administration.[6] Now he told Bess that next year he was going off to "Harvard, fair Harvard," which he had long considered "the flower of the academic world."[7]

All that wishful thinking collapsed entirely that spring when the regents turned down his request for leave. Now that he was committed to A&M for the coming year, Harvard would have to wait. In the meantime, he had the summer free and the means to enroll at the University of Chicago for the so-called half-term in July and August. Nothing transpired in their courtship so dramatic as the episode in Cuernavaca with Shirley Green, but by the time he left, he and Bess were exchanging love poems, and they had taken a long walk to the top of Mt. Bonnell, from which came a mutual understanding, short of pledging engagement, that they were serious about each other.

In Chicago, Lomax took a cozy room all to himself at the Phi Delta Theta house on Monroe Street, in a quiet neighborhood adjacent to the campus and only a few blocks from Lake Michigan. His classes included English composition, the early Romantic poets, and a seminar in Tennyson and Browning, by this time familiar, comfortable companions. He attended other lectures as well, went to an occasional opera, and learned to play golf, but spent most of his spare time roaming about the city and keeping up with the daily reading—"about 200 pages"—required by his courses. "The work at the University [of Chicago] outclasses ours," he noted with satisfaction, and resolved to study rather than socialize. Relishing "my Bohemian way of living," he wrote Bess that he took his meals in colorful little diners wherever he happened to be—in dark greasy spoons and large crowded cafés, occasionally in a nice restaurant on the ninth floor of the Pullman building, where he could sit by a window and look out on Lake Michigan and "beyond to the land I love."[8] He had obviously taken along his poetic license; open land was scarcely visible in any direction from that point on the lakeside. But of course his reference to "the land I love" was merely to remind Bess that he was still a country boy at heart, unsullied by urban blight.

However, he took to the city enthusiastically and wrote movingly of its energy, its thronged streets and bright lights, its grand skyline. It was not the lighted boulevards or swarming crowds that caught him in their spell, but the high, silent skyscrapers "in their somber greys and browns [that] are alive to me with mystery and wonder."[9] This was the once-poor farm boy reaching out to the dazzle of civilization and respectability, the same man who had long extolled the virtues of plain and woodland, to whom the conditions of his rustic boyhood were evidence of strong character and moral fiber. That summer was on the whole a pleasant time, free from the burdens and annoyances that had dogged him for years. His health was still not good—he suffered frequent headaches and spent several weekends in bed with a high fever, but missed no classes.

Early in the term he had traveled up to Highland Park to visit a friend, and while listening to a concert in a park by the shore, he wrote to Bess to assure her that the beauty of the place already had him on the mend. He described a particularly attractive "Japanese lady" who had caught his eye: "I am ravished with [her] beauty and I am not unhappy."[10] Bess may not have found news of the "Japanese lady" particularly comforting—or appropriate—but she turned it nicely, in a newsy little note reporting, among other things, that she had bought some silk dress material for her mother, silk that no doubt came, she said, from the same Japan which had sent the lady to please him. For this, Bess wished from the very depths of her heart that she could thank the lady, as she wished to thank "all the beauties that touch your life and make it happier."[11] It would not be easy to one-up Bess Brown.

By early September the term was winding down. Lomax took one final exam and turned in papers on composition writing, the time scheme in *In Memoriam,* and the prose of the Romantic period, the last of which "got praised by the best man in the English Literature Faculty." He spent another week in Chicago, resting, playing golf, and traveling up to Zion, north of the city, to hear a flamboyant revivalist preacher who called himself "the Second Elijah." (The trip was a rudimentary sort of folklore fieldwork; Lomax said he went partly out of curiosity and "partly to study the people who are hoodwinked by [the revivalist's] pretensions."[12] He also had hopes of getting material for a magazine article he could sell—the first in a long line of such schemes that rarely came to fruition.)

He wrote to Bess that when he got back to Texas he would teach her to play golf and they would take a buggy trip to Mt. Bonnell and spend evenings in quiet talk on her front porch.[13] He arrived in Austin on September 17, carried out those plans over a long weekend, and set off for College Station on the following Monday.

· · · · ·

Having had the summer to recover from the imbroglio at the University of Texas, Lomax now had to face an unhappy reality. Going off into the sticks to teach English at the state's "cow college" was a comedown from being registrar at its major university. Although he'd left of his own accord, he couldn't help feeling that he'd been banished, and he would always look on his years at A&M as time spent in exile.

With an enrollment scarcely a third that of the University, "the A&M" was both smaller and more remote, tucked off on an undeveloped campus generally considered "unhealthy and malarial." Established as a technical school for farmers and engineers (both subject to mandatory military training) it was dismissed by the haughty University crowd as "an institution devoted largely to sowing oats and raising cain."[14] Critics of its agricultural programs pointed out that A&M's experimental farms were located on the poorest soil in the state, while business leaders complained that the engineering students were too far from the centers of professional industry.[15] Academic excellence was hardly one of the things A&M was known for; the all-male student body was generally considered a collection of castoffs, clodhoppers, and boneheads. The nearest town was Bryan, which, with a population of 3,589 in 1900, was little more than a village. In his first weeks at A&M, Lomax complained that the isolation there was a great trial for someone like him, "used to the active stir that has been mine for so long."[16]

A&M's inferiority was rooted in the strange circumstances of its origin in 1871, when the legislature established it as "a branch" of the then nonexistent University of Texas. When the upstart Austin campus finally came into being a dozen years later in the shadow of the capitol, constitutionally ordained "a university of the first class" and backed with an appropriation many times that of the Agricultural and Mechanical College, the folks over at A&M, toiling amid the canebrakes of rural Brazos County, had reason to feel abused and put upon.

Anxious to shake the onus of inferiority, they challenged the upstarts on several fronts, most visibly on the playing fields, where they failed dismally. Between 1894 and 1903 the two football teams met in ten games; the Texas Longhorns won eight of them, often by lopsided scores of forty and more points. Lomax, like many college men of the day, equated his alma mater's athletic prowess with her natural superiority in other areas. It was an exaggerated sense of allegiance to the institution rather than any deep interest in athletics which made him a ready rooter, but at the University he'd attended all the home games and followed the team's fortunes with keen interest. During the 1903 season, his first semester at A&M, he watched in silence as Texas trounced the Aggies 29 to 6, a spectacle that did nothing to ease his feelings about leaving Austin. It was not merely a matter of divided loyalties; to all appearances he had signed on with a loser, and the champions he'd left behind were rubbing it in.

He took even less comfort in A&M's reputation as a dumping ground for delinquents, derived from its general character as a military school.[17] All students were automatically enlisted in the cadet corps, which required that they wear uniforms on campus, march in a body to and from classes, stand twice-daily inspections, and otherwise endure the regimentation and Spartan rigors of soldierly life (thanks to the tightfisted Texas legislature, a number of them lived year-round in tents). The majority were practical-minded students of farming or engineering, with little interest in such frivolities as art, philosophy, or literature.

There was also the matter of salary. The $1,500 he had been paid at the University at least allowed him to move into the upper levels of genteel poverty. Taking a three-hundred-dollar cut was no small concern, with old debts lingering and the growing prospect of domestic responsibilities, now that Miss Bess Brown was a presence in his life. In recent years he'd saved enough from time to time to invest in small insurance policies, dabble in a land venture, and back his brother in the general store partnership at Meridian. Now all that had to be put on hold.

In disagreeable situations in the past, his habit had always been to bury himself in his work, and that was just what he did now. He wrote Bess that he had nothing to report about himself, only that "I am doing my work with all my heart."[18] He was assigned a teaching load of sixteen hours a week ("not counting consultation periods"), ten of which were in freshman composition. For the six additional hours, he conducted a senior seminar in Shakespeare and a general survey course for sophomores. The classes were large—thirty-five and more—but Lomax pitched in enthusiastically. He discovered that he had a great deal in common with his students, and the similarity in their backgrounds made him more sympathetic than he would otherwise have been. He dedicated himself to their cause, saying that he believed—"like a good Methodist"—that he had a special call to help them. "They shall have my best," he said.[19] Habitually insecure, he worried that the boys would not like him; habitually egotistical, he was sure that his proto–Dale Carnegie tactics would prevail. He needed friends among the students, he told Bess, but he would have to be patient in finding them. It wouldn't do to rush anything "when a college vogue is in question." Still, "I shall win them yet."[20]

At A&M all faculty lived on the campus in housing provided by the college. Lomax was assigned austere quarters in Bachelor Hall, the residence for unmarried faculty, all of whom were of course male. His mornings were devoted to classes ("recitation periods") and his afternoons spent reading student papers, interrupted by a game of tennis three or four times a week. Preparation for the next day's classes took up most of his evenings, so that he had little time to fret over the lack of social activity. Still, he missed it.

The puckish Judge Clark wrote with news of doings in Austin, including the state guard's annual summer camp: "The Encampment is in full blast, and lovely woomun is yielding, pro. tem., her fluttering heart to the irresistible charms of brass buttons. I have seen your Miss Brown once or twice, this vacation. She is ne plus ultra, sine qua non, e pluribus unum, and altogether lovely."[21]

Once her summer school classes were over, Bess had enrolled as a full-time student for the fall, taking a course in German and twelve hours of English, including a class with Lomax's old nemesis, Morgan Callaway. She was also on the yearbook staff, as assistant to Harry Steger, who had returned to do graduate work and edit the *Cactus.* Both she and Steger urged Lomax to send material for the *Cactus.* Bess herself was thinking of doing something light and frothy, but "Harry is firm for *local color,*" she said, and Steger implored John: "Why can't you write me some allegories that would have a 'local application,' to quote the legend on my vaseline bottle?"[22] But the only writing Lomax had time for were routine news stories from A&M for the *Houston Post,* which paid him five cents per column inch as their correspondent at College Station.

Lomax had no Saturday classes. As soon as he felt he was firmly settled in and couldn't be accused of neglecting his duties, he was frequently aboard the Friday night train to Austin, to spend Saturday and Sunday in Bess's company, then he would take the late train back, often riding all night and arriving on campus at sunrise on Monday, only minutes before classes began.

His blossoming romance was not without its problems. For a time the major obstacle was Bess's mother. In October Bess celebrated her twenty-third birthday (Lomax had just turned thirty-six), and on the morning of that occasion, contemplating her prospects, she sent off a sprightly letter to John that spelled out the situation. Her mother, she said, called John "that man" and "grinds her teeth." Further, Mrs. Brown resented John's being a Methodist—the Browns were Presbyterian—and objected most of all to the way Bess seemed to fling herself at him. Bess, her mother said, was just a child and didn't know what love was.[23]

Never at ease with matrons of commanding presence, Lomax shrank from dealing with the denture-grinding Mrs. Brown, hopeful that Bess and her father would somehow save him from the situation.[24] Having found an ally in Mr. Brown, he told Bess, "To your father I may be able to say a word soon."[25] By mid-December he had worked up his courage and sent off a carefully composed letter of proposal, then waited in suspense for almost a month. When Brown finally wrote (the delay, it turned out, was caused by illness, a Civil War wound from which he had never fully recovered), it was to give his approval, "with a view to surrendering unto your keeping the treasure of our home—the happiness and future of our daughter."[26] Vague plans were laid for a June wedding.

It was, on the whole, a happy match. Despite the thirteen-year difference in their ages and their dissimilar backgrounds—her family was solidly, if not always prosperously, middle-class and urban—John and Bess were as suited to each other as two people are likely to be. Even their occasional variances tended to mesh well. Although she was lively and fun-loving where John inclined toward moodiness and solemnity, she too had a deep streak of practicality, which was to emerge more and more solidly over time. She saw through to his essential nature, in a way other women hadn't; what she liked best about him, she told John, was "a certain quaint, old-fashioned soberness that is *you* at heart."[27] He also understood the ways in which they complemented each other. While he was often capable of considerable self-delusion in personal affairs, he accurately described their relationship when he compared them to "two friends who agreed *enthusiastically* and disagreed *sympathetically.*" On the other hand, he complained that she sometimes agreed with him when he didn't want her to, as when he remarked that he should have waited to declare his love until she had finished her work at the University. Her reaction to that was emphatic: "You behaved just like Tar Baby," he said, "and Tommy 'lay low' and changed the subject."[28] ("Tommy" was her pet name for him, derived from the Little Tommy Tucker of Mother Goose, who sang for his supper and fretted that he couldn't marry. For years John would sign his letters to Bess, "Your boy, Tommy"; the nickname was still current among his grandchildren in the 1940s.)

• • • • •

When he first arrived at A&M, Lomax had felt uneasy about his relationship with the head of the English department, Dr. C. P. Fountain, but after a few months he reported that "Prof. Fountain has come to think highly of me." Classes were going well and his students were enthusiastic—except in the matter of evaluations. Lomax complained that the monthly reporting system caused students to exaggerate the importance of grades, and he hated to think that his students might consider him unjust. If it were up to him, he would make every student happy at least once a month by giving them all high grades.[29] In at least one instance he did just that, and had to confess to telling "an untruth."[30]

Reporting this to Bess set off a lengthy discourse on ethics and social conduct in general. The ravages and humiliations of his own schoolboy experiences were clearly behind his attack on harsh discipline and the "artificial rules" of society. He rejected the rigid militaristic codes of behavior prescribed at A&M and opted for a warmer relationship with his students: "I *will* not pose or assume a chilling unfriendly attitude."[31]

After several months he felt that he was making solid progress with his students, and he set great store by their approval. His visions of married life with Bess, spelled out for her over and over, depicted the stern but kindly headmaster, Texas variety, and his gracious wife, surrounded in their paneled and book-lined quarters by grateful and devoted students. He and Bess would find ways to make life pleasant for downhearted boys. If this weren't possible, he would quit teaching instantly: "I've got to be a human being, else I won't play."[32]

That fall Bess had been busy with her classes and the yearbook. She successfully tested out of English 2 and was allowed to enroll in upper level courses, although for a time Lomax fretted that her fate was in the hands of Morgan Callaway, who directed the program—"His Doctorship," Lomax called him sarcastically, but admitted that he did not know the source of his intense dislike for the man.[33]

When the fall semester ended, Bess dropped out of school—more than a little reluctantly, as her "Tar Baby" response to John indicated—to prepare for the wedding and spend time with her mother, who was still not reconciled to the match. John took the high road, assuring Bess over and over that all would be well in time. Still she was troubled. She had to face the fact, she told him, that their marriage would inevitably break her mother's heart, adding sharply, "And I shan't ever tolerate your schoolmaster air of knowing it all."[34]

John argued that he wouldn't be taking her far from home—"College Station is only four hours from Austin (normally)"—and manfully assured her that there would be money for her to visit her parents and room in their home for her mother (a promise he was destined to keep). After all, what if he wanted to take her to the Philippine Islands, where he once thought of going? What if she had fallen in love with some handsome Presbyterian missionary to China?[35] To her mother's complaint about his religion (now more nearly an absence of religion), he remarked that, while it was certainly a pity that he wasn't born a Presbyterian, he could become a Presbyterian now as easily as he would ever again be a Methodist.[36]

Meanwhile, they went on making plans. He favored a June 1 wedding, after which they would go by steamer to New York and Boston and take a walking tour of New England. Then Harvard summer school was a possibility, but he tended to favor the University of Chicago, where he knew his way around, and also because "Harvard does not, I fear, have much summer English."[37]

Contrary to later stories of pioneer folksong collecting during this period, his major literary efforts that spring were directed toward a more prosaic scheme for producing a series of textbooks for the public schools. These well-illustrated readers would introduce pupils to the familiar world they saw every day but tended to take for granted—flora and fauna and "the whole of the out-of-door." Two of his colleagues were already coauthors; Bess was to become a third, putting to use her writing ambitions and valuable experiences with preschoolers. If the series was adopted by the state board of education, their fortunes would not only be made but they would accomplish work that would be "monumental in its power for doing good." For a time this proposition played a major part in their summer plans—they would "botanize together," write songs, do nature study (perhaps at the University of Chicago), and work on the project with such energy that nothing could stop them.[38] However, enthusiasm dwindled and nothing more was heard of the textbook scheme.

Bess said June 8 was the earliest possible date for the wedding, but concurred with his plans for "camping and tramping rather than sticking to the large cities." Primarily, John was concerned for his pocketbook, but he frequently waxed poetic over the splendors of nature and complained about the stresses of city life (little of which he suffered at College Station), telling Bess how he longed for the sylvan tranquility of their "playtime in June" and assuring her that life would be free of care and woe once they were married. Through all the turmoil of future years, he never stopped predicting that tranquility would descend, any day now.[39] It rarely did. Years later, a Lomax daughter-in-law laughingly but accurately observed that "the Lomax family lived always from climax to crisis."[40]

In mid-February 1904, Bess fell ill with "hysterics and a nervous rigor."[41] There had been signs earlier—references to being "sensitive and high strung," talk of depression, fretting about her mother, snapping at John over trivial matters. Now she cried for days, pronounced herself well for a few hours, then lapsed back into tears. For the present, he was forbidden to visit or write (undaunted, he resorted to the telephone, assuring her she could talk freely because "Central is too busy to listen"). She wanted to be his wife "in all beauty and sweetness," but all she could feel for him was "dread and fear and distress" and she could not marry him in that frame of mind . . . although, she insisted, that did not mean that she would never marry him or that she did not love him.[42] It seemed like the Shirley Green affair all over again. The difference this time was that John never wavered.

He tried philosophy, he tried psychology, he tried soothing words and silent support, he tried (or said he tried) to ignore the whole thing—but he never gave up. Earlier he had told her that he didn't believe in theories: "It is safer to . . . respond to the natural impulses of the heart."[43] Bess countered that they were too much alike: it was a hazard to pair two people whose temperaments were so similar, "each possessing *possibilities of morbidness.*"[44] John could do little but urge her to rest and let matters take their course. He also stepped up his predictions that once married, they would idle away the summer, spend their time outdoors, do as they pleased, read the classics, write great books, "dream and love each other." On the other hand—if their energies were restored in time, he said, they could "drift over" to the University of Chicago for the summer term.[45] His streak of practicality and great need to be active at *something* could not be entirely suppressed.

He may have understood from the beginning the cause of Bess's malaise, but it was only after several months that he pronounced judgment, choosing his words carefully. He had concluded that her conception of love and marriage was simply too idealized, and she had not clearly faced "the real, material side of such a union."[46] In that way he not only illuminated the problem but assured her he understood, and that helped matters materially. She responded also to his enthusiastic descriptions of their "playtime in June," the sea voyage to New York, and tramping through the hills and villages of New England. Very soon she reported, "Your lady grows stronger and happier daily." Theirs had been a chaste but ardent courtship;[47] in the end love conquered all.

It helped too that Bess's younger brother, Will, had recently been married in Dallas. Her mother, in the spirit of that occasion, welcomed John into the family, and everyone's spirits were lifted. For all too long John and Bess had had only each other for company, under trying circumstances. Her hysteria, like John's sudden resignation from the University, was not normal behavior. Ordinarily, stoicism and practicality were her dominant traits, and she was the sort of person who once praised a tennis opponent because she played just as Bess did—"with all her heart and to *beat* if she can."[48] In the very letter that she wrote to John announcing the onset of her crying spells, she had coolly added a postscript analyzing in detail the merits of a financial investment he was considering.[49] In the days before the wedding, now scheduled for June 9, she would suffer a minor relapse or two, but the worst was over. If, in the years afterward, she ever shed a tear for herself, no one knew about it.[50]

Plans for the wedding and honeymoon resumed in full swing. Bess ordered four hundred invitations, then had to add another hundred when Lomax, who so often railed against pomp and ceremony, informed her that he would need at least 250, for all the officials at A&M, his "numerous kinnery," his friends at Weatherford and Meridian, and "the widely scattered individuals who have claims on me."[51] This was the man who had earlier complained to Bess that he was friendless and alone in the world.

As the spring semester at A&M came to a close, he was caught up in the usual flurry of social affairs and final exams. Only a few days before the wedding he was sent by President Houston to Prairie View, some fifty miles away, as Houston's delegate to the graduation exercises of Prairie View State Normal and Industrial College (later Prairie View A&M), a branch institution for Negroes that amounted to little more than a vocational training school. At Prairie View he inspected classes, ate sumptuous meals (the "cooking department" was a mainstay), and attended a student concert which moved him deeply. His comments on the experience, written to Bess, shed important light on later events and attitudes:

> The singing is perfect, the rhythm, modulation and perfect time I have not heard excelled; yet the old time negro trill is gone. These blacks are civilized. Still it is pitiful, pitiful. With my heart all tender and softened by the two days I had with you, something I find in these faces, the impossible barrier, so plain to me, that bars them perpetually from the highest achievements of civilization, the almost hopeless struggle before them (it is hopeless in its larger meaning),—with a thousand thoughts like these the day and its experiences have moved me highly. And their singing, Bess; I wish you might hear the voicing. They have thrilled me through and through, with the hymns I love.[52]

From his point of view, it was not a compliment (nor even a well-meaning condescension) to say that "these blacks are civilized." Social progress, he was convinced, had robbed their singing of "the old time negro trill" and replaced it with art and artifice. On the other hand, he was tragically close to full sympathy and understanding of their terrible oppression, and tragically close to seeing its remedy. Yet he fell short, as he would forever fall short. So far as he could see, the barrier *was* impossible, they *were* perpetually and absolutely barred from "the highest achievements" of civilization. Their struggle was not "almost" hopeless but, as he parenthetically made clear, entirely and totally hopeless. Assaulted as he was by genuine sympathy for blacks and at the same time loaded with an absolute view of the world, it is no wonder that the issue of race was to create such terrible anomalies and distortions for him in years to come.

· · · · ·

The marriage of John Lomax and Bess Brown took place on June 9 in the Free Presbyterian Church in Austin. They had talked of a honeymoon trip by train to St. Louis and the World's Fair, then on to the summer "half term" at the University of Chicago, where John could take a course or two in English literature and "a stiff training in composition" which he felt he needed to improve his teaching at A&M. Then, just before the wedding a letter had come from an old classmate, "Captain" E. P. R. Duval, who was at Harvard, doing graduate work in mathematics. Duval spoke warmly of the situation there and reminded Lomax that he had promised to visit.[53] When John learned that he could get the courses he wanted—eighteenth-century English literature and the basic composition course ("Comp B")—at Harvard, he returned their train tickets to Chicago and booked passage on the SS *Lampasas,* sailing from Galveston on June 15 for New York.

After three days in Manhattan, the newlyweds took a leisurely trip up the Hudson Valley to Lake George, then on to Cambridge. Lomax had at last reached "Harvard, fair Harvard," mecca of his dreams. But between the natural commotion of his newly married state and the considerable demands of his studies, he had little time to savor the place. Classes met six days a week between July 5 and August 10. In that scant period, Lomax turned in at least twenty-five papers, averaging between five and ten pages each, for Robert P. Utter in Comp B; he had wanted "stiff training in composition," and he certainly got it. He wrote another five or six papers of equal length for Professor H. H. Holmes's course in eighteenth-century literature.

Once the term was over, John and Bess were quickly on their way back to Texas. By taking the train to St. Louis, they got to see the World's Fair after all, and during the stopover there purchased furniture to be shipped to their new home at College Station. (Shrewd John, never one to pay retail if he could avoid it, went directly to the manufacturer and for $364.75 got all the essentials, including a mahogany dinner table, a brass bed, two rockers, and an office chair.)

They arrived back in Austin in mid-September to find Bess's father suffering another bout of ill health. After courtesy calls on relatives of both families in Dallas and Meridian, Bess decided she was needed in Austin to nurse her father while John went on College Station to organize their new household and, in effect, formally close out his long bachelorhood.

CHAPTER SEVEN

The Boston Come All-Ye
1904–6

Married life required surprisingly little adjustment. Lomax's lengthy status as a bachelor, after all, had been more a matter of circumstance than anything else; if Shirley Green had yielded, he would have been married long before. Now, even with Bess off in Austin attending to her father, he settled into the domestic routine at College Station, attending to all sorts of household matters.

A&M's faculty lived in college housing on campus. Lomax's first task was to inspect the two small houses available and decide which was best. He chose a small bungalow, known as the Sanderson cottage, near the far edge of the campus, rejecting the other because it was too close to the chapel and "the center of gravity." Also, the Sanderson cottage had stables and a chicken yard, which the other lacked. The farm boy in Lomax yearned to own animals, both as pets and to stock the larder. Very soon he acquired laying hens, two pigs (which he named Jim and Jennie), and Princess, a nondescript but lovable pup who followed him to his office every day and slept beneath his desk while he was in class. A milk cow and a cookstove were ordered through the Lomax Mercantile Company in Meridian, but because of a shipping error the cow wound up at the rail depot in Bryan, and Lomax had to walk the five miles into town and lead her back on foot. The stove also went astray; in late September, he reported that it was still "somewhere between this place and Meridian."[1] In the meantime he took his meals in the Mess Hall, a huge, centralized facility that fed the student body.

Except for a few overnight trips to College Station, Bess was kept in Austin until early December by her father's condition. Deciding that groceries were cheaper in the larger city, she stocked up on essentials and had them shipped to A&M, along with sixteen quarts of preserves put up by her mother and a supply of John's "nerve medicine tonic," which he took for periodic headaches and general agitation. He asked about spending four dollars for a bathtub—"nearly long enough for you"—to which Bess responded that she definitely wanted a tub, but "one *you* can flop over in."

Far more troublesome was the servant problem. John quickly learned that he would have little luck locating help until the cotton-picking season ended. Shortly he reported to Bess that "a chocolate colored female has been hovering about," wanting work as a cook, but her terms included board for her, her husband, and their three-year-old child. Thrifty Bess concluded that would be too expensive for the little help they needed. In time, they were able to hire another black woman, Mary Evans, who would serve them ably through most of their time at A&M, patiently accepting layoffs during summers when they were away and returning whenever needed to clean, cook for John in Bess's absences, and otherwise attend to the small household.

Soon Lomax's attention was diverted to the students arriving in droves for the fall term—"the new men already number 200," he wrote to Bess. He was busy through the day helping Houston with administrative matters, and they worked late at night reading all the English entrance exams. "I am writing this between breaths," he said.

He complained that he was not getting enough to eat—the Mess Hall had only half enough servants and "their food is nearly as limited"—and he began to fret over Bess's absence. She was home by early October, but within a few weeks both her parents took sick and she had to return to Austin. By this time Mary had come to cook, and most of Lomax's spare hours were occupied with seeing after their thriving menagerie of barnyard stock. Bess worried that they had too many animals and would soon be spending all their time attending to them. Their other extravagance was books; now the guardian of their household expenses, she lamented, "I expect we'll be poor all our lives from buying books." Both were constant readers. In late November, still by her parents' bedside, Bess noted that while John was reading to his boys at A&M, she was reading Kipling to her "invalids" and added that she was proud of him for his generous devotion to his students. "Thou art so much a man," she told him, "so strong, so gentle, so wise, so merry hearted."

He was not always merry hearted. One dreary winter day in early December, the dog ran away, the pigs escaped from their pen, and John came down with a case of the blues. The next day, however, he was able to announce that "Princess and the pigs reported this morning early," and things were looking up. Soon the "invalids" in Austin had improved, and Bess, now complaining of an ailment of her own, returned to John at College Station for the first Christmas of their marriage. For some days she had been nauseated all the time. The reason for her queasiness was soon apparent; the Lomaxes were going to be parents.

Bess was called back to Austin on several occasions by the illness of one or the other of her parents. In February 1905, her mother took sick, and Bess was by her side most of that month. Some members of the family, sensing that Mrs. Brown was still not fully reconciled to Bess's marriage, gossiped that her condition was not so much a matter of health as one of temperament—her way, deliberately or otherwise, of holding on to her daughter as long as possible.

Back at A&M, John fretted that the junior class was "stiff and offish with me." Ever opportunistic, he fell back on an old strategy, telling Bess that he and she would cultivate the freshmen and sophomores and then "come into favor again" when these men took over the upper classes. Except for the unfriendly juniors and occasional cold snaps, things were peaceful enough. The cold wind made the pigs squeal lustily, Princess got lonely and ran away to visit the neighbor's dog, John and President Houston smoked cigars together and "placidly readjust[ed] the universe—all things run smoothly, no jar or ferment (nothin' don't never happen)."

To celebrate Bess's return, John planned a weekend theater outing in Houston. They attended Melba's *Tosca* and saw *The Two Orphans*, starring Clara Morris, Louis James, and James O'Neill (father of Eugene O'Neill). Lomax's good friend Roy Bedichek, who was teaching high school in Houston, handled all the arrangements, reserving their hotel suite and securing theater tickets. The trip meant that Lomax, the diligent company man, had to take a day from his classes, but the respite would be good for both students and teacher. The promise of seeing her, he told Bess, "makes me thrill as I did when getting ready for June Ninth"[2] (the date of their wedding).

The spring of 1905 brought the newlyweds their first sustained period of domesticity. Although it was a happy time, it was hardly calm and restful. Setting up and running the household was something they undertook enthusiastically, but also with such industry and plotting that one might think they were organizing a business. In many ways the Lomax household *was* a business. Both John and Bess were money-minded, keen with a dollar, and both had—or fancied they had—an entrepreneurial eye for tactics that might turn a profit. They were forever poised to take up any scheme that promised to stretch John's salary, now $1,300 annually.

Their cow and chickens were immediate, if modest, sources of income, in the form of excess milk and eggs sold to neighbors. Soon the demand for their fresh milk was such that they had to add another cow, named Beauty. Then there was the income from newspaper "stringing." During the previous year John had earned occasional small sums by sending news items from College Station to the *Houston Post,* which paid a few cents per column-inch for whatever they printed. Bess soon made a similar arrangement with the *Galveston News* (and later with the *Houston Chronicle*). She put the "stringer" operation on a business footing, establishing for herself and John a monthly goal for the number of column-inches which they would submit, and she bought a journal in which to keep careful track of all income and outgo. The newspapers did not always print everything they sent in, but in some months their efforts as stringers paid them as much as thirty or forty dollars. Bess also regularly sold off clothing they had outworn; her journal contained almost monthly entries of three or four dollars earned from "old clothes," along with occasional small sums for "copying" or "typewriting." From all this cottage industry, together with a windfall of several hundred dollars from John's stock in the Lomax Mercantile Company in Meridian, their income in 1905 was increased by almost 50 percent.

One disastrous enterprise was an investment in the Oklahoma State Loan and Trust Company—founded, promoted, and ultimately folded by Bess's younger brother. Will Brown, like Richard Lomax, was a likable, happy-go-lucky dreamer constantly on the trail of instant riches. He had managed a scheme for franchising fruit orchards, sold memberships (at fifty cents a head) in something known as the Modern Order of Praetorians, and peddled insurance for various fly-by-night companies. In early 1904 he had gone into Oklahoma, then still Indian Territory, with grandiose plans for a savings and loan operation that, despite his enthusiastic proclamations, was badly undercapitalized. He wrote at length to Lomax, outlining the infinite possibilities of the scheme and offering to let John "in strictly on the 'ground' on stock issue."[3]

John consulted Bess, who was at the time in the throes of her breakdown just before the wedding. In a letter otherwise filled with an account of her "hysterics and nervous rigor," she coolly added a postscript saying that her brother's proposal was "as safe as any that promises larger return than 8% or 9%." But the decision was John's, she insisted, and included a warning from her mother, who said plainly, "The Browns are no good at making money."[4] Undeterred, John invested a thousand dollars he'd somehow managed to put away after paying off Richard's old debt.

For a few years there were small dividends from the Oklahoma Loan and Trust Company, then suddenly Will was in Dallas, running an auto parts agency, and soon after that in New York, peddling real estate and window ventilators, fending off creditors. Many years later, Lomax, counseling one of his own children on financial matters, recalled that the first thousand dollars he and Bess saved after paying off Richard Lomax's debt "was stolen from us by her brother and never repaid."[5] Will Brown was a tragic victim of his own schemes and a relentless economic system he never quite understood; he died, broke and defeated, in the influenza epidemic of 1918, leaving a destitute widow and small child who would have suffered mightily if John Lomax had not come to their aid.

In late June, with nothing to keep them at College Station, John and Bess went to her parents in Austin to await their baby's birth, which came on August 7. It was a girl, whom they named Shirley—"in honor of Father's old girlfriend," his older daughter would say in later years, somewhat ruefully. But Shirley Green had been Bess's dear friend also; naming the baby was as much Bess's idea as John's.

· · · · ·

Almost since the return from their honeymoon and the six weeks in Cambridge back in 1904, there had been plans afoot for a year's leave of absence that would take them back to Harvard. They had high hopes of success with President Houston, himself a Harvard alumnus, who in the past had offered encouragement. Those hopes suffered a setback in the summer, when, following the sudden death of President Prather of the University of Texas, Houston was offered the presidency there—the job for which he had been passed over three years earlier.

On the very day Prather died, John had left Austin and his new family and returned to College Station to deal with various matters, chief of which was a meeting with Houston to discuss the leave. After a sumptuous dinner at the home of C. P. Fountain, head of the English Department, John joyfully reported to Bess that "Mr. Houston looks kindly on the year at Harvard" and would support his cause.[6] But within a month, Houston had gone back to the University of Texas as president and was replaced at A&M by H. H. Harrington, a dour, elderly chemistry professor who showed little interest in advancing the literary arts.

The setback proved only temporary. Harrington, if not entirely sympathetic, was at least fair-minded, and he allowed Lomax to present his case for leave to the board of directors, with the support of Dr. Fountain and other colleagues. The issue was in doubt throughout the fall and winter, but even by November, Lomax thought approval likely enough that he applied to Harvard for admission and after Christmas began boning up on his German, "should the Harvard scheme prosper."[7] In April he and Bess were still speaking of "the projected Harvard trip" and waiting to hear from Cambridge. Word of acceptance came the following month, and A&M's directors approved John's leave for the 1906–7 school year, beginning in September. It was an unpaid leave, but the directors, in an uncommon gesture, voted him a third of his salary—$36.11 each month—to defray moving costs.

Bess went to Austin to break the news to her parents ("Mother behaved better than I expected . . . so that ordeal is over"). To John, still her "Tommy Tucker," she wrote an enthusiastic projection of the trip to come, by steamship to New York, where they might go sightseeing (she would be happy with even half a day there, she said), then on to Harvard for the winter. She was overjoyed that John had at last achieved his heart's desire; he was, she said, her Galahad who had long searched for his Grail through "such dolerous [*sic*] ways."[8]

His exuberant reply was filled with typical Lomaxian dreams and schemes. They would spend far longer than half a day in "dear old New York," and they would have the best of times there and everywhere, soaking up culture and reading great books. He would join the Southern Club and the Graduate Club in order to meet important men, and she would go to the clubs with him if that was permitted; in any event, she would get an outing to the opera for every time he went to his clubs, and she would be in the receiving line when they entertained. "Yes ma'm we are going to have some happy, growing days," he said brightly.[9]

Lomax had been awarded one of Harvard's prestigious Austin Teaching Fellowships, which carried a stipend of $500.[10] Still, he needed employment for the summer if they were to survive a year in Cambridge. A&M had no summer sessions, so he turned to the University of Texas. From W. S. Sutton, dean of the Summer Schools, he learned to his considerable discomfort that any decision would be in the hands of his old adversary,

Morgan Callaway, Ph.D. Dreading the worst, John told Bess that "I have sent his Doctorship a letter—after some fear and trembling."[11]

That spring there was one more A&M-related task to perform. As Houston had done in 1904, President Harrington sent Lomax to Prairie View to attend graduation exercises at the Negro branch. Again John wrote a detailed account to Bess: "I have had the unique experience of being overnight the sole white man (wholly so) among nearly a thousand negroes. I dined in solitary state last night and this morning, attended by a courtly colored gentleman imported from the Rice Hotel in Houston. Last night I was lulled to sleep to the soothing strains of plantation melodies sung as only they can be sung when there are a sufficient number of falsetto voices to give the songs local color. There is an overpowering amount of aforesaid 'local color' at every turn." A young male student was delegated to shine his shoes and attend to his every need, and the principal and faculty were "pitifully obsequious in their attentions." One night he suffered from mosquitoes and a stomachache, but next morning "a sour toddy, a good breakfast, and an excellent and philosophically smoked cigar" restored him.[12]

The summer teaching job at the University of Texas did not materialize, but with President Houston's intercession, he was given work in the business office, auditing accounts. He earned some $320, which meant that the Lomaxes eventually netted within fifty dollars or so of John's regular salary for the year. They would have to do without the extra income from cows, chickens, and newspapers, but with their inventive ways of making and saving money, it was not hard to fill the slack. On September 5, they sailed from Galveston, on a rough sea that in no way diminished their high spirits.

• • • • •

John Lomax's journey from Granbury to Harvard, over the course of twenty years, was an immense one, greater than time or distance. Cambridge, in contrast to the arid, flimsy-new Texas villages and towns Lomax had known, reeked of substance and an honored past, burnished in its broad brick streets and the elegant (by Texas standards) high, spacious old houses, turreted and verandaed and set on deep green lawns under leafy elms. Harvard represented everything he wanted: achievement, authority, recognition among the elite. Other men from the frontier went back East for an education; Lomax went there to be anointed.

Harvard, with an enrollment of nearly 3,000 that year, was more than twice the size of the University of Texas, six times larger than Texas A&M.

But numbers were really beside the point; what mattered was Harvard's prestige, its luminous aura—"the flower of the academic world," as Lomax so often put it. And it very nearly was, after almost forty years under the inspired leadership of Charles William Eliot, who in 1869 had taken the reins of a small regional school with no real claim to the title of university and moved it, in the words of George Lyman Kittredge, "from a provincial college into a national seminary of learning."[13]

Of course not everyone found Harvard ideal. Henry Adams damned it with faintest praise as "only the least harmful institution in America."[14] Other critics charged that it was insular and snobbish—"provincial" was Henry James's lofty slur—and there was truth to that. Quietly confident of its place in the scheme of things, Harvard could be chillingly high-minded. But its stuffiness was as much New England reserve as anything else. In any event, elitism was not something John Lomax would quarrel with.

At the time he went there, near the end of President Eliot's long and eventful tenure, Harvard's faculty included many of the nation's most distinguished academic names of that era—among them William James, Josiah Royce, George Lyman Kittredge, Barrett Wendell, Irving Babbitt, Frederick Law Olmsted, George Pierce Baker, and Alexander Agassiz. Never mind Henry James's prattle about Harvard's "provincialism"; to John Lomax it was as near to the center of the universe as he could hope to get.

The Lomaxes' initial visit two years earlier had been exhilarating but all too brief; moreover, as a mere summer student in ancillary classes which awarded only a "certificate," Lomax had scarcely felt himself a true Harvardian. Now he was a bona fide graduate student there, properly admitted to a full-time degree program.

The Lomaxes arrived in Cambridge on Sept. 12 and found rooms in a small but comfortable boardinghouse at 67 Oxford Street, a few blocks north of the Yard. On September 26, three days past his thirty-ninth birthday, John enrolled in English 1, "Chaucer," taught by Professor F. N. Robinson; English 2, George Lyman Kittredge's "Shakespere" (as Kittredge insisted it be spelled); and English 5, "Advanced Composition" under L. B. R. Briggs, who was dean of the Faculty of Arts and Sciences. These were all full-year courses. In addition, for the fall term, Lomax took English 3a, "Anglo-Saxon," under Dr. K. G. T. Webster, and English 33, Barrett Wendell's "Literary History of America."

Among his classmates were a number of men who later established academic and literary reputations and became names familiar to generations of English graduate students: Joseph Warren Beach, Oscar James Campbell, Tom Peete Cross, James Holly Hanford, and Jay B. Hubbell. T. S. Eliot entered Harvard as a freshman that fall; Van Wyck Brooks was an undergraduate in Briggs's English 5. Among the juniors was Charles Seeger, destined for a significant role in Lomax's life (and Lomax in his) thirty years later.

The role of George Lyman Kittredge and Barrett Wendell as Lomax's guiding lights at Harvard is well known. A role every bit as important, although less publicized, was that of Dean Briggs, who was to rescue Lomax from a serious crisis the following spring and who over time became in many ways a closer friend and benefactor than either Kittredge or Wendell.

There were many seeming differences between the two men—Briggs the austere but amiable New Englander, erudite, upper-crust, descended on his father's side from John Alden and Priscilla Mullins; Lomax the rough-cut Texas farmer's son, with a veneer of savoir faire but beneath it bumptious, moody, insecure—but it was not as unlikely a relationship as some thought. Of course, at the time they met, Lomax had scarcely any professional standing or social position and was in effect a nobody, while Le Baron Russell Briggs was not only Harvard's distinguished dean but also Boylston Professor of Rhetoric and Oratory, an illustrious post whose previous occupants included John Quincy Adams, Edward T. Channing, and Francis James Child.[15] But Briggs was not a man who relished rank and title; he served as dean because he genuinely cared about students regardless of their social position or origin and devoted a large part of his time and energy to their welfare.

Slight, still boyish in appearance (although he was twelve years older than Lomax), Briggs beneath his plain Yankee countenance was a warm man, more relaxed and genial than either Kittredge or Wendell, and he drew the affection as well as the respect of his students and colleagues. He had begun as a lowly teacher of English and classical languages at Harvard in 1878. Despite various honorable elevations into the administrative ranks, he remained essentially a teacher—"a teacher," said one who knew him, "who loved youth and had a genius for letting youth love him."[16] At the time, Lomax might have wished to describe himself in exactly the same way. Just what Briggs saw in Lomax—ambition, intelligence, energy—is unknown, but he took him up at the very time when John most needed support and encouragement. One measure of the relationship is that, of all his course work at Harvard, the only papers Lomax saved were those he wrote for Briggs.[17]

Briggs's English 5 course in composition, since its inception in the late nineties, had become a Harvard institution, and Lomax was to find it both exhilarating and demanding. Enrollment was set at thirty—large for a writing class—and consisted mainly of mature graduate students, some of whom might already have published in minor fashion (as indeed Lomax had done). Briggs's interests were not limited merely to expository writing; his students were encouraged to submit fiction and poetry as well.

Briggs personally read and wrote comments on every paper, and each Tuesday and Thursday at 2:30 P.M. he met with the class in Sever Hall for an hour of criticism. He read aloud from their work, then called for discussion. That was followed by a session of impromptu writing, during which each student wrote a criticism of what had been read or discussed. At the next meeting, Briggs read from the criticism, and that in turn was discussed and written upon; the cycle went on and on. Between October and March, when he began to suffer health problems, Lomax wrote over thirty major papers for Briggs, not counting all the "dailies," which were written in class. Additionally, there were regular conferences between the dean and each student, during which Briggs went over the man's work and offered his appraisal. Under such "beneficent but penetrating watchfulness," said one of them, every student "experienced an incessant scrutiny of soul. . . . It was a liberal education just to be going around with oneself in that frame of mind day after day."[18]

Lomax submitted a few of his poems (Briggs thought them essentially "mediocre") and also the account of his Christmas visit in 1898 to Shirley Green in Cuernavaca, redolent of bad Poe but suitably disguised as fiction. His nonfiction topics divided into two or three categories. He wrote a number of papers on literary figures—Meredith, Kipling, Browning, Dryden, Tennyson—subject matter that was a natural outgrowth of his studies in literature, past and present. Several papers dealt with his responses to Harvard, valuable for what they reveal of the cultural clashes that he experienced—or, with his talent for self-abasement, only imagined. In an early and no doubt politic effort, he wrote of his great surprise at finding his Harvard instructors cordial and accommodating, lacking "the coldness of the d——d Yankees" he was prepared to face. But that happy attitude changed when he went alone to a meeting of the Graduate Club at Phillips Brooks House and no one there offered to introduce himself. Lomax came away feeling slighted and wrote an account of the event for English 5. Briggs, who found the essay "correct but rather stiff," responded to Lomax's complaint with the obvious question: "Why didn't you speak to somebody yourself?"[19]

Closely related to the Texan-goes-to-Harvard papers were two or three which focused strictly on Texas or on the South. Here Lomax took up an old pose that seemed to surface whenever he left the Lone Star State. As early as his University of Chicago days, for the benefit of his northern professors he had subtly depicted himself as a hard-bitten ex-cowboy, now turned civilized and sophisticated, dressed up in coat and tie and gone East. Essays on such topics as "An Old Range Bull" and "How to Rope and Tie a Steer in Thirty Seconds" included invariable references to "my father's ranch." Nor was he above recycling his themes; one that he had first submitted in summer school two years before, a melodramatic tale of a cowboy shoot-out that began "Not very far from what was once my father's ranch door . . ." was now refitted and turned in to Briggs (who thought it "solid but undistinguished"). In a similar manner Lomax reworked several times the story of a lynching, probably based on an event from his youth, in which a black man on trial for raping a white woman is attacked by a mob, hauled from the courtroom, and hanged. It seemed to be a story he couldn't quite finish or let go of; from a first draft—with the puzzling title of "Ebony Fascits" [*sic*]—through successive versions entitled "The Courtroom," "Mob Vengeance," and finally, for Briggs, "A Southern Scene," he kept every copy.

Clearly, racial issues held for Lomax a greater than ordinary interest. He also wrote papers dealing with miscegenation and black convicts. In one essay—it does not appear to be fictionalized—he recounted an event which he had witnessed in San Antonio the previous summer. As he sat on the veranda of his hotel, police officers marched up a chain gang of prisoners and halted them in the street while the sergeant went inside for a beer. Lomax, watching a stoic black convict at the head of the line, began to reflect that from earliest boyhood some of the most tender associations in his life involved "negro friends." The prisoner vaguely resembled Nat Blythe, and his beaten, dejected look aroused Lomax's sympathy. When a fly landed on an open wound on the man's neck, he raised a weary hand to brush it away, and spied Lomax watching him with a look "partly of grief, partly of protest, partly of remorse." For a moment the man gazed silently at Lomax, then muttered to him, "I ain't never had no show, boss; I ain't never had no show."

Good English teacher that he was, Briggs picked a few nits—Lomax had written that the fly "lit" on the man, and Briggs preferred one that "lighted"—but he found the piece on the whole satisfactory. "The ending is particularly good," he said, and indeed it was. How accurately or honestly it represented Lomax's true feelings remained to be seen.

In broader fashion Lomax examined the racial problem—as he saw it—in an ambitious essay entitled "The Solid South." An effort to explain the domination of the South by the Democratic party, it was in many ways a perceptive analysis, but one which ultimately ran aground on the matter of race: "overstepping every question that moves the South is the shadow of the black race." "Instead of the relation of master and slave, however unwise, there is now two peoples [*sic*] separated more and more widely by distrust and fear. Education has thus far only widened the gulf, making the negro more discontented and the white man less tolerant. So long as the black man is there and so little understood by his northern sympathizers, the work of the southern politician will be easy. There will always be a 'Solid South,' and the South, sad to say, will continue to be sectional."[20]

It all seemed quite reasonable—Lomax was careful to keep his language moderate, his generalizations rooted in one reality or another—but what gradually emerged was the viewpoint of the unreconstructed southerner, convinced that northerners didn't know or understand blacks, distrustful of all efforts to educate the minority, and supremely confident that the South—the old, white, paternal South of his childhood illusions—would go on and on. In pointing to the predilection of southern politicians to prey on racial conflict to their advantage, he was accurately predicting the course of the next forty years or so—but it would happen in the face of increasing resistance and change that ultimately resulted in the overthrow of that system. The South is still sectional, as he said, and it is still sad to say that, but the South is no longer solid, at least not in the way Lomax thought. Breaking up the old attitudes and prejudices that had bound it together, however, was the work of future decades. In the meanwhile, John Lomax would go on his racial way, proclaiming on the one hand his earnest sympathies for the individual black and asserting on the other the absolute necessity of keeping all blacks segregated while their white superiors worked to "civilize" them.

Otherwise, Dean Briggs's composition class was a liberating experience. Lomax already wrote well, with a deliberate, if sometimes musty, flair, and thus it was easy for Briggs to give him praise—praise he badly needed. It was in Barrett Wendell's course in "Literary History of America," however, that Lomax was to discover his true métier.

CHAPTER EIGHT

The Highly Educated Man, Part 2

1906–7

In contrast to the homely, often rumpled Dean L. B. R. Briggs, Barrett Wendell cultivated the appearance of a dandy, dressed invariably in a cutaway coat and spats, with a walking cane extended from his little finger. He parted his hair carefully in the middle, grew a pointedly "English" beard, and paced pompously back and forth on the lecture platform, twirling his watch chain and issuing grave proclamations in a high-pitched pseudo-British accent that dazzled and terrified earnest boys from the New England countryside. Forward-thinking in matters of dress and learning, conservative to the point of reaction in all else, he had, said one student, "the air of an Anglicized Boston man of letters who had crossed the Charles to speak to the boys about life."[1] Apologists for Kittredge, who was in some ways even more flamboyant and frightening, could point out, correctly, that much of "Kitty's" arrogance was an act, covering up an essentially warm and generous nature, perhaps even a certain insecurity, but the most said for Wendell was that beneath the fancy togs and magisterial bearing "he was a man of great simplicity, irreproachable motives, and profound devotion."[2] Wendell and Briggs, to the surprise of many and the amusement of others, were close friends, a circumstance which probably owed a great deal to the fact that they were near the same age, had worked together from their early years on the faculty, and were jointly responsible for having brought Harvard's composition curriculum to its present state of excellence.

In the fall of 1906, Wendell was fifty-one years old and in the prime of his Harvard career, which he began as an undergraduate there in the 1870s.

As a teacher he had covered broad ground, passing from English composition to Cotton Mather to Shakespeare. He wrote major texts on those subjects as he went along, steadily widening his scope in what was just then becoming known as "comparative literature"—the attempt to study simultaneous relationships in the literary matters of many cultures and nationalities. In the late 1890s, drawing on his interest in the nation's colonial literature and history, Wendell had developed what was, in effect, the nation's first course in American literature, Harvard's famous English 33—"Literary History of America." It was in this class that John Lomax came to a revelation—or it came to him—which would profoundly affect the course of his life. He recounted the key event in his autobiography: "I chose American Literature among my English courses at Harvard in 1906. At the beginning of the second term the instructor, Professor Barrett Wendell, asked each man to select examples of regional literature for study until the end of the session, and to prepare a thesis to be read in class. 'I am worn to a frazzle,' Professor Wendell declared, 'with reading, year in and year out, dissertations on Emerson, Hawthorne, Thoreau, Holmes and Poe. You fellows come from every section of the country. Tell us something interesting about your regional literary productions.'"[3]

Lomax seems to have confused the timing of Wendell's momentous pronouncement—"Literary History of America" was offered only in the fall term—but there is no doubt of its consequences. For the first time, Lomax had gotten official confirmation that there was meaning and value in his native culture—the raw, uncouth life of the frontier.

Each student met with Wendell in his office in Grays Hall to discuss a possible subject for the term paper. Lomax first suggested that he could write about Negro music, but when he also mentioned cowboy songs and said that he had in mind songs which the cowboys "made up" while they worked, "Professor Wendell sprang from his chair, and, in his enthusiasm, came around the table to shake my hand."[4]

So enthusiastic was Wendell that he arranged an audience with the eminent George Lyman Kittredge, whose background in comparative literature was even broader than Wendell's. Moreover, Kittredge taught "The English and Scottish Popular Ballads," a course which derived from the vast, pioneering work of Kittredge's mentor, Francis James Child (1825–96), who had been Harvard's first professor of English. It was Child who had introduced to the English-speaking countries the notion of bringing together folksongs as a means of studying the culture of those who created and sang them.

By no accident was the definite article "The" the first word in the title of Child's masterwork, *The English and Scottish Popular Ballads* (in five quarto volumes, the work of a lifetime). So exhaustive was its scope and so overpowering its scholarship that for years folklorists merely took for granted that Child had found and brought together all the traditional ballads in English that ever were. They numbered exactly 305 and anything beyond that, however much it might seem like a ballad, look like a ballad, or sing like a ballad, simply could not, by virtue of Child, exist as a ballad of tradition. Child's work lived on in Kittredge's ballad course, essentially the only one of its kind at any major university and thus a seminal focal point for anyone interested in folksong. (It is worth noting that the course, although regularly scheduled, was not being offered during the 1906–7 academic year, and Lomax seems neither to have known nor been concerned with that circumstance when he went to Harvard.)[5]

The meeting between Lomax and Kittredge took place prior to Christmas of 1906.[6] Kittredge expressed immediate interest in what Lomax told him about cowboy songs and suggested ways that Harvard—or at least Wendell and Kittredge—might support his efforts to increase his stock of material, which at that time apparently consisted of little more than the few verses he had published in "Minstrelsy of the Mexican Border" eight years before, coupled with vague memories of songs he had heard growing up.[7]

Despite the confused chronology of Lomax's autobiography, it is certain that he had met with George Lyman Kittredge by late December. On the twenty-third of that month he wrote to Bess, who was visiting relatives in New York: "I am just back from Prof. Kittredge. He was cordial and is genuinely interested in my work. We are to extend the collection over the entire West, through printed circulars to newspapers and teachers of English. He will join me in issuing the circulars and they will be printed at the Harvard Press at no cost to me—or rather to us, for you are really my precious little partner in all that I do. I must not forget to add that he gave me a fine cigar. We smoked and chatted for more than an hour."[8]

Barrett Wendell's call for regional literature marks a turning point, an event that significantly changed the course of Lomax's life by opening to him possibilities for his talents that earlier he had only remotely considered. It is fitting that the first step in this new direction should have taken him to George Lyman Kittredge, at forty-seven already a gray eminence at Harvard, a man very different from Lomax and yet in certain ways much like him.

Like Briggs and Wendell, Kittredge was Harvard to the core, having also begun his career as an undergraduate there. Although he was the youngest of the three, by the time he was in his mid-forties his brilliant, far-ranging scholarship and imperial manner had made him Harvard's most famous personality—"character," some said—and arguably the greatest teacher of his time. Indeed, for most of his adult life, he was America's best known literary scholar here and abroad.

Kittredge, who was only seven years older than Lomax, had graduated at the top of his class in 1882. Although he was eager to begin graduate study at Harvard, lack of funds forced him off into rural New Hampshire, where for a few years he taught Latin to the "manly boys" at Phillips Exeter Academy, an episode he regarded in much the way that Lomax looked upon his exile to Texas A&M—with the significant difference that the essentially upper-crust student body of Phillips Exeter bore little resemblance to the coarse plowboys and mechanics at A&M.

A year of study abroad (1886–87) qualified Kittredge to return to Harvard in 1888 as an instructor in English, and his climb to prominence was rapid, despite the fact that he was among a band of young conservatives on the faculty who opposed President Eliot's programs to modernize the university. By 1895 (when Lomax, at twenty-eight, finally got to the University of Texas as an undergraduate), Kittredge had reached the rank of full professor, having the previous year succeeded Child as chairman of the Division of Modern Languages. He was to hold that post for two decades. By the mid-nineties he had already become something of a legend, the object of endless stories, anecdotes, and rumors.

Many of the stories centered around his famous English 2 course—"Shakespere"—conducted for years on Monday, Wednesday, and Friday mornings at 10:00. So dramatic was Kittredge's appearance that it became a custom of the class each morning for a vanguard of students to spill out onto the steps or grass in front of Harvard Hall to catch a first glimpse of "Kitty" as he made his progress from his spacious Victorian home on Hilliard Street, a few blocks west of the Yard, down Brattle Street to Harvard Square—where, legend has it, he would raise his cane as a signal against the traffic and march boldly across, impervious to the shouts and honks of passing drivers.[9]

Striding on through Johnston Gate toward Harvard Hall, he was unmistakable—a tall, lithe figure in a light gray suit and matching gray fedora, mottled cravat, and a luminous white beard (it made him look a great deal like G. B. Shaw, although Kittredge disdained the resemblance).[10] He was a passionate cigar smoker and invariably puffed away at a large *Elegante* on his way to class, at the last moment tossing the remnant off into the shrubbery with a grand flourish as the students scrambled up the stairs ahead of him. With a majestic air, he swept past those who lingered in the hall, a keen eye peeled for any head still covered by a hat (spying one, he would shout at the offender to remove it; there were stories that he had doffed student headgear himself with a swipe of his cane or umbrella).

The "Shakespere" class was always large—sometimes as many as two hundred, although there were only ninety-four men in Lomax's section that fall of 1906—and the work was rigorous. Students read six plays intensively and were required to memorize lengthy sections—as many as six hundred lines altogether. The final examination also covered a broad range of supplementary reading.[11] Kittredge was a tough grader. To the disgruntled parent who complained about a son's C, Kittredge replied, "My own daughter got a D in my course in Shakespere some years ago."[12] Lomax earned a respectable B.

Kittredge's method was essentially that of close textual reading, augmented by his own vast knowledge ("ruthless and superb," one contemporary called it) and his powers of imagination. Striding back and forth on the platform, he examined every line, every significant word in detail—often without a text—and kept up a running commentary on language, history, etymology, theater, whatever seemed relevant to the explication of Shakespeare's intention and artistry. From time to time he would pause, frame a question, and pick a name from the class roll, thereby, in the words of a former student, "making that name uncomfortable for three generations."[13] Woe to the man who had no answer, or merely hesitated. One poor soul began, "Well," then paused to indicate that he was formulating a response. Kittredge roared, "The grave yawns, the Devil waits."[14]

Undergraduates knew one Kittredge, graduates another. The histrionic Kittredge, many say, was a deliberate pose, calculated to strike terror into undergraduate hearts. Graduates, although not immune to his scorn, knew him as a mostly warm and genial man who treated them as fellow scholars. He often held his graduate seminars in the evenings at his home, where he passed around cigars and listened quietly as papers were read, offering at the end trenchant commentary and, very occasionally, restrained praise.

Kittredge's eminence belied humble beginnings. Son of a storekeeper and sometime farmer, he had earned his way largely through merit and hard work, with the occasional help of benefactors and a talent for stretching a dollar—circumstances which John Lomax could certainly identify with. On a personal level they shared a fondness for fine cigars and good whiskey, an essential shyness often masked by arrogance and theatrics, and a thoroughly conservative view of the world. As young men both suffered frail health and weak eyes from long hours of study; in later years both were robust autocrats who tolerated no fools and allowed no one's attention to drift away in their presence.

There were of course significant differences. Even in their political conservatism, there was little common ground between Kittredge's mainstream Yankee Republicanism and the reactionary tenets of a southern Democrat like Lomax—and Lomax, bright as he was, would never quite become Kittredge's intellectual (or social) equal. But these were not crucial matters where the collecting of cowboy songs was concerned, and that, after all, was what had brought them together.

· · · · ·

Soon after Wendell's call for "regional literary productions," Lomax had begun writing to possible sources in Texas. Now, in the wake of his first meeting with Kittredge, there were still other plans to "extend the collection over the entire West," as John had told Bess. Kittredge and Wendell considered means of financing research in the field and discussed the possibility of applying for a grant from various benefactors, notably the Carnegie Institution, where Wendell had (or thought he had) connections.[15] At their urging Lomax stepped up his letter-writing to Texas and drafted a circular that would advertise the quest among editors and teachers throughout the Southwest.

In the midst of all this activity, coupled with the approach of examinations for the fall term, Lomax somehow found time to socialize. His Chaucer professor, F. N. Robinson, encountered him in the post office one day during the Christmas holidays and took him to a tea at the Phillips Brooks House, where Dean Briggs introduced him to President Eliot. "We chatted quite a chat,"[16] John reported glowingly to Bess, who was still visiting in New York. He went to see Bertha Kalish in *The Kreutzer Sonata* and yielded to an invitation to a night on the town with "a band of congenials" from Texas known as the Musketeers.[17]

Constantly troubled by his dead-end situation at A&M, he also found time to start looking for a job that might get him away from College Station. Through the Clark Teacher's Agency ("New York, Chicago, and Boise"!), he applied for positions in the English departments at Oberlin and South Dakota's A&M (now South Dakota State University). Further, he still had hopes that something might open at the University of Texas and kept up correspondence with its president, David F. Houston. Houston sent occasional reports on the University's continuing skirmishes with the state legislature, dealt patiently with Lomax's apprehensions about life at Harvard, and largely ignored hints about job possibilities (when the position at racially integrated Oberlin failed to materialize, Houston said only that it was probably for the best: "I do not believe you would enjoy teaching black men.")[18]

Despite Lomax's newfound enthusiasm for cowboy songs, his health, always precarious, began to suffer from long hours and the bleak New England winter. Still he struggled on, memorizing Anglo-Saxon declensions for Kittredge's *Beowulf* class, writing dull papers such as "Karsish and Cleon" and "Meredith's Themes and Characters" for Briggs. Bess was also plagued by colds, earaches, and general depression from the weather. Moreover, she was approaching the seventh month of pregnancy with their second child. In late March it was decided that she would take little Shirley, now a toddler, and return to Texas to await the baby's birth. She had hardly gone when John was afflicted with an inflammation of both eyes and with stomach trouble, a debility so serious that he began to worry about finishing the term. Bess wrote a long letter of support and encouragement, with some typically practical advice, urging him to enjoy all the pleasures he could, "join the union and play in the gymnasium," and, most of all cultivate the friendship of Briggs, Wendell, Kittredge, and the students who were sympathetic to him. If his work suffered, she said, so be it. She also urged that he renew his efforts with Houston by having his Harvard professors write letters of recommendation. John replied that her advice was "clear-minded and sensible," but she was forgetting that he wouldn't have anything to say to Houston "should I dawdle along with my courses."[19]

There was also the business of ballad collecting to attend to. With the help of Kittredge and Wendell, Lomax prepared a form letter to be sent to western newspaper editors. In mid-April, one thousand printed copies of the circular letter arrived from the Harvard Press, and Lomax, despite his disabilities, set about trying to get them addressed and in the mail. The circular, dated April 12, 1907, and addressed "To the Editor," identified the writer as a member of the faculty of Texas A&M on leave for graduate study at Harvard, where as part of his work he was endeavoring to "make a complete collection of the native ballads and songs of the West." He described the sort of thing he wanted, pointing out, significantly, that they were for the most part songs which had never been in print, but "like the Masonic ritual, are handed down from one generation to another by 'word of mouth.'" They were, he said, "attempts, often crude and sometimes vulgar, to epitomize and particularize the life of the pioneers who peopled the vast region west of the Mississippi River." Insisting that such "pioneer ballads *do* exist," he asserted that he had already collected a hundred from Texas and called on the editors to help him preserve "this expression of American literature" by soliciting such material from their readers, which was then to be published "in book form."[20]

The circular carried the endorsement of Wendell and Kittredge—"Mr. Lomax's plan has our hearty approval"—and indicated in passing that whatever he collected would be placed in the library at Harvard. (Nothing more would be heard of this for many years—until Lomax, in old age and nursing a slight from the Library of Congress, threatened to leave everything to Harvard.)

By early May, with most of the circulars in the mail, replies were coming in in such numbers that Lomax gave up trying to acknowledge them. One respondent, interestingly enough, was his old nemesis at the University of Texas, Morgan Callaway, who sent him some twenty songs, had the circular letter published in the *Texan,* and wrote to Barrett Wendell enthusiastically endorsing the project—acts strangely at variance with Lomax's story that Callaway had stifled his interest in cowboy songs a dozen years earlier.[21]

His eyes and digestion continued to plague him. For relief he went to hear Caruso in *Aida* but had to squeeze his way through the crowd (and lost his only gold sleeve-button "to some light-fingered dago" in the crowd). He didn't much care for Caruso, he wrote Bess. "Emma Eames and [Pol] Plancon were better." During the spring vacation he went to see the stage presentation of *Brown of Harvard* and to watch the Boston Marathon ("It was won by an Indian"), which so invigorated him that he felt he should have been among the runners. But later, "a touch of my trouble" returned, and for a remedy he took hourly doses of one-tenth of a grain of calomel (mercurous chloride, a purgative and fungicide). Still later, "some quinine and a good deal of my usual medicine [a whiskey toddy]" improved his condition considerably, although his eyes were soon bothering him so much that he could no longer take notes in most of his courses.[22]

This tumultuous time had its lighter moments, although Lomax, with his sober, dead-ahead outlook, was scarcely aware of them. One day while busy trying to get the cowboy song circulars into the mail, he was interrupted by a visit from a Colonel Pierson, the Boston relative of a Greenville, Texas, lawyer whom Lomax knew only slightly. Pierson, in the spirit of looking after expatriate Texans, invited John to his lodgings for dinner. Lomax remembered the street address but on his way to keep the engagement realized that he'd forgotten the man's name. He paced back and forth in front of his host's house at 31 Chestnut Street for nearly half an hour before finally going to the door. In desperation, he rang the bell and told the maid "I wanted to see COLONEL wangy-wangy (deep down in my throat)." That ploy worked for the time being; the maid fetched the master of the house and the evening proceeded without incident. But now the man was coming to return the call, and Lomax feared that all was lost unless Bess could rescue him in time. Perhaps, he said, he would have to wire her.

"Your man's name is Colonel Pierson," Bess wrote back dryly, and, with John's priorities in mind, added that she hoped the news reached him in time "to save your life and a telegram."[23] Lomax's notorious confusion with names apparently developed early; he was absentminded about friends and relatives as well as important figures and was forever sending mail to the wrong people and places. He once addressed his good friend H. Y. Benedict as "Roy Benedict" and sent a letter to his mother in Oklahoma, a state where she'd never set foot. He often thought the North Carolina folklorist Frank C. Brown was "J. C. Brown" and years later, when it really mattered, he insisted on addressing Librarian of Congress Herbert Putnam as "Frederick W. Putnam." (Putnam, an eastern aristocrat in the mold of Wendell and Kittredge, alluded mildly to the mistake once or twice, but when Lomax failed to take the hint, he coldly remarked, "My preference is to be addressed by my correct name.")[24]

• • • • •

In the midst of getting out the cowboy ballad circulars, suffering increasing problems with his eyes and facing preparation for the end of the term, Lomax came up with still another research project which he was sure would interest Kittredge even more than cowboy songs—a study of Negro dialect as he had experienced it among country people in Brazos County. Drawing on his old affinity with blacks, he was convinced that such a study would shed important light on eighteenth-century English idioms. Blacks who had not mixed with whites had, according to his theory, preserved the language they learned as children—the language of the early planters ("men of culture," according to Lomax) who had brought them from Africa in chains. "This idiom I hold the negroes still speak," he said, and Dean Briggs had told him that if even half of his theory could be demonstrated, the work would make him famous. Loyal Bess urged him on but suggested that the scheme looked terribly complicated; to her it seemed more reasonable to think that the speech patterns and vocabularies learned from the first slave masters would have become "hopelessly entangled" in the mass of cultural influences imposed upon blacks through the centuries.[25] Nothing came of the project, but it held the germ of a notion that later formed the basis and design of most of Lomax's folksong collecting—the idea that black society, because of the special nature of its separation and isolation from mainstream culture, was the purest transmitter of American folkways, especially folksong, having passed the material down from generation to generation unadulterated by change and "progress" in the larger society. It was his perception of this circumstance that would eventually take him to prisons, whose black population endured the most severe segregation and isolation of all, and was thus, he felt, the purest of all sources.

As Lomax's printed request for cowboy songs reached newspapers all over the West and Southwest, the mail brought a rising flood of replies. "Letters poured into my Cambridge address," he recalled, but among them were dozens of dead ends and negative responses, many from "cranks and plain damn fools," as he said later.[26] An editor in Denver who claimed to have lived for thirty-five years among cowboys and Indians wrote to propose that he and Lomax collaborate on the work, and Lomax, who was suffering more and more with his eyes, thought the arrangement sounded promising. Kittredge immediately advised against it and so did Bess, reminding John that he had all the support he needed in her. He would supply the head for the project, she said, "and I the eyes therein, and the hands."[27]

Then it all seemed to fall apart—Harvard, his health, the folksong search that was to make him famous. For weeks following the dinner with Colonel Pierson, he'd been bothered with a recurrence of digestive trouble. His eye trouble grew increasingly worse, compounded by the general stress of approaching examinations. For the first time ever, he'd gotten behind with his work. He was scrambling to catch up, but the task seemed overwhelming. Already he'd begun to think the unthinkable, warning Bess that "you must not tell my friends I expect a degree."[28]

Finally one night in early June while hard at work over his books, he collapsed and woke up the next day in Stillman Infirmary without knowing, he said, how he'd gotten there. As he lay in a mild daze, suffering from what he later referred to as a "brain lesion," the future looked bleak indeed.[29] It now seemed certain that he would not recover in time for final exams, which meant that he would return to Texas "with no evidence . . . that I had ever been to Harvard University."[30]

In stepped Dean Briggs, who came to the infirmary immediately. He was back every day to check on Lomax's condition, and soon other faculty members began to appear, all sent by Briggs—Fred Robinson and Barrett Wendell and "finally Jove himself, George Lyman Kittredge, to wish me a speedy recovery."[31] Then, as Lomax was improving but still at his lowest spiritual ebb, Briggs returned with the information, in a note slipped under the door lest he disturb the patient, that he had made the rounds of Lomax's instructors and all agreed—contrary to the rules—that he be given full credit for his year's work without taking final examinations. He was free, said Briggs, to return to Texas whenever the doctors would release him.

Years later, Kittredge told Lomax that he had been out the night before and returned home at 2:00 A.M. to find Briggs on his front step, waiting to report to Kittredge, as chairman of the division, that Lomax had met the requirements of Briggs's English 2 course.[32] Lomax then realized that the dean had scarcely slept that night, for he had been at Lomax's hospital door as the sun came up the next morning.

On June 11, Kittredge made the faculty's decision official: "I hereby certify that John A. Lomax has completed a full year's work with high credit for the degree of A.M., and that he is not required to take his final examinations, since the Division has ample evidence without such records."[33] The evidence in terms of grades—three A's and three B's—was only average, but it was a credit to both Harvard's enlightenment and Lomax's ability that despair turned to triumph and his year there ended with a bright flourish.

• • • • •

Lomax left Cambridge toward the end of the first week in June, while the term was still in session, taking with him a toy train for Shirley and assorted gifts for Bess and her family.[34] He arrived in Austin in ample time for the birth of his son, John Jr., on June 14. While Bess and the baby were still in confinement in Austin's Seton Infirmary, he took two-year-old Shirley—"the happiest, jolliest, smartest little witch or elve or fairy that ever was"—to visit his mother and other relatives in Meridian.

The peace and quiet of Bosque County was a good tonic, and as his health slowly began to improve, his thoughts turned again to the search for cowboy songs. Back at Harvard he had made ambitious plans to spend the summer traveling on horseback through the cow country in the Big Bend region of the Rio Grande, but now his health prevented that. "My physician will not agree to my projected trip," he wrote to Barrett Wendell, so he would have to pursue his ballad collecting by other means. From responses to the circular letter, he had identified three likely informants scattered about in Arizona, Texas, and Oklahoma, all very old and unable to write down any songs to be mailed. These he proposed to visit by train. One was an ex-scout for the army ("under Custer," Lomax said) now living in Arizona but expected to be in Texas that summer. The second was a black cook in Wichita Falls, who had worked on many trail drives and cooked for Teddy Roosevelt's hunting parties, and the last an old-timer in Guthrie, Oklahoma, who reportedly could sing every Texas cowboy song known in the early days. But Lomax couldn't afford train fare to any of these places, and he hoped that Wendell would be able to come up with money from the Carnegie people or other sources which he and Kittredge had blithely proposed in their initial burst of enthusiasm.[35]

Wendell and Kittredge had been discussing this very subject between themselves and were beginning to see that their efforts with the Carnegie Institution were not likely to succeed in the immediate future. Wendell turned his attention to possible private sources, writing to Lomax to ask what funds he would need, at minimum, for the summer. Lomax responded that the ex-scout had already come and gone from Waxahachie, where he'd hoped to meet him, but said he could visit the other two for "something like Fifty dollars." For another fifty, he could spend the rest of the summer pursuing other sources, now that his health was improving. His only expense would be for railroad fare, because it was the custom for ranchers to meet their guests at the train, even a hundred miles away, and provide all the amenities. "The welcome never runs out," he said. He had recently talked with a group of geological surveyors ("all of them graduates of eastern universities," he added for effect) who were interested in his work, and he was arranging with the U.S. Department of Agriculture to have field-workers aid in the search, along with various historical and folklore societies throughout the West. He told Wendell that he was daily more and more convinced of the importance of the project, remarking that "Everywhere there is interest and even enthusiasm for the undertaking." He had even received, he said, many orders for the book—a book he had scarcely begun to put together.[36]

Word came that the Carnegie trustees had declined to consider their informal proposal, submitted on short notice. Bess remained optimistic. "We will be all right," she consoled John. "They'll come through another year."[37] Even more encouraging, Wendell sent Lomax fifty dollars of his own money, and shortly he persuaded his brother Evert to do the same.[38] Lomax responded with effusive thanks, saying that he was almost ashamed to take the money and acknowledging that his debt transcended the financial support they were giving him. He scarcely understood, he said, why men like Robinson, Kittredge, Briggs, and Wendell had taken him under their wing; Briggs had given him more care and attention in his illness than his own father would have, and they had all been instrumental in convincing Harvard to "give me a degree which I had not really earned."[39] He found this all the more embarrassing in light of the way his efforts were shabbily ignored in Texas, a feeling no doubt reinforced a few days later when A&M turned down his request for a modest increase in salary.[40]

The projected folksong collecting trips were postponed for several weeks, while Lomax went camping up the Colorado River with a band of old friends and professional men from Austin. Among his University of Texas cronies were H. Y. Benedict, professor of mathematics and astronomy, William S. Sutton, soon to be Dean of Education, and C. S. Potts, who had taken a year's leave of absence from A&M to enter the law school at the University. Lomax's attention was also drawn to the presence of H. C. Pritchett, a state educator whose cousin, Henry Smith Pritchett, was president of the Massachusetts Institute of Technology and a trustee of the Carnegie Institution. Always convinced of the importance of knowing the right people, Lomax set about making an ally of Pritchett, whom he felt might speed access to the Carnegie officials. At the opposite end of the social spectrum, he was also attracted to Albert, the entourage's black cook, who had spent many years on the chuck wagons of cow camps and cattle drives. Albert didn't know any songs, John told Bess, but he told many good stories, and he had given Lomax the names of several people who might be good sources.[41]

• • • • •

The campers hunted and fished, loafed, ate watermelons by the wagonload, and spent their evenings around the campfire, sipping whiskey and telling tall tales. For Lomax the scenery and easy life were great restoratives. To Bess, at her parents' home with the children, he wrote detailed accounts of the natural beauty of the place, its cliffs, mountains, waterfalls, shaded paths, and the big river "which buoys me up like a gentle mother" when he went swimming morning and night. "I roll out of my cot at daybreak, walk 20 steps in soft sand to the edge of the bluff, and then take a header into the Colorado." The nights were cool and he slept well; although he still awoke at times in the night, "I am not restless or uneasy and I grow stronger."[42]

When the camping trip ended, he spent a few days in Austin. Then, while Bess took the children to visit in Meridian, he was off to San Antonio to see a University acquaintance, John Lang Sinclair, who in his undergraduate days had penned the mighty "Eyes of Texas" and fancied himself a connoisseur of folk poetry and song. From San Antonio, Lomax went to Fort Worth and Wichita Falls. Although he reported that he was "mighty busy" and "having good luck with the ballads," there is no record of just what, if anything, he turned up.[43] By the middle of September he was back in Fort Worth, visiting with his brother Richard. Bess wrote to him there: "Come on to me and lets go home [to College Station]."[44] Their yearlong odyssey from the Texas backwoods to Harvard was over, but it had brought with it a change of fortune, and life would never be quite the same again. Nor would John Lomax.

CHAPTER NINE

John Was A-Writin'

1907–10

At long last Lomax had a sense of mission. But momentous as his Harvard experience had been, the change it brought about was neither sudden nor dramatic. He was still "marooned" at lowly Texas A&M as an underpaid and little respected teacher of English to plowboys and engineers.[1] Higher education in Texas had little use for anything so trivial and common as folksongs (even worse: *cowboy* songs). A&M expected him to diagram sentences, lecture on punctuation, and, occasionally, extol the splendors of Shakespeare, Chaucer, and Browning.

Now at the age of forty and with a family of four to support, Lomax had little choice that fall of 1907 but to straighten his shoulders and go back to the isolation and tedium of College Station. He went back grimly determined to find a way out.

As soon as his degree had been assured in June, he set about marshaling recommendations and renewed his assault on David F. Houston at the University of Texas. As Bess had urged, he got Kittredge, Wendell, Briggs, and Robinson to write to Houston in his behalf. Robinson, whose letter was typical, told Houston that while Lomax's talents were obvious, "The fact that he was given his A.M., though he was unable to take his final examinations, shows that we regarded him as a man of exceptional quality." He ought to be encouraged to go on for his doctor's degree, Robinson said, but regardless, "I should expect him to be an enthusiastic and productive scholar. . . . I liked him thoroughly, and I know that Briggs and Wendell and Kittredge did also."[2]

Another avenue of escape lay in obtaining a substantial grant to fund the cowboy song project, to free him for as long as a year, or at least allow him to devote his summers to song collecting. Wendell and Kittredge renewed their efforts to gain the support of the Carnegie Institution in Washington. Wendell set Lomax to work in October on a preliminary proposal so they could get the necessary application forms, but it was not until January, after the exchange of many drafts and letters and anxious inquiries from Cambridge that he and Kittredge finally had Lomax's letter in hand. Then, "Mr. Wendell and I are moving in your matter," Kittredge assured him.[3]

Lomax outlined the project in much the same way as in the circular sent to newspaper editors, indicating that for some years "in a desultory fashion" he had been collecting songs and ballads of the Southwest. The circular had produced, he said, hundreds of songs, of which only a few had ever been in print and many existed only through oral transmission. The two dozen or so "specimen titles" which he cited provide for the first time some indication of the progress of his collecting efforts; the list includes such now-familiar ditties as "Jesse James," "The Old Chisholm Trail," "The Zebra Dun," and "A Home on the Buffalo Range" (presumably "Home on the Range," although the chronology of his autobiography suggests that he did not come upon "Home on the Range" until later that year). Like "Home on the Range," many of the songs that came to him would prove to be less "folk" than "composed"; still, they were valuable artifacts of a vanishing culture and would have disappeared were it not for Lomax. The nature and significance of this material he saw with considerable vision, and he grew eloquent in expressing that vision to the Carnegie trustees. The songs he sought would forever be of interest to historians and sociologists, for they expressed the native mind of the frontiersman and captured every element of the Old West. The narratives they contained, however "crude and unpolished," formed ballads as authentic as any found among English and Scottish sources. The music was as original as the words, shaped and formed by the conditions of western life—Indian war cries, the movement of the cattle trail, the vast emptiness of the prairies.

Lomax took some pains to point out the element of crudeness—both social and aesthetic—in the songs he sought, alluding to the "raciness" and "unprintable" quality of many (although the cowboy's coarseness, he primly insisted, "is rarely unwholesome"). It was because of this that the songs were rarely written down but instead passed along orally among the "elect"—men who shared the same cultural values and could be trusted both to appreciate such songs and to protect them from widespread dissemination among outsiders, who might be offended or otherwise find reason to disparage the material. In turn, it was this circumstance which required that the collector be a native, someone of the same cultural and social background—in other words, an old cowhand like John Lomax, who never hesitated to paint himself in that manner when it suited his purpose. In listing his qualifications for the robust, outdoor task of canvassing ranches all over the country by horse and train to gather songs, he looked straight past a long history of physical ills and his recent collapse at Harvard, baldly asserting that he was "in good health, and accustomed to the sun and horseback riding"—and once more gave his age as thirty-five, five years younger than he really was.

If the Carnegie Institution would supply the necessary funds, he planned to visit the larger ranches in every major cattle-raising state—he named seven, stretching from Texas to Washington, "and perhaps other states and territories." There he hoped to collect both the words and the music of every typical western song he could identify. He stressed the importance of tracking down sources in person—the typical westerner was uneducated and ill at ease with bookish matters, many could not write, and the few who could were not inclined to answer letters. But their very reliance on oral traditions meant that the most ignorant of them remembered things which the educated had forgotten.

To support this work, Lomax requested travel expenses and $2000 for a year's leave from A&M (he said $2000 was his annual salary, but like many grant applicants he fudged a bit; even after his promotion to full professor the following spring, he was paid only slightly over $1700). Alternatively, he would teach during the regular terms and collect songs over the next three or four summers, mostly by horseback. That would cost "$750 and possibly as much as $1000."[4]

In support of this proposal were strong recommendations from Kittredge, David Houston, H. C. Pritchett (the "connection" Lomax had courted while camping), Morgan Callaway (oddly enough), George P. Harrison, professor of history at the University of Texas, and H. H. Harrington, president of Texas A&M.[5] Conspicuous in its absence was the name of Barrett Wendell. Perhaps Wendell did not want to trade on his friendship with Weir Mitchell, who was one of the trustees, or perhaps he was being saved for later, in case they needed an all-out assault.

Lomax was eager for all the help he could muster. Always one for thinking big, he tried to enlist the support of President Theodore Roosevelt (who had been an undergraduate at Harvard with Kittredge and who had, as Lomax knew, strong ties to the Carnegie Institution). But this produced only a terse one-line rejection from Roosevelt's secretary: "In reply to your letter of the 18th instant I regret to say that the President is unable to give you any assistance in the matter to which you refer."[6] The effort was not entirely in vain, however; a year later, when Wendell tried again in Lomax's behalf, he found Roosevelt interested and supportive.

In 1908 the president of the Carnegie Institution was Robert S. Woodward, an astronomer, geographer, and former dean of the School of Pure Sciences at Columbia. The board of trustees was composed mainly of scientists and engineers. With that in mind, Kittredge in his letter of support emphasized that "Professor Lomax's investigations are of great scientific interest." Obviously employing "scientific" in its broadest sense, he quickly turned to the "historical, literary, and sociological significance" of the project, asserting that its ultimate importance lay in what it would reveal about "certain problems now much discussed in Europe and America"—specifically, the nature of oral tradition and the origins and transmission of folk ballads and folk poetry.[7]

The Carnegie technocrats were unimpressed. Two weeks later Woodward replied to Lomax, enclosing the application forms, but offering little encouragement: "I deem it a duty to inform you . . . that so many applications are filed with the Institution that no one of them, whatever its merits, can stand a high probability of being granted." He raised the question of whether such a book as Lomax proposed would have general appeal, complaining that "many of our publications do not appear to be needed by the public"; they had to give many away or, indeed, "pay people to read them." Unless they could recover some of the costs of publication, the Carnegie Corporation was not interested in funding the work, "even if the ballads in question might thus be lost to the world."[8]

Kittredge was not amused by Woodward's lofty tone. Woodward's letter, he told Wendell, "strikes me in very bad taste. There is a kind of labored and supercilious jocosity about it which indicates that he is a man in the wrong place." Kittredge and Wendell agreed that the book would probably sell enough to cover half the printing costs, which was essentially what Woodward wanted, and they discussed ways and means of conveying that opinion back to the Carnegie board and generally stepped up their campaign in Lomax's behalf.[9]

· · · · ·

Back in Texas, Lomax's efforts to move on with the cowboy song project were suddenly interrupted in early February by a brief but dramatic incident, eventually famous as "The Great A&M Strike." This momentary insurrection among the student body was apparently rooted in grievances harbored by various members of the senior class—straight-arrow types rather than oppressed radicals and reformers—who felt they weren't getting their share of special favors from the administration. Initially, the furor focused on a disagreement between President H. H. Harrington and the campus physician, Dr. Joe Gilbert, who was popular among the students. As the seniors lined up behind Gilbert, there came a flow of charges against the administration, suggesting at worst fiscal mismanagement, at best high-handedness and insensitivity to student complaints. All this was exacerbated by the nature of all-male life at A&M, isolated as it was in the backwoods, subject to Spartan conditions, strict military discipline, and a rigid caste system. In a secret midnight meeting on February 7, the seniors—as leaders of the cadet corps—ordered all undergraduates not to attend classes or participate in any college function.

Lomax discovered what was happening the next morning, when he arrived at his classroom to find it vacant. He looked out the window and saw the usually swarming parade ground also deserted. These ominous signs worked on him instantly; writing about the event years later, he supplied omens, lest the import of the scene escape his reader. At that very moment, he said, the huge American flag flying above the Main Building ceased to wave in the breeze and dropped motionless on its standard.

Walking across the empty parade ground to the dormitories, he found two students whom he considered to be friends, but neither would discuss the matter, except to tell him they had been ordered by the seniors to remain in their rooms. One said he would dig a redoubt if Lomax ordered him to, but he wouldn't walk across the parade ground with him for any amount of money. Lomax went back to his office, having learned nothing from talking with "these two fine Texas boys" about the culprits who, he felt, were trying to destroy the institution.

Part of his dilemma concerned his role as campus correspondent for the Dallas and Galveston newspapers. He conferred with his friend and colleague, C. S. Potts, who was the *Houston Post* stringer. They agreed that the public had a right to know what was going on, but decided their loyalty to the college was greater than that to the papers, or to the citizens whose taxes supported the college. Learning that the students had pledged not to write home about the strike, he and Potts conspired, according to Lomax's own account, to prevent any news of the uprising from reaching the public. It would no doubt have shocked him to realize that in their own safe, stolid fashion, they were also, in effect, "striking."

The faculty as a group was also divided; a later investigation by the board of directors blamed "the professors and their families" for failing to support "constituted authority."[10] But for Lomax the issues were not clear, or simple. As the strike continued, he went to his office one day to find there a prominent faculty member, who closed the door and in conspiratorial tones told him that the whole thing was President Harrington's fault; he had to be fired. The faculty member was there, he said, to find out how Lomax would "line up."

Stalling, Lomax attempted to defend Harrington, pointing out that the president had made possible his year at Harvard and always treated him kindly. The visitor said Lomax was obviously unaware that Harrington and his wife never missed a chance to ridicule the Lomaxes, and cited a number of such instances. Struck in a sensitive spot, Lomax wavered, recalling, now that he thought about it, that Harrington had always been a bit aloof. The dilemma grew, through a painful maze of efforts to resolve it: Gilbert, Harrington's foe, was the Lomax family physician, had seen little John Jr. through a serious illness, and thus was owed a certain allegiance; yet what were the motives of the man before him, who was trying to enlist him in a conspiracy against the president? He represented the faculty supporting the strike—that elite band of full professors to whom Lomax was a mere underling and outsider ("I with my $1300 a year salary didn't belong").[11] But if the senior faculty treated him badly, he reflected, so did the students, sticking to their tight little cliques and refusing his efforts to cultivate them. As he silently pondered all this, the "prominent member of the faculty" went away, bidding Lomax to reflect on their conversation and give him a decision. But he never returned, and Lomax was off the hook—or so he wanted to believe. The affair tormented him for years, until, late in life, he attempted to write out an account of it, possibly for his autobiography, and struggled through a dozen or more pages in several drafts before giving it up, no more certain of its meaning than he had ever been.[12]

Lomax's immediate superior, C. P. Fountain, showed no such irresolution. Fountain, whom the students called "Deacon" behind his back because of his sanctimonious manner, angrily insisted that the rules and regulations be enforced and called for the immediate dismissal of any student who refused to submit. "The school can get along without you," he shouted at a group of strikers. "There are twenty thousand other young men wanting to enter the College." Whereupon the students mockingly hailed the creation of "The Twenty Thousand Club," supposedly instituted by

Fountain and "his two trusty assistant organizers, Messrs. Lomax and Junkin [another English instructor]" to handle the phantom flood of eager replacements.[13]

There is other evidence that Lomax stood with Fountain in support of "constituted authority." Among the students' complaints against Harrington were charges that state funds were being mishandled. A student publication, the *Sophomore Battalion,* offered the following sarcastic commentary:

> For any information regarding the appropriations made to the College and the expenditure of same, apply to Prof. Lomax. He is extremely well posted on this subject and declares that there is no possible chance for grafting to be done here. He is so full of his subject (or something else) that he even gives his English classes free lectures once in a while, to their great delight (?) In his enthusiastic praises of the openness and absolute accuracy of all money transactions here, his beloved "Chaucer" is for the time forgotten and he gives himself entirely to his pet theme.

When Lomax was elevated to full professor in June, four months after the strike, another student publication reprinted the passage above with the headline, "What Probably Gave John A. His Promotion to the Faculty."[14]

News of the strike finally reached the public on February 11, when the *Dallas News* ran a front-page story: "College Clash Involves Cadets; Senior Class Mutinies." Similar reports continued through the week, from information supplied by Lomax but written by staff editors.[15] By the end of the second week, the seniors had been joined by the other classes in a united front, and the board of directors was hastily convened. All across the state prominent citizens, especially Texas Aggie alumni, were horrified by the thought that their bastion of old-line Texian values—God, flag, soil, and sword—had been breached by what were surely bomb-throwing anarchists and revolutionaries. Yet the students were not without support. Among their sympathizers were officers of the state's stock and swine associations, many of whom had ties to the college.

Many of the lowerclassmen, however, had no real stake in the argument. Upset by the interruption of their education and fearful of reprisals, great numbers began to drift away home. The hard-core continued to resist, disregarding orders to either return to class or stack their arms and leave. With the situation deteriorating, the board of directors was forced to act. On February 14, they announced a quick decision: Harrington was upheld; Gilbert and three others, including the football coach, were fired.[16] Order slowly returned, but the issue refused to die. Students claimed that the exoneration of Harrington was a whitewash, and newspapers around the state fiercely continued to argue the matter.

Having weathered the worst of the storm, Lomax went back to teaching Chaucer and collecting cowboy songs. For the latter, he was still depending largely on what came in the mail; except for a few days the previous summer, when he'd gone to San Antonio and one or two other places nearby to pursue possible sources, his "collecting" had been largely limited to material sent in response to newspaper notices of the circular letter he'd mailed to editors from Harvard the previous year. Many responses contained popular printed songs, duplicates of what he already had, useless fragments, or merely hasty jottings from people who had nothing to offer but took the time to write and say so.[17]

Some opportunity for rudimentary "fieldwork"—at least getting out and traveling around the state—came that spring in the wake of the Great Strike, when Lomax was sent on a two-week speaking tour of the public schools to repair the damage done by the uproar. Informal conversations with teachers, students, and parents enabled him to put out feelers about song material (there's no evidence that he got any). But in general he found his delegated duties disagreeable, especially when called upon to address large groups, an undertaking which even later, as an accomplished lecturer and storyteller, he genuinely dreaded. But he proved so good at it that the board of directors, responding to continuing turmoil over the strike and Harrington's handling of it, decided to repeat the tour that summer, again utilizing Lomax's talents for a recruiting trip whose itinerary this time included the normal schools at Huntsville, Denton, and San Marcos, as well as high schools around the state.

In his efforts to depict A&M's situation in a favorable light, he faced a formidable task. Newspapers around the state continued to fan the flames of controversy; that was most discouraging, he wrote Bess from on the road, but he was forging ahead. He felt that he was surely building up his stock with his superiors by taking on such a difficult venture. Pledging Bess not to tell anyone, he reported that a member of A&M's board had told him to be patient, that he was highly favored by the administration and "The Board will be generous with me."[18] It was not the first time that management had stroked an ambitious underling. In time the board's shoddy treatment of him would show just how willing he was to believe whatever they told him.

By this time the Lomaxes were A&M's official correspondents for the *Dallas News,* the *Galveston News,* and the two Houston papers, the *Post* and the *Chronicle* (Potts having again returned to Austin to complete his law degree at the University). John and Bess worked to increase the size and frequency of their dispatches, in some months adding as much as forty dollars to John's college salary of $150. And as usual, Bess had other business plans in mind, writing him while he was on the road in March that she was planning a new "scheme for a little extra money."[19] Whatever that "scheme" amounted to, it was eclipsed a few months later when he took up the notion of buying property in Austin and forming a partnership to establish a boys' school there. Busy with his public relations tour for A&M, he sent Bess to evaluate the situation, telling her that now would be a good time to leave College Station. She reported favorably on the proposition, but it was clear that neither of them liked the idea of a partnership or the burden of debt it would require. Bess thought they might try it for six months or a year, then sell out and move the school to a better location and "change its scope to one more like our ideal."[20] The projected boys' school was a subject of much discussion, planning, and negotiation for months, but like so many of their schemes for making money, nothing came of it.

The controversy surrounding Harrington and the A&M strike continued to grow, and Lomax's goodwill tour failed to stem the tide of public opinion. By August, Harrington had no choice but to resign. The board, responding to agitation rather than dealing with the real issues, replaced the president with one of its own, Colonel Robert T. Milner, a former commissioner of agriculture whose qualifications were managerial rather than scholastic. Milner did not know much about colleges, but he knew Texas politics, and he knew how to ride herd on a bunch of uppity farm boys. His appointment was a singularly Texas solution to a singularly Texas problem.

Lomax, who also knew something about politics, meekly returned to College Station and went about preparations for the next school year, keeping a low profile and hoping that his defense of Harrington had not placed him in jeopardy with the new administration. He and Bess turned their attention to such routine matters as getting a fireplace for their house and various ways of gaining the approval of his students, a subject of frequent concern. As the fall semester neared, Bess and the children went to visit her parents in Austin, and Lomax fretted that he was left alone to face the new cadets, who were certain not to like him. Bess wrote to placate him, again proposing grand plans for the future: they would do great work in the coming year, she said—"teach well and love the boys and cultivate friendships and work on the ballads."[21] Those were comforting words, very much what he wanted to hear—especially that business about cultivating friendships among the boys, for, as he frequently reminded her, "So much of our happiness depends on this attitude."[22]

In December Lomax made slight revisions to the Harvard circular and sent out another mailing to newspapers in Texas, Arizona, Idaho, and Montana.[23] His application to the Carnegie Institution was due for formal consideration in January. With that in mind, Wendell and Kittredge stepped up their efforts to apply whatever pressure they could. Wendell wrote to his friend on the board, Weir Mitchell, "urging the claims of Lomax." Should that fail, he proposed to Kittredge that they offer a series of literary lectures in Boston to raise money for the cowboy song project. "The fact of our professional standing would combine with the unusualness of our appearance in public" to insure success, he said. Three or four such lectures, he speculated, might raise as much as a thousand dollars at five dollars a ticket. An alternate suggestion was for "one general meeting somewhere, to which a good many people would be invited, where we should appeal for money in aid of Lomax's work."[24] But Kittredge was forced to decline; he had been chosen to deliver the prestigious Lowell Lectures during the coming year and was busy preparing his talks on five tragedies of "Shakespere."

In January, Wendell scored what seemed, briefly, to be a great coup. He had dined at the White House, he wrote Lomax, and struck up a conversation with Secretary of State Elihu Root, who "happened to mention that he is a Carnegie Trustee." Wendell promptly brought up Lomax's project, and Root was interested; more importantly, the conversation was overheard by President Roosevelt, who was also enthusiastic. He took down Lomax's name and, having assured Wendell of his support, wrote right away not only to Woodward but to other Carnegie trustees as well, urging that the project be funded.[25]

Unfortunately, the decision had already been made, and Wendell's sortie among friends in high places went for nothing. On January 25, Woodward wrote President Roosevelt to tell him that the Carnegie's executive committee had found it "inadvisable" to give Lomax the grant. "Since the Institution must live within its income, a majority of applications must necessarily fail to receive subsidies," he said in the chilly language of stiff-necked patrons down through time, adding loftily, "It appears to be highly desirable also, in the interests of due progress, for the Institution to avoid dissipating its income in aid of a multitude of minor issues which should be left to individuals and to other institutions."[26] Transmitting all this to Lomax, Wendell said bluntly, "It is pretty clear to me that Woodward's sentiment is that of a somewhat bigoted man of science who regards anything not technically scientific with suspicion."[27]

Disappointed, Lomax took comfort in Wendell's assurances that both Roosevelt and Root would continue to support his work and press his case with the Carnegie people. Lomax was particularly pleased that the president, through Wendell, had asked to see some of the material he had collected and reported that he was sending "more stirring songs" as thanks for Roosevelt's interest and encouragement, which later events would prove to be more than mere political pleasantry.[28] Inspired by the president's attention and eager to get a book into print, Lomax in early 1909 began to test the publishing waters, even though his cowboy song collection was still in rough form. It was, in fact, only one of a number of projects he hoped would interest publishers.

By February, he had written to several publishing houses in New York. One reward of these inquiries was renewed contact with his old friend and former assistant, Harry Peyton Steger, now an editor at Doubleday, Page & Company. Initially, Lomax proposed to Steger a book on George Meredith (he had finally finished his M.A. at the University of Texas in 1906 with a thesis on the novels of Meredith, and his offering it to Steger is further evidence that he was still not focused entirely on folksongs). Steger told him to send along a chapter, but added quickly, "The work you contemplate doing with cowboy ballads is, of course, more appealing to me than Meredith. It seems to me that you have a chance there to do something worth while."[29]

Lomax thought so too, but he needed reassurances. A few days later he wrote to a new and very small New York publishing house, Sturgis and Walton, asking if they would be interested in seeing a manuscript he called "Characteristic Western Poetry," alluding also to a book of cowboy songs he was working on. Like Steger, the publishers expressed mild interest, adding, "We should also be glad to see the 'Collection of Cow Boy Songs' whenever you have it completed and ready for publication."[30]

Lacking experience in such matters, Lomax took this as tantamount to an offer to publish, and hoping to impress his mentors at Harvard he sought their advice. Wendell said only that publication would be "abundantly worth while" and deferred to Kittredge, who had already told Lomax, "By all means publish."[31] But there was as yet no book to publish, and thus no real offer from either Doubleday or Sturgis and Walton.

Lomax regrouped, sending newly collected songs off to Wendell for his evaluation and laying plans to do fieldwork in the summer. He hoped to be able to travel through Texas, Arizona, and New Mexico for material that he had located but which could only be had by personal contact. "That, as you know," he told Wendell, "is the only way I can secure the music of the songs," and getting the music for each song was something he was more and more concerned with.[32]

. . . . .

On the home front, it had been a year of much illness. Although John's health was improving, Bess continued to suffer from the effects of John Jr.'s birth, and the children were afflicted with a variety of ills—Shirley with flu and "catarrhal fever," John Jr. with pneumonia and severe dysentery. In May Bess was confined to bed for several weeks—"a general breakdown," she said—then went to her parents in Austin to recuperate. All this, combined with his summer teaching duties, severely interrupted Lomax's work with the cowboy songs.

Bess took the children to visit her brother Will and his wife, Anna, in Dallas where Will was trying to sell stock in an auto supply business. Bess, impressed that Will was now the proud owner of a snappy new Maxwell touring car, blithely reported that her brother was "making lots of money at last." Earlier she had shown a healthy skepticism toward Will's business schemes; now, even in the face of his recent failure in the savings and loan business in Oklahoma, she urged John to invest in the auto parts enterprise, telling him that Will "guarantees 20% [return] and might be as much as 50%." Also, while in Austin she had located several vacant lots on West 26th Street near the campus and was trying to convince John they should buy them. Prices for property around the University were going up, she said, and "the old Varsity" was sure to keep expanding. Thrifty John resisted, telling her that people like her who were anxious to buy always paid too much. He urged her to take a ride with Will in his new car "and let him enthuse you with his big schemes."[33]

He changed his mind about the lots when they managed to haggle down the price from $4000 to $3600, then floated a loan from her father to make the down payment. It was more than just a good business deal; the notion of owning real estate in Austin had strong appeal to Lomax, who still felt that somehow, someway, they would return there permanently. It would be a safe investment, he assured Bess, and it did him good to know that she would have a home in Austin, adding wryly, "Then, too, we shall both enjoy paying for it."[34]

Bess was no less mindful of the debt they had taken on, having also prevailed in touting the auto parts stock. She recorded in her household journal that they bought ten shares in Will's company, paid $1500 down on four lots in Austin, "turned off the cook, & went in for saving." The Austin real estate proved a wise investment. As for the auto parts venture, scarcely a year later Will Brown was bankrupt and destitute, trying to peddle office ventilators in New York.

In Bess's absence from A&M, John again took his meals in the Mess Hall and occupied himself with domestic matters, one of which involved a continuing effort to get a fireplace for their house—or another house. A colleague who lived across the street was leaving, and Lomax fretted about asking the directors to assign it to him. Although he thought they would give it to him, it was much larger than their present place, and if that meant Bess would work herself sick taking care of it, he would be sorry he'd ever brought it up, he said. The barnyard menagerie continued to thrive; he reported that Beauty, the cow, was giving five gallons of milk daily, so much that he had to pour it out to the chickens.[35]

His ambitious plans to travel through the Southwest that summer collecting songs did not materialize, probably for lack of funds, but in August he was able to spend several days living and working with the cowboys on a ranch northwest of Austin, while Bess and the children vacationed at a campground on the Colorado River near Kingsland. He instructed Bess to tell Shirley that someday soon he would appear on a big brown horse and take her riding. He had just ridden with the ranch hands to drive up a cattle herd and was now going to help load them on the railcars.[36]

In September they returned to College Station and moved into the house across the street. Lomax returned to the manuscript of cowboy songs and efforts toward publication. He was increasingly convinced of the importance of obtaining the music which accompanied the songs he had collected. "In many cases the tune is the real life of the ballad," he wrote Wendell, and he was afraid there would be little public interest in his cowboy songs unless each one was accompanied by music. He had, he said, enough ballads to fill a "comfortable-sized volume" but music for fewer than half of them.[37]

A fresh source of possible funding had presented itself, in the form of a research award newly endowed at Harvard by the widow of alumnus Frederick Sheldon ('42). The Sheldon Fellowship, with an original endowment of almost $350,000, was a prestigious appointment designed to provide time and research support for postgraduates traveling or living away from Cambridge. Dean Briggs chaired the selection committee, and Wendell was prompt to nominate Lomax and sent both Briggs and President Lowell a letter full of high praise for the cowboy song project, telling Lomax at the same time that while he and Kittredge were not on the committee, "Be sure that we will do all that is in our power." Pressing the point, he added: "Your researches, when they first came to my knowledge, seemed to me of extraordinary interest and importance, both as revealing and saving from destruction matter interesting from both its literary and its historical aspect; and also as throwing unique light on the questions of how popular literature arises."[38]

Wendell had also praised the project to his former assistant, Charles Read Nutter, who was now an editor at D. Appleton and Company in New York. Nutter wrote to Lomax and invited him to submit his manuscript of cowboy songs for consideration.[39] Elated at having aroused the interest of three publishers, Lomax saw visions of large advances and imminent publication.

In early November, Briggs notified him that the Sheldon committee was prepared to award him $1,000, assuming that A&M would give him a year's leave on half pay. Lomax submitted a written request to the A&M board, outlining plans to travel by horseback through the more thinly populated areas of West Texas and spend a year living "with the type of westerner who has not forgotten the old border songs." Emphasizing the advantages to A&M, he stressed that he would represent the college in his travels and whatever he published as a result would reflect glory on the institution.[40]

Once again he called out the big guns at Harvard to back him up. Briggs, Robinson, and Kittredge all wrote to President Milner to extol Lomax's virtues and praise the project.[41] Kittredge, high on the Mount, gently appealed to A&M's sense of identity—"the results of [Lomax's] year's investigations will be extremely creditable to the institution with which he is associated"—and cannily asserted that "this particular piece of work should be done by a Texas man."[42] All to no avail. The confidence Lomax had expressed, in the wake of the Great Strike, that "the Board will be generous with me" was unfounded. His request for leave was rejected unanimously, without a word of explanation.

Happily, the faith of Lomax's supporters at Harvard remained unshaken. Although Wendell told him that the Sheldon committee considered it vital that A&M contribute something to the project, he also assured him that "If you can't meet this condition, do not despair of something less."[43]

The committee went into huddle again and decided to go ahead and appoint him a Sheldon Fellow for 1910 and simply give him $500 outright. "Lomax is straight goods," said one committee member, "and we ought to see him through."[44] When Lomax got the news he went back to A&M's directors—properly polite but no doubt more than a little triumphant—to ask if they would at least release him from his commitment to teach summer school the coming year so that he could travel. That request was also promptly rejected, but by the time summer came around, his circumstances had changed, and what the board of directors of A&M College did no longer mattered.

· · · · ·

Meanwhile, there were other affairs to deal with. When Lomax left Harvard in the spring of 1907, he had asked Kittredge what he might do to repay him for his help and support. Said Kittredge, "Go back and organize a Texas branch of the American Folk-Lore Society." As far as Lomax was concerned, the only place where such an organization might take root and flourish was the University of Texas—it was clear that A&M had no use for such folderol—and he set about locating someone on the Austin campus who would help him follow through on Kittredge's injunction. The most likely prospect was L. W. Payne, a newly arrived English professor with an interest in folk speech and regional dialects. On learning of Lomax's cowboy song collecting, Payne had supplied one or two ballads from his students, and on several occasions the previous year the two men had talked casually about forming a folklore society. Finally, on Thanksgiving Day in 1909, when Lomax was in Austin for A&M's traditional "Turkey Day" football bout with the University, he called on Dr. Payne to see what they could do about organizing the society. "I nominated and elected Dr. Payne as the first president," Lomax wrote later, "and he nominated and elected me as the first secretary of the fledgling organization. As I recall, I was to do the active soliciting of members, while Dr. Payne was to act as cheer leader in Austin."[45] Their immediate plan, realized in due course, was to draft a constitution, solicit charter members (at $.50 a head) and then formally launch the society at the annual meeting of the Texas State Teachers Association in Dallas in December. Sixty-six dues-paying members were initiated at that time, and some thirty more joined by the end of April.

The Texas Folk-Lore (later "Folklore") Society was the second of all such state organizations to be formed, preceded only by the Missouri society, founded in 1906. Within only a few years, the Texas group was one of the larger and more significant of its kind, in some years enrolling more members than the national organization itself.[46] Lomax and Payne later developed a sort of Alphonse-and-Gaston routine in which each tried, publicly at least, to give the other credit for founding the Texas Folk-Lore Society. At the time, however, Lomax wrote to Wendell: "I am the originator and practically the only promulgator of the society" (he had organized it, he said, to help him with his song collecting—"in fact, that is my only interest in it.")[47] Ironically, as it turned out, neither Lomax nor Payne was present in Dallas for the official debut of their brainchild. Payne's wife was about to give birth; Lomax, largely through the good offices of George Lyman Kittredge, had been invited to present a paper on his cowboy songs at the annual meeting of the prestigious Modern Language Association, convening that year at Cornell.

At this juncture, feeling the weight of greater honor than the occasion actually warranted, Lomax might have preened a bit—but fame had its fearful side as well, and he characteristically went into a dither at the thought of addressing so lofty a group as the MLA, the preeminent organization of scholars and teachers of modern languages and literatures ("modern" as distinct from "classical"; in the title of the organization it means "since 1500"). What should he say to this august body? It was to Wendell, more accessible than Kittredge, that he took his apprehensions. Wendell replied that he felt himself "little competent to advise," but offered the suggestion "that you make clear then—in twenty minutes or so!—two things: first, the actual quality of your collection; second, the manner in which it illuminates conjecture concerning old balladry. For the former purpose, you have treasures. For the latter, the thing which occurs to me is a typical example of how fragments of a quasi-epical ballad are known to different people, no one of whom knows the connection[,] if not wholly consistent and coherent, which formed by putting the fragments together."[48]

These remarks show Wendell dutifully following the accepted line of ballad scholarship in his day—Francis Gummere's now musty and mostly discarded theory of "communal composition." Both Wendell and Kittredge, as friends and former classmates of Gummere, subscribed to the theory, but they were lukewarm disciples at best.[49] In offering Lomax advice, Wendell, for all his pedantry, knew that the course of human events was not likely to be altered by a single paper delivered before the MLA, and he wanted to put Lomax at ease. "Very likely," he added, in what for him was an unbuttoned moment, "some better means [i.e., other than ballad theory] of interesting the learned—as distinguished from the human—will occur to you."[50] That struck a responsive chord in Lomax, who was even less a theorist (although he would pay feeble respects in that direction), and far better suited to catch the interest of the "human" rather than the "learned" elements in his audiences.

No copy of his paper to the MLA at Cornell survives, and thus the extent to which he followed Wendell's advice—either scholarly or jocular—cannot be determined.[51] What *is* clear, however, is that he was a great success. It was one of those rare instances in which a single paper before a learned society did in fact have significant bearing on the course of cultural history. "Cornell, 1909" stands as a major turning point in the career of John Lomax.

His own autobiographical account of the event, composed three decades later, is characteristically taut with drama and spotted with misremembered dates and facts: "On a bleak wintry afternoon in late December 1911, a timid and uncertain young man stood on the platform in a circular auditorium in Cornell University to read a paper on 'The Songs of the Cowboys.' My book with the same title had just been published to a frozen-faced academic audience in Texas."[52] In fact, the year was 1909, the "young man" was forty-two, the title of the paper was "Cowboy Songs of the Mexican Border," and the book which evolved out of it was yet unpublished.

Possibly he was thinking of the circumstance that, in his absence from the Texas Folklore Society, which was meeting simultaneously in Dallas, Bess took his place to read the same paper—but hardly to a "frozen-faced" audience. Reporting that event to him, Bess described an audience of "about 50 appreciative people," many of whom came up afterwards to praise the work. "Your paper read mighty good," she said.[53]

It read mighty good to the gentlemen at Cornell, too. In *Adventures of a Ballad Hunter,* Lomax related the episode in wonderfully theatrical detail—how no one had greeted him when he appeared, "forlorn and lonely," to give his talk, how most of the audience had melted away when his paper was announced, how he had pushed on in the face of their indifference and gone into a big finish by "singing the dogies to sleep," giving "the long, eerie, lonesome night-herding yodel" which brought forth a surprising roar of applause—then afterward all sorts of compliments, dinner invitations, and general hoorays. It was all true enough, but his letter the next day to Bess was far more revealing. He had shown up for the session in his old brown suit, he told her, and was called to the podium sooner than he'd expected, dry-mouthed and stiff-tongued, needing a drink of water. He did not read well, he said, but got more attention from the room than the distinguished professors who had preceded him, Cook of Yale and Schofield of Harvard. The audience laughed so hard at his stories that he had to stop several times and wait for them to settle down. At the end he was "enthusiastically cheered" and had now become the center of constant attention—a hundred men or more had come up to congratulate him, several accosted him on the streetcar and took him to meet their wives, at dinner in the hotel his companions called on him to sing some of his songs, and he was such an impromptu success that the toastmaster for the association's smoker also insisted that he perform for that group. He sang "Git Along, Little Dogies" with what he termed "my bunch of cowboy professors" joining in on the chorus. Over and over he sang it; they wouldn't let him stop until his voice gave out. Even then, "the cheering kept up."

All sorts of extravagant things had been said to him, but they were not about him, he generously told Bess, giving her her due—they were praise for the "stuff that you have kept believing in and plugging away at."[54]

Late that evening Lomax took the train down to New York, and the celebrations continued. More than thirty years afterward, Prof. Raymond Weeks, a former president of the American Dialect Society, recalled the train ride: "Five or six of us sat in the smoking compartment of the Pullman, and none of us wished to sleep while John Lomax was awake. [He] sang dozens of cow boy songs, and we joined in on the chorus. A more delightful ride I never took."[55] Lomax's paper caught the attention of the *Nation,* which reported its substance in some detail, particularly intrigued by one song with so many stanzas that it seemed "intended to last from one end of the trail to the other." Pleased with the "remarkably poetic" quality of some of the songs, the writer noted that they were fast disappearing and emphasized the importance of collecting them.[56]

Lomax's work had been legitimized, however tenuously, by a national forum. In the wake came attention such as he'd only dreamed of—flurries of song texts, tips on likely sources, letters of encouragement and congratulation from important scholars, dozens of invitations to lecture. "After Cornell," he said, "I never lacked for friends among the Modern Language Association group." By his own count, "During the following ten or fifteen years I spoke to more than two hundred institutions of learning, in every state except three, for a total of more than five hundred engagements."[57] After Cornell, there came increasing attention to lecture tours, administrative posts, and book promotions, less and less talk of making friends among students and educating the poor boys and girls of Texas.

CHAPTER TEN

Git Along, Little Dogies

1910–11

In May 1910, Sidney Mezes, who had succeeded David F. Houston as president of the University of Texas, wrote a brief note to Lomax at College Station, asking him to stop by on his next visit to Austin to discuss "a matter of mutual interest." Lomax carefully preserved Mezes's message for posterity, scribbling across it, "This is the letter that brought me back from A&M College to the University."[1] His exile—at least for a time—was over.

The circumstance which finally rescued him from College Station was the offer of the newly created position of "Secretary of the University Faculties and Assistant Director of the Department of Extension," a title, one wag remarked, "almost as long as that of a Spanish grandee."[2] Just what was behind this unusual turn of events is not clear, but David Houston probably had some hand in it, even though he had departed from the University two years earlier to become chancellor of Washington University in St. Louis. Lomax had kept up a steady campaign to advance himself with Houston, who no doubt felt a lingering sense of obligation. Their relationship went back to Lomax's student days in the late nineties, when Houston had been one of his professors, and of course it was Houston who as president at A&M had taken him away from the Winston mess in the University registrar's office and thus was largely responsible for his going to College Station in the first place.

The new University president, Mezes, was also an old U.T. hand, and a Harvard man to boot, well acquainted with Lomax's considerable skills and his capacity for hard work. It is not difficult to imagine Houston leaving a strong recommendation in Lomax's behalf and Mezes, who was himself a capable administrator, agreeing that when some opportunity presented itself, Lomax would be an asset to Mezes's rather considerable plans for the University.

In the waning days of 1909 and the first weeks of 1910, Lomax had scored a series of distinct triumphs: his rousing performance before the MLA at Cornell, Harvard's bestowal of the prestigious Sheldon Fellowship, and most recently, a contract with Sturgis and Walton to publish his collection of cowboy songs. If Lomax strutted a bit, he had good reason.

Ironically, all this carried little weight with those who made the decision to bring him back to Austin. Writing of this period afterward, and thinking of the hardships he later endured while finishing the cowboy song collection, Lomax recalled, "Very few of my associates in the University of Texas expressed sympathy or took the project seriously. For them this crude product of the West had no interest, no value, no charm whatever."[3] Yet at the time he could write to Bess that the people at the University, even those with whom he had been at odds, "are genuinely glad to have me back."[4]

Although his duties (and titles) were to change from time to time, initially he was responsible for keeping the minutes of faculty meetings, printing and disseminating committee reports, and attending to all official correspondence. As time permitted, he assisted the director of extension, Dr. H. Y. Benedict, with what today would be called "outreach" matters—recruiting, publicity, and alumni affairs. Eventually these duties came to occupy him more and more, but at the outset he was essentially a sort of aide-de-camp to Mezes, to be on hand with whatever logistical support the president required. When the occasion arose, he was even expected to cover for Mezes. An article in the *Alcalde* dubbed him "John Avery Lomax, Utility Man," observing that whenever the president left town, Lomax "becomes president—indeed he becomes any place he undertakes to fill."[5]

Lomax had accepted the job with the stipulation that during his first summer he would be allowed to go on leave—the leave A&M had so contemptuously denied him—to pursue the objectives of his Sheldon Fellowship. In February, before the University of Texas job was offered, he had told Wendell that he hoped to get away by June 1 and spend up to four months traveling through the Rio Grande country of Texas, then into New Mexico and Arizona—"partly by horseback."[6] His change of employment caused some delay, which in turn shortened the length of time for the trip. Mezes told him to take his time settling into the job and agreed that he could leave on his collecting trip around the first of August.[7]

The legend has persisted—fed to some degree by his autobiography—of John Lomax roaming the Southwest that summer by horseback, an Edison cylinder recording machine strapped to the saddle horn, traveling from ranch to ranch to collect cowboy songs. In fact, the manuscript of the book he had been calling *Cowboy Songs of the Mexican Border* was essentially completed the previous fall. Just after the first of the year he signed the contract with Sturgis and Walton for its publication, and production was already underway in May.[8] He persuaded Wendell to write an introduction, and by July it was in hand. By that time also he had decided to call the book *Cowboy Songs and Other Frontier Ballads.* The original title—*Cowboy Songs of the Mexican Border*—carried an allusion to Scott's *Minstrelsy of the Scottish Border,* but Lomax decided that it "sound[ed] a bit affected and literary."[9]

The summer trip got underway on July 28. Lomax saw Bess and the children off to North Carolina to stay with relatives, then boarded the westbound train, traveling as far as El Paso in the company of Mrs. Benedict and her young son, who were on their way to meet Benedict in Los Angeles, where he was attending a meeting. Following a day or two in El Paso, Lomax set out to visit several places in southern New Mexico and Arizona, after which he planned to go on to the West Coast and up to San Francisco, to do library research across the bay at the University of California.

His first stop was in Deming, New Mexico, where his old friend from University days, Roy Bedichek, was homesteading on a tract of land some eight miles south of town. Since working in the U.T. registrar's office under Lomax, "Bedi" had spent time as a newspaper reporter in Fort Worth, taught school in Houston and San Angelo, tramped around Europe one summer with Harry Steger, and undergone a variety of other exploits. Once described as "artist, scholar, and primitive all in one,"[10] he was handsome and affable, known to clench a literary pipe in his teeth and affect the flowing neckerchief of poets (one photo of the period shows a resemblance to the young Robert Frost). In 1908, at the age of thirty, still single and still ripe for bold deeds, Bedichek headed west, not by wagon train but on a bicycle, to stake out a homestead in the shadow of the Florida Mountains in southern New Mexico. To survive, he was forced to take an ill-paid job in town as secretary of the Deming Chamber of Commerce, walking the eight miles from his farm and back each day (the bicycle had suffered a terminal accident) accompanied by a loyal but wonderfully loopy Airedale named Hobo.

"Bedi is wholesome, breezy, and sane," Lomax reported to Bess. He walked to and from town each day with Bedichek, slept out under the stars, hiked up into the nearby mountains the first weekend, and got a bad sunburn that peeled and made him look, he said, "homelier than ever." After a few days of this, he turned to work; in typical Lomax fashion, he had brought along a batch of University paperwork as well as his own. The immediate objective, however, was to complete his introduction ("Collector's Note") to *Cowboy Songs.* He also hoped to pick up a few additional songs in the area. Those hopes soon faded. Prospects for cowboy songs were not promising, he reported, but at least he absorbed a lot of local color that would help make his introduction to the book "somewhat livelier."[11]

Within a week he had completed the introduction, which, he told Bess, combined the "most forceful things" they had both been saying about the songs, with a few new observations of his own, inspired by the picturesque region where he was traveling. Pointedly acknowledging her contributions to his work, he told her that the introduction contained "some of your best sentences." Bedichek praised the manuscript, but Lomax modestly noted that Bedi was always inclined to be "too generous over my performances."[12]

With the "Collector's Note" out of the way and some University work done, Lomax renewed his efforts to locate new songs. He had been "seining saloons" and other low hangouts, but with only limited success. There were plans to visit a man he'd known in Bosque County who now owned a ranch near Silver Spring, northwest of Deming. Then came an invitation to visit the huge Apache Teho ranch further up in the Elk Mountains, near the Arizona border.

To Bess he wrote a colorful and detailed account of the trip, which had taken him further and further from civilization. On his arrival by train, he was driven out to the ranch headquarters in a buckboard by a Mexican who spoke no English. The foreman was a taciturn westerner with a charming wife. They gave their visitor a big welcome and provided him with another buckboard, pulled by a span of sorrels, and a driver who took him some miles away to a canyon where several hundred men were building a smelter. Most of the cowboys were away on a cattle drive, but he was able to find the two he was searching for, and as word of his presence got around, a dozen or more men gathered in the tent where he was trying to work. The net result was "a couple of new songs [and] several new tunes." Back at the ranch house that night, he went quickly to sleep in a fine big bed beneath three blankets (it was still summer, but the elevation there was above five thousand feet). Lomax was especially grateful for the comfortable bed with lots of pillows—comforts notably lacking back at Bedi's homestead.[13]

Roughing it with Bedichek meant sleeping on a cot out in the chill night air, losing sleep to the howling coyotes and the strange antics of Hobo, suffering more digestive problems, and tramping those long, three-hour walks to and from town. On the other hand, he responded to Bedi's hearty companionship, and the climate and exercise were good for him. Nearing the end of his three-week visit with Bedichek, he concluded that he had "never known a more delightful combination of business and pleasure."[14]

In his autobiography, Lomax made no mention of the colorful trip to the Apache Teho spread. He did include, however, an account of riding out of Deming on a livery-stable horse to visit a ranch known as the Diamond A, reportedly owned by William Randolph Hearst's father. In this later account a fifty-pound recording machine suddenly appears, balanced on the pommel of his saddle, while "tied up in a slicker behind the cantle of the saddle was the recording horn."[15] Curiously, his many long and detailed letters of the time contain no reference to the recording machine or to what must have been the considerable difficulty of managing it and the fragile cylinders over time and distance.

Several stops in Arizona had been planned, but if he made them, they are not chronicled. He left Deming on August 17 bound for Albuquerque and within a day or two was in Los Angeles, perhaps mindful of his late start and anxious to please the Sheldon committee, although Briggs had assured him that he need be in no hurry: "Do not worry if you fail to spend all the five hundred dollars before October 1. Also try not to be worried when all the five hundred dollars is gone, for I have an impression that there is more behind it. We are not afraid of your pursuing the quest with luxurious extravagance."[16]

Luxurious extravagance was scarcely a part of John Lomax's nature, whether he was spending his money or someone else's, but in California he took time to relax, go sightseeing, and dine leisurely, if not expensively, with people he knew there. In Los Angeles he was reunited with the Benedicts and with C. S. Potts, his old friend, student, and colleague, who was finishing his law degree at the University of Texas and doing research that summer at colleges on the West Coast. Potts and Lomax traveled together up to San Francisco, where they spent a few days touring the bay area and going to the theater. In the Bancroft Library at the University of California, Lomax discovered a bundle of early "California songsters" in which he found "Sweet Betsy from Pike" and "Days of Forty-Nine." These two songs alone, he felt, "repaid me for the long trip from Texas."[17] They were scarcely cowboy songs, but he sent them off to Sturgis and Walton to be included in the book.

On August 28 Lomax embarked on the last and most important leg of his journey—a visit to the famous Frontier Days Celebration in Cheyenne, Wyoming. This event, which he described as a gathering of "cowboys, broncho busters, buckaroos, rangers, and Indian fighters of the West," had been a part of his plans for several months. In May he'd told Barrett Wendell that he could imagine no better place for his song collecting than among this crowd.[18] And there was another, even greater reason for going: Theodore Roosevelt was one of the featured speakers at the celebration, and Lomax saw this as an opportunity to meet and cultivate the eminent figure who had so generously, if unsuccessfully, supported his Carnegie application. A month earlier, eager to pave the way, he'd written to Roosevelt asking permission to dedicate *Cowboy Songs* to him, and wondered if, just perhaps, the former president might write an endorsement for the book. He'd also asked Barrett Wendell to use his influence to arrange a meeting with Roosevelt in Cheyenne.

Lomax turned up at Roosevelt's hotel early on Sunday morning, August 28, and sent a note to the former president's room, asking for a brief interview. Roosevelt, who was preparing to go to church, came down to the lobby immediately, greeted Lomax in his famous hearty fashion, and apologized for having been too busy to respond about the book dedication. Could Lomax come to his room at two o'clock and bring a sheet of paper on which he, Roosevelt, could compose a testimonial for the book? Lomax could, and did.

Roosevelt received him promptly at the appointed time. When the former president asked him what he should say about the book, Lomax launched into his standing complaint about the general lack of appreciation for his work, remarking that even westerners failed to understand how important his cowboy songs were in illuminating and preserving the traditions of their region. Yes, of course, said Roosevelt, adding that the songs further helped to illustrate that the West was a reproduction of life in the Middle Ages (a pet theory which he tended to offer as holy writ). Lomax promptly suggest that "such a happy phrasing of the truth" was just the thing for Roosevelt's endorsement of the book.[19]

Except in general outline, neither of them really knew what he was talking about—nor was either deterred by that. "Every man a ballad scholar, and bully for it!" Teddy might have shouted, to Lomax's beaming approval. As far as Roosevelt was concerned, the notion that Jesse James had taken the place of Robin Hood in songs expressing "sympathy for the outlaw" was proof enough of what Roosevelt termed "the curious reproduction of mediaeval conditions in the West."

The former president chatted on as he wrote, musing over a line expurgated from "Jesse James" ("The G—— d—mn coward who shot Mr. Howard"), joking about his poor handwriting and complaining of the American public's indifference to cultural and historic preservation. He complained also of the poor response to his massive *The Winning of the West* (published in four volumes between 1889 and 1896) because he had declined to romanticize the pioneers as knights and instead made them out to be the "free-booting Vikings they really were." He had, he said, too much respect for a forty-niner to call him a knight. Lomax, who could transform cowboys into cavaliers, had no such reservations, but he was not inclined to press the point with a former president of the United States and a man just then in the process of doing him a big favor.

Roosevelt's fondness for the Viking image resurfaced when they moved on to talk about Texas history. Lomax flattered the ex-president by urging that he write a history of the state. Roosevelt modestly agreed that the subject cried out for an author such as himself, especially in view of the fact that it had been so badly treated by northern writers. "They all say that Texas was settled from a desire to extend the slave territory, when the truth is that Sam Houston and his crowd would have conquered Texas in just the way they did had there never been a slave in the South. It was again the old Viking spirit pressing westward and overcoming and dispossessing an inferior race."[20] He was probably right about Houston and the Texians, but such grand simplification overlooked the early and pervasive element of Texas's southern character, permeated as it was by the social, political, and cultural effects of slavery and slaveholding. And eventually that "inferior race" of Mexicans, blandly assumed by Roosevelt to have been overcome and dispossessed, would have something more to say about its rightful place in the history of the state, past, present, and future.

It was a curious event, this meeting of East and West, this brief encounter between the upper-crust statesman-soldier-sportsman and the Texas farm-boy schoolteacher. They had both been at Harvard, but thirty years apart and under vastly different circumstances; beyond that, they had little in common except their romantic visions of the Old West and the happy assumption that cowboys had something to sing about.

Lomax was untroubled by any of the anomalies. He had met the Hero of San Juan Hill, they had spoken cordially, and he had gotten what he wanted: a ringing endorsement for his book—"You have done a work emphatically worth doing and one which should appeal to the people of all our country." Roosevelt's page-and-a-half-long message was promptly mailed off to Sturgis and Walton, who reproduced it exactly by line engraving, to preserve the authenticity of the former president's pen, and placed it just ahead of the table of contents, where through the years it has given imprimatur to the many editions and reprintings of *Cowboy Songs.*

From Cheyenne, Lomax headed south through Colorado. After a short trip to Boulder, he made a jog eastward again, to Kansas City, then up to Lincoln, Nebraska, and back across to Columbia, Missouri, for a long-anticipated visit at the University of Missouri with Professor Henry M. Belden, who'd also been one of Kittredge's students at Harvard. They had a fine time, chatting late into the night, comparing folksongs and folklore societies and laying plans for future work. Belden brought two deans to meet Lomax at lunch the next day, and they dazzled each other with bright conversation and witty stories ("What egoists we are!" John told Bess). He had already reported that he had gotten more information than he could use; now he told her he was "plum, jamfull of University information" about California, Colorado, Kansas, Nebraska, and Missouri, "to say nothing of New Mexico."[21] There was yet a man or two to see in Oklahoma on his way to Texas, but he was homesick and anxious to finish the trip. Most of all he missed Bess, telling her that he would never again travel so far away by himself. On September 16 he met her in Meridian, to spend a few days relaxing with Lomax relatives in Bosque County before heading on to Austin to resume his new job at the University and await the publication of *Cowboy Songs,* due in November.

• • • • •

Cowboy Songs and Other Frontier Ballads occupies a vital place in American cultural history, but locating that place precisely is tricky business. Lomax's own statements about what he had achieved with the book and how he had gone about it are both plentiful and contradictory. That ought not to trouble anyone who understands the man himself.

In some ways it is easier to say what *Cowboy Songs* was not rather than what it was. It was not, contrary to what Lomax wrote in his autobiography, "the first collection of native American folk songs ever printed along with the music of the songs," nor was it, as he wrote in another place, splitting other hairs, "the first copyrighted collection of American white folk songs, containing music, printed in the United States."[22] In James McNutt's rather stern judgment, *Cowboy Songs* was comprised of material that was "neither so western nor so cowboy as [Lomax] asserted," but rather "the synthetic products of folk, popular, and elite composers."[23]

Fine points and invidious distinctions aside, one hazards the plain assertion that what *Cowboy Songs* amounted to was—if not in fact, then certainly in substance and in effect—simply the first important collection of American folksong.

True, it dealt with a fairly narrow band of "folk," confined more or less by definition to those of a single gender and a single, rather minor occupation. But of course men who drove cattle for a living still exerted vast pulls on the public imagination, out of all proportion to the realities of cowboy life, and so despite its limited focus, the work had broad popular appeal, exactly as Lomax intended. It is also true that some of the entries were not exactly "pure" folksongs, or at least not the original discoveries Lomax thought they were. A few owed their existence to prior publication, others were amalgamations blithely put together by the collector himself. But if Lomax's methods of research and compilation were something less than those of a careful scholar—or even those of a reliable antiquarian—*Cowboy Songs* was nevertheless a major influence on fledgling cultural studies in that era. The very fact that it had been done, warts and all, gave encouragement to many who had similar ambitions and faced similar obstacles.

The ultimate value of *Cowboy Songs* is measured not in scholarly abstractions but in what it gave us all, in those lovely, sad, and funny bits of tune and line now embedded in our lives: "Whoopee Ti Yi Yo, Git Along, Little Dogies," "The Old Chisholm Trail," "Jesse James," "Sweet Betsy from Pike," and of course, "Home on the Range," among dozens of other American favorites which Lomax saved from doom or otherwise helped preserve and popularize.

The bulk of these had come to him through the mail, from friends, former students, businessmen, teachers, and local officials, mostly in Texas, to whom he had written after Wendell expressed enthusiasm for the project.[24] Other songs were gleaned from scrapbooks and newspapers, especially the *Dallas News.* A very few had come, as Lomax wrote, "from the lips of ex-cowboys, now in many cases staid and respected citizens."[25] Following his return to Texas in the summer of 1907 he began making short trips out of College Station whenever he could, to track down leads to possible sources and interview those already located. This rudimentary fieldwork had continued at sporadic intervals during the next two years, mostly during the summers of 1908 and 1909. Lomax recounted these activities in great detail in his autobiography: how he had gotten "Whoopee Ti Yi Yo" from a gypsy woman near the Fort Worth Stockyards, eighty-nine verses of "The Chisholm Trail" from a cowboy in the White Elephant Saloon, "The Buffalo Skinners" from an old buffalo hunter in Abilene, Texas, and "Home on the Range" from a Negro saloonkeeper in San Antonio. Although he indicated that he had collected songs from practically every state west of the Mississippi, "fully seventy-five percent of the songs have come from Arizona, Texas, and New Mexico."[26]

By the early fall of 1909 he could report to Wendell that he had enough songs to fill a "comfortable-sized volume." Getting the music for each song had become a matter of increasing concern, and at this point he had the music for less than half of them, "much of that on phonograph cylinders [i.e., not transcribed]."[27]

At the outset, Lomax's guiding principle had been to include only unpublished songs or those which seemed "to most nearly fit Professor Kittredge's definition of a real ballad."[28] Kittredge's definition—"a story told in song, or a song that tells a story"—was certainly loose enough, but even that standard was casually amended or ignored according to the merits of a particular song or the circumstances of its discovery. Lomax knew, for example, from Henry Belden that "Jesse James" had been published in one form or another, and several of the songs he printed, even "Whoopee Ti Yi Yo," are composed of only vaguely related stanzas which have little or no sense of narrative. If the definition of a "real ballad" required the further refinement of anonymous authorship, Lomax set that aside also in accepting such songs as "Days of Forty-Nine" and "Sweet Betsy from Pike," which he had traced to what he felt were fairly certain origins.[29] And of course he did not consider what he found in newspapers to have been published and thus could blithely claim, in his introduction to the book ("Collector's Note") that the songs it contained were "never before in print."

Dutiful pupil that he was, he must have felt a twinge or two of conscience whenever he violated the boundaries of the nebulous ballad territory that his mentors had charted, but ultimately it is to his credit that he did it, whether deliberately or by simple misdirection. The matter of "the

Ballad" was academic in more ways than one; cowboy songs, whatever they were, were something else, spawned in a climate and a culture far distant from the miasmic communes vaguely imagined by Child and Gummere. If Lomax had held himself strictly to their tenets, we might well have lost "Git Along, Little Dogies" and "Home on the Range" and "The Dying Cowboy."

His methods of handling the material were to cause him more trouble than his standards for selecting it. When a reader of *Cowboy Songs* wrote to suggest an error in orthography and question certain terms describing cowboy gear, Lomax defended himself on the grounds of textual purity and higher authority. At the outset, he said, Kittredge had told him to pay no attention to anything "except to get the stuff." He had followed that advice, he claimed, and printed the material just as he found it, "spelling and all."[30] Yet he was determined to have it both ways, admitting even at the time of publication that he had tinkered with the texts and "violated the ethics of ballad-gatherers" in some instances by discarding lines, editing others to soften the "coarser elements," and patching together several variant versions.[31] All this, of course, was done in the name of aesthetics, to improve what was given. Writing in his autobiography about "Home on the Range," which by that time had reached the status of a hallowed national artifact (it was supposedly President Franklin Roosevelt's favorite song), Lomax admitted to having compiled his version from several sources and worked it over to make it better: "Yes, I know I did wrong, but I rephrased some unmetrical lines."[32]

All this roughshod scholarship was quite at odds with the intellectual ambitions of his youth which had placed him in the sway of such men as Wendell and Kittredge. Indeed, he now sometimes seemed at pains to distance himself from the scholarly world, writing sharply to one correspondent at a university, "I am not of academic work myself." To another, who had ventured a mild correction to *Cowboy Songs,* he sniffed that he was pleased to learn that his book of "rough ballads" had attracted the attention of true scholars: "I make no claim for membership in that charming company."[33] This was Lomax at his most cavalier, an altogether curious attitude from the man who only short years earlier had gotten quite puffed up at being called "Professor."

The cowboy song collection, building in fits and starts, had begun to take final form by the middle of 1909. Since early that year, Lomax had been corresponding with prospective publishers. Flouting the unwritten rule prohibiting multiple submission, he sent copies of the manuscript to

Lawton Walton at Sturgis and Walton, to Charles Read Nutter at D. Appleton, and, in all probability, to Harry Steger at Doubleday, Page & Company.[34] On New Year's Day of 1910, Nutter wrote to Lomax: "I find a general disinclination in the house toward publishing [the collection]. In one case it is, perhaps, due to a lack of imagination; in [another editor's] case it is due to a general disinclination to publish any form of poetry."[35] Steger at Doubleday had likewise been unable to prevail with that firm's senior editors on behalf of his friend.

By this time, however, Lomax was already in serious negotiation with Sturgis and Walton, and while traveling back from his triumph at Cornell, he had taken the opportunity to stop off in New York to call on Lawton Walton. Although Sturgis and Walton was a new firm, with "more nerve than capital," as Lomax said later, Walton had earlier indicated not only interest in the book but also in printing the music with the songs, a major concern to Lomax.[36]

Two days after his meeting with Walton, he wrote to Bess from Plymouth, Massachusetts, where he was visiting Dean Briggs at Half-way Pond, the Briggses' retreat southwest of the town. After a lengthy account of a dozen other matters, he added, almost as an afterthought, but with his usual careful attention to finances, that Sturgis and Walton had accepted the book and would publish it in the fall—"10% to us on the retail price."[37]

Elated over the book's pending publication, he was moved to pay debts of gratitude, especially to Barrett Wendell. Apparently feeling that what he had to say might only embarrass them both, but intent on saying it nevertheless, he wrote a long and almost poetic letter to Wendell's wife. It was an act quite uncharacteristic of Lomax, and one made all the more touching by the fact that he was never comfortable with Mrs. Wendell, a Boston Lady of most exquisite sensibilities whose presence had always been a source of quiet terror to him. Bravely he set forth the occasion: perhaps she knew of her husband's interest in Lomax's work from the time of their first meeting in Grays Hall over three years earlier, but whether or not Wendell had told her about it, he wanted to pass on "a few words of appreciation." It was a great deal more than "a few words"; he detailed at length Wendell's work in his behalf—writing at least a hundred letters, contributing money of his own and soliciting funds from others, and spending endless hours in otherwise promoting the project to people who were in a position to help. Lomax would not always be so generous in acknowledging the efforts of others; in fact he may have even overstated the case here. But if his remarks are accurate, Wendell deserves even more credit than history generally recognizes. Lomax told Mrs. Wendell that her husband had always had more faith in the project than he himself: "In truth, [Wendell] discovered it, and is yet pushing it along." Lomax himself, he said, had never been more than an "automaton," occasionally brought to life by Wendell's generous and enthusiastic letters.[38]

• • • • •

Cowboy Songs was published in November, to sparse but mostly favorable reviews. Lomax complained that the notices were "none too flattering or numerous" and cringed when the *Boston Transcript* called it "vulgar and cheap trash."[39] But in fact the book got considerable early attention for a work of its kind, and most of it was positive. The *St. Louis Post-Dispatch* praised it at length, and the *New York Times* commended not only the collection but Lomax's commentary as well, "a model in the way of just and modest appraisement of his own work." The book was favorably noticed by the *Independent,* the *Dial,* and the *Bookman;* English newspapers generally praised the British edition.[40] "Frankly, the volume is meant to be popular," Lomax had asserted in his introduction, and by and large that hope was fulfilled. *Cowboy Songs* did not appear on any best-seller list, and Lomax's boast that "my first royalty check was half my annual salary" was an exaggeration,[41] but initial sales were strong enough to warrant a second printing in April 1911, and the book continued to bring steady and not inconsiderable cash to the Lomax household for decades, passing through more than a dozen printings and at least three revisions with major additions—in 1916, 1938, and, most recently, 1986, almost eighty years from its point of origin. It did not instantly make Lomax, in James McNutt's words, "a national figure," but it certainly laid the foundation for his eventual reputation as a major force in the cultural history of the United States.[42]

PART THREE

• • • • •

One Man's Family

'Mid pleasures and palaces though we may roam
Be it ever so humble, there's no place like home.

—John Howard Payne, "Home, Sweet Home" (1823)

CHAPTER ELEVEN

• • • • •

Man on the Flying Trapeze

1911–15

In his autobiography, Lomax slipped past the years between 1911 and 1917 in a single paragraph:

> When my income was no longer increased by the annual Sheldon Fellowship grant from Harvard University, the demands of a growing family forced me to give up active folk song collecting. Salary increases were small and came slowly to a frontier university striving to win public favor in the wide empire of Texas. My work as Registrar [he never officially held that title after 1903] and Secretary of the University of Texas kept me busy the year 'round except for a month each winter when President Mezes allowed me to attend the Modern Language Association meetings and to lecture on Cowboy songs at colleges and continue to collect folk-song material.[1]

If he misremembered some of the details, he nevertheless caught the essential character of that period, a time pleasantly given over to domestic matters and his new job at the University of Texas. But it was not quite as calm and simple as he made it sound.

The Sheldon stipends, which boosted his annual income by as much as 25 percent, lasted through three consecutive years, the last payment of $500 coming in late 1911. Although the award periods were only loosely defined, the last entitled him to advertise himself as a "Sheldon Fellow of Harvard University" through 1912; in any event, it supported considerable collecting activity, including in May a new call (via another circular letter) for "songs of the Negro." By September of 1913, he had gotten two substantial raises—one of which he called so generous "that I am at this time almost making a living"[2]—bringing his annual salary from the University to $2,700 (roughly $35,000 in present-day dollars, and worth even more than that because it was all tax-free—the federal income tax became law that very year, but married couples earning less than $4,000 paid nothing). Moreover, the lecture trips to which he barely alludes were becoming a frequent and fixed part of his annual schedule, as well as bringing in steadily increasing sums of money. In 1913 his lectures and the sales of *Cowboy Songs* earned him over $600.00. In financial terms at least, Lomax had reached that comfortable middle-class niche to which he had long aspired.

Among the tangible evidence that he had arrived was the fine new home the Lomaxes built on the Austin property they had purchased in 1909. Located a few blocks from the campus on West 26th Street at what was then the western edge of the city, it was a spacious two-story bungalow of yellow brick, with two baths, four bedrooms, and a large screened sleeping porch extending across the rear of the second story. At the top of the interior stairway was a window seat in an alcove, looking out on a grand view of Shoal Creek and Mt. Bonnell across the river on the west. Construction began in the fall of 1911, and the Lomaxes moved in shortly after Christmas. The house was a frequent topic in Lomax's conversations and correspondence for many months, an object of justifiable pride and a locus of the domestic tranquility which he was always trying to impose on his life (and sometimes convinced himself that he had succeeded). In August, long after the house was completed, he wrote to Benjamin Wyche, an old friend who had been head librarian at the University when Lomax was a graduate student, describing their "pretty, big brick cottage" in detail, along with the backyard menagerie of chickens, turkeys, and cows. The children were thriving, and he himself had become so involved in his work and "my life in the University" that he could not imagine ever doing anything else.[3] Those words would come back to haunt him in only a few short years.

For now, however, the telling phrase was "my life in the University." To say that he was absorbed in his job was to put it mildly; as always, he went at the work the only way he knew: with fierce industry and seemingly tireless energy. As secretary of the University, he attended every meeting of the several department faculties and the administration—as many as four a day—kept the minutes, recorded vital statistics, and saw to it that committee reports and other key documents were printed and distributed—in addition to the routine affairs of his office, which included processing all official University correspondence, administering loan funds, editing the

University Bulletin, greeting parents and visitors when they appeared on campus, and dealing with whatever other odd jobs the president might throw his way.[4] But the work did not end there; as an alumni report observed, "Perhaps the activity dearest to Mr. Lomax's heart has been the raising of funds to assist worthy students." He established several loan funds and was relentless in soliciting contributions from alumni and other sources. When no other money was available, he loaned—or gave—students his own.[5]

As assistant director of extension he dealt with curricular matters related to "self-study" classes conducted at various places around the state. In this capacity he introduced, in 1913, an extension course called "Folk-Lore and Balladry" as a tentative step toward an extended program in folklore at the University. Lomax also hoped that it would further the aims of the Texas Folklore Society and serve as a conduit for his collecting efforts, but the course failed to attract sufficient enrollment and was discontinued.[6]

A natural outgrowth of his work in the Department of Extension was issuing publicity and recruiting for the University, and that in turn led to his being elected secretary-treasurer of the Alumni Association, an organization which then existed in little more than name, propped up by a few former students whose sentimental attachment to the institution exceeded both their managerial skills and their operating budget. As a University entity, the association was neither fish nor fowl. Its more ardent supporters—notably Will Hogg and Dexter Hamilton, both old friends and schoolmates of Lomax—wanted to think of it as an independent organization, yet they very much needed backing from the University, which offered little more than its indifferent sanction, a filing cabinet for membership records, and occasional clerical help. Lomax, who found the work congenial and had little patience for doing things halfway, set out to change all that. Very soon, the Alumni Association began to thrive, and its growth and influence over the years owed much to his organizational abilities and his firm, if not always felicitous, hand.

One of his ploys for enlarging the membership involved a change of name for the association, from "Alumni" to "Ex-Students." The move, supported by Will Hogg and other powers within, was a seemingly trivial matter of terminology, but it had far-reaching effects: "alumni" had been interpreted to mean "graduates," while "ex-students" included anyone who had ever enrolled in a class. In that era in Texas, hundreds of young men and women found their college careers interrupted by various circumstances, and many might accumulate several years of credit at the University only to leave finally without a degree, but with their loyalty to the institution intact. The name change—informally it became simply "Texas Exes"—increased the pool of prospective members by many dozen.

Very early Lomax recognized the need for a regular publication that would serve as a focal point and source of esprit for the organization. Recalling the short-lived student newspaper he had worked on briefly as an undergraduate, he realized that its name—*Alcalde* (Spanish "mayor," chief, leader)—was far more appropriate to an organ aimed at older, and presumably wiser, graduates of the institution. Thus sprang forth in April 1913 the new *Alcalde,* a slick monthly alumni magazine that in time earned a reputation as one of the best of its kind, noted for its attractive design, liberal use of graphics, comprehensive coverage, and generally lively style. Lomax shrewdly saw to it that some prominent alumnus, often residing in a distant city, was named editor-in-chief, but the position was largely pro forma; most of the work of compiling the magazine and seeing it through the press was done—or delegated—by Lomax himself.

Similar political instincts gave him a clever penchant for setting up all sorts of directing boards and executive councils and coordinating committees, composed of affluent former students scattered about the state, who got their names in print and were allowed to think that they were running the affairs of the association, while Lomax kept a low profile and did the work. In this manner he created a power base that put him on familiar terms with politicians, businessmen, and other movers and shakers around the state. Power, however, was never his primary goal—or if it was, he acquired it haphazardly and tended to handle it ineptly whenever he got it. What he wanted most was prominence, and that, ironically, is what he got from his behind-the-scenes manipulation and management of the Ex-Students' Association. John Lomax became known across the state as a loyal and dedicated supporter of the University, an organizer, a solid citizen, a man who "got things done."

His public image was further enhanced by his increasing activity on the lecture circuit and his reputation as the author of *Cowboy Songs,* which brought further notoriety (although in time it would prove to be notoriety he could do without, when the governor publicly ridiculed his song collecting and lambasted the University for employing what the state's chief executive considered to be an educated fool).[7] In any event, the nature of Lomax's job was such that by 1915 that part of his official title which named him "Assistant Director of Extension" had been changed to "Chairman of the Division of Public Lectures and Publicity." (He was not only "chairman" but the division's sole member.) His colleague in the Texas Folklore Society, Dr. L. W. Payne, was probably correct when he referred to Lomax simply as "general publicity agent for the University."

It was in large part Lomax's function as "publicity agent" which persuaded Mezes to give him time off once or twice a year for the lecture tours which eventually became a central part of his professional life (as well as a sustained source of income). Lomax even implied that Mezes planned these trips for him, to coincide with the annual conference of the Modern Language Association, which, then as now, met in December each year. But the first such tours, in 1911 and 1912, which essentially set the pattern for later ones, were quite unrelated to the MLA. His round of lectures in 1911 took place in late spring rather than in December and was mostly instigated by Lomax himself, to augment his current song-collecting interests.

Early that year, he outlined an elaborate scheme to scour the Mississippi Valley for folksongs, traveling by "several steamers" upriver from New Orleans to St. Louis and meeting expenses by lecturing along the way at colleges and universities. To a prospective sponsor he explained that his purpose in undertaking the trip was to "make converts to the cause of collecting American folk-song." The sincerity with which he espoused the cause at this early stage is reflected in what was for Lomax a remarkably casual attitude about the money he was to be paid. His usual fee was twenty-five dollars, but if no funds were available, he would speak anyway if there was a chance he might stir some interest in folksong among his audience and enlist any of them in his collecting efforts.[8]

Turning to his old-boy network—then still a modest one—for lecture dates, Lomax confided the plan to Albert Granville Reed, a professor of English at Louisiana State University who had been his colleague at Texas and a classmate at Harvard. The lectures, Lomax said, would interest and entertain audiences not because of his "grace of delivery" as a speaker but because of "the uniqueness and liveliness of my material," a note of seeming modesty he was to sound over and over.[9] Reed was only lukewarm to the idea, and in any event L.S.U. had no funds to pay for a lecture there. Undeterred, Lomax looked to the East once more. Harvard too had no money with which to pay him, but Kittredge enthusiastically urged him to come anyway (Wendell was abroad, touring the world with Mrs. Wendell). At Kittredge's suggestion, Lomax got in touch with William Lyon Phelps, who was Kittredge's counterpart at Yale—or the nearest thing to Kittredge that Yale could manage. "Billy" Phelps (or just plain "Bil," as he liked to sign himself) quickly took to Lomax, eventually arranging for him not one but two lecture dates in New Haven, paying $100 and the speaker's expenses while there.[10] This enabled Lomax to tell Kittredge that he would come to Harvard whether they paid him or not, flattered merely to be invited there.[11] Setting aside the Mississippi River scheme, he began a flurry of correspondence with institutions throughout the South and East which, after much debate and negotiation, resulted in speaking engagements at more than a dozen schools, scattered across Kentucky, North Carolina, New York, Vermont, Connecticut, and Pennsylvania.[12] Accompanied by Bess, he set off in late April.

For a man determined most of his life to travel about bullishly all over the place and under the most difficult conditions, Lomax showed a blithe disregard for clocks, maps, and timetables. After his talk to the Cornell (Alumni) Club in New York, he tarried too long, then had to rush frantically to Grand Central without his luggage to catch the train for Poughkeepsie, where he was to lecture at his old summer school, the Eastman Business College. Whenever Bess was at his side, she managed the details and kept him on schedule, but on this occasion it had been decided that she would remain in New York while he went upstate. Fortunately, a member of the Cornell Club told him of a short cut to the station and helped retrieve his luggage from the hotel and get it to the train on time. He made the date at Poughkeepsie "by a hair," he reported. Although he missed breakfast in the rush and had to speak on an empty stomach, he did manage to secure a half pint of "good Texas booze," which "carried me through the ordeal in fine form."[13]

For his appearance before the Yale graduates at the University Club, he asked Phelps to arrange for four or five Yale students who could sing to dress like cowboys and join him on the stage, but Phelps stiffly pointed out that undergraduates were not allowed in the University Club, and thus instructors who taught the Glee Club would have to be substituted. Lomax was less concerned about their singing voices than that they looked enough like cowboys "to bring out the local color." The Glee Club instructors probably didn't *sound* much like cowboys, but that didn't matter—least of all to Lomax, whose notions of what singing cowboys sounded like derived as much from his vivid imagination as from actual experience. He was there to provide an evening's entertainment and drum up support for folksong collecting.

Reviewing his Yale performance self-critically, he wrote later that his first appearance, at the University Club, was successful enough, but when he spoke to a general convocation of undergraduates the following evening, he did not feel he'd ever really reached his audience. Typically, he tried to shoulder the blame and simultaneously reject it, saying that "the fault was mine entirely, of course, and yet not mine, because I did my best." Phelps, however, was highly pleased: "Both of your lectures were bully and greatly appreciated; people are still talking with immense enthusiasm." If the audience was perhaps a bit small, it was because of the timing—"The men will not turn out to lectures . . . later than the middle of April, Heaven knows why."[14]

The audience at Harvard was also small and disappointing, perhaps due in part to the absence of Wendell. Lomax's visit there was otherwise uneventful. The Lomaxes were guests of Dean and Mrs. Briggs for a few days, then sailed on May 27 for Galveston and home.

• • • • •

There were still other lectures that year. Promoting himself at some length to Harry Steger, Lomax wrote that he was to give two lectures on ballads at the University of Chicago in August, and he had more invitations to speak in Texas than he could accept. The same letter proudly heralded news of his third consecutive Sheldon award and a long, favorable review of *Cowboy Songs* in the *Dial.* He further reminded Steger that he had the strong support of Kittredge and Wendell, to which was now added that of ballad theorist Francis Gummere (who had appeared together with Lomax as guest of honor at the Franklin Literary Club when Lomax spoke at the University of Pennsylvania in May).

All this was merely preliminary tub-thumping for what was really on Lomax's mind: a proposal to Doubleday, Page and Company for a comprehensive, six-volume set of American folksong, which he coolly assured Steger he would have done "by the end of 1912."[15] In one form or another—and it went through many permutations—this was a project very much on his mind for the next quarter of a century, contrary to his statement in *Adventures of a Ballad Hunter* that during this period "the demands of a growing family forced me to give up active folksong collecting."

This ambitious plan for a folksong anthology was quickly reduced in size and scope, probably through Steger's wise counsel. It shrank to one volume and took as its immediate focus the music of American blacks, a subject which had held a fascination for Lomax long before he turned to cowboy ditties. It was "Negro songs," in fact, which he had first proposed back in 1907 when Wendell called for papers on "regional literary productions." Had Wendell not rejected that topic in favor of cowboy songs, the course of Lomax's life and career might have been quite different. In any event, his interest in the music of blacks predated even his encounter with Wendell by several years, documented as early as 1904 by the enthusiastic letters he had written Bess from his inspection trips to the state college for blacks at Prairie View.

Even on his return from Harvard, when his immediate objective was the cowboy song book, he had continued to pursue his interest in black music and black culture. The chairman of his department at A&M, C. P. Fountain, owned a small plantation along the river some ten miles from College Station; Lomax often accepted invitations to visit there and "observe the negro in his raw state." References to collecting Negro songs in the Brazos river bottoms are found throughout his papers of this period.[16] There were also return trips to Prairie View, where the black students' music was an increasing attraction.

After one such visit in early 1910, while he was in the midst of seeing *Cowboy Songs* through the press, he wrote at length, and with considerable perception, to Barrett Wendell. He had collected some one hundred "mating ballads" from the students; most were only fragments but all of great interest, he said. More importantly, they were evidence of Kittredge's belief that black folksongs and folklore had never been collected by anyone with a genuine interest in preserving them in their native forms. White people—he named Joel Chandler Harris as an example—"dressed them up for literary purposes," while literate blacks sought to polish them in order to present their race in the best possible light. In either case, said Lomax, the material was rendered useless for serious study, while at the same time its most attractive elements were destroyed. Negro folksong was obviously a subject of considerable scope and complexity, he said, "the most natural and distinctive [music] of any America has produced." Observing that it was a field untouched by scholars, he told Wendell that he was increasingly drawn to it, although it would probably involve the work of a lifetime.[17] Certain themes that first surfaced here—the lack of serious attention to Negro music despite its important cultural significance, the corruption of "Negro ideas" by whites for literary purposes, and the regrettable efforts of educated blacks to suppress or refine their race's lively and authentic vernacular music—were to be repeated over and over by Lomax in coming years.

In the face of these circumstances, his interest in the subject only intensified. In May 1912 he sent out to newspapers his last circular as a Sheldon

Fellow, calling for "songs of the negro—his 'reels,' his spirituals, and his play songs." Within months he was at work on a lecture entitled "Negro Plantation Songs" (delivered at both the MLA and AFS meetings for 1912),[18] and he announced that Doubleday, Page and Company would shortly publish his book of that title.[19] The title was altered for a time to "Ballads of the Cotton Fields and Back Alleys" ("or some such"), and the publication date extended from "shortly" to a year, then eighteen months, until finally, following the untimely death of Harry Steger in January 1913, the book faded into limbo. But Lomax went on with the work, seeking out black informants, traveling around to interview them, collecting and preserving bits and shards of songs, although more than twenty years would pass before any substantial result found its way into print.

That Lomax should devote so much time, energy, and emotion to investigations into black music and black culture was all the more curious in light of the mossback racial attitudes he was frequently criticized for. Those attitudes, although indefensible from an enlightened point of view, were nevertheless commingled with a sensibility which complicates any effort to dismiss him as a simple racist. One way of understanding him, if not excusing him, is to see him as merely representative of his age—it was, after all, an age when the president of Harvard University sought to limit the enrollment of Jewish students (and men like Kittredge agreed with him on the "Jew problem"),[20] an age when the term "nigger" was a commonplace in print and on the lips not only of the unwashed but of the nation's white elite, from the White House to the Great White Way, an age when the laws of the land and its highest courts drew rigid lines between black and white, thereby feeding the notion, all too readily harbored by human frailty, that one was superior to the other. In Texas, the prevailing attitude was expressed by a University alumnus who considered himself "progressive," extolled the virtues of education, called on the legislature to fund schools of the first class for Negroes, and in the next breath stated, "Because of fundamental differences between the white man and the black man, there is little danger of the negro ever being in a position in the South to demand social equality. The Southerner resents to the very last drop of his blood and last ounce of his strength even the slightest suggestion of social equality with the negro, and will never do anything for the negro race if what is done tends in that direction."[21] Some men and women born into this culture with no more vision and intelligence than Lomax could somehow escape it and transcend its limitations, but he did not. He was no less than a product of his time; he was, alas, never more than that either.

As time passed and the social order began to change, however slowly, Lomax was constantly banging his head on the matter of race, and he never understood why. That very fact points to a disarming innocence, a sad naivete in his character that lies at the heart of his attitudes toward blacks. It appears over and over in his papers, both published and private, but the most succinct evidence is in a letter he wrote to an acquaintance in Middletown, Connecticut, where he had lectured on several occasions at Wesleyan University. On his first visit there, about 1915, he had delivered his talk on cowboy songs to a highly enthusiastic audience. When he returned a year or two later, his subject was Negro music, and the response quite different. He had made his share of failures, he said, but this was the worst; the students seemed to think he hated Negroes and was making fun of them, when in fact he genuinely loved the black man "despite his many weaknesses" and had been more moved by black songs than by any other musical form.[22]

It was all true, and the most terrible thing was that, through all his days, Lomax understood neither the voice of condescension nor the inherent contradiction expressed by that seeming casual little condition: *despite his many weaknesses.* In a draft for the paper which became "Some Types of American Folk-Song," he wrote that the Negro as he had observed him was "a simple, emotional, imitative, human being," a childlike creature with "a child's eager and willing adaptableness to his environment." Although those lines were struck from the final copy, he would repeat them, in one version or another, over and over through the years. That sweeping and tragic misconception was his earliest, most deeply held notion of blacks, and it would always prevent him from seeing the basic contradiction: if they were inferior, how could they create the exalted art that he so cherished and respected?

Such an analysis may seem to reduce Lomax's racism to fairly simple and standard form. But very little about his character and personality was ever simple or consistent. He was earnest when he said, "I speak as a sympathetic friend of the negro race," pointing out that he had always been concerned with the progress of blacks. On several occasions an honest perception of their plight set him at odds with his own shabby dogmas; one of his more tangled convolutions arose when a northern correspondent took him to task for what may or may not have been a racial slur. Defending himself, Lomax sputtered that he did not want anyone to think "that I do not believe that 'it is hard to be a niggah.'"[23]

If he had his problems with the larger racial question, he was on surer ground in his pursuit of black music. When he sent out his circular asking for "songs of the negro," the yahoo leader of a small-town municipal band wrote to inform him that "the negro as 'songster' is all a myth," advising that "If it is your desire to obtain negro songs go to some opera house leader who plays minstrel business and he will write negro songs that are sung by white people in an imitation of what the negro should do but don't. The negro has no song and never has had any." Lomax replied tersely that it was needless to say he disagreed. He would not argue the matter, he wrote, but felt confident that the book of Negro songs which he expected to publish "in the next 12 months" would prove him right and his correspondent wrong.[24]

But the book did not appear. Other than a very brief piece in the *Nation* entitled "Self-Pity in Negro Folk Songs," the only published result of Lomax's interest in black life and music during this period derived not from the indigenous African-American culture he found so compelling but from the distant folk life of Nigeria, about which he knew, and probably cared, very little. But he took a personal interest in his source, a young Nigerian student whom he had met and befriended on one of his visits to the State Normal and Industrial College for Negroes at Prairie View.

The boy's name was Lattevi Ajayi (which Lomax persistently misspelled, even in print, as "Ajai" or "Ajaji"), whose grandfather, according to Lomax, was "king" of the Yoruba tribe in west central Africa. The boy had apparently been given some tribal military training and other preparation as heir-apparent, but he was sent to this country in his early teens to study agriculture, under the auspices of one J. Wesslay Hoffman, an instructor at Prairie View who formerly had been employed by the German government to teach agriculture in Nigeria.

At his first meeting with Ajayi, Lomax was impressed by the lad's demeanor and appearance, quite unlike that of the local blacks with whom Lomax was familiar and fancied he knew so well. The boy had come into his room quietly, he wrote, "and stood with some embarrassment before me, erect as a soldier, while I questioned him. Although plainly ill at ease, his dignity was impressive. His bright eyes met my look squarely, and he gave my questions prompt, thoughtful answers." To Lomax, the "African prince" was a more exotic specimen than any African-American he knew, and the quality which distinguished the boy was patently obvious: "[Ajayi] has not learned to dissemble any more than has a wild animal suddenly taken captive."[25]

Although Lomax expressed an interest in the songs which Ajayi's people sang, he curiously seems to have set aside that investigation in favor of the folk tales told among the Yorubans—perhaps because the stories were more easily translated than the songs. Moreover, as Lomax later realized, many of the stories bore resemblance to those of Joel Chandler Harris and other popularizers of black folklore, a circumstance he noted without comment when he eventually published them.[26]

Lomax and Ajayi corresponded over a period of several years, and Lomax occasionally sent along a few dollars to encourage Ajayi to send him more tales. In December 1911, the young man was invited to spend the Christmas holidays with the Lomaxes in Austin, a move motivated by genuine altruism but also by the notion that this would be an opportunity, as Lomax said, for the boy "to finish writing out my Folk-Lore stories for me."[27] A further consideration was that Lomax was about to be elected president of the American Folklore Society for 1912 ("through the partiality of Professor Kittredge")[28] and clearly felt the need to broaden and intensify his folklore work. To his dismay, Ajayi wrote that he couldn't come because "the faculty have decided that no student should spend the Xmas no where, except in Prairie View."[29]

Lomax promptly investigated the matter through Hoffman and was told that the real reason Ajayi wouldn't come was that he had heard stories about blacks being beaten by University hooligans.[30] Lomax was indignant, saying there was not the slightest chance the boy would be harmed, and he insisted that Ajayi be put on the train as planned. But he was also willing to go out of his way to accommodate the boy, assuring Hoffman that he would meet Ajayi at the train and look after him. In all his time at the University, he said, he had never known of any incidents such as those which seem to have frightened the boy.[31] He was no doubt sincere in this regard; it was simply not his nature to know things—word of racial turmoil, for example—that he didn't want to hear.

In any event, Ajayi and Hoffman held out, and the trip was never made, although Lomax invited him again later. Ajayi was grateful ("Dear Professor Lomax I could not find the word in english to tell you how I thank you, so I will tell you in Yoruba—*modupe*"), but he negotiated an arrangement whereby he would remain in Prairie View and, for a modest price, send his stories to Austin by mail. During one week in June of 1912 he turned out three stories each day, for which Lomax paid him $7.00. Lomax eventually put together sixteen of the stories for his presidential address to the AFS in December and published them in the *Journal of Amer-*

ican Folklore under the title "Stories of an African Prince." He tried to persuade Ajayi to dress up in native costume and pose for a picture to illustrate the article, even offering to stand "any reasonable expense" for the picture, but Ajayi politely declined.[32]

• • • • •

Throughout the spring of 1912, Lomax shuffled a lot of paper trying to launch the projected book on Negro music, issuing public announcements and writing letters to solicit material, but there is scant evidence of any fieldwork, and mail response was meager, in marked contrast to the flood of letters produced by his search for cowboy songs. The folk tales he'd gotten from Ajayi provided material for a paper at the Texas Folklore Society meeting in February, and he added the lecture, "Ballads of the Cotton Field," to his repertoire for a second major lecture tour in the East in March.

En route he spoke to an enthusiastic audience at the University of Kansas, reporting to Bess that the chairman of the English department told him he had a fortune in his cowboy song lecture and could make $20,000 a year with it on the lecture circuit.[33] Then it was on to New York, where, momentarily, he lost his laurels. Steger had arranged for him to speak at a Doubleday, Page function for employees and their families, and the date turned out to be "a fizzle," in Lomax's words. The night was cold and wet, and his audience was mostly composed of giggling teenagers and their mothers. "The hour was supreme torture," he reported to Bess, "about as bad as you can imagine."[34] With heavy heart he headed toward Poughkeepsie for dates at Eastman Business College and Vassar the next day. At Eastman he was on familiar ground and things went better; with his confidence restored by a generous reception there, he was feeling his old self by the time he faced an audience of six hundred at Vassar. The applause there was so enthusiastic that he again began to feel, he told Bess, that people were really interested in "the stuff I present."[35]

Back in New York, he was again a success at the Cornell Club, patriotically noting that "a lot of Texas men [among the membership] were there to hear me."[36] Seeking a respite from his hectic schedule, he wired Dean Briggs and invited himself to the Briggses' retreat at Half-way Pond, near Plymouth, where the dean and his family were spending the winter vacation. Failing to hear from Briggs, Lomax went on to Plymouth anyway, on the chance of finding him, then in the chill dusk of a mid-winter day tramped all the way out to Half-way Pond, some eight or ten miles from town. There he found the Briggses at home, was seated to a big dinner before a roaring fire, and went for a sleigh ride through the woods.

Briggs escorted him to Cambridge for a week of engagements in the Boston area. First was a dinner in his honor given by Barrett Wendell, followed by a motorcar trip to Andover to lecture on cowboy songs, then back to Harvard to meet with Dean Briggs's English 5 class and to Boston for a round of social events. The pressure and excitement were almost too much. Late in the week he wrote to Bess that he was about to appear before a society audience at the Wendell residence and dreaded it more than anything he had ever done. One problem was the Wendells; they did not wear well. She was the sort of woman who made him nervous, and Wendell's obsession with genealogy bored Lomax "dreadfully."[37] He drew a sad conclusion, saying that, much as he regretted it, "they are not my kind of folks"—while still acknowledging that no one had ever done as much for him as Wendell.[38]

As usual he wanted to have everything two ways at once, complaining that the Boston lectures were wearing him down and in the same breath dropping names and puffing his own importance. At the dinner given him by Wendell, he reported, he was seated next to Ellery Sedgwick, editor of the *Atlantic Monthly,* who invited him to write an article for the magazine. At his lecture to the Thursday Evening Club he met a number of Boston's "leading musical and literary people," including George Whitefield Chadwick, president of the Boston Conservatory, and Frederick Shepherd Converse, "one of the leading American composers."[39] Both men followed him around, he said, firing tiresome questions at him. And on and on.

After another round of lectures in New York, he left on March 30 for appearances in Chicago and at the Universities of Wisconsin and Illinois. The trip had scarcely made expenses, but Lomax felt he was "getting some mighty good advertising," and after all, his avowed purpose for the lecture tours was to stimulate interest in folksong and augment his own collecting efforts.[40] In a further effort to salvage some profit from the trip, he arranged on the way home to visit in Iowa with a woman who reportedly had valuable Negro songs. He was enthusiastic, saying he was convinced that if he and Bess could find the material that was out there, "the negro book will go."[41] But within only a few months, he was telling Steger that they should not expect a manuscript of "Ballads of the Cotton Fields and Back Alleys" for at least another year.[42]

Another venture with Steger involved efforts to purchase the rights to *Cowboy Songs* from Sturgis and Walton for a new edition to be published by Doubleday, Page. After the book's first year in print, sales had begun to dwindle, following a fairly normal pattern in the publishing business. But Lomax, following a fairly normal pattern among authors, didn't see it that way. As far as he was concerned, it was all the fault of his publisher, whose poor business principles and cold unconcern were allowing his grand opus to slip into obscurity. Negotiations for reprint rights dragged on and on; whatever their merits as publishers, Sturgis and Walton drove a hard bargain over the republication of *Cowboy Songs.* In the end, about all Lomax ever got was their agreement to undertake a new, revised edition of their own, and by the time that was finally in the works, in 1915, the company was heading into bankruptcy.

As in the case of the projected book on Negro music, the immediate fate of *Cowboy Songs* was affected more by the unexpected death of Harry Steger than by anything else. Steger, not yet thirty, was just at the outset of what promised to be a brilliant career in publishing. His initial claim to fame had come as editor and confidant of William Sidney Porter ("O. Henry"), and following Porter's death in 1910, Steger scored a great literary coup when, as Porter's executor, he had discovered a valuable lode of back issues of the whimsical newspaper, the *Rolling Stone,* which Porter had published in Austin in the 1890s.

Just after Christmas in 1912, Steger had taken a fall from a New York streetcar and suffered what ultimately proved to be a fatal head injury, although at the time he insisted that it was not serious and refused to have it treated. Lomax was among the last to see him alive. Passing through New York on his way to Philadelphia to attend the MLA meeting and deliver his paper on Negro plantation songs, he visited Steger in his apartment at the Caledonia Hotel. Steger was in bed, his head wrapped in a huge, turban-like towel, surrounded by manuscripts and papers which he shuffled through restlessly and incessantly. He complained only of a slight headache, vigorously resisting anyone's efforts to tend to him or seek medical aid. After a brief, inconclusive visit, Lomax came away, attributing Steger's condition to his bohemian habits and perhaps a night on the town. Only a few days later the young editor collapsed and died.[43]

• • • • •

Lomax's proposed lecture tour that winter of 1912–13 never got off the ground. After delivering his "Negro Plantation Songs" paper before the American Folklore Society in Cleveland, he went on to Cambridge to speak to Kittredge's and Briggs's classes and try to line up further appearances. There were firm invitations from Yale and the University of Maine, but other dates failed to materialize, and Lomax began to worry that Mezes and others back at the University of Texas would take a dim view of his gallivanting around the country. There was also the matter of money. He cautioned Bess not to tell anyone he was lecturing; his best prospects had faded because he couldn't work out a profitable itinerary. Except for Harvard, he wasn't going to lecture anywhere he couldn't make money.[44]

His trip home was routed through the South to accommodate scattered lecture dates in South Carolina, Virginia, and Alabama, justifiable as an extension of his work for the American Folklore Society, which had just taken the unprecedented step of reelecting him president for a second successive term.[45] Otherwise, he fretted about being away from his job, delegating Bess to keep a weather eye on Mezes and assure the president that he would cancel the tour and take the first train to Texas if he were needed.[46] After a few more days, the pressure was too much for dutiful John; he announced that he was coming home ahead of schedule "to look after my job." But he'd no sooner gotten on the way than he was sending Bess long lists of prospects for a summer lecture tour, with instructions to start soliciting them right away.[47]

Once home, he decided to take the lecture business even more seriously. He signed up a Boston theatrical agent (Glenn Palmer of "The Players"), printed flashy playbill announcements, and doubled his price to $50 a lecture. When he realized that the agent would pocket 20 percent of that, he promptly raised the rate to $60. From time to time he took less, depending on various circumstances, but from now on, talk of lecturing for the sake of fostering interest in folk music faded beneath a growing volume of financial discourse. In typical Lomax fashion, he boasted of his steadily rising fees while at the same time indulging in self-deprecation. In due course he was telling a prospective sponsor that, surprising as it might seem, his price for his lectures was a hundred dollars. Feigning modesty, he said that even he thought it "absurd" that anyone would pay him that much, but added quickly, however, that he was scarcely willing to appear for less.[48]

He also spent considerable time that year arranging with Harvard for George Lyman Kittredge to visit Texas and deliver the keynote address at the Texas Folklore Society's 1913 meeting.[49] Arriving in Austin in early April, the indefatigable Kittredge gave four lectures in three days, charmed one and all with his best Yankee behavior, and, after being treated to a number of Lomax's big black cigars and the hospitality of the Lomax household, went off to cap his trip with similar successes in Waco and Dallas.[50] Lomax basked in the reflected glory for months.

It was no doubt his success in promoting Kittredge's Texas trip that led him to enlist his former mentor's help in getting on the MLA program that year, acknowledging that it was "neither graceful nor modest" of him to again ask Kittredge for help "in securing for me a place." If his proposed paper added little to scholarship, he said, he felt it would at least be entertaining.[51] That was an odd approach to take with a man of Kittredge's solemn intellectual bearing, but whatever the Great Man's reservations, it worked. In December Lomax went East for the MLA meeting in Cambridge and for AFS in New York, giving the same paper, entitled "Typical American Folksongs," at both meetings (published as "Some Types of American Folk-Song" two years later in the *Journal of American Folklore*).

Before his audience at the MLA, where the typical paper was twenty minutes long and the maximum never more than thirty, he droned on for almost an hour. Lomax thought he was a great success—"I had to stop repeatedly and let 'em cheer," he wrote to Bess—but the organization's secretary issued him a reprimand for "overrunning [his] time."[52] It was very much like him to misread the situation, and to suffer more and more from ambivalent feelings about the whole business of lecturing. As the tours lengthened and intensified, he swung from mood to mood, one minute reporting a great triumph, in the next burdened by doubts and anxieties. "The way I hate [lecturing] is dreadful," he told Bess repeatedly, and he meant it. At Johns Hopkins on the current tour, he said, his sponsors pronounced him a huge success, but to him it was "positively excruciating."[53] Yet every triumphant performance—real or imagined—sent him soaring; and at same time he complained most loudly of how he suffered, he was busy trying to sign up more dates.

Some engagements went better than others. He ventured off to the University of Maine in twenty-below-zero weather, but his lecture was well received and he chanced upon some new songs among the students which encouraged him to feel that there were still rich pockets of material to be mined. In Baltimore he was fussed over and taken to dinner by a group of Johns Hopkins professors and their wives. His hosts included the famous and respected scholar of Anglo-Saxon, Professor James W. Bright, under whom Morgan Callaway had studied. Lomax couldn't wait for the news to reach his old tormentor; word that the author of *Cowboy Songs* had dined on equal terms with an intellectual of Bright's stature would surely to put the detested Callaway in his place. "You know how much I enjoy such lionizing," Lomax crowed to his wife. Still, there were difficulties—the event was ultimately marred by the presence of "a Beacon Hill Boston Mrs. Wendell pattern of a woman," who made him exceedingly uncomfortable throughout the dinner.[54]

Even back in Cambridge the air sometimes grew too rarefied to suit him: the Kittredges ("that is, the ladies," he said) were "just a bit too, too [*sic*] for me to enjoy thoroughly."[55] Presumably he was referring to Mrs. Kittredge and the Kittredges' youngest daughter, Dora. If he was ever less than devoted to Kittredge, his criticism is not recorded.

• • • • •

The extent of Lomax's travels that winter of 1914 is reflected in a letter he wrote promoting himself to Arthur Page, who since Steger's death had become his target of opportunity at Doubleday, Page. He had spoken to the Modern Language Association and read a paper as president of the American Folklore Society, he told Page, as well as appearing four times at Harvard, twice at Yale, at Johns Hopkins, Wesleyan College, the Universities of Maine and South Carolina, and Alabama A&M, among others.[56] There was at least one additional appearance he did not mention, before the Washington Women's Club in the nation's capital. This date was arranged by the wife of the U.S. Representative from Texas's Twelfth District, Oscar Callaway (no relation to the iniquitous Morgan). Oscar Callaway and his wife, Stella, were old friends of Lomax's, having known him since his days as registrar at the University when the Callaways were undergraduates. This occasion also gave Lomax the opportunity to renew briefly his friendship with David F. Houston, who after five years as president of Washington University now occupied the lofty position of Secretary of Agriculture in the Wilson administration.

Once again, Lomax came away with mixed feelings, reporting widely divergent reactions to his talk. Mrs. Houston and Mrs. Callaway told him he was a great success, he wrote to Bess, but to him, it was "the most harrowing experience of my life."[57] Years later he recalled it as the worst of all his lecture appearances. The legislators' wives were "rudely inattentive," he said, and spent the whole time appraising each other's wardrobes and chattering furtively. Torn between his hunger for the limelight and the nagging sense that he was lowering himself to the level of literary huckster, he blamed himself for the whole affair; the audience had rightly perceived him to be just another publicity seeker, he said, willing to sell himself for a trivial fee to ingratiate himself. Worst of all, "That excruciatingly mortifying hour didn't sell a [single] book."[58]

The previous year, Lomax had had to cancel a lucrative engagement at Chautauqua when an appropriations battle emerged between the University and the Texas legislature. Now he succeeded through his Boston agent in getting the Chautauqua appearance rescheduled for the summer of 1914. He went there for a week in August, giving talks along the way at various state universities, including those of Oklahoma, Kansas, Missouri, and Vermont. While in Burlington he also gave two lectures at the New England Chautauqua, but these dates in Vermont were his least successful. He once complained about his New England audiences—they were polite, he said, but "you know how a New Englander can be polite and still dislike you."[59] A friend at Virginia Military Institute, Prof. Robert Kerlin, commiserated: "About these Burlingtonians—I've tried my best jokes on them; I have sparkled and scintillated and sizzed [*sic*] like newly-opened champagne bottles before them while they sat like saints in alabaster. It's no use—the damned Yankees. You gave them yodeling when they had their beaks open for Emersonian oversoulism."[60]

Bess was traveling with him that summer, and thus the record is deprived of the flood of lively letters—sometimes two and three a day—which passed between them when he was on the road by himself. Her household ledger reveals, however, that the summer lecture tour "cleared 400 dollars." There is also skimpy evidence of a brief lecture tour that fall, but it seems unlikely that he was accompanied this time by Bess, who was expecting their third child in January.

In any event, between November 17 and 26, he bounced from St. Louis to New Bedford, Massachusetts, back across to Minneapolis and down to Norman, Oklahoma. When the Men's Dinner Club in Norman failed to give him the warm reception he'd gotten at the University of Oklahoma, he complained that it was because they were old and conservative—his cowboy songs were appreciated only by those who had "young blood, enthusiasm, [and] a spirit of adventure and endeavor."[61] By this time his repertoire had solidified around five lectures, two of them cowboy-oriented ("The Songs of the Cowboy" and "Songs and Poetry of the Frontier"), two on black music ("Plantation Songs of the Negro" and "Negro Spirituals"), and the catchall entitled "Types of the American Ballad." His mainstay, however, continued to be the general talk on cowboy songs, which he described as a "lecture reading" that included material portraying the cowboy at work and play, "in his communion with nature and in developing his philosophy of life." For this, Lomax quoted numerous passages from songs, read some in their entirety, and—whenever his audiences seemed sufficiently warm and sympathetic, he said—often sang a few of his favorites.[62]

Two letter fragments, mailed from places unknown, suggest that he was on the road briefly in the period just after Christmas, perhaps on his way to Dean Briggs's home at Half-way Pond.[63] But he did not attend the meeting of the MLA in New York that year, and his major project at the time was an early draft of the somewhat curious volume entitled *The Book of Texas,* which he compiled in collaboration with his friend and colleague Harry Benedict. In any event, he was home in Austin in time for the birth of his second son, Alan, on January 31, 1915.

CHAPTER TWELVE

Long Summer Day

1915

A new baby in the house was symbolically appropriate to the interlude of domesticity that marked the relative calm of Lomax's life in the middle teens. While he might seem to complain about the demands of a growing family, his flourishing household was a source not only of great pride but of renewed vigor and a sense of well-being. This would prove to be his last quiet time for many years.

Although Bess's health suffered after each birth, the children seemed to thrive. In 1915 Shirley was ten, John Jr. eight, both of them sturdy, handsome, and intelligent. Lomax had described his small daughter, fulsomely but not incorrectly, as the "happiest, jolliest, smartest little witch or elve or fairy that ever was."[1] She would grow up to be the family beauty, lively and fun-loving, although she also inherited her share of Lomaxian quick-wittedness. From a sickly babyhood, John Jr. was growing more and more athletic every day, a lithe, active little boy with his father's boundless energy and his own clean good looks. Little Alan, precocious almost from birth, quickly became his father's favorite, although true to form, it was several years before Lomax settled on the correct spelling of his youngest son's name, writing it variously as "Allen" or "Allan." Perhaps that was an unconscious reflection of the fact that he had wanted to name the boy "Will Hogg Lomax" after his old friend (a further incentive was that the baby was born on Will Hogg's birthday). But Bess rather understandably balked; as it happened, her brother, Jack Alleine Brown, also shared the same birthday, and the baby thus became the namesake of "Allie" Brown ("Alleine" was a family name, pronounced "Alan" and transferred in that form to the littlest Lomax).

The Lomax household might be characterized as "child-centered," insofar as both John and Bess prided themselves on being progressive and up-to-date on matters of child-rearing, hygiene, and education. Bess drew on her considerable experience as a teacher of kindergarten, and she was an early advocate of Montessori (whose first book appeared in English in 1912). Since her school days she had been writing stories and songs for children and attempting to publish them. John had shown a special affinity with children dating at least as far back as his bachelor-teacher days at Clifton, when he romped and rambled with Cousin Lon Cooper's boys, and later, when Shirley Green's little nieces, Maude and Bess Prather, were the apples of his eye. He'd been a big brother to young Lewis Winston when Lewis's father, Dr. George Winston, was president of the University of Texas, and he carried on an affectionate correspondence with the boy long after the Winstons left Texas. At A&M he formed a similar relationship with David Houston's son Franklin, often looking after the boy when his parents were away.[2] Given Lomax's drive for upward mobility, a cynic might look for sycophantic motives, conscious or otherwise, but there is nothing to suggest that. To the contrary, his interest in the youngsters seems genuine, to which is added the evidence of his clear devotion to his own children.

The world of the child—nursery rhymes, fairy tales, play songs—dovetailed with Lomax's folksong-collecting interests, as in a letter he wrote to Shirley—addressed to "My Dear Little White Kitty-Cat" and enclosing in a post script a new song he had found, with the lines, "When yo pappy come home, / He bring you a purty little pony." On that occasion, he had returned briefly to College Station on business, and took a nostalgic stroll around the campus that carried him past the house they had lived in there. It had made him terribly sad, he wrote Shirley (who was only five at the time), when he approached the house and didn't see her and John coming out to meet him.[3]

Such letters to his children, which he wrote regularly whenever he traveled, brought lively responses. On one occasion, when she was eight, Shirley wrote: "Dear Farther [*sic*] We are wanting you mighty bad. I wood like you to bring me something for Halloween. It is the 30 of October. John wants a box of blocks that he can build houses with like those up in Cambridge. I send you 15 kisses and 3 bear hugs." At the same age two years later, John Jr. showed different concerns but similar orthography: "Dear Farther, The corn has some roastn ears on it. It is raining now. Your tirky is nearly well. Two of the tomaters are blooming. The squash are blooming like fire. I have a stocking cap now. Me and Sam went fishing and didnot catch a thing. John Lomax Jr."[4]

Lomax wasn't joking when he'd promised Shirley he would "bring you a purty little pony." And the horse—"Daisy"—was soon joined by all sorts of other range and farmland creatures. The family was hardly settled in their new Austin home when Lomax was building chicken pens, inquiring about prices for "one Bronze Turkey Tom and two or three hens" for breeding and ordering grape cuttings suited to the rich black soil on West 26th Street.[5] "Everywhere we lived," said John Jr. later, "there sprang a miniature farm. . . . When we lived in Austin, Father utilized the land surrounding our home for a fruit orchard, an over-sized garden, and a corn patch. We also raised turkeys, chickens, and pigeons, and kept a cow and a pony on the lot. . . . For many years Father milked the cow himself."[6]

One outgrowth of this "miniature farm" was that it became, in effect, a home business, and on a fairly large scale. Sales of milk and eggs were resumed, and soon Bess's ledger was showing regular monthly income from "Hens, wood, milk," "Calf, hens, & milk," "Milk & eggs & old clothes." Just before they moved from Austin in 1917, Bess noted that during the previous year "the place earned $530.00"—almost one-third of the $1874 it had cost to run the household.[7]

Another enterprise of the Lomaxes' cottage industry involved selling copies of *Cowboy Songs.* Initially, Lomax had pushed local stores to stock the book and referred inquiries to them. But as time went by and he got more and more letters asking about the book, he began to order small lots from the publisher at a discount and mail them out himself. When that proved to be a bonanza, he started placing small ads in rural newspapers and various cattlemen's magazines. Soon he was selling more copies of *Cowboy Songs* than the publisher and earning, through his author's discount, a whopping $.60 per copy instead of the $.15 his royalty contract paid. In 1914, Bess noted that the book had brought in about $300 (while "cow" earned only $120). That year Sturgis and Walton sold some four hundred copies of *Cowboy Songs* and paid Lomax a royalty of slightly over $50.00.[8]

He also continued to dabble in a number of small investments, the mainstay of which had always been that notorious golden fleece of the middle class, insurance. His correspondence during this period grew thick with premium notices, loan applications, payment stubs, and countless letters from half a dozen insurance companies—all despite his populist's fundamental suspicion of financial institutions. He complained to one of his several insurance agents that there was so much chicanery and outright thievery "in high financial circles" that he distrusted all of them. A man in his position was an easy mark, he said, and "we gullible folks" enabled the money men to operate schemes no sensible person would support.[9] It was another instance of the bifurcation of his character: he was not nearly so gullible as he feared, yet he feared it mightily, and (as in matters social and racial) was even at times in jeopardy of acting irrationally on that fear. Considering the insecurities bred into his background, such an outlook was understandable, but also an altogether strange attitude for a man who would himself shortly become a bond broker and bank executive.

Lomax rushed about from task to task, toiling through office work, milking cows, wheeling and dealing and generally giving off the air of a besieged man of affairs, but it was Bess who remained the firm rock and anchor of the household. Despite recurring bouts of ill health—excruciating earaches in addition to the various disorders then lumped together under the euphemism of "female troubles"—she ran the house and helped as well to manage John's multifarious business affairs, all the while radiating calm and good cheer. "She was a very vigorous and active woman," her daughter Bess recalled, "and she was enormously stoical. Her message was very much that you were supposed to put up with things."[10] That included teaching the children at home (John and Shirley attended public schools only sporadically while they were growing up), nursing them through illnesses while Lomax was away, handling his lecture correspondence, tending to the stock, and taking care of all sorts of other family business, in addition, of course, to the routine matters of keeping house, sewing, canning, and attending meetings of her various clubs, where she usually held one office or another and carried more than her share of the organizational load. Still, "I like busy days," as she told John at the end of a typical one, "and I am not too tired to love you."[11]

The steadfastness of their marriage, now into its second decade, is reflected in the affectionate, often ardent closings of her letters. At the end of one she said she was going to bed, "tho it isn't much fun when you aren't here"; in another she told him that all her nervous tension would disappear if he were there to put his arms around her: "I'm not fit for anything but just to be your girl." Especially revealing of the team-like nature of their relationship was her "Goodnight, dear Big Partner, the best Partner a girl ever had."[12] In his letters to her, John still signed himself, "Your loving boy, Tommy Tucker."

The decision to educate the children at home had been made soon after Shirley reached school age. "I started in the first grade," she said later, "and

I'd get sick about every week and come home and John [Jr.] would catch it—and [Mother] decided . . . to teach me at home. I didn't think anything about it. Everybody else went to school and we were free!"[13]

By this time Bess also had the care of her aging parents. Soon after the move to West 26th Street, the Lomaxes built adjacent to their new home a small three-room cottage for Mr. and Mrs. Brown on the same property. Lomax—at considerable expense to his peace of mind as well as his pocketbook—had not only kept his promise not to separate mother and daughter but also arranged privately to contribute a monthly sum for his in-laws' living expenses, without their knowing the source.[14] This drain was offset to some extent by another enterprise which Bess put into operation about this time: renting spare bedrooms in the big new house to University students and single faculty members (among their eventual tenants was the young folklorist Stith Thompson, fresh out of Harvard with a Ph.D.).

But all their business schemes paled momentarily beside the Great Magazine Subscription Contest of 1916. John Jr., then only eight, had for some time been a distributor for the Curtis Publishing Company, delivering copies of the *Saturday Evening Post, Country Gentleman,* and the *Ladies Home Journal* to customers on an established route in the neighborhood. In December 1915, Curtis announced a sales contest, offering a grand prize of $1,000 to the boy who sold the most new subscriptions by the end of August. Turmoil and industry descended immediately on the Lomax household—only little Alan, not yet a toddler, was spared. Bess drafted sales letters to potential customers; Shirley, mounted on the brave little pony, Daisy, was delegated to make deliveries while her younger brother devoted himself to hustling new customers. John Sr. enlisted the aid of the Texas Exes, drew up mailing lists of prominent persons, and ran ads in the *Alcalde.* Among the respondents—testament to Lomax's renown—were such prominent Texans as Major George W. Littlefield and Will Hogg, along with dozens of banks, railroads, and other major businesses around the state.

The contest was soon at fever pitch, with fifty thousand boys around the country knocking on doors, phoning, and pulling every promotion stunt they (and their parents) could dream up. Bess wrote "sales talks" for John Jr. which were models of the "go-get-'em" commercialism of that era, heavily laced with positive thinking, point-of-sale appeal, and the spirit of Horatio Alger. She worked out a plan for bulk sales to local businesses, which gave away the magazines as premiums, and she discovered ways to wangle free publicity. "She was into everything," daughter Shirley said later[15] (and "everything" included regular complaints to Curtis that the rules favored boys in big cities, that the term of the contest was too long, that bulk sales weren't counted sufficiently, etc.). "I think day and night of the Curtis publications," Bess told her husband, which proved to her that the Curtis people were smart businessmen; by offering such a prize, she said, they were putting to work not just their 50,000 delivery boys to market the Curtis magazines but shrewdly enlisting "the brains of each mother and father" as well.[16]

To Bess, it was all a part of making men out of boys, an integral element of the American Way. She was confident, she told Lomax, that John Jr.'s participation in the contest was "toning him up" and making him better at other tasks he undertook. "He sells Posts hard, he plays hard, he studies hard," she said.[17] Considering John Jr.'s later life as an apparently confident, serene, and successful individual, there is little evidence that she was wrong.

• • • • •

In 1915 Lomax had managed to schedule only a few scattered lectures. There were prosperous seasons yet to come, but he rightly saw the decline that year as a sign of changing times, complaining to a friend that lecturers were declining in popularity: moreover, "the Lyceum stage is over crowded," and moving pictures were capturing the public fancy.[18] The national depression of 1913–14 was a factor as well. In August he addressed the convention of University Alumni Secretaries at the University of California and booked a few random lectures on cowboy songs while touring in the West, but the trip was a bust as far as making any money was concerned.

Freed for a time from the lecture circuit, he found other outlets for his nervous energy. Sturgis and Walton had finally agreed to issue an expanded edition of *Cowboy Songs,* and the raw material he'd turned up in the meantime had to be put into shape. He was also busy gathering facts and figures for the quasi-encyclopedic *Book of Texas,* another piece of cottage industry which he hoped would add to the family coffers, undertaken in collaboration with his friend and colleague H. Y. Benedict (who was now dean of the College of Arts and Sciences at the University).

There was considerable work for Lomax that fall in arranging speaking tours of Texas for two of his friends back East. William Lyon Phelps swept through in November, lecturing in Fort Worth, Austin, and Corpus Christi and, in the fashion of Kittredge two years earlier, created a mild stir among the Texas literati. Through Lomax's maneuvering—in a flurry of correspondence between Austin and Cambridge for some months—Barrett Wendell was invited to come the following spring to address the University's celebration of the tercentenary anniversary of Shakespeare's birth.[19] Then prospects for a winter lecture tour of his own began to improve, and by the time Lomax went off to Cleveland for the MLA meeting in December 1915, he had almost two dozen bookings in the East and Midwest that would keep him on the road until early February.

From Cleveland he wrote to Bess that he had been elected to the executive council of the Modern Language Association, adding a self-congratulatory "Ahem!" The MLA's executive council was scarcely a hot center of power, but membership clearly implied recognition among one's peers. Puffed up as he was, however, the prestige of such a position could not tempt the frugal Lomax into any show of extravagance. Next morning he notified Bess that he was moving to a hotel "less pretentious and costly." Still, he could force himself to enjoy the privileges appertaining thereunto, expressing considerable satisfaction at having had an MLA underling call him and "wish to begin to do things for me."[20]

Arriving in New England, Lomax paid his usual visit to Dean Briggs at Half-way Pond and spoke at Radcliffe (reporting that "the Cambridge folk-lore people" liked his talk and afterwards Kittredge praised him "until I turned a turkey red").[21] He spent a night in New York and dined with his former boss, Dr. Mezes, who had left Texas to take the presidency of C.C.N.Y. Mezes seemed reserved and distant, in a manner that Lomax associated with easterners (Mezes was "transforming his interest from Texas to New York," but despite that, he still liked him).[22] Then Lomax was off to New Hampshire and Down East to Maine in twelve-below-zero weather. He took a bad cold and fell into the old depression that public speaking always caused him, complaining constantly to Bess that he didn't want to make speeches and if it weren't for the money, he would "chuck the whole business and come home."[23]

His itinerary was a maze of loops and backtracks. The New England dates were interrupted by a hasty excursion into the South, but there the weather and his audiences improved. From Richmond in mid-January he wrote of an extravagant reception at Lynchburg, where he had been a hit with an audience of six hundred at Randolph-Macon Women's College. Girls from Texas thronged around him afterward, he said, some actually brought to tears ("of excitement or pleasure or what not") by his talk. The applause went on and on until he finally brought it to an end by asking the crowd to join him in singing two or three songs. When that was over, the audience stood, at the college president's direction, and as a body invited him to come again.[24] He began to report that he was now hitting his stride, and after returning to Cambridge and a warm reception at Harvard, his mood shifted. Dean Briggs told him he was the first man Briggs had ever known whose physical appearance was improved by "privation, loss of sleep, nights on trains, etc." According to Briggs, he said, he looked 50 percent better than he had two weeks before when he left for the South. His condition was no doubt further improved by the roaring success of his talks at Harvard and Yale—"ovations from beginning to end," he told Bess.[25]

Kittredge took him to the Adams House Hotel for an elegant dinner (at the same table, said Lomax, where Kittredge and his father had lunched together once a month for ten years). Thrifty Lomax was awed by Kittredge's generosity with tips—he gave a quarter to the man who helped Lomax out of his coat and another to their taxi driver; their waiter and a messenger bearing a telegram were each rewarded with a dollar. Lomax had never seen such largesse, and he reported the details of their meal with gusto: cocktails and oysters for appetizers, then fresh codfish, venison, and a variety of vegetables, followed by nuts, aspic, coffee, and Rose of the Rancho cigars. Best of all ("save Mr. K. himself") was a quart of Moselle champagne; Lomax said he drank his full share and enjoyed every second of the two hours he spent with "this rare man."[26] At Yale it was much the same—"only more," said Lomax. He was treated to a formal dinner at the University Club, and William Lyon Phelps gave him such a glorious introduction that Lomax wanted to hug him; all in all, it was one of his most memorable lecture evenings.[27]

Bess, whose support never wavered in adversity, took good news equally in stride. All along she had been cheering him on: "Of course I knew you would succeed." And as always, she was awash in grand schemes. When he got home, she told him, they would compile and edit his lectures for publication, and Doubleday, Page would be fools if they didn't take it. If the *Book of Texas* was a success and they could get "the Negro book" out by summer, he would have four books on the market, and that would mean a tidy boost in their income.[28]

By this time the Curtis circulation contest was gathering momentum, and Bess's entrepreneurial zeal was focused on that as well. When he returned from his lecture trip, she told the boy's father, he would have to help her and John Jr. "scheme some *big killin's*" that would add a couple of hundred sales to the total.[29] John Jr. was caught up in her enthusiasm, and whatever he lacked of her talent for commercial maneuvering he made up for in energy and hard work. Accustomed to going barefooted most of the year, he shunned shoes even in January, eager to make his sales rounds. In spite of the cold, he was off one morning by six, Bess wrote to John Sr., wearing an extra shirt and sweater under his coat and a pair of Shirley's shoes and stockings. "These last he discarded by breakfast time."[30]

By spring, he was emerging as a serious contender in the contest, to the surprise of everyone but the Lomaxes. Could it be that a boy not yet nine years old, in a little town like Austin, Texas, was seriously competing against 50,000 boys, most of them teenagers, in major cities all over North America?! The Curtis magazines printed tallies weekly and monthly, and many national newspapers carried daily standings. In early July, John Lomax Jr. took over the top spot, and each week he lengthened his lead, holding on through August and to the finish line. In addition to the first prize—and considerable national publicity—he had earned more than two hundred dollars for his savings account, which totaled almost $800 by August, and along the way he accumulated enough Curtis savings stamps to buy a bicycle for his sister.[31] She was not much taken with the suggestion that the bicycle would come in handy when she helped deliver the new subscriptions he'd sold.

Later Shirley laughingly related how John Jr.'s prize money was delivered to their door in gold pieces, and how it was transferred to the bank: "it came from the express company in a sack, and they delivered it to our house—we didn't have a car—and John and I sat on the floor—we'd never seen a gold piece before, of course—playing with it, and it had to go to the bank, and [Mother] decided that the safest way to send it to the bank was to put it inside John's shirt and put us on the pony, so we rode downtown—John holding on to me and the gold pieces jingling." Some years later, John Jr. asked his father what had happened to the money. According to Shirley, "Father said, 'Well, son, I'm real sorry, but I had to pay it on the house.'" John Jr. was disappointed but took the news in stride—only to learn much later, when he was about to enter Harvard Business School, that his father had been joking. The money had been in the bank all along, drawing interest, to pay for his education and start him in business.[32]

In the midst of the Curtis circulation wars, the boy had implored his traveling father to "answer me a few letters." Waiting for his train in a drafty depot in Bangor, Maine, Lomax did his best, but it was almost all he could do to cope with his cold, the bad weather, and the relentless demands of his schedule. Following his brief triumphs in the East, he headed back to Cleveland for a public lecture at Western Reserve, and the old gloom descended again. Once he wrote home just as he was about to undertake what he characterized as the most difficult and trying event of his trip—a lecture to a group of "Cleveland highbrows—not students but sated sensation seekers." He apologized to Bess for complaining so often about the lectures; they were a cross he must bear and had only one redeeming feature. "Tonight it is $100."[33] Feeling his age, he observed that "grey hairs don't fit with ballads" but summoned up his last bit of energy and optimism as he went off to fill his remaining dates in the Midwest, assuring Bess that he would survive it all, reminding her that the one thing he had was persistence, "however lacking I am in sense and judgment."[34]

In the coming months, his capacity for perseverance would be tried to the sticking place. Trouble was brewing back in Texas.

· · · · ·

Politics—of either the official or office variety—had played a natural role in Lomax's life for some time. Although he scarcely thought of himself as a politician, he had been involved in various kinds of political maneuvers actively or behind the scenes almost from his undergraduate days at the University, when the law school was in its first generation and turning out an array of men who would become influential officeholders. His schoolmates included a future governor, Pat Neff, a future lieutenant governor, Edgar Witt, and several lower-level politicos. Fritz Lanham, '00, who had been one of his students back in Weatherford and helped him revive the *Alcalde* at the University in 1913, was in the Texas legislature from 1919 to 1947. Lomax's best friend in his University days, Tom Connally, entered local politics in 1906 as a county attorney, went to the U.S. House of Representatives in 1916, and eventually became one of the most powerful and distinguished members of the U.S. Senate, serving six terms there. Another influential senator from Texas, Morris Sheppard, earned his law degree the year Lomax graduated, spent six terms in the Texas legislature, and went on to the U.S. Senate in 1913, where he remained until his death in 1941. Years later, Tom Connally, Edgar Witt, and Morris Sheppard were to figure prominently in Lomax's career in Washington.

The political nature of the environment at the University of Texas had only intensified for Lomax when he returned there from College Station. His new job was inherently political, in the sense that it involved paying court to governing powers and placed him in frequent contact with the state legislature. It was political at the personal level as well, requiring a sensitivity to key issues and considerable shrewdness in managing, contriving, wheeling and dealing, qualities Lomax possessed in abundance (although he was noticeably deficient in one vital element of the successful politician—tact—and that would cause problems later). As his interests and energies shifted to the Alumni Association, it became ever more important for him to cultivate close working relationships with movers and shakers at various political levels around the state. Announcing his intention to attend the state Democratic convention in San Antonio in 1912, he told a friend that he was not really interested in politics but simply wanted to be where he could "meet as many University men as possible in a short time," and they tended to be found at such places as political conventions.[35]

But his involvement in politics was stronger than such a casual disclaimer would indicate. He was scarcely back at the University in 1910 when his support was enlisted in the successful campaign of his friend Oscar Callaway for the U.S. House of Representatives, and he even contributed to a campaign biography of Callaway.[36] His counsel was sought by would-be candidates for the Texas legislature, and various political groups around the state often asked him to give his talks on folksongs at their gatherings.[37]

During this time, relations between the University and state government had drifted into an unusual period of tranquility. The governor in office when Lomax returned to Austin, Oscar Colquitt, was a mild neo-Populist, a watered-down version of Will Hogg's father, Gov. James Hogg, who had fought the out-of-state trusts and whipped the railroads into line in the early 1890s. Times had turned more prosperous after the turn of the century, and the fashion for governors was to act common, speak broadly for social justice, and at all costs avoid offending the many complicated local interests which prevailed in a state as large and diverse as Texas. Colquitt, like the majority of Texas governors in the twentieth century, was essentially content with the status quo.

Following his reelection in 1912, however, Colquitt embarked on a program of modest reform of state institutions, including a bill which would increase appropriations to the badly underfunded University, toward the goal of making it, as the state constitution had decreed, "a University of the first class." There were later accusations—from, among others, Lomax and Benedict in *The Book of Texas*—that Colquitt's motives were self-serving, that he had attempted to allocate funds he privately knew the state did not have, in order to win favor with the public.[38] But in the meantime, giddy supporters of the University, unaccustomed to such favor from the governor and emboldened by the prospects, decided the time was also ripe to strike against their old adversary, the Agricultural and Mechanical College. Written into the bill of amendments—formally titled "Senate Joint Resolution No. 18"—and buried deep in a paragraph of technicalities was a seemingly innocuous provision allowing the University to establish, among other new departments and programs, its own "agricultural and mechanical college."

When the ploy was discovered, A&M officials began to circle the wagons, calling the provision "a bug under the cow chip" and crying out in anguish. University backers of the amendments pointed out, correctly enough, that A&M, according to the state constitution which established it, had never been more than a branch of the University (despite the curious fact that when A&M opened its doors in 1876, the projected "University of Texas" was yet only a phantom, seven years from realization). Bill No. 18 would do nothing to change the official relationship between the schools, said its supporters, and besides, in a state like Texas where farming was the leading industry, every school in the state should be empowered to teach agriculture. It was nonsense, they said, to think that the bill would set up a school of agriculture at the University which, as the bill's opponents feared, might "in time overshadow the A. and M. College and bring about its removal or ultimate destruction."[39]

That's what they said for public consumption, but privately the University crowd intended not merely that A&M suffer and decline. If they had their way—if the amendments in Bill No. 18 were passed by the electorate and put into law—A&M would be shut down permanently, moved lock, stock, and parade ground to Austin, and consolidated with the University. John Lomax was in the very midst of the fray—if not, indeed, leading it.

Drafts of the Colquitt-sponsored amendments were being circulated among prospective supporters and University alumni soon after the governor's reelection in the fall of 1912. Within weeks, the plan to consolidate A&M with the University had caused such a clamor that it was separated from Joint Resolution No. 18 and written into an amendment bill of its own. By December, Lomax, as secretary of the Alumni Association, had gone to work alerting all ex-students by letter and telephone, setting up alumni representatives in each senatorial district to coordinate lobbying efforts, and compiling statistical information to support the proposed amendments. Drafting a broadside letter for the signature of the alumni president, C. K. Lee, he called for unified action and pointed out that for years ex-student support of the University had been "spasmodic and individual rather than general and intelligently organized."[40] Lomax, with his penchant for running things, hoped to avoid the errors of the past.

He almost instinctively understood the value of the press and how to cultivate its support. From the beginning of his tenure as publicity agent for the University, he had established close personal relations with a number of powerful editors and writers around the state, many of whom were alumni of the University or had reasons otherwise to support its interests: George W. Brackenridge, owner of the *San Antonio Express*, and his editor, Joseph Emerson Smith; Frank Holland of *Farm and Ranch;* George Bailey of the *Houston Post;* D. P. Toomey and Alonzo Wasson of the *Dallas News.* Now Lomax made the most of those contacts, working quietly behind the scenes to feed them inside details and keep them posted on the latest developments.[41]

The proposed amendments were approved in due course by the state legislature and scheduled to go before the general electorate on July 19. Lomax's office became the command post and communications center for the pro-consolidation forces, a focal point for strategy meetings, straw vote tallies, promotional mailings, and rousing messages to the troops in the field. Much was at stake, and combining the state's two most prominent institutions of higher learning was only part of the issue; passage of the amendments would also bring the University a $3,000,000 bonanza which it badly needed for new buildings to replace the fourteen "temporary" wooden shacks that had been hastily thrown together around the campus to meet growing enrollments since the turn of the century.

For many weeks victory seemed certain. From the outset there had been little opposition, save the outraged cries of a few isolated Aggies here and there—and Aggies were always upset about something. Lomax had mounted a smooth and efficient campaign which appeared to reach the key constituencies and inspired great confidence among backers of the amendments. Then, in early June, a backlash began to build, and soon reports of serious opposition were filtering in from out west, where A&M's supporters were most numerous and vocal. With the level of opposition intensifying, Lomax was forced to shorten, then postpone, and finally cancel his summer lecture tour, pleading that his superiors were "unwilling for the University to take the risk of letting me go" in the midst of the battle.[42]

Despite all he could do, the turning tide gathered into a great wave. On July 20, the *Austin Statesman* announced the results of the election in an eight-column banner headline across the top of the front page: "ALL AMENDMENTS ARE DEFEATED."

That was not the worst of it. Colquitt, embarrassed by the affair and disgusted with the University for what he perceived to be excessive greed and attempts to broker power, proceeded to veto the institution's entire appropriation for 1915, threatening to deprive it of some $700,000 of expected revenue. The University was not only in danger of failing to get its three-million-dollar building fund but now could not even afford more of the cheap, ugly pine shacks which dotted the campus and were already filled to overflowing.

There matters stood when James E. Ferguson succeeded Colquitt in January of 1915.

CHAPTER THIRTEEN

• • • • •

Hell in Texas

1915–17

Like Morgan Callaway and the Great A&M Strike, "Farmer Jim" Ferguson remained an enigma to John Lomax and worried him practically to the grave. Late in life he wrote: "I have never understood why I was included among the seven faculty members who won the displeasure of Governor James E. Ferguson." And again: "The underlying motives of the savage attack . . . have as yet to be made clear."[1] In his autobiography he said only that Ferguson "didn't like me,"[2] again passing off a tempestuous and traumatic episode in a single sentence.

Ironically, Lomax and Ferguson were shaped by many of the same forces and had a great deal in common. In childhood they were separated by scarcely sixty miles and only four years (Ferguson was the younger); both were Scotch-Irish farmers' sons of modest means whose mothers had the dominant role in their early lives (Lomax's father was simply aloof and withdrawn; Ferguson's died when the boy was four). Both men grew to be relentless Texans, both were ambitious, keen-minded, hardworking, and egocentric. Both struggled for an education and achieved it relatively late. After a roustabout, jack-of-many-trades youth, Ferguson "read law" on his own and was admitted to the Texas bar in 1897, the same year that Lomax graduated from the University of Texas.

Socially, politically, and philosophically, their similar experiences and temperaments made them both "folk-conservatives" in the peculiarly Texas fashion characterized by a fervent espousal of "the common man" (by which they meant men like themselves) and an abiding belief in the power of the individual to shape his own destiny. Added to this were distrust of government and a professed hatred of moneyed interests, especially those in which they did not participate—and typically self-contradictory in view of the fact that Ferguson was a banker and Lomax later became one. They were instinctively opposed to most social reform, especially prohibition, which was the big issue of their day, and civil rights, which wasn't.

Despite the similarities in their origins, as adults their paths quickly diverged. One difference was external—Ferguson married money, while Lomax had to scrabble for it—but the element which most set them apart was in their psychological makeup: Lomax's ego, commodious though it was, constantly suffered from insecurity and self-doubts, while, by all accounts, Farmer Jim's high opinion of himself never wavered. His tendencies ran to the absolute and tyrannical; indeed, at times he seems to have exhibited symptoms of classic megalomania. "I don't have to give any reasons!" he was known to storm. "I am the Governor of Texas!"[3] J. Frank Dobie described Ferguson as having "the brutal self-assertiveness of a man used to forcing men, because of his financial power, to their knees."[4]

The historian T. R. Fehrenbach defended "the most colorful governor since Jim Hogg" in this fashion: "Ferguson threw up a completely confusing image to some people, but the pattern of his own career was quite simple. He was typical of a whole breed of Texas politicos in the 20th century. Ferguson liked office, but was a man without a mission; having no particular program, he tailored his principles to the electorates' foibles and desires." He was, in other words, an opportunist, with little regard for fixed principles. His devoted daughter assured the public, however, that he loved his family and was "uncommonly kind to animals."[5]

Physically, Ferguson was tall but otherwise unimpressive, with a bland countenance and a weak chin that kept receding as he aged. But his gunmetal gray eyes could bore holes, and on the stump he turned into a demon, possessing a style described as "equal parts of wit, slander, and sarcasm."[6] That and his pseudo-populist support of tenant farmers, convicted moonshiners, and "the little schoolhouse on the country road" made him immensely popular in rural areas of the state. He strengthened that support by cleverly stepping around the prohibition issue and promising to uphold the status quo in such matters as women's suffrage (anti) and deregulation of corporate wealth (pro), in effect giving Texans a rest from the liberal reforms of the Hogg era. To his credit, however, in his first term—1915 to 1916—Ferguson was responsible for a number of genuine improvements in the penal system, public education, and farm tenancy laws.

For a time after he took office, Ferguson and the University circled each other warily; in the eyes of academicians, the new governor was clearly an ignoramus. Yet education had been a major plank in his campaign. In his first message to the legislature, he called for a central governing board for the state's colleges, which sparked the hopes of Lomax and others who still dreamed of consolidating A&M and the University. The consolidation-backers probed cautiously to determine what was really on Ferguson's mind, but he remained characteristically vague. Then, out of the blue, the governor proposed the largest University appropriation in the institution's history—$1.6 million. Lomax and Benedict, at that time busy with the manuscript of *The Book of Texas,* wide-eyedly set down Ferguson's name as a strong claimant for the title of "Texas' greatest educational governor"—and were dejectedly munching on those words by the time the book saw print.

Ferguson, godlike, had no sooner given than he took away, striking down the proposed appropriation in a fit of anger because the board of regents foiled his efforts to fire the University's acting president, Dr. W. J. Battle. Battle was a distinguished professor of classical languages and former dean, who had agreed to fill in when Sidney Mezes resigned to go to C.C.N.Y. Ferguson charged that Battle, widely known as a man of unimpeachable integrity, had deceived the legislature and lied to the governor about the previous appropriations bill. (Of Battle, a senior member of the faculty said he was "true as steel and honest as sunshine. He couldn't tell a lie if he tried.")[7] Lacking any evidence to support Ferguson's charges against Battle, the board declined to act, pointing out that in any event, the budget had been drawn up and the appropriation made before Battle took over as acting president. But the whole affair so disconcerted Battle that he asked not to be considered for the permanent presidency, although he had been the leading contender. Lomax, because of his proximity to the president's office, knew that something foul was going on, but many details he learned only from campus rumor. It was with both consternation over the gathering storm and a certain relief at being away from it that he went off that winter to Cleveland and points east to lecture.

Ferguson, his imperial will thwarted, was still seething in early 1916, when the University's regents named Dr. R. E. Vinson to the permanent post of president. For reasons never clear, Vinson, a minister and respected educator who headed the Austin Presbyterian Theological Seminary, immediately aroused the governor's ire. Ferguson fought Vinson's appointment, but the chairman of the board at that time was Will Hogg, a power in his own right who influenced the majority on the board and had little use for the Ferguson administration. "I had rather go to hell in a hand-basket," Hogg told the governor on one occasion, "than to submit meekly to your demands."[8]

Ferguson's only firm ally on the board was Dr. A. W. Fly, a crusty old character who weighed three hundred pounds and once, as mayor of Galveston, had single-handedly held off an angry mob in the streets, waving his six-shooter and defying the crowd to take another step. Fly vehemently but unsuccessfully opposed Vinson's appointment. "Do you mean to tell me that you have gone to a preacher factory," he railed at the other regents, "and got a president and are going to put him in charge of the University? I am going to record my vote against it; there ain't a damned preacher I ever saw I could vote for University president; not that I am against preachers as a whole, but I am against a sectarian minister as head of the University." Fly said later that those were his exact words—"I am a verbatim sort of a bird."[9]

Although Fly's case against Vinson never quite acquired the stature of an argument for separation of church and state, it seems to have been the same as the charge lodged by Ferguson—that a minister was not suited to be president of the University. "Vinson is a failure," the governor told Major George Littlefield, one of the regents. "He has wrecked this Theological school out here, and he is not the proper man for this place." But Vinson's real sin, in Ferguson's eyes, was that he wouldn't "stand hitched"—that is, wouldn't take orders. Littlefield tried to argue—or reason—with Ferguson, but he would have none of it. "Governor Ferguson just seemed to want his way entirely as to Dr. Vinson; he just had to get him out," Littlefield testified later in court.[10] Thwarted again in his efforts to remove a University president he didn't like, the governor grew increasingly obsessed by the affair, and it quickly degenerated into an acrimonious conflict not of issues but of personalities.

Farmer Jim intended to have his way. If he couldn't get rid of Vinson, he could certainly control him—make him "stand hitched" and do what the governor wanted. That motive seems as good as any other to explain Ferguson's next move. Following a regents' meeting in June, he took Vinson aside and told him that there were several men on the faculty that he wanted fired. Somewhat astonished, Vinson replied that appointments for the coming year had already been approved by the regents. When the governor continued to insist, Vinson said only that he would investigate and present the facts to the board of regents. Whereupon Ferguson pounded the desk with his fist and shouted that the men had to go.

Vinson stood his ground. A slight, scholarly man who looked as if he had been supplied by Central Casting, down to his winged collar, primly pursed lips, small steel spectacles, and hair parted in the middle, Vinson nevertheless came equipped with more than the ordinary college president's share of backbone. He told Ferguson, he later testified, "that I intended to be free to act upon my own understanding of the facts, and that I never had been accustomed to acting upon any man's dictation, and did not propose to begin then." Ferguson's heated retort was that if the men weren't fired, "you are going to have the biggest bear fight that has ever taken place in the history of the State of Texas!"[11] The affair was soon known as "the Big Bear Fight" and in such manner passed into the state's annals of tragicomic buffoonery.

To this point the names of the targeted faculty members remained unknown. But the rumor mills had begun to grind, and Lomax, naturally paranoid anyway, soon had proper cause to suspect that he was on the list. In the meantime, there were welcome distractions from the gathering turmoil.

• • • • •

In late April the Barrett Wendells arrived for the University's Shakespeare Tercentenary. In addition to evening lectures, a week of great social activity was arranged to show the eastern visitors that Austin was as civilized as any other city when it came to luncheons, teas, country club dinners, and afternoon excursions by motor car to see the local sights. Although Lomax had engineered Wendell's appearance, the honor of hosting the distinguished visitors was given to Mr. and Mrs. Lewis Hancock—Hancock was prominent in real estate and "investments"—and the Lomaxes got scant (and noticeably neutral) attention in the careful record kept by Mrs. Wendell in her diary. "Mrs. Hancock, Prof. Lomax and Mrs. Lomax and their children met us at the depot"—but "We went to the Hancock's charming house to stay." She and Mrs. Hancock lunched at the country club, she and Mrs. Hancock had "a very beautiful drive," she and the Hancocks went to see *She Stoops to Conquer,* and when the visit was all over, "BW & I regretfully left the delightful Hancocks at [the] 1:20 train to San Antonio." The single entry for the Lomaxes was noncommittal—"We dined with Prof. & Mrs. Lomax [and] went to see the "Comedy of Errors"[12]—but of course Mrs. Wendell, impeccable Brahmin that she was, would never have deigned to remark on social distinctions, even in her diary. Lomax was no doubt glad to be relieved of the strain their presence caused.

The visit at least provided Lomax an opportunity to confide to his aging mentor some of the details of the looming Big Bear Fight, but Wendell, in ill health and soon to retire from Harvard, could offer little but sympathy. Later, when the situation at the University had intensified, he put Lomax in touch with his son, Barrett Wendell Jr., a Boston financier, with important consequences. Meanwhile, accustomed to the regularity of civilized New England conservatism, the Wendells must have found a man like Ferguson thoroughly confusing—and even more confusing as the antagonist of so cautious and solid a citizen as John Lomax.

Another major—and more than a little ironic—event that year was the publication of Benedict and Lomax's *The Book of Texas,* which contained no fewer than four glowing references to Ferguson, including a full-page picture effusively captioned "GOV. JAMES E. FERGUSON—Who first brought the evils of tenantry to the attention of the people, who enthusiastically signed the million-dollar appropriation for rural schools, and who is the only governor of Texas who ever shipped a carload of cattle to market."[13] But that was in keeping with the book's general tone. It was an unabashed hurrah for Texas, 448 pages of press agentry covering every wonder of the state from Alamo to Zinc. The authors even apologized for their cheery outlook, noting that "inclination and the orders of publishers both conjoin in making the 'Book of Texas' optimistic." Yet they did not shrink from a lengthy paragraph on laziness ("common enough in Texas") or a pragmatic discourse on tenant farmers: "Incapable, untrained, careless, often lazy, affected with hookworm, eating poor food very badly cooked, living in uncomfortable and crowded 'shacks,' victims of typhoid and ignorance, and money lenders, these submerged tenants are the modern representatives of the 'poor whites' of the old South. The major evils of tenantry are largely confined to this group and to the negroes and Mexicans."[14]

Queried about this passage nearly thirty years later by a scholar who wanted to quote it in an economic and social history of Texas, Lomax stood by what he and Benedict had written. He did not know, he said, how to turn "Po' white trash" into "self-respecting human units" but was convinced that any improvement in social and economic conditions must come from within the individual and could not be imposed by external forces—to wit, government.[15] In the intervening years, the horrors of the depression and the programs of the New Deal had only hardened his resistance to social reform.

At the book's opposite extreme was more romantic nonsense about cowboys, carried over from *Cowboy Songs:* "Mr. [Theodore] Roosevelt has pointed out that the days of free grass were essentially similar to the days of medieval England, Jesse James taking the place of Robin Hood. The songs of the cowboys correspond to the ballads of the Scottish Border, and the roping and riding contests of to-day are the lineal descendants of courtly tournaments. The Knights of King Arthur's Round Table and the Texas broncho busters have been poured from the same mold."[16]

Despite its flagrant boosterism, however, *The Book of Texas* offered on the whole a comprehensive and fact-filled account of the state at that time. As recently as the 1970s it was still being cited as a reliable source by scholars and historians.[17]

• • • • •

Another round in the Big Bear Fight began in September, when Vinson wrote the governor a polite note, reviewing their June meeting and asking him again to specify his charges against the faculty members he wanted fired, so that Vinson could investigate and report to the board of regents. Vinson offered to come to the governor's office so they could discuss the matter. In a haughty reply, Ferguson denied that he'd ever said he had charges to make; he simply wanted the men fired. He added tersely: "I think for the future it will be better for us to remain in our respective jurisdictions, and no good purpose can be subserved by any further relations between us." He would deal with the regents, said Ferguson, and "I shall promptly and surely meet the issue which it is apparent from your letter that you intend to force on me."[18]

Stunned by the governor's hard line, Vinson wrote what he hoped was a conciliatory letter, assuring Ferguson that he wasn't forcing any issue but only doing his job according to the regulations of the University. Once more he made it clear that he was willing to fire anyone who was "incompetent or unworthy" but only when sufficient evidence had been presented.

Ferguson ignored the letter and instead began badgering members of the board, accusing them of conspiring against him. He demanded the resignation of any regent who did not support him against Vinson. "It is quite apparent that the issue is going to be decidedly drawn," he wrote. "The time has come when I must know who is for me and who is against me."[19]

The matter appeared to be coming to a head at the regents' meeting in October, when Ferguson turned up and, "in a speech of unparalleled violence, bristling with misstatements,"[20] named names and offered his complaints against them. The alleged culprits, in addition to Lomax (who was far down the list) were Dr. Battle; C. S. Potts, Lomax's friend and colleague; R. E. Cofer, a law professor; Dr. A. Caswell Ellis, a psychologist in the Education Department; Dr. William Mather from the Science Department; and Will H. Mayes, a newspaperman and former lieutenant governor who headed the newly instituted School of Journalism.

Ferguson's shotgun accusations, which varied widely from one man to the next, were vague and unsubstantiated, ranging from his old charge that Battle had mishandled the previous appropriation to the complaint that Cofer once presided over a county convention of Democrats which only reluctantly supported the Ferguson administration. Several accused faculty members, including Lomax, were said to have profited from the manner in which their travel expenses were paid by the University, although—as the regents' investigation quickly proved—the complicated reimbursement procedure was in fact required by the state auditor, a solid Ferguson man.

Lomax's inclusion on the list seemed directly related to his high profile as de facto assistant to the president, publicity agent for the University, and secretary of the Ex-Student's Association (a group which Ferguson eyed warily—and with good reason, as it turned out). Otherwise, the board of regents' concluded that "the Governor's disapproval of Mr. Lomax is obscure" and the charges against him "so trivial that it is hardly believable they represent [Ferguson's] real reasons."[21]

Former U.T. president Mezes had gotten out just ahead of the Ferguson mess, but his long years in Texas had given him a fine understanding of the political machinations involving the University. From the safety of his post in New York, he counseled Lomax: "My information is that the Governor has nothing against you personally, but has conceived the foolish notion that there is a small clique [including Lomax] who are running the University, and he has it in for all of you."[22]

In any event, the governor's appearance before the regents, ranting vague charges and carrying on about the "unholy spree of the educated hierarchy out there" made one thing clear: his real objective was not merely to have seven men fired, but to bring the entire University to heel and assert absolute control over it.

It was something of an irony that as a candidate Ferguson had campaigned for better schools, and he was probably earnest in his efforts to improve the conditions and standards of public education in Texas, particularly in rural areas. But education to a man like Farmer Jim meant simply "the little schoolhouse on the country road"—teaching the 3 R's that were basic to the pursuit of a livelihood in those days. Like many who are themselves unschooled, he distrusted and perhaps even feared the high-minded and fancy talking professors just down the hill from the capitol, and they, who perhaps understood him even less than he understood them, were equally irrational and panicky in response to his threats.

The governor got nowhere in his initial assault on the regents. The board's investigation, chaired by the tough and feisty Will Hogg, promptly exonerated all seven men by majority votes. In two cases the count was seven to one for retention, the lone holdout for dismissal being Ferguson's die-hard henchman, the obstreperous Dr. Fly, who had boasted that "I stick by my friends—as long as there's a pea in the dish."[23]

Ferguson also refused to give up. He only widened and intensified his attack, now threatening to fire the entire faculty and bullying the University like a mean dog with a rag doll in its teeth. For him the conflict had become a personal vendetta. Once more repulsed by the regents, the governor's only consolation for the moment lay in knowing that time was on his side. The terms of three anti-Ferguson regents (including Hogg) were about to expire, and Ferguson was confident that in the coming year he could somehow force the resignation of one or two more.

Roy Bedichek, now city editor of the *San Antonio Express*, told Lomax there was widespread disgust with the University. "Of course," he added wryly, "I have that lingering affection which I am told men still feel for wives who have proven unfaithful—but respect—no. There are no guts in the institution." The school was simply producing "a lot of trickster lawyers, plodding pedagogues and whispering politicians," said Bedi, and Ferguson, "that ignorant wretch at the capital," had instinctively taken its measure.[24] But as Ferguson's attacks continued, University resistance stiffened and the "guts in the institution" soon renewed Bedi's respect. A few months later he was writing that "The faculty looks so brave, loyal, and true. . . . There's many a fine belly in that bunch."[25]

Bedi's perceptive analyses of the situation did little to lift Lomax's spirits. But Lomax was scarcely in a mood for optimism anyway. Despite the regents' vote of confidence, he felt the die had been cast—Ferguson was out to get him, and it was only a matter of time. Years later, he vividly recalled "the old excited feeling of dread" that haunted him, "the instinctive human fear, the protective cowardice of the salaried man."[26] With scathing (and perhaps unconscious) honesty he had phrased what was for him the greatest social and economic horror of all, the plight of the "salaried man." It was a term which reeked of servility, dependence, and gutlessness, describing those hapless souls who were bought and paid for but whose payment—indeed, their very selfhood, in Lomax's view—was always at risk, according to the whim of their employers. The hobgoblin of the "salaried man" haunted him much of his life; he was never quite free of it even when he'd gone off on his own and become independent of bosses and institutional authorities.

That fall, in a spell of gloom, he set about lining up lecture dates. Feeling that his platform talents might soon be his only source of income, he tried to enlist Barrett Wendell's help in being chosen to give the prestigious Lowell Lectures at Harvard but was quietly rebuffed. He then intensified his efforts to fill as many dates as he could during January and February, after his appearance at the MLA meeting at Princeton.

There he would present a new talk on "Poetry of the Cow Camp and Cattle Trail," drawn from material largely culled from printed sources but which he saw as a natural extension—he called it "a by-product"—of *Cowboy Songs.* Enlarged and expanded, it became the basis for his next book, *Songs of the Cattle Trail and Cow Camp,* which Macmillan published in 1919.

New appeals went out to Wendell, Mezes, William Lyon Phelps, and a dozen others in high places, alluding to the Ferguson situation, asking for help to increase his lecture dates, and, incidentally, angling for any job that might be open.[27] Instead, he got fulsome letters of rhetorical support, pointing to his supposed great fame and stature (Phelps: "through your publications you have become something of a national figure"),[28] telling him to laugh off "mere politics" and ignore the whole dirty business. Lomax, much as he loved praise, must have felt the gap between appearance and reality, the irony of a "national figure" about to be kicked out in the cold.

· · · · ·

After so many years, Lomax's annual lecture tours had become like baseball seasons, one fading into another in a blur of dates and places and numbers. Invariably, the trip would begin, in late December, with a few scattered bookings on the way east to wherever the MLA was meeting. After that, there would be a quick visit to Dean Briggs and his family at Halfway Pond and a luncheon with Kittredge at the Parker or Adams House, then Lomax would seem to ride off in all directions at once, scattering over New England like a starburst. The route home stretched through the South, and a weary Lomax usually tottered back into Austin in late January or early February, considerably worse for the wear of what was always announced as his "vacation."[29]

In late 1916 the Ferguson affair hung over the trip like dark cloud. Various elements of the University—regents, alumni, faculty, and even the student body—had called on the legislature to make a full investigation, and Lomax no sooner boarded the train for the East after Christmas than he was worrying about what might happen in his absence. He instructed Bess to see if she could get his December paycheck from the University and told her to remove all his personal correspondence and lecture files from his office in case of an investigation by the legislature, fretting that he should have done all this before he left.[30] He had much on his mind, and the uncertainty of his precarious situation had him thoroughly distracted.

This lecture tour differed from the others in one respect: Lomax was job-hunting. He'd been feeling out Sidney Mezes about the prospects at C.C.N.Y., and Barrett Wendell had arranged for him to meet while in the East with Wendell's son, Barrett Wendell Jr., a Boston banking executive with the firm of Lee, Higginson and Company. Headed toward New York, Lomax was also heartened by the prospect of talking things over with Will Hogg, who would be there on business. Hogg was a man of power and influence, and although his term as a regent was expiring, Lomax looked on his old friend as an ace in the hole, someone he could trust his fate to; at least Hogg would offer wise counsel. From a distance, the situation in Texas seemed less grim; he told Bess optimistically that, having gotten away from the turmoil, he was sure they would be all right even if the worst came, and the worst might even prove to be a blessing.[31]

Bess, as usual, ran the home front with the precision of an adding machine and the energy of a dynamo. "Me and Belgium, we are buffer states," she said, likening her continuing role as John's go-between and factotum to the war situation in Europe. Lomax wrote asking her to find out "how Dr. Vinson seems to view my absence" (he was anxious to stay in Vinson's good graces and wasn't quite sure where he stood with the administration). She dutifully saw Vinson and reassured her husband that the president seemed quite pleasant and agreeable, and told her that "you were to stay your full limit of Feby 4."[32] She also baked, cleaned, milked the cow, gathered and sold eggs, tended to the children, nursed her ailing mother, went to meetings, mailed out copies of *Cowboy Songs,* tended to a dozen of John's routine office affairs—and still found time to plan and execute strategies for increasing the Lomax treasury. She had more business "schemes" for him when he returned and was certain, she told him, that she could devote all her spare time to helping him with the ballad work, which might make them money and "certainly [add] to the glory of the

Lomax name." Her goal was a lofty one; by setting their minds and energies to it, she said, not only would the two of them free themselves from the petty nuisances of people like Ferguson, they would establish John's reputation once and for all as a folksong scholar of Francis James Child's magnitude.[33]

On the road, Lomax urged her to hire help for the house so she would have more time for the ballad work. He also fed their dreams with talk of applying for another Sheldon Fellowship, adding that there was a movement afoot at Harvard "to get me on the Carnegie Foundation for ballad collecting."[34] One plan—quietly put forth by Bess—was for him to take what he termed "a 'loaf' of absence" from the University to do nothing but lecture and collect ballads; that too could lead to a national reputation and perhaps also "some money for our grandchildren." For the time being, however, it was necessary that they keep silent about such schemes; indeed, Lomax was even concerned that word of his current bookings would leak back to Texas, and when he sent Bess money, he cautioned that she should consider it hers so there would be no appearance of his turning a profit on the trip. "We must be wise as serpents, etc.," he said—she should tell everyone at the University that he was merely at Harvard, which is where he would actually be, he said, by the time she got his letter.[35]

Moreover, the thought of lecturing full-time reminded him of how difficult it really was and how much he dreaded failure. If any of his lectures suffered a flop, that might convince her that he lacked the "stomach for such work." Again he cautioned Bess about the need for secrecy—"Anyway, let's not talk it outside ourselves."[36]

His stomach wasn't improved by the fish he had during his lunch with Kittredge at the Adams House, but his lectures went well, and soon he was sending back the usual glowing reports, telling Bess that when he gave his first talk in Cambridge, the hall was jammed and the "universal praise" so profuse that he was downright ashamed. There was more of the same all along the line; on the train between Akron and New York, he wrote, "As for my lectures, Bess, spare me blushes!"[37] He was spared no blushes when he heard from one of his hosts, Professor J. M. Telleen at the Case School of Applied Science in Cleveland, that his lectures were much better attended than those of the eminent Charles Hall Grandgent of Harvard, who'd appeared there recently before a sparse audience. Said Telleen sarcastically, "The tremendous attendance that [Grandgent] drew was undoubtedly due to his subject, 'The Ladies in Dante's Lyrics.' After all, we of the day are more interested in Cow Punchers and Niggahs."[38] On the other hand, Lomax had carelessly made himself "a wretched schedule," with more than the usual number of doglegs and switchbacks. To get certain bookings he'd even agreed to give unpaid talks at points along the way. The long jumps between dates ate up his profits, he complained, and the free lectures "do not swell them."[39]

Bess meanwhile had to contend with various household stresses. Since the death of her father the previous November, her mother had become increasingly difficult to care for, and they had moved her from the small cottage next door into their own home. That left the cottage to be rented, but first it had to have a new stove, which in turn required an extension of the gas line, for which Bess had to petition the city. Alan came down with the measles, she and her mother quarreled, talk of America entering the war was everywhere, prices were going up (perhaps the most severe threat to Bess's equanimity), and if all that weren't enough, one day she reported that she'd even been deprived of her newspaper, when Billy, the dog, ate the *Daily American.*[40] She decided that, regardless of what came of the Ferguson mess, some of the Lomax livestock had to go. Much as she hated to sell them, Daisy, their horse, and her colt, Juno, would bring $125 and "stop the leaks of 8% interest." Bess said she'd get rid of the cow if she had to give her away; the three quarts of milk she gave each day was costing them fifteen dollars a month for feed. The problem, she felt, was one of priorities. She and John were "too good material" to waste as much of their time as they did over such trivial matters as the livestock.[41]

The lecture tour was wearing thin, but in New York Lomax was revived by talks with Mezes, Will Hogg, and Arthur Page of Doubleday, Page and Company, all of whom he saw in one very busy day. Page was receptive to publishing a new volume of cowboy "verses," and they made plans for the volume that would appear as *Songs of the Cattle Trail and Cow Camp* (although Macmillan, not Doubleday, Page would eventually publish it). A day later he discussed job possibilities with Barrett Wendell Jr. and other officials of Lee, Higginson, the venerable Boston financial firm, which had branch offices in New York and Chicago. The talks were inconclusive, but both Wendell and Charles Schweppe, head of the Chicago office, encouraged Lomax to "stay in touch." Mezes had been less optimistic about Lomax's chances at C.C.N.Y. He and Will Hogg both counseled patience and good cheer in dealing with Ferguson, but Lomax's heart was far from light on that score. "My lectures go well," he'd written to Bess as he made plans for the homeward trek. "That ain't what worries me."[42]

Bess did her best to set his mind at ease. Still promoting the idea that they devote full time to his lectures and ballad collecting, she declined to hire a housekeeper, assuring him she enjoyed the work and the money she saved by doing it. Employing a bit of wifely psychology, she referred to the new plan of lecturing and song collecting as "your scheme" (of course it was her idea), and praised it as a singular opportunity to make a reputation for him and produce "a flock of books to stay our old age." Above all they must complete his ballad collection; he owed that to Harvard, if not to himself and posterity.[43]

But later the same day she heard a bit of heartening news from the campus rumor mill. President Vinson supposedly had told Dan Williams, editor of the student newspaper, that Ferguson was willing to give up the fight and had even promised the University a liberal appropriation. That meant the Lomaxes could stay with the University if they wanted, she told her husband happily. Like John, she had Texas deep in her heart; expressing the reservations she'd had all along about his plans to find a job elsewhere, she added that it would give her "a green feeling" to leave Texas for good. New England or New York seemed awfully foreign, and for her part, she thought "we'd best cast our lot with our own sort of folks and country."[44]

· · · · ·

It would be several months before she would learn the terrible irony of those words, for other events conspired to put the Big Bear Fight temporarily on hold. A much bigger fight took its place in April, when Congress declared war on Germany. Martial frenzy swept the country in the early weeks, and Lomax's office was deluged with paperwork. There were wires and letters from hordes of ex-students asking for school records and recommendations that would get them into officer's training camps, along with a constant stream of mail to congressmen and other officials assuring the University's unconditional support of the war (and often containing unsolicited advice, courtesy of Lomax, on how to conduct it). No little of this activity involved scare talk about German spies and saboteurs, relating to Texas's considerable German population, dating back to the days of the republic and concentrated around such places as Fredericksburg and New Braunfels, less than forty miles from Austin.

A minor dustup had begun on campus just prior to the country's entry into the war, when a student editor of the campus magazine wrote an article with decidedly pacifist overtones, arguing that the U.S. ought not to go to war under any circumstances. This did not set well with True Texans, notably one D. A. Frank, a former law student at the University in Lomax's days as registrar, now general counsel for Southwestern Bell Telephone in St. Louis and a staunch member of the Texas Exes. In Frank's view, the writer's name—Bercowich—was decidedly un-Texan, and Frank was especially outraged when he learned that Bercowich was from New York—so far as Texans like Frank were concerned, a foreign and probably hostile country. He wrote the young man a letter that stopped just short of accusing him of being a traitor. Bercowich had asserted that the U.S. should not go to war even if an American ship were sunk by German submarines and American lives lost. "If such a statement as that meets your approval," wrote Frank, with scarcely controlled rage, "then I say that you are not a true American or a representative of the University of Texas, and have not caught the spirit of the history and achievements of Texans in every field of endeavor. Your sentiments seem to be inspired more by contact with certain classes of Europeans than to have anything in common whatever with Americanism, and especially with the ideals of the average Texan."[45] And of course True Texans knew what was meant by "certain classes of Europeans."

Frank sent copies of his Bercowich correspondence to Lomax, calling for the student's dismissal from the magazine and suggesting that Higher Authorities ought to be informed; Bercowich's activities were probably treasonable. Lomax, to his credit, thought Frank had overreacted, but he did send the offending article to both the U.S. Attorney in Dallas and the Attorney General in Washington (perhaps motivated in part by his job-hunting efforts at the time and the hope of some sort of government service).

The U.S. Attorney in Dallas replied, "Thanks for the paper. The articles marked do not constitute treason, but are so near to it that this party will bear watching, and we will have it done." The Attorney General's office took a calmer view, merely thanking Lomax for his "patriotic attitude" and indicating that they would keep him in mind in case anything else turned up "wherein your services can be utilized."[46]

Once war was declared, Bercowich fell in line, literally if not philosophically—Lomax mollified Frank by reporting that the young man had joined the rest of the male student body in marching up and down on the football field to hone their military skills. Harrumphed the disgruntled Frank: "I think about 12 or 18 months of good hard drilling and standing at 'attention' before the flag twice a day at 'retreat' will materially change his viewpoint."[47]

Lomax's friend Roy Bedichek had a more enlightened view (as well as a *mitteleuropäische* last name which placed him in as much jeopardy as Bercowich). Within days of America's entry in the war, the Texas legislature began purging state offices of employees suspected of pro-German sympathies, including a friend of Bedichek's named Muensinger. Attacking what he called "this crazy paroxysm of pseudo-patriotism," Bedi told Lomax that, "To cut off all these poor fellows and starve them and kick them around is perhaps the easiest thing to do, but it is not the wise or humane thing to do. We keep talking about making war only on the Prussian military autocracy, and immediately attack most viciously the only German *people* we can lay hands on. That is rotten."[48]

If Lomax rose to the defense of any victims of patriotic zeal and prejudice, it is not recorded. He was, in fact, caught up in his own plans for making war on the "Prussian military autocracy." The minute America entered the conflict, Teddy Roosevelt, aging but indomitable, with visions of San Juan Hill dancing in his head, had immediately announced his intention to raise and equip as many as two divisions of men privately, in the old, nineteenth-century fashion, assuring President Wilson he would have them trained and in the field—in Europe!—in thirty days. When word of the plan reached Lomax, he wrote Roosevelt, his erstwhile acquaintance and endorsement-writer, to volunteer his services—the services of a man approaching fifty (although still pretending he was five years younger). He had, moreover, a wife and three young children, a house heavily mortgaged (something he complained of every time the Ferguson conflict heated up), a balding dome, several excess pounds around the waist, any number of health problems, and absolutely no military training whatever.

His friends were naturally dismayed. Tom Connally was about to resign from the U.S. House of Representatives to take a commission in the army, but he was ten years younger than Lomax. Connally wisely counseled, "With reference to your own enlistment, beg to say that my advice to you is to remain at home and take care of the babies."[49] From Bedi came more of the same, in his uniquely jocular vein: "In the first place, if you really want to serve your country, you can do so much more effectively with a hoe and Daisy hitched to a garden-plow than you can with a rifle or boosted on a war-charger in Teddy's immortal cavalry. In the second place, it is patriotic to allow those with no dependents to do the actual fighting, as when they are killed we are through with them, whereas a man with a family embarrasses the government by leaving a family to support when it is taxed to the utmost to support an army on the firing line."[50]

Lomax had feared that Roosevelt might not remember him, but the Hero of San Juan replied with a personal and quite flattering letter. "Of course I recall you," he beamed. "Why, I think you have done as good work as any of us have been doing of recent years! It will give me great pleasure to get you in the division."[51] But there was to be no such division. President Wilson firmly rejected the Roosevelt proposal, not only because it was based on hopelessly outdated notions of warfare and military organization but also because Wilson and the Democrats had no intention of sharing the national spotlight with their old Republican-Bullmoose adversary, who they felt had been showboating at their expense for much too long.

In the midst of all this, the war on the home front erupted again, and Lomax was more certain than ever that he would lose his job any day. "It is hard for me to realize that you are really to be fired," Bedichek wrote to him in April, "but I suppose you have the right dope on the situation." Bedi advised him to get a job in the English Department of some small New England college, at whatever small salary the Lomaxes could live on, and devote himself to ballad collecting and lecturing.[52] That suited Lomax fine—but where was such a job? He'd been trying for nearly a year, putting out feelers to every college on his lecture tour list, and all he'd gotten were empty words encouraging him to stand up to Ferguson.

He kept looking to his Friends in High Places for help, and was invariably disappointed. Tired of the mess at the University, C. S. Potts had resigned and gone off to Washington to work for David F. Houston, now Secretary of Agriculture in Wilson's cabinet. Lomax indicated he'd like to do the same, but Potts sent back a discouraging report on their old boss at A&M: "I have had one talk with Mr. Houston—we lunched together at the Cosmos Club one day. He is greatly absorbed in his multifarious duties but is mildly interested in our turmoil. . . . while Houston does smile, he is very reserved and stiff as compared to the Houston of A&M days."[53] When Lomax enlisted the aid of his representative in Congress to pull strings with Houston, the secretary coolly offered his sympathy but little else. "I have known Mr. Lomax for a number of years and have a very high regard for him," Houston told Rep. James Wilson. "I was very sorry to learn that he was one of [Ferguson's] victims. I do not know of any way in which this department could utilize his services."[54] Mezes at C.C.N.Y. offered the odd suggestion that Lomax find "some work of the kind that is being done by the Y.M.C.A. troops," and from Yale "Billy" Phelps insisted one more time that Lomax feel free to call him by his first name.[55]

· · · · ·

Although the Ex-Students Association had earlier asked the state legislature to conduct a full investigation of Ferguson's charges against the University, the lawmakers were reluctant to stir up the governor and offered instead a weak resolution supporting the regents' vote to retain the men he had tried to fire. Ferguson's tactic was to lay low and let everyone think he'd given up the fight. It was largely in this manner that he got the legislature to approve his nominees for new vacancies on the University's board of regents.[56] Confirmations came in May; two members of the newly constituted board were solid Ferguson men, and a third was thought to be. Coupled with his old supporters still on the board, that was likely to give him a majority, but no one yet knew. The new board was expected to hold its first meeting in early June. Several weeks prior, however, Ferguson tried to steal the march by suddenly calling the regents to meet privately in his office on Monday, May 28, intending to coerce any reluctant members into doing what he wanted.

On the Saturday before that, Lomax and his family were at a faculty picnic and had just boarded an excursion steamer for the trip up Lake McDonald when President Vinson appeared on deck, took Lomax aside, and told him of the governor's plan for a secret meeting of the regents. "After next Monday," Vinson said, "I will no longer be president of the University of Texas. Governor Ferguson now has a majority on the Board." Visibly upset, Lomax left his family, hurried down the gangplank as it was being lifted, jumped ashore, and took the trolley into town. He knew that if Vinson went, so would he and the other men on Ferguson's list. But fear for his job ran second to anger; he was infuriated to think that the governor would resort to such an underhanded tactic as calling an irregular, and no doubt illegal, meeting to carry out his vendetta against the University.

Lomax talked things over with Harry Benedict and Judge R. L. Batts, an eminent Austin lawyer, federal judge, and former University law professor. Together the three of them decided, in desperation, that the least they could do was sound the alarm. It was now late Saturday night, but Lomax, wrestling with the quirks of long distance phone lines in those days, finally got through to his contacts at the major metropolitan newspapers around the state. The story of the "Secret Session with the Board of Regents" made front page headlines in Sunday editions.

Lomax also aroused the leadership of the Ex-Students Association, and on campus he put to work the editor of the *Daily Texan,* Dan Williams, who arranged student protest committees and began organizing a giant rally and parade to the capitol. Dozens of banners were painted, reading "DOWN WITH KAISER JIM," "STOP 'PRUSSIANISM' HERE FIRST," and other slogans "most insulting to the Governor," as Ferguson's daughter recorded it.[57] Monday's classes at the University were canceled, and the president of the Student Association, already on army duty at an officer's training camp in nearby Leon Springs, was somehow furloughed and sent back to Austin to lead the protest parade. (Rumor had it that the student's commanding general was a Texas Ex and had ordered out his personal staff car and driver to get the young man to Austin. According to another story, the orders came directly from President Wilson, whose cabinet included three Texans with University ties—Watts Gregory, Albert Burleson, and D. H. Houston.)[58]

The ensuing uproar and public demonstration in front of the capitol on Monday effectively dampened Ferguson's planned gathering of regents—what action they took, if any, was never recorded. Farmer Jim went into a rage, shaking his fist and shouting at the protesters from his office window. Later he denounced the students as a mob of hoodlums and declared that their leaders should be lined up and shot.

The University forces had yet another salvo to fire. On June 1, a lawsuit was filed in the District Court of Travis County (Austin), naming as principals "John Avery Lomax vs. [Regent] G. S. McReynolds et al" and asking for an injunction against the board of regents of the University, restraining them from acting against or removing those at the University whom they opposed. Lomax implied that he had known nothing about the suit, that it had simply been "brought in my name while I was away from Austin," although there is evidence to suggest otherwise.[59] He later boasted, however, that it was the first link "in a long chain of successful happenings" that eventually brought down Ferguson, "a consummate scoundrel."[60]

But now the consummate scoundrel still had plenty of fight in him. Although the Lomax faction was successful in obtaining a temporary restraining order against the board, they got little respite from the heat of battle, and ultimate victory seemed as far away as ever. The governor went back to plotting rump meetings of the board, issuing threats, and generally making life miserable for everyone. And each time Ferguson made a move, the Lomax backers hauled out their lawsuit, brandishing it like a cross before a vampire. All through June alarums and excursions rang out across the state.

Earlier, Ferguson had emphatically rejected the notion that the faculty members had any legal rights in the matter. "They are tenants at will," he ranted at the regents, "just like any man that is working . . . in Major Littlefield's bank. For the good of the bank he can discharge and the discharging is done and does not call for anything further."[61] By this time the roster of accused had changed a bit—Battle had removed himself by resigning to take a prestigious position at the University of Cincinnati, and Potts's name had been taken off the list (some said through the intercession of Major Littlefield) even before he resigned and went off to do war work in the U.S. Department of Agriculture. To the list was now added the name of Dr. George Butte, a professor of law, whose crime against Ferguson was that he reportedly had been seen clapping as the student protesters marched around the capitol on May 28. Ironically, it was Butte who had succeeded Lomax as registrar when he resigned in 1903, and the two had never gotten along. Now they found themselves reluctantly linked as comrades-in-arms.

The state legislature that year had budgeted almost two million dollars for the University. On June 30, the last day for the governor to approve or veto the appropriation, Lomax was suddenly called to President Vinson's office. That was most unusual—it was a Saturday afternoon—but he was scarcely prepared to find there, in addition to Vinson, Regents Littlefield and Allen, both supporters of Ferguson against the University. Present also were D. K. Woodward and John Brady, Austin lawyers described by Lomax as "two stalwart and courageous ex-students." Together Woodward and Brady headed the committee of Texas Exes which had petitioned the legislature for a public investigation of Ferguson's charges. The atmosphere was strained; no one shook hands, and the six men sat down in chilly silence. Then Major Littlefield opened with the blunt statement that he and Allen had just come from the governor, and Ferguson was about to veto the entire University appropriation unless Vinson and Lomax resigned immediately.

Vinson stiffened and said—"dramatically and emphatically," according to Lomax—"I will not resign." Littlefield thundered back that it was the only way to save the University, that Ferguson's veto would close the institution down without a cent. At this, Vinson became even more heated. The charges against him were false, he said, and he would rather work the next two years for nothing than resign. They—he and his faculty—would find some way to run the University, and he would never resign—never, *never.*

At this point John Brady stood and began to deliver an emotionally charged speech ("his eyes filled with tears," Lomax reported). Dearer than life, said Brady, he loved "that old Main Building that crowns University Hill," but he would rather see it pulled down, "ground into powder and scattered to the four winds of Heaven than to have President Vinson do this shameful act [of resigning]." All were moved, but in different directions. Littlefield and Allen rose to go. The meeting was over.

Lomax, who had been totally ignored, now thought to complain of that fact, but the others were leaving. Following after them, he assured Brady that he loved Old Main every bit as much as any man, and by george, he wasn't going to resign, either. It was a grand and typically Lomaxian anticlimax, and all the more grand because Lomax told the story on himself (without seeing, perhaps, the full extent of what it revealed).[62]

The Big Bear Fight rushed to a finish. Within hours Ferguson had vetoed the appropriation bill and declared to Major Littlefield, "If this Board doesn't get rid of those fellows I will have a Board that will."[63] He had maneuvered to appoint Wilbur Allen to the board and have him made chairman; he now had four regents solidly behind him and one (Allen) who could be counted on to abstain in any crucial situation. Less than two weeks after Vinson and Lomax refused to resign, the reconstituted board met in Galveston and, on motions introduced by Littlefield, summarily dispatched the same men who had been retained by the old board the previous October.

There is evidence that Littlefield had no personal animosity toward any of the men and simply felt that he was acting in the best interests of the University, but Lomax never forgave him for leading the charge in this final, decisive battle. Although Littlefield had probably interceded for Lomax's friend Potts, and although Lomax could usually find some reason to think well of legendary Texans like the Major, many years later, when he learned that Vinson had spoken approvingly of Littlefield ("a Prince of Israel," Vinson had said), Lomax wrote a harsh note to the former president, castigating him for having publicly praised a man who had voted to fire without cause six members of the faculty whom Vinson himself had said were blameless. Every informed Texan, Lomax told Vinson, knew that was a terrible injustice, motivated by political and probably even financial expediency. Casting a scornful glance at Littlefield's philanthropy and his Civil War service, he added in closing, "Millions of money and love for the Confederacy will never sweeten that record."[64]

. . . . .

The men who'd been fired were notified immediately and told to clear out. Official word of their dismissal came from the president's office on July 16; Vinson, although still locked in combat with the governor, had no choice but to follow the decision of the regents. "This action," he told Lomax, "was taken by the board notwithstanding that . . . [s]o far as I have been able to see, your services to the University have been eminently satisfactory in every way." Vinson further expressed his regret, "both officially and personally," that the regents had acted as they had in Lomax's case.[65]

That was small consolation. What Lomax had feared for two years had finally come to pass. He was without a job, bereft of a regular income. To a man like him, nothing could be more dreadful. To be gainfully employed was not only the means of paying the bills and getting on but the source of one's identity in the world, the very wellspring of being. To be unemployed was shameful and terrifying. "I owned a home only partly paid for, into which all my savings had gone," he said. "I had a wife and three small children and no experience at hunting for jobs. Moreover, I had absorbed the feeling of financial helplessness that seems to flourish in an academic community."[66] That was all true except for one minor detail: over the past two years he'd acquired a great deal of experience at hunting for jobs, although right now he had little to show for it.

Even before the official firing had come down, Will Hogg—in a move to appease a disturbed minority of alumni—had already asked Lomax to resign as secretary of the Exes. Then there had been some talk among Lomax's friends of hiring him as full-time head of that organization, entirely independent of University politics. Attractive as that notion was, he stiffly put it aside, telling a prominent alumnus that the Exes weren't obligated to him in any way, nor did he think it wise for them to offer him any sort of job. It would be best for him to "clear out of Texas," he said, not to avoid conflict but because his presence would most likely do more harm than good.[67] Weary and dispirited, his ego wounded, he had resolved to let them see—all those factious, wrongheaded folk who didn't appreciate him—just how hard it would be to get along without John Lomax. And indeed they would.

CHAPTER FOURTEEN

• • • • •

Good-bye Old Paint

1917–19

For Lomax, there were two centers of the universe—one in Texas, the other in the East, emanating from Harvard. It was entirely in character that, when Texas failed him in the summer of 1917, his instinctive response was to look eastward. Distraught to the point of panic, he wrote to Dean Briggs the day after he got word of the firing, outlining a bizarre new scheme that was quite contrary to Bess's feeling that "we'd best cast our lot with our own sort of folks and country." After recounting the history of the Big Bear Fight and ensuing turmoil in Texas higher education, he told Briggs that he had decided to return to Harvard for a year of study and bring his family with him. He would work primarily with Kittredge, to whom he had also written, asking to be considered for any available scholarship or appointment and hoping to earn what he could "through my pen and an occasional lecture."[1]

But before this highly improbable plan went any further, rescue—of a sort—came through Barrett Wendell Jr. and Charles Schweppe, in charge of Lee, Higginson's Chicago office.

Lomax's negotiations with Lee, Higginson had begun back in January, when he met with Barrett Wendell Jr. and other officials in the firm's New York offices near Wall Street.[2] A month later he made a clandestine trip to Chicago to meet Schweppe, and they discussed the possibility of Lomax becoming Lee, Higginson's man in Texas, operating out of Austin or Dallas, and acting as agent for bond transactions with major financial institutions around the state. Accordingly, when he got home, Lomax began an extensive survey of business prospects in Texas, writing to dozens of bankers and businessmen to solicit their opinion regarding the demand for high grade bonds in the state. The responses he got were not encouraging, and there the matter rested for several months.

The war, however, produced an immediate manpower shortage on the home front, and draft-exempt men like Lomax were in demand. In June, Schweppe suggested that they talk again about a job: "I think it would pay you to come to Chicago in the near future to see me. . . . We may be able to find an opening for you in our office as we feel a man of your intelligence and ability would probably be useful to us."[3] At that point Lomax was up to his ears in the Big Bear Fight, but once the firings took place, he hastily got in touch with Schweppe and arranged an appointment for August 6 in Chicago, where the deal was concluded. Lomax would be based in Chicago; whatever initial reluctance he had about moving was quickly overcome by the $5,000 salary Schweppe offered him. And there would be an annual bonus, based on sales. From salary alone he would be paid more than the governor of Texas, which of course gave Lomax more than a little satisfaction.[4]

Most of all, in going to Lee, Higginson he was at last connecting himself with a first-rate institution. The firm had national standing, a long history, and an excellent reputation; it backed "some of the biggest financial undertakings on this continent," as Lomax told John Brady, citing the example of the thirty-million bond issue of the Federal Farm Loan Banks. As with all its holdings, he pointed out, Lee, Higginson purchased the issue outright as evidence of their confidence in the securities before attempting to attract other investors.[5] Lomax had hardly stepped off the train back in Austin when he was sending out letters to his banking contacts in Texas, trying to sell them Federal Land Bank bonds. He was now a member of the business world, he told a correspondent, and in a position "to sell you bonds as well as sing you songs."[6]

The farfetched Harvard scheme was immediately given up. To Barrett Wendell, Lomax wrote that "through the good offices of your son," he would now be with Lee, Higginson in Chicago, and he declared he would do all he could to succeed, if only "to prove the wisdom of his judgment."[7]

Lomax himself never stopped exclaiming over the anomaly that he had turned financier. "I knew nothing of high finance; I know even less today," he said, somewhat disingenuously, in his autobiography. "At that time I don't think I could have defined accurately the difference between a stock and a bond."[8] Yet he wasn't totally unprepared for the business world. He'd taught accounting several summers at the University, handled the finances of numerous organizations, and for years had been dabbling in all sorts of small investments. Then, too, he prided himself in being a polymath, or at the very least a fast learner and a living refutation of the saw about old dogs being unable to learn new tricks.

By late August the Lomax entourage was on the Texas Special to Chicago—John, Bess, twelve-year-old Shirley, ten-year-old John Jr., Alan, not yet three, and Bess's mother, Mrs. Brown. Billy the dog was left behind for the time being; all the other animals in the backyard menagerie had been sold. The Lomaxes had tried without success to sell or rent their house, but whatever sadness they felt at leaving it locked and vacant was more than offset by their Lomaxian optimism and spirit of adventure. Shirley and John, excited to be traveling to a big city on a "real train" (they'd ridden only the rickety local to and from Meridian), prowled from car to car, hung out the windows, and stayed awake in their Pullman berth all night, peering through the shade and counting cars on the passing trains.[9] Bess organized the move and saw to everything, with the same enthusiasm as always, regardless of whatever private feelings she may have had.

The Lomaxes quickly absorbed the cultural shocks of the move, which were considerable. Chicago, with a population approaching three million, was almost a hundred times the size of Austin and a truly metropolitan city of great variety and extremes, splendid in many ways, rough and wretched in many others—"queen and guttersnipe of cities."[10] The blustering, specious William Hale "Big Bill" Thompson was then in his first term as mayor, slowly tightening a shifty grip on the city and leading it toward the crime, corruption, and general civic blight for which Chicago would become famous in the twenties. But Lomax had little time for politics and even less interest in local affairs; he was busy settling his family into the large house he had rented in the North Shore suburb of Highland Park, which was, he boasted to Harry Benedict, "much more quiet and rural" than Austin. He was determined to shield them from the worst aspects of big-city life, and even then planning, however vaguely, to get them back to Texas. The children had seen Chicago only in passing through, and he hoped to bring them back to Texas someday "as unsophisticated as ever."[11] Very soon he was reporting that the children were in school and Bess was "busy making the home pleasant for us all."[12]

Lee, Higginson's Chicago offices were in the magnificent Rookery Building—"one of the final monuments of the art of masonry architecture"—on LaSalle Street in the heart of the Loop.[13] Lomax's home in Highland Park was, he said, "twenty-six miles from my desk," and he commuted on the Northwestern Railway, quite a change from the eight blocks he'd walked to work in Austin. He complained of the high cost of living up North and in an effort to hold down expenses initially declined to have a telephone installed, claiming that he hated telephones and could now live without one.[14] But Bess soon convinced him that a phone was vital to their business interests—renting spare rooms, dealing with tradesmen, and operating John Jr.'s magazine business, which was promptly resumed in Highland Park. Bess could take care of many of her errands over the phone, she said, "and still not break my cash and carry home scheme of marketing," but she thriftily opted for a two-party line at $2.00 rather than a private one that would cost $3.00.[15]

They had hardly gotten settled in Illinois when—to the chagrin of everyone, especially Bess—it turned out that they probably could have stayed in Texas after all. Farmer Jim Ferguson's arrogance and high-handed tactics had made too many enemies, and his attack on the University finally convinced the state's power elite that he had to go. Earlier, the legislature had investigated charges of fiscal chicanery, in particular the matter of a 1914 "loan" of $156,000 which had been made to Ferguson by a person or persons unknown and never repaid—all of which suggested that the money constituted illegal campaign funds or, at worst, an outright bribe. Ferguson first refused to divulge the source of the so-called loan, and when it was eventually revealed to be the Texas Brewery Association, he steadfastly continued to claim that it was legal and aboveboard, strictly a business transaction. His fellow politicos, none too pristine themselves, were willing to look the other way—until Ferguson began his vendetta against the University. His indiscriminate attacks angered professional men and women across the state and aroused a sleeping giant that was only beginning to realize it was a giant. The University Ex-Students Association, largely John Lomax's creation, now numbered in the thousands, many in positions of power and influence, and all of them loyal partisans of their alma mater. The first test of their strength as an organization lay in rising to meet the threat posed by Farmer Jim.

Opposition to Ferguson spread through the rank-and-file membership of the association, but it was those alumni in the power structure of the state legislature, inspired by Will Hogg's fiery opposition to the governor, who brought him down. Nor was Ferguson's standing enhanced among his Baptist tenant-farmer supporters when it was revealed that he had accepted a small fortune from the beer interests. Organized prohibitionists, suffragists, and progressives were already calling for his hide.

Impeachment proceedings began in August, less than a month after the University firings, and three weeks later the state senate upheld ten of the twenty-one charges submitted by the house of representatives. Farmer Jim delivered a final rambling and defiant outburst to the assembly before being removed as governor and barred from ever again holding a state office.

On September 18, President Vinson wrote to Lomax: "It gives me great pleasure to inform you that the action taken by the Board of Regents at Galveston on July 12–13 removing you from the faculty of the University of Texas was rescinded by the board on yesterday, and that you and all the others discharged at that meeting have been reinstated."[16]

Lomax responded magnanimously that he would always look back on his years with the University of Texas as the happiest time of his life. Despite the recent upheaval, the University was, he said loyally, "sound to the core," and he predicted great things for it in the future. But of course he couldn't accept the reinstatement, having obligated himself to Lee, Higginson and Company, "who offered me employment in an honorable business" (in pointed contrast, of course, to the shabby transactions of the University's board of regents). It was clear that he was duty-bound to remain in Chicago.[17] High-mindedness aside, it was important to Lomax that everyone know he'd been vindicated, and toward that end he sent copies of Vinson's letter and his reply to the major daily newspapers in Texas.

He'd also taken care to see that his connection with Lee, Higginson was widely publicized throughout the state. Among the many papers which ran the story, the *San Antonio Express* was unusually laudatory, due in part to Roy Bedichek's presence as city editor. Large headlines, accompanied by a photograph of the subject himself, announced that "John A. Lomax Accepts Position With Big Industrial Bankers—His Many Years' Labor for University of Texas Can Never Be Compensated—Has Performed a Lasting Service to All the Great Southwest." The story, reaching back to Lomax's Harvard days, recounted how he had been inspired there to collect and preserve "the rich ballad lore of the Southwest," only to have his work ridiculed by Ferguson. As for his accomplishments as alumni secretary, "His place in the Ex-Students' Association cannot be filled. He perhaps knows more men personally than any other one man in Texas."[18]

To which Potts added his praise, telling Lomax, "[Bedi] might have said that but for your work during the last five or six years the fight that has saved the University might never have been made. You waked the sleeping alumni—and press—and they turned the trick."[19] E. T. Miller, another prominent alumni from Weatherford, sent Lomax his account of "how the 'bear fight' finally turned out." Ferguson—whom he characterized as "the dishonorable one"—"got it put to him good and plenty. His speech in his own defense was full of the typical Ferguson stuff—inordinate conceit, venom, and ungrammatical demagoguery." According to Miller, Ferguson's lawyer had quit, saying he didn't mind defending a thief, but he hated to defend a damn fool.[20] Friends in Texas jokingly told Lomax they'd tried to rent his house to the ex-governor, but "Jim hung up the receiver."[21]

· · · · ·

Part of Lomax's arrangement with Lee, Higginson was the understanding that he'd be traveling to Texas from time to time to call on major banks there. Within only a few days after the move to Chicago, he was back in the Lone Star State, making the rounds of business accounts and tying up personal affairs (including the retrieval of Billy the dog).

Another matter, one which he no longer controlled but continued to follow closely, concerned the Texas Exes Association. At the height of the Big Bear Fight, Will Hogg had persuaded him to step down as secretary, planning, it seems, to have him reinstated when the smoke of battle had cleared. But Lomax's move to Chicago forestalled that plan, and now the alumni organization, despite its moment of glory in the Ferguson affair, had begun to flounder. Fritz Lanham was offered the secretaryship and declined; Roy Bedichek and others were considered but for one reason or another moved out of reach.

Hogg remained the association's strongest and most influential backer, but he was a busy man with important business and civic matters vying for his time. He had also come to realize that the organization was seriously handicapped by its precarious, ill-defined relationship with the University. In the lull following Ferguson's ouster, he began to campaign quietly to get the Exes office moved off campus and set up independently, supported entirely by the membership fees and donations of ex-students, so that "we can freely fight any politician who dares put the putrid paw of politics on the University of Texas."[22] Moving the association out of its University quarters seemed relatively insignificant at the moment, but it would have long-term impact on the organization, as well as on the future of John Lomax.

For a time the Exes moved, as one member said, "from one hole to another like a restless prairie dog." Day-to-day operation had been taken over by a young alumnus named Sam Polk, and Hogg instructed him to look for suitable property nearby which the Exes might purchase—or which he might purchase and make available at a price they could afford.[23] But Polk soon left to join the staff of Sen. Morris Sheppard in Washington. A young woman who worked downtown was paid $5.00 a month to open the association's mail and sweep out. When she left, the job of caretaker fell to the reluctant Roy Bedichek, who drew no salary and whose duties in the Department of Extension required most of his attention. Bedi shortly lost the key to the alumni office, and the Texas Exes Association, for all practical purposes, faded into the ether. News of these events reached Lomax regularly, often from Hogg himself, and he followed the story with dismay. All his efforts to build the organization seemed to have been wasted.

He was back in Texas on business several times that fall. On one occasion, Lee, Higginson loaned him to the Federal Reserve Bank of Dallas to oversee a month-long Liberty Bond drive, touring the backwoods of East Texas and Louisiana by rail. The train carried dramatic exhibits of war and weapons fresh from the battlefronts along with a motley aggregation of personnel that included two drunken French soldiers, a wounded Canadian lieutenant, and Roy Bedichek, on leave from the University, as publicity agent. Coming and going along the way was an oddball assortment of politicians, preachers, and patriots whose job it was to mount the platform at each whistle-stop and hawk war bonds to the wide-eyed country folk who gathered from miles around.[24]

Again Lomax had been picked for his special skills—organizing, promoting, managing, manipulating. He worked out the routing of the tour from day to day, saw to it that the conductor moved the train on time, arranged the speakers' schedules, and wired a daily report to Dallas giving their location and progress. He viewed this work, rightly, as service to his country in wartime. Lee, Higginson had given its approval by placing him on paid leave for the tour and no doubt felt, along with Lomax, that it was good for business, both in terms of goodwill and in the opportunities it gave him to meet future stock-and-bond prospects along the way.

With cotton bringing a record forty cents a pound, even backwoods sharecroppers and laborers were flush. They made easy targets for the tour's pitchmen, who combined razzle-dazzle show biz with emotionally charged appeals to patriotism—and, in cases where they met resistance, some rather dubious sales tactics. One speaker shamed a prominent citizen into buying a $2,500 bond by accusing him in front of his family and friends of being a miserable slacker who did not deserve "to live in a country where the law protects you and your selfish and unpatriotic greed."[25] Lomax took it upon himself to arrange segregated meetings with black audiences and "counsel" them on the finer points of Liberty Bonds, baldly asserting that "President Wilson has sent me from Washington" for that express purpose. Through one maneuver or another, the tour sold more than a million dollars worth of bonds in slightly over a month on the road.

Business also took Lomax to Boston in late November, where he visited Lee, Higginson's home office. With the outbreak of war, the economy had boomed; on Christmas Eve Lomax found on his desk—as he reported in his autobiography—an envelope containing four hundred dollars as his bonus for less than four months on the job. "Such generosity humiliated and shamed me," he said, aware that the company had earned less than half that amount from his sales. He took the money back to Charles Schweppe and told him he couldn't accept it. Said Schweppe (according to Lomax), "Lee, Higginson and Company think they know how to run their business. You take that money and go back to work."[26]

But all was not stocks and bonds. That same month he went up to Madison, Wisconsin, to attend the annual meeting of the Central Division of the Modern Language Association and deliver a paper, entitled "Two Poetic Interpreters of the West."[27] He got invitations from various colleges to lecture on folksongs, and Lee, Higginson generously allowed him to accept many of them. There were no major, concentrated tours, but during his time in Chicago he spoke throughout the Midwest—at Oberlin, Hiram College, Denison University, Indiana University, and others—and on at least one occasion traveled out west to lecture at Stanford and the University of California.

He had other avenues for keeping up what he termed "my interest in folk stuff" while "submerged in the financial vortex of Chicago."[28] Always a clubbable man, he joined the University Club of Chicago and there renewed his friendship with an old Harvard classmate, Tom Peete Cross, now at the University of Chicago. Cross was another native southerner (from Virginia) and a scholar of Irish literature with more than a passing interest in ballads and folk music.

Through Cross, Lomax met two men with similar interests, businessman Alfred MacArthur and Lloyd Lewis, a Chicago newspaperman, later famous as editor of the *Chicago Daily News* and author of several books, including *Myths after Lincoln* and a biography of Sherman. Lewis in turn introduced him to a fellow staffer on the *Daily News,* a tall, rawboned, mop-headed Swede named Carl Sandburg, who'd gained some notoriety from the publication of his *Chicago Poems* a few years earlier. All of them were from farms or small towns, "all getting a little sick of the efficiency, the mechanism, the culture of the big industrial cities of the 1920's," as

Lewis told Lomax later. They had had their fill of "sophisticated programs and artists," he said. "We were ready for realism, for the genuine folk-music, and it seemed important, seemed nostalgic, and natural when you sang it."[29]

The men met in the evening from time to time at Lewis's apartment on Dorchester Avenue to sing and swap stories over a convivial dollop or two of rye. On weekends they traveled to the sand dunes on the Indiana shore. Lomax, with his cowboy songs and animated, dramatic way of singing them, was an instant hit. Lewis told him that "you had what we took to be pitch, you could hit the sharp, often piercingly right note that gave the song character, made it descriptive, made it a picture of somebody, or some mood. We could see the characters who were singing—the buffalo-skinners killing old Crego, the Negro woman when her apron got too high." "The Buffalo Skinners" was one of their favorites; Lewis recalled how during a particularly moving rendition of it one evening, Sandburg had shut his eyes, rocked his head to and fro in time with the music, and made "whistling little 'ohs'" of pleasure. When Lomax finished, he said "That's a novel, a whole novel, a big novel. It's more than a song." Lewis liked "Git Along, Little Dogies," and he remembered a particular time when Lomax

> cut loose with that yodel at the end—the yodel just after the cowboy has assured the little doughies [*sic*] that Wyoming will be their new home. It was one of the damdest pieces of transporting of the imagination I had ever experienced, and I had before that and since seen a lot of actors and heard a lot of singers. It was the same sort of thing Bert Williams and Mary Garden did—the song without singing—the role established without great technical display—the singing voice made a medium and not a goal—the singing voice which isn't mechanically remarkable (possibly not even good) but capable of making the listener get up and go where the singer wants him to go, and feel what the singer feels.[30]

Sandburg, who was already collecting songs for what became *The American Songbag* (1927), said, "That Lomax, ain't he something, when he drives the doughies?"[31] Despite their differing views, especially on politics and race, Sandburg and Lomax became fast friends and kept in touch for many years.

With their interests in the rustic past—sometimes sentimental, sometimes scholarly—Cross, Lewis, MacArthur, and Sandburg had all become occasional collectors of folksongs, and their enthusiasm for such activity renewed Lomax's interests in putting together what he termed "an overflow book" from the material left from *Cowboy Songs,* along with what he'd acquired in a desultory fashion in the meantime. That eventually became *Songs of the Cattle Trail and Cow Camp* (Macmillan, 1919), although, unlike *Cowboy Songs,* it contained no music and consisted mostly of poems which, as John I. White has remarked, "probably had never been sung by cowboys or anyone else."[32]

In the meantime, *Cowboy Songs,* almost nine years after publication, was still selling at a steady if unspectacular pace. For the six-month royalty period ending in April 1919, the publisher paid Lomax $133.91 for almost a thousand copies sold here and abroad. From the volume of individual orders which found their way haphazardly into Lomaxes' files, it may safely be assumed that he himself sold another five hundred copies that year to readers directly through the mail, netting on each copy half of the book's current price. Publishing royalties were augmenting his already respectable salary by at least 10 percent.

While Lomax sang songs with his cronies and traveled for Lee, Higginson, Bess rolled bandages for the Red Cross, found renters for their spare rooms, cleaned house mercilessly, and tended to the accounts with her usual zeal and energy. Her letters to John were peppered with numbers: bank balances, insurance payments, income from renters, questions about checks he might or might not have written. With prices rocketing because of wartime inflation, she prized a bargain more than ever and discovered she could save five cents a dozen on eggs (thirty-three cents versus thirty-eight cents) by going in with her neighbor to buy them by the case—and they were "the loveliest big, fresh eggs" she'd seen since they left Texas, she told John. She tried to heed the government's calls for "meatless Tuesdays" and other household economies proposed by U.S. Food Administrator Herbert Hoover, but they offended her Texan sense of abundance, and three growing, energetic children made it difficult. Shirley, said Bess, ate like a wolf, "and I don't see how I can feed her and Hooverize too." News from the western front was gloomy, and neighborhood rumors said the war would go on for five, maybe even ten years.[33]

John had his own money matters to contend with. The "financial vortex" at Lee, Higginson worked heavily on his feelings of inferiority, and he was plagued with any number of nagging financial concerns. Many were trivial, but they kept him in a constant state of distress over his pocketbook. To his brother-in-law, lawyer Gene Pedigo, who was looking after his affairs in Texas, he complained that rent payments on the Austin house were late, that he couldn't transfer his household insurance to Chicago, that the furniture wasn't worth what it cost him to ship it, and that the woman who had bought his heifer calf in Texas had skipped town and never paid for it. Pedigo offered little comfort from the law: "The idea of a man with sense enough to work for Lee, Higginson & Co. not taking a note and mortgage, or some contract in writing, from a woman obligating her to pay for property in the county where she purchased it!" Pedigo had located the miscreant cow-napper in a town some miles away, but she was "a veritable she-cat" and refused to answer his communications. "You can bring suit against her, of course, and recover the price or get the calf back, if she still owns it, otherwise, not so, but you will have to go to San Bonito to do it and the price won't even pay the R.R. fare one way. . . . Didn't you even take a written memorandum on the deal?" All this occurred about the same time that Lee, Higginson was blithely tendering Lomax a generous bonus for his business acumen.[34]

After six months on the job, Lomax began to hit his stride. Touring Texas again in February, he reported to Bess that in Dallas he'd sold $77,000 worth of bonds in under two hours and some orders had to be canceled because the issue had been oversubscribed. The ensuing paperwork kept him toiling most of the night and gave him a lasting headache. In Houston a few days later, he admitted that, until his success in Dallas, he'd been sick with worry that he wasn't paying his way with Lee, Higginson. Being "non-productive," he said, "has been on my nerves to an extent not known to you." He was feeling much better now that he'd turned a substantial profit for the firm—a profit which amounted to more than his yearly salary at the University.[35] One sign that things were better was his return to the familiar old closing: "Your lover, Tommy."

In his heart of hearts, Lomax longed to be back in Texas permanently. It wore on him that he had been panicked into taking the job with Lee, Higginson. Despite many solemn declarations, then and later, of his sense of obligation to the firm, by the spring of 1918—after scarcely nine months in Chicago—he was sending out feelers to the University and trying get a line on the now-moribund Texas Exes Association. When this appeared to arouse interest among various alumni, who began considering what it might take to get him back, Lomax wrote in May to his old friend Professor Eugene Barker at the University, and offered to pay Barker's expenses if he would go to Dallas and meet with prominent Exes in Lomax's behalf. Ultimately the sticking point was money; Lomax would agree to take a 25 percent cut in his $5,000-a-year salary at Lee, Higginson, but the "interested parties" in Texas "speak of only $3,000."[36]

Much as he wanted to return to Texas, he shrewdly concluded that the Exes would respect him more if they had to pay him a high salary. So he stuck to his guns for another six months, while the alums muttered and dallied and counterproposed and the association continued to slide downhill. Under a succession of caretaker managers, its functions one by one had come to a halt. Even the *Alcalde* had ceased to publish, despite Will Hogg's insistence that "The *Alcalde* must be preserved!" Loyal Roy Bedichek had taken it up and managed to get out two more issues before the money ran out. Said a bemused alum, lapsing into rhyme: "Like the boy that stood on the burning deck / Again the only fellow left was Bedichek."[37] The war, which restricted funds and manpower, had contributed to the collapse, but the real cause was simply that the Exes had been deprived of John Lomax—there was no one left with his talent for management and promotion. Dexter Hamilton, one of the more prominent alumni, began to court Lomax vigorously that summer, assuring him that "you are the only man in a position to understand how to pick up the broken threads and knit the Association compactly together again."[38] But nothing happened.

• • • • •

Despite Lomax's newfound enthusiasm for selling bonds, business tailed off, and by mid-year Lee, Higginson's operations had slowed considerably—Barrett Wendell Jr. complained that they were "limping badly."[39] In early November, with the end of the war in sight, Lomax was on the road again and having little success. From Muskogee, Oklahoma, he wrote Bess that he had been all over town that day, but prospective customers had little else on their minds other than "the great issues at stake across the seas." He couldn't blame them; with matters in such flux, it was a poor time to convince people to make permanent investments. Still, he had schemes of his own, including some "big gamble" (undivulged to anyone but Bess) that sparked a certain optimism.[40]

The pleasant fall weather made him ache all the more, wishing they were back in Austin, with a job that wouldn't keep him on the road so much and away from his family (whose "wholesome home life" was a source of great strength for him). The extent of his desperation finally surfaced; he confessed that he was traveling not merely on Lee, Higginson business but in the hope of finding something in Texas "that will call us all back." If that didn't happen, he was ready to return anyway, confident that he could find a job of some sort.[41]

Such drastic action proved unnecessary. Two days after he wrote those words, the war ended. Hamilton and Hogg counseled a little more patience, until the country settled down and normal conditions were restored. In January, Hamilton convened what he called a "Revival Meeting" of some sixty Exes in Dallas, where plans were laid for a new Texas Exes Association, to be financed by subscriptions from the membership. Their goal was to raise $25,000 a year through five hundred pledges of $50, and each subscriber was committed to pay that amount annually for ten years, to insure the stability of the organization. Reaffirming their independence, the Exes declined a University offer of facilities on campus, and rent-free office space was located in the YMCA Building at 2200 Guadalupe Street, facing the southwest edge of the campus. After they had "resoluted and resolved and whereased" at great length (as one of them put it), Hamilton wired Lomax offering him the job of running the operation at a salary of $4,000, starting in March. It was roughly the equivalent of what a full professor at the University earned. But Lomax had raised the ante and now held out for $5,000 *and* his moving expenses. Nine of his friends—including Roy Bedichek, Harry Benedict, E. C. Barker, and C. S. Potts—signed a letter imploring him to take the job, even suggesting that they might try to make up the difference in salary themselves.[42] Still, Lomax refused to commit himself.

In February, Will Hogg brought him to Houston for more arm-twisting, but he continued to hedge. He wrote Bess that the Exes were trying hard to raise the $5000 salary he wanted, adding wistfully that he would never be satisfied anywhere away from Austin. Finally, after a four-hour session with Hogg and a "ripping headache," he agreed to take the job, with the understanding that he would be paid the additional $1,000 if and when it was raised. The association would pay his moving expenses and dispose of the lease on their house in Illinois. "I have cut the bridges and we are off on another voyage," he told Bess.[43]

There were certain formalities to be observed. Mindful of his obligation to Lee, Higginson, he wired Barrett Wendell Jr. with details of the offer (but cited an inflated salary figure clearly contradicted by his correspondence with Bess). Not to be overlooked among his motives for wanting to return to Texas was a matter that had irked him since his firing by Ferguson: "Return measurably vindicates my former course," he told Wendell. But Wendell was away on business and the message was delayed. Eventually he replied that Lomax was perfectly free to take the offer with the firm's blessings, but in the meantime Lomax had already wired Dexter Hamilton: "Accept secretaryship gladly. And now your real troubles begin."[44] Lomax, perhaps to justify himself vis-à-vis Lee, Higginson, always spoke conveniently of his time in Chicago as a period of "nearly three years,"[45] but in fact scarcely eighteen months had elapsed since the Lomaxes left Texas.

In his autobiography, Lomax has the family merrily singing "The Eyes of Texas" as they cross the Red River heading for home. They may have, but the return trip to Texas, undertaken in haste and confusion, was a haze of discomfort; in addition to everything else, four-year-old Alan was suffering from tonsillitis and had a raging fever. Lomax was so distressed over the boy's condition that he forgot to file his income tax that year and later had to go hat in hand to the Internal Revenue to avoid a stiff fine.[46] But by March the family was happily settled back in Austin at 910 West 26th Street, and Lomax had set about rebuilding his "farm in miniature." He sent word to an old crony that he was in the market for live turkeys, pecans, and good old country sausage, adding, with his usual financial shrewdness, that he was interested in these items only if the friend would exercise his renowned "canny judgment," thereby "getting a little the best of the other fellow in prices."[47] It was good to be home again.

CHAPTER FIFTEEN

• • • • •

More Hell in Texas

1919–25

In the wake of the war that had saved democracy and ended war forever, a spirit of optimism launched America into the Harding "normalcy" of the 1920s. The country was victorious and thriving, maybe even a bit smug. It was very much in this same spirit that John Lomax returned to Texas—in triumph, he felt, having at last achieved the place of prestige he had spent his life preparing for. His exile in Chicago had been not unlike that at A&M, if mercifully briefer: "All along I seemed happier than I really was in the bond game," he had told Bess.[1] Now he was restored to the best of the several positions he'd been fired from at the University, that of heading the newly independent Texas Exes' Association[2]—no despotic governors to fear, no imperial college presidents to run errands for, no capricious faculty to cater to, no dull paperwork to shuffle. He answered only to the association's directors, and they were all friends and former classmates, sympathetic to his ideas and his way of doing things—or so it seemed at the time. In place of the cluttered, dingy quarters he'd occupied on campus, there was a modern, roomy office in the YMCA building just across the street, for him and a secretary who would handle the trivia and detail he'd been saddled with before. Of course there was plenty of work—raising the association from the dead would not be easy—but his efforts were to be concentrated on the Big Picture, as Dexter Hamilton had outlined his duties at the time he was hired: "Re-organizing the association on a solid basis; directing the publication of the Alcalde; directing the raising of the memorial fund [for veterans and needy students], and co-operating and handling it after it is raised." Fifteen thousand dollars was at hand for the first year's budget, and, said Hamilton, "we expect you to use it all."[3]

As usual, Lomax had his finger in more than one pie. His deal for returning to Austin had been sweetened by Lee, Higginson's willingness to have him continue to represent them "on the side" in Texas, operating a Mom and Pop bond business out of his home, for which he was paid the nominal sum of $150 a month, to be deducted from whatever commissions he earned. In the event, it was Bess who did most of the real work, answering the phone, handling correspondence, keeping the books, and before long making most of the sales herself, by telephone or mail solicitation from prospect lists that Lomax compiled while traveling on alumni business.

Within weeks he had breathed life into the dying alumni association. The *Alcalde* resumed full-scale publication,[4] a vigorous membership drive was begun, and by summer Lomax was juggling the usual dozen or more balls in the air at once. Early on, he tried to revive sentiment for the A&M consolidation movement, but the time for that had passed, and he went on to more tangible matters. When Will Hogg succeeded Dexter Hamilton as president of the association in late 1919, he told Lomax to run ads in every Texas newspaper stating that the Texas Exes would supply money to any returning veteran who wanted to attend the University. Applications flooded in, and Lomax in a panic asked Hogg where the money was coming from. "That's my problem," Hogg boomed. "You get the soldier students; I'll get the money." Lomax learned later that much of it came from Hogg's own pocket, anonymously.[5] This was entirely separate from the Exes' "Million Dollar Student Loan Fund" which Lomax had been given the responsibility for raising and administering. At the same time Lomax was also trying to keep his stock going in the East by serving as point man at the University for the Harvard Endowment, soliciting contributions from the twenty or so Harvard men on the U.T. faculty (most of them turned him down, citing the meager salaries paid them by the State of Texas). He was more successful in raising a modest sum for a personal cause—the welfare of his old teacher at Weatherford, D. A. Switzer, who was in ill health and dependent upon what his wife and daughters could earn giving piano lessons. Lomax started a relief fund for Switzer with $50 of his own money and took time from his busy schedule to track down former students of Weatherford College for donations. More than $1,000 was shortly raised and presented to Switzer as a "Christian gift."[6]

Lomax also fell back into his old habit of looking after struggling students—loaning them money, finding them jobs, helping them cope with homesickness and poor grades. These days the objects of his attention were often problem offspring of the affluent, or from some branch of the multitudinous Lomax family tree. Somehow he found time to counsel and comfort, investigate difficult cases, and reassure anxious parents. This often required considerable tact, as Lomax sought to provide, for those who were paying the bills, an accurate account of what their lackadaisical sons and daughters were doing, yet at the same time found himself temperamentally inclined to side with the students and excuse their wayward habits.[7] He would never be quite so indulgent with his own children, whom he was constantly lecturing about grades and self-discipline.

Lomax urged concerned parents to send their troubled or troublesome youngsters to him any time for a "chat," and—reminiscent of those days when he and Bess had served in loco parentis to the cadets at A&M—frequently issued folksy invitations. He told one anxious father to encourage his wayward son to drop into Lomax's office anytime he needed to talk, and added that Bess would be happy to have the boy come to their home whenever "he wishes to eat some home-grown chicken and blackeyed peas."[8]

• • • • •

Before leaving Chicago, Lomax asked William Lyon Phelps at Yale to write the foreword for his book-in-progress, *Songs of the Cattle Trail and Cow Camp.* Phelps obligingly cranked out three paragraphs in praise of Lomax, cowboys, and even Harvard. It was something Phelps could have done blindfolded, and may have; his huffing and puffing about these verses being "closer to the soil" than any others and sketching campfire visions of "the men who first sang them"—cowboy *volk,* of course—showed that he shared Lomax's romantic notions of the range and knew even less about the material in the book, which, as noted earlier, had probably never been sung by cowboys or anyone else. Lomax had at least shown some awareness of this fact by first calling the book *Poetry of the Cattle Trail and Cow Camp.* In July, perhaps to link it with *Cowboy Songs,* or even deliberately to have the two books confused by the public, he suddenly asked Macmillan to substitute "Songs" for "Poetry" in the title. In his own introduction he said nothing about folksongs; although he would have the reader believe that most of the material had been passed on to him directly by some honest-to-gosh cowpoke out on the range, he admitted that his sources were not oral but printed—scrapbooks, newspapers, and "lifted from the collections of Western verse" written by such men as Charles Badger Clark and Herbert H. Knibbs. Ultimately, the best he could do for the material as "songs" was to suggest that some of it had been set to music by cowboys.[9]

Later, Lomax would have to contend with critics who seriously questioned the origins of the material in his cowboy books. Writing in the *Saturday Evening Post,* Will C. Barnes said, "Prof. John Lomax of the University of Texas, who has delved into the history of cowboy songs and done much to preserve them, is sure he can detect in them a genuine cowboy music," but Barnes's considerable musical education and forty-five years on the cattle ranges of the Southwest led him to different conclusions. In his opinion, such songs were "not distinctive or particularly original in any way," and the best-known of them had been imported to the West from distant places and were "written by college men who knew little or nothing of the real life and work of the ranges."[10] Still others, who shared Lomax's vision of the Old West, defended him. These tended to be academics or journalists somewhat remote from the life of the frontier, writing for a more polite or domesticated audience. *Better Homes and Gardens* ran an article, reprinted in the *Reader's Digest,* which asserted, "People who still have the storybook picture of range life ought to read the songs the cowboys made and sang. From [the collections of] Professor John A. Lomax, of Texas University [*sic*], one gets a more complete record of the life than a hundred conventional 'Westerns' could give."[11] Clearly, popular notions of just what constituted an accurate picture of cowboys covered a wide spectrum.

Published in November 1919, *Songs of the Cattle Trail and Cow Camp* was favorably, if obscurely, reviewed in publications ranging from *Booklist* to the *Times of London.* Typical was the *New York Times Book Review,* which praised the collection for being unpretentious, robust, and natural, in an omnibus review of poetry anthologies headed "Poetry of Last Year and Today."[12] No one seemed to fret much over a distinction between "songs" and "poetry."

· · · · ·

In February 1920, Lomax declared suddenly to Will Hogg that he had been on the job for a year with only two weeks off and was "tired to the bone, irritable, and unfit for human intercourse." Thus, he was leaving March 2 for a month's rest.[13] His idea of resting was to embark immediately for New York by way of Chicago, lecturing at some half a dozen colleges and universities along the way and spending a busy week in Manhattan. He met with book publishers, looked up old friends and Texas alumni, and spoke at several public schools. One day in New York he "knocked about town" with his old friend John Lang Sinclair, now publishing tax manuals in Manhattan. With J. Keith Torbert, a Texas Ex who was an editor at E. P. Dutton, Lomax talked over a book idea that had been resurfacing through the years, one that he and Torbert had discussed by mail earlier. He was, he told Torbert, especially interested in "the songs of the world [*sic*] Negro," which were "vital expressions of the negro's mind and soul" but had been largely neglected by scholars. If he could accomplish what he had in mind—an anthology of black secular music—he was sure it would be a best-seller.[14] But the plan was too vague, and Lomax admitted that he did not yet have enough good songs to make such a book. After traveling upstate to Hamilton College and Syracuse to lecture, he headed toward Texas by way of Columbus, Ohio, to attend the MLA's annual convention.[15]

During his absence, he'd assured Hogg, the office affairs of the Exes would be in the capable hands of Bess, Mrs. Harry Benedict, and Lomax's secretary, with the faithful Roy Bedichek coming in to put out the next issue of *Alcalde.* As usual, the bulk of the work fell to Bess—perhaps because she wanted it that way. She reported to John that she had read most of the proof for the next issue of the magazine and spent several hours at the printers' making up pages. She attended to their personal financial business, called on prospective bond customers, and concocted a shrewd deal for selling their house and lots—she was opposed to the idea, but John wanted to test the market, so she went at it full tilt, cannily telling a prospect she guessed they could be tempted to sell but certainly weren't in the mood to give the property away. The price she fixed would have returned them a profit in excess of 30 percent, but even at that her heart wasn't in it, and the thought of giving up her dream home made her increasingly apprehensive. She had planned the house with the idea of living in it the rest of her life, she said, just as she had married John Lomax for good, with no thought of changing her mind if she saw a better course down the line. He shouldn't have chosen "a girl with such tenacious affects," she told him, if he wasn't willing to have them attached to a home as well as to him.[16] It was a pretty convincing argument, and after John returned from his trip there was no more talk of selling the house.

They would need all the space and comfort of the old place, anyway, for it was soon evident that there was to be another addition to the family. Lomax had arranged to tour and lecture again that summer, this time to the West Coast, and Bess had planned to accompany him, but her pregnancy (added to the multifarious affairs she normally looked after) kept her at home. Instead, he took along young John Jr., now thirteen, following a crowded itinerary that carried them to campuses and lecture halls in Idaho, Oregon, Washington, California, and Arizona.

He gave more lectures after returning to Texas, often accompanied by six-year-old Alan. In August they went up to Commerce for an appearance at East Texas Normal School, where their hosts included the young dean of women, Miss Ruby Terrill. Alan, lively and precocious, was popular wherever they went; he made a special friend of Miss Terrill, who was a fan of *Cowboy Songs* and a loyal Texas Ex. She took father and son on a drive around the town and was more than a little surprised when Lomax deposited Alan with her and went off, as she said, "to hobnob with the faculty."[17] She did her best to entertain the small boy but felt he did most of the entertaining. Fourteen years later, Ruby Terrill would become the second Mrs. John A. Lomax.

The following January Lomax went east again and risked missing the birth of his fourth child but returned a few days ahead of the baby's arrival on the twenty-first. Lomax insisted that she be named after her mother, and she was "Bess Brown Jr." to the family long after she was grown.

· · · · ·

The nation's economy inched into a postwar depression in 1921, and the University's appropriations suffered at the hands of a cautious legislature. But the Texas Exes who'd pledged continuing support to the association were loyal to their commitments, and Lomax went on building and promoting and traveling far and wide. In April he was off to Cornell for the annual convention of college alumni secretaries, visiting prominent Exes and lecturing, from Oklahoma City to Chicago to Cleveland to Baltimore. In Washington he was wined and dined by congressmen Tom Connally, Fritz Lanham, and Sam Rayburn and a swarm of other Texas politicians whom he publicized at length in a later issue of the *Alcalde.* It was much the same in New York, where it seemed that every office he entered contained an old Texas friend or two, and every other person he met on the street turned out to be an ex-student of the University, now raised to eminence in the big city. His long account of the trip for the *Alcalde*—"The Editor Takes a Holiday"—contains not a single mention of what went on at the convention in Ithaca, but the names of the lofty and distinguished Texas alums en route, the dates their of graduating classes, their positions of esteem and vast accomplishments, all went into the *Alcalde* for everyone, including themselves, to see and admire.[18] It was Lomax at his most Lomaxian.

Throughout the early 1920s he kept up a regular correspondence with Carl Sandburg, whom he genuinely admired despite their widely differing social and political views. Once, when Sandburg referred to himself in a letter as a "Red" and spoke vaguely of the need for a revolution in this country, Lomax took vigorous exception, saying that he didn't like Sandburg calling himself a Red even as a joke, nor did he want the word "revolution" applied to America; for him it was a terrible word associated with bloodshed and misery. Sandburg's reply is not known, but it was apparently rather glum, for Lomax told him he hoped the exchange of views hadn't affected their friendship. It was merely, he said, that when he looked at his children and thought about Russia and revolution, his heart sank. He didn't know how serious Sandburg was about Soviet communism, but he'd always liked him without knowing or caring, he said (adding that another reason he liked Sandburg was that he didn't talk about his poetry all the time, as most poets did). Part of their differences, Lomax felt, grew from the circumstance that Sandburg lived in a big city and took its problems too seriously; remember, he said, that "the greater majority of the American nation" were untouched by such problems. Meanwhile, he suggested that they drop the subject until they could get together and "talk it through" in person.[19]

Some time would pass before that opportunity came, but in the meanwhile Sandburg kept up his end of the correspondence, sending Lomax news of his lecture tours and sharing songs he collected along the way.[20] The public's interest in folk music was being stimulated by his activities and those of other literary figures in the twenties, and Sandburg encouraged Lomax's plans—vague at this stage—for a comprehensive work on native folksong, as well as a revival of *Cowboy Songs*.[21]

Some of Lomax's closest relationships were those he maintained through correspondence with people like Sandburg and others who shared similar interests. After the financial debacle with his brother Richard twenty years earlier, he had steadily distanced himself from his siblings, and long periods went by when he rarely saw or communicated with other members of the family, except for his aging mother in Meridian, to whom he remained a dutiful son. In the early twenties, however, his brother Rob (now "R. P. Lomax") resurfaced, this time as "President and Manager" of an enterprise known as the Citizen's Loan and Investment Company of Denton. In a manner uniquely his and Richard's, he managed to prevail on John for a loan of four hundred dollars, by simultaneously conveying the dichotomous news that (a) his business was prospering and (b) he was in sore need of cash. To make the loan, John had to borrow the money himself and would be in dire straits if Rob didn't repay it. (He pointed out to his brother that he was the sole support of a wife and four children—"one of them a babe in arms"—as well as his mother-in-law.) Rob made payments for a time, but inevitably the Citizen's Loan and Investment Company began to sink. Yet Rob was unshakable. His recourse, as matters grew more and more grim, was simply to intensify his optimistic predictions and continue his appeals to John for loans.

Lomax, finally tired of carrying unpaid notes and fending off Rob's other creditors, advised his younger brother to take bankruptcy. That of course was advice he himself had declined in the earlier affair with Richard, but he was older and wiser now. Still Rob persevered. Even before the national economy self-destructed in October 1929, Lomax was telling his brother-in-law, Gene Pedigo, that in his judgment Rob was broke and had done nothing for years but run around borrowing and reborrowing to pay the interest on his loans.[22] Rob died a few years after the Crash, leaving an impoverished widow and children and a mountain of unpaid notes, many held by his brother John.

Other Lomax enterprises thrived. Through Orville Bullington, his lawyer friend in Wichita Falls (and another Texas Ex, law class of '05), he made investments in oil leases, mechanics liens, and related businesses.[23] In the early twenties, income from rental property, interest payments, and real estate profits alone was bringing Lomax around $2,000 annually. By 1924, his salary from the Texas Exes had risen to almost $6,000; that year, with Bess's commissions of $420 from Lee, Higginson, they earned a total of $8,193.30, including $550 from lectures and book royalties. (Per capita income in the U.S. in 1924 was about $500.) But thanks to Rob and other defaulters, Lomax also wrote off bad debts of $2,600 that year, although he later sued one of the dead beats and won a judgment for $3,374.51.[24] Macmillan, which had issued a cheap edition of *Cowboy Songs* in 1922, reported that both it and *Songs of the Cattle Trail and Cow Camp* were selling steadily, and Lomax made a deal with the director of the University Glee Club, Oscar J. Fox, which allowed Fox to use any text in *Cowboy Songs,* set it to music, and publish the results.[25] Lomax asked for and got 40 percent of the royalties, including those from records and films, as well as "proper credit."

The "farm in miniature" no longer had much impact on the Lomaxes' gross income, but their garden and other cottage industries contributed to the larder and provided Bess and the children with spending money. In the summer of 1921, Lomax wrote to Dean Briggs that Bess was busy canning peaches and plums from their garden, "while Allen [*sic*] and John are marketing our surplus vegetables."[26] Alan took over magazine sales and John Jr. devoted himself to their latest enterprise: selling Texas papershell pecans through the mail. This set off another blitz of sales letters, brochures, and strategically placed advertisements, reminiscent of the Great Magazine Contest. Texas papershells were poetically but not unreasonably hailed as "Condensed Sunshine," and one flyer asked dramatically, "Did you know that a pound of pecans did you about as much good as ten pints of milk or forty-five eggs?" John Jr.'s name was affixed, but the "angle" was clearly Bess's. Orders poured in from the Harvard Club in New York, from Barrett Wendell Jr. and other officers of Lee, Higginson, from the Naval Academy, and from Texas Exes all over the country. Whenever Lomax wanted to stroke the high and mighty and invoke a bit of Texas color, he sent them a modest parcel of papershells. Nearing Christmas one year, Lomax wrote to Lee, Higginson to ask for a list of the firm's current officers; the staffer who responded remarked, "Sounds like pecan time in Texas."[27]

• • • • •

In late 1921, as he'd done regularly throughout the prewar years, Lomax began planning a trip to the MLA meeting in December (the site was Baltimore that year) and set about lining up a lecture tour in the East for the following month. Accordingly, he sent out appeals to anyone of prominence whom he felt might be in a position to secure bookings for him. Previously he'd declined to help schedule a Texas tour for Carl Sandburg, telling Sandburg's agent that he felt he should "stay out of the date making for Mr. Sandburg in Texas."[28] He gave no reason, but it was clearly protectionism—Sandburg was about to invade his territory—as well as professional jealousy over the fact that Sandburg got $200 per lecture, while Lomax's fees were generally $50 to $100. Sandburg came to Texas anyway, and they had a grand time together.

In any event, Lomax never hesitated to enlist the aid of anyone who might help *him.* One of his more seemingly improbable appeals, in light of his uneasiness with grandes dames, was to the formidable Amy Lowell, doyenne of Boston literary ladies, she of ample girth and Cuban cigars. They had met once in Waco when Baylor University gave Miss Lowell an honorary degree, and now he wrote in the hope that she had not forgotten "the Texas Cowboy" or her invitation for him to call when he was in New

England. If she knew of any group that might like to hear him talk on cowboy songs or Negro spirituals, he told her, "I am in the market for a reasonable honorarium." Miss Lowell replied warmly, but cautioned that "Boston is not a happy field for lecturing." The Lowell Institute, for which he had been angling, was out of the question, and other groups she knew of did not pay.[29] She promised she would do what she could for him, but there is no evidence that she succeeded. On his own he obtained a date with the Boston City Club and secured another at Harvard, as usual, through Kittredge and Briggs (Barrett Wendell had died the previous February). He arranged to call on Miss Lowell when he reached Boston, but there is, unhappily, no record of what must have been a lively and numinous meeting of East and West.

Other friends in high places were of little help—Sidney Mezes at C.C.N.Y. told him that his trip would coincide with exams there and "the students . . . would not be in a mood even for anything so good as cowboy and nigger songs"[30]—but eventually he was able to put together an itinerary of some eight or nine schools, including such prestigious ones as Cornell, Yale, Harvard, Haverford, and Smith.

His efforts to mount another campaign on the lecture circuit that summer were less successful, and he finally settled for two appearances at UCLA, only because he was determined to go to California and could get part of his expenses paid. By this time his fee was $100, and he was still announcing it with the same old mixture of arrogance and humility. To a Fort Worth matron who inquired about his appearing before her club, he said that he had recently lectured at Southern Methodist and they were generous enough to give him a hundred dollars, even though "my talk was not worth fifteen cents." But there was a bit of puckish humor in his remark that he would rather lead a charge against a German machine gun nest than face the Women's Wednesday Club of Fort Worth. The only thing that could compel him to do that, he said, was the money it took "to keep my large and growing family from starvation."[31] That was only half a jest; he was forever haunted by the fear of another reversal of fortune that would spin them into destitution. Just such a possibility arose—at least in his darkest imaginings—when discord again broke out on the University of Texas campus.

• • • • •

Lomax was never far from trouble. The controversy which erupted around him in the spring of 1923 had been building almost from the time he returned from Chicago. He was an instinctively political animal, if sometimes inept, and he'd no sooner taken over as secretary of the Exes when he was dabbling in political matters, more or less behind the scenes. As he saw things, it was part of his job to act as a shadow lobbyist for the University, and he relished the notion that he was in a position to cultivate higher powers and help secure jobs and other favors. During the Harding and Coolidge years, he was sometimes obliged to deal with local Republicans (what few there were), although consorting with any "black-leg Republican" would have been anathema to most unregenerate southerners of his kind. Lomax seemed not to mind. He disavowed having ever been a Republican, but told a correspondent that from time to time there were matters within a Republican administration "in which I have the interest of any good citizen."[32] There is, however, evidence that he voted for Harding and Coolidge in the election of 1920,[33] and he appealed through Republican channels in quest of a postmastership for one of his cowboy song sources, J. E. McCauley, whom he jokingly promoted as "my greedy Republican friend."[34] But he worked the Democrat side as well. Since going broke twenty years earlier, his brother Richard had had a sinecure in the state comptroller's office; when it looked as though he might lose it if the incumbent comptroller stayed in office, Richard campaigned for the challenger and enlisted John's help to line up influential Exes. The challenger won, and Richard got a promotion.[35]

Lee, Higginson was not above calling on Lomax's political resources, even after he'd left Chicago. Barrett Wendell Jr. asked him to use his influence with Texas officials in Washington, notably old friend Congressman Tom Connally, to prevent Henry Ford from obtaining control of the power development project at Muscle Shoals, Alabama. Lomax wrote to Connally and "about a dozen good friends" in the Senate and House of Representatives, including Morris Sheppard, Fritz Lanham, and Sam Rayburn.[36] What effect this had is unknown, but in due course the government rejected Ford's proposal.

As political wheeling and dealing went, this was all rather low level; it generally made friends for Lomax among those he could accommodate and only rarely involved him in open controversy. But working back and forth among so many factions made him both visible and vulnerable when the issues were closer to home and involved "politic" in the sense of being "carefully tactful."

One of his first acts on returning to Texas from Chicago had been a short-lived attempt to revive the A&M-University of Texas unification issue. Soon afterward, when the regents proposed to move the main campus of the University some miles away to a 440-acre site on the banks of the Colorado river, he found himself in the midst of a fierce squabble that extended all the way to the legislature. Factions were realigned, old friends divided into opposing camps, and the Exes split between those who were for "progress" (moving the campus) and those who looked upon old Forty Acres as hallowed ground, to be kept intact and inviolable forever. Lomax as secretary assumed a public stance of neutrality, but he was clearly one of the Hallowed Grounders. They eventually raised such a ruckus that the regents were forced to reverse themselves and leave the University of Texas undisturbed on its original perch behind the state capitol. On the losing side were several stalwart Exes, among them Lomax's old lawyer friend, D. A. Frank, and a lumber magnate with the ominous name of H. J. Lutcher Stark, both of whom had been among the Exes who met in Dallas in 1919 to select Lomax as their secretary. Stark, especially, was beginning to have second thoughts.

Lomax did nothing to mollify Stark and other ruffled alumni when he appeared at their annual March meeting (on Texas Independence Day) and chided them for not appreciating what the legislature was doing for the University.[37] Soon after that, he became embroiled in a statewide dust-up when a national publication, the *Outlook*, wired and asked him for a short piece on the current U.S. senatorial race in Texas. Six men had entered the first Democratic primary, but none won a clear majority. The runoff pitted Earl Mayfield, backed by the Klan, and the relentless Jim Ferguson, making the first of several attempts at a comeback. Mayfield won the runoff by a substantial majority, whereupon—in one of those bizarre twists that only Texans can make sense of—the liberal Democrats of Texas deserted the ticket and nominated a candidate who was promptly endorsed also by state Republicans.

In his dispatch to the *Outlook*, Lomax pointed out that 100,000 fewer voters had turned out for the runoff than had cast ballots in the first primary, the obvious conclusion being that "the two least desirable men had been chosen." Writing in haste and assuming that the magazine's editors would polish his copy, he implied, not incorrectly, that both Mayfield and Ferguson were scurrilous frauds, neither of whom deserved to win. But the editors printed his remarks verbatim, headed the piece "MERELY A CHOICE OF EVILS," and concluded on their own that "There does not seem to be even one lone star of any magnitude among the candidates." That caused tremors back home among the high and mighty, who were sensitive to any criticism of Texas, and Lomax was at the epicenter. To no avail, he fired off a letter of protest to the magazine, complaining that they had added erroneous details and offended "some in Texas who may try to use this to discredit me."[38] Calm eventually descended, but his reputation for public relations had suffered damage.

He had also managed to alienate two powerful factions within the student body—fraternities and athletes—whose ranks, once graduated, tended to supply the most active and influential Exes. Given his elitist tendencies, his change in attitude toward fraternities was curious, having swung a hundred and eighty degrees since his undergraduate days as a dutiful, ambitious Phi Delt. Writing to his friend Norman Crozier about John Jr., he said he hoped his son would become "a leading barbarian" and not join any fraternity, not even his father's. In addition to being a waste of money, said Lomax, fraternities interfered with study, created class feeling, and "do little, if any good."[39] That view can only be explained as a symptom of his latent populism, which was inclined to surface in unexpected places. His dislike for fraternal organizations grew through the years until, in old age, he angrily and bitterly rescinded his membership in Phi Delta Theta.

• • • • •

The quarrel between Lomax and the campus athletes was even more complex. An avid sports fan, he took his family to almost every track and field event at the University, and rooted lustily from the stands—"took on like a Comanche," in the words of his daughter Shirley.[40] He was something of a sportsman himself; in his younger years he played a fair game of tennis, later took up golf, and enjoyed hunting when he had time. As secretary of the Exes he spent considerable effort planning their social activities around sports events, and among the alumni he was the man to see for tickets and special accommodations.

But as college athletic programs expanded in the 1920s, drawing dollars and attention away from the classroom, Lomax grew disturbed by what he considered an excessive emphasis on sports. He also had to contend with campus politics and personalities while the athletic department went about building its empire. He said very little about this openly, but letters and articles by alumni began to appear in the *Alcalde* which were critical of U.T.'s sports program. More often than not the complaint was simply that the Longhorn football team wasn't winning enough games, which was certainly accurate in the early twenties. But no one was supposed to criticize the brave sons of the gridiron, and whenever the *Alcalde* did, Lomax got the blame—if he hadn't written the piece himself (and many readers attributed unsigned articles to him), as editor he'd allowed the offensive item to be printed. The athletic director, L. Theo Bellmont, grumbled that the alumni ought to replace Lomax on the grounds that he was disloyally opposed to athletics at the University. There was brief consolation for U.T. sports fans when the Longhorn eleven finally whipped their archenemy, the hated Aggies, in the fall of 1923, after having lost to them the three previous years.

Unhappily for Lomax, a bigger and much more political issue had emerged back in the spring, involving the incumbent governor, Pat Neff. Neff, a member of the law school class of '97 and the first graduate of the University to occupy the governor's office, was then in the second of two terms allowed him by statute. The lieutenant governor, T. W. Davidson, was expected to announce as a gubernatorial candidate for election in 1924. Rumors began to surface that a deal had been cut between the statehouse and the University's board of regents, whereby Neff would resign and be named president of the University by the regents—whom he had appointed—leaving Davidson to succeed him as governor and take the inside track toward election.[41] Many Exes, John Lomax among them, rose up in alarm. Neff, a lean, stiff-necked Baptist, was not popular with the University crowd—few governors were—and they shuddered at the thought of the University in the hands of a man they considered little more than a Philistine and a prohibitionist and—even worse—one who would resort to political skulduggery to get the job.

From Lomax's standpoint, all these rifts and strains began to coalesce in the person of H. J. Lutcher Stark, who had been a University regent since 1919 and was currently serving as chairman of the board. Stark was not only one of the wealthiest and most vocal supporters of the athletic program (read "football team"), he was openly behind the proposal to make Pat Neff president of the University—in fact, there were well-founded rumors that he had engineered the deal in the first place, with the understanding that if Davidson succeeded Neff, Davidson would then resign and throw his support to Stark for governor.[42] To make matters worse for Lomax, Stark was still mad at the Texas Exes for opposing the regents' attempt to move the main campus of the University back in 1921.

Lomax, with the best of motives but bad timing, managed to walk straight into the Stark windmill. Perhaps with an eye to mending fences, he proposed a special issue of the *Alcalde* to honor Mrs. Homer Hill, a University institution—known affectionately as "Granny" by generations of students she had taken under her wing—and, coincidentally, Lutcher Stark's mother-in-law. Following pleasant meetings with Mrs. Stark to discuss this honor for her mother, Lomax arranged to have the cover of the special edition printed in color, with the understanding—via telegram from Stark—that the family would pay a hundred dollars toward the cost of the cover. When the person Mrs. Stark selected to write the introduction failed to deliver, Lomax even sat down and wrote it himself, saying later that he had "never done a better or more sincere piece of writing." When the issue appeared, Mrs. Stark wrote to thank him and express her approval. Lomax billed Stark for the cover, Stark paid the bill, and Lomax assumed the matter was closed. Then he heard from Will Hogg, "one of those icy cold letters he had in his system." Hogg could be as fierce with his friends as with his enemies; Stark was spreading the story that Lomax had billed him for the entire cost of the special issue of the *Alcalde,* and Hogg demanded an explanation. Lomax was able to supply documents to mollify Hogg, but the damage was done.[43] Through no fault of his own, his reputation for smooth management had slipped another notch with his alumni constituency.

Stark was a powerful enemy. Immensely wealthy, he was heir to one of the country's greatest lumber fortunes and held interests in a dozen other industries, from agriculture to steelmaking. He donated liberally to the University (often with strict conditions), but most of his support went to sports rather than to academics. In the early twenties he spearheaded the drive to build a new stadium for the football team, and the *Alcalde* later observed that "he has been a liberal subscriber to funds for carrying on baseball, football, tennis, and other activities."[44] Over time he was to serve—some said "buy"—six four-year terms on the board of regents, and if his bumptious, high-handed manner offended some, he did not lack for support among those who responded to money, power, and a winning football team. On campus this included the fraternities, most of the student body, the athletic department, and the newspaper, the *Daily Texan*—all evolving as natural enemies of the secretary of the alumni association.

As an example of *boobus Texicanus,* Lutcher Stark was an unlikely-looking specimen, with his little round bookkeeper's spectacles and his hair parted in the middle, but he could be as rowdy and crude as any Good Old Boy. Lomax referred to him as "that young man with his money, cowboy suits, Longhorn blankets, and other showy gifts," adding wryly that money and energy would take anyone a long way even if they lacked brains.[45]

Student criticisms of Lomax began airing in the pages of the *Daily Texan* early in 1923. The situation reached a crisis on May 25 when the senior class convened and voted to call for the secretary's firing or resignation (as it happened, that same day Stark was at a regent's meeting trying to sell Governor Pat Neff as University president). "Seniors Unanimously Adopt Resolutions To Oust Lomax At Called Meeting of Class," read a large headline on the front page of the next day's *Daily Texan.*

The students complained that Lomax was away too much and that he catered to the older generation—Exes of his own era—rather than taking an interest in current student affairs. It was claimed that he had refused to schedule the Exes' annual reunion to coincide with a big fortieth anniversary celebration planned by the student body, and he was said to lack enthusiasm for the fund-raising campaign to build a new student union. These vague and trivial charges appear to have been hastily trumped up to strengthen support for the real issue, athletics: the secretary of the Exes had taken a cavalier attitude toward the football team, failed to support the drive for a new stadium, and allowed what was termed "antagonistic criticism" of athletics in the *Alcalde.*[46]

Lomax did not help the situation by first going into high dudgeon, then refusing to make any public statement on the matter. Word went around that he was in a rage and had "cussed out" a young woman reporter from the *Daily Texan* who tried to interview him (he probably told her only that he wouldn't talk to "any damned *Texan* reporter," but in those days that was strong enough to give offense and, once he'd thought it over, inflict pangs of guilt on his southern gentleman's conscience).[47]

As the crisis built, support for Lomax rallied among his old friends and classmates. Orville Bullington, current president of the alumni association, was by virtue of his position and close friendship with Lomax the person best placed to help him, but as luck would have it, Bullington was traveling abroad at the time. Affairs of the association were temporarily in the vice-presidential hands of one D. C. Bland, who seemed as colorless as his name. Bland was sympathetic but cautious. When Ed Crane, '06, a prominent attorney in Dallas, more sympathetically asked for Lomax's side of the story in order to compose a public defense, Lomax responded at length, launching, as he was inclined to do, into the whole story of his life and hard times.

He recounted his long struggle to get away from "a rocky little farm in Bosque County" (one notes the disappearance of "my father's ranch") and spoke of his enduring ambition to help students gain a college education and avoid the hardships he'd endured. In leaving Lee, Higginson to work for the Exes, he said, he had thrown away his chance to become rich, and he enumerated his accomplishments since becoming secretary of the association: the Exes had money in the bank and no debts, collections were good, membership was steadily increasing, and some one hundred University Clubs had been organized around the state.

He was forthright in saying that the seniors were probably right to charge him with neglecting student affairs, but he pointed out that no one person could attend to everything that the alumni membership, the student body, the administration, and the public expected. Of course, he said, he had serious faults, but the students' complaints against him simply weren't true—adding, however, in still another change of tack, that he was glad they didn't know the whole truth about him. In retrospect, if he had it to do over he would not act differently: "I ain't sorry for anything I have done," although he was "terribly humiliated and distressed" by the public uproar and bad publicity the University was getting. This brought him to graphic recollections not only of the Great A&M Strike and the Big Bear Fight but of the precarious state of his health, all the way back to his breakdown at Harvard in 1907. Now he feared he lacked "the nervous and physical strength" to bear up under the present crisis.[48]

Derailed by memory and anxiety by the end of his outpouring to Crane, he had drifted far and wide from the student's charges. Evidence was offered to exonerate him from the fortieth anniversary business, but beyond that, explanations of the situation were, he said, simply too numerous and complex to deal with. Nonetheless, with what Crane learned from Lomax and other sources, he constructed a long and eloquent letter to the *Daily Texan,* carefully repudiating the charges against the secretary—but it was never published. The student editors maintained that they had only one more issue before the semester ended and it was already full.

Copies of the Crane letter were circulated among the alumni, however, and in the meantime others had risen to Lomax's defense. Bullington, upon his return from abroad, wanted to "make Christians forever" of the upstart seniors, but there was a general feeling among Lomax's supporters that the students were only being used by Stark and that it would do little good to take them on directly. Crane counseled, "Don't dignify [the students] by responding any further."[49] Lomax agreed. Taking the high road, he saw to it that the student resolutions were published in the *Alcalde* but wouldn't allow the magazine to print Crane's rebuttal. Nor would he make public his own report to the Exes' president and executive council, of which he was a member, at their next meeting on June 11.

This situation prevailed for some time—an increasingly uneasy alliance between Lomax and his directors, continuing conflict with the student body, growing concern that Governor Neff would become president of the University, and Lutcher Stark still lurking about, possessed, said Lomax, of a "rampant and irresistible spirit," waiting for an opportunity to strike.

More skirmishes erupted in the following months, as when Lomax and the *Alcalde* applauded the dean of the law school, George Butte (the same George Butte who had replaced Lomax as registrar in 1903 and was fired along with him in the Big Bear Fight) when Butte issued stricter class attendance rules directed at law students active in athletics. Bellmont, the athletic director, protested, and Lawyer Crane, expressing a view that Lomax also held, told Bellmont bluntly, "I heartily concur [with Butte], that a man's major activities at college should be devoted to his studies." Butte, he said, was merely asking for more work and less play from a few students "who have heretofore experienced difficulty in finding the law building."[50] But then Lomax confused matters by defending Bellmont—"he has about the meanest job about this place"—although Bellmont had been one of the loudest calling for Lomax's head because of items criticizing the football team in the *Alcalde.* Nor had Lomax made friends among the law students when, in a controversy over adopting the Harvard case system, the *Alcalde* declared, "When [a student] graduates in law from Harvard, if he is well prepared in law, in our opinion, it is in spite of the Case System, and not on account of it."[51] Lomax, of course, was the resident expert in matters Harvardian.

In time, a form of the case system was adopted, the regents forced Butte to back away from his tough attendance rules, and Lomax, exhausted and shaken by so many lost battles, asked the Exes for a vacation—"I have stayed on this job too constantly and must have a rest."[52]

• • • • •

By the mid-1920s the University of Texas bore little resemblance to the raw little state college that Lomax had come to thirty years before. The four original buildings he had found scattered across the prairie in 1895 were now crowded among new halls and classrooms of stone and steel (and still a number of the ugly wooden shacks that had been thrown up in the teens as "temporaries"). Forty Acres was crisscrossed by streets and sidewalks, businesses catering to students lined the campus on the south and west, and Texas Memorial Stadium, Lutcher Stark's concrete playground, was taking shape on its eastern edge. Three hundred miles away, out west in Reagan County, oil had been discovered on University lands, and while that was not the windfall most people thought (only interest on income went to the University, and it had to be shared with A&M), oil money would in time help to loosen the legislature's budgetary grip on the school and shape it into the modern "multiversity" of today. In 1924 the student population of 9,250 was almost double what it had been when Lomax returned from Chicago five years before. Although he was always one of the University's biggest boosters, now even he complained that the campus had become "big and complicated, and everyone is busy, or thinks he is."[53] The Exes, despite recent upheavals, had purchased the home of former president (and Lomax's old Shakespeare mentor) Leslie Waggener, a stately residence at 2300 San Antonio Street, one block west of the campus, and that was now Lomax's center of operations.

In 1923 the redoubtable Dr. Vinson had resigned in mid-semester to take the presidency of Western Reserve University in Cleveland, having headed the University of Texas longer than any previous president. Vinson's shoes were large and not easily filled. Dr. W. S. Sutton of the Education Department was named acting president, and it was his lame-duck situation (and rather lame management) which gave rise to the notion that Governor Neff could work a deal with Lutcher Stark and the regents to become president. Rumors to that effect persisted well into 1924, fueled by the regents' repeated delays in acting to name a permanent president. The board was divided and faced with growing opposition to Neff from political leaders and powerful newspapers in the state. Meanwhile, Stark continued to stalk Lomax; in May, Ed Crane wrote to the Exes' secretary to tell him that "the 'rich grandson' [i.e., Stark] is again at his old tricks of trying to get your executive scalp."[54] Crane was confident that he would fail, but Lomax was not reassured.

There were other reasons for pessimism. The University, for all its growth and vaunted "progress," was still a hotbed of reaction, resisting the intellectual and social complexities of the twentieth century with all its might. The board of regents passed a resolution denying employment to "atheists, agnostics, and infidels" and requiring that all faculty and staff sign a statement professing belief in "a supreme being" or be fired. This act was promptly applauded by D. A. Frank in the *Alcalde*—the same D. A. Frank who had called a student war protester a traitor and who thought he was being progressive when he proposed a state college for Negroes while at the same time baldly stating that blacks must never be given social equality.[55] Opposition to the religious test for employment was raised by a few people, notably R. R. "Railroad" Smith, one of the more colorful Exes (and a longtime friend of Lomax), who argued for separation of church and state and asserted that the regents had exceeded their powers in requiring University employees to believe in God. Whereupon Frank smugly pointed out, correctly, that it was not the regents but the Constitution of the State of Texas which ultimately imposed such a requirement.[56]

Only slightly less depressing as a sign of the prevailing intellectual climate in Texas was the attitude of one student's father, a prominent San Antonio lawyer, who was upset that his daughter couldn't transfer to Sweet Briar because she'd had only two years of Latin at the University of Texas. "If I had my say about it," he told Lomax, "I would prohibit the study of Latin or Greek in the University of Texas, except that it might be a course that a student could take by paying extra for it. The idea that a Girl's School should require four years in Latin before allowing a student to enter is really worse than silly."[57]

Ed Crane spoke for the enlightened minority when he observed that the University had "lost all sense of perspective" and protested the prevailing notion that "its major function is to develop super-gladiators." Responding harshly to a leading alumni who had asked him to help raise funds for the new stadium, Crane attacked "the 'Athletic oligarchy' headed by [Lutcher Stark,] that spoiled and petulant grandson of a very rich woman, whose sole claim for scholarly distinction, so far as I have been able to ascertain, is based upon the fact that thru his generosity the [University of] Texas band has been able to make a few trips over the State with our Athletic teams, and our foot ball boys have, by his gifts of thanks, been able successfully to avoid the chills of winter weather."

Moreover, said Crane, the faculty was underpaid and students had to attend classes in buildings in "which no self respecting dairyman would house cows." In view of all this, he had no enthusiasm for building a concrete playground for the athletes, who were, after all, only a small minority of the student body.[58]

To the relief of almost everyone—except perhaps Pat Neff and Lutcher Stark—the quandary over a president for the University was finally resolved in the summer of 1924, when the regents, in Ed Crane's view, "hit upon the happy solution of the problem" by electing Dr. Walter M. Splawn to head the institution. Crane was not happy long. An economics professor who had also served with the Texas Railroad Commission, Splawn initially had the respect of the faculty and the legislature and used his influence to increase appropriations and strengthen graduate programs. He was particularly qualified to deal with the University's new oil bonanza, setting policy and procedures that would guide future development. But problems emerged and dissension set in again. Splawn lasted only three years before resigning (later he was to have a long and illustrious career in Washington with the Interstate Commerce Commission, where he gained a reputation as the "father" of modern regulatory legislation).

In any case, Splawn's appointment did not alleviate Lomax's problems with Lutcher Stark, who was still on the board of regents. Very shortly, Orville Bullington warned Lomax that Stark was again trying to get control of the Texas Exes by devious means. Stark had just paid a big fee to D. A. Frank for legal services, and Bullington drew the obvious conclusion that Stark was trying to co-opt Frank, who to this point had supported Lomax. "You know how a big law retainer sometimes has a bad effect in changing the opinions of some people," Bullington told Lomax darkly.[59]

More gloom descended from elsewhere. There seemed to be no relief from Farmer Jim Ferguson, who had reappeared again—in a big way. Rejected three times by voters since his impeachment and now barred by law from running for governor, he had put his wife up for the office and waged a fiery populist campaign. When portly, plain "Ma" Ferguson swept into office, vying with Nellie Tayloe Ross of Wyoming as the first woman elected governor in the United States, her jubilant husband set up shop in the suite next door, and it was clear to everyone that he was in charge.

Ferguson may have been crude and even corrupt, but he was no fool. He'd struck at the University once before and drawn back a nub; now he circled it cautiously and politely. In January, only days after he and "Ma" moved into the governor's mansion, he sent communications to both President Splawn and the alumni association, expressing what the *Alcalde* termed "a most commendable spirit of co-operation between the [Ferguson] administration and the friends of the University."[60] It was a good sign, but no one was taken in, least of all John Lomax. He knew that the Fergusons wielded the ultimate weapon—power over budget appropriations. Indeed, "Ma" would shortly demonstrate the extent of her "commendable spirit of co-operation" when in only a month or two she reappointed Lutcher Stark as chairman of the board of regents and struck over a quarter of a million dollars from the University's budget. While this was not a direct threat to Lomax, it did nothing to make him feel that there was much future in what he was doing.

More evidence of that came the following month, when he was relieved of his duties with the *Alcalde,* his pride and joy, and replaced by a young alumnus named Reavis Cox. It was asserted that this change would allow Lomax to "spend considerable time in visiting the ex-students over the state."[61] Another explanation was that someone wanted Lomax out of town, one way or another.

He took the hint, realizing that his effectiveness as promoter, manager, and general trail boss for the Exes had ended. Alienated students were turning away from the association upon graduation, and without a steady influx of new members it would wither. "My local influence was gone," Lomax said later. "I was on a greased toboggan, no brakes working."[62] For the third time in twenty years he was being driven away from the University of Texas under pressure.

Now approaching sixty, he saw that his dream of a great reputation as an educator and benefactor of "the poor boys and girls of Texas" had gone glimmering. *Cowboy Songs* and his lecture tours had earned him modest renown, but that field was pretty well plowed by now. His activity as a folksong collector had been dwindling for several years; there was little money in it anyway, and he had, as he kept reminding everyone, a family to feed. It seemed that everything he had worked for for thirty years had come to nothing. That was a bitter pill to swallow, but he faced the situation squarely: it was time for lowered expectations, time to pull back and seek shelter for his old age—if only he could somehow get off this "greased toboggan" on its downhill slide.

When rescue came, it came again in the form of the son of a former teacher, a Texas version of the Barrett Wendell father-son combination that had moved Lomax to Chicago in 1917. Leslie Waggener Jr., son of the long-ago University president, had been a tennis-playing man-about-campus in the law school during Lomax's days as registrar. In the years since his father's death in 1896, Waggener had dropped the "Jr." from his name, moved to Dallas, and gone into high finance. Now he was on the board of directors of the young and prospering Republic National Bank, and an active vice-president of its subsidiary, the Republic Trust and Savings Bank. Business was good, and the officers had decided to open a bond department. They needed a man with John Lomax's abilities.

CHAPTER SIXTEEN

Fare Thee Well, Babe

1925–32

The Republic National Bank of Dallas was the brainchild of one Colonel Eugene DeBogory, a 1907 graduate of the University of Texas law school, who in 1920 saw opportunities for a "working people's bank" which would cater to the throngs of prosperous small farmers and new wage earners created by the wartime economy. To accommodate such customers, who were busy at their jobs during conventional banking hours, DeBogory kept his doors open as late as 10:00 P.M. and tried to avoid the cold, formal atmosphere of big-city banks, which intimidated small depositors. His hero was that great American entrepreneur, James Cash Penney, who admonished, "Never turn your back on the front door, because that's where the customers come in." DeBogory's desk was in the lobby, where he could greet everyone who entered.

DeBogory's bank, then known as the Guaranty Bank and Trust, was hardly open when the national economy went into a severe postwar decline, but the "day and night" bank was an immediate success, attracting not only small depositors but, as DeBogory had foreseen, the payroll accounts of the large companies which employed them. Within seven weeks of opening, the bank's original capital of $100,000 was increased to $1,000,000, and in nine months its deposits had grown to almost five million dollars. As DeBogory succinctly put it, "A small idea made a hell of a big bank." By 1922 Guaranty had begun to suffer from the limitations of its state charter. The officers applied for a national charter, which required a change of name. One of the directors was awarded a prize of $100 for suggesting "Republic National Bank of Dallas," honoring, it was said, both the Republic of Texas and the Republic of the United States, in that order.

The institution had outgrown not only its state charter and old name but also its original quarters. Negotiations were begun to buy the adjoining eighteen-story Scollard Building, owned by Leslie Waggener and two partners, who represented the Travelers Insurance Company and operated a mortgage company. The deal provided that Waggener would become a director of Republic, with the bank's services at the disposal of his insurance clients. Waggener and his partners also wanted Republic to take over their farm and ranch mortgage business, but banking laws at that time restricted national banks in transactions involving real estate loans. To circumvent these restrictions, Republic rearranged its lobby and constructed within it a separate entity, complete with its own teller windows and enclosed offices, to be known as the Republic Trust and Savings Bank, under a state charter. The similarity in names and the odd situation of a bank-within-a-bank may have caused confusion at first, but for most people it amounted to little more than semantics. In any event, it is worth noting that it was Republic Trust and Savings Bank, not Republic National Bank, which originally employed John Lomax. Three years later, with a change in banking laws, Republic National reabsorbed Republic Trust and Savings, tore down the bank-within-a-bank, and resumed business, no less confusingly, as Republic National Bank and Trust. (In 1937, it finally reverted to the original: simply "Republic National Bank of Dallas.")[1]

Both Republic operations grew so rapidly in the early years that they had difficulty finding qualified people for executive positions. In early 1925, when Leslie Waggener, as vice-president of Republic Trust and Savings, began looking for someone to run the newly established bond department, John Lomax was an obvious choice. Lomax knew the bond business and had contacts with businessmen and bankers all over the state, as well as a reputation for shrewd dealing, cautious management, and hard work. There were a few problems—controversy seemed to follow him around like an old coon dog, for one thing—but his assets outweighed his liabilities. One could overlook his rough manner and occasionally sharp tongue, and as for the trouble at the University, that was what one expected from fuzzy-headed academicians, state politicians, and football-crazed alumni. Lomax was certainly none of those; deep in the calm and sedate chambers of high finance, the bank's directors felt, he would be fine. And, for the most part, he was.

Later he complained in passing that the situation at Republic was one "where cross-currents of clashing ambitions and jealousies thrived,"[2] but sensing potential conflict everywhere was part of his nature. Republic, like any large organization, had its share of office politics and internal stress, but there is no evidence that Lomax's tenure there was subjected to any unusual upheavals.

He and Leslie Waggener had preliminary discussions about the job as early as February 1925, involving, said Lomax, "a salary much larger than any I had ever earned."[3] He was immediately receptive to Waggener's proposal—stimulated no doubt by the fact that "Ma" Ferguson had just taken office as governor the previous month—but he had commitments which he felt prevented him from accepting the job immediately. These were both professional and personal; he was scheduled to attend the annual meeting of the National Association of Alumni Secretaries at Lehigh University in April, and he had arranged several lecture dates along the way. But then he was relieved of his duties as *Alcalde* editor, and when Mrs. Ferguson made Lutcher Stark chairman of the regents and cut the University budget, that was the last straw.

A face-saving arrangement with the Exes made it possible for him to resign silently, take up his banking duties in Dallas, and still continue as secretary until the appointment of a successor, thus gliding quietly from one job to the other.[4] When he went East that spring to the Alumni Secretaries meeting, he was both a representative of the University of Texas and, sub rosa, an active vice-president of Republic Savings and Trust. His resignation from the Exes was publicly announced in May, long after the fact. (Critics later noted with some satisfaction that the date of his official departure had been All Fool's Day.) The *Alcalde* limply observed "The Passing of Lomax" with a conventional statement of regret and best wishes, but later the Exes' executive council adopted a laudatory resolution praising his contributions and voted to make him the organization's first lifetime member.[5]

In July the *Alcalde* reported that William B. Ruggles, '11, former sports editor of the *Dallas Morning News*, had been named to succeed Lomax as secretary of the Exes.[6] Coincidentally, the same issue carried news of the appointment of Miss Ruby Terrill, late of East Texas Normal, as the new Dean of Women at the University of Texas, coming from Columbia University, where she had completed course work for her doctorate in classical languages.

Republic's new bond department, "in charge of Mr. John A. Lomax" officially opened on May 11, but Lomax had gone to Dallas immediately upon his return from the East in mid-April. He was joined there in June by Bess and Bess Jr., now four. The other children were scattered far and wide. Shirley, grown into a young woman of beauty and popularity, had entered the University of Texas in 1921 ("a flapper freshman," her father said, "the flappiest flapper you ever saw"),[7] then transferred to Goucher College in Baltimore for her senior year—"sent away," she felt, by her anxious father to discourage what he considered her too-intense interest in a young Texas medical student. John Jr.—"Johnny" to the family—was a handsome and athletic freshman at the University, already known as the most stable and dependable of the Lomax children. Ten-year-old Alan, who had suffered one ailment after another from infancy, had been sent to live with old friends of the family, Oscar and Stella Callaway, on their ranch in Comanche County, southwest of Fort Worth. Lomax, imbued with the legend of his hero Theodore Roosevelt, placed great stock in the restorative powers of the great outdoors as a cure for sickly boys. Spindly, asthmatic Alan confirmed the prescription; he rode ponies across the prairie, chased cattle, chopped cotton, and in due course gained weight and a healthy tan.

· · · · ·

Like the pull of the moon on ocean tides, the University of Texas had ruled the ebb and flow of Lomax's life for thirty years. Now he had left it for good. That severance was bound to work its grief and inner turmoil on a man as emotional and tradition-bound as he was. Yet he said little about his feelings and, uncharacteristically, never invested this radical alteration in his life with the high drama and fulsome rhetoric that he gave to his exile at A&M or the Big Bear Fight. He was weary of battle and weary of time, weary of his old dreams of some nebulous grand place in education or literary scholarship. He'd given his best to academia and it had only spurned him, again and again. *Cowboy Songs* had brought him a modest reputation in certain circles, but he'd never quite been able to build on it. There was no real money in that sort of thing, anyway, and he always seemed to be too distracted or disorganized to focus on song collecting. It was time to put away old dreams forever, time to think of his family and storing up for old age. He was going to take care of business, very literally, to the exclusion of all else—devote himself, with a vengeance, to making money. And with his connections, Dallas at that time was a good place to do it.

If "Big D" in 1925 was not exactly a boomtown, it was certainly in a period of accelerated growth, an emerging commercial metropolis. Additions that summer to its already impressive skyline included the new offices of the Republic National Company, a $1,500,000 Cotton Exchange Building, an expansion of the swank Adolphus Hotel complex, and the five-million-dollar Baker Hotel. Clearly the business of Dallas was business: banks, insurance companies, savings and loan institutions, brokers, agents, and accountants. Daily pages of the *Dallas News* were devoted to stock markets, oilfield exploration, and residential real estate developments. The city's two radio stations broadcast seven market reports daily and a plethora of "businessmen's talks." The Dallas Power & Light Company claimed 400 new customers monthly, adding 4,800 families and as many as 25,000 Dallasites annually to the city's estimated population of almost 200,000, fast closing on San Antonio as the state's largest city. Dozens of new subdivisions were extending the city's boundaries in every direction, sporting names flavored with the suburban catchwords of that era: "Oak Lawn Heights," "Lisbon Acres," "Country Club Estates," "Forest Hills," "San Jacinto Lawn."

Yet for all this influx and movement, Dallas was growing up as a place distinctively Texan, immune to the diversity and cosmopolitanism that characterized rising cities in the North or East. The people who flocked to Dallas in the 1920s were by and large natives of the state, often only a generation and a hundred miles or so from their roots—and as historian T. R. Fehrenbach has noted, "They kept their roots."[8] In the city, their lives were not much changed from what they had known on the farm or in small towns; they remained insular and politically conservative, welcomed progress but not change, worked hard, practiced thrift, and identified themselves first of all as Texans. They were, in other words, people very much like John Lomax. He felt at home in Dallas.

• • • • •

At Republic Savings and Trust, Lomax's title was Manager of the Bond Department. Initially, he was not only chief of the department but its sole Indian. Shortly, however, Waggener brought in his young son, Leslie Jr., recently returned from Dartmouth and Harvard Business School, and gave him a desk next to Lomax's. (Technically, he was the third Leslie Waggener, but his father had long ago given up the "Junior.") Lomax referred to young Waggener as his "understudy and close associate," but at first he was more than a little apprehensive about the boss's son looking over his shoulder. Sensitive to the pecking order and never quite secure with superiors, he was only too aware of the senior Waggener's power in the organization. "In any controversy with his young son, I would be at a complete disadvantage," he noted cautiously.[9]

Happily, he and Leslie Jr. got on famously. One clue to the source of their fast friendship lies in Lomax's later praise for young Waggener as "a charming boy [who] seemed to have caught up into his life and personality all of the worthwhile graces of the old South"[10]—in other words, those values and attitudes which Lomax himself most respected and cultivated. There were also similarities between Leslie Waggener Jr. and John Lomax Jr.—they were about the same age, both dutiful sons, bright, handsome, well-mannered, and attracted to careers in finance (in fact, they eventually shared an alma mater; John Jr. would attend Harvard Business School in 1928). Young Waggener was a playboy—in Lomax's words, he "belonged to the debutante group, and often came to work when he had slept not a wink the previous night"[11]—but that was merely part of his southern charm. What mattered to Lomax was that he got to work on time, whether he'd slept or not, and performed well on the job. He responded immediately to Lomax's avuncular style and seemed oblivious to any special privilege as the boss's son. The two of them occasionally made out-of-town business trips together and soon formed a strong relationship. "Neither of my two sons had ever talked so intimately with me," said Lomax. He may have honestly felt that way, despite unusually close bonds with both of his sons, but it seems clear that young Waggener found in Lomax some element missing in his relationship with his own father—which made the tragedy all the greater when Leslie Waggener Jr. died suddenly in a bizarre accident in the summer of 1928. Lomax was one of the first to learn of the tragedy; arriving shortly at the Waggener home, he was told by the boy's father, "Lomax, you have lost your best friend."[12]

Lomax's work at Republic was essentially that of locating sound bond investments, recommending their purchase by the bank, and in turn reselling them to the bank's clients and other local investors. He and young Waggener followed the securities markets closely and prepared a daily list of prospective bonds for the bank's purchasing officers. Leslie Jr.'s particular job had been to compile the monthly offering sheet, which contained those bonds available to the bank's customers, while Lomax solicited sales by telephone, mail, and personal contact. Business boomed in those later years of the decade, at the crest of the Roaring Twenties. No records of Lomax's income survive, but he was obviously doing well.

One indication was the fine home which he built shortly after moving to Dallas. Famous in family lore as "The House in the Woods," it was a sprawling, nine-room bungalow, set deep among elms and white oaks and pecan trees on several acres of timberland in what was then known as the Forest Hills development, some six or seven miles northeast of downtown Dallas. Lomax called it "a lovely refuge amid towering trees" and for him "the end of the trail." An elaborate prototype of the design later so widely copied (and deprecated) as "ranch-style," the House in the Woods was designed by David Reichard Williams, a young Texas architect just then at the beginning of a long and distinguished career. From extensive study of early Texas homes, many built by German and Czech settlers, Williams developed a sturdy, highly functional design adapted to the special needs of the region, with an emphasis on roomy comfort and features which captured summer breezes while protecting against the glare of the sun. Other architects throughout the West and Southwest adopted Williams's ideas; by the late 1940s, his indigenous Texas-style ranch house—or some shabby mutant of it—had become one of the more pervasive features of the nation's suburban landscape.

But there was more to Williams's involvement in Lomax's House in the Woods than the usual architect-client relationship. As one might suspect, Williams had attended the University of Texas. He also happened to be the Lomaxes' closest neighbor in Forest Hills, off through the trees and down San Benito Way, where he had built a showplace for his ideas, with an oak tree growing in the center of the huge living room and a balcony stretched across it—something quite radical in 1925. Further, Dave Williams's twin brother, Dan, had been editor of the *Daily Texan* at the time of the Big Bear Fight and had vigorously supported the Lomax forces against Farmer Jim Ferguson. When Dan Williams taught English at the University briefly in the early twenties, he often invited the Texas Exes' secretary to visit his classes and demonstrate cowboy songs. A decade or so later, as a prominent newspaperman on the staff of the *New York World Telegram,* he would host—and help promote—Lomax and his new folk-singing sensation, Huddie Ledbetter, when they made their foray into the big city.

But that was still years away—and a cataclysm or two. In the late 1920s, Lomax's days as a folksong collector were over, it seemed. From his time at Harvard on, he had kept files labeled "Ballad Search Correspondence"; for the period from 1925 to 1932 they are essentially empty. Even before he moved to Dallas he was declining requests to write articles for folklore journals and telling those who inquired about his long-planned book of Negro songs that he had no idea whether it would ever appear. He had to make a living, he told one, and books of ballads were not a very profitable means of supporting a large family.[13] When J. Frank Dobie expressed concern about infringing on Lomax's cowboy song territory by writing an article on the subject, Lomax told him that "you have about supplanted me in everything pertaining to the Southwest." That was the way it should be, he said; he—Lomax—was too busy trying to make a living for six hungry mouths. When Dobie had that many, he added, he would know what a struggle it was.[14]

Except for a cowboy song lecture now and then in the Dallas area and an occasional appearance at meetings of the Texas Folklore Society (he'd never officially renewed his membership since returning from Chicago), Lomax's only involvement with literary matters during these years had to do with helping to establish the Book Club of Texas, and even that, one suspects, was as much business as pleasure—the club's founder and principal backer was Stanley Marcus, of Neiman-Marcus, someone obviously worthy of being cultivated by a vice-president of Republic Trust and Savings. There was also a Harvard connection, for it was as a student there that young Marcus had acquired his interest in fine bookmaking. On his return to Dallas, he determined to set up a nonprofit publishing operation that would preserve important but neglected Texana in volumes elegantly printed and bound. Among the directors of the Book Club were two old Lomax compadres, Will Hogg and Dr. Harry Benedict (risen to president of the University of Texas in 1927, having survived so many of the wars in which Lomax had fallen). Lomax mother-henned the Book Club of Texas operation, drawing on his Exes experience to compile lists of prospective members and using his contacts with newspapers all over the state to get publicity. Otherwise, his time and effort went to Republic; as he told one of his former sources, "This busy Bank so utilizes all my physical energy that I have no time to keep up my ballad collection work."[15] The secluded study that he'd had built in the rear wing of the House in the Woods was little used except as an occasional playroom for young Bess.

• • • • •

It was, on the whole, a life of comfort and tranquility—certainly more tranquil than any time in recent years. Only a short distance from the House in the Woods was White Rock Lake, with its miles of shoreline, parks, country clubs, and boat docks. Nearby also was Tenison Golf

Course, where the Lomaxes frequently played a round on Sundays. The days of the "miniature farm" around the Lomax homestead were over, but John saw to it that there was a small barn on the property to house a pony for the children, and he still cultivated a flock of chickens, his favorite farm animals.

Bess found outlets for her high energy in a number of social and cultural groups; she was especially active in the Women's College Club, which she'd helped establish as an alternative for women who, like her, had attended college but lacked a degree or school affiliation and were thus denied membership in the American Association of University Women. Lomax, to the contrary, increasingly shunned all organizations, even those that might be professionally beneficial—he made no effort, for example, to rejoin Rotary, which had drummed him out in Austin for missing too many meetings. By this time complaining of busy-ness was an ingrained habit with him, but it is true that he devoted long, hard hours to his work at the bank. He even declined to have his name put forth as an appointee to the board of regents of the University—a position he surely coveted—because he couldn't take time from his job.[16]

Upon graduation from Goucher College in 1926, Shirley came to Dallas and took a room with her parents, waiting for her young doctor to finish his internship in the Navy so they could be married. Through her father's connections with his old classmate, Norman Crozier, now superintendent of schools in Dallas, she got a job as grade school playground supervisor, where she taught the children games and physical activities. Her duties at the House in the Woods included driving her father to work and young Alan to school at Terrill Preparatory. Shirley bought a used Ford for $100; when it was time for her to go to Philadelphia to meet her fiancé and on to New York for their wedding, Lomax refused to let her drive the Ford. Instead he arranged for her to travel by rail in the private car of her "Uncle Allie" Brown, Bess's older brother, who was now a vice-president of Missouri Pacific Railroad. "I'll buy the Ford from you," her father told her. "I need a trade-in, anyway, and I'll give you the best price you can get." Eventually he sent her twenty-five dollars, Shirley recalled years later, laughing ruefully.[17]

But that was all in the family. The children took a patient, often bemused view of their sober, thrifty, hardworking father. In New Orleans on a summer job one year, Johnny wrote home that he and his friends had gone "to a saloon—I mean a soft drink stand—and drank a cock-tail apiece at 50¢ a smash with real whiskey in it"; mindful of Prohibition's inroads on his father's habits of relaxation and economy, he added, "Tell father that he should visit New Orleans, for they sell whiskey openly and at a cheap price."[18] From Cambridge during his year at Harvard Business School, Johnny took a mild dig at his father's admiration for Herbert Hoover by telling him of meeting Herbert Hoover Jr., then a faculty member at Harvard: "He was just a common person in every way. We had a nice chat about his father's chances in Texas, which I painted up rosier than I knew them to be."[19] Hoover's chances in Texas were rosier than Johnny knew; defying conventional political wisdom, he carried the state by some 26,000 votes and became the first Republican presidential candidate to take Texas's electoral votes. In the same election, Texans sent Democratic congressman Tom Connally to the U.S. Senate, where he would remain until 1952. Connally was the only freshman Democrat elected to the Senate in 1929.

Careful as Lomax was with a dollar, he had never spared expense when it came to Alan, his favorite. After Alan's junior year at Terrill Preparatory, he was sent to the prestigious Choate School, in Wallingford, Connecticut, which counts among its alumni such distinguished names as those of Adlai Stevenson ('18) and John F. Kennedy ('35).

Renewing acquaintances with an old friend, Elizabeth Darley, in early 1931, Lomax dotingly traced the achievements of his far-flung family and their whereabouts. After graduating from Goucher, Shirley had married her medical student scholar, who was now practicing in Lubbock; John Jr. graduated from the University of Texas, attended Harvard Business School for a year, and was now managing the investments department of the City National Bank in Corpus Christi. Lomax said he had great hope that Alan, who resembled his father, would accomplish some of the things "in the world of scholars" that he had once dreamed of for himself but had started too late to achieve. Bess, then ten, reminded him of pictures of his mother when she was a girl. All of them, he said, were normal children, although Shirley was so pretty that she had had more boyfriends than he was comfortable with until he'd seen her safely married. John had always been "steady as a church"; Alan was "volatile and explosive," and there was no predicting what he might do. Young Bess was "a darling," he said, and their home would be quite empty without her happy nature.[20]

· · · · ·

At the end of the decade of the twenties, Lomax was sixty-three years old, an age at which most careers are normally expected to be nearing their end. He had come a long way (as he so often liked to remind everyone) from a small farm in Bosque County to—well, to whatever he now was. Former teacher, lecturer, song collector. Former "utility man." Now bond salesman, banker, third vice-president of the Republic National Bank of Dallas. Whatever it was, it was a position of some prominence. He knew, and was known by, people in high position and low; his acquaintances included poets, senators, business moguls, and college presidents all over the country. His name was on the title page of books, and no less an eminence than Theodore Roosevelt had pronounced one of them "bully." His life was insured for some $15,000, no paltry sum in those days, and he had money in the bank, an impressive portfolio of stocks, and a fine home in a big city. His children attended the best schools.

To Lomax, it didn't seem to amount to much. He had aspired to something far greater. In his letter to Elizabeth Darley, whose mother had boarded him on credit in those long ago years when he was a struggling school teacher at Clifton, he earnestly turned aside any exalted notions she might have of his achievements, for once speaking with little of the false humility or breast-beating that often marked such ruminations. She was mistaken, he said, to think that he had achieved any success in life. Looking back, he saw that all his hard work and efforts to accomplish something significant had been mostly in vain. She must not forget, he said, that he'd been fired from the University by the governor, and he and his family had had to live "as exiles" in Chicago because he was not considered worthy of being connected with the University of Texas. Even now, he added, he was merely one more "busy, hard man" among several hundred others in a large institution, and in view of the uncertain economy, no one's job was secure.[21]

By this time the Wall Street Crash had come, but the real effects of the depression would not be felt in Texas for several years. There was another, greater misfortune presently in store.

• • • • •

For some time, Bess Lomax's health had been declining. In addition to the myriad disorders diagnosed in those days as "female trouble," she suffered excruciating earaches caused by mastoid infections, which seemed to run in her family. But she was a woman of great fortitude, a stoic who disdained any show of weakness or incapacity, and for years she had maintained a vigorous life of hard work at home and involvement in many social and cultural affairs outside it. Since moving to Dallas, much of her time and energy had gone to the Women's College Club; for several years she had served as the club's secretary, edited its journal, planned programs, and served on a number of committees. It was at a meeting of the College Club in late February 1931 that she suddenly collapsed and was rushed to hospital. Doctors eventually offered a vague diagnosis, alluding to "overwork" and a possible thyroid deficiency as the cause. Her mind remained clear, but she suffered dizziness and eventually began to lose the use of her hands. After a week or two in the hospital with no noticeable improvement and only more confused medical advice, she was taken home to the House in the Woods and placed in the care of a private nurse.

Doctors who were called in for consultation talked, without much conviction, of this or that operation. In light of their continuing indecision over the cause of the problem, she and John decided that rest and seclusion was the best course of action, with the notion of building up her strength before deciding about surgery. By early May there seemed to be signs of improvement, and Lomax even ventured the hope that she might be on the way to full recovery. Then suddenly she suffered a relapse and died on the morning of May 8. In five months she would have observed her fifty-first birthday.

For John the only consolation was that there had been some warning, however brief. His own health had not been good, and Bess's death all but crushed him. For almost thirty years she had been, as she often told him, his "partner," in the thick of it with him every day, shoulder to shoulder, the two of them like a sturdy plow team in harness, uphill and down through hard rock and root, through thin crop and rich harvest. She had written his speeches, typed his books, kept his accounts, run his house, raised his children, and remained, to the end, his true love. And she had done it all—most importantly, perhaps—standing neither in his light nor in his shadow. From start to finish, Bess Brown Lomax was very much her own person.

During her mother's illness, Bess Jr. had been sent to stay with Shirley and her husband, Dr. Chris Mansell, in Lubbock, three hundred miles away to the west. Alan, at the still-tender age of sixteen, was already a freshman at the University of Texas, struggling with an insensitive English instructor and trying to arrange a scholarship to Harvard for the following year. Johnny, after some time as an underling in his father's office, had recently taken a promising job with the City National Bank in Corpus Christi, on the Gulf Coast. They all assembled in Austin on May 10 for their mother's funeral and burial.

Afterward, Shirley and Bess Jr. accompanied their father back to Dallas in the Pierce-Arrow limousine which Leslie Waggener had generously sent for their use. Lomax returned to his office the very next day, in what was clearly an effort to show as much composure as he could muster. Hiding the extent of his grief, he wrote a subdued but encouraging note to Johnny, in the spirit of looking after his flock and putting the best face on the situation. It would be hard for them to bear up and go about their daily routine, he said, but they had no choice but to do that, adding, "In fact, under such circumstances work is a blessing."[22] Alan and Bess Jr. would need careful attention, he said, but he was sure they were made of stern stuff and would do well. As for himself, he was going to heed Johnny's advice and take afternoons off from the bank to exercise and "harden up physically." He knew this would strike a responsive chord with Johnny, who after many illnesses in early childhood had acquired a serious interest in physical culture, almost literally rebuilding his once-frail body through strenuous exercise.

John's hope of getting himself back in condition that summer was sadly frustrated. Instead, his health grew steadily worse, assaulted by numerous afflictions—indigestion, insomnia, headaches, nervousness, and a particularly troublesome inflammation of the skin diagnosed as erysipelas. In May he wrote Johnny that he was still not up to "the grind of office work," but, fortunately, his employers were understanding and urged him to take time off until he improved.[23] He spent time with the Callaways at their ranch in Comanche County and began planning a long trip with his sons as soon as Alan finished spring exams at the University, "a vacation for the three Lomax males" that might even include an ocean cruise from Corpus Christi to Miami. Johnny quietly dissuaded him from that on the grounds that it would cost too much, and they settled for "a jog around in our little Ford" down to Monterey, Mexico, then up the Rio Grande Valley and out to the South Plains, where Bess Jr. was visiting the Mansells in Lubbock. But his ailments only intensified. Throughout the summer he spent days at a time in bed. In September he wrote to Johnny that he was making "little progress towards getting well" and could spend no more than half a day at a time at the office, even then unable to get much work done.[24]

As his health failed, so did his financial fortunes. The effects of the depression had been rippling toward Texas for many months. As long ago as the previous November, Lomax was complaining of uncertain business conditions and "the daily anxieties and problems" which were wearing him down. People weren't willing to buy long-term securities at any price, he told his old friend Sidney Mezes, and there was no profit in short-term securities.[25] The yield to investors on U.S. government certificates was 1 percent; they gathered dust in the vaults.

Under Lomax, Republic's bond department had thrived during the late twenties. Now the day came when the bank's president, F. F. Florence, walked into Lomax's office and instructed him to sell every bond they had, at any price. Wiring New York, he was chagrined to learn that for some of Republic's securities, there was simply no market at all. "No buyers, only sellers," he was told. Republic weathered the storm, but Lomax was left to face old friends and customers to whom he had recommended investments that were now worth less than half what they'd paid for them—or nothing. For a man with his rigid sense of integrity and his poor-boy's attitude toward money, that was not easy. Even worse, in flusher times he'd backed—verbally or with his signature—various private loans and transactions that were now going into default, leaving him responsible.

One such case was that of the Rev. J. Abner Sage, an impecunious man of the Methodist cloth whom Lomax had known when Sage was studying for the ministry at S.M.U. in Dallas. It was that acquaintance, presumably, which had led Lomax to recommend him to the bank for a loan of $150, giving verbal assurance that Sage would pay. Instead, Sage broke down under the strain of his debts, then lost his church. When he took bankruptcy, he was relieved of legal obligation for the debt—but John Lomax, in the view of the bank, was not. At least that's the position Republic took with Sage, telling him, "If you do not pay this note, John Lomax will. He has lost his money, wife, health, and present business connection with the bank. When he has regained his health, he will be with us again, but, in the meantime, he is in very poor condition to pay out $150.00 because he has had implicit confidence in a friend. The obligation against you is not legal at present, but only moral."[26] Privately, the bank told Lomax that the debt had been written off, but Sage, "a very pitiful and distressing piece of literature," was not to know; let him stew. Little people, said a Republic official, don't worry enough about owing a big bank, which they think can afford to lose.[27] Lomax, it seems, was the only person in the whole shabby affair who acted honorably; as in the case of his brother Richard years earlier, he paid Sage's note in full although he had no legal obligation to do so and although he had to eke it out over several years. When the last installment was made long afterwards, he at least had the satisfaction of praise from Republic president Florence: "We appreciate, very much, the fine position you have taken. . . . We would not have made any claim against you . . . so having it come from you voluntarily is just an indication of your innate fineness and consideration for fairness at all time."[28] But these words of comfort were far in the future. At the time, Sage was only one of many such aggravations he had to deal with.

His relatives could always be counted on to add to his troubles. Brother-in-law Gene Pedigo, caught short by the depression, appealed to him for a loan, and Lomax came up with it, although wearily pleading for security (he'd had to borrow some of the money himself) and pointing out, one more time, that he, too, had a family to feed. Rob Lomax's tangled financial affairs were another drain; John was still paying the interest on Rob's notes, supporting his family from time to time, and trying to get his younger brother on firmer ground.[29]

For more than a dozen years, since the death of Bess's lackadaisical brother, Will Brown, Lomax had been helping his widow and young daughter, Virginia, who were left practically destitute. In the mid-twenties, he'd used his connections to get Anna a secretary's job with the Missouri, Kansas & Texas Railroad in San Antonio, for which she had written, "I thought it splendid of you . . . to concern yourself and . . . use your influence in my behalf. . . . Please believe me that Virginia & I are the most sincerely appreciative folks anywhere, and we truly like you for this for we see in it a real expression of yourself—a big kind self."[30]

By 1931, Anna and Virginia Brown were living in Dallas, where Virginia was teaching school, and soon after the death of Bess Lomax, they moved into the House in the Woods with Lomax and young Bess Jr., the idea being that they would help fill the large empty house and provide welcome company, while at the same time reducing expenses. The move seemed to offer a solution to another problem. Bess Jr. had been attending the exclusive Hockaday School, which was now proving too expensive; according to the plan, she would transfer to the ward school in south Dallas where Virginia taught, and travel back and forth with her each day. But Lomax, in physical and financial pain, was not a very pleasant companion, and the arrangement did not last long, although he initially reported that "Miss Anna and Virginia are proving to be treasures."[31] Bess, however, took to the new plan immediately; having resented the high-toned atmosphere at Hockaday, where she was something of a misfit, she found an exciting new world in the school where Virginia taught—a "slum school," as she said, with a heavy enrollment of Mexican-American children. In contrast to the snobby students at Hockaday, she found her new classmates warm and open—"they were used to dealing with and caring for the 'lame, halt, blind, elderly, and idiotic,'" she said, "and so they just adopted me. I was well ahead of them in school terms, but they were ahead of me in life terms. It had a very profound affect on me—it developed my social attitudes for the rest of my life."[32]

The steady decline in Lomax's fortunes continued unchecked through the fall of 1931. One day in early October he went down to the bank and told Leslie Waggener that he could no longer do his job properly. Waggener suggested that he take a leave of absence for a year or so to recover his health, then they would see what might be done. The bank couldn't afford to pay him, of course, but Waggener generously offered to keep him on salary for the next two months, to get him through Christmas. Lomax went home, weary and disconsolate, and took to his bed. For the time being, he told no one but Johnny that he had left the bank. He was sixty-four years old, sick, and out of work. His adored wife was dead, his family scattered, his spirit gone.

• • • • •

As it happened, John Lomax Jr. had also lost his job that fall, when the City National Bank in Corpus Christi went into receivership (or, as he said, "exploded in my face"). But Johnny had an entirely different attitude about the situation. He was young and healthy, with no family to support, and he had some money saved up. Since childhood he'd been pounding away at one job or another. Now, "having nothing to do was a new experience," he said. Besides, in those darkest days of the depression, he was hardly besieged by offers of work. "Loafing a spell enticed me," he said. "I loafed and enjoyed loafing."[33] He loafed through Christmas in Dallas, hoping merely by his presence to comfort his troubled father, who kept more and more to himself, moving slowly about in a kind of daze, rarely leaving the House in the Woods.

On New Year's Day of 1932, Johnny persuaded his father to go with him to a benefit football game at Southern Methodist University's Ownby Stadium, pitting the "S.M.U. All-Stars"—"football idols of bygone days"—against a similar group of alumni from other colleges and universities in the Southwest. The sharp winter air acted like a tonic, and even more invigorating was the local team's 16 to 9 victory.[34] Over dinner that night, Lomax talked enthusiastically of the days when he had toured the country lecturing and searching for folksongs. Sensing a change of spirit in his father, Johnny reminded him of all his old plans and schemes—a comprehensive anthology of American folksongs, a book about the music of blacks, perhaps even more cowboy songs—projects he'd never had time for, until now. A lecture tour would bring in some badly needed dollars and provide the means for renewing his contacts among other collectors and scholars. Johnny ventured these notions cautiously, for he knew that no one made up his father's mind for him.

It was clear that the older man had been thinking along similar lines, but still he hesitated. "I need every penny I can earn," he said, "but giving lectures is a hard grind for a man in my shape. I'll need help—someone to drive me around and help me arrange the dates."

Johnny grinned. "Your obedient servant," he said. "At least until I can find a job that pays."

It was, as historians like to say, a turning point. John Lomax had, in effect, gotten up from his deathbed and was about to set out upon the work which would occupy him for the remaining sixteen years of his life—the work which would finally bring him the rewards he had long sought.

John Lomax's parents, James Avery Lomax and Susan Frances Cooper Lomax. (All photographs courtesy Shirley Lomax Duggan except where noted.)

John Lomax, age six.

John Lomax (left rear) with three of his brothers, George and Robert (front row) and Jesse, about 1879.

Lomax as a student at the University of Texas, 1897.

Bess Brown, about the time of her marriage to John Lomax in 1904.

John and Bess with baby Shirley and part of the "miniature farm" at Texas A&M, 1905 (Lomax holds a chicken, one of his favorite animals).

Bess Brown Lomax, 1910.

Lomax as secretary of the University Faculties at the University of Texas, ca. 1910–12.

The Lomaxes (center, under umbrella) at a gathering of University of Texas alumni, 1911.

Bess Lomax with Shirley, Alan, and John Jr., 1915.

Shirley Lomax, “the flapper-iest flapper of all,” 1920s.

John Lomax as secretary of the University of Texas Alumni Association, about 1914.

John Lomax Jr. and John Lomax Sr. in New York during Lomax's transcontinental lecture tour, 1932.

"The House in the Woods," Dallas.

Lomax surveys his garden from the back door of the House in the Woods.

The wedding of John Lomax and Ruby Terrill, 1934.

Alan Lomax, 1942. (Courtesy Alan Lomax and the National Archives, Washington, D.C.)

Bess Lomax Hawes, 1950s. (Courtesy Bess Lomax Hawes.)

In retirement, Lomax with produce from his garden at the House in the Woods.

A pause for refreshment, with his grandson, John Lomax III.

John Lomax on his eightieth birthday, looking through a volume of letters from well-wishers.

PART FOUR

• • • • •

High Roads, Hard Roads

The true way goes over a rope which is not stretched at any great height but just above the ground. It seems more designed to make people stumble than to be walked upon.

—Franz Kafka, *The Great Wall of China*

CHAPTER SEVENTEEN

• • • • •

Johnny, Won't You Ramble?

1932

His spirits revived by plans for a return to the lecture circuit, Lomax lost no time. The very next day he dug out his old lectures and set to work polishing them up, while Johnny typed out inquiries to colleges and universities, military schools, social and fraternal clubs—any group that might form a paying audience to hear about cowboy songs. The list of prospects ran into the hundreds—Johnny said that on his best day he typed "sixty-two identical letters"—and the process of answering interested parties and working out the details required a flurry of mail that dragged on for several weeks.[1]

They faced numerous obstacles. Not only were lecture tours fast becoming a thing of the past, having been replaced by radio and talking movies, but in that time of deep economic depression, some schools had dropped all extracurricular events, while others had already filled their meager programs for the year. Many responded that they would like to have Lomax come but had no money to pay him. Setting aside his pride, he bargained and bartered, accepting whatever the traffic would bear: ten dollars here, twenty-five dollars there, merely food and lodging if a paying date could be arranged nearby. Nevertheless, by the middle of February, they had "bagged," as Johnny put it, fifty-three confirmed, paying engagements that included twenty-eight colleges and universities, nineteen women's clubs and high schools, and six boys' schools. From these, father and son worked out three itineraries—two in Texas that would serve as shakedown cruises, and a long, involved national tour that would take them first to the East Coast, where they would pick up Alan, now at Harvard; from there the three of them would travel across the nation to California, then home to Texas, zigzagging and backing and filling all the way.

The Texas trips, beginning February 20 and extending into April, took John Sr. and John Jr. the length and breadth of the state, from Brownsville at the southern tip to Dalhart near the top of the Panhandle, from the piney woods of East Texas to the windy plains out west. Their conveyance was affectionately dubbed "Nancy Ford"—a 1929 tudor sedan of faded robin's egg blue, with 43,000 miles already on the odometer and well past her prime. Bulging with baggage top and sides, Nancy Ford appeared to be just another migrant rattletrap, joining the procession of displaced and dispirited people lining the roads in those depression days. "To the effete colleges we later visited in the East," Johnny wrote, "the entourage certainly must have looked appropriate for an itinerant cow-waddie lecturer."[2]

Earlier, Lomax had resumed the sale of copies of his books through the mail, advertising them in various farm and ranch magazines. With boxes of books already on hand, he loaded a supply onto Nancy Ford in the hope of peddling them to lecture audiences, having decided, as Johnny facetiously put it, "that ethics would not be seriously trampled" by such an endeavor. *Cowboy Songs* and *Songs of the Cattle Trail and Cow Camp* were offered at $1.75 a copy; purchased by Lomax from his publisher at the standard author's discount of 40 percent, they netted him $.70 on each transaction. The sale of one or two books often covered traveling expenses for the day.

In the further interests of economy, Lomax arranged to stay with friends and relatives along the way. Passing through Austin, they were guests in the home of J. Frank Dobie and his wife, who served them a "sumptuous" lunch and invited old friends Roy Bedichek and Dr. W. J. Battle. By this time Dobie's popular course on life and literature of the Southwest was becoming an institution at the University; Lomax happily accepted Dobie's invitation to speak to the class on cowboy songs as a warm-up for the tour ahead.

On the road, response to his lectures was mixed. Students were generally enthusiastic, but attendance was sparse when not required. At a high school in South Texas, where a hundred or more students lolled about in the spring sunshine outside the auditorium, he waited until long past the appointed time and finally dismissed the few who had gathered inside. But he was roundly cheered at the Women's College in Denton, and the cadets at A&M, steeped in school tradition and drilled to mind their manners, gave the former Aggie instructor a standing ovation.

Johnny began a journal of their travels, later famous in the family as "The Log," written in present-tense-bulletin style that managed to be both breathless and deadpan, reflecting Johnny's dry wit, even temper, and eye for telling detail. His flat, sometimes cryptic entries were frequently punctuated by graphics drawn in the margins. After a disappointing turnout at Mission, in the heart of the lush citrus-growing region of the Rio Grande Valley, he wrote, "A poor crowd that night is forgotten later when Father visits Reynosa, Mexico." Drawn beside the entry was a whiskey bottle with a question mark in it.

Perhaps the low point of this trip was a long swing into North Texas where, after a dismal two-hour visit with Rob Lomax and his family, they drove on to the hamlet of Valley View as a cold March "norther" descended. Johnny's log entry: "A dimly lighted hall on the second floor of the school building, inadequately heated by gas stoves, housed a few dozen coughing school boys and unbending club women. One tough audience! Gross receipts—$6.60 . . . book sales—None."[3]

Forging on to the western plains and up into the Panhandle, they encountered howling sandstorms and more northers and added 1500 miles to Nancy Ford's odometer in less than two weeks. Johnny recorded that "The two Scotchmen . . . spent the wasteful sum of $21.20 for all expenses during the 11½ days on the road." In Lubbock, they stopped to pick up Bess Jr.—"old baby bambino"—at the Mansells, then headed back toward Dallas, detouring to visit Orville Bullington in Wichita Falls ("the Siberia of Texas," as John Jr. accurately characterized it). Bullington was running for governor on the Republican ticket in that overwhelmingly Democratic year, and although his chances for election were roughly those of the proverbial snowball in hell, Lomax actively supported him, possibly inspired by the fact that the opposition, yet once again, was Miriam A. "Ma" Ferguson—with Farmer Jim standing by, of course, to "carry the wood and tote the water," as canny Texans told each other with a wink.

With Bess Jr. along for company on the next outing, they embarked on a whirlwind circuit of East Texas, covering more than six hundred miles in five days. Wrong routes accounted for considerable mileage, because Johnny navigated the same way he drove—with happy abandon. Still, father and son found time to play several rounds of golf along the way, and Bess entertained them with spelling contests, limericks, and word games. In Jacksonville, Johnny noted cryptically, "Father struggles vainly with East Texas society women." Lomax's burdens were society women and Johnny's driving. Nor did Johnny endear himself to his father when he left behind a box of *Cowboy Songs* on their last day out. Lomax roared; Johnny appeared properly contrite but went on his merry way. That was the pattern for the long haul coming up.

• • • • •

Back in Dallas they rested, caught up on correspondence, packed, bought supplies, and readied Nancy Ford for "THE BIG JAUNT," as Johnny's log termed it. With warm weather approaching, it was Lomax's plan to camp out along the way—for his health, he said—with only occasional respites at what were then known as "tourist cottages." Accordingly, Johnny stocked the car with bedding, cots, and a tarpaulin. Golf clubs were a further health-and-recreational necessity. Cooking utensils and dishes were stowed in a carpenter's tool box for which he had paid $1.00 in a pawn shop on Dallas's "Deep Ellum" Street. The rattling, clattering tin box was an object of derision throughout the trip, but Johnny was firm in defense of its utility. Shirley came and took Bess back to Lubbock, and on April 18 father and son were packed and ready to go.

There is a mental image of their departure: casually dressed, Johnny takes the wheel and with a jaunty wave, steps on the gas; beside him, grave as a mortician and wearing his inevitable dark suit, vest, tie, white shirt, and rumpled fedora, Lomax holds on for dear life, clutching his hat, his coattails swirling around him. Away they go.

The depression notwithstanding, it was a glorious time for an open-air tour of the nation, before the age of mind-dulling interstates and commercialized homogeneity, a time when each region, each city, still had its own distinctive character, architecture, vernacular, newspapers, hamburger stands, and roadside attractions. Everything was cheap, even by Lomax's standards, and when you went from Texas to New England to Idaho, you experienced something very different, as different as if you'd gone to Holland or Russia. Only a generation later it was all fading into comfortable sameness.

Lomax's itinerary called for a couple of stops before leaving Texas, both "washouts" in terms of attendance. In Weatherford, hard rains kept people away, but after his talk, he salvaged something from the day with a sentimental visit to one of the daughters of David S. Switzer, his mentor many years before at Weatherford College. After another poorly attended lecture at Bowie, north of Fort Worth, they headed off into the night, crossing the Red River near Waurika, Oklahoma, and pitched camp beside the road for the first time. The next day, "Father struts his stuff in two talks at Oklahoma Women's College. Six books sold!" Johnny recorded triumphantly. In Oklahoma City they were put up in style by the Charles Johnsons, University of Texas alumni, who took them golfing and to dinner. Johnny's log chronicled other fun and games: "Father has late date with an elderly widow, keeping Mr. Johnson up to a late hour."[4] It was a sure sign that Lomax was on the mend from the previous year's disasters.

At the College of the Ozarks in southwestern Missouri the students were "raw mountain angels," but they received Lomax warmly. After his talk, he and Johnny faced what Johnny termed "an impossible task"—a hard journey of "560 strange miles" to Nashville, Tennessee, in the next thirty-six hours. They drove south into Arkansas that night before bedding down beside the road, then rose at 4:30 "in the cool, grey mountain mist" to strike out over winding gravel routes through the Ozarks. Still, they had covered 204 miles by noon. Lomax, seeing a ray of hope, took the wheel while Johnny napped. Long after dark, they settled fitfully on cornshuck mattresses in a shabby "tourist camp" east of Memphis, only sixty miles from their destination. But a rainstorm in the night fouled both Lomax Sr.'s digestion and Nancy Ford's ignition system. Next morning, their only recourse was to push the baggage-laden little car up hill and down until, just as they were about to despair, she sputtered and sprang to life. They rolled into Nashville and up to the campus of Ward-Belmont School for Girls with only minutes to spare before the morning assembly at which Lomax was to speak. Johnny practiced his golf swing outside the chapel, while "Father, inside, gets all the Texas girls homesick" and "as a result the book racket breaks all hoped for records: wowie! and whoopee! forty-one books sold!"

Forty-one books sold put $28.70 into the coffer. A few days later, crossing the Ohio River into southern Indiana, they made camp and Lomax bought staples for their supper and breakfast. These included two pounds of tenderloin steak, eight eggs, a quart of milk, a tin of kippered herring, a tin of deviled ham, two grapefruit, and a box of strawberries. Total at the checkout: 86¢. (The most expensive item, as one would expect, was the steak; it cost 33¢.) Big Cuban cigars topped off their repast, and they climbed into their cots to count the stars, then sleep as all men hope to. No hint of his old insomnia for Lomax on nights like this.

They were on the road constantly, for stretches averaging as much as three hundred miles a day over primitive highways, through rain, heat, cold, up hill and down. "All this is *work*," said Johnny, but that was the closest he came to a complaint. In the Finger Lakes region of central New

York, they gave in to fatigue and a beckoning sign: "Quiet Tourist Home With Feather Beds." Conversation with the farm couple who were their hosts turned to such rustic matters as crop prices and duck egg fertility—"*some* contrast," said Johnny, "to the furrow-browed money changers of Wall Street only 200 miles distant, sweating over vanished billions!"[5]

Deflected southward into Pennsylvania for an appearance at Bucknell, they were warmly received by the college president, Homer P. Rainey, a former Texan, who hosted a special dinner in his home for father and son. Then they struck out for the East Coast, speeding through the night along the Susquehanna River. Long after midnight they made camp "on some unknown burgher's hillside" but were soon awakened by sprinkles of rain. Certain that a downpour was looming, Lomax insisted they dress and be on their way. At dawn, nursing a cup of coffee and bone-weariness in a cheap Hamburg diner, Johnny noted glumly in his log: "No real rain falls, branding Father at least a stranger" (an allusion to the Texas saw that only fools or strangers predict the weather).

· · · · ·

By June 7 they were in New York. Lomax's later account of the momentous event that day made it all sound quite casual: "One morning I drifted into the offices of The Macmillan Company at 60 Fifth Avenue." Behind this seemingly offhand visit lay weeks of thought and preparation; much of his motive for coming east was the hope of a book contract with some prestigious publisher, preferably Macmillan, which had been publishing *Cowboy Songs* since 1919. To H. S. Latham, a Macmillan vice-president, he made his pitch: a proposed anthology of American folksong, with music, from all walks of life and as big and thorough as he could make it. To the fruits of his sporadic labors over thirty years would be added all the new material he could locate in a year, from library sources and from intensive fieldwork that he could undertake if he had a contract in hand. Lomax watched the publisher's face for any sign of response. "I was desperate," he said later, "and I think he realized it."[6]

Latham had liked Lomax's cowboy song books, but while they sold steadily, they certainly weren't big money-makers. He listened to Lomax read samples of the songs he had in mind, and, after what seemed an interminable pause, said he would take Lomax's proposal to his editorial council. Two days later, a contract for the book, with an advance of $250, reached Lomax at the home of Dan and Jean Williams on the Upper West

Side, where he and Johnny were staying. "That's the moment," he wrote in his autobiography, "at which I turned the corner to where a little light was shining."[7] The restoration was not yet complete, but he had come a long way from the terrible dark days of the previous fall, when it had seemed that his useful life was over.

A mishap three days earlier dimmed some of his elation over the book contract. Johnny, driving up Broadway alone one night, failed to execute a left turn quickly enough and was struck by an oncoming car, flipping Nancy Ford on her side. Johnny was surprised to see passing New Yorkers calmly pocket their tabloids long enough to gather round nonchalantly, lift the car upright, and push it to the curb. He suffered a badly bruised elbow but could think of nothing but how grateful he was that his father wasn't there to see what had happened. The next day he nursed his swollen arm while "Father views wreck of Nancy ruefully." The damage seemed substantial—a broken wheel, a shattered window, three bent fenders, and a ripped molding—but despite his injury, resourceful Johnny again saved the day: "I learn plenty about New York City methods, chiseling all over the East Side keeping the repair bill down to $9.00."[8]

Back in January, Lomax had asked Sen. Tom Connally about the possibility of getting Johnny a position with the newly formed Reconstruction Finance Corporation, one of Hoover's belated attempts to deal with the banking crisis.[9] From New York, Lomax appealed again to his old friend in the Senate, and Connally arranged an appointment with the chairman of the board of directors of the RFC, Jesse Jones, another Texan. The two Lomaxes drove down to Washington on June 8 and were Connally's guests in the Senate Gallery "to hear Democrats roast Hoover." At 10:00 A.M. the next day they met with Jones and "other officials who promise to do what they can for poor, jobless Johnny," as the Log put it.[10] The bureaucrats offered encouragement but no job at the moment. We'll be in touch, they said.

While in the nation's capital, Lomax visited the Library of Congress to examine folksong holdings there. Not one to linger about with underlings, he went immediately to the office of Librarian Herbert Putnam, announced himself, and was given a cordial reception by the aged, stately Putnam, whose vision and long reign had developed the Library of Congress into a truly national repository, "a university of the people with the staff as its faculty."[11] Putnam took him to the office of Carl Engel, chief of the Music Division, who found working space for him and saw that he was given a special pass admitting him to the Library on Sundays and holidays. "Thus began," said Lomax, "my unusually pleasant relations with the Library of Congress."[12]

From Washington, father and son headed for Providence, Rhode Island, where Lomax was scheduled to lecture at Brown University. By mid-afternoon they had skirted New York City, gotten lost twice in Connecticut, and encountered endless detours. "Father (strongly!) upbraids Johnny for carrying him thru rough trafficky Newark street."[13] They were both out of sorts, and upon learning, at a gas station, that they had taken yet another wrong turn, Lomax declared a halt, disembarked, and stretched out on a patch of grass nearby for a nap. "An old hag at the filling station," said Johnny, was sure that they were "truly loco Texans."

Refreshed, they drove on to Providence and the secluded, palatial home of Brown University Professor Cletus Oakley and his wife, Louise. The Oakleys, "sympathetic Texans," alumni of the University, knew just what the weary travelers needed. "Alcoholic bitters and steaming baths," said Johnny, "loosened our cramped limbs." But the combination of "alcoholic bitters" and an abbreviated nap left Lomax so groggy that at his lecture that evening he attempted to pour water into the wrong end of a glass and flooded the podium. Happily, it served only to break the tension; the laughing crowd gave him a good-natured round of applause, and Johnny enthusiastically reported that "Father knocks 'em clear off their chairs into the aisles!"[14]

After four days of much-needed rest with the Oakleys, father and son drove to Harvard, where Alan was finishing his spring exams. For some time Lomax had voiced strong concerns about his younger son's liberal sympathies, which his year at Harvard had, it seemed, only intensified. The closeness of their relationship made this disagreement all the more poignant. Although they would find various accommodations that would enable them to live and work closely together for years, their differences of political opinion were never to be reconciled, despite all of Lomax's earnest efforts to "save" Alan from what he considered dangerous socialistic tendencies. Johnny was happily neutral in the fray, merely recording the current standoff wryly in his log—"We repair to Charles River bank to try to settle Alan's communistic activities. Still at loggerheads at 6 P.M."[15]

On June 16 the three of them left Cambridge, headed west. By interesting coincidence of geography, a beeline in that direction from Massachusetts took them to Canada (at Niagara Falls), where they added certain medicinal beverages, prohibited in the U.S., to Nancy Ford's ever-swelling baggage stores. Johnny quoted a roadside billboard:

Once upon a time, feeling rather dry,
Three Yanks went to Canada to get a case of rye;
When the rye was opened, these Yanks began to sing,
We're loyal to our country, but God save the King!

To which he added: "Those were our sentiments, especially of the Pater, who has been craving good beer since we left Matamoros, Mexico, in March."

Two days out of Boston they camped at the rear of a rambling, deserted old country mansion on the shore of Lake Cayuga in central New York. Arising at his customary hour of 6:00 A.M. and feeling unusually hearty, Lomax, according to Johnny, "gave vent to several fine imitations of the fine old time Comanche war-whoops, which echoed in the hills across the lake." Caught up in the spirit, Johnny and Alan joined in with whoops of their own. A few minutes of this aboriginal chorus aroused the Swedish farmer-caretaker just down the road, and he quickly came roaring up, yelling at the top of his voice. Lomax attempted "mild rejoinders," but the fierce Swede would have none of it—"If you don't getta hell out of here qvick, I'm agoin' call State Poliss!" In minutes the "Texas trio," as Johnny called them, were vanishing down the road.

Beside an Ohio country lane they encountered opposition of an even fiercer sort. Offered easy access to a well-cropped pasture, enclosed by only two strands of barbed wire, they slipped through as night fell and set up their cots several yards inside the fence, ate a hasty dinner, and were soon fast asleep under a warm, clear sky. Some hours later, Johnny, an extremely sound sleeper, was shocked awake by a terrible noise, "the most awful, blood-curdling, death-sounding bellow I have ever heard." His father, now also awake but more accustomed to sounds of the countryside, diagnosed it as a bull who had caught their smell downwind. Upon hearing that news, Alan hit the ground with both feet churning and made a blur to the fence, some yards away. Said Johnny laconically, "It isn't even close. Alan wins not by a nose but by a full lap. In fact he loses one of his socks, not to be found until daylight; nor does he return to help lug the cots."

No sooner were their beds relocated in the lane outside the fence and the bull pacified than an amorous cow in the field on the other side began to call out, and the bull resumed his bellowing. Johnny's report: "We are in between the two lovers, leaving our technical position not strong. . . . By now Father has *his* dander up. Night-gowned he takes his stand on the rim of the hill and with best war-whoop challenges el toro. He and that bull blood-curdlingly destroy the calm of the night; all the dogs for miles around take up the argument. . . . Father wanders along the lane trying to locate the Jersey, alternately talking in soothing tones, calling 'sook, sook,' or chunking rocks as she coyly flees her sweetheart and departs for regions unknown."[16] Watching the fierce antics of their father, clearly visible in his white nightshirt, the boys were struck by the farce of it all and broke into loud laughter. Lomax was not amused. A cowboy on foot is no cowboy at all.

Across mid-America, between Berea College in eastern Kentucky and Billings, Montana, out west, Lomax gave only one lecture, at Northwest Missouri State Teachers College in Maryville. Otherwise, their journey through the Heartland was a long, uninterrupted stretch of "plain and fancy traveling," in "rough and ready style," as Johnny put it. Lomax, revived by the open air and feeling more and more robust as they went along, cast off his coat and tie and occasionally even—mirabile dictu!—his shirt, joining the boys in bare-chested comfort on the warmest days. They shaved only every four or five days and rarely combed their hair—Johnny cut most of his off, while Alan grew long and tangled locks.

The two brothers were getting to know each other, as adults, for the first time; since Alan's childhood they had been together only rarely, separated by geographic distance as well as by dissimilar personalities and the difference of seven and a half years in their ages. John Jr. had once written to his mother, "From the temperaments of Alan & John and from their hobbies and inclinations, you certainly would not recognize or guess them to be brother beans, would you? If we are to be beans, I suppose Alan would qualify more as a brittle but active 'snap-bean' while I would best be a big and strong but fairly substantial 'lima.'"[17] It was an astute characterization.

Now the brother beans got on famously, playing golf—"cow pasture pool," they called it—swimming in lakes and streams along the way, and "buzzing" for girls in Nancy Ford. After their father's appearance in Billings, they picked up two who had attended the lecture: "One . . . makes a crack about how bum it was. We draw her on, never letting on that we are THE SONS." Johnny recorded with equal glee (and clearly some exaggeration) other outings, depicting the two brothers as South-of-the-Border desperadoes: "In inspection tours of strange towns these tough 'Mehoxicans' [i.e., Alan and Johnny] don black corduroy pants, longhorn belt buckles and boots, swagger along sort of scowling and usually bluff the natives into making way on the sidewalks."[18] Lomax swam with them, joined their golf games, and cast an envious eye on their "buzzing" expeditions, but otherwise entertained himself and found no more elderly widows to court. As the Democratic National Convention began in Chicago during the last week in June, he tuned in the car's radio each evening and followed the proceedings carefully but said little, silent on the nomination of Franklin D. Roosevelt for president.

In Yellowstone Park they loafed and fished for four days. Johnny recorded an outing on the river: "Father in the stern handling awkwardly a rod and reel for the first time in his life." Attempting to land a trout by yanking the line instead of reeling it in, Lomax lost both the trout and his fishing equipment. "Yes, there we were with no tackle, only one fish, and way down stream. Alan & Johnny certainly poured the jeers in a heartless manner upon Father's bloody and bowed head." Reequipped, they landed fourteen rainbow trout, but Johnny's "artless cooking" over the campfire that evening reduced them to "fish hash."

Camped out on the Fourth of July near Old Faithful, they wore all their clothes to bed, surprised to find that (at an elevation of almost 8,000 feet), even the summer nights could be bitterly cold. "At 4:30 A.M. Father, unable to stand it any longer (although he has on 2 pair of socks, 2 pair of winter underwear, shirt, pants, and sweater—all topped by the irrepressible nightgown) arises, wraps our Indian blanket around his shoulders, departs, hoping to find hot coffee in the nearby lodge. Puffed out all over, swarthy, five days of whiskers, a towel around his head, he looks like old Sitting Bull himself." Approaching the darkened lodge in this getup, he was accosted by a park ranger who, suspecting that he was some aged renegade up to no good, turned him away. Shortly he was back in camp, cold, grumpy, and sans coffee.

On the eastern shore of Lake Pend Oreille in Idaho, accessible only by boat from across the water, was the summer home of Prof. and Mrs. George Miller of the University of Idaho. The thrifty Lomaxes shunned an expensive trip by steamer and instead elected to rent a rowboat. It was a large, sluggish affair, big enough to hold their luggage but slow and unwieldy in the water. For what seemed like hours, they took turns at the oars, hauling and pulling and grunting, steering an erratic course across the rippling waves. "While John rowed, Alan and Father gave directions and jeered. While Father rowed, Alan and John gave directions and jeered. And when Alan rowed, there was no time for jeering." Their destination proved worthy of the struggle. For a week they loafed with the Millers in the idyllic village of Lakeview, at the rim of the ice-blue lake, nestled between steep mountain canyons and shaded by pine and cherry trees. Then it was time to resume the tour.

When they reached Ellensburg, Washington, for Lomax's lecture at Washington State Normal, they found waiting for them a telegram from Sen. Tom Connally in the nation's capital: "HAVE JOHN JUNIOR REPORT HERE AT ONCE STOP HAVE SECURED POSITION FOR HIM WITH IMMEDIATE EMPLOYMENT." Glad to have a paying job again but disappointed that he would miss the Olympics in Los Angeles, Johnny departed on the midnight train for Pasco, 125 miles away, where he could catch a commercial flight aboard a Ford Tri-Motor that would take him eastward.

Lomax's engagement at Ellensburg was an all-day affair, involving an informal talk on folklore with the faculty in the morning, a luncheon hosted by the dean of women, and a public lecture that evening. While he took care of business, Alan attended to Nancy Ford and their gear. Then came a distraught call from Johnny; he had carried with him no cash but only Post Office money orders and had arrived in Pasco only hours away from his scheduled flight to discover that he lacked the necessary identification to cash them.

It was always Lomax's instinct to start at the top in such matters; he went immediately to the president of the college and asked that the institution advance him the necessary cash—$150—so he could get his boy on the plane to begin his important government job. Lomax's idea was that he would give the president his personal check to hold, then redeem it as soon as Johnny had returned the money orders which his father, having proper identification, could cash. But this was all very complicated and unusual; the president had not risen to his position of eminence by acting rashly or irregularly. To Lomax's surprise, the man hesitated, hemming and hawing. The more Lomax thundered, the more obdurate the official became, pleading that he could accept such an arrangement only if he had security of some sort. "All I have with me is my car," said Lomax. The president thought that over, then reluctantly accepted the deal—on the condition that the car be chained to the college gate post and the key to the lock held by the college bursar. Lomax huffed and fumed and seethed, his face a purple rage. He had no choice but to agree to the terms.

His lecture that evening was a tour de force, "a howling success," in Alan's words. At its conclusion, the college president came up to extend congratulations and invite him to a reception in his honor, where the regents, their wives, and other officials were awaiting his presence. Lomax fixed steely eyes on the man. "I am leaving," he said, "and I want the keys to that padlock." Well, said the president, I'm giving a party for you; surely that can wait until afterward. "I am leaving!" roared Lomax, turning on his heel and marching to the bursar, where he again demanded, and got, the key that freed Nancy Ford from the gatepost.[19] Next day, according to the Log, "Father and the president, stiff with personal pique and offended virtue, walked around and around each other, tips of conversational tails barely moving in courtesy."

With Johnny's departure, Alan had taken over the Log, pedantically vowing that he would abandon Johnny's use of the energetic present tense and describe events and scenery only in the past tense, which he felt was more "truthful." Whatever the Log may have gained in accuracy, it suffered the loss of Johnny's wit and liveliness. One entry, omitting intriguing details, recorded that Alan and his father (described as "two bourgeois") had had a lively conversation about Alan's communist associations during a hot drive through the parched hills of southern California. From this, Alan said, he gained insight into his father's political philosophies and "the roots of his dilemmas." A more revealing vignette—lapsed back into the present tense—is that of the two of them playing records in a music shop, sampling items from Beethoven to Cab Calloway's "Minnie the Moocher" ("the latter both of us like—tremendously"). It was the only chronicled instance of Lomax listening to jazz, which he professed to loathe.

In Los Angeles by early August, they spent three days at the Olympic Games, recording for Johnny their impressions of the track and swimming events. Lomax went to the libraries at UCLA and Southern Cal to look for folksongs and had a daylong outing with his old schoolmate, Bates McFarland, now a prominent California attorney. Disdaining the company of his elders and their reminiscences of long ago, Alan went swimming in the ocean and admired golden beauties on the beach (the Log tough-mindedly calls them "dames"). Later he took a drive to Long Beach, ate a watermelon, and, upon seeing ships on the horizon, sadly wished that he had the courage to go to sea. When he returned to Hollywood, where his father was picnicking with Bates McFarland and McFarland's two sisters, he found Lomax still holding forth with endless stories about the old days at the University of Texas.

Father and son started for Texas on August 11, camping near Needles, Arizona, on the first night out, then driving on in torrid heat to the Grand Canyon. Alan noted that only a Homer could do justice to its spectacle ("or Santayana," he added, paying homage, perhaps, to Harvard). He was not only moved by the grandeur of the landscape of the Southwest but much taken with Native Americans they encountered along the way. At Taos, New Mexico, they stopped to visit with Orville Bullington, who owned a ranch there. That evening strange music rose in the hills around them—distant drums, then from several directions voices chanting in unison. Stirred by the ancient rhythms of the natives, he vowed that someday he would return and record that music on a phonograph.[20]

On August 19 father and son slept under the stars for the last time in a pasture south of Amarillo and the next day reached Lubbock and the Mansells.[21] Unpleasant news awaited them; Dr. Chris Mansell had lost his job with the student health service at Texas Tech, and later, when they drove on to Comanche and stopped to see Oscar and Stella Callaway, they found them "old, weary, and discouraged" by the depression. The Log reported the tired travelers in a similar mood when they finally reached Dallas and the House in the Woods on August 30, some six and a half months and 25,000 miles after John Sr. and John Jr. had set off in mid-February. Alan's last entry may have been influenced to some extent by Hollywood or simply the melodramatic language of those grim depression days, but one also remembers that he had undertaken to make the Log "a little more truthful." In any event, there is no denying his youthful earnestness as he closed out the account of the travels and travails of himself and his father that summer of 1932, writing in the third person: "They know nothing of the future, even ten days ahead. They are homeless, jobless, and have no expectations. Let the curtain fall upon this woeful last scene."

· · · · ·

Happily, it was not the last scene, nor was it all that woeful. On the homeward leg of the journey, Lomax's outlook had been markedly different from Alan's. True, he was tired of the road and apprehensive about the future, but he was also abuzz with plans and reaching down into his old store of optimism. After all, the trip had made him some money—the total gross was slightly over two thousand dollars, including his advance from Macmillan, and they had spent less than half of that, coming home with a net profit of $1,035.22—in a day when, as Johnny observed later, "a dollar *was* a dollar."[22] The gain was not merely monetary: Lomax's health had been restored, and he had a contract for the book he had long wanted to do. For the first time in years, he had a purpose in life.

From Lubbock he had written to Johnny with all his plans: Bess would remain with the Mansells and go to school there, the house in Dallas would be put up for rent, and he and Alan would make their headquarters in Austin, where Alan would return to the University of Texas and he himself would write and lecture wherever an opportunity arose. Meanwhile, he said, he was back among friends, where he would have the best chance to find "something permanent."[23] Although times were still hard, he found all sorts of positive omens: the cotton crop on the South Plains was good, Bess was thriving, and Macmillan had written him enthusiastically about the proposed book. He was in such good spirits that he would continue to support Orville Bullington for governor "regardless," despite the fact that Ma Ferguson's victory seemed certain (she defeated Bullington by a plurality of 184,500, out of 770,844 votes cast). He even had a piece of advice for Johnny that sounded remarkably like the old John Lomax, telling his oldest son to "cultivate your superiors" and do his best until they could find him a job "outside Government service." In light of what was in store for Lomax himself, there was more than a little irony in that remark.

CHAPTER EIGHTEEN

Hallelujah, Bum Again

1932–33

Ever since he'd gone off to Granbury College, forty-five years before, Lomax had sought the safe, ordered life of middle-class respectability. Now he had discovered that he liked bumming around. Of course he'd always had a wanderlust, but never had he traveled quite so close to the ground as he had that past summer, earning his living as he went along, directing his own destiny, as unbuttoned and bohemian as he'd ever be—five days' beard on his face, shirt and tie cast aside, stirring a pot of stew over an open campfire and whooping like a Comanche in the early morning dawns. It wasn't bumming in the truest sense—he still had a permanent address and money in his pocket, and he donned a coat and tie now and then to make his lectures. But he'd had a taste of the open road and thrived on it. Happily, the book of folksongs he'd proposed to Macmillan gave him both motive and means to hit the trail again, as soon as he could catch up on his business affairs and plan an itinerary.

The restoration of his health was confirmed that fall of 1932 when he went to his doctor for a physical. There was the minor matter of slightly elevated blood pressure, but Dr. Neighbors assured him it was no cause for concern. The essential systems—heart, lungs, liver, kidneys—were as sound as those of a man half his age. A mild tonic was prescribed for a nagging digestive complaint. What the patient needed most of all, said Neighbors, was to lose some weight, twenty pounds or so over the next six months. He recommended a lean-meat, starch, and vegetable diet that excluded butter, biscuits, gravy, fried chicken, and anything else cooked in grease.[1] It was medical advice Lomax had been getting, and ignoring, for years. He never bothered to fill Neighbors's prescription for his intestinal upset, and the doctor's diet presumably got similar attention.

Meanwhile, Lomax's desk bubbled and boiled with maps, letters, plans, projects. He wrote far and wide to request copyright permissions for songs from other collections, queried the National Broadcasting Company about doing a regular program on cowboy songs (NBC politely declined), sent out form letters supporting Orville Bullington for governor, and searched for a recording machine that would stand up to the rigors of fieldwork.[2] He devoted renewed energies to ferreting out lecture sites and trying to line up dates, wherever and whenever. Initially the results were meager, and Johnny urged him to concentrate on the proposed book, warning against taking just any lecture engagement: "The way we used every possibility to get a date last spring at any price does your rep[utation] no good; another year of this may ruin your future opportunities in the field."[3] But Lomax persisted. With the eventual help of lecture agencies, he lined up two tours for the coming year, a brief one in early March to the West Coast and a more extended trip in the East and Midwest later that fall.

Johnny, still based in the nation's capital, was delegated to scout out lecture possibilities in the Washington-Baltimore area. He netted only one firm engagement—an assembly program at American University for $35—but wrote his father enthusiastically that "the eye-opener is that *each and every one* [his emphasis] of the dozen professors I have interviewed, all total strangers to me, either knew of you or knew you personally. May the Lomax name carry on as you have borne it!" Impressed by this unsuspected glimpse of his father's stature, Johnny dropped his opposition to the lectures and pledged all his spare time to working on a schedule.[4]

Returning from Baltimore one day in December, Johnny stopped by the Library of Congress to meet Robert W. Gordon, who had been more or less directing the Library's Archive of American Folk Song since its inception in 1928. The Archive was, in fact, largely Gordon's creation, aided and abetted by Carl Engel, the sympathetic chief of the Library's Music Division. Johnny went to see Gordon with the hope of enlisting his aid with lecture dates, but he quickly found their roles reversed. Gordon was in trouble, and the Archive along with him. "His project is at the end of the rope financially," Johnny wrote home, "and he doesn't know what is going to become of [it] after the end of the year." Gordon, as desperate as Lomax had been the previous spring, welcomed anyone who might be a source of aid or comfort. "He received me most cordially," Johnny told his father, "stating that he would rather see *you* than any other person in the country. . . . Therefore he was most delighted to find that you are coming soon." Johnny warned his father that Gordon had a "bad case of halitosis" but would gladly offer "a shake-down bed in his house while you are here."[5] Lomax was not due in Washington for several months, but he took careful note of the situation, and not merely because he'd been offered a free bed.

At forty-four—twenty-one years younger than John Lomax—Robert Winslow Gordon was a tall, disheveled man, with thinning hair, a dark bush of a moustache, and, increasingly these days, the stale fragrance of something stronger than coffee hanging about him—the adumbration of a seedy journalist or an absentminded professor.[6]

Gordon had been traveling a difficult path for some time—but he was a difficult man, his career largely one of fits and starts and unfinished business. In his youth back in Bangor, Maine, he had seemed destined for great things. At fourteen he'd won a scholarship to the prestigious Phillips Exeter Academy, a school otherwise beyond the means of his ne'er-do-well family, and entered Harvard as a freshman in 1906 (the year Lomax went there for his M.A.). But after graduating Phi Beta Kappa in 1910, he stayed on at Cambridge for another eight years, sometimes attending graduate classes, sometimes waiting tables, selling magazine subscriptions, getting married, teaching English to freshmen, and doing research for a dissertation that never got written.[7] A tinkerer and a dreamer from youth, he'd become a man of compulsions and obsessions, a perfectionist, a loner. At Harvard, under the influence of men like Kittredge and Wendell, what he got mostly was an intense interest in folklore and folk music and the conviction that therein lay his life's work.

That conviction, along with a wife and daughter, was about all he took when he left in 1918 for the University of California, where he had been hired, sans dissertation, as assistant professor of English. He was an excellent teacher, but his colleagues found in him certain troublesome idiosyncrasies. One was his increasing involvement with folksong study and collecting, which, as John Lomax had discovered, still lacked academic respectability in the hinterlands. Gordon's other annoying traits included desultory work habits, bad breath, and a disinclination to tolerate fools. There was also his continuing failure to publish scholarly work—or what was worse, publishing in a common pulp magazine called *Adventure,* where he conducted a monthly column headed "Old Songs That Men Have Sung."

Forced from his job in 1924, Gordon took his family back East, ostensibly to finish his degree at Harvard. But within weeks he was in the wilds of

North Carolina, doing fieldwork among the mountain folk there. When his funds soon ran out, he transferred his base of operations to Darien, Georgia, on the Atlantic coast south of Savannah, lured there by cheap living and the prospect of rich folklore gleanings among the region's large black population. In Darien, Gordon and his family subsisted for more than four years, living hand-to-mouth while he rushed about in the field, interviewing, photographing, and recording, meanwhile formulating intricate "scientific" theories and searching for some holistic system that, like the peevish Mr. Casaubon's "Key to All Mythologies" in *Middlemarch,* would explain every question that might arise concerning the "evolution of folksong."

Gordon was not without his supporters in scholarly and cultural circles. Among those he impressed was Carl Engel, who had succeeded the great Oscar Sonneck as chief of the Music Division of the Library of Congress. At first glance, Engel, a classically trained European musicologist, seemed hardly the sort to become the benefactor of some errant collector of American folksong. Born in Paris of German parents and educated at the universities of Strasbourg and Munich, he had the bearing of a maestro and spoke with the accents of *Kultur.* But he'd lived in America since 1905, was thoroughly nationalized, and as a serious student of music deplored the lack of interest in systematic and critical musicology in this country. Engel envisioned a center of musicology at the Library of Congress, devoted to analysis, theory, and historical study, or, as he told Gordon, to "the *research* (not the making or faking) of music."[8] Gordon's methods were, at least in Gordon's view, scientific, and that appealed to Engel.

By 1927, Gordon was well known around the Music Division of the Library, having interrupted his fieldwork from time to time to do research there. He had also struck up a regular correspondence with Engel, laying out his ambitious plans and exploring possibilities for financial aid. Tiring of poverty and neglect, he had begun to look for some sort of institutional refuge. As it happened, his ideas seemed to coincide with the research center that Engel had been thinking about. Money was the obstacle, but after months of discussion, planning, and proselytizing, by mid-1928 Engel had raised sufficient funds from private sources to enable the Library of Congress to offer Gordon a one-year appointment as "Specialist and Consultant in the Field of Folk-Song and Literature" with a stipend of $300 a month. It was his first regular salary in four years.[9]

This was the beginning of the Archive of American Folk Song, although that did not become the official title for some months. At first the institution was rudimentary in the extreme; except for Gordon's private collection of recordings and song texts, which he guarded carefully, there was very little to archive. For some time the Archive of American Folk Song existed mostly in Gordon's head.

Both Engel and Gordon embarked upon their new collaboration with high enthusiasm, but trouble developed almost from the start. Gordon was immediately conspicuous by his absence; instead of settling in at the Library of Congress and going about the business of building a national repository of folksong, he disappeared back into the remote reaches of southern Georgia and resumed his fieldwork. He had gotten what he wanted: the sanction—and financial support—of a national institution. He also convinced himself, and thought he had convinced Engel, that he could fulfill his new duties for the Library while continuing his own work in the field.

That was not the way Engel saw it. Soon he began to send out inquiries to Darien. Where was Mr. Gordon? What were his plans? When did he expect to establish his headquarters in Washington? Pushed, Gordon would respond with a report of sorts, setting forth optimistic schemes for the future and trying to justify his continuing absence. Variations on this theme went on for months. Eventually the impasse reached the attention of Engel's superior, the venerable Librarian of Congress, Herbert Putnam, who made *his* displeasure known. But more than a year elapsed before Gordon was finally persuaded, none too gently, that it was in his best interests to move to Washington.

Once Engel had Gordon where he could keep an eye on him, he may have wished he'd left him in the field. Gordon was not, to put it mildly, a company man. He performed his duties, but in his own erratic and fiercely unconventional fashion. The stress level went up several degrees on the top floor of the southwest pavilion of the Library, where the Archive had been established in a large but mostly empty room.

Gordon's work showed some progress in the next year or two. He made serious headway with the thorny problem of copyrights as related to folk materials and archives, and he conducted important pioneering experiments with recording equipment for fieldwork. These efforts extended even to magnetic wire and tape prototypes, and they constitute some of the first experiments with such equipment in this country. A small but significant innovation was his use of movie film to record and store manuscripts and print documents—a pioneering step toward microfilm. He undertook the major task of cataloging and indexing the holdings of the Archive to date, consisting initially of his own collection (which he had agreed to place on deposit but which remained his property), together with what materials the Library acquired from a few other collectors and individuals.

But nothing ever seemed to get finished. Gordon's efforts to find suitable recording apparatus is typical. There were machines that would work, but none was perfect, so rather than attempting modifications or making do with something less than ideal, he kept bringing different models into the laboratory, testing, fussing, experimenting, instead of going into the field and making records. Near the end, he did take an Amplion machine into Virginia, West Virginia, and Kentucky and supposedly returned with nearly a hundred metal-disc recordings. But few if any of them seem to have made their way into the Archive. Harold Spivacke, who shortly afterward joined the Music Division as an assistant, said that Gordon "told me that he made about thirty records, but I never found them, and neither have I found any evidence they were here, not that I mistrust Gordon's word." Regardless of what happened to the records, the pattern was cast. In the minds of Engel and Putnam, Gordon was difficult and unproductive, and he had to go.[10]

By this time—nearing the end of 1931—private funds for the Archive were drying up, and Gordon was told that his job would end in June 1932, at the close of the fiscal year. Then, discovering that his work on indexing the Archive was still far from complete and aware that he was probably the only one who knew what was there, Engel and Putnam came up with a last-minute reprieve. An $800 grant provided earlier by the American Council of Learned Societies was extended, and Gordon was given six months, until the end of 1932, to complete the job, with the understanding that if he didn't meet the deadline, he would work on without salary until the index was finished. Gordon—accustomed to living on thin air anyway—not only agreed to the arrangement but offered to stay on indefinitely for the nominal sum of a dollar a month, even after the index was completed, with the hope that he might be rehired when the economy improved. Engel listened to this proposal without comment; however weary of Gordon he might be, he was hardly willing to literally throw the poor man out of the building, and no one knew what might become of the Archive when Gordon left.

When Johnny Lomax visited the Archive that day in December 1932, Gordon was in the last throes of finishing the index, fretting and wondering where his next dollar was coming from. As it turned out, he managed to hang on in limbo for several months longer, a spectral shape haunting the halls of the Library, but he spent most of his time trying to eke out a living with free-lance articles and dreaming up more grand projects that never came to be. At one point he considered pulling his collection out of the Archive and transferring it to Harvard.[11] Harvard was not interested.

Eventually, after Lomax was named "Honorary Consultant" to the Archive the following September, rumors surfaced that he had conspired to move Gordon out, but there is no evidence of that. Gordon's connection with the Library of Congress was already about as tenuous as it could get, and Lomax would not reach Washington for another four or five months. If anyone attempted to pull strings, it was Gordon. "Meanwhile, much as I detest it, I'm getting drawn into politics," he told a correspondent in January 1933. "Certain friends of mine have started a quiet but determined lobby. I shall, I think, have a fairly good personal standing with our new president [Roosevelt] after March 4th."[12] As a delusion of grandeur, it outstripped anything Lomax could come up with.

· · · · ·

In early March, Lomax made a quick trip to the West Coast, where he lectured and probed the libraries at the University of Southern California, Pomona College, Cal Tech, Stanford, the University of California, and Mills College. Then he hurried back to Texas to resume preliminary work on the book and laid plans for hitting the road with Alan as soon as the spring semester at the University was over.

The search for a suitable recording machine had begun as early as the previous fall, when Lomax appealed to Macmillan to help him get a Ediphone cylinder machine on loan from the Edison Company in exchange for the material he would record. But Edison was closing down its phonograph and recording operation and had no use for the records. The company offered to sell him a machine, but that was not what he had in mind. By spring he had had no luck in borrowing a recorder from either the American Council of Learned Societies or from RCA Victor, so he traveled to Washington to see if he could enlist the help of the Library of Congress.

There he learned that the Amplion machine used by Gordon had been sold, but Putnam suggested that the Music Division might consider having a portable machine built to order for his use, in exchange for copies of the records he made. At Engel's urging, Lomax hurried off to New York to visit the showrooms of Fairchild, Amplion, and others to see what was available. There, as he said later, he "fell among thieves."[13] He named no names, but the culprit he had in mind was apparently one Walter C. Garwick, an otherwise well intentioned gentleman who had been an engineer for Fairchild and was just then setting up his own business for designing and manufacturing sound recording devices.

More than ten years earlier, commercial phonograph companies such as Okeh and Victor had developed cumbersome but portable equipment for making wax master recordings in the field. But turning these masters into usable, permanent records was a complicated process that had to be done at the factory.[14] The technology for what Lomax wanted—disc records that could be played back immediately upon recording, from equipment that was simple and easy to carry—was in its very infancy in 1933, and almost no one else had envisioned the uses for which he intended it. At this early stage, Garwick undertook to convince Lomax that he could build a recording machine that was smaller, lighter, better, *and* cheaper than anyone else's. Lomax was not totally taken in—he cautioned Engel that "Of course [Garwick] has something to sell and wants to sell it"[15]—but initially he thought that Garwick had the experience to produce what they wanted. It took him a year or more of tangles and frustrations to realize his mistake. Meanwhile, he was impressed by Garwick's estimated price of $450, which was cheaper than either Fairchild or Amplion, and by Garwick's assurance that his machine would weigh half as much as another other available.

Alan had returned to the University of Texas in the fall of 1932. By May of the following year, Lomax was also in Austin again, "back in the old familiar scenes," rooming with Alan and waiting for the end of the school year.[16] He had printed and sent out several hundred copies of a form letter, similar to those he'd used for the earlier books, announcing his new project and soliciting songs and advice from correspondents. "I plan to print in one volume what seems to me the best Folk Songs indigenous to this country and to include certain Ballads from other sources, to which have been added words and music such as to give them a distinct American flavor."[17] Recipients of the letter were asked to seek material from their colleagues and students and send him a list of songs already in print which they felt ought to be included. In addition to the form letters, during a period of three or four days of intense activity he composed and Alan typed some fifty personal letters also asking for material. Just what he got from this is difficult to assess—as usual, he showed little interest in keeping track of sources and origins—but one tangible result was that he set off a wave of folksong preservation around the country, as dozens of song enthusiasts both amateur and professional went to work digging out old songs for him and sought to establish their provenance.

By late May Lomax was in the midst of frenzied preparations, hoping to get on the road with Alan by June 10. Their itinerary, he wrote to Engel, would take them to "chain gang camps" in Texas, Louisiana, and Mississippi, as well as the black districts of New Orleans, Vicksburg, Memphis, and St. Louis.[18] He hoped to visit other black enclaves along the way, traveling by river steamer from New Orleans to St. Louis. A trip up the Mississippi by boat had been a dream of his as early as 1911, when he mounted his first lecture tour. For one reason or another it had never happened, and now such a journey again had a prominent place in his plans.

Prior to departing, Lomax found time to renew his acquaintance with Miss Ruby Terrill. Since that occasion a dozen years earlier when she had entertained young Alan at East Texas State Teachers College while his father lectured there, she had gone off to Columbia University for course work toward her Ph.D., then returned to Texas in 1925 to become dean of women at the University. By 1933 Ruby Terrill was an institution in Austin—an attractive, vivacious maiden lady of forty-eight, known for her intelligence, quietly forceful character, and active involvement in campus, church, and social organizations. Lomax's daughter Bess described her as "a witty, lady-like figure, short and stout and twinkly, very attractive." (On one occasion, traveling with her by car, Bess was fascinated when, during a lull in the conversation, Miss Terrill doffed her driving glove, probed into her purse, and brought out a tiny harmonica, which she popped into her mouth and played while driving along.)[19] Coincidentally, Miss Terrill was Alan Lomax's Latin instructor and personal favorite on the campus. The two of them had developed a fast friendship; she occasionally loaned him her car for dates, in return for which he chauffeured her around town on errands. From time to time they were joined by the young man's father, who took to dropping into Miss Terrill's office to invite her to lunch. Flowers began to arrive at her desk. Dinner dates ensued.

J. Frank Dobie, who lived on Park Place up the street from the rooming house where Alan and his father were staying, told of encountering Lomax one afternoon just about the time of day that they often shared, as Dobie put it, "the better adjuncts of water." Lomax seemed unusually cheerful, but Dobie allowed as how they could both use a drink and was more than a little surprised when his offer was declined. That had never happened before. Pressed for an explanation, Lomax beamed from ear to ear. "I'm on my way to take Miss Terrill to dinner," he said. "She does not approve of whiskey."[20] Clearly, Lomax was taking the situation seriously. More seriously than Miss Terrill, as it turned out.

· · · · ·

Near the end of May, Lomax and Alan packed Nancy Ford and drove to Lubbock, where they spent a few days relaxing with Bess and the Mansells before taking off on their big collecting expedition. Garwick's proposed recording machine was still being built, and although Lomax was delighted that the Library had finally decided to buy it and loan it to him in exchange for copies of whatever he recorded, he was anxious to get going and urged Engel to use "what pressure is wise" to speed Garwick along. Engel replied that the machine would not be ready until early June.[21]

In the meantime, Lomax had been corresponding with Mrs. Janice Reed Lit, a wealthy and enthusiastic amateur folklorist in Haverford, Pennsylvania, who thought she might obtain a machine for him through RCA Victor or the Edison Company. Both deals fell through, but at the last minute she managed to arrange with the Dictaphone Corporation in Philadelphia to ship him one of their cylinder model dictating machines, equipped with a spring motor.[22] Lomax now decided to start the trip with the Dictaphone, then, once Garwick's machine was ready, have it shipped to reach them somewhere along the way. He and Alan left Lubbock on schedule June 10 and picked up the Dictaphone in Dallas, then headed for Huntsville, site of the state penitentiary.

They found little they could use in Huntsville, but a week or two later they were at Prairie View and the state school for blacks, familiar to Lomax from the days at Texas A&M when he'd been sent there on inspection tours. That June seven hundred black teachers from rural Texas were gathered at Prairie View for a convention, and Lomax thought song pickings would be ripe. Instead, he found the assembly distrustful of whites and not inclined to perform the raw and more primitive music that he was interested in.

Two days of hard going netted only one song, although Lomax felt it to be it to be so entirely unique that it might "go sounding down the ages." This was important; he had learned only recently that one of the frontier songs he'd collected back in 1909 was becoming a hit around the country, and it irked him that he hadn't tried to stake some sort of claim to it. As it turned out, he was lucky his name wasn't on it—the song was "Home on the Range," and it shortly became the subject of a half-million-dollar legal wrangle, which led to the discovery that it was scarcely a folksong at all but had been "composed" in 1873 by a doctor out in Kansas and appeared in print the same year. Still, Lomax hated the thought of losing out on some unsuspected bonanza, and he clearly stated his intention to "protect for our benefit"—presumably through copyright—any promising material they turned up that summer.[23]

The music instructor at Prairie View, who styled himself "Professor," took the Lomaxes down into the Brazos River bottoms to look for a spiritual entitled "Deep River" that they had heard about. There a mulatto woman sang it for them with such power and beauty that it transported Lomax's imagination to the "turgid, slow-moving rivers in African jungles."[24] The local people, despite their uneasiness with whites, welcomed them hospitably, spreading out a fine supper that included fried chicken, corn on the cob, fresh milk, and peach preserves. That night Lomax and Alan set up their cots under the mulberry trees in the front yard.

The next day they dispensed with the services of the "Professor"; he had too many cultural pretensions to suit Lomax, who felt he belonged to that segment of blacks who were ashamed of their heritage and blind to the true artistic value of their vernacular music. They simply made fools of themselves, said Lomax, when they tried to imitate white music, with all its artifice and class snobbery.[25] Far more to his tastes was a guitar player they encountered. They accompanied him to a party that night, where he played for a throng of dancers who kept going until after midnight. As Lomax sat in the car outside and listened to the music and the dancers, he was again "carried across to Africa," envisioning tom-toms and savage bodies leaping and turning in the night. It was a rich and entirely new experience for him and Alan, he said, "amid a people we really knew little about."[26] This was a rare insight; only once or twice would he ever admit that in spite of his almost obsessive interest in blacks, there were profound differences between black and white culture that he couldn't understand.

From the river bottoms Lomax and his son drove to Galveston, slept on the beach, and treated themselves to breakfast at an oceanfront hotel. While Alan napped, his father visited with a woman he had known in his youth back in Bosque County. His hope of getting material from black longshoremen was ruined by the Fourth of July holiday; they went instead to a Negro church and spent the day listening to rousing sermons and many fine spirituals.[27]

Lomax observed that Alan was inclined to romanticize the conditions of the poor and rustic, and thus was disappointed that many of the blacks they had visited owned their farms and were relatively prosperous. Lomax himself was determined to penetrate further into more remote areas in his quest for "the folk songs of the Negro," whose great virtue, he felt, was that they were songs that "in musical phrasing and in poetic content, are most unlike those of the white race, the least contaminated by white influence or by modern Negro jazz."[28] So far he had had modest success with the blacks along the river bottoms, noting that their isolation from white society made them a good source for the sort of material he was searching for, but he was convinced that more fertile fields lay in the penitentiaries and prison farms, where the black convicts were kept in strict segregation from whites, and where the mere condition of their imprisonment isolated them from mainstream influences on the outside.[29]

The first large prison farm they encountered was Imperial, near Sugarland, Texas, where they spent a grueling day and evening adding several dozen songs to their collection. One of their best sources was a sixty-three-year-old convict named Iron Head—"a black Homer," as Lomax described him, whose singing moved him more than any he had heard in years. Another elderly prisoner, Clear Rock, knew enough songs, as Lomax said, "to fill a volume of 500 pages."[30]

The next day, from Darrington Prison Farm south of Houston, Lomax wrote to Engel at the Library of Congress, asking for a letter of introduction ("put on your seal and make the document as overpowering officially as possible")[31] for his use at other institutions down the line. He was anxious also to get the disc recording machine which Garwick was building; arrangements had been made for it to be shipped to Baton Rouge in time to meet them when they arrived there in mid-July. Meanwhile, the Dictaphone appeared to be working satisfactorily, although Lomax was staking a great deal on technical expertise back at the Library to salvage and reproduce the faint signals they'd managed to record on the fragile cylinders.

Headed east toward Louisiana, they visited a sawmill town and a turpentine distillery near the state line, deep in the piney woods of East Texas. There they located Henry Truvillion, a black worker of some prominence in the community. Truvillion, who headed a railroad track crew and preached on Sundays, would become one of Lomax's more abundant and enduring sources of work songs and chants, but their first session together was anything but auspicious. Initially, Mrs. Truvillion insisted that her husband sing only spirituals or "sanctified" songs, although her objections were shortly overcome. But the night was sultry and Truvillion would perform only inside his small house, with the doors and windows closed, for fear he would be expelled from his church if the members heard him singing "low-down blues."[32]

Still counting on a steamer trip up the Mississippi, Lomax worried that Alan wouldn't like traveling by boat, then realized that they didn't even know if passenger boats were still running on the river. And what would they do with the car? One of the things he loved about the trip, he said wryly, was that they had made little effort to find out such things in advance, and they never knew what the next bend of the road would bring.[33]

At Angola State Prison Farm near Baton Rouge, Louisiana, the two collectors spent several days recording both men and women inmates among the black population. They could work only in the evenings, because the prisoners were not allowed to sing in the fields. This circumstance also inhibited the process of creating new songs and transforming old ones; Lomax complained that at Angola "the fountains were drier" than they had been in Texas. But he told Miss Terrill that one man, who knew many songs, "almost supplied the deficiency." This was Huddie Ledbetter—known to his fellow prisoners as "Leadbelly"—around whom would later center one of the more glorious and stormy episodes of Lomax's career.

Lomax was so moved by the "restraint and sympathy" with which Leadbelly sang that he deliberated about trying to get him released from prison so that he could travel with the Lomaxes.[34] Unanswered was the question of just what function Lomax had in mind for the black songster. Was Leadbelly simply to join the Lomaxes as a part of their happy band, singing and strumming as they rolled across the country? Or would he constitute another hand to help with the driving, toting, and lifting and also, perhaps, put on a performance from time to time—for a paying audience? Or had Lomax almost instantly conceived the notion of making Leadbelly a "star" of national prominence? The only hint lies in a remark he wrote to Miss Terrill (deleted when he excerpted the letter for *Adventures of a Ballad Hunter*): "He sung us one song which I shall copyright as soon as I get to Washington and try to market in sheet music form."[35]

Just now, whatever plans Lomax had for Leadbelly would have to wait. He later said only that "the prison records proved . . . unfavorable," suggesting that Leadbelly was serving a long sentence with little chance of parole.[36] In fact, the Louisiana Board of Pardons had just recommended that Leadbelly's original six-to-ten-year sentence be commuted to three to ten years, which, with credit for time served, would make him eligible for parole within a year. What may have caused Lomax to hesitate was his discovery that Leadbelly had also been convicted of murder in Texas and had served part of a thirty-year sentence there. He would have to give more thought to this business of traveling around with an ex-convict prone to violence. Meanwhile, it was obvious that Leadbelly was a rich source of material, and they definitely wanted to visit him again later, especially in light of the uncertain results they were getting with their new recording machine.

. . . . .

Garwick's recorder, which had reached them in Baton Rouge, was an immediate disappointment. Described by its designer-manufacturer as "the first really portable recording instrument ever built," it weighed over three hundred pounds, in contrast to the one hundred pounds or less that Garwick had promised, and initial tests in a laboratory at Louisiana State University were unsatisfactory.[37] A week later the machine was still not working properly; as soon as they got one thing fixed, another conked out. Lomax urged that the Library not pay for the machine until it was operating correctly, and he insisted, to no avail, that Garwick meet them in Memphis and straighten everything out.[38]

In New Orleans, an old friend of Lomax's from the University of Texas got them admitted to the New Orleans Athletic Club, where they could swim and relax. He also supplied "a Plain Clothes man" to go with them into black districts in their quest for music from the "seamy side of negro life in the city."[39] But the sources of such music proved elusive—or wary of white men with strange recording machines. Alan reported only frustration and failure after a determined search of the red-light district, the French Quarter, and the steamboat docks; people were constantly telling him there was a singer just around the corner, but when he arrived with the recorder, the singer was gone or too busy to cooperate.[40] Father and son were already behind schedule—"but for the best of reasons," Lomax had been saying (i.e., they had struck rich lode, and working it took time).[41] Now the vein had thinned out, and to make matters worse, Lomax fell ill with a high fever and had to be taken to Tulane Hospital. He made a bad patient; Alan wrote to Miss Terrill pleading with her to use her "nimble pen" to persuade his father to stay in bed.[42] On another occasion, Alan reported that his hospitalized father had decided he was well enough to leave and asked for his clothes; when the nurses refused to bring them, he called a taxi and, in his bare feet and wearing only his nightshirt, marched downstairs, through the lobby, and into the waiting cab. "That's Father," said Alan, resignedly.[43]

Lomax's illness was a touch of malaria, complicated by what Alan referred to as "a bad attack of grippe," as well as neuritis, indigestion, and sciatica.[44] After several days of high fever, he began to show improvement—just as Alan took sick also and had to be hospitalized. Lomax got out of bed to nurse his son, but apparently suffered no lasting effects from this premature return to duty. He reported to Miss Terrill that he had had a fever of 104 for a solid week, but was now recovered except for "a drawn and somewhat pale face" and otherwise as hale and hearty as ever.[45] But plagued by so many setbacks, he gave up once more on his plan for a picturesque journey up the Mississippi by riverboat. It was just as well; by this time very few boats were still carrying passengers, and a vessel that would ferry Nancy Ford along with them was out of the question.

New Orleans had been a bust, "miserable in every respect."[46] As soon as Alan was well enough to travel, they took the highway north out of town, headed for prison farms in Mississippi. Arriving at Oakley, between Jackson and Vicksburg, on Sunday, August 6, they were able to record a number of fine spirituals sung by convicts in the dining hall. Garwick's machine was working better, but efforts to record choruses of a hundred or more were so muddled and distorted that Lomax began to experiment with smaller groups of eight or ten, with better results. On learning that each convict was given a permanent nickname as soon as he arrived—"Tight Eye," "Rat," "Breadline," "Log Wagon," "Iron Jaw," and so on—Lomax went to work gathering 5,000 examples for Kittredge, whose philological interests extended to unusual monikers.[47]

At Parchman State Penitentiary, northeast of Greenville, Lomax was moved by a sinister-looking inmate who sang "Midnight Special": "The simple directness and power of this primitive music, coupled with its descriptions of life where force and other elemental influences are dominating, impress me more deeply every time I hear it."[48] As each prisoner recorded, others drew around, forming an attentive, sometimes rapt, audience. But Lomax noticed that the white guards took little interest, watching the proceedings "condescendingly, sometimes with amused tolerance."[49] It puzzled him that the music which struck him as so rich and soul-stirring had no appeal for the jailers.

· · · · ·

Although Parchman proved to be fertile with material, conditions for recording it were poor. Because the male prisoners were in the fields from 4 A.M. until dark, they were available to the Lomaxes only at noon and in the brief period between supper and lights out. It was no wonder that the inmates were often reluctant or even silently hostile, for asking them to perform meant interrupting their mealtimes and rest periods. The Lomaxes put in long hours, munching quinine tablets and perspiring freely in the humid Delta heat, setting up their equipment in the mornings in the huge, open sewing-room, where the women inmates were allowed to sing spirituals while at their sewing machines, then moving on to the dining room to record at noon and again after the evening meal, often working until the men were sent to bed at nine o'clock. These sessions were grueling, Lomax complained, understandably if somewhat uncharitably, because the singers were often "timid, suspicious, sometimes stubborn, and of no help whatsoever."[50] He thought it would take a month or more to obtain everything available there, and that was time he and Alan didn't have. But of course their sources at Parchman were quite literally under lock and key, and many would be there for a long time to come. Parchman, like Angola, held buried treasure that they could come back to and dig up later.

Memphis, birthplace of the blues, seemed to offer great potential, but their street work in the black districts there produced even less than in New Orleans, probably because Lomax was in a hurry and had come to prefer prisons, where he literally had a captive audience and, to his mind at least, a purer strain of folksong. The Shelby County Workhouse and later the Tennessee State Penitentiary at Nashville yielded some results and "made a considerable addition to our store of 'ballets,'" as Lomax wrote to Miss Terrill.[51]

In Harlan, Kentucky, they rendezvoused with Harvey H. Fuson, a local lawyer and ballad enthusiast, compiler of *Ballads of the Kentucky Highlands* (1931), who put them up in his comfortable home and drove them about the countryside to look for song sources. With Fuson's help they found a rustic balladeer, James Howard, described by Lomax as "the blind bard, with a good voice, for whom we had been looking since we left Texas." Howard so enthralled them with his fiddle playing and "blood-stirring ballads of love and life in the mountains" that Alan filled all their remaining record blanks with his music.[52]

Alan had other pursuits as well, among them a beauteous country maiden, described by Lomax as "a mountain rose just emerging from the bud." She had appeared in the doorway of a remote cabin where they were recording one day, and "it was all over for Alan." He had a girlfriend back in Texas, of whom his father strongly disapproved, and all along the way Lomax encouraged any sort of dalliance that might weaken the attachment. With some glee he noted that upon espying the "mountain rose," Alan had disappeared that afternoon and again that night. "Now he is busy with plans to help her with her education, for she turns out to be artistic." Lomax resolved to urge matters along from a distance and "not to be intrusive."[53]

He was pushing his own *affaire de coeur* with even greater vigor. From the outset of the trip, back in June, he'd been writing long and effusive letters to Miss Terrill, invariably slipping some profession of his undying love into the detailed accounts of his and Alan's activities. Almost any excuse—such as the dangers of Alan's driving—would set him off: "Because Alan will drive recklessly and because you are a lovely person, I say now that I love you."

It had all the marks and reverberations of the Shirley Green affair thirty years before. Miss Terrill sent polite replies, addressed him as "Mr. Lomax," occasionally expressed concern for his welfare—the concern of a friend, nothing more—and carefully avoided any further familiarity. In the Shirley Green mode, she began to write to him of her "reticence and buried self," and he carefully set himself to drawing her out, promising patience, assuring her he wouldn't misjudge anything she cared to tell him. Another ploy was to ask her repeatedly if he should continue writing to her. She couldn't say yes, but she didn't want to say no. Eventually he elicited from her the mild assurance that if she continued to receive letters from him, "they will not be returned unopened." That kept him going, but by the time he and Alan reached Washington on August 23, she was still addressing him as "Mr. Lomax" and he was still complaining about "our one-sided correspondence."[54]

· · · · ·

In Washington, Lomax and his son found rooms in a boardinghouse on First Street S.E., four blocks from the Library of Congress. The recorded results of their travels—some one hundred songs on twenty-five aluminum and fifteen celluloid discs[55]—were deposited in the folksong archive at the Library, "where we have been provided every facility."[56] Right away they set to work compiling and refining their material for the book which would become *American Ballads and Folk Songs.* Engel, anxious to publicize any activity in the Archive, arranged what Lomax termed a public "recital" in the Coolidge Auditorium of the Library, during which Alan played records they had made and discussed their collecting activities. The demonstration was so well received that he was asked to repeat it, and Lomax glowed with fatherly pride.

Working on the book long hours each day to have it ready for the publisher by early October, Lomax made only vague plans for the future. Once the book was done, Alan might return to the Callaways' ranch in Texas, he wrote Miss Terrill, but definitely would not go back to the University; the boy needed to build up his health, and he would certainly benefit from being separated from the "extreme radicals and rebels against society" that he had associated with at college.[57] In light of later events, that seems to have been a father's wishful thinking more than anything else.

As for himself, Lomax told Miss Terrill only that, eager as he was for her company, he didn't know when he would get back to Texas. He had no clear professional plans beyond finishing the book, but was keeping various options open. All summer he had been promoting himself with Engel and Putnam, sending them newspaper clippings, publicity blurbs for his lectures, and any other news that depicted him in a favorable light. Had Gordon's connection with the Library not already been so insubstantial, this activity might be seen as part of a deliberate effort to force him out and take his place. But in fact Gordon had already forced himself out, even if he hadn't yet quite found the door. Lomax was simply positioning himself to fill a place already vacant. And while he may have coveted the prestige of a connection with the Library, his first priority was income, a source of steady salary, and he had no illusions about getting that as Honorary Curator of the Archive of American Folk Song, which he later referred to as "the biggest title and the smallest pay in the Government."[58]

Prestige seems about all he could have had in mind when, in early September, he set the wheels in motion by writing to Engel and offering to serve "without compensation" as a consultant to the Archive. This gave Engel the very opportunity he had been waiting for. If Lomax's offer was acceptable, he told Putnam, Gordon should be officially notified, by letter, that his services—volunteer or otherwise—were no longer needed: "This should terminate Mr. Gordon's 'Semi-official' status in which, I believe, he regards himself to be at present."[59]

· · · · ·

Two days later Putnam confirmed the appointment in a letter to Lomax, naming him "Honorary Conservator [*sic*] of our Archive of American Folk-Song, incidentally continuing, with our machine, at your own expense, to record and collect material in the field, and, while in Washington, assisting in the response to inquiries involving the Archive itself."[60] Regulations required that he be paid one dollar a month—a pittance but considerably more than the "dollar-a-year" men the Roosevelt administration was famous for—and the Library was given rights to copy any material Lomax had made prior to the appointment.

All this came as a great disappointment to Gordon, whose reclusive habits and consumption of alcohol steadily increased in the days that followed. It was only the most recent blow he had suffered. A few months earlier, Macmillan had rejected a book on which he had been collaborating, and, as his biographer suggests, he may have had reason to suspect that Lomax had some part in that affair as well. But, again, the evidence indicates only that Lomax was looking out for his own interests, anxious that his book in progress not be jeopardized by Macmillan's consideration of the Gordon project.[61] In any event, Gordon seemed to have forgotten what he had said to Engel when he first proposed the Archive of American Folk Song: "Let the best man have charge over it. I'll *bid* for the place, but cheerfully resign all claim if a better man can be found."[62] Engel and Putnam felt they had found that better man.

The provisions of Lomax's arrangement with the Library are worth noting. Critics eventually would accuse him of using government facilities for his own gain, to produce material that he later sold or leased. In fact, he was only continuing the arrangement originally put in place by Gordon. Lomax's original understanding with the Library, he wrote later, was simply that once the material they had gathered was archived, the Lomaxes would have first access to it and permission to transcribe it for publication (initially, in *American Ballads and Folk Songs*), in return for their contribution of "the fruits of our time, upkeep and other expenses."[63] Informal though it was, the agreement was from the beginning legal and aboveboard, an arrangement mutually beneficial to both parties. For essentially nothing, the Library got not only Lomax's expertise and labor but copies of everything he recorded—and felt it had gotten the best of the bargain. Lomax, in return for a nebulous title, the loan of a recording machine, and office help, was able to go on with his work of preserving rare and vanishing elements of American culture, while retaining control of his original recordings, to do with as he pleased. In the beginning he had paid all his own expenses, including the costs of record blanks and supplies. A year later, he began to receive minimal reimbursements for travel and supplies—administered through the Library but paid by private corporations, such as Carnegie and Rockefeller, not from government funds. Eventually, he was able to collect modest sums for his travel expenses from the Music Division budget, but only after he'd practically begged for allocations and then waded through endless red tape to get his money.

• • • • •

In early October, Lomax went to New York, accompanied by Alan and the manuscript of *American Ballads and Folk Songs* in a launderer's shirt box. He had insisted on delivering the manuscript to the publisher in person, and his editors at Macmillan responded by arranging a small ceremony in the office of vice-president H. S. Latham. Among those present were two prominent musicologists, Charles Seeger and Henry Cowell, whom Macmillan had brought in to look over the manuscript and offer their opinion on its merits. This did not set well with Lomax, and Alan's hackles immediately went up; he was already on edge from fatigue and the day's excitement, and he had no intention of putting their work in the hands of a couple of dreamy intellectuals. Seeger recalled the incident years later: "Part of the ceremonies was a presentation to us of the material by John and Alan, who was a young man and extremely belligerent once he saw these two highbrow musicians who were going to pass on something they knew nothing about." But Seeger and Cowell were so enthusiastic about the book that "John's truculence was immediately mollified, and even Alan came around eventually."[64]

Macmillan catered to them in other ways, or as Lomax said, "made a to-do over us."[65] They were guests of honor at a cocktail party, along with Charles and Mary Beard, whose new edition of *The Rise of American Civilization* had just appeared in the spring, and they were invited to play some of their records for a gathering in the home of James Putnam, assistant to Macmillan president George Brett Jr. They lunched with what Lomax termed "a group of distinguished musicians and music publishers of New York City" and were, in his estimation, big hits. He wrote Miss Terrill that his publisher thought the manuscript of *American Ballads and Folk Songs* "fascinating, even a great book." To Engel he said that was "blarney, perhaps; but pleasant to hear."[66]

Macmillan's Brett suggested that the Carnegie Corporation might be interested in contributing financial support for Lomax's future plans for field recording. He sent Lomax off with a letter of introduction to Frederick Keppel, Carnegie's head man in New York. Lomax was wary, remembering his failed efforts to get Carnegie money for *Cowboy Songs,* but he and Alan paid a visit to the corporation's offices on Fifth Avenue. Robert Lester, the executive to whom they talked, was not encouraging, but on their way out, he suggested that they submit a written application and indicate what their needs were. Lomax later sent him a request for $2,400, or two hundred dollars a month for the coming year, to defray travel expenses and pay for recording supplies.[67]

After the hectic events of the past several months, Lomax admitted to "frazzled nerves" and the need for rest and relaxation. At the same time he could hardly wait to get back into action. On their last night in New York, about to depart for the seclusion of suburban Rumford, Rhode Island, and the Oakleys' beautiful, roomy old New England manse, he dashed off for Miss Terrill his schedule of coming events. After resting briefly in Rumford, he said, they would squeeze in a visit to Harvard, then back to New York to work on publicity for the book; there he would read proofs, write five or six articles which he had sold, and set out to give a few lectures in various places. After Christmas there would be a hurried trip to St. Louis, where he was scheduled to read a paper at the annual meeting of the Modern Language Association.[68]

It was a daunting schedule for anyone half his age. Just one item on that busy agenda—those seemingly innocuous "few lectures"—would alone involve more wild and hectic adventure than most men experience in a lifetime. To Lomax, tearing around all over the country for weeks in a jitney Ford through raging blizzards was all in a day's work. He didn't even mention it in his autobiography.

CHAPTER NINETEEN

• • • • •

Wedlock

1933–34

Lomax's courtship of Ruby Terrill had been, if not entirely private, at least discreet. Miss Terrill, as dean of women of the University of Texas, a single woman of mature years and a prominent figure in local society, quite reasonably felt she had to observe the proprieties. But despite her strict silence on the subject of Lomax's attentions, Austin was already twittering with rumors. Campus gossips would like nothing better than to learn that the very proper and dignified dean of women, long held to be a confirmed spinster, was carrying on a flaming romance with none other than John A. Lomax, elderly literary lion, bon vivant, notable Texan.

As the pace of Lomax's professional activity quickened in the fall of 1933, so did his pursuit of Miss Terrill, despite his long absences from Austin. By October he was writing her almost every day, sometimes twice a day. All this mail coming from him to her office, she told him, would cause talk "and do me no good." But she didn't want him to stop writing, and after much consternation she decided that perhaps he should address some letters to her office and some to the Women's Faculty Club, where she lived. There was also the problem of his sister, Alice, whose pretensions to high society and yearnings for southern aristocracy were even greater than Lomax's. Alice Pedigo moved in many of the same church and social circles as Miss Terrill, and at a recent tea, "Mrs. Pedigo," as Miss Terrill always referred to her, had unwittingly confided that brother John was "happy over something else besides his book." Miss Terrill wanted to know how much Lomax had told his sister, "because fencing is not one of my accomplishments, especially fencing in the dark."[1]

Lomax may have recalled with dismay those long-ago tiffs with both Shirley Green and Bess Brown, who had also tried to keep their romances with him quiet; in any event, Miss Terrill's concern for appearances sent him into a livid huff. So long as he wanted to write to her, he stormed, and so long as she was willing to receive his letters, it was no one else's concern, and he cared not a whit what anyone said or thought. He hadn't breathed a word to Mrs. Pedigo, he said, and besides, "a hundred years from now who will bother about it?"[2]

In the face of this outburst, Miss Terrill's levelheadedness prevailed. She wrote him sternly that he was taking the whole thing much too seriously and tried to insist that she wasn't much concerned about secrecy.[3] But this bold front was largely for his benefit; she was far less comfortable with the situation than she would admit. In resolving this little spat, however, they had moved one step closer to becoming, openly and publicly, a Couple.

· · · · ·

In mid-October, Lomax's restful interlude with the Oakleys in Rumford drew to a close. Unhappy with the recording machine, he arranged for Garwick to meet him at the Library of Congress to discuss an overhaul—and then took the machine away with him to Cambridge because he couldn't resist showing off his work to Kittredge. While there he scheduled lectures at Brown and Yale for the coming week, but his biggest coup involved his old mentor. Kittredge, "the great George Lyman," agreed to write a foreword to *American Ballads and Folk Songs,* Lomax wrote elatedly to Miss Terrill.[4] He may have been less elated to find, months later, that Kittredge's foreword amounted to a single very perfunctory paragraph (which began, "Professor Lomax needs no introduction").

On the first of November, he lectured and Alan sang at the monthly luncheon of Manhattan's Texas Exes. That night they entertained at the National Arts Club and the next day headed north, retracing their route to Harvard, where Kittredge had arranged for Lomax to speak at a conference of modern language scholars. Kittredge introduced him, he told Miss Terrill, with more effusive praise than he had ever expected from the Great Man. "Hear me strut!" he said.[5] Dean Briggs reported the event to Johnny Lomax, who was in Kansas City with the RFC auditing crew: "Your father looks like a new man. . . . His search for ballads evidently agrees with him; I hope this book will give him not fame merely, but good royalties."[6]

From Cambridge, Lomax and Alan drove through the snow-clad Berkshire hills to Poughkeepsie for a lecture at Vassar, where Alan "made a hit with the Vassarites," and a coed from Texas flattered Lomax no end by telling him she was sending a 300-word report of his lecture to the *Dallas News.*[7] Then they were off on the sort of dizzy, loop-the-loop itinerary that only John Lomax could devise. Hurtling into the night for a 400-mile trip to northwestern New York state, they got only as far as Albany before running into heavy snow. A lecture was scheduled there at the State College two days hence, but in the meantime Lomax's itinerary called for a swing west to Rochester and points beyond, then back through the Finger Lakes district for other lecture dates. Their rescuer in Albany was Prof. Harold Thompson, who had volunteered to do the bibliography for *American Ballads and Folk Songs;* Alan and Nancy Ford were left in the care of Thompson and his family while Lomax caught the train and rode all night to Rochester. There he took a bus to Brockport, twenty miles away, for a lecture at 10:00 A.M. From Brockport he went helter-skelter by several busses to Keuka College, in the Finger Lakes district, to lecture that evening. The next morning, "three kind ladies" drove him over icy roads to a distant bus station. He rode all day to get back to Albany in time for his lecture at 8:00 P.M. Alan, he said, "made the hardship worthwhile by forgetting himself and hugging me."[8]

After Albany, they were all over the place—a 500-mile, five-day drive south to West Virginia Wesleyan College at Buckhannon, in a snowstorm and raging wind "that threatened to blow us down the mountain,"[9] then north again, into mountainous western Pennsylvania—and the worst November blizzard in the history of the region. Their objective was Allegheny College at Meadville, three hundred miles away in the far northwestern corner of the state.

Lomax complained of Alan's madcap driving, missing no opportunity to play on Miss Terrill's sympathy with images of a crashed and crumpled Nancy Ford, sirens and flashing lights, carnage on the highway. But as Alan guided the trusty little car through the howling storm and into Meadville on time, Lomax spoke admiringly of his son's steady hand at the wheel.[10] Their visit to Meadville yielded a small bonus in the form of a previously uncollected stanza of "The Ballad of the Erie Canal," discovered in the college library.[11]

By this time Lomax had covered so much ground in so short a time that he scarcely knew where he was. Passing through Maumee, Ohio, he wrote several letters datelined "Maumee, Illinois" and sent random pages from two different letters to Carl Engel, who couldn't make heads or tails of what Lomax wanted him to do. This was scarcely a sign of approaching senility; Lomax had been doing the same kind of thing for years.

The weary travelers got a brief respite along the way to Chicago when they stopped off in Harbert, Michigan, to visit the Carl Sandburg family at their home nearby on a high bluff overlooking Lake Michigan. It was the ideal place, Lomax wrote Miss Terrill, for "a dreamer who loves water and trees and graceful sand dunes." Sandburg, "quiet, laconic, kindly," greeted them warmly, and shortly Alan was calling him "Carl" and deep into arcane discussions of literature and philosophy. Lomax was mightily pleased when Sandburg remarked that he appeared healthier and more energetic than ever, a circumstance which Lomax attributed to "a single fact"—namely, Miss Terrill.[12]

Lomax had left Washington and New York with the understanding that he would return for a week or so to clean up unfinished business. Now he was "tired of the automobile" and anxious to see Miss Terrill, and for a few days he entertained hope that the trip back East could be deferred. But Engel kept sending out anxious inquiries, addressed to Macmillan or Texas or wherever he thought Lomax might be, wanting to know what the new honorary curator's plans were, when he would return to Washington, and just where was he, anyway? It was not much different from the days when Gordon was in charge of the Archive.

Finally, Lomax had to backtrack into Michigan for a lecture at the Detroit Institute of Arts, and once there he decided it would be easier to return to the East and take care of matters at Macmillan and the Archive than have to interrupt his collecting work after the first of the year. He hoped to be back in the field in Texas by the middle of December, recording inmates he and Alan had located at various prison farms during the summer.

The Detroit date turned out to be a disappointment. "Extravagant advertising" (which Lomax claimed was an embarrassment) turned out a large crowd, but they were markedly cool to his lecture. Nor was it any comfort to reflect that after proclaiming his love for Miss Terrill for six months, he was still lying awake at night fretting that he had "failed to evoke from you any response."[13]

By Thanksgiving he and Alan were back in Manhattan. There they went over the recording machine carefully with Garwick, who again assured them that its faults were minor and would be corrected. Then they drove to Washington so Lomax could straighten out the confused instructions he had mailed to Engel while on the road. Among other things, he wanted Engel's approval for Garwick to ship the recording machine to him in Texas, and he hoped to enlist the Library's support in squeezing money from the Carnegie Corporation or the Rockefeller Foundation—or any other source—to support his collecting efforts. Engel would see that the machine was shipped, but he was noncommittal on the matter of financial support, having been through all that with Gordon. By December 7 the Lomaxes were on their way to Texas by way of Tennessee, to catch up again with rambling Johnny Lomax, who had just been dispatched to Nashville by the RFC.

A week later they passed through Austin and spent the night with the Dobies. Lomax called briefly on Miss Terrill, and the next day father and son were on the road to Lubbock to spend Christmas with the Mansells. There Nancy Ford was retired from active service, replaced by a new blue sedan of the same make, the color of which, said Lomax, he had selected because it was "the favorite color of my favorite lady."[14] Although his visit with Miss Terrill had lasted only an hour or two, much transpired in that time. The next morning, as he sped west toward Lubbock, she composed for him a summary of their discussion the night before: "You love me, and I am not without some feeling of interest in you." She was still addressing him as "Mr. Lomax," but her tone was decidedly warmer, and a few days later she wondered if the lyrical feeling inside her was "in response to you, love in general, or to you, John A. Lomax, my lover in particular."[15] Figuratively, Lomax pitched his hat in the air; he knew he was home and dry. But Miss Terrill still resisted any public announcement, and Lomax himself was much concerned about breaking the news to his family.

· · · · ·

Back in November, Johnny had written from Kansas City, "Father, I am certainly proud of you. I have never known anyone who has shown such courage and ability to pull himself together after as many discouraging reverses as have you. A mere 2 years ago you were at the lowest ebb of your life, but now you are not only back on your feet but have accomplished some of the best feats of your already outstanding life."[16] To which Lomax might well have responded, in the manner of Al Jolson in *The Jazz Singer,* "You ain't heard nothin' yet."

The next triumph came just after Christmas. The scene was St. Louis and the annual meeting of the Modern Language Association, which Lomax had not attended in years. Now he was on the program, to discuss his recent fieldwork and present a paper entitled "Songs from Negro Convict Camps." In addition to Alan (who was to sing and demonstrate the equipment), he brought with him "the girls"—Bess Brown Jr., Shirley, and Shirley's two-year-old daughter, Patricia, who would visit with Uncle "Allie" and Aunt Louise Brown while Lomax and Alan attended the meeting. Allie Brown had risen through the ranks to become a senior vice-president of the Missouri Pacific Railroad in St. Louis; as in-laws, he and Lomax had always gotten along well, and their fondness for each other was undiminished by Bess's death.

Immediately following his talk on the morning of December 29, Lomax was taken aside by a distinguished gentleman who turned out to be David Stevens, director of the Humanities Division of the Rockefeller Foundation. Stevens offered his compliments on the talk and said, "I wonder if you would like to have the Rockefeller Foundation finance your project?" Stevens was vague about the terms, but Lomax was nevertheless elated. It was the best Christmas gift he'd gotten in years, he told Johnny, although it placed him in the quandary of having to decide whether to base his operations in Dallas, Austin, or Washington, D.C.[17]

Like so many Lomax episodes, this one turned out to be part serious drama, part opéra bouffe. When he returned triumphantly to the Browns' home to report the good news, he walked into a family fracas. At the center, apparently, was little Patricia, who from all accounts was a handful, in the throes of the "terrible twos" and much accustomed to having her way. This did not accord well with Aunt Louise, who, as Lomax later stated bluntly to Johnny, "could not stand Pat." Lomax's tolerance for Aunt Louise was equally thin. In a fit of pique, he "loaded up my crowd" and drove away in the middle of the afternoon—a clear sign, among Texans of his generation, of the depth of the insult, even though it meant putting up "the girls" at an expensive hotel.[18]

The funding situation began to have ludicrous moments of its own when the news came from the Carnegie Corporation, through its director, Frederick W. Keppel, that the Carnegie board had responded almost simultaneously to Lomax's application with a one-year grant of $3,000. Suddenly there was an embarrassment of riches—and more than just embarrassment for officials at the Library of Congress, who worried that Lomax was drumming up support on his own and accepting deals from one benefactor without telling the other. The fear was that he—and the Library—would be accused of double-dipping, and they would lose both sources of support. Herbert Putnam insisted that Lomax straighten things out immediately (although Engel was already plotting ways to spend both grants and fretting over which to keep if they could have only one). Lomax, who rightly felt that his dealings with both Carnegie and Rockefeller had been aboveboard, was mostly worried about where he was going to be based—Stevens had approved the present arrangement with the Library of Congress, but also hinted that Lomax might be attached to either Harvard or the University of Texas. Confusion reigned; memos and letters flew—all further complicated because Lomax was now back in Texas and rambling around from place to place; most of the time no one knew where he was.[19]

When the dust settled some weeks later, it all seemed quite pointless. Initially Engel and Putnam had favored Stevens's offer over the Carnegie's (if they couldn't have both), for while Stevens had not yet mentioned a figure, there was the clear implication that support from the Rockefeller Foundation might be long-term, while the Carnegie grant was for one year only. In the event, however, there was an considerable gap between what Stevens promised (or appeared to promise) and what Rockefeller delivered. It turned out to be a one-time, lump sum payment of $350, rather than the five-year grant Stevens had hinted at.[20]

Lomax wistfully acknowledged the Rockefeller's modest gift, clearly let down but careful not to bite the hand that fed.[21] In the end, the Carnegie grant, doled out through the Library in quarterly installments of $750, paid for a substantial part of Lomax's travel expenses, while the Rockefeller money went for recording accessories and rebuilding the back of his new Ford to accommodate the recording apparatus on a solid framework.

It is worth noting that while the Carnegie grant was eventually (and only by chance) administered through the Library of Congress, in his original conversation with Carnegie executive Robert Lester, Lomax had been told that he was free to deposit his material wherever he wished, and Lester had even suggested either the University of Texas or Harvard. In Lomax's eyes, it was only a matter of circumstance—and convenience—that the Library of Congress became the depository, largely because of "the friendly attitude of Mr. Engel and Mr. Putnam."[22] In later years, whenever he grew disenchanted with the Library, he would not hesitate to remind its officials of that circumstance.

· · · · ·

Meanwhile, production of *American Ballads and Folk Songs* was moving along, with publication expected sometime in the spring or summer. Galley proofs began arriving in January, and by the end of the month Lomax had submitted all the front matter, including his introduction and Kittredge's brief foreword. With the help of Engel's assistant, Edward Waters, in the Music Division of the Library, he had located a Washington, D.C., music teacher, Mary Gresham, to do the musical transcriptions for the book. That work also seemed to be progressing well. Later there would be problems, and the arrangement with Gresham was one that both Waters and Lomax regretted. She proved to be poorly qualified, particularly with African-American music, and the transcriptions in *American Ballads and Folk Songs* are the weakest of any Lomax book. Asked about Gresham many years later, Waters said only, "Terrible woman."[23]

As he worked on proofs and other details of the book, Lomax had additional literary matters to deal with. His lecturing and collecting activities during the past two years had revived the notoriety that had been his for a few years in the teens, in the wake of *Cowboy Songs*. Mail came from dozens of collectors and scholars, as well as from a vast panoply of would-be collectors, enthusiastic old-timers, oddballs, and dilettantes—typified by one Ethel Matthews Casey of San Antonio, who had heard Lomax speak and was inspired to write a piece on "ranch life and cowboy songs" for the Scribbler's Club of the Junior League.[24] Would he be interested in seeing it, and could he advise her about publication? He wasn't, and he didn't.

By this time Lomax had become a habitual nomad, "living in a Ford with a lot of machinery and two rusty valises" (as he told Johnny),[25] carrying his work with him and holing up here and there to read proof, answer mail, and have his laundry done. The House in the Woods was leased, and his mailing address had become simply "c/o University Station, Austin, Texas." He was rarely there, but more often there than any other place—to see Miss Terrill, of course.

When he drove out to Lubbock in mid-January, he had more than routine business on his mind. Shirley noticed that her father seemed unusually preoccupied and silent. After a time, he indicated, rather mysteriously, that he wanted to talk to her—alone. So alone, in fact, that she was instructed to drive them out of town, off across the open plains, and down a deserted country road. At last he told her to stop, miles from anywhere. Solemnly he began: "You know, I've been seeing Miss Ruby Terrill. I must ask you very seriously—Miss Terrill refuses to marry me unless she has your consent and John's."

Shirley, who had been much disturbed by his behavior and expected the worst, almost burst out laughing with relief. She was delighted, she told him. "We were all just crazy about Miss Terrill," she said later.[26] In due time Johnny wrote from Chicago to give the match his blessing as well and to praise Miss Terrill for her "wonderful spirit of sacrifice" and "true nature and character" in agreeing to marry his father. Reporting this to Lomax, Miss Terrill said, "Does one make a sacrifice when she takes to herself the most delicious piece of fruit in the bowl?"[27] When she at last told her office assistant that she was marrying John Lomax—ending weeks of speculation and rumor—the woman blurted out, "Well, *that* ought to be an interesting experience."[28]

If Miss Terrill had had little exposure to domestic matters, she learned fast. As the time approached for Lomax and Alan to appear in Austin for a lecture and demonstration at the Women's Open Forum, of which she was a member, she reminded Lomax to dress well and wear the dark suit that she liked, with black shoes. Pointedly she remarked that she wouldn't be on the platform with him, where she could brush the cigar ashes off his vest. But perhaps it was enough for him to know that as a member of the audience, "I shall have to assume my pokerest of faces, but all the time I shall be loving you."[29] Lomax told her to inform the "program lady" not to expect him until the very last minute, protesting that he dreaded the time just before he was to go on and hated anything connected with speaking in public or the stage.[30] It was a protest he'd been making throughout a quarter-century of lecture engagements.

• • • • •

Ten days later, in early February, he and Alan and their recording equipment were on the road again, headed for San Antonio and other places in southwest Texas where they hoped to record Hispanic material. In the San Antonio area he planned to record some of the local *Pastores,* folk material depicting the events of the Nativity in song and recitation and handed down within families for many generations. Initially their luck ran foul; in Cotulla, south of San Antonio, the recording machine wouldn't work, and Alan fretted over it endlessly while their timid group of singers milled about and Lomax stood around and tried to look important. With them was Frank Dobie's brother, Richard, an old cowman who was fluent in Spanish and who, according to Lomax, sang better than some Mexicans. Richard Dobie was suspicious of the whole affair, especially when the machine wouldn't work and the other singers drifted away. But finally a loose connection was located, and they were able to record Dobie singing two fine songs. That night they made several records of *Los Pastores,* although Lomax felt that the singers were "constrained, timid, impassive."[31]

The next day they drove to Laredo. Alan was anxious to record the vaqueros on the King Ranch, so after a leisurely lunch across the border in Nuevo Laredo, accompanied by liberal glasses of Mexican beer, they went on to Corpus Christi, where Lomax enlisted the aid of his old college roommate, Edward Kleberg, a distant relative of the King Ranch Klebergs. This brought them an invitation to lunch with another socially prominent

Kleberg relative, as well as an introduction to Robert Kleberg, general manager of the ranch. But they drove to Kingsville in a cold rain only to be politely turned away. Lomax appealed to Carl Engel for help—Robert Kleberg's brother, Richard, was a member of the U.S. Congress and supposedly a fancier of Mexican folksongs; Lomax was sure that if Engel would only invite him to lunch at the Library, Richard Kleberg would pull strings for them. And perhaps Sen. Tom Connally ought to be courted as well, said Lomax: "He is helping me in other directions."[32] But nothing came of these political maneuvers. According to Frank Goodwyn, who grew up in Kingsville and traveled with Lomax in the late 1930s, Lomax "never did get on the King Ranch" despite several attempts.[33]

From Kingsville, Lomax and his son went to Port Aransas, located on San Jose Island off the Texas coast, hoping to find old fishermen who had learned sea shanties in the course of their travels, but that trip was also a failure. They had dinner with friends in Port Aransas, then beat a hasty retreat to San Antonio and the comforts of the Menger Hotel. Two days later Lomax was back in Austin, "tired and half-sick."

Miss Terrill made amends. In the spasmodic diary he was trying to keep, Lomax recorded that he saw her twice, had lunch with her in the country, "and enjoyed her to the utmost." And on Valentine's Day, two days later: "Miss Terrill has asked me to eat sandwiches . . . with her on top of Mt. Bonnell."

For some time Lomax had been working on the itinerary of another crazy-quilt lecture tour in March, beginning with a Texas Exes dinner in Comanche on March 2, then extending to eastern Kentucky and back to the Midwest. This tour was still taking shape in late February when he announced to Miss Terrill that he was entering Baylor Baptist Hospital in Dallas for an operation "to correct a minor ailment."[34] He would spend only four days in the hospital, he said.

A week later he was still there and in no condition to leave.[35] It fell to Alan explain to Miss Terrill, matter of factly, that his father been operated on for hemorrhoids. The early prognosis was good, and Alan assured her that his father's doctor was the best in Texas. The morning after surgery Lomax was still planning to leave the hospital a day early to keep his lecture date in Comanche. Then it became obvious that the operation had been a greater ordeal than he'd expected. And, as Alan and Miss Terrill knew only too well, he was "the worst patient in the world."[36] As the days and nights of pain and sleeplessness dragged on, he announced that he had absolutely no confidence in the judgment of the doctor Alan thought the best in Texas, and the hospital was "the cruelest place on earth."[37] One consolation was a dutiful black orderly whom Lomax, for whatever reasons, had dubbed "Boll Weevil." There was also Alan. Despite a recent spat with his father, Alan stood by loyally, spending hours every day at the hospital, reading proofs on their forthcoming book whenever there was a lull, and doing his best to cope with the world's worst patient. Boll Weevil assured Lomax that he was making a speedy recovery, but Lomax grew increasingly fretful and difficult as the pain lingered and it became clear that he would have to cancel several of his upcoming lectures. He denounced his doctor as being "cruelly inattentive."[38] The four-day hospital stay grew to five, then seven, and finally nine.

Still shaky after ten days but well enough to leave, he took Boll Weevil with him as a private nurse and checked into a tourist camp, which he said was "1000% better than the cross, cruel, impolite Baylor Baptist Hospital."[39] The doctor had told him that he couldn't ride in a car for at least another week, but by this time Lomax was so sure that the man was a quack that he paid little heed to anything he said. In fact, almost two weeks went by before Lomax could pull himself together and get back on the road—and only then because he was scheduled to give the prestigious Moody Lecture at the University of Chicago. With Alan at the wheel, he set out on the 1,000-mile journey still weak and in severe discomfort.

Despite a spring blizzard and other hazards, his lectures along the way went well, and the Moody Lecture, highlighted by Alan's singing, was enthusiastically received. The only disappointment was that they missed seeing Johnny, who had been working in Chicago but was transferred to Brooklyn just a few hours before they arrived in the Windy City.

Because of the weather, Lomax decided to leave Alan and the car in Chicago while he took the train to fill lecture dates through the upper Midwest. The plan was for Alan to meet him at Des Moines, where they would travel on to Omaha in the car and then home to Texas.

All that was seriously jeopardized the night after Lomax left, when Alan parked the new Ford momentarily outside Burton Hall at the University of Chicago, went inside for a few minutes, and came out to find the car stolen. He reported the theft to the police, then went to bed troubled and dispirited. Informed the next morning that the car had been recovered, he streaked off to the storage garage where it had been hauled, to discover that while the car was essentially intact except for a slashed tire, everything in it was gone—his suitcase and all his clothes, books, sheet music, and guitar. (Fortunately, the recording machine had been left in Texas for repair work.)

Putting the car back on the road cost Alan $18.66—$14.16 for a tire and tube and the rest for hauling and storage ("excessive," he thought, "but there was nothing to do").[40] Lomax later counted the cost at $150 and complained that the incident further spoiled a trip he had undertaken on nerve alone, "in pain almost constantly." Nevertheless, he reported triumphantly to Johnny that he had delivered ten lectures in seven states, traveled more than 4,000 miles, grossed $750, lost seventeen pounds, "and yet have a little life left."[41] But he was through lecturing for the year; he and Alan, he told Engel, "will give through 1934 all our time to folk-song collecting."[42]

• • • • •

On Saturday, March 31, some eighty of Austin's most socially prominent women and a dozen out-of-town guests gathered in the new union building of the University of Texas for a gala luncheon, the purpose of which was to announce the engagement and forthcoming marriage—"early this summer, the definite date to be set soon"—of Miss Ruby Terrill to Mr. John A. Lomax. The groom-to-be was not present; it was strictly a women's "do," and, anyway, he avoided such events, whether he was the object of attention or not. Fittingly, however, the University Men's Glee Club sang "songs of the range" taken from his books. The story was carried next day (alas, April Fool's) in all the Texas papers; the *Fort Worth Star-Telegram* called it "an event of statewide interest."

In honor of the occasion, Lomax tarried in Austin two days, then he and Alan were on the road again, making the rounds of Texas prison farms. This time they carried a note of introduction from Lee Simmons, head of the farm system, which Lomax hoped would open doors and insure cooperation. Despite this strongly worded message to all farm managers—"I am expecting and am sure you will cooperate with Mr. Lomax in every respect"—father and son still met with a great deal of what Lomax termed "cold indifference" and even "badly concealed contempt."[43] Their warmest reception was at Clemons Prison Farm near Brazoria, where they were guests of the manager and his wife. But collecting efforts among the inmates produced only fair results; they found numerous variants to lyrics already collected, but few new tunes.[44]

Lomax's efforts to keep a diary of this trip lasted only a few weeks. Invigorated by the resumption of fieldwork in April, he made a few more entries, then gave it up entirely. The man who habitually scribbled off five or six long, detailed letters almost every day of his life had found that the task of keeping a diary, "for one so unmethodical," was next to impossible.[45]

One event that may have interrupted his diary-keeping was the annual meeting of the Texas Folklore Society in Austin on April 19 and 20. The society celebrated its twenty-fifth anniversary that year, and the meeting climaxed with a Founders' Dinner honoring Lomax and L. W. Payne for their organizational efforts in the fall of 1909. Ninety-one members and guests—the largest assemblage in the society's history—gathered at the University YMCA for the dinner and program, which included a talk by Dr. Payne on the history of the society. J. Frank Dobie generously characterized Payne's talk as "charming and vivacious" (elsewhere he was known to remark that "nothing can be duller than Dr. Payne").[46] Lomax gave an account of his recent travels in a paper entitled "Folk-Lore Trails." Payne and Lomax were made Life Members of the society, and a copy of *American Ballads and Folk Songs,* much heralded but yet unborn, was awarded to the guest who offered the best old-time saying or proverb.

Unhappily for Lomax, there was to be no picnic on Mt. Bonnell with Miss Terrill this time. In a momentary reversal of roles, she was the gadabout traveler now, off to St. Louis for a convention of the American Association of University Women, while he cooled his heels in Austin and settled for nostalgia with the TFS. But she sent a wire that reached him just before the dinner—"It breaks my heart that I can not be present"—and that was consolation.

There was little comfort, however, in news from Macmillan of continuing problems with the production of *American Ballads and Folk Songs.* A major cause of delay was the preparation of the music, which had to be handset from a limited supply of type, and the type which was set into forms could not be reused until proofs had been made, sent out for corrections, and returned. Lomax's hectic way of life and desultory habits contributed to the problem; an assistant at Macmillan finally had to tell him bluntly that his failure to return music proofs was holding up everything.[47] Lomax tried to foist off the blame on Ed Waters, but Waters insisted that he never kept proofs more than one day before passing them on to Mary Gresham. Finally on May 3, Waters was able to wire Lomax: "MARYS PROOFS OFF TODAY IN TOUCH WITH MACMILLAN DELAY ENDED." But the difficulties with *American Ballads and Folk Songs* were far from over.

Another continuing problem was Garwick's now-infamous recording machine, which had never worked properly for any length of time. While his father fretted with music proofs and other matters, Alan ("in despair," said Lomax) had taken the machine to the physics department at the University of Texas. There he had the good fortune to meet a young adjunct professor named Paul Boner, who in time would become recognized internationally for his work in acoustics. Boner looked over Garwick's device and pronounced it "something resembling junk." The amplifier design was outdated, the transformers were of poor quality, the switches were too small for the currents involved, and the wiring was badly done. Moreover, the system was designed for a carbon microphone, poorly suited for the kind of recording Lomax wanted to do. The whole thing, said Boner, was so cheap and in such bad shape that no amount of work would make it operate properly.[48]

Reporting all this to Engel, Lomax hoped to impress him by attributing Boner's expertise to the fact that he was "a Ph.D. graduate of the Physics Department of Harvard University."[49] (Boner had been a Whiting Fellow at Harvard in 1927–28, but all his degrees, including the Ph.D. in 1929, were from the University of Texas.) Engel's initial response was to defend Garwick: "Whatever the initial faults of the machine may have been, I daresay that the roads of Texas may have had something to do with the final breakdown."[50] Garwick mounted a sustained defense of his own, and although Lomax told Engel at one point that Boner was building them a new machine, it turned out that he had only reconditioned and rebuilt the old one.[51] The Lomaxes were still struggling with Garwick's apparatus as late as November, and Garwick was still sending instructions to Lomax in the field, explaining the operation of his machine, and insisting that "your professor is wrong."[52]

While Lomax visited relatives in Meridian, Alan attended to the myriad details of preparing for their next field expedition. There were notes from the previous trip to be brought up to date and records to be transcribed. He helped Boner with the recorder, got their camera repaired, and ran tests to see that everything worked. The back seat of the car was removed and a rack constructed to hold the recorder—no easy task in the confined rear end of the small tudor Ford.

• • • • •

By early June they were in southern Louisiana, headed for the area around New Iberia—"the Evangeline country," as Lomax romantically reminded his correspondents. It proved to be a fertile area for folksong collecting, and they spent several busy weeks there.

At Avery Island, some six miles south of New Iberia, they were guests of E. A. McIlhenny, maker of McIlhenny's Tabasco Sauce and a dedicated ballad hunter who had previously given a collection of spirituals to the Library of Congress. He was veritable lord of the domain at Avery Island (which, despite its name, is not an island at all but a massive upraised salt dome, surrounded by marshlands and covered with fields and meadows). There McIlhenny presided over the pepper fields which produced his family's famous hot sauce, a huge rookery populated by thousands of egrets, herons, and ibis, 250 acres of tropical gardens which he had planted in exotic vegetation, and a large salt mine, reputedly the oldest in the western hemisphere.[53] Through an exchange of letters, Lomax had learned also that McIlhenny had gone on scientific expeditions to the Arctic, where he lived six years with "the Esquimaux." He knew dozens of their songs and promised to record them on Lomax's machine.

They had no sooner arrived and set up operations on the McIlhenny estate when a violent rainstorm soaked all their clothing and equipment except the recording machine. When the clouds had passed, McIlhenny sent them off to the home of an elderly black woman, Alberta Bradford, who had been a slave, "a right big girl when the Yankees came down," she said. Alberta knew many Negro spirituals and had once sung with another ancient ex-slave; between them they were reputed to know more than a hundred "before the War" songs. But the other woman's whereabouts were not clearly known, and it was not even certain that she was still alive. Alan drove off with Alberta to look for her, leaving Lomax beside the road because there was no room for him in the car ("Alberta is hefty," he wrote to Miss Terrill). After waiting several hours, he sat down and wrote some letters, then walked five miles to a country café, had a glass of orange juice to cool off, and went to see a John Barrymore movie. There was still no sign of Alan, so he walked on two miles to the place where they were making their camp.[54]

Activity picked up considerably in the days following. They eventually spent four or five weeks in Louisiana and returned with several dozen recordings.[55] Getting these involved grand adventures among colorful sources; among those reported to Miss Terrill were Ovide, an accordion player who also sang; a blind Cajun minstrel; a Negro play party; a four-foot hunchback—"a merry old maid of 45 years"; and a rural quartet of accordion, guitar, violin, and "iron," the latter played (or struck) by a sad-eyed little boy. At one event a large blond woman of German extraction kept the crowd entertained with her antics, while her daughter, "fourteen, handsome, dimpled, fully grown," attracted Alan's attention. The Negro play party, "a wild barbaric scene such as I have seldom witnessed," kept them up, recording, until two A.M. The pace intensified as time passed; on their last day in the New Iberia region, Lomax got up early to drive to a plantation twenty miles away with their chief songster, who produced four English and three French songs of considerable interest. An elderly Cajun sang songs his grandmother had taught him, and in the afternoon they drove thirty miles in a different direction to meet another group of promising informants. At six P.M. Lomax was finally back to camp, "where our engagements will likely keep us going until midnight."[56]

Near the end of their time in Louisiana, their car overturned on a country road, damaging the recording machine and spilling battery acid on most of their clothing. Everything was restored to working order within a few days, and they resumed their recording work.[57] At the end of June, they packed up and headed for the Angola Prison Farm, where Lomax had unfinished business with Huddie "Leadbelly" Ledbetter, the talented black singer they had encountered there the previous year. A week later, on July 6, Lomax wired Miss Terrill from Houston, "HARD TIMES DONE . . . HOME AND YOU PERHAPS TONIGHT."

. . . . .

The wedding date had been set for July 21. As the time approached, Lomax again sought to clarify his relationship with the Library of Congress. From New Iberia he had written to Engel that the prospect of again making a home for Bess Jr. and Alan once more raised the question of where he should base his operations. Gingerly, he indicated that he might be willing to live in Austin *or* in Washington, according to Engel's preferences, but "wherever this home is, I as a field worker must stay in the field," and he pointed out that Texas was more centrally located for his work than was Washington. He ventured also to ask that Engel elevate his position from that of mere "Honorary Curator" to "Archivist," presumably with the assumption that the latter would carry with it a regular salary, instead of the token $1.00 a month he was being paid as honorary curator. But this proposal was also cautiously voiced. If this was not a good time to discuss such matters, he said, Engel should just ignore that part of his letter.[58]

Engel thought this was as good a time as any for discussion. Taking up the matter with Librarian Putnam, he acknowledged the value of Lomax's fieldwork and more or less endorsed the idea of making him archivist—but with certain conditions. The overriding need, he said, was for someone permanently based in Washington to administer the Archive of American Folk Song, and Lomax's "heart is evidently with the University of Austin [*sic*]." It was much the same problem he'd had with Robert Winslow Gordon: "With Mr. Lomax's avowed preference for field work and with his obvious inclination to restrict his work to the Southern states [Engel told Putnam], he would not be in a position to *direct* the work of the Archive such as we have conceived it. There should be someone in charge of the whole enterprise who will not only attend to the necessary correspondence *from here,* but who will be able to direct *other workers* in *other* regions than those covered by Mr. Lomax, so that the entire country may eventually be canvassed."[59] This did not rule out Lomax's suggestion about being made archivist, Engel said, so long as there was a qualified assistant, "permanently in residence here," to handle administrative matters.

"Archivist" was Lomax's own term; Putnam interpreted it as "Director of the Archive" ("which is, I suppose, what Dr. Lomax would have in mind"). He concurred with Engel's view of the matter, but in any event the question was moot. There was no money in the budget for the coming year to pay Lomax a salary, in any capacity. Putnam would continue to request funds for an assistant's position in future budgets, but as long as Lomax was getting support from outside sources, Putnam saw no way of "assigning to him a place upon our regular roll, or a compensation." Thus, "There would seem no propriety in dropping the honorary."[60] So long as Lomax was willing to work for a dollar a month and a mostly empty title, the Library of Congress was happy to have him.

Engel conveyed this to Lomax in the best possible light, generously allowing that, since the Library wasn't paying him anything, it could hardly tell him where to live. "Naturally, we should welcome having you nearer at hand; but whether or not you choose Washington is a matter for you to decide irrespective of your connection with the Library."[61] Given Lomax's announced preference for Austin, that would seem to have settled the matter. But what Lomax did was entirely typical; having convinced Miss Terrill to marry him, he set her up in Austin in a rented house with a ready-made family (Bess and Alan), maintained his old forwarding address at the University, and took to the road again. During the next two or three years he spent far more time in Washington (or "nearer at hand" to it) than in Texas.

· · · · ·

Lomax's relationship with the Library of Congress was no sooner simplified than it became complicated again. In early July he learned that Engel had resigned as chief of the Music Division and would be succeeded by his assistant, W. Oliver Strunk. Engel, of course, had been the motive force behind the formation of the Archive of American Folk Song, and although he would continue to serve the Library in an advisory capacity on musicological matters, there was serious concern that Strunk lacked his commitment to the Archive.

Strunk, who was only thirty-three, almost twenty years younger than Engel, was something of an unknown quantity, although he had been in the Music Division for six years. A shy, extremely reserved man, he was the son of Cornell English professor William O. Strunk, famous coauthor, with E. B. White, of *The Elements of Style,* and there were rumors of bitterness between father and son. The younger Strunk had left college without a degree to play the piano in movie houses before returning to the serious study of music.[62] He studied abroad for a year at Berlin University, then joined the Library of Congress in 1928.

Although Strunk had been Engel's second-in-command, Lomax had had few dealings with him. Upon learning of Engel's departure, he wrote diplomatically to Strunk: "Mr. Engel has been courteous and thoughtful always; while I am welcoming you I am also missing him."[63] There was a note of suspicion in that greeting, and it proved to be justified. Much later, in a passage deleted from his autobiography, Lomax wrote of an early meeting with Strunk and of Strunk's indifference, "an indifference that later grew into downright opposition, unfortunately intermingled with double-dealing."[64] Their relationship over the next three years, until Strunk managed to get himself fired, was not a harmonious one. Perhaps Lomax's disappointment was all the greater because Strunk had initially written to him with seeming enthusiasm, asserting "my keen interest in all that you are doing."[65]

Lomax's trials with Strunk were yet to come. At the time he was too busy getting married and wrestling *American Ballads and Folk Songs* through the press to pay much attention to Archive matters. Ed Waters was having second thoughts about some of Mary Gresham's music transcriptions, and Waters now insisted on seeing final proofs of the music, reminding Lomax that the prestige of the Library of Congress was on the line. There were also early signs of copyright problems, the first when Macmillan cautiously raised the issue of "Home on the Range," reportedly the favorite song of President Franklin Roosevelt, Admiral Richard E. Byrd, and millions of others who were hearing it over the radio and on jukeboxes all around the country. Had Lomax obtained permission to use the song when he first published it in *Cowboy Songs* back in 1910? It was news to Lomax that any permission was needed; so far as he was concerned, it was a folksong, in public domain. But an Arizona couple, William and Mary Goodwin, now claimed authorship and had filed a half-million-dollar lawsuit against the National Broadcasting Company, Warner Brothers, and others for infringement of copyright.[66] Lomax ducked for cover, and "Home on the Range" was pulled from *American Ballads and Folk Songs* before it reached the press[67] (although there was not time to delete his lengthy mention of it in the acknowledgment section). This was only the opening shot in a protracted series of copyright skirmishes that would plague the book and delay its publication.

• • • • •

Lomax's wedding was as hectic and harried as most of his other undertakings. He had returned from Louisiana scarcely two weeks earlier, loaded with field notes that had to be put into shape and recordings to be transcribed and copied. He also had a huge backlog of correspondence and no end of miscellaneous matters to attend to. Then, just three days before the marriage was to take place, on July 21 at the home of Miss Terrill's sister in Commerce, his brother Richard suffered a massive stroke and was hospitalized in a coma. Miss Terrill had already gone on to Commerce; Lomax planned to take care of some business in Dallas and join her there the day before the wedding. Now, with Richard lingering near death, everything seemed in jeopardy. To make matters worse, Texas was sweltering in the grip of a terrible heat wave, and tempers were short.

Richard Lomax died on the morning of July 18. His funeral was held the next day, which left Lomax only one day to do everything he thought would take two. Somehow he also found time to write to Oliver Strunk, take a cooling dip at Barton Springs, arrange transportation from Dallas to Commerce for the minister, and commiserate with Miss Terrill over the heat. He and Alan arrived in Commerce on Friday night, almost on schedule.

The ceremony the next day was attended only by family and close friends. The newlyweds planned to leave immediately on their honeymoon trip and Lomax, assisted by Alan and a few other relatives, went out in the midday heat to load the car. Accustomed to traveling light, he installed his small bag and a suit on a hanger, then watched with increasing dismay, mopping his face and growing redder and redder, as Alan and the others brought out suitcase after suitcase belonging to Miss Terrill. The back seat was filled, then the space between the seats, the luggage rack, and every other available nook. At long last, Alan, who was keeping an eye his father with silent amusement, appeared with two folding chairs. Lomax could stand no more. "Miss Terrill," he boomed, "what the very devil are we carrying *chairs* for?" Miss Terrill sweetly allowed that she thought they might want to stop beside the road and look at the scenery, and chairs would be handy.[68] Lomax sighed heavily, onlookers tittered, and the chairs were dutifully tied to the top.

Lomax had been putting great thought into an itinerary for their honeymoon, but the route changed almost every time he considered it. At one time or another he had proposed a motor tour of the region around Santa Fe, New Mexico, a visit to his recent field sites in Louisiana, a trip by steamer from Houston or New Orleans to New York. But Miss Terrill remained noncommittal, and by the time of the wedding, their only plan was to head west and motor "somewhere to a cooler region for a few weeks," precise route and destination unknown.[69] The only problem with that was that for months Lomax had been setting all sorts of wheels in motion, initiating deals, making plans that involved other people. Now, as the weeks passed and July turned to August, August to September, no one knew how to reach him.

Macmillan was frantic to get the book out, but a dozen last-minute problems had erupted. The song Lomax had sent to replace "Home on the Range" was too long and they didn't know how to cut it. Advance orders for the limited edition he'd talked them into printing were disturbingly low, and they needed him for promotional appearances. When would they get Professor Thompson's bibliography for the book? And where were they to send the autograph sheets of the limited edition for Lomax to sign? Elsewhere, at the offices of the Modern Language Association, the deadline was approaching for action on a resolution which Lomax had sponsored at the previous meeting, but no one seemed to know what it was all about. His fiscal-year report on the activities of the Archive of American Folk Song was past due; Strunk's repeated requests for it grew less and less polite. The Rockefeller Foundation was trying to send him money, but all the addresses he'd given them were old, and the checks kept being returned.

And Huddie Ledbetter, fresh out of prison, was looking for him.

CHAPTER TWENTY

Prison Moan

1934

On September 5 Lomax finally resurfaced in Austin. "JUST HOME FROM WEDDING TRIP," he wired Strunk; "WILL PREPARE AND SEND REPORT IMMEDIATELY." The newlyweds had driven nearly eight thousand miles through the West, eventually spending most of their time in Lakeview, Idaho, the idyllic mountain resort which Lomax and his sons had first visited in 1932. His fiscal-year report on his activities for the Archive of American Folk Song went off, in installments, to Strunk, and within days he'd attended to everything else that had piled up.

A song entitled "The Killer" was successfully squeezed into the book in place of "Home on the Range"; a publication date was set for fall, and advance orders for the limited edition were picking up. Professor Harold Thompson in Albany completed the bibliography for the book and sent it to Macmillan with a playful headnote extending "compliments to John A. Lomax, with New York's greetings to Texas and a loud shout for Professor George Lyman Kittredge of Harvard." In the midst of all this, Lomax also dealt with reprint permissions, sent off a new batch of songs to *Wild West Weekly* ("a poor medium, but good pay," he called it) to which he had been contributing, helped find a job for a young woman who had done typing for him, and attended to the myriad details of his regular routine.

Then it was time for Leadbelly.

Lomax had been mulling over his earlier notion of traveling around with someone like Huddie Ledbetter, a black who was not only a musician and himself a fertile source of songs but who was also familiar with prisons and the low-life haunts of blacks and knew the sort of secular music Lomax was after. Lomax had contacts for getting into Negro schools and prison farms, but once there he often encountered the black man's inherent distrust of any white, especially one with foolish ideas about "worldly songs" and a strange machine for capturing voices. Someone like Leadbelly would not only help to bridge the cultural gaps, his presence might also offer additional incentive to prison inmates and other down-and-outs: if Leadbelly could get out of jail and travel around in a fine car with a prosperous-looking white man, there was hope for them, too. Moreover, Lomax was going to need a driver for his field trips; Alan, who'd still not fully recovered from illnesses the previous year, had had enough of the road for a while.

Back in July Lomax's last stop in Louisiana had been a return visit to Angola to see Ledbetter, whom he and Alan had first encountered on their trip there the previous summer. During the return visit in 1934, on a "drizzling rainy Sunday" (probably July 1), Leadbelly played and sang for several hours while Lomax and his son took turns operating the recording machine. At the end of the day, the singer persuaded them to let him record a song he had written for Louisiana governor O. K. Allen, asking to be pardoned. A similar ploy had worked for him in Texas back in 1925, when on the strength of his performance and eloquence he'd persuaded Governor Pat Neff to release him from prison after serving six and a half years of a thirty-year sentence for murder. Now he prevailed on Lomax to take the new recording to the state house in Baton Rouge.

Recalling this episode and its ensuing consequences for reporters in New York six months later, Lomax compressed both time and reality, perhaps in the interests of simplifying a rather complex story. There was no mention of having met and recorded Leadbelly a year earlier, in 1933; Lomax's momentous "discovery" of the singer coincided with Ledbetter's dramatic plea to the governor. After that everything fell colorfully into place: "I took the record to Governor Allen on July 1. On August 1 Leadbelly got his pardon. I was sitting in a hotel in Texas when I got a tap on my shoulder. I looked up and there was Leadbelly with his guitar."[1] This account, which implied things it did not quite say, instantly gave rise to numerous misconceptions. Most notable was the enduring myth that Lomax was responsible for Leadbelly's release from prison, a story repeated in similarly ambiguous form by Lomax and others many times, until it achieved the force of holy writ. Three years later, so eminent a popular authority as *Life* magazine was still asserting that "Lomax sent the [Leadbelly] record to musical Governor Allen who promptly pardoned the persuasive petitioner."[2] Even today, after more than half a century, the notion that "Lomax got Leadbelly out of jail" continues to be a central element of Lomax-Leadbelly lore.[3]

In fact, Huddie Ledbetter was released from prison solely by virtue of having accumulated enough "good time" to reduce his sentence by some five and a half years. Lomax must have suspected as much; later, when the first, heady days of Leadbelly's fame in New York were over, he wrote to Angola's general manager, R. L. Himes, asking for an official version of the release. Himes sent him Leadbelly's prison record and stated unequivocally, "Huddie Ledbetter was not pardoned in Louisiana, but was released by operation of the 'good time' laws." It was true that his original sentence had been commuted the previous year, reducing it from "6 to 10 years" to "3 to 10 years," thus cutting the minimum time in half and making him eligible for parole on August 1, 1934. But as Himes pointed out to Lomax, "Since he was about to be discharged fully by allowance of good time, he did not apply for parole, but let matters take the same course they would have taken in any case."[4] Five years later, Angola's warden offered further confirmation: "This man [Ledbetter] has been the recipient of wide publicity in various magazines of national circulation, the story usually being that he sang or wrote such moving appeals to the Governor that he was pardoned. Such statements have no foundation in fact. He received no clemency, and his discharge was a routine matter under the good time law."[5] Lomax had merely been in the right place at the right time. Although he did take Leadbelly's recording to the governor's office in Baton Rouge, Allen was in a meeting with Senator Huey Long and the disc was left with a secretary. There is no evidence that "musical Governor Allen" ever actually heard it. But for months to come, Lomax was to use his version of the story to good advantage, with both Leadbelly and the public. Ultimately, in his own published account, *Negro Songs as Sung by Leadbelly* (1937), Lomax himself was moved to acknowledge, in a small footnote, his letter from Himes: "Gen. Mgr. Himes has since written to me that Leadbelly's pardon was due to his 'good time.'"[6] In the meantime, that was not what he told Strunk at the Library of Congress. He had promptly driven to Baton Rouge, a hundred miles away, he said, with Leadbelly's recorded petition for pardon. "The Governor listened to it," he wrote Strunk, "and then pardoned Leadbelly," who then came to Texas where he "attached himself to me."[7]

The story of that "attachment" was not so simple, either. Newspaper accounts, quoting Lomax, gave the impression that after obtaining Ledbetter's release, Lomax had gone on his way and then, some months later, was taken by surprise when Huddie turned up in a hotel lobby in Texas, tapped him on the shoulder, and pledged himself body and soul to Lomax's service for life, as repayment for Lomax's role in getting him out of jail.

Lomax was on his honeymoon when Leadbelly was released from Angola. Ten days later, from his home in Shreveport, Leadbelly wrote to Lomax, referring to a previous arrangement, loosely defined, to meet him in Dallas, where Leadbelly's daughter lived. "If you get there Before i do i will Be in Kildgo [Kilgore] Texas," Huddie said in his letter. "But i am looking for you i am going to work for you. your Servan, Huddie Ledbetter."[8] Lacking any word from Lomax, he wrote again on September 4 and 12. Shortly after this Lomax in turn began trying to reach the singer, but there was another mix-up involving addresses. Then he tried and succeeded by wire, telling Leadbelly to meet him at the Plaza Hotel in Marshall, Texas, on September 22: "COME PREPARED TO TRAVEL. BRING GUITAR." Marshall was chosen as a meeting place because Lomax considered it neutral territory, far from Austin yet close enough to Leadbelly's home in Shreveport that the singer would have no trouble getting there.

The meeting in Marshall did not take place until September 24.[9] Lomax arrived the day before, driving Miss Terrill's new Plymouth, and out of sorts from "a hard bed after a cold bath" in a cheap room the previous evening. By phone from the relative comfort of the Plaza Hotel in Marshall, he contacted Leadbelly, who was probably in Dallas or Kilgore, and made attempts to record him over the phone line but soon gave up. Leadbelly appeared in Marshall the next day—for a scene that would later be re-created and memorialized on film and in print—and said, according to Lomax, "I've come to be your man, to drive your car and wait on you."[10] Lomax wrote Miss Terrill to send one of his secondhand suits and other clothing for Leadbelly, assuring her that her apprehensions about her husband traveling with an ex-convict were groundless: "Don't be uneasy," he said. "He thinks I freed him."[11] If that was Leadbelly's delusion, Lomax's lay in thinking that the ex-convict's gratitude would forestall trouble between them. The scales would fall from their eyes soon enough, but without such illusions the two men might never have formed an alliance.

Leadbelly was immediately delegated to do the driving, which Lomax hated and which had been the root of much discord between him and Alan on earlier trips. The two of them set off for Little Rock, Arkansas, in a region that was largely virgin territory for Lomax. The ubiquitous Johnny Lomax was also there, still auditing banks for the RFC, and he may have encouraged the trip and even suggested likely song sources to his father.

Lomax and Leadbelly were, as Lomax himself discovered, "a queerly assorted couple"—a stern, old-fashioned white southerner hunting for folksongs and a black ex-convict still in the cheap prison clothes he'd been given when he was released. In the back seat of the car they carried what appeared to be the portable laboratory of some mad scientist from the movies, five hundred pounds of dials and wheels and wires and batteries that constituted Lomax's recording equipment.

Lomax installed himself and the recorder in a comfortable "tourist cottage" a few miles outside Little Rock, somewhat secluded yet convenient to town, chosen because it seemed a good place to bring black singers from the city to record. Leadbelly was left to shift for himself in town, although he had friends there and made new ones easily. It was, in fact, a part of his duties to circulate on his own in the black sections and look for possible song sources, demonstrating by his own playing and singing what Lomax wanted. Ledbetter took to this with considerable enthusiasm, working the streets and cafes, sometimes earning small amounts by passing his hat. He also rounded up several street singers for Lomax's recording machine.

Johnny Lomax brought a girlfriend out one evening to the tourist camp for a Leadbelly "concert," but Huddie was tired and in poor voice, which Lomax attributed to all the singing he had been doing in town. Otherwise, Lomax was much pleased with his traveling companion and assistant, although he worried that Leadbelly's longing for his "Shreveport woman" would eventually cause him to leave for home. Lomax's compassion as well as his cupidity is couched in another rare admission of racial bewilderment: "If I understood the nature of a Negro, I could perhaps do something with him to the end that I could sell his product. But he is too much of a child to wait."[12]

Lomax had been arming himself with letters of introduction to southern governors, including several from his old friend and classmate, Edgar E. Witt (U.T. '00), now lieutenant governor of Texas. This gained a pleasant reception from Arkansas governor J. Marion Futrell and, in turn, from officials at Cummins Prison Farm, southeast of Pine Bluff. As guest of the warden there, Lomax was given a private room and bath, with meals cooked by black women convicts. He said he preferred a hotel room, but there was none within fifty miles, and much of his recording work was done after dark, when the inmates returned from the fields. Leadbelly's demonstrations proved a valuable asset in turning up songs and singers;

Lomax told Miss Terrill that Leadbelly played much better whenever he was in the vicinity of a penitentiary, "perhaps [because that was] his native environment, poor chap."[13] As their time at Cummins grew to an end, the recording machine began to malfunction again, requiring numerous trips to Pine Bluff for parts and repairs. The last three days were especially hectic, with both Lomax and Leadbelly rising at 5 A.M. and putting in sixteen-hour days struggling with the machine and trying to make all the records they could. Among the treasures they found was "The Rock Island Line," later made famous by Leadbelly and recorded by many others through the years.

· · · · ·

After two weeks in Arkansas, they treated themselves to a brief respite, Leadbelly in Shreveport and Lomax in Austin, then took to the road again, headed east to Alabama. Once more, the way was being prepared by Johnny Lomax, who had just been posted to Birmingham and sent word that if he couldn't find folk singers, he'd at least treat his father to the Alabama-Tennessee football game. Lomax decided he might as well go, since so many other things were on hold. The publication of *American Ballads and Folk Songs* was imminent but still being delayed by copyright problems; Lomax was anxious to start an extended trip through the South that would eventually take him to Washington, then to Philadelphia for the MLA meeting in December, but he wanted Alan for that excursion, and Alan was laid up in Lubbock, suffering from some mysterious bodily ailment and a severe ear infection. While his son recovered and the book struggled toward publication, Lomax resumed his adventures with Leadbelly.

In New Orleans they worked the docks and listened for unusual material in the singing of the stevedores. But Leadbelly said, "I don't seem to like these New Orleans niggers much," which Lomax interpreted to mean that he wasn't impressed and was ready to move on.[14] Results in Birmingham were only fair, and Lomax, who had looked forward to the football game with Johnny, pronounced it "stupid."[15] Initially things went no better in Tuscaloosa—the whites were indifferent and the blacks "unusually stupid and unfolksongy"—but then their fortunes changed for the better. On October 28 Lomax reported to Miss Terrill that they had had their most successful day since leaving Texas.[16] But despite all his careful preparation and the letter of introduction from Lieutenant Governor Witt, the Alabama state penitentiary at Huntsville dealt with him harshly. The warden and his staff were "coldly hostile to my project and brutally insulting,"

Lomax told Miss Terrill indignantly. He had to deal mostly with the executioner, he said, and the executioner eyed him as though relishing an opportunity to strap him in and throw the switch.[17]

At this point more important matters intervened. *American Ballads and Folk Songs* had appeared at last, and Alan seemed to be on the mend. Lomax headed back to Texas to prepare for what would turn out to be his biggest—or certainly most sensational—trip of all.

· · · · ·

American Ballads and Folk Songs was published in late October to generally enthusiastic reviews. *Books* called it "a rich depository of ballad knowledge, and the largest single collection of ballads we possess," obviously applying "ballad" in the same loose sense as Lomax had.[18] Mark Van Doren in the *Nation* observed that the book was neither final nor entirely representative as an "American" collection, due to the omission of Indian songs, traditional Spanish ballads of the Southwest, and traditional English ballads of the Southeast (Lomax himself admitted as much in his preface), but went on to praise it as the best anyone was likely to produce for years to come.[19] Said Dorothy Scarborough in the *New York Times*, "Here is a book to read with eager enjoyment, to keep safe from would-be borrowers, to cherish permanently"[20]—words which were no doubt flattering to Lomax, who had followed Scarborough's rise in the academic world from the time she taught freshman English at Baylor. (In *American Ballads and Folk Songs* he printed several songs from her *On the Trail of Negro Folk-Songs;* whether or not this influenced her review is merely a matter for speculation.) Only the *Christian Science Monitor* cast a critical eye, calling attention to the Lomaxian habit of patching some songs together from multiple sources. This was a two-edged sword, as the *Monitor* noted—"a heresy for which scholars will wish to pillory the compilers and for which the general reader, not being interested in variants and origins, will rise up and call them blessed."[21]

Ostensibly, *American Ballads and Folk Songs* was a collaborative effort between father and son—Alan's name appears on the title page as co-collector and co-compiler, and he was responsible for much of the spadework in both field and laboratory that went into the book. But the final product bears the unmistakable stamp of John Lomax. He is the "I" (otherwise unidentified) who surfaces from time to time in commentaries and notes, and the tone of the introduction—at once defiant and defensive—is also singularly his. "Alan complains of [my] stiffness in the rather long Introduction to our book," he had told Miss Terrill when they were working on it.[22] Equally open to criticism is the eccentric apparatus and wild sprawl of material, hallmarks of nearly all the Lomax books.

Most worrisome is the format—or lack of format. Some songs have commentaries in headnotes, some in footnotes, some in both, some none at all. There is no consistency in size, shape, or content of the apparatus, nor in the method of annotation. Songs and commentaries are glossed at random, apparently only when Lomax happened to know a fact or detail or was interested in it. Some songs in foreign languages are translated, others are not; sources are identified in a variety of ways, some not at all—Slim Critchlow is variously "R. R. Critchlow (Slim Slocum)" and "Slim Critchlow of the Utah Buckaroos"—the address of a source is given in one place as "R.F.D. No. 1, Clayton, Mo.," in another as "Vicksburg, Mississippi." All this reflects the fact that the material was compiled over a period of years and never quite assimilated; it is further evidence also of Lomax's complex persona and his cavalier disregard for scholarly detail.

Apparently he intended to group the songs by occupation, but the categories are arbitrary and inconsistent, hence mostly meaningless. In one case an entire "nonoccupational" chapter ("The Great Lakes") is composed of a single brief song which logically seems appropriate to the chapter on "Sailors and Sea Fights." Trivial matters, Lomax would say—and he would be right if *American Ballads and Folk Songs* were only intended to serve as a national songbook, as it so admirably does. But he typically wanted it both ways; his introduction is a mighty effort to legitimize folk music as an academic discipline, and all the starred and daggered notes at the bottom of many pages are his bow, however feeble and erratic, in the direction of scholarly documentation and annotation. At best the "apparatus" is merely better than nothing, at worst it is a needless distraction. Only Harold Thompson's thorough and extensive bibliography justifies itself as a useful addition to the book.

For the book's most serious shortcoming, Lomax was only marginally responsible—for placing economy over expertise in selecting someone to annotate the music. As Ed Waters of the Library of Congress's Music Division told him later, "You were the unfortunate victim of a musical transcriber who had no realization of how a melody should be written down for common use and no experience in this kind of work." If Mary Gresham's errors were not quite the "fantastic monstrosities" that Waters thought them to be, they were bad enough to damage the book's reputation with serious students of music. Even the usually supportive Carl Engel was critical of the book when it appeared, citing numerous errors in musical notation "that absolutely defeat Mr. Lomax's intention."[23] A decade later, when Lomax was considering a new edition and asked Waters's expert opinion about having the music redone, Waters told him that while this might make the book more acceptable to a general audience, "I don't think you can raise it very much in the eyes of scholars and academicians."[24]

Flawed musical transcriptions and clumsy apparatus aside, the core of the text itself—the body of collected folksong presented in *American Ballads and Folk Songs*—is quite another matter. It too was a cobbled affair—tossed, thrown, and hammered together from every imaginable source among the hundreds Lomax had encountered since he began work on *Cowboy Songs* almost thirty years before. Credited are previously published collections, scholarly and amateur, old and new; pulp magazines; authentic field recordings; an anonymous "old newspaper clipping"; second- and third-generation "recollections"; radio performers; family lore (especially the Lomax family); and even literary sources such as Carl Sandburg, Willa Cather, and Robert Frost. Many songs are acknowledged to be "composites"—amalgamations of verses collected or sent in from hither and yon, in some cases made of words from one source and music from another. Purists may view the result as so much musical goulash, but its rich and sprawling mixture produced one of the first truly great collections of American song, in its rough, robust, distinctly American character as well as in the range of titles that have become national classics: "Casey Jones," "Frankie and Albert (Johnny)," "Jesse James," "Down in the Valley," "Rye Whiskey," "Little Brown Jug," "Shortenin' Bread," "Cotton-Eyed Joe," "Sweet Betsy from Pike," "Yankee Doodle," "Dixie," "Amazing Grace," "Swing Low, Sweet Chariot," and dozens more whose place in our culture was established by the work of John Lomax.

• • • • •

Publication of *American Ballads and Folk Songs* gave rise to a flurry of letters from readers around the country purporting to identify otherwise anonymous authors of songs in the book, and also a flood of requests from singers and compilers of anthologies for permission to use various pieces in their work. Close on the heels of this onslaught came other, less favorable mail—complaints from people who claimed *they* had written such-and-such uncredited song, and were going to sue the pants off John Lomax and Macmillan. Some of these were merely cranks, but one or two were not.

The book had scarcely reached the stores when, in early November, Macmillan wired Lomax in a panic: Shapiro-Bernstein, the large New York music publisher, was threatening to sue over "Zeb Turney's Gal," which Lomax had "collected" from Slim Critchlow, assuming that it was an old folk tune. Now Shapiro-Bernstein asserted that it had been composed by Carson Robison, prolific hillbilly tunesmith and performer, and copyrighted in 1926. The ubiquitous Vernon Dalhart (Marion Try Slaughter) had recorded it for various labels, which Lomax might have known had it not been for his aversion to radio singers, contemporary hillbilly bands, and anything that appeared to be "commercial." He temporized, saying that he thought maybe Robert Gordon had collected a version and could be invoked as an authority on the matter. But Gordon did not respond to Macmillan's inquiries, and the publisher had to take the book off the market and issue Lomax an ultimatum: either establish without doubt that the song was in public domain prior to 1926, or send them new material to replace "Zeb Turney's Gal." Lamely, Lomax scribbled off his response: "Evidence inconclusive yet. Sending air mail substitute material."[25] Fortunately, the book had been selling so well that Macmillan was about to order a second printing anyway, so the correction was made with a minimum of trouble and expense.

In the meantime, Curley Fletcher, a sometime performer and collector of cowboy lore in California, had written Lomax a furious letter claiming that he'd been the first to publish "The Strawberry Roan," back in 1915. Later, Fletcher wrote to apologize for his harsh, impulsive letter, saying that he now felt the song should remain in the book for "it belongs there," but his music publisher demanded a permission fee, then after extracting it insisted that "The Strawberry Roan" be deleted from future editions.[26]

Less easily disposed of was a complaint from John Jacob Niles which followed directly on the heels of "Zeb Turney's Gal" and "The Strawberry Roan." Niles, whose own penchant for borrowing material became legendary, complained irately that Lomax had used three songs which appeared in Niles's *Songs My Mother Never Taught Me* (1929). Demanding that his publisher, Macaulay and Co., protect his interests, Niles stormed, "This business of making up a book by pasting up a dummy from other existing books might as well stop here as anywhere else."[27] Somewhat wearily, Macmillan's H. S. Latham again wired Lomax asking him to prove that the songs were in public domain or provide new material for yet another reprinting. Lomax replied that he had gotten Niles's written permission—

"afterwards confirmed while a guest in his rooms in presence of witness." Niles had even said he would notify his publisher of the arrangement; Lomax was at a loss to understand why he was now making a fuss. Besides, he said, the songs were probably in public domain anyway.[28]

Macaulay and Co. remained adamant. Back came a wire from Macmillan: "SEND COPY NILES PERMISSION LETTER IMMEDIATELY MUST SHOW HIS PUBLISHER."[29] Unfortunately, by now Lomax was on the road again—doing field recording through the South with Leadbelly and Alan on their way to the East Coast—and had no access to his files. Macmillan managed to obtain a temporary truce with Niles and his publisher, but advised Lomax to go straight to Niles's apartment the minute he reached New York and try to settle the matter. "The book trouble looks very serious," Lomax told Miss Terrill.[30] Finally, in the midst of Leadbelly's sensational debut in New York in January, an unspecified amount of money changed hands, copious credit was given to Niles, his coauthors, and his publisher in the next printing of *American Ballads and Folk Songs,* and the issue was at last put to rest.

· · · · ·

By late November Alan's health had improved enough for him to rejoin his father and Leadbelly. A short time earlier, Roy Bedichek had encountered Alan on the street in Austin and reported to his father that he was "as picturesque and belligerent a vagabond as I ever saw." Alan reminded Bedi of European university students of long ago, "the intellectually elect young scallywags drawn from hut and castle who thronged the classrooms of Abelard . . . forming a sort of Aristocracy of Scorn." Walt Whitman, he said, would have liked Alan: "bare-throated, bearded, rough, but clean inside and out."[31] Alan assured his concerned father that Bedichek's description was no longer accurate, "even though my undershirt does show at my collar,"[32] but he was much flattered by Carl Sandburg's remark that "[Alan] is intensely American and flagrantly and vagrantly modern, somewhat of my own trend except that I could never begin to catch him in certain areas of mental efficiency. Whatever jails he may land in I am still for him as a character witness."[33] Lomax beamed as well, but he needed no such reassurances; Alan was his favorite and could do no wrong—except of course when it came to political ideology. But that was a private matter between the two of them and brooked no interference from outsiders. Time would straighten out his son's politics, Lomax felt. Meanwhile, his trusty aide-de-camp and traveling companion had been restored to service, and that was what mattered most. The big tour with Alan and Leadbelly was about to begin.

Lomax's primary objective was the MLA meeting in Philadelphia, beginning December 27, where he was to appear on the program with Leadbelly, his "dusky song-bird."[34] But he had laid ambitious plans for working prisons along the way, in Georgia, the Carolinas, and Virginia. To prepare ahead, he sent out another form letter, on Library of Congress stationery and with the imposing endorsement of Librarian Herbert Putnam, to penitentiary wardens around the country, explaining the object of his quest—"songs 'made up' by the prisoners and passed around by 'word of mouth.'" Prison officials were asked to send him any such songs that turned up, "no matter how crude or vulgar," so he could determine whether to visit and record the songs in person. This brought mixed responses. Some officials patiently did their best to comply; others were abusive or indignant, telling him that "Vulgar documents of any nature are immediately destroyed" and inmates caught with them were promptly punished.[35]

The trip began with a stop in Palestine, Texas, to visit the white Gant family, who had recorded for Lomax before. Afterward, passing through south-central Alabama, near Montgomery, they came upon a colorful gypsy camp, and Alan insisted they stop. Because the gypsies had no written language (as Lomax happily announced), all their songs were folksongs—that is, none were in print because their language was entirely oral. No copyright problems here. The aged gypsy queen was persuaded to sing, and Lomax was as taken with her gestures as with the haunting music. Then, when the three men started to leave, they were surrounded by the gypsy women, begging for money or whiskey and offering to read fortunes. One of them attached herself to Leadbelly, "to his consternation and fright," and pursued him "all over the glade" until Lomax finally interceded and got Leadbelly and Alan safely into the car. As they drove away, with the women of the camp still swarming after them and the men looking on impassively, the old queen raised her arms in a grand gesture of blessing. Lomax found out afterward that Alan had given her money.[36]

A day or so later the trio was in Atlanta, where Lomax reported that everything was going well. Alan's appetite had returned, and Leadbelly was "a treasure so far." He did most of the driving for Lomax (relieving that source of conflict between Alan and his father), rose early each morning to make coffee before waking the others, and kept the car in top condition.[37] Despite letters of introduction, they encountered resistance in Georgia prisons, which Lomax attributed to northern writers coming down and writing lurid stories about conditions there. Still, they found all the material they could handle. At the central penitentiary in Milledgeville, black prisoners sang more than two dozen songs for them and kept Lomax recording throughout the day. Alan fell ill again, but recovered in a day or two. Lomax blamed a recurrence of malaria and the hectic pace at which they were working.

At the South Carolina State Prison at Columbia, the letter which Lomax had sent out under the aegis of the Library of Congress produced a rather startling result. Ushered into a room where the warden sat with five or six other men, all silent and grim faced, Lomax was greeted coldly. No one offered a handshake, and the warden flung a copy of the form letter at him. "Are you the man that wrote that letter?" he demanded. Lomax admitted that he was. "Then you're the very man we're looking for. You get out of here, and don't tell anyone who you are. And go quickly."

It turned out that Lomax's letter had created conditions for an incipient riot. The inmates, learning that a "man from Washington" was coming, had become convinced that the government was sending someone to hear their grievances, issue pardons, and bring Roosevelt's New Deal to the convicts. Six prisoners were already in solitary for trying to rouse the rabble, and Lomax's presence—in quest of nothing more than folksongs—threatened all-out rebellion within the walls.

As Lomax turned to leave, the warden fired a final blast. "I notice, too, that in your damned letter you asked us to send the Library of Congress all the 'vulgar' songs these men know. What in the hell do you want with dirty songs? And did you think we would violate postal laws to send indecent stuff through the mails?" Lomax reflected that it was Professor Kittredge, a man of great cultivation, who had told him to collect *every kind* of folksong; but not even the great Kittredge would have been able to calm that angry and indignant warden.[38]

Alan's health was better, for the time being, but Leadbelly suffered an agonizing toothache and tried to extract the tooth himself with a pair of pliers before Alan finally succeeded in getting him to a dentist. As for Lomax, he assured Miss Terrill that "riding continues to be the most tiring work that I do."[39] They were all exhausted, he said, but things were looking up with the end of the trip in sight. After two days at the state prison in Raleigh, North Carolina, they were on the road to Washington to report to Strunk and perhaps rest for a day or two. Lomax complained that the hectic pace had worn him down, but on Christmas, two days after they arrived in the capital, he made several calls on business acquaintances, took Leadbelly to the zoo, had a late dinner, and went to a movie. But the effects of nearly a month of hard traveling and arduous work were catching up with him. "Alan's sickness, Leadbelly's rebellions, rebuffs from Governors and other officials, then the strain of handling the Negroes"—all that, he said, had left him "limp."[40]

· · · · ·

Throughout the fall Lomax had been laying plans for his arrival with Leadbelly in the East. Through Dick Fleming, the Manhattan attorney who'd been his office boy when he was secretary of the University of Texas alumni, he'd arranged a date to perform at a New York luncheon of Texas Exes,[41] and L. E. Widen of the Parnassus Press in Greenwich Village issued a similar invitation, writing that "Leadbelly seems to have no end of possibilities." With more prescience that he could have imagined, Widen added, "It wouldn't be impossible for him to become the rage overnight here, on the vaudeville stage" and told Lomax to read Leadbelly the invitation "if you think it wise to begin his 'ruin' so early—or suppress, as you prefer."[42] Whether Leadbelly knew of the invitation or not, the conditions of his "ruin" were already at work.

By the time Lomax reached Philadelphia with Leadbelly and Alan for the meeting of the Modern Language Association, a busy schedule had been set up and publicity sent out. News of a Negro convict attending the meeting of the staid MLA caught public attention, and almost from the time of their arrival, Lomax was complaining that reporters were taking up all his time.[43]

Early on, he had secured a place on the program of the Comparative Literature section and proposed to the planning committee at Swarthmore, which was host for the meeting, that Leadbelly perform at the annual smoker, a popular event that Lomax knew would attract considerable attention to his new discovery. The committee's chairman, Townsend Scudder III, replied that they "welcomed your generous suggestion that your talented aborigine 'nigger' sing for the guests."[44] The program for the smoker, which took place at the Benjamin Franklin Hotel on Friday evening, December 27, surely rates high in the all-time annals of cultural collisions. For good or bad, it set the tone for the events of the next several months.

The evening began with an English madrigal—"Elizabeth Ayeres to the Virginals"—sung by Mary Peabody Hotson, wife of Professor Leslie Hotson of Haverford College, followed by informal addresses by Henry Seidel Canby, editor of the *Saturday Review of Literature,* and Marjorie Nicholson, dean of Smith College. Then John and Alan Lomax presented "Negro Folksongs and Ballads" with demonstrations by Leadbelly, identified only as "a Negro minstrel from Louisiana." The program closed with "Songs and Chanties by the Diners," with Professor Hotson as master of singing. The next morning at the session of the Comparative Literature section, Lomax read his paper, "Comments on Negro Folksongs," which was "illustrated with voice and guitar of Negro convict Leadbelly of Louisiana."[45]

Lomax referred to these appearances as "shows"; Leadbelly passed his hat both times, even among the lofty audience of Comp. Lit. academics, who were variously amused and appalled that Lomax would allow such a thing. Leadbelly happily collected $47.46 for his efforts.[46] He was clearly a hit, although perhaps not quite the sensation that Lomax later reported in *Negro Folk Songs as Sung by Leadbelly,* or in the preface to his autobiography, where he said that Leadbelly's "dramatic rendition of raw folk songs shocked his hearers in attention."[47] At the time, he told Miss Terrill merely that "the two shows here went off fairly well." Except for noting Leadbelly's take from passing the hat, he was much more concerned with his and Alan's performance, assuring Miss Terrill that he himself was dressing properly and doing his job; Alan complimented him on his "spiffiness" and told him he had never spoken so well. As for Alan, "He himself looked like a young Prince."[48] There was also much praise from the Library for *American Ballads and Folk Songs,* and Lomax was flattered that his old Harvard professor, Fred Robinson, greeted him "like a son." Professor S. B. Hustvedt of UCLA urged him to write his memoirs, insisting that his experiences were unique and compelling. All this was heady, indeed, to the man who had long sought the approval of his peers. Although he wouldn't boast of it openly (he said to Miss Terrill), his two appearances at the MLA had gotten more publicity than all the other activities of the meeting—"I who hate publicity."[49] If he truly hated publicity, he would spend a lot of time being angry in the next month or so.

· · · · ·

On Sunday afternoon, Lomax, Alan, and Leadbelly drove out to Bryn Mawr, where Janice Reed Lit had gathered what Lomax reported as "a very distinguished audience of Philadelphia literary and artistic elite."[50] The occasion was a holiday tea, given in the imposing building known as the Deanery, former home of the college president and now the alumnae house. Lomax was normally wary of social situations such as this, but he and Leadbelly had been invited as guests of honor as well as to perform, and he was anxious to maintain the momentum of publicity generated by the MLA meeting.

All went well except for one seemingly minor mix-up over Leadbelly's long-established practice of passing the hat after his performance. This was to be the source of much criticism of Lomax as time went on, but in fact the hat collection was a routine part of Leadbelly's "act," something he took for granted. To Leadbelly, it was not only the means by which he was paid for his performance but it had become part of the performance itself—a genial way of closing the show by sweeping off his hat and passing it around, good-naturedly hustling the crowd, chiding the timid, bantering and haranguing his audience to part with their cash. There was a lot Lomax didn't understand about Leadbelly, but he understood the hat collection. Mrs. Lit, unfortunately, did not. Concerned that it appeared to be demeaning, she asked Lomax to dispense with it, offering instead—generously, she thought—to pay Leadbelly ten dollars herself. Lomax, aware that Leadbelly's hat might garner three times that from the "literary and artistic elite," simply ignored her.

For the moment the matter seemed closed, but later Mrs. Lit insisted on pressing the point. Although she praised Lomax as "a genius" for having discerned Leadbelly's talent, she sternly took him to task for allowing the hat collection. Said Lomax, "This finishes her!" When she wrote later offering $25 if Leadbelly would play for a private party, he ripped the letter in two.[51] Lomax and Leadbelly had gone on to bigger things in New York.

CHAPTER TWENTY-ONE

• • • • •

Yankee Doodle

1935

Lomax admitted that he never understood Huddie Ledbetter. As they drove along toward New York, he often wondered what his black "driver and assistant-in-general" was thinking. "I did not know then. I do not know now."[1] This came as no surprise to those who criticized Lomax for patronizing Leadbelly or, worse, for exploiting him. But others, even many who resented Lomax and sympathized with Leadbelly, found the black songster often moody and incomprehensible. To some he would not talk about his past; to others he gave conflicting and inflated accounts. It seems likely that no one really knew him, and that Leadbelly relished being a man of mystery. For years the essential facts about his life were missing or blurred by rumor and error.

Huddie (pronounced "HUGH-dee") Ledbetter was born near Mooringsport in northwestern Louisiana, not far from the Texas line, in 1888. His father was a small landowner of comfortable circumstances, his mother half Cherokee. Their only child, Huddie was pampered and indulged as a boy. He learned to play the guitar in his teens and soon became a favorite at local parties and dances, earning a reputation both for his skill as a musician and his popularity with the ladies. This naturally led to small-time altercations with other young sports who resented his talents; Huddie, physically adept and strong of will, gave as good as he got—or better. He was quick to anger and, by his own admission, "terrible with women, terrible rough."[2] Whiskey, women, music, and his temper eventually brought more serious trouble. Still in his early twenties, he drew a thirty-day sentence on a county road gang in Texas for beating a woman who had rejected him. He escaped, went to New Orleans, and later turned up back in the Lone Star State under the name of Walter Boyd.

In a quarrel on the way to a dance in late 1917, "Walter Boyd" shot an assailant through the head and fired after another one, leading to his arrest for murder and assault. Sentenced to thirty years in the Texas penitentiary, he was anything but a model prisoner, challenging his guards, attempting several escapes, and even trying to drown himself. But along the way he became the prison farm's best worker and acquired the nickname "Leadbelly" because of his powerful build and ability to outwork all the other prisoners. In time, he was allowed to take his guitar around to other camps on weekends to entertain. When Governor Pat Neff visited the prison farm in 1924, Leadbelly was called to perform for him, and he ended with a song he had "made up," asking the governor to pardon him. Neff promised he would do that—when he left office. Another year passed before Leadbelly was set free.

In the ensuing five years after his release, he went through several jobs, numerous romantic alliances, and at least three violent encounters with other men, each time warned by the law and let go. The events leading up to his eventual return to prison in Louisiana were never quite clear—Leadbelly insisted to Lomax that he had merely defended himself against six blacks who were harassing him, but court testimony shows that while drunk he attacked a white man with a knife. Convicted of assault with intent to murder, he was sentenced to hard labor "for a period of not less than six years nor more than ten years" and sent to Angola Prison Farm on February 26, 1930. He worked first as a tailor and then as a waiter. On two occasions he was punished by being whipped with the "Black Betty," ten lashes for "laziness" in 1931 and fifteen for "impudence" in 1932. That was not unusual; most prisoners felt Betty's sting from time to time. In June 1933, the Board of Pardons recommended that Ledbetter's sentence be commuted to three-to-ten years, making him eligible for parole the following year. He was working as a waiter with trusty status in "A" Camp at Angola when John and Alan Lomax first came there in July 1933, with their recording machine.

If there were many ambiguities surrounding Leadbelly, one thing was certain: he was already a powerful and accomplished performer when Lomax came along. Despite his rough and rowdy past—or perhaps because of it—he had acquired a broad, culturally diverse repertoire of songs as well as considerable expertise with the twelve-string guitar. More importantly, he had also developed that ineffable quality at the heart of every great performance, the ability to reach and respond to his audiences, and to manipulate them, in the best sense of the word. If at first he seemed, to northerners at least, something of a primitive, that was part of his appeal—but it was also the source of his artistry, rooted in the natural vigor and simplicity of his material and performances. Lomax, to his credit, at least understood this and tried to make the most of it—one of his early difficulties with Leadbelly was trying to keep him "pure" and prevent him from slickening up his act with pop songs and commercial stage business.

• • • • •

When Lomax and his folk-singing ex-con arrived in Manhattan on the eve of the new year 1935, people were still talking about another exotic phenomenon which had descended upon them less than two years earlier. *King Kong,* the landmark fantasy-adventure movie released in March 1933 for a long run in Manhattan, had captured the public's fancy as few other films have; the story it set forth seemed to strike at some archetypal nerve deep in the public consciousness. The relationship between Hollywood and real life—that is, the often tenuous and always complex ways in which films capture essential myths or create new ones and thereby shape our thoughts and actions—is a subject best approached with caution. But certain key similarities between *King Kong* and what was about to be reported in the press are unavoidable, and perhaps help to explain the sensation which Leadbelly created among New Yorkers: a savage being, primitive and violent, is discovered by a white man, put in bondage, transported to Manhattan, and placed on public display. A further intrinsic element—the beauty-and-the-beast motif—was shortly added when Lomax sent for the convicted murderer's tall, attractive sweetheart, Martha Promise, and brought her north to marry Leadbelly.

In any event, it was surely Leadbelly's exoticism which first captured public attention. "Lomax Arrives with Leadbelly, Negro Minstrel," read a headline in the *Herald Tribune* on January 3. "Sweet Singer of the Swamplands Here to Do a Few Tunes between Homicides." *Time* labeled Leadbelly a "Murderous Minstrel," and the *Brooklyn Eagle* referred to him as "a Virtuoso of Knife and Guitar."[3] "This nigger," said Lomax, four days after their arrival, "has captured the imagination of New York."[4]

News of Leadbelly first reached the public as a result of a social event the day after he and Lomax arrived in New York. Margaret Conklin, a reader in Macmillan's editorial department, invited Lomax to bring Alan and Leadbelly to a New Year's Day party at her apartment at 181 Sullivan Street, where the guests were mostly literati—writers, artists, and journalists. Leadbelly sang, and, as Lomax told it later, "Keen minded reporters scented a story."[5] Instantly, headlines were proclaiming, "Negro Convict Sings Himself out of Two Penitentiaries and Captivates New York."

Cohostess for the affair was Miss Conklin's roommate, Mary Elizabeth Barnicle, who taught folklore and literature at New York University's Washington Square campus. Like Conklin, Barnicle was already a great admirer of Lomax's work and had written him several fan letters ("It must be a joy beyond expression to collect these songs as you and your son are doing").[6] Barnicle, whom Lomax described as "about 50," was a large, hearty woman of many enthusiasms, mostly intellectual and literary. Although born in Massachusetts, she had a passionately romantic attachment to the South: "I wish I had been born and brought up in the South—New England was too rock-ribbed. . . . Perhaps it is good for Anglo-Saxons, but poor old Celts pay an awful price for that chilly, controlled heritage."[7] Rhetoric of this sort captured Lomax right away; he was also taken with Barnicle's "merry laughter" and her flattering attention to his stories. Margaret Conklin, an attractive woman in her early thirties, was equally winning. The Misses Barnicle and Conklin made a great fuss over Leadbelly, to whom they were instantly "Mis Bonkle and Conkle"—a phrase happily picked up by the Lomaxes.

Very shortly, "Bonkle and Conkle" had taken in Alan and his father as guests in their apartment. Lomax said that he had hoped to keep Leadbelly with him, fearing that the songster would get into trouble if left alone. But no hotel south of 110th Street, he said, would accept the racially mixed party, so Leadbelly had been lodged at the Negro YMCA in Harlem. He did nothing to relieve Lomax's anxieties when he got drunk his first night there, went on a "terrible debauch," and turned up late for an appointment with Macmillan brass the next day.

Some events for Leadbelly had been scheduled far in advance, including the special luncheon of New York's Texas Exes on January 4, where among the audience were such prominent Texans as newspaperman Stanley Walker and Tex Ritter, who had come under the influence of *Cowboy Songs* while a student at the University of Texas in the 1920s and was now pursuing a radio career in New York. By this time new invitations and offers were coming in right and left. In the next three weeks, Leadbelly was put on display for officials at Macmillan, the *Nation, Time,* and the Rockefeller Foundation; he entertained at half a dozen parties, auditioned for Rudy Vallee's NBC radio show, broadcast on the *March of Time* program, performed at the Bookseller's League Dinner, and recorded the first of some forty sides for the American Record Company. He was in *Time* magazine and every metropolitan newspaper, and the *New Yorker* published a long poem about him, "Ballad of a Ballad-Singer," by William Rose Benét (it was rather pedestrian stuff, as this sample attests: "Leadbelly drives the Lomax car / And he is never tired; / He's a better man, John Lomax vows, / Than any he ever hired").[8]

The air was full of deals—proposed book contracts, movie offers, concerts, night club engagements. Everyone, it seemed, wanted Leadbelly. Lomax complained that it was all happening so fast he couldn't keep track. He threaded his way carefully through all the hoopla, suspicious one moment that he was surrounded by New York sharpers, then certain that the next person to wave a contract in his face was going to make them rich. He was equally ambivalent about the media uproar. "Publicity proclaims me the most famous man in New York City," he wrote home, then insisted that he sought no notoriety and was in fact trying to avoid it.[9]

Five days after arriving in New York, he and Leadbelly drew up an agreement, unwitnessed, that made him Leadbelly's exclusive manager and agent for a period of five years, for which he was to receive 50 percent of all earnings. A month later, a "supplement" was added which in effect made Alan a third partner, with each of the three principals receiving a one-third share. Another way of looking at it was that Leadbelly's management was now taking two of every three dollars he earned (although, it should be noted, Lomax invariably "performed" alongside him, introducing the songs and commenting on them). Leadbelly would eventually repudiate both documents, insisting that he had never agreed to such terms.[10]

The most tangible project at the moment, so far as Lomax was concerned, was a contract with Macmillan for a book, tentatively entitled "Leadbelly and His Songs," for which they were to receive an advance of $500. A second hot prospect was the *March of Time*, which in recent weeks had been experimenting with a movie newsreel version of its popular radio program and was now considering a Leadbelly segment for its first release, scheduled to be in theaters on February 1. Toward this end, following Leadbelly's appearance on the *March of Time* radio show, he and the Lomaxes were invited to a party in the home of Roy E. Larsen, the handsome, dynamic young *Time* executive responsible for developing the newsreel series.

Lomax's Texas farm boy sensibilities were less than impressed by the crowd of sophisticates on hand. He enjoyed meeting John Martin, *Time*'s managing editor, but sniffed that Marcus Loew of Loew's Theaters was "hard-faced, almost repulsive," along with "some of his women and others of their ilk."[11] Leadbelly found it a difficult audience as well, but he won them over. At the end of his performance the crowd was begging for more and stuffing his hat with bills.

The more successful Leadbelly was, however, the more he worried Lomax, who noticed that he was beginning to "show off," exaggerating his delivery, adding bits of stage business, and generally departing from the plain, natural style that Lomax felt to be his real strength. All along, Lomax had feared that Leadbelly would be "contaminated" by northern society and mores; if left alone in Harlem he would succumb to what Lomax considered primitive lusts for liquor and women, and unless he was protected from the public and press, all the attention and flattery would go to his head. To Miss Terrill, Lomax complained that he had his hands full trying to keep Leadbelly away from admirers and had to rush him away as soon as he had finished singing and passed his hat.[12] Added to this tense circumstance was the singer's growing homesickness and longing for Martha Promise, back in Shreveport. Lomax was beginning to fear that, lest Leadbelly simply take off on his own, they might have to send him home to Martha and cancel their New York activities. It wouldn't be quite like killing the goose that was laying golden eggs, but it was a possibility Lomax dreaded to think about, considering what he'd invested in the operation.

Just as the pressure was reaching a bursting point, the Misses Conklin and Barnicle came to the rescue. They had a small summer home in Wilton, Connecticut, less than fifty miles from the city, which they offered to Lomax as a place where he could take Leadbelly and keep him more or less in seclusion, away from the turmoil and temptation of the city. To further persuade Leadbelly, Lomax promised that once they were settled in Wilton, he would arrange for Martha to join them.

This plan was no sooner underway than it occurred to Lomax that they would all be in jeopardy of violating the Mann Act if he transported Martha across state lines to cohabit with Leadbelly without benefit of clergy. Such things were understood in the South, he muttered, but up north among the puritans, they would have to be on their best behavior. Possibly he had another motive as well. Concluding that there must be a marriage, he told Miss Terrill that he and Alan would no doubt stage "a wedding affair that will again stir emotional New York."[13] Reporters and photographers from the Associated Press and *Time* would attend, and he expected "quite a crowd" to fill the house at Wilton.[14] This was, of course, the man who hated publicity.

Martha's arrival created more headlines. Lomax and Leadbelly were waiting for her at Pennsylvania Station; when the scheduled train arrived and she was not on it, Lomax in a panic had visions of a poor simple black woman, unaccustomed to the ways of the city, having gotten lost and come to harm. After meeting another train or two, with Leadbelly growing distraught, they discovered only by chance that Martha had actually arrived on an earlier train and was sitting patiently in the waiting room. "Leadbelly Gets a Bad Scare as Fiancee Rolls In," read one headline. "Homicidal Harmonizer at All the Trains from Dixie but Martha Arrives Early."[15] Even as a comedy of errors it was not much, but the *Herald Tribune*'s story ran to almost twenty column inches, surely the leading nonnews of the day.

A more telling scene, witnessed only by Lomax, occurred on the commuter train back to Wilton. In the seat just ahead Leadbelly huddled with Martha, telling her with high drama of his recent successes and his happiness at having her by his side once more. Then, caught up in his excitement, he suddenly broke down and cried. "He is a strange combination of emotion and vacillation," Lomax observed, a man with "impulses . . . stronger than his promises."[16]

After less than three weeks in New York, Leadbelly was the toast of the town. Lomax noted just how sensational his climb had been: in August he had been wearing stripes, and now he was on network radio, signed for a movie, interviewed by *Time,* the Associated Press, and all the New York newspapers. Reporters were lining up to cover his wedding, a major publisher had contracted to publish a book about his life and songs, and invitations were arriving daily from universities and scholarly groups.[17] Of course, Lomax shared in the achievement. Pointing out to Miss Terrill that Leadbelly's glory invariably reflected on him, he modestly confided that he felt he was at last earning "a permanent and honorable place in the history of American literature."[18] That, in one form or another, had been his goal for forty years.

Leadbelly and Martha's wedding took place in the living room of the house at Wilton on Sunday, January 20, with sleet and snow falling outside. Lomax had assembled a small group of blacks from the A.M.E. church in nearby Norwalk, including three deacons and the Rev. Overton, who performed the ceremony. "Bonkle and Conkle" attended the bride, Lomax gave her away, and Alan served as Leadbelly's best man. In addition to a crowd of reporters and photographers, the audience also included the much-traveled Johnny Lomax, who seemed destined to turn up on an RFC assignment (now in New York) wherever his father was making news.

Leadbelly serenaded his new bride with a sugary little love song, then shocked the minister with a "sinful blues" ("Dark-skinned woman makes a jack rabbit hug a houn' / Makes a brown-skin preacher lay his Bible down").[19] After the disappearance of "several plates of sandwiches and some liquid refreshment," the principals, accompanied by Lomax and sons, departed by train for Brooklyn, where Leadbelly was to perform at a cocktail party that afternoon in the home of M. Preston Goodfellow, president and publisher of the *Brooklyn Daily Eagle,* whose guests included New York Mayor Fiorello LaGuardia. If either Leadbelly or Martha objected to this event as an intrusion on what rightly should have been a very private day in their lives, there is no evidence.

· · · · ·

Life at Wilton was both routine and bizarre. The house, reportedly a former home of Frances Perkins, Roosevelt's secretary of labor, was a thoroughly New England white cottage, described by Lomax as "quaint, 200 years old . . . built into the side of a high hill," surrounded by trees and ancient green stone fences, with the view of a picturesque lake from the sitting room window.[20] Wreathed in snow most of that winter, it looked like something out of "White Christmas." Into this lyrical all-American setting were installed a crusty old Texan and his intellectual young son; a middle-aged, melodious, and violence-prone black ex-convict; and tall, sweet-faced Martha Promise, a laundress from Shreveport who had never been out of Louisiana before Lomax summoned her north to help him tend to things.

Once Martha arrived, they settled into a pattern that seemed pleasant enough, although it was clear from the beginning that the Lomaxes were masters—"Big Boss" and "Little Boss"—and the black couple mere servants.[21] Initially this was an arrangement that everyone more or less accepted and took for granted—Martha cooked and cleaned; Leadbelly did the laundry, made the fires, shoveled snow, pressed Lomax's suits, shined his shoes, and kept the car in prime condition. Lomax drove Martha into town to do the shopping and have her hair done; he paid the bills, arranged everyone's schedule, and in general performed the role of grand seignior. Alan, when he was well enough, attended to paperwork and chummed with Leadbelly, who was teaching him to play the guitar.

For a few days all was calm, but soon they were back to the hectic routine of trying to maintain the momentum of Leadbelly's big splash. This required frequent trips into New York at irregular hours, complicated by the bitter winter weather, a return of Leadbelly's terrible toothache, and the mysterious fevers that sent Alan to bed for days at a time. Despite Martha's calming influence and the apparently rosy prospects for his future, Leadbelly grew daily more morose and dissatisfied. However willing he had been in the beginning to be Lomax's "man," as his fame grew Leadbelly rightly resented being kept a menial, washing dishes, toting water, and polishing the car between engagements. Lomax understood little of this; he saw only the precariousness of the situation and fretted that Leadbelly was getting "uppity" and hard to handle. "This card house can blow over from only a small puff of wind," he told Miss Terrill.[22] Worn down by the long hours, hard work, and multiple responsibilities of promoting Leadbelly's career and looking after him, Lomax was also troubled by nervous indigestion and the perennial problem of his weight, which had gotten up to two hundred pounds.

Having booked Leadbelly to play for a "swank wedding party," he took Alan and Johnny along for company and was chilled when the hostess greeted them archly and ignored Leadbelly. Worse still, she had them hang their hats and coats in the servant's closet, then sent her husband to show Alan and Johnny to a vacant room upstairs, out of the way. Lomax stepped forward. "You mean then that you want us *all* to leave?" he said coldly, drawing himself to his full height. The flustered host apologized, and the boys stayed with the party, but later the "loutishly arrogant" hostess swept by again and put them off in a corner. Lomax was little mollified to learn that the hostess was not only from Texas but the granddaughter of Burke Burnett, the oil millionaire. She clearly had a devious reason for not telling anyone she was a Texan: "She is evidently trying to break into high New York society" and felt that her background would be a handicap.[23]

There would be no high society for John Lomax. Miss Terrill gave him the names of her friends in New York, but he repeatedly told her that "I cannot accept social engagements."[24] On his way to New York, she'd arranged for him to have dinner with an acquaintance of hers in Houston, and he'd complained that the woman was the sort of "nervous hostess" that always made him uncomfortable, and he couldn't stand society women who giggled after every remark.[25] Long ago he'd asserted his independence from what he considered the hypocrisies of social life, and in this, as in so many other elements of his life, he was torn between extremes. Most people grumble occasionally about the hollowness of social conventions but for the sake of approval accept the formalities. Lomax, although he was desperate for that approval, genuinely despised the appurtenances of social intercourse. As an early biographer observed, "To make his point more emphatically he would go so far as to eat peas with a knife, yawn and stretch before the assembled diners with never an apology, help himself to the entree without utensils, etc."[26] Willing to deliberately offend others, he was at the same time alert to every slight, real or imagined, that might be aimed at him.[27]

· · · · ·

Originally, a Leadbelly segment had been planned for the premier *March of Time* theatrical film, but the deadline was missed and the segment rescheduled for the second film of the series, to be released on March 8. Alan labored away on the script, with some collaboration from his father.[28] There was talk of flying Lomax, Leadbelly, and the film crew to Angola and Marshall to reconstruct the now-historic meetings of folk song collector and his famous protege, but Lomax's fear of flying and the pressures of time and money finally ruled that out. On Saturday, February 9, most of those who had attended the Leadbelly wedding—including Bonkle and Conkle, Johnny Lomax, and the black group from Norwalk—were brought back to Wilton to reenact the ceremony before the *March of Time* cameras. Although they shot and reshot for nearly twelve hours, from late in the afternoon until 3:30 the next morning, only a few feet, showing Leadbelly singing to Martha, made it into the finished film.

The next day Lomax, Leadbelly, and the film crew went to south Norwalk, where Lomax had located a hotel which he felt would serve as a reasonable facsimile of the one in Marshall where Leadbelly had met him. The Angola scenes were reconstructed in a darkened garage, with Leadbelly and a group of local black men dressed in prison stripes, the extras looking on grimly as Lomax "recorded" Leadbelly's plea for Governor Allen to pardon him. Although the performances are wooden and the dialogue embarrassing, the film is altogether typical of its time, neither better nor worse than the "reconstructions" of news events that the *March of Time* became famous for in the 1930s and 1940s. Numerous existing outtakes, consisting of both master shots and closeups, repeated over and over, are evidence that the producers were making a serious effort to do the best work possible under prevailing conditions. They did go to the trouble of traveling to Washington, D. C., to film Lomax playing records of Leadbelly for officials at the Library of Congress. Special permission had to be obtained, and Lomax fretted that this would cause him trouble, because Librarian Putnam was "old-fashioned, courtly, and dignified" and Strunk was "young and nervous and afraid."[29] In a shot lasting for scarcely ten seconds of the finished film, Putnam and Strunk both smile broadly while Lomax operates the record player. Then, as narrated by the intensely dramatic voice of Westbrook Van Voorhis, "Leadbelly's songs go into the archives of the great national institution—along with the original copy of the Declaration of Independence."

That was not only a jarring but ironic juxtaposition, for by the time this footage was shot, Leadbelly was having his own ideas about independence. The scenes purportedly shot in Marshall are unintentionally an almost obscene parody of Uncle Tomism, with Leadbelly, dressed in bib overalls and neckerchief, pleading with Lomax to "let me be yo' man," so that he can tie the massa's shoes, drive him around the country, and take care of him in every way. Lomax declines, on the grounds that Leadbelly is a "mean boy," but when the black man persists, Lomax asks if he has a gun. "No suh, but I got a knife." The knife, he explains, handing it over, is for Lomax's protection—"I use it on anybody try to bother you." When Lomax is persuaded, Leadbelly literally breaks into a shuffle, clapping his hands and dancing a jig. "Thank you, suh, thank you, suh." However faithful the scene may be to what had happened six months earlier, by the time it was filmed Leadbelly could no longer be subjected to the idiocies of racial stereotypes and the worldview of well-intentioned but woefully wrongheaded white southerners. Lomax would pay for his failure to see that.

The *March of Time* "reenactments" of historical events were sometimes deplored by later generations of historians and critics who were unaware that intercutting actual news film with footage of actors recreating key scenes was a standard practice of the day. Commentators have leaped to the conclusion that this was just another shoddy example of the Luce organization's journalistic manipulations, but in fact, many "documentaries" and newsreels of the period employed the same device.[30] Although some naive audiences may have thought they were seeing the real thing, the *March of Time* never attempted to conceal the fact that much of its footage was staged after the fact. Stiff and awkward as the Leadbelly episode may be, it was at least performed by the original cast. Lomax and Leadbelly were spared the fate, suffered by many famous people, of being impersonated on screen by amateur actors of the caliber often employed by the *March of Time.*

Re-creating events for posterity was nothing new to Lomax. In his first report to the Library of Congress (1934), he remarked that when it was impossible to make recordings of work songs on the spot, "we have successfully staged groups, with axes or hoes in hand, and secured on our records precisely the same musical effects of concerted blows with voice accompaniment."[31] Miss Terrill recalled that Henry Truvillion's timber calls could not be satisfactorily miked outdoors, but Lomax was able to get "some good facsimiles when we set up our machine inside a building."[32] Charles Seeger remembered Lomax instructing convict workers to blow out their breath and make the "hunh" sound at the end of each line.[33] And anything in a song or performance that carried even the whiff of jazz was quickly weeded out. Folksong purists complained that this was a distortion of the material, but Lomax, like the *March of Time,* made no bones about presenting his sources in the best possible light, the way *he* thought they should be recorded.

• • • • •

Despite the initial uproar over Leadbelly, his notoriety in New York was shortlived. Jaded New Yorkers soon turned to other novelties, and within six weeks the momentum was slowing. Lomax's dreams of big-money contracts and lucrative stage tours vanished. With an invitation from Harvard already in hand, he began trying to put together college dates. That, at least, was something he knew how to do.

In mid-February, he and Miss Terrill were reunited briefly in Atlantic City, where she was attending a conference of university deans of women. As a present for Bess on her fourteenth birthday, Lomax had instructed Miss Terrill to bring her along; Alan took his young sister for a "wild and wonderful" tour of New York while Lomax holed up in his hotel room in Atlantic City, trying to work and complaining about the $8 room rate and Miss Terrill's constant social engagements.[34] In Lomax's absence from Wilton, Leadbelly, drawing on the Big Boss's credit, bought a new set of wheels and tires for the car, with matching hub caps. "A black Uriah Heep," Alan called him.[35] Lomax was livid, but said nothing to Leadbelly.

When the Atlantic City conference was over, Miss Terrill came to Wilton for a week. Lomax had hoped to take her to Cambridge—he wanted her to see him "in my Harvard setting"[36]—but the Harvard date kept changing, and she returned to Texas on the same day that Lomax and

Leadbelly set out on a circuit that would take them to Albany, Rochester, Buffalo, and finally Harvard—and to the end of their shaky alliance.

Trouble began in Rochester. Leadbelly had grown moody and silent along the way; the next day, hoping to humor him, Lomax told him to take the car and visit friends in the black section of town. Leadbelly failed to return at the appointed time, and after more hours had passed, Lomax went to the police. Before they could locate the car or driver, however, Leadbelly turned up back at the college dormitory where he and Lomax had been lodged. He was drinking and had with him what Lomax described as "a penniless black tramp" he'd made friends with. His performance that night was weak—"not even his second best," said Lomax—but the novelty of his material was enough to please the crowd. Afterward, Lomax tried to get Leadbelly to bed but he refused, insisting that he'd promised to take his friend to a party. For the first time, he flatly ignored the Big Boss's orders.

The situation continued to deteriorate in Buffalo. Leadbelly put Lomax on notice that *he* was making decisions now and would go on future tours only if Martha were brought along. Then, the next afternoon, as Lomax worked alone in a small room at Buffalo's Grosvenor Library, Leadbelly suddenly appeared and demanded money, which he felt he'd earned and was rightfully his. When Lomax refused, Leadbelly pulled a knife and threatened him. Little wonder then that the knife played so persistent and prominent a role in all of Lomax's later telling of the Leadbelly saga: the object which Leadbelly had first presented as a weapon to protect Lomax—the loyal retainer's sword on which he had pledged his oath of fealty, as it were—had now been turned against the lord of the manor.

This tense scene was interrupted by the arrival of Judge Louis Hart, president of the library's board of trustees, who had come to see Lomax. Leadbelly, according to Lomax, turned affable again, for the moment. But the damage was done. Leadbelly's sullen moods had troubled Lomax before, but his strongest complaint to this point was merely that Leadbelly had failed to show any gratitude for all he had done for him. Now the black man had gone far beyond that, and literally realized Lomax's worst fear. Leadbelly had frightened him, he told Miss Terrill a few days later, and "the humiliation of that will be lasting."[37] Lomax had convinced himself that by taking up Leadbelly's cause and "looking after him," he would somehow transform the man—Leadbelly would be so amazed by Lomax's largesse and so grateful for it that he would give up forever his violent ways and revert to the faithful, obedient, shuffling darky that Lomax expected him to be. Now Lomax had been betrayed to the core of his belief and his very personhood threatened. For that he could never forgive or forget.

The last concert in Buffalo, at the University Club on March 9, was a failure. Leadbelly had been up all night, singing for his new-found friends in the black district, and his voice was nearly gone. Afterward, the pair made their way uneasily back to Albany and the home of Professor Harold Thompson, where Alan was waiting to join them. By the time they arrived, Leadbelly's voice had improved and his performance that night at the teachers college in Albany was well received. In the midst of the concert, however, he took out his knife and used it to fret his guitar, in the manner often called "bottleneck" playing. To Lomax, brandishing the knife was Huddie's way of reminding him that all was not well. Harold Thompson's daughter, Katy, twelve years old at the time, later remembered the incident: "Instead of his pick, [Leadbelly] was using his knife and it was really frightening the Lomaxes. He switched in the middle of the concert. He was just burned up about something. I imagine that my father knew what it was, but I didn't. As soon as the concert was over and they got to my house, John said to Alan, 'Get hold of Martha and tell her to take the next bus. We've got to have Martha here, right now.'"[38]

At a party at the Thompson home following the concert, Leadbelly refused to join the group in the living room and spent the evening in the kitchen with Katy Thompson, showing her how to play the guitar. Later, she spoke of the tension in the air that night and the source of Lomax's behavior: "I think that he was frightened. I heard my father talk about it since and he said that John was one scared man. I guess that Leadbelly did have a terrible temper."[39]

There was to be one more harmonious outing for Lomax and Leadbelly, and happily enough for Lomax, it came at Harvard, two days later. "Staid New England broke down its reserve," as Lomax reported to Miss Terrill, and the Harvard audience applauded the two performers at length. (A point overlooked by critics of Lomax who blame him for exploiting Leadbelly is that Lomax was almost always part of the act, introducing the songs, commenting on their origins, and discussing the cultural dimensions of Leadbelly's work—all for no additional fee.)

Presenting Lomax to the audience of six hundred, Professor Kittredge told the crowd that "Lomax and Ballads" were as recognizable in world literature as were the works of Shakespeare. At dinner Lomax sat between Kittredge and Fred Robinson and regaled them with stories of his ballad collecting. Leadbelly was at his very best, said Lomax, and the Harvard appearance "exceeded my wildest dreams."[40]

But he had already realized that his venture with Leadbelly was over. "He is either an embarrassingly servile nigger or an overbearing boasting brute," he wrote to Miss Terrill. After the incident in the library at Buffalo, Lomax decided that for the time being he had to let Leadbelly have the upper hand, for fear that if he didn't, the singer would desert the tour, embarrassing Lomax with his friends and colleagues who had helped arrange the concerts. But after Harvard, he told Miss Terrill, his association with Leadbelly was over.[41]

The return to Wilton was more pleasant than the outward trip. Leadbelly, subdued by the calming influence of Martha and perhaps a bit contrite, went back to his chores amiably. Alan took him to one more performance, at the Providence, Rhode Island, Arts Club on March 20. Then Lomax told Leadbelly and Martha that he was sending them back to Shreveport on the bus. They were "jubilant," he said, and went off to celebrate with friends they had made in south Norwalk. For his part, Lomax was disappointed at the way things had turned out, "for I could have grown really fond of Lead Belly."[42] Scarcely three months after the New York adventure began with such high hopes, it was over.

· · · · ·

Much has made of the obvious differences between Lomax and Leadbelly, the oppositions in race, culture and temperament that led to the inevitable tragedy of their association and its equally inevitable end. But in fact their problems may have been rooted in the circumstance that, as mere human beings, they really were more alike than different, as Lomax unwittingly detailed when he described Leadbelly as "an unbelievable combination of a brute, a poet; a shuffling servant and a supreme egomaniac; . . . an amazing mixture of craft, guile, cunning, deceit, ingratitude, suspicion, fawning, hypocrisy, and at times a charming companion and entertainer."[43] Lomax's harsher critics might have used the same language to describe him. Both men were complex individuals, beset by social and cultural currents neither could comprehend, much less control, and the question of race plays back and forth in their relationship in strange and sometimes ironic ways. If, for instance, Leadbelly had been a shiftless white man with about the same musical talent, Lomax would likely have taken little interest in him—or treated him any better.

Lomax came under fire early for his role in Leadbelly's abortive career. Even before they had reached New York, controversy erupted in the pages of *New Masses* when Lawrence Gellert accused the Lomaxes of bribing prison guards and resorting to other chicanery to get songs from convicts.

Gellert, a folklorist, scholar, and left-wing activist, was also incensed that Lomax had taken up the cause of Leadbelly, a convicted murderer, but had shown no similar sympathy for the Scottsboro boys, who were widely held to have been railroaded into jail on false charges.[44] Lew Ney of Parnassus Press defended Lomax by pointing to his national reputation as "the most painstaking, conscientious literary collector of folksongs in all America." He was, Ney admitted, "a Southerner with a Southerner's racial prejudices," but son Alan had been arrested a few years earlier for making Communist speeches at Harvard—a point aimed at establishing Lomaxian credentials with the *New Masses* audience.[45]

Gellert would have none of it. "Getting 'our niggers' out of difficulties with the Law when we need them to work or to entertain our crowd is a time honored custom with the Southern landlords," he said. Lomax ignored the Scottsboro Boys and aided Leadbelly for the same reason: "He embodies the slavemaster attitude intact" and therefore "failed to get to the heart of contemporary Negro folk lore." Leadbelly had only killed others of his race ("The fact that he's still above ground is ample proof he killed no white man"), while the case of the Scottsboro boys raised political and racial questions that "good niggers" were expected to keep quiet about. Gellert closed his polemic with a remark that from today's perspective seems brave, optimistic, and almost touchingly stupid, a musty reminder of the extremities of political division in the 1930s: "Look for the complete liberation of all the Negro masses only under a Soviet America."[46]

Other complaints against Lomax followed, a major one being that he exploited Leadbelly financially, trotting him out to play and sing for money, then kept more than a fair share of the take. Even Harold Thompson, who was fond of Lomax, thought he was "kind of pushing it" when it came to money dealings with Leadbelly.[47] It certainly may be objected that the three-way split, with two-thirds going to the Lomaxes and one-third to Leadbelly, was inequitable, even immoral. But of course Lomax also appeared in front of every audience, performing alongside the singer. Further, as he pointed out privately (he apparently felt that a public defense would be unseemly) he had provided all of Leadbelly's living and traveling expenses for the three-and-a-half months from the time they met in Marshall until they reached New York. After that, he kept rather careful records of income and expenditures connected with Leadbelly, and an inspection of these accounts, along with correspondence relating to paid performances, indicates that he was scrupulous in handling the finances (although the complete record can't be reconstructed). From December

20, 1934, to March 20, 1935, Leadbelly's one-third share of the proceeds amounted to roughly $650, slightly more than $200 a month, at a time when the average family income nationwide was about $150 per month. He and Martha went home with cash and checks from Lomax totaling $298.94 as their share after living expenses had been deducted. But the books weren't closed; Lomax would hear more from Leadbelly about money in the coming months.

Although Lomax regretted the Leadbelly experience the rest of his life, he seems to have learned little from it, then or later. Astonishingly, within a day or two after he had sent Leadbelly packing, he began trying to secure the release of another black man convicted of murder, a Tennessean named Allen Prothero. For this he enlisted the aid of Richard Kimball, a prominent Chattanooga insurance executive, an old friend, former Meridianite, and fellow graduate of the University of Texas ('03). Kimball was not particularly eager: "I do not feel so sure as I think you do that every darky with a golden tenor voice has a golden heart, but if you really believe that Prothero, colored, is another Caruso and should be saved to the South, I will cooperate with you in making the rescue." Prothero died in prison of tuberculosis before his parole could be obtained, but Lomax's adventures with black ex-convicts did not end there.[48]

• • • • •

There was at least one happy distraction for Lomax as the Leadbelly episode was coming to an end. Almost out of the blue, he learned that the Carnegie Corporation had renewed his grant and increased it to $4500 for one year. He'd applied for this sum back in January, submitting a highly ambitious three-year plan that would have taken a dozen men to carry out.[49] The American Council of Learned Societies, through which he applied, offered little encouragement. "I had abandoned hope for this grant," he told Miss Terrill when the news finally came, "so it finds my plans chaotic."[50] He was still picking up the pieces from the Leadbelly debacle and trying to get to work on the book, under contract to Macmillan as "The Songs of Leadbelly." Back in January he had optimistically predicted that the book would take at most a month (nearly two years would pass before it finally appeared). Alan's immediate plans were also indefinite. He was thinking of returning to the University of Texas in the fall, but Mary Elizabeth Barnicle was trying to convince him to undertake a recording expedition of his own—with her assistance—and he hoped to fit that in during the summer months.

By early April they were gone from Wilton, ensconced in adjoining rooms at the Earle Hotel in New York, and working on the book (which Lomax was now saying would be finished in a week!).[51] Macmillan had agreed to publish it largely on Lomax's assurance that they could get it out while Leadbelly was still in the news. That hope had gone glimmering, and the publisher was more than a little unhappy. One problem had been to find someone to transcribe Leadbelly's recordings into musical notation. In February Alan had gone to see Professor George Herzog, an anthropologist at Yale who was also prominent in the field then becoming known as ethnomusicology—the study of the music of non-European cultures. Herzog was immediately interested in the project and had agreed to do the transcriptions for $100, anticipating that he could be finished by April 1.[52] That date came and went. But the Lomaxes hadn't finished their part of the book either. Macmillan reluctantly offered a two-week extension on the deadline, then a second, indefinite extension. Matters tottered on. Lomax decided to head for Texas.

By early May he was again giving Austin as his address but in fact running all over the state. With fresh money from the Carnegie Corporation and a new recording apparatus, he had returned to "living in a Ford with a lot of machinery and two rusty valises," as he had told Johnny earlier.[53] Miss Terrill had scarcely seen him since their honeymoon eight months earlier, but he wrote her almost daily—long, effusively romantic letters lamenting that his work kept them apart, depicting rosy scenes of domestic bliss, just the two of them in a vine-covered cottage someday, somewhere. Any time now, he was forever assuring her, things would settle down and they would be together. Miss Terrill smiled patiently and kept the home fires burning.

CHAPTER TWENTY-TWO

Rambled the Country Early and Late

1935–36

When he and Miss Terrill were married the previous summer, Lomax had insisted that a household be established in Austin—something that would at least have the appearance of an official domicile, even if he was rarely there. Toward this end, he further decreed that Bess must leave the Mansells in Lubbock and take up residence with Miss Terrill, whom she hardly knew. This precipitated a serious family squabble. "I didn't want to leave Shirley," said Bess, "and she didn't want me to go either. That was a real family fight."[1] Although the children sided against their father, Miss Terrill tactfully remained neutral, and Bess eventually joined her in Austin.

It was an uncomfortable situation for everyone—except Lomax, perhaps, who made a show of being troubled by the arrangement, offered fulsome advice to all concerned, and stayed on the road for months, safely out of the way. Despite being strangers who were suddenly pronounced a family by fiat, Deanie and Bess (and later Alan, who joined them the following year) got on far better than might have been expected. Although she and her stepmother were never close, Bess felt from the beginning that Deanie did a remarkable job against great odds. Shirley said later that Bess was not happy with some of the restraints imposed by Miss Terrill's Baptist attitudes—"all Bess could do on Sunday was read the Bible, and she didn't think what she did on Sunday was any of Deanie's business"—but Alan found Miss Terrill remarkably liberal and tolerant. She knew more stories than even his father, he said, she had a winning laugh, and for a dean of women and elder in the Baptist church she was unusually broad-minded.[2]

Miss Terrill had much to cope with. Until she married Lomax, her job had been her life. She remained committed to it, even in the face of increasingly trying circumstances within the University of Texas administration. But now she was pulled in other directions. Did Lomax want her to continue working, or did he expect her to travel by his side and be the "dear little partner" he was always talking about? He was not much help when it came to answering this question; in one letter he would tell her to do as she liked about her job, in the next he would say she ought to keep it, and sometimes he didn't seem to know what he wanted.[3] Her constant round of club socials and teas and professional meetings made him groan, louder and louder, and became a growing source of irritation between them. When he met her in Atlantic City during the Leadbelly adventure, he laid down the law: he would work alone in their room with no interruptions while she socialized, went to committee meetings, "and finally and certainly fixed up the co-ed universe."[4] He would listen anxiously for her return to the room, he said, but he wouldn't promise to attend any parties.

They slept in separate beds but from all indications enjoyed a healthy and robust physical relationship.[5] On one occasion, when he was doing fieldwork in San Antonio and she was on her way to Tucson for a meeting, he intercepted her at the station and whisked her away to his hotel for a bit of midday romance. "That is the outstanding 'caper' of our career," she wrote him from the train later. "Bless your heart, I am the happier and more contented for it, and I hope you are."[6] As time passed, Miss Terrill was drawn into the day-to-day details of his activities, taking over business correspondence, helping arrange schedules, packing and shipping recordings to the Library of Congress. Lomax's second marriage was very much like his first.

• • • • •

The first repercussions from Leadbelly came before Lomax reached Texas in May. Even as he was sending Leadbelly packing, Lomax couldn't refrain from trying to look after him, clumsily, in the only way he knew: he had paid him off with three checks made out jointly to Huddie and Martha and postdated so that one came due on May 1, one on June 1, and the last on July 19. This, Lomax had explained to Martha, was for her protection, so that Huddie couldn't spend the money all at once. But Leadbelly was no sooner back in Shreveport than he hired a lawyer to demand that all the money be paid to him immediately.[7] There were serious legalities involved in writing postdated checks to settle a debt, and Lomax knew it; as a countermove he immediately wired the sheriff in Shreveport, claiming that Leadbelly "threatens my life" over the checks. Whether he really believed that or was just being dramatic seems a toss-up, but he arranged to send Leadbelly the cash.[8]

That matter was scarcely behind him when Leadbelly's lawyer raised the issue of royalties for the records the singer had made for the American Record Corporation. The records had not sold well, but Leadbelly had no way of knowing that, because ARC's contract was with Lomax (who insisted, however, that the recording deal had cost him "more trouble, worry, and expense" than anything he'd ever been involved with).[9] The company paid an advance of $250, to be charged against royalties, and Leadbelly had already gotten his one-third share of $83.34. There would be no more income for anyone until the advance was returned from sales, which seemed a long way off—or never. At this point only two records had been released,[10] and the initial response was not promising.

By now Leadbelly had also seen himself on the screen in the *March of Time* movie and wondered why *that* wasn't making him rich. The payment for the film had been a flat $200, and in this case Leadbelly may have had a legitimate complaint. The full $200 was paid to Lomax by Roy Larsen on March 2; Lomax gave Leadbelly only fifty dollars at the time, although he sent the rest at some later date, after they parted.[11] In the meantime Leadbelly became convinced that Lomax—or someone—owed him money, and he hired another lawyer, in Dallas, to look into things. The lawyer's inquiries to Lomax, Macmillan, and *Time* were polite at first—"Mr. Ledbetter does not want to throw any monkey wrenches into the machinery anywhere"—but when there was no prompt response, he notified Macmillan that Leadbelly would file suit to prevent publication of the book unless Lomax made a suitable settlement.[12] Curiously, at almost the same time, Leadbelly was writing cordially to Lomax and trying to revive their old partnership: "Boss we have a lots of money to make But i could not tell the Peoples any thing untill i see you so Boss come over Here [to Dallas] if you can i will tell you of it then you can Decide what you want to do. We are looking for you Boss, got some new Songs i no [you] will like when you Here them."[13]

When Leadbelly went to a third lawyer, Dallas attorney (and one-time Texas A&M football star) Joseph Utay, Lomax thought he saw a silver lining. Not only was Utay a student of his from long ago, but as a white man and a Texan, he surely saw things from Lomax's viewpoint. He was "all right," Lomax told Alan, indicating his intention to "tie up" Utay so that Leadbelly would stop making trouble.[14] What Lomax apparently had in mind was a sort of gentlemen's conspiracy, whereby Utay would appear to be Leadbelly's lawyer but would in fact be looking after Lomax's interests.

Utay at first seemed pliable. Following Lomax's instructions, he summoned Leadbelly to his office and convinced him to get rid of the other lawyers, making Utay his sole representative. But after examining the case, Utay proved to be his own man and stood by his client. He notified Lomax that Leadbelly emphatically denied having agreed to the management contract which Lomax held and insisted that Lomax owed him money from what he'd earned in the East, amounting to $661.77. Publication of the book was threatened unless Lomax settled in thirty days. If no agreement was reached by that time, Leadbelly would sue.[15]

George Brett at Macmillan did not take this news calmly. He had warned Lomax in the beginning that trouble was possible, and Lomax assured him that he had an airtight arrangement with Leadbelly. Now there was a serious case against the only document Lomax had, the unwitnessed—and highly suspect—"contract" he had drawn up with Leadbelly back at Wilton.[16] Brett told Lomax, "If you [and Macmillan, of course] are going to benefit from the Ledbetter book it must be gotten out quickly. Unless the fall and Christmas sale is to be ruined this legal hurdle must be jumped instantly."[17] Toward that end, Lomax offered to accept all responsibility and indemnify Macmillan against any action by Leadbelly if they would go ahead with the book, but Brett declined. "I should dislike very much seeing you lose anything," he wrote, "and the anything might be a substantial sum, in defending yourself against Ledbetter's attack, or in defending us against Ledbetter's attack. I think your Texas lawyer simply must be instructed to make some settlement."[18]

Lomax's Texas lawyer was his old friend and classmate, Dallas attorney Ed Crane, who had been called upon when Utay defected. He handled Lomax carefully, telling him what he wanted to hear—that Leadbelly was blind to his own interests and a brute for making such trouble—while at the same time guiding his client toward an equitable settlement. After much negotiation, Lomax finally bit the bullet and agreed to pay Leadbelly $250 for all rights to the book, with the stipulation that Leadbelly waive further claims against him.[19] Leadbelly accepted, and on September 12, Crane wrote to Lomax that "your alliance with Ledbetter is at an end."

Almost, but not quite. Later in the year, Leadbelly wrote to Lomax at least twice, in need of money and imploring the Big Boss to take him on the road again. He wasn't mad at Lomax, he insisted, and assured him they would make more money than before if they got together again.[20] Lomax turned a deaf ear.

Two more years passed before the final curtain came down. Leadbelly had returned to New York with a new "manager" to make another attempt at the Big Time, only to realize that whenever he sang any of his old songs, he was trespassing on the property of the Lomaxes and Macmillan, to whom he had sold all rights. At Macmillan's instigation, an agreement was drawn up giving Leadbelly permission to use the material in his performances.[21] In return for that permission and an additional ten dollars, paid to him by the Lomaxes, Leadbelly renounced all claims against them "from any cause whatever." John Lomax's association with the King of the Twelve String was finally over.

• • • • •

There were other lingering aftereffects from the Leadbelly affair that were to cause Lomax considerable grief. The most serious of these involved Mary Elizabeth Barnicle, whose name was not her only resemblance to the infamous marine crustacean. Initially she had attached herself firmly to the Lomax-Leadbelly convoy, perhaps genuinely impressed by the importance of Lomax's work but also alert to prospects for promoting her own interests. In addition to providing lodging and maneuvering the threesome among New York's literati, she took them to perform for her classes at NYU and began to lay plans for future projects that would involve her in their work. Early on, she objected to the way Lomax treated Leadbelly, but kept silent; Alan's liberal attitudes made him her best hope, and she cultivated him assiduously. There may have been other attractions. Apparently oblivious to Freudian overtones, she blithely wrote to his father: "[Alan] is what I wanted in youth when I was a young woman and what I seek each year with each new class—to find young men and young women who along with their beauty and strength, have understanding and the courage to be free. When I think I have found these creatures of light, these youths whose minds seem to flower again with the Attic splendor, I lift their tunics and find the hair cloth shirt—things of the womb after all fearful of the air and light. But Alan is strong and knows the secret of Medusa."[22]

Leadbelly's arrival in New York had also attracted the attention of Zora Neale Hurston, the young black writer of exceptional talents who had just published an important volume of folklore, *Mules and Men,* and was gaining attention as a novelist and scholar. With few resources beyond a strong will and her considerable wits, Hurston had gotten admitted to Barnard College, earned a degree there, and come under the influence of Franz Boas, Columbia University's eminent anthropologist. She was in Florida, her native state, collecting Negro work songs when the Lomaxes and Leadbelly arrived in New York, but she wrote to Lomax to say that she admired his work "and knowing what I am talking about, feel that it is something fine and necessary to American culture and art." She asked to meet with him and Alan on her return and "have the pleasure of listening to Leadbelly."[23]

Hurston knew Barnicle, although distantly, and she and Alan quickly formed a warm friendship. Barnicle had been working on Alan to set up a field expedition of his own and break away from what she viewed as the heavy-handed influence of his father. When Alan and Barnicle evolved a plan to take a recording machine that summer to Georgia, Florida, and the Bahamas, they invited Hurston to join them, aware that as a black woman and a native of the South, she would be a valuable guide. From the field Barnicle wrote rapturous reports to Lomax: "It is so beautiful here I wish you were with us. You would be nothing but smiles and laughs and shining eyes. . . . Almost everyone is a Leadbelly or Aunt Molly [Jackson]."[24] But all did not go well between Barnicle and Hurston. They argued frequently, and Hurston at last left the expedition in Florida after Barnicle insisted on photographing a black youth eating a watermelon[25]—highly ironic in light of Barnicle's criticism of Lomax for his racial stereotypes. Alan and Barnicle went on to the Bahamas, where Barnicle wrote that they were having great success and Alan "is brown as a berry and so handsome, especially when he tips one of these island hats on the side of his beautiful head, that he really makes my heart stop beating."[26]

Hurston also thought Alan was "a lovely person" but in August, after leaving the expedition, she wrote to Lomax from a perspective quite different from Barnicle's. Carefully avoiding any mention of the trouble between her and Barnicle, she dwelt instead on her concern for Alan's well-being—a matter she knew was also close to Lomax's heart. She sought to assure him that Alan remained loyal to his father, despite having gone off on his own: "[Alan] says he is just seeing you as you are and appreciating your bigness and your tenderness. On another occasion he repudiated the Communist Party for the same reason. . . . He kept me up until four o'clock one night talking John Lomax." Alan had told her he had gone to see Boas and gotten a cold reception; as evidence of her admiration for both Lomaxes, she assured him she would use her influence with Boas to Alan's advantage.[27]

Then, two weeks later, Hurston could restrain herself no longer. "I thought once that this letter would not be necessary, but what I heard two nights ago makes me feel that it is," she wrote to Lomax. "Miss Barnicle is not the generous disinterested friend of yours that *you* think." What she had heard two nights before came from Alan; he told her that he did not intend to return to school in Texas in the fall, although he knew that was what his father wanted him to do. Instead, with Barnicle's help, he would stay in New York and risk a complete break with his father. All this, said Hurston, was Barnicle's fault:

> If she has her wish, Alan will not be back with you for years to come, if ever. . . . For one thing [Barnicle] has a certain attachment for the boy and the next, she is trying to build herself a reputation as a folklorist thru the name of Lomax.
>
> When she proposed that I go on this trip with them one of the things she earnestly urged upon me was that I must help her to get this lovely young man out of his stifling atmosphere. He had a backward father who was smothering Alan with fogy ideas both of mind and body. I heard how you took that gentle poet and artist Leadbelly and dogged him around and only her sympathetic attitude and talks with him (when you were not present, of course) kept the poor fellow alive and believing in himself. Leadbelly got no ideas of persecution from the Negroes in the village as you supposed. He got them right there in the house in Wilton. Why? She was attracted to him as a man by her own admission. And next, she like all other Communists are making a play of being the friend of the Negro at present and stopping at *absolutely nothing* to accomplish their ends. They feel that the party needs numbers and the Negro seems to be their best bet at present.[28]

Hurston further accused Barnicle of plying Alan with alcohol and encouraging the notion that drinking on the job was the best way to collect folksongs—"Horrible to me from the view point of a worker who feels that one needs all one's faculties plus every mechanical help to do the job," said Hurston. "And then from my small town Florida background to see a fifty year old woman plying a twenty year old kid with likker."

The charge that Barnicle was a communist was probably exaggerated, but her "attachment" to Alan is clear. Even to his father she said, "All summer long he shared everything he had with me and gave me open and beautiful the treasure of himself. . . . For the first time in my life he made me feel how pleasant it is to be a woman."[29] Hurston pointed out Barnicle's ultimate treachery: "The works of John and Alan Lomax are being deviously diverted to the works of [Mary] Elizabeth Barnicle," who was telling Alan that he must build his own reputation, independent of his father—but the credit would go to Barnicle, said Hurston: "all these activities will center around the English Dept. at NYU."

Hurston's case was a strong one; she insisted that she had ample proof of her charges and urged Lomax to take his time and investigate on his own. Barnicle no doubt felt secure, Hurston told Lomax, because "you are a white Southerner and I am a Negro and so I am certain that she feels she could be daring and you would never believe me."

Unhappily, if Barnicle thought that, she was right. Lomax had had mild doubts about her all along—"For many of her judgments I am in disagreement," he had told Miss Terrill back in March[30]—but ultimately he found her "wholesome and honest" and a good influence on Alan. (Miss Terrill ventured to say only that if Barnicle was a deceiver, she was a very clever one.)[31] "She has a merry heart," Lomax decided, "and as silvery a laugh as many sixteen year old girls," and he found her company refreshing.[32] For him, Barnicle was an epitome of eastern intellectualism, while still being just earthy enough to dispel his distrust of New Yorkers. It didn't hurt, either, that she had once flattered him and catered to him (he never forgot that she introduced him to her class at NYU as "a man who is a ballad in himself").[33] Much later, Barnicle turned on him openly, maliciously telling him that everyone in New York bitterly condemned him for his treatment of Leadbelly.[34] He would have railed at anyone else who said that, but in Barnicle's case, it only made him sad, and he long held the wistful hope of winning her approval again.

As for Hurston, it appears that rather than disbelieving her charges, Lomax simply ignored them. There are almost no clues to his reasoning. Whether he questioned her accusations, distrusted her because she was black (and a woman), refused to hear bad news about Alan, or was simply under the spell of Barnicle are all only matters for conjecture.

• • • • •

During the time Lomax was trying to shelter himself from Leadbelly's lawyers and the Barnicle business—roughly from April into the early fall of 1935—little work got done on "Leadbelly and His Songs." Herzog had finished the musical transcriptions in June, with assistance from Ed Waters at the Archive of American Folk Song,[35] but faced with Leadbelly's threats to stop publication and a dozen other interruptions, Lomax drifted on to other projects. That summer he obtained the loan of a second recording machine (Alan had the original in the Bahamas) and took it to the mountains of southwest Virginia, with only meager results. Later he attended the annual folk festival at White Top, Virginia. Back in Texas, he began work on a projected book about the Chisholm Trail, with the notion of rounding up his three favorite old cowboys, Tom Hight, Ed Nichols, and Jeff Hanna, and taking them on a trip to Montana over the route of the trail.[36] But all three were getting up in years and eventually declined to go. Tom Hight told him he could get all the information he needed at the Cowboy and Old Settler's Reunion in Stamford, Texas, that summer. Nichols and Hanna were able to travel in the car with him from Meridian to Stamford, and there they all had a grand time, reminiscing with old friends and reliving frontier days. Lomax was flattered when Texas governor James Allred, carrying a copy of *Songs of the Cattle Trail and Cow Camp,* sought him out and introduced him to Will Rogers.[37] The three westerners had a long chat, perched on a cattle pen near the picnic grounds.

At Stamford, Lomax made new friends among the stockmen, renewed old acquaintances, and came away with invitations to half a dozen Texas ranches for material about the Chisholm Trail. Once the problem with Leadbelly was settled in September, he rushed through the manuscript in three weeks, mailed it to Macmillan, and set off around the state to locate cowboy informants. For this trip, the Archive of American Folk Song had shipped him a new recording machine, which initially proved as troublesome as Garwick's erratic apparatus.

One of his first stops was at the sprawling headquarters of Henry Zweifel's ranch near Cleburne, southwest of Fort Worth. Zweifel was a large, energetic lawyer and businessman whom Lomax had first met in 1932 when they worked as volunteers in Orville Bullington's unsuccessful campaign for governor. Lomax was attracted to Zweifel's hearty manner and (as Lomax saw it) his success as a self-made man; Zweifel liked showing off the fruits of his labor and playing lord of the demesne among the families of tenants who worked his land and tended his cattle. He also had a nerve-wracking, social-climbing wife with cultural airs he didn't understand; acting as a sort of patron to Lomax was Zweifel's way of both catering to and countering his wife's literary pretensions. Lomax was famous for writing books, but they were books a man could understand. And Lomax wasn't some prissy, high-falutin' author; he still behaved like one of the boys.

For Lomax's recording machine, Zweifel called in his hired hands and their families and even started things off by singing a few bars that everyone happily agreed were "rotten." But that broke the ice, and Lomax added to his song collection a large store of new tunes and variant versions. There was little in the way of cowboy material, however, and he went on to the S.M.S. Ranch at Stamford and the Swenson Ranch near Throckmorton. He rode for two days with the cowboys, sleeping under the stars and working alongside the cattlemen as they herded, doctored, and loaded for shipment. (The cattle were being sent to Missouri, he told Miss Terrill with mild sarcasm, to be fattened into steaks to feed "impoverished schoolmarms attending one convention or another.")[38] It was all great fun, but there wasn't much to be found about the Chisholm Trail. The book on that subject soon evaporated.

From Throckmorton Lomax went to attend a rodeo in Midland and then on to the Spur Ranch, on the high plains. The weather had turned cold and windy, and he soon gave up. After a day or two with the Mansells in Lubbock, he headed back to Austin, where a letter from James Putnam at Macmillan awaited him. The Leadbelly manuscript was much too long and would require drastic cuts. Their contract specified 150 to 200 pages; Lomax had delivered over six hundred. And he had to make the cuts quickly, said Putnam, because Leadbelly's notoriety was fading with the passing of time, and "every month's delay in bringing out the book means so much less interest in the subject on the part of the general public."[39] Within a week Lomax was back at Zweifel's ranch with blue pencil and scissors, set up in a private room with every amenity at his disposal, struggling to trim out at least three hundred pages—half of everything he and Alan had written about Leadbelly over the previous year.

As 1935 drew to a close, Lomax had at least one accomplishment that gave him great satisfaction. Since rousing himself from his sickbed four years earlier and going on the road to lecture and collect folksongs, he had paid off debts of some $9,000, and his remaining liabilities were covered by collateral in the form of eight hundred shares of Republic National stock and other securities. On the debit side, several friends and family members owed him money that they were repaying only slowly, if at all. He was cosigner on Oscar Callaway's note for $2900, money borrowed to help the Callaways through the depression. Brother-in-law Gene Pedigo still owed him $750 and made small payments from time to time. Rob Lomax was being supported almost entirely by a daughter, who'd assumed her father's six-hundred-dollar debt to Lomax, but on a schoolteacher's salary, she could pay him nothing on it.[40] Lomax reported all this to Johnny philosophically. What mattered most, he said, was that his health had been restored, and he looked forward to getting on the road again with the recording machine.

• • • • •

Christmas of 1935 brought more turmoil with Barnicle. Alan had had the bright idea that the Lomaxes—he, his father, Miss Terrill, and Bess—should spend the holidays in Saltillo, Mexico, where Alan would soon be doing fieldwork, accompanied once more by Barnicle. He suggested that Barnicle fly to Texas and join them for the trip south for Christmas. His father, still eager to cultivate her, quickly agreed, even though there had already been some rumpled feathers when "Bonkle and Conkle's" offer of the free house at Wilton had turned out not to be so free.[41] In the meantime Barnicle and Conklin had had a falling out, and no one was quite sure just where the allegiances ought to be. But things went reasonably well in Mexico until Barnicle discovered that she was not an "out and out guest" (as Miss Terrill put it), but was expected to pay her own way.[42] The whole thing was highly unpleasant. Lomax dodged the fallout by scurrying off to Cincinnati for the MLA meeting and then back to Texas to start another round of field recording.

In San Antonio to make another attempt to record *Los Pastores,* he nervously enlisted the aid of priests and nuns at Our Lady of the Lake College to help him find singers. Sent to confer with two nuns, he found himself a stranger in their midst, and an unsteady one at that, unsure just how one was supposed to act among these garbed religionists so foreign to his native Methodism. Then Sister Joan of Arc, who seemed shy and withdrawn, suddenly offered him a hearty handshake and astonished him by suggesting that they all have a drink before discussing folksongs. A table was set with tasty morsels, Lomax had a beer, and the three of them, "a most friendly trio," worked out plans for finding and recording singers. He was especially impressed by Sister Elaine, whom he described as "a tall, willowy, blushing, dimpling, beautiful blond" who laughed like Martha Promise.[43]

The priests at the college also won his esteem. They accommodated him in every way, served him wine, and fed him exotic dinners that included stewed kidneys and "a queer and delicious Italian dish," which he could not identify.[44] He made friends with Father Silva, "a sub-junior pastor," despite great differences in their backgrounds. Father Silva spoke no English and Lomax no Spanish, yet they somehow managed genial conversations over bottles of Mexican wine.[45] Father Silva helped record *Los Pastores* and then performed for Lomax the Blessing of Animals, a ceremony which involved hundreds of animals and birds of every description—dogs, cats, burros, sheep, chickens, parrots, ducks, canaries, guinea pigs—brought by their owners to the church courtyard to be blessed. The rite was frowned upon by Father Silva's superior, who thought it a survival of Indian paganism, but Lomax was so impressed that he devoted several pages of his autobiography to a description of the event.[46]

Lomax spent many days in San Antonio over a period of nearly two months. They were busy days, with full schedules devoted to a variety of materials, recording white musicians, fiddlers "of the old school," Mexican singers in the market square, Negroes at the WPA.[47] In mid-February he came away with over a hundred records and more than his usual store of warm memories. Of the priests and nuns he had met, he said, "I shall not see their like again." But it was his fate to keep moving on, "like the poor Wandering Jew."[48]

By early March his wanderings had taken him back to the Zweifel ranch, where he was struggling again with more revisions on the Leadbelly book. The work was push-pull—cut some, add some—and he hated it, complaining of many distractions, including the Fort Worth Livestock Show, which he wanted to see, and hunting trips with "Will," Zweifel's hired hand. (They feasted on "broiled birds," he said, "I the Nimrod.") Worst of all was Mrs. Zweifel and her crowd. She was obsessed, he said, with "shining in the blab blab ilk of women's clubs," dressed in ostentatious diamonds and rushing about to luncheons and bridge parties.[49] All this, of course, was partly a cautionary tale for the benefit of Miss Terrill. He assured her that, in the presence of Mrs. Zweifel, he was careful to mind his manners and not speak his mind—"thus far."

At last he finished the revisions on the Leadbelly manuscript and sent them to Macmillan. The book had, he said, "cost me many a tortured hour, much humiliation and chagrin," thinking of what he had suffered with Leadbelly to get the material as well as the struggle he'd had in shaping it to Macmillan's requirements. But now it was done, "and other jobs beckon."[50]

One of those involved a scheme he'd already tried to his dismay. On earlier trips to the prison farm at Sugarland, Texas, he had struck up an acquaintance with a black prisoner named James Baker, nicknamed "Iron Head" by his fellow convicts. Impressed by Iron Head's repertoire of "sinful songs" and his colorful stories—"a black Homer," Lomax had called him—he visited the convict whenever he was in the area and sent him small gifts of cigarettes and money. In response to a Christmas card from Lomax in December, Iron Head had written, "I have often wandered as I am a lone some Prisnor and glad to know that some one in Old Texas is taken me as thier old Friend yet."[51] Iron Head's job in prison was to weave corn shucks into horse collars and door mats; he sent one of the mats to Miss Terrill as a Christmas gift.

Lomax investigated Iron Head's record and learned that he was merely a burglar, although a habitual one, serving ninety-nine years as a repeat offender. Trading on his passing acquaintance with Texas governor James Allred, Lomax undertook to have the black prisoner paroled in his care for four months, with the understanding that he would provide employment for Iron Head during that time. A further condition was that, if all went well, Lomax was to set him up in the business of weaving rugs from corn shucks.

Iron Head's major duty while traveling with Lomax was to perform Leadbelly's original function—acting as a go-between with black musicians and demonstrating the kinds of songs Lomax was looking for. Lomax apparently had no illusions about trying to make him a "star" in the Leadbelly fashion, for while Iron Head was an able musician with a large repertoire, he lacked Leadbelly's flair for performance as well as Leadbelly's ambition. Moreover, Iron Head's publicity value as a mere burglar could scarcely match that of a convicted murderer.

The timing was more than a little ironic: Lomax finished his revisions on the Leadbelly book one day and drove to Austin to arrange Iron Head's parole the next. The pair set off in Miss Terrill's 1935 Plymouth—Iron Head pronounced it "Primer"—and created a mild stir in Fort Worth when they stopped to visit Henry Zweifel at his office. Local police were suspicious of a black man loitering around a new sedan and were on the point of tossing him in the pokey for auto theft when he finally convinced them that the car belonged to his boss.[52]

On April 6, armed with Governor Allred's letters of introduction to the governors of Mississippi, Florida, and North Carolina, Lomax and Iron Head were off, "going so fast East and so far," Lomax told Miss Terrill, that he scarcely knew when she would hear from him again.[53] The day before, perhaps mindful of his experience with Leadbelly, he had cautiously written out a will, making John Jr. his executor and leaving everything to Miss Terrill.[54]

At Vicksburg, Lomax settled them in high above the Mississippi at the Abe Lincoln Tourist Camp, apparently undeterred by the management's

Yankee sympathies. They walked down to the levee to watch roustabouts unload sugar from the *Tennessee Belle,* just up from New Orleans. Lomax had hoped to catch some colorful riverboat songs but heard none; the heyday of the old-time river traffic had passed, and workers on the levee were not likely to reenact a scene from "Showboat" merely for his benefit. Of his new charge, Lomax reported to Miss Terrill that Iron Head was good company and to this point "graded 100% as to obedience and care of me." Yet Lomax found himself in the same old quandary; he sensed that he could not keep a tight rein on Iron Head indefinitely, but who knew what might happen if he relaxed his grip?[55]

At Parchman prison farm in the Mississippi Delta—Lomax's second trip there—they discovered a cornucopia of songs. Even Iron Head said he had never seen "such a mess of singing niggers."[56] After four long, hard days they had mined most of the ore. (While Lomax was recording convicts, back in Austin Miss Terrill tuned in to Lily Pons and Wayne King, "The Waltz King," on the radio.)[57] From Parchman Lomax and Iron Head drove south to the Gulf, passing through Lomax's birthplace in Holmes County. Iron Head, Lomax noted ruefully, was "developing some Leadbelly ways."[58]

After a delay of several days while waiting for more record blanks to be shipped, they arrived at the Florida State Penitentiary at Raiford on May 1. Lomax was gratified to learn that the superintendent was a Texan, who put him up in grand style and provided "too much to eat." But material was thin, and as recording activity slowed, Lomax had more time to reflect on domestic matters—and write endless letters filled with his thoughts on the subject. Asserting himself, albeit by long distance, as master of the household, he issued all sorts of precepts and proclamations: telephones were "destroyers of the peace and quiet of home," Alan's "headstrong blindness" was ruining him, Bess spent too much time with her friends, Miss Terrill had wounded him by going to church on his last day in Austin rather than being with him. Her constant flurry of teas and meetings and social calls was beyond comprehension. His home was not a home, he pouted; whenever he was there, it was too noisy and disordered—implying, of course, that this was all Miss Terrill's fault. Most of all, he complained repeatedly that she never heeded his advice. (He praised her extravagantly for being steadfast, indomitable, and lovely, then moaned, "Why can't you be reasonable and obedient when I speak to you?")[59]

This sort of thing grew more frequent and less jovial, until finally Miss Terrill had had enough. "I merely repeat that on occasion you can make the most exasperating remarks," she wrote. She had cut her social engagements by half in the past two years, she would have him know, and she wouldn't stoop to respond to his babble about telephones; she hated telephones as much as he did. His most reckless charge was that she had failed to make him a home; how could he possibly expect perfect quiet there with two lively teenagers like Alan and Bess Jr. around?[60] The situation would not improve, she said, as long as she had to keep working—which he had been insisting, off and on, that she do.

Caught flat, he knew when to retreat. He didn't want to argue with her, he said huffily, and claimed that, when he got wound up, what he said was "never personal but only institutional"[61]—whatever that meant. Soon everyone's wounded feelings were soothed, and Lomax's letters resumed their normal tone and content: he stopped issuing orders to Miss Terrill and went back to logging his daily activities.

From Raiford, he and Iron Head made a loop down through central Florida, reaching as far south as Belle Glade, near Lake Okeechobee. Outside town, they stopped beside the road and had lunch under a canopy of huge moss-covered live oak trees. Iron Head made the meal—steaks, coffee, and strawberry dessert—while Lomax rested from the previous night's work, a long recording session among migrant Negro bean pickers. But he lamented that all he could get from them were "jazz tunes" and made the curious observation that the churches were mostly full of "Holy Rollers," whose "songs are only a form of sublimated jazz."[62] Their circuit through Florida took Lomax and Iron Head to Lakeland, on the west side of the peninsula, then back up to Jacksonville, over three hundred miles with little to show for their efforts.

Lomax's old friend, Reed Smith at the University of South Carolina, had invited him to lecture there, and Lomax hoped to find and record songs at the state penitentiary in Columbia, where he and Leadbelly had been turned away two years earlier. This time he gained limited access to a few prisoners, but then the recording machine broke down, and he retreated to avoid further problems with prison officials and the governor, who was "too busy to stop and help a Texan."[63]

Thus it went, up the eastern seaboard, Lomax and his black parolee Ping-Ponging from squalid prison camps to tony college campuses, from cheap tourist courts to the homes of university professors. At Duke University, Iron Head sang for two classes and collected six dollars in his hat. There and at the University of North Carolina Lomax spoke to attentive groups and was fussed over, invited to dinner, and driven about the countryside. At tourist courts where they stayed, Iron Head slept on a pallet on the floor beside Lomax's bed; when that could not be arranged, he would sleep in the car, despite a great fear of being alone in the dark. He insisted that Lomax lock him in the car, so that no intruder could reach him but he could get out if he needed to. Lomax reported these oppressive arrangements as if they were entirely normal.[64] On one occasion, he wrote Miss Terrill that after a few days of relative comfort in Columbia, S.C., "Iron Head, the patrician," had complained about a small tourist cabin in the pine woods, "where I slept soundly."[65] Iron Head, "the patrician," might have slept soundly, too, if he'd had a bed rather than a pallet on the floor beside the Ole Massa.

They reached Washington, D.C., on May 20. Lomax took a room at a small residential hotel on E Street NW and went to dinner that evening with two old Texas friends, Senator Tom Connally and Edgar Witt, now chairman of the Mexican Claims Commission. Iron Head's arrangement went unrecorded, but presumably he was lodged among other blacks. Lomax remarked merely that "in a city he is only in the way."[66] Iron Head didn't know it yet, but he was about to be shipped back to Texas.

When Lomax went to New York on business a few days later, he took Iron Head with him, to show him the sights. The weather was grand, with hundreds of children playing in Central Park and New Yorkers stretched out everywhere in the sun, but Fifth Avenue filled Iron Head with terror, if Lomax's later account in his autobiography is to be believed.[67] Iron Head was put up at the YMCA in Harlem, while Lomax spent a busy four days visiting old friends and attending to myriad business matters. Among the people he saw were Carl Engel, David Stevens of the Rockefeller Foundation, and Dan Williams, now an editor at the *New York World-Telegram.* When Lomax phoned Barnicle, she said she was busy, which, he admitted, disappointed him and hurt his feelings.[68] He called again later and she finally saw him for a few minutes; they chatted politely about unimportant matters. "She has no further interest in our family," he told Miss Terrill.[69] A further disappointment was the news that the Carnegie Corporation would not renew their support for his work.[70]

Iron Head behaved himself but grew restless. Lomax reported that he was as difficult as Shirley's daughter, Pat—"say Pat at one year old about hits him."[71] It was particularly disturbing that Iron Head, like Leadbelly, failed to show the gratitude Lomax felt was his due. As with Leadbelly, Lomax fretted over his seeming failure to change the man and, in Lomax's view, make him see the error of his ways. Disgusted, Lomax gave up. They were getting along all right, he said, and he wouldn't complain, "only I know now that you can't make a silk purse from a sow's ear."[72]

When Lomax told Iron Head he was sending him back to Texas, the black man's temper flared. To Iron Head this meant that his newfound freedom was in jeopardy—his parole depended on Lomax's sponsorship—and he rightly resented being hauled away to a far-off place and then unceremoniously dumped. As he got out of the car at the bus station and dragged out his bundle of belongings, Lomax reminded him to take the old overcoat Miss Terrill had sent him. Iron Head sneered and threw it back in the car. "I got plenty a junk already," he said.

To Miss Terrill, Lomax speculated that Iron Head was angry at him merely because he resented Lomax's role as "a sort of brake and watchman of his conduct," missing the point that Lomax had appointed himself to the role of "brake and watchman." He felt also that he had contributed to Iron Head's uppity attitude by unwisely allowing him to keep some of the more generous collections from passing his hat after singing. In any event, Iron Head made veiled threats as he departed, and Lomax was less interested in Iron Head's motivations than in "the possibilities of peril to my family."[73] But what really annoyed Lomax was that, in the bus station as he was leaving, Iron Head spent a large part of the money he'd made for a five-thousand-dollar traveler's insurance policy—and flauntingly named as beneficiary not Lomax but Captain Gotch at Sugarland Prison Farm.[74]

Lomax instructed Miss Terrill not to give Iron Head any money when he returned to Austin or let him stay at their place, and he told her to call the Board of Pardons and turn him in if he made any trouble. Miss Terrill was more sanguine; she sent Alan to meet Iron Head at the bus station and gave him odd jobs around the house for a few days. Then she and Alan appealed to a friend of the family to find him a job on a farm. Unfortunately, that lasted only a short while. Less than a year later, Iron Head was behind bars again, having once more resorted to daylight burglary, or "porch-climbing," as he called it.[75]

Back in Washington, Lomax had matters more serious than Iron Head to deal with.

PART FIVE

• • • • •

Twilight's Last Gleaming

Our journey is ended in the land of our dreams.

—"Sioux Indians"

CHAPTER TWENTY-THREE

• • • • •

White House Blues

1934–36

Oliver Strunk had been a problem for Lomax almost from the time that he replaced Engel as chief of the Music Division at the Library of Congress in the summer of 1934. Initially, Strunk told Lomax that he looked forward to "furthering your work as best I can," but his best turned out to be no better than indifference—indifference, said Lomax, that was later "unfortunately intermingled with double-dealing."[1] Only weeks after Strunk had taken charge of the Music Division—and after the Lomaxes had produced some 150 records from their field expeditions, almost doubling the Archive's holdings—Strunk complained that "we have here at the Library so little [from you] to show in the way of positive accomplishment."[2] He went to work on Herbert Putnam, the venerable Librarian, to convince him that Lomax was not carrying his weight.

Shortly after the Carnegie Corporation renewed its grant (and increased the stipend) to Lomax in early 1935, Putnam told Lomax that he was concerned "over the relatively small accumulation to date of your two years' efforts." He would be embarrassed, he said, to admit to the Carnegie people that the results of Lomax's work amounted to "only about 200 records." In fact, the figure was considerably more than that, according to a report verified by Strunk himself. In 1934 the Lomaxes had deposited 280 records and by the end of 1935 another 261, for a total of 541. At the time Putnam was complaining of "only about 200," the figure was roughly double that.[3] Putnam admitted that the value of the collection was not necessarily measured in numbers; still, "two hundred seems a small result from so long a period of activity."[4] Lomax must have wondered why he had spent so many long days and weeks roaming the country under all kinds of adverse conditions, flushing out song sources in remote places, cajoling singers, making records far into the night on a rickety machine, and, at his age, regularly pushing himself beyond his limits. To Johnny, Lomax lamented that he got no encouragement for the work he was doing—"among strangers, driving exhausting journeys, on a mission for which few have any sympathy."[5]

His work as honorary curator of the Archive of American Folk Song had been more or less put on hold while he toured with Leadbelly and attended to other business affairs afterward. Then he came to Washington to catch up with Archive matters and get back into the traces, but Strunk greeted him coldly, even rudely. Lomax grew despondent, telling Miss Terrill in May that Strunk had plans for the Archive which didn't include him. He had about a month's work to do there, taking care of routine paperwork, copying and cataloging recordings, and making out his final report. Then he would come home. "This is the end of the trail for me in the Library of Congress."[6]

Personal finances were always a worry. He'd earned no salary for five years, and while his books sold well—especially *American Ballads and Folk Songs*—they had not produced any substantial amounts. Grants helped to underwrite the costs of his collecting work, but there were still out-of-pocket expenses. Money to maintain a household and live on had come from stock dividends and book royalties, the consumption of which bothered him no end because they were all he had for retirement; approaching seventy, he worried increasingly that he would outlive his money and become a burden to his family, haunted by the fear of becoming "a helpless old man dependent on the charity of others."[7] All along he'd held out hope for some sort of salaried position with the Library of Congress, but that seemed no more likely now than in the beginning. The only financial solution, he told Miss Terrill dejectedly, was to live on his meager savings while he worked to produce more books. If she was committed to living in Austin, he would rent some shanty out near Mt. Bonnell where he could work: "Me for the hills and no more telephones and receptions and banquets." (If Miss Terrill visited him there, he added, she'd have to bring a cot to sleep on.)[8] One hope lay in the material he had collected for the Library; if he and Alan could get to it before anyone else, they might make some money, but they'd have to hurry, because all of it was available to the public. That was only one of several schemes that ran through his troubled mind. Whatever the outcome, he said, "my heart's in Texas."[9]

Then, to his even greater dismay, he learned why the Carnegie Corporation was withdrawing its support—he had been betrayed from within the very walls of the Library of Congress by a conspiracy hatched by Oliver Strunk, "young, greedy for power, selfish, arbitrary, and vain."[10] Through Strunk's connivance, the Carnegie people had been told that the Library would no longer support Lomax, because he had limited his attention mostly to the South at the expense of the rest of the country and recorded mostly blacks. There was worse news still when Lomax discovered that Putnam, "the urbane and courtly and apparently saintly Head of the Library," was Strunk's willing accomplice and had approved the action to cut off the Carnegie funds.[11] Lomax's mistake, others told him, was merely that he failed to flatter Strunk sufficiently.

Lomax had taken to having breakfast frequently with Sen. Tom Connally and Edgar Witt and pouring out his troubles with Strunk. Sometimes they were joined by Texas's other senator, Morris Sheppard, who, like Connally and Witt, was an old friend and had served in the Senate even longer than Connally. Staunch Democrats in the New Deal government, both men wielded considerable power on Capitol Hill. When they heard how Putnam and Strunk had cut the ground from under Lomax with the Carnegie Corporation, Connally and Sheppard strolled across the Capitol grounds to the Library of Congress and called upon the Librarian.

The next morning a pale and obviously upset Strunk appeared at the cubbyhole in the basement where Lomax worked and told him Putnam wished to see him. Ushered into the librarian's office and given a plush chair, Lomax heard himself generously praised by Putnam, who had somehow taken a sudden interest in his work. Lomax fixed a cold gaze on Strunk and told the librarian just how the division chief had been treating him, whereupon Strunk began to offer extravagant assurances that no harm had been intended. Putnam oiled the troubled waters, heaping praise on Lomax and ignoring Strunk. The Library would reopen discussions with the Carnegie and Rockefeller people, Putnam said; meanwhile, Strunk and Lomax would work out a budget and seek funding for a new recording machine, a secretary, a car, traveling expenses, and even a salary for the head of the Archive—pointing to Lomax. Putnam took him by the arm, leaving poor Strunk behind, and guided him into the exclusive Round Table dining room where he was given the place of honor between Putnam and the head of Cornell University's music department, who was visiting. Throughout the meal, all sorts of attention was showered on Lomax, and when it was over, Putnam insisted that he drop by more often. There was no mention of the role that had been played by Connally and Sheppard ("No reference to my friends, the Senators!" Lomax pointedly told Miss Terrill).[12] His many years of playing scrub politics had not been wasted.

A week later, more manna fell from the skies, and again Texans played an active role. In addition to Senators Connally and Sheppard, there was David Williams, who had designed Lomax's Dallas home and was now an official with the National Youth Administration, involved with planning government housing projects. Through these men, word of Lomax had reached yet a fourth Texan, Luther Evans, youthful head of the New Deal agency known as the Historical Records Survey, part of the depression-born Works Progress Administration. Thirty-three-year-old Evans, son of an East Texas sharecropper, held two degrees from the University of Texas and a doctorate at Stanford and had taught political science at Dartmouth and Princeton before joining the Roosevelt administration. Beyond politics and the Texas connection, however, Evans had a genuine interest in Lomax's work and realized that he had talents and experience the Historical Records Survey could use. In particular Evans had in mind projects involving a national survey of historical records in county courthouses and the collection of interviews with several thousand ex-slaves. Lomax was offered a salary of $3200 to serve "part-time as advisor on Folk-Lore collecting," with the understanding that the job would dovetail with his own fieldwork and allow him both time and money to continue his expeditions for the Archive of American Folk Song.[13]

Shortly, Lomax would don still another hat when he was drawn into the operations of a sister agency, the Federal Writers' Project, headed by fifty-nine-year-old Henry Alsberg, a rumpled, avuncular New Yorker who had roamed the world as a newspaperman, written and produced plays, and dabbled in left-wing politics. The major focus of the Writers' Project was the now-famous state guides—volumes not unlike Lomax and Benedict's earlier *Book of Texas.* Alsberg had been quick to realize that, with offices and field-workers in every state, the Writers' Project had the potential for collecting American folklore on a grand scale. At his direction a manual had already been distributed to field offices with instructions on how to go about such work.[14] This soon produced far more material than Alsberg or anyone else had anticipated. The project needed someone with the knowledge and experience to help channel all this information and supervise its collection. Lomax had the credentials and was readily at hand; moreover, there was a natural overlap with the work he had already been assigned for the Historical Records Survey.[15]

Lomax was eager for the job, but he hesitated because he was still hoping for money from the Rockefeller Foundation. If a Rockefeller grant would pay him as much as the WPA, he would much prefer that, he told

Miss Terrill, expressing his instinctive disdain for government service. Moreover, the national election was coming up, and strange as it now seems, the result was far from certain: "Should Roosevelt be defeated, the [WPA] job will only last until January 1." For once, Miss Terrill did not defer to his vacillations. "By all means accept the WPA offer unless you KNOW the Rockefeller is forthcoming," she fired back.[16] He promptly accepted Evans's offer, deciding it was best "from a practical standpoint—I mean a sure income"[17]—and showed up for work at the WPA office early on the morning of June 25.

• • • • •

For many Americans the WPA was simply the lengthened shadow of the man largely responsible for its creation—a tall, horsefaced Iowan named Harry Hopkins, who combined a head full of fanciful dreams for bettering mankind with the practical skills of a businessman. The dreams were sometimes out of focus, but his good heart and level head accomplished a great deal for humanity. So it was with his brainchild, the WPA. Cherished by those whose lives it almost literally saved from starvation, reviled by others to whom it was the ultimate governmental boondoggle, the WPA had but one purpose: to provide jobs for people who had none, in the midst of the nation's worst economic upheaval of modern times.

After a successful career of administrating large social programs, Hopkins had caught the attention of incoming President Roosevelt in early 1933. With the help of Secretary of Labor Frances Perkins, he got an audience with the president to present his plan for federal unemployment relief, channeled to the states through grants-in-aid and directed toward small local projects employing ordinary workers, such as day laborers, clerks, secretaries, and teachers (as distinguished from the Public Works Administration [PWA], which funded massive group projects). Roosevelt was immediately enthusiastic about Hopkins's plan for distributing jobs and relief to individual workers—later to include artists and writers—through the agency which became known as the Works Progress Administration. The WPA's umbrella was large enough to accommodate even itinerant folklorists like John Lomax.

Together, the four arts programs of the WPA—Art, Music, Theater, and the Writers' Project—officially constituted an entity known as Federal One. At the time Lomax went to work for Evans and Alsberg, the staffs of Federal One were housed in a massive Florentine mansion at 1500 Eye Street NW which had once been the home of Evelyn Walsh McLean, owner of the

Hope diamond. It was an extravagant setting for the plain and often mundane work that went on there, amidst "elegant chandeliers dripping with the opulence of the twenties, silken walls and mahogany paneling, a veritable museum of life-size statues emulating the ancient Greeks, and a mammoth fireplace supported at each side by big-muscled, stooping men of stone," as one staffer described it. It had the air, he said, "of some Russian palace during the Revolution that had just been seized by the proletariat."[18] Lomax was assigned to one of the fifty or more desks that had been squeezed onto the floor of the ballroom where surrounding statuary served as hooks for hats and coats. All seemed chaos: clattering typewriters, constantly ringing telephones, conversations shouted across the room. "Nobody introduces you to anybody," Lomax said, "which situation suits me precisely."[19]

One of his first responsibilities was to draw up guidelines for workers in the field who were interviewing former slaves for the Historical Records Survey. This resulted in what was termed a list of "detailed and homely questions" designed to "get the Negro thinking and talking about the days of slavery."[20] With his lifetime interest in blacks and their way of life, Lomax was well prepared for the task and came up with a set of questions that elicited valuable information. In time the project produced more than two thousand vivid and comprehensive narratives that provide an invaluable eyewitness account of slavery and its terrible ramifications. Deposited with the Library of Congress, these narratives later formed the core of the anthology, *Lay My Burden Down: A Folk History of Slavery* (1945), compiled and edited by Lomax's successor, Benjamin Botkin.

• • • • •

As "National Advisor of Folklore and Folkways" for the Writers' Project, Lomax reviewed material gathered for some of the state guides and helped Alsberg plan for wider collecting efforts. Folklore for the guides remained the major goal, but workers in the field were encouraged to collect other information on local lore and customs. Lomax sent out detailed instructions about the type of material the project wanted; it included tall tales, local geographic eccentricities (e.g., "lovers' leaps," "proposal rocks"), table manners, religious customs, epitaphs, accounts of people with supernatural powers, stories about animal behavior.

Some state directors thought the whole thing was ridiculous—"the biggest piece of malarkey we'd ever seen," one said—and critics of the WPA used Lomax's folklore index as evidence that the project was a pathetic waste of taxpayers' money. "Animal behavior is being studied intensely and before long our people will know why a rooster crows and a dog barks," read one derisive editorial.[21]

In other states, however, staff members were enthusiastic and generated considerable support in local communities. Collections of valuable material were amassed in Nebraska, Idaho, and Indiana, among others; throughout the South the project turned up vast amounts of long-forgotten lore just in the nick of time. Jerre Mangione, Alsberg's assistant and later historian of the Writers' Project, assessed its folklore collecting efforts: "While it existed, the Project was able to salvage for posterity a rich and significant part of the American past that was in danger of being lost."[22]

At first Lomax felt mildly intimidated because the whole staff—even the secretaries, it seemed to him—were professional writers and "extra versatile."[23] Nor did he endear himself to Alsberg, a fervent liberal, when he wrote him a rather pointless and certainly tasteless memo recounting an experience he'd had earlier (probably in the summer of 1933) while recording convicts at the Tennessee State Penitentiary. One enormous Negro prisoner, Black Sampson, had a large repertoire of work songs, but would not sing them because they were "sinful." Lomax complained to the warden, and Black Sampson was ordered to sing whatever Lomax wanted. The prisoner began to pray aloud, explaining to God that he was just a poor black and had to do what the white man told him. Lomax recorded both the prayer and the vigorous work songs which Sampson then sang. Oblivious to the consequences of having coerced a man to act against his conscience, he told Alsberg, "I call this my prize record."[24] And yet at almost the same time, presuming upon his slight acquaintance with Governor James V. Allred of Texas, Lomax wrote to Allred asking him to investigate the convictions of black prisoners in the state and issue pardons wherever warranted, saying that his sympathies had been intensely aroused by these men, "many of whom are only victims of misfortune."[25] Lomax could see no contradiction in ordering a black man about one instant and acting in his behalf the next. According to his southern heritage, it was merely a part of doing what was best for an inferior race that was incapable of caring for itself.

Henry Alsberg was apparently willing to overlook Lomax's racial attitudes—or chose to see them in their full complexity. He and Evans praised Lomax's work for the Writers' Project and, as Lomax reported to Miss Terrill, listened so attentively to everything he said that he decided his job was secure.[26] In addition to his new duties with the WPA, he was still spending time at the Library of Congress, working with the raw materials he and Alan had collected on their many field trips. Strunk, newly chastised, went out of his way to assure Lomax that the Music Division wanted him to continue as honorary curator of the Archive, and Lomax relished his victory: "My attentions from Mr. Strunk are almost embarrassing," he told Miss Terrill, adding that he missed no opportunity to make Strunk and Putnam offer further assurances that they were delighted to have him continue as director of the Archive.[27]

• • • • •

Buoyed by these successes, he set aside his normally reclusive habits and began to enjoy a bit of social life. One of the first—and perhaps most important—friendships he made on returning to Washington that summer was with Charles Seeger. From the beginning theirs was an odd relationship. About all they had in common was that both had attended Harvard and both were full of contradictions. A major difference was that unlike Lomax, Seeger was aware of his contradictions, relished them, and in a certain sense made a career of them.[28]

Born in Mexico City in 1886, Seeger was the son of a wealthy Yankee businessman who wanted him to follow a career in commerce. Instead, he went to Harvard in 1904 to study music composition (and read Chaucer under George Lyman Kittredge). After a season abroad as conductor of the Cologne Opera, he returned to the U.S. as chairman of the music department at the University of California when he was only twenty-six. An experience with migrant farm workers opened his eyes to social and economic realities; converted to left-wing politics, he vigorously opposed America's entry into World War I and lost his job as a result.

From 1921 to 1933 Seeger taught in New York at what is now the Julliard School of Music and was a lecturer at the New School for Social Research during 1933–35, where, with composer Henry Cowell, he introduced the first courses in ethnomusicology, the study of music within its social and historical context. It was Seeger and Cowell who had recommended that Macmillan publish Lomax's *American Ballads and Folk Songs* because of its impressive scope and cultural importance.[29]

In November 1935, Seeger eagerly accepted an offer to join the Resettlement Administration (RA), a federal emergency agency established to deal with rural poverty and the problems of farmers and others displaced by the depression. His job was music technical advisor to the head of the Special Skills Division, charged with the laudable if perhaps naive notion of consoling rural people in their poverty and upheaval by giving music programs, reviving and disseminating the folk music heritage of those in resettlement communities, and otherwise serving the "expressive needs" of down-and-out families. This work allowed Seeger to merge his developing affection for American folksong with his fervently New Deal politics. Significantly, his first official act was to obtain a recording machine to collect folksongs in the field.

Such activity quite naturally drew Seeger to John Lomax, despite the fact that, as one who knew them both said later, Seeger was a "New England Connecticut aristocrat" and Lomax "a kind of Texas roughneck, who wished he were a plantation owner and occasionally played the part of the big white man."[30] Their temperaments were certainly similar; each held himself in high regard and had scant tolerance for fools. It was said of Seeger that he divided the world into three categories of worth: "The Seegers, friends of the Seegers, and everyone else."[31] Lomax held a similar view of the Lomaxes, who were soon admitted to the inner circle, "friends of the Seegers."

Sidney Robertson, a young California woman (later married to Seeger's colleague Henry Cowell) who worked for Seeger at the RA, thought his association with Lomax was strictly political: "It was like many Washington relationships; you were friends because there was something to be gained." In other words, Seeger, an energetic leftist, tolerated Lomax's oafish racial and social attitudes (and joked about them behind his back) because he felt he could gain professionally from the association. There was nothing particularly blameworthy about this, Robertson felt; it was "just the way Washington worked."[32]

Lomax was introduced to Seeger at lunch one day by Harold Spivacke, Strunk's chief assistant, shortly after Lomax arrived in Washington with Iron Head. Seeger made an immediate impression—in Lomax's letters to Miss Terrill he was invariably identified as "a famous musician [and] collector," "a distinguished musician," "an accomplished musician and a very fine gentleman"—although Lomax for the life of him couldn't get Seeger's name right. He was variously "Seegur," "Sigur," and "Cigur." Lomax's handwriting was partly to blame; Miss Terrill complained that "we couldn't decipher the musician gentleman's name in your letter," then Lomax spelled it out carefully, ending all doubt about his confusion: "My friend's name is SEE-gur [*sic*], a distinguished composer and a most charming man."[33] It was months before he got it right.

Seeger and his second wife, Ruth Crawford Seeger, and their two small children lived a rather bohemian existence out in the woods of northern Virginia, some distance from Capitol Hill. Ruth Crawford Seeger, an accomplished musician and composer in her own right, was an important ingredient in the fast-forming Lomax-Seeger friendship. "She was a very warm person, very kind," said Sidney Robertson Cowell. Touched by Lomax's stories of longing for Miss Terrill and Texas, Ruth Seeger fed him dinner frequently and did her best to lessen his homesickness.[34]

There were other social diversions, which caused Miss Terrill, from a distance, to fret about his wardrobe and remind him to brush the cigar ashes from his vest. Lomax was careful to assure her that he was dressing properly, decked out "in my fresh grey suit, white shirt, and speckled tie," all harmoniously coordinated.[35] At one gathering the ladies complimented him on his new suit, and some days it seemed that he was being lionized everywhere he turned. Invited to dine at the home of John Vance, chief law librarian at the Library, he was flattered to learn that Vance was a fan of *American Ballads and Folk Songs* "and heroized me embarrassingly."[36] He was taken to lunch frequently by Spivacke, who unlike Strunk had a genuine interest in him and his work. There were regular breakfasts with "Tom and Edgar" (Connally and Witt), dinners with the Spivackes, with Mr. and Mrs. Ed Waters, with the Williams brothers, Dan and David, and their wives, and with the Otto Praegers. Praeger, who had been assistant postmaster general in the Wilson administration and later served as an adviser to the Siamese government for many years, was an old University of Texas classmate whom Lomax had seen only once or twice since their days together on the *Texas University* magazine. The Praegers were Washington insiders and entertained widely. "So you see," Lomax told Miss Terrill, "I'm in the middle of things, especially socially."[37]

Another blossoming friendship that was to pay both personal and professional dividends was that with Harold Spivacke, who would replace Strunk the following year. Like Engel and Strunk before him, Spivacke came from an eastern background, born in New York in 1904 and educated in classical music. A Ph.D. from the University of Berlin and his orientation toward art music did not prevent him, however, from becoming an ally of John Lomax. "I'd always studied music," Spivacke told an interviewer later, "and of course it was the music of Aeolian Hall, Town Hall, Carnegie Hall. I had never heard any of this sort of [folksong] stuff, and I fell in love with it."[38]

In mid-June, Lomax set aside other work to make a field recording trip to a prison farm near Richmond, Virginia, for the Archive of American

Folk Song. Spivacke arranged to accompany him and had an adventure he never forgot. "[Lomax] took me into a prison," he said. "I'd never been in a prison. I was scared stiff." On the way, Lomax sought out "liquid refreshment" from a local bootlegger, and Spivacke marveled at his expertise in dealing with a service station attendant "who seemed to know exactly where the dispensary was."

Spivacke was even more impressed when he saw how Lomax handled the recording session at the prison farm. They arrived to find the warden and his family on the veranda, while on the lawn before them was a black quartet which broke into song the minute Lomax and Spivacke appeared. On the steps sat a blind prisoner plucking a banjo. "This is trouble," Lomax said, sotto voce, and only later Spivacke realized the problem: the warden's quartet was terrible. He watched with growing admiration as Lomax tactfully set about getting rid of them without offending the warden. That took an hour or so. Then Lomax sat down on the steps with the blind banjo player, and to Spivacke's amazement, did nothing but talk to him for hours. That, said Spivacke, was when he realized just what "a consummate artist" John Lomax was, as he encouraged the blind musician to tell his life story, "swapped songs with him, [and] did everything but make records." Spivacke impatiently suggested that they ought to start recording because time was short, but Lomax waved him away. They returned to Richmond that night without having made any records at all.

Back at the prison the next morning, Spivacke witnessed the fruits of Lomax's labor. When the equipment was set up and the blind singer brought in, Lomax told Spivacke to do the recording while he went off to visit a neighboring camp. Spivacke felt, he said, "pretty much like the boy who was being taught to swim by being thrown in the water," but he quickly saw what Lomax had accomplished the previous day. The performer "had been so well prepared by [Lomax] . . . that all I had to do was ask him to sing one song after another and turn over the records and set the needles, etc." Spivacke had seen Lomax at work and learned firsthand the trials and tribulations of field collecting. When he took over as head of the Music Division the following year, he was one of Lomax's firmest allies.[39]

· · · · ·

Lomax had scarcely begun his work for the WPA when it was interrupted for an extended field recording trip. This time he was off to North Carolina, where he had been invited to accompany Duke University's noted folklorist, Frank C. Brown, to record musicians in the area around Brown's home in the northwest part of the state. This coincided with a project overseen by Charles Seeger, who wanted recorded evidence of the songs which resettled families had sung in their original communities. The Resettlement Administration had at last gotten a recording machine, and Seeger arranged for Sidney Robertson to travel with Lomax to gain experience in operating the machine and working with song sources. Robertson, young but worldly, was amused by Lomax's old-fashioned provincialism and his determined efforts to "show me a good time." Like many New Dealers of her generation, she was appalled by his attitudes toward blacks, but attributed what she termed his "special form of arrogance" to deep-rooted insecurities. Despite his being "sort of a scamp," she liked him and was particularly impressed that he was kind and helpful to her even though she was a mere underling and had no power, "nothing he could use." One thing she could do was drive the car, which he was always anxious to avoid. But Robertson was perplexed by Lomax's odd ideas about it—he wanted her to take the inside of all curves, she said, and asked her to rest the car at the top of every hill (which she attributed to his days of driving horse teams). Seeger was also struck by Lomax's idiosyncrasies about cars, recalling that he once asked why Seeger drove as fast going uphill as down.[40]

In North Carolina they found Brown accommodating but cautious. He was eager to see the recording machine in operation and have access to the results but protective of his territory, afraid that Lomax and Robertson might poach his material. Their initial progress was slow, and Lomax reported that Brown was difficult but felt things would improve.[41] Lomax responded to Brown's fussiness just as he did to Miss Terrill's perfectionist tendencies—he ignored them both. While Brown puttered, Lomax sat back in his seat, took in the magnificent scenery, and said nothing. He found small things to entertain him—a flock of chickens, a new straw hat, two ancient mountain ladies with squeaky voices who sang about Lord Thomas "a-riding his milk white steed up yanders (to rhyme with gander)." As the work drew to a close, Lomax fretted that he had done his job poorly, but decided they had accomplished what they set out to do.[42] He and Brown recorded a hundred songs in their ten days together, and Lomax, anxious to counter the charge that he was interested only in blacks, noted with satisfaction that all but a dozen or so had come from white singers. At least twenty-five were Child ballads, few of which had previously been collected on record for the Archive.[43]

From North Carolina, Lomax set off for a brief visit to Texas, leapfrogging around the Southeast on inspection trips to field offices of the Historical Records Survey. In Arkansas he recorded nearly a hundred songs in the repertoire of a blind mountain woman, seventy-five-year-old Mrs. Emma Dusenbury, then traveled to Austin to load up Miss Terrill and bring her back to Washington for a short visit. On the way he consulted with Writers' Project staffs in states along the way and visited various song sources, including Mrs. Genevieve Chandler of Murrell's Inlet, South Carolina, who became one of his more valuable contacts for Negro spirituals.

Throughout all this activity, Lomax kept up with his usual flood of correspondence, writing as many as half a dozen letters a day for sustained periods, even when on the road. His family staggered under the load, for he expected a reply to every letter, and grew morose or testy when he didn't get it. Daughter Shirley wished he would slacken. "I never saw such a man to write letters!" she complained.[44]

One letter of note was to Bess as she began her first year of college (precocious like Alan, she was entering the University of Texas four months before her sixteenth birthday, just as he had done). Five pages front and back, Lomax's letter to her was that of a doting parent, full of Horatio Alger advice: take only a normal load, join an organization or two (no more!), read at least one good book a month (his old friend, Dr. Benedict, now president of the University, would happily make a list for her if she would ask him), keep and file alphabetically all her letters, invitations, dance cards, and so on, avoid "grievances" against her professors. Touchingly, he spoke of what a vivid adventure it had been for him when he first came to the University of Texas, "gratifying a life-long desire." Now, overcome with memories and far from everything he loved in Texas, he could hardly avoid a note of self-pity. Bess needn't answer this letter, he told her, but could dismiss it as the mutterings of a lonely old father, feeling neglected and sometimes saddened by the hard life that fate had dealt him. Thinking of Bess revived his spirits, however, and he closed with a page of glowing compliments on her grace, intelligence, and loyalty. "I am a proud father and I love you very much."[45]

• • • • •

Miss Terrill spent two weeks in Washington, then returned to Texas in early September to start the school year. Once she had come and gone, Lomax was bluer than ever, despite a continual round of socializing that included an elaborate dinner given by his landlady in honor of his sixty-ninth birthday. He stayed busy at both offices—the Writers' Project and the Archive of Folk Song—putting into finished form the material from his latest trip, copying recordings, and giving a series of programs for various government officials to demonstrate the results of his expeditions.

These demonstrations often extended to social occasions. Harold Spivacke said later, with some exaggeration, "The whole Archive was in John's suitcase . . . and at the slightest provocation—such as an invitation to your home—he would bring it along and play it on your phonograph. . . . And he would play [the records] and tell these marvelous tales. He was a marvelous storyteller."[46] But, as Spivacke noted, the records were often worse for the wear caused by the typical home phonograph, with its heavy tone arm.

At the Library, the equipment frequently failed and Lomax's demonstrations had to be canceled. Mrs. Roosevelt was reported several times to be on her way to attend a demonstration but never turned up. Lomax dressed in his new winter suit "so as to look nice for my show," then the weather turned hot and he was miserable, so disturbed in fact that he paid his room rent ten days before it was due, which only upset him more when he realized what he'd done.[47]

In October he fell ill. The doctor identified high blood pressure as the cause and put him on a strict diet of "pink pills and milk toast—no meat, except white fish," as he complained to Miss Terrill.[48] But it was clear that the trouble was partly psychological. To Johnny he had confided that he was so lonesome for familiar faces and his beloved family that it made him physically ill—"indigestion and sometimes slight fever."[49] Skeptical of the blood pressure diagnosis, he wrote to his doctor in Austin, relating his symptoms and enclosing a copy of his urinalysis. The doctor in Washington had mentioned Bright's disease, but Lomax pointed out that he still worked his usual long hours, maintained his normal weight and appetite, and "do not drink." Dr. Weller in Texas told him it was impossible to offer a diagnosis from evidence supplied by mail, but he didn't think there was anything seriously wrong.[50] The diet seemed to help; he lost five pounds and his blood pressure dropped eight points. In any event, he assured Miss Terrill that he did not have "the disease you say afflicts so many men 'past 55.'"[51]

Feeling better, he began to make new plans for a book of folklore in a "huge volume to cover the country" and got Alsberg to authorize his travel to Cambridge with the hope of convincing George Lyman Kittredge to serve as editor-in-chief. If he succeeded, he told Miss Terrill, his name anywhere near Kittredge's on such a book would make him, at last, "a distinguished person." But Kittredge turned him down. His old mentor was gracious, but "the *no* was definite and clear cut and final." The next day in

New York, the business people Lomax wanted to see were either busy or out of town. He called on Margaret Conklin, got a frosty reception, and fled to John Lang Sinclair's apartment when it became clear that he was still persona non grata with Bonkle and Conkle because of the Leadbelly affair.[52]

Alan arrived in Washington in early November. He'd been doing fieldwork in Mexico and had applied for a fellowship at the University of Texas to sustain the project. But despite his considerable credentials and all the strings his father could pull (a recommendation from Herbert Putnam, for example),[53] the application was turned down, and he had come to Washington with the hope that either Seeger or Alsberg could find a place for him in their operations. Meanwhile, he was more or less employed by his father to work with him in the Archive, making copies of their recordings and organizing material from their earlier expeditions. Lomax advanced him living expenses, sums which were to be repaid from the profits of their joint enterprises—books, radio royalties, reprint rights, and other means of "cashing in on the folk music we have collected."[54] This was the beginning of what Lomax humorously referred to later as "the racket I run with the Ballads."[55] It was also during this time that he began to envision a second volume of *American Ballads and Folk Songs,* the work which eventually emerged as *Our Singing Country.*

Roosevelt's stunning reelection that month brightened many lives, especially those on the government payroll, although Lomax in reporting to Miss Terrill tacitly refrained from mentioning the name of the president, who in time would become his bête noire. He said only that "The election with its amazing outcome makes us all feel more cheerful."[56] The cheers had hardly died when the realization set in that Roosevelt intended to make good on his campaign promise to balance the budget. That meant cuts in government programs and jeopardized Alan's chances of going to work for either Seeger or Alsberg. Lomax felt scarcely more secure, and he again considered shifting his base of operations back to Texas. To some extent, that depended on Alan's progress in making copies of their recordings in the Archive. Once that was done, Lomax told Miss Terrill, he could take them back to Texas to work on for publication, while Alan went his own way. Eventually, he felt, "our various schemes ought to make some money and reputation" for both of them.[57]

An earlier such scheme came to fruition when *Negro Folk Songs as Sung by Leadbelly* was finally published on November 24. Against Lomax's opposition, Macmillan had changed the title from "Leadbelly and His Songs" because too much time had passed and Leadbelly was no longer an attraction.[58] As the publication date neared, Lomax warned Miss Terrill to prepare herself "for criticisms in the North of a Southern man writing about a black,"[59] but there was little of that. Most reviews were ambivalent and bland, focusing on Leadbelly's exoticism and the brief sensation he had created. Black playwright and composer James Weldon Johnson praised the Lomaxes for letting Leadbelly tell his own story, which resulted in "one of the most amazing autobiographical accounts ever printed in America."[60] Similarly, Harry Hansen in the *New York World Telegram* dealt almost exclusively with the details of Leadbelly's life rather than his music or the Lomaxes, but mentioned finally that the book was "a valuable contribution to folk lore."[61] Asserting that it was "not for the casual reader," the *Saturday Review of Literature* concluded that "[the book's] final appeal may prove to be that of a historical record of certain elements in the growth of jazz"[62]—a judgment which, in view of Lomax's distaste for jazz, must have jarred him. Although the Lomaxes originally felt they had scored a coup in obtaining the services of so eminent a musicologist as George Herzog for the book, many reviews were critical of Herzog's musical notation, and even Lomax later complained that the music was "so meticulously done" by a Yale scholar (Herzog was at Columbia by the time the book appeared) that no one else "has ever been able to translate it into melodies."[63]

If he expected money or reputation from *Negro Folk Songs as Sung by Leadbelly,* Lomax was doomed to disappointment. Macmillan submitted the book to the Pulitzer Prize committee, but it was not even nominated. Six months after publication—usually the period of most concentrated sales activity—it had not sold enough to cover the advance paid by the publisher.[64] Sadly, Lomax hoped that this information might at least change Mary Elizabeth Barnicle's opinion of him, "though I hardly suppose she . . . can ever think well of me." In the meantime, busy socializing in Washington, he consoled himself with the notion that the book's publication had not damaged him with the people he knew there.[65]

All was not as harmonious as he thought. Although he and Alan were frequent guests in the apartment of Strunk's assistant, Ed Waters, Waters and his wife were privately critical of the way Lomax had treated Iron Head. Despite her husband's small income, Mrs. Waters was famous for her culinary efforts and, to Lomax's delight, regularly set out elaborate buffets for their gatherings. Lomax noted sympathetically that Mrs. Waters had to work door-to-door for a city directory firm to supplement her husband's meager salary,[66] but he contributed little to remedy that situation, although Waters had helped with both *American Ballads and Folk Songs* and *Negro Folk Songs as Sung by Leadbelly,* at first in his official capacity, but gradually spending more and more time outside office hours on work for Lomax. All he got was a credit among the acknowledgments. Finally, after making many new musical notations and writing an introduction for an enlarged edition of *Cowboy Songs,* he declined Lomax's offer to collaborate further, and Lomax told Seeger that Waters had "refused in the rudest terms" to help him. When that got back to Waters, he turned against Lomax for good; years later, he insisted indignantly that he had not been rude, but admitted to being "irritated by the smallness of the amount" he got for all his work on *Cowboy Songs.* Lomax had paid him twenty-five dollars.[67]

There was sudden turmoil on the domestic side as well. For two years now, almost from the time of their marriage, Lomax and Miss Terrill had been debating whether she should quit her job. They had never quite been able to get synchronized; when she wanted to quit, he told her not to, and when he said she should do as she liked, she opted to stay. But the University of Texas was going through another period of strain, and by late 1936, Miss Terrill had decided she had had enough. Still, Lomax felt they needed her salary, and he was offended that she wouldn't take his advice and cut down on her social obligations. In a long, rambling letter, he complained that she had said "No" to him rather than to the organizations she belonged to. As long as she was supporting herself, she could do as she liked and consult with no one (i.e., himself) about how she spent either her time or her money. But what she would do with him was entirely something else. This sounded vaguely as though he were thinking of some sort of estrangement, present or future. He would always love her, he said, and would come to see her whenever she would let him—as if their marriage had reverted to a courtship arrangement—and added oddly, "I'll always wish that you could have been my partner."

For some time she had been hinting that she'd like to join him for Christmas—wherever he might be. She knew he was planning a recording trip into the South, and she suggested they meet in Richmond, where he could attend the MLA meeting during the holidays. He responded that "the M.L.A. may go where the whangdoodle whineth," confiding that, despite his many appearances before that learned body, he had always appeared there with "a depressing sense of inferiority," because his own school, the University of Texas, had never thought him good enough to teach even a freshman class there.[68]

Even if that were true—in fact, he had taught summer school accounting classes at the University of Texas in the teens—there's little evidence that he was eager to teach freshman classes anywhere. Further, his sense of the MLA's response to his presence was quite at variance with the opinion of Stith Thompson, who was never exactly a Lomax partisan. After Lomax died, Thompson wrote, "For many years his appearance at the Modern Language Association of America afforded a welcome contrast to the solemnity of most of the papers presented, and always drew large audiences and great applause."[69] Clearly what was on Lomax's mind in this imbroglio with Miss Terrill were thoughts of mortality, complicated by ego, stress, and distance from familiar places and people. To her credit, Miss Terrill understood and, as usual, took a calm and reasoned view of it all. "I believe that we could understand each other if we could look into each other's eyes, touch each other's hands and lips, feel each other's arms," she wrote. At practically the same time he was mourning his dashed hope of her ever joining him as his "partner," she wrote again to plead that he let her come "and walk by your side and help you."[70] Once she was no longer dean, she promised, she would give up all her activities except church, the AAUW, and her sorority, Delta Kappa Gamma.

Lomax responded as though nothing had happened. "I do not know what I was trying to say," he wrote. He was feeling better and had more practical matters to face. With government agencies cutting back their work forces, he took an uncharacteristically philosophical view of the possibility that he might be the next to go. The nation could certainly get along without folklore, he told Miss Terrill; maybe the whole world would be better off without it.[71]

Nevertheless, Miss Terrill—feeling perhaps that the time had come for at least one of them to act decisively—resolved at last to quit her job and join her husband in whatever pursuits might come his way. Her resignation would take effect at the end of the fall 1936 term. But arranging their Christmas plans remained a problem. Lomax was anxious to get on the road with a recording machine by early December, but there were delays in obtaining equipment. Then John Vance asked him to talk at a retirement dinner honoring a Library official on December 17. Lomax decided he'd leave on the recording trip (if the machine arrived), then backtrack to Washington for the dinner. The machine failed to arrive and he changed those plans. Then a machine came and he went ahead scheduling his itinerary only to discover that the machine wouldn't work. Miss Terrill threw up her hands. "One day I am spending Christmas in Washington, the next in Mobile, the next in Charleston, and today again in Washington. Now I know all the train schedules of the Middle West and East."[72]

At last the Library agreed to purchase a machine that would work, although it couldn't be delivered until after Christmas. That settled matters. Miss Terrill was finally instructed to buy her ticket for Washington. They had Christmas dinner with the Vances in Chevy Chase, the new recording machine arrived on schedule, and four days later they drove away together, headed for Richmond and the MLA.

CHAPTER TWENTY-FOUR

• • • • •

Ten Thousand Miles from Home

1936–39

By late 1936 the Archive of American Folk Song had become a functioning reality. Despite Harold Spivacke's witty remark that it existed entirely in Lomax's suitcase, in mid-1937 the Archive contained some 1,314 cylinder and disc recordings with over four thousand folk tunes. The Lomaxes had supplied almost a thousand of these recordings—over three thousand songs—in the period since Lomax became honorary curator in 1933.[1] Although the Archive lay largely fallow for extended intervals while Lomax was in the field, there was always a flurry of activity whenever he returned to Washington, and the growing collection was gaining favorable attention from Library officials. With the national economy improving, Putnam was able to secure for the first time a small appropriation from Congress to support the Archive in July 1936, and that fall Alan Lomax became its first paid staff member, hired on a temporary basis to undertake an extended collecting trip to Haiti in December.[2] For the first time also, government funds were used to purchase a recording machine for Lomax's use, when he took to the road just after Christmas with Miss Terrill as "chauffeur, valet, buffer, machine operator, disk-jockey, body-guard, doctor and nurse, wife and companion," as she later described herself, "a timid successor to Alan and Leadbelly."[3]

After attending MLA sessions in Richmond and Williamsburg (the conference was divided between the two cities that year), they set off on a long, convoluted journey through the South and all over Texas during January and February, a trek that eventually put nearly seven thousand miles on Miss Terrill's Plymouth. Much of this was a scouting expedition, in preparation for work Lomax would undertake after their return to Washington in March and April.

By early spring Lomax was complaining that work was "pouring in" at his WPA office. Despite the heavy load, there were rumors of budget cuts, and he was sure he would be one of the first to go. That wouldn't bother him, he said, because there was so much work at the WPA that he could hardly keep up with it and run the Archive at the same time.[4] Still he found time to resume the social whirl—more lunches with important people, dinners at small hotels in the country, concerts, movies, plays (at the Belasco he saw *Ecstasy,* "a naughty, naughty play open only to adults").[5] Mr. and Mrs. Ed Waters hosted a meeting in their home of the Musicology Society that included a talk by Charles Seeger entitled "The Future Strategy in American Music." Lomax made a point of attending and taking a front seat, but muttered later that Seeger's paper was "long drawn and wearisome," on "a commonplace subject" unnecessarily obscured by jargon and abstractions.[6]

Miss Terrill returned to Washington in late April and they were off on another field expedition. In August Lomax reported to Spivacke from Texas that since the first of the year he and Miss Terrill had filled nearly two hundred records (each containing as many as twelve songs) from sources in Texas, Mississippi, Alabama, Florida, and numerous sites in South Carolina. He had the sources staked out and waiting, he told Spivacke, enabling him to gather more good material than he'd ever been able to do in so short a time.[7]

One of their more fruitful trips was to Livingston, Alabama, where a local woman, the redoubtable Ruby Pickens Tartt, had played a material role in helping locate sources. As a $56-a-month local field-worker for the Writers' Project ("chairman" of its Sumter County operation), Mrs. Tartt was one of those who had answered Henry Alsberg's call for folklore material and so inundated the project's Washington office that Lomax had to be called. Once he spotted the rich variety of rare Negro songs and stories from Mrs. Tartt, he quickly set about arranging to visit Livingston with a recording machine.

Ruby Pickens Tartt's interest in Negro life and culture reached back almost to her childhood, when she accompanied her father, a prominent landowner, to visit his black renters. Talented as a painter, she had attended the Chase School of Art in New York, then returned to Livingston to teach art at the local college and later married her childhood sweetheart, Pratt Tartt, a clerk in his father's bank. But keeping house and playing the young southern matron held little attraction for her. Involving herself in community issues, she took a particular interest in improving conditions among blacks, who constituted almost 80 percent of the county's population. Like her father, she loved the preaching and singing in black churches and was especially drawn to the spirituals that had been handed down orally through the years.

Mrs. Tartt eventually acquired a reputation as the town character. She scoffed at the accepted notions of social and racial behavior and spent much of her time visiting among black families, observing their habits and rituals, writing down their folktales, proverbs, party and play songs, blues, and spirituals. Her relationship with blacks was paternalistic, not unlike Lomax's, but she was genuinely incensed by the injustices they suffered, and she worked to improve their lot whenever she could.[8] Blacks and whites alike fell under her sway; as a storyteller and raconteur, she was very nearly a match for John Lomax.

In the depression of the early 1930s the fortunes of the Tartts were drastically reduced. The family bank failed, and the lands and fine home that had belonged to Ruby's parents were lost to creditors. She and her husband, now in their fifties, were almost without income. Pratt Tartt was ill much of the time and could scarcely work even when a job was available. Ultimately, they were among the thousands saved by the WPA. After that agency was created in 1935, Mrs. Tartt at last found work on a federal sewing project in nearby York, Alabama, although her salary was barely enough to pay their living expenses. When they lost the estate that had been in her family for generations, they were forced to become renters, moving into a large but shabby old house known as Baldwin Hill. At one side, surrounded by shady oaks and boxwoods, was a rose arbor that became Lomax's favorite place for recording the black singers and storytellers that Mrs. Tartt brought for him and Miss Terrill when they came visiting that spring of 1937.

For the first day's recording, Mrs. Tartt had chosen two cousins, Dock Reed[9] and Vera Hall, whose voices blended beautifully. Reed, who had a dreamy, faraway look in his large eyes, sang only spirituals, but his cousin's repertoire included "worldly" songs as well. In time, Lomax—and many others—thought of Dock Reed and Vera Hall as perhaps his finest discoveries, although they never gained the notoriety of Leadbelly or Iron Head.

Initially, the singers were ill at ease in the presence of white strangers and the unfamiliar recording apparatus. Mrs. Tartt was also apprehensive, but Lomax quickly put her fears to rest. Long attuned to such situations, he saw to it that everyone was seated and comfortable, then suggested that they listen to a record he had made recently at Parchman prison farm in Mississippi. When Dock Reed heard the familiar strains of "I Don't Mind the Weather," a song he knew well, he grinned broadly, and Vera Hall began to hum an accompaniment. Soon they were all laughing and talking easily, and Lomax's warm manner with the singers made a lasting impression on Mrs. Tartt.[10]

From these and other singers she brought to Baldwin Hill, Lomax and Miss Terrill came away from their week in Livingston with more than a hundred outstanding tunes.[11] They came away also with lasting friendships both among the singers and with Mrs. Tartt, who had felt she was toiling alone and unappreciated until Lomax took an interest in her efforts to preserve the black culture of her region. In him she had found the kindred spirit she badly needed. Later, he helped her publish some of her local-color stories, and they kept up a lively correspondence until his death. He and Miss Terrill returned to Livingston to record on three future occasions, so rich was the lode of folk material which Mrs. Tartt mined for them.

An important development had taken place at the Library of Congress while Lomax was roaming around the country that summer. Oliver Strunk, who was an annoyance not only to Lomax, had finally managed to get himself fired. Disdaining blatant philanthropy, he casually mislaid a check from one of the Library's more prominent patrons. His superiors were apparently waiting for just such a lapse; when the matter was brought to Librarian Putnam, he told the patron simply, "If you don't like Strunk, we'll find someone with whom you *can* work."[12]

That someone turned out to be Harold Spivacke, who had been Strunk's chief assistant since joining the Music Division in 1934. Spivacke was efficient and well liked by everyone at the Library (with the possible exception of Ed Waters, who tended to feel he should have gotten Strunk's job).[13] When Lomax heard the news of Spivacke's promotion, he told the new chief that he felt much warmer toward the Library of Congress, "now that you are where you are."[14]

Lomax happened to be back in Washington on the day Spivacke officially took over the division. "Things were *very* difficult," Spivacke remembered, "and Lomax dropped in, sat down, with a cigar, hat on, feet on my desk, and said, 'Spivacke, why do you look so sad?'" When Spivacke explained his woes, Lomax replied with a story. Back on the Texas frontier when he was a boy, he said, "an old Indian friend" came every day to visit

Lomax's mother. One day the Indian went into the kitchen, sat down on the hot stove, and was too polite to move until his pants caught fire, whereupon he leapt up and ran away. He finally came back again after several weeks, but in all the years that followed, he would never sit down on anything in the Lomax home. Lomax paused and looked at Spivacke. "That's the trouble with you, Spivacke," he said. "You get more out of an experience than there is in it." Spivacke loved the story. "I like to be put in my place," he said later. "This [story] I have never forgotten."

Spivacke and Lomax had worked together harmoniously for two or three years prior to Spivacke's appointment as head of the division. Despite the differences in their backgrounds, Spivacke developed a genuine affection for the old Texan, along with a growing interest in the folk music that Lomax was adding to the Archive. Like others of his generation around the Library, Spivacke was much taken with Lomax's Texas background and accepted the romantic notion that he had once been cowboy. "He never took his hat off," said Spivacke, "except when he took it off with a great flourish to greet a lady—but then he put it on again. In your home. He was an old cowboy and, although he later went to Harvard, he never grew out of his cowboy habit of wearing a hat." Spivacke was amused on one occasion when, as he left the office on an errand, Lomax sent for a nickel cigar, claiming that "I can't smoke any of these expensive ten-cent things." Years later, when a portrait of Lomax was painted for the University of Texas, Spivacke praised the likeness, but said it lacked realism—the big corona in Lomax's hand was too expensive.[15]

· · · · ·

By midsummer, Lomax could see that his WPA job was ending (his more or less official departure from the Writers' Project would indeed come in October). He had plenty of other work—a new, enlarged edition of *Cowboy Songs,* a sequel to *American Ballads and Folk Songs,* and a proposed autobiography, all under contract to Macmillan—but he was, as he told Spivacke, "tired down to the inner recesses of the marrow of my bones."[16]

For some time he'd been having repairs done to the House in the Woods in Dallas, with the notion of moving there permanently to "write books and lecture and otherwise take my ease," as he'd told Johnny.[17] First there were plans for a trip to Europe, perhaps for as long as a year, accompanied by Miss Terrill and all of his children who could be persuaded to go—but like all of Lomax's plans, this one was subject to much backing and filling. In June he told Johnny that he was determined to go—"only a general European war can stop me"[18]—but in August glumly wrote Spivacke that he wasn't up for such a trip, for "I don't like the prospect of being buried at sea," voicing a premonition of death that was beginning to haunt him. He also told Spivacke that rather than settling in Dallas, he might return to Washington and "join with you to shake down the Carnegies or the Rockefellers."[19]

What he finally did was a bit of both. Looking ahead six months, he booked a European departure for early 1938 and in September took Miss Terrill and Bess with him back to Washington to work on what he termed "the second big ballad book" (eventually *Our Singing Country*). That same month he observed his seventieth birthday with little fanfare, and soon after, with even less ceremony, he quietly withdrew from the WPA, his departure eased along by controversy rising within the ranks of the American Folklore Society. Elitists within the AFS, which had twice honored Lomax by electing him president, now declared him unacceptable as a folklorist because he lacked a Ph.D. Some observers attributed this action to the jealousy of certain academics over the commercial success of Lomax's books; there was also widespread feeling that the Lomaxes were trying to stake a claim on the whole of American folksong and keep everyone else out.[20] Whatever the motive, at its annual meeting in December the AFS adopted a resolution distancing itself from the material assembled by the Federal Writers' Project under Lomax's direction. It would be acceptable, said the association, only if collected under "expert guidance" (in other words, by an academic with specialized training).[21] Lomax, always painfully sensitive to charges, real or imagined, that he was a mere amateur, said little. Perhaps weary of the whole business, his only response to the AFS's snub was the wry observation, sometime later, that "perhaps the collector must go out among the people dressed in cap and gown."[22]

After a few months, Alsberg named as Lomax's successor Benjamin Botkin, A.B. Harvard (*magna cum laude*), M.A. Columbia, Ph.D. University of Nebraska, editor, professor at the University of Oklahoma, and contributor to learned journals. At its next annual meeting, the AFS "noted with interest" the appointment of Botkin, "a trained folklorist" and now expressed a willingness to cooperate with his WPA projects.[23]

Harold Preece, a WPA staffer in Texas who had arranged recording tours for Lomax, once asked him, "What do you know and think about Botkin in Oklahoma?" Botkin's work was interesting, responded Lomax, but it wasn't the sort of thing he did; moreover, "how much is Botkin and how much is folklore, only he knows."[24] Ironically, despite Botkin's impeccable credentials, within a decade he had also earned the enmity of academics for publishing "popular" books and was cast from the fold.

Lomax had at least one consolation in the wake of all this discord with the AFS. Earlier in the year, he had written Johnny that "I owe no man any money," adding, "for your ears only," that his net worth amounted $80,000, entirely aside from the value of his books. The result, he said, was that he was happier and stronger than he had been in years.[25] The foundation and major part of this modest fortune was Republic National Bank stock; over the years Lomax had wisely increased his holdings from a few hundred shares to more than a thousand. In the pit of the depression the stock had sold for as low as 18½—when there were buyers. Now it was in the mid-50s and climbing in an active market. Lomax also held miscellaneous other stocks, and additional assets included paid-up insurance policies, his home in Dallas, and the income from his books, which in 1938 produced some three hundred dollars, a substantial sum at a time when few Americans earned that much a month.[26]

· · · · ·

On February 9, 1938, Lomax and Miss Terrill sailed from New York aboard the *Queen Mary,* accompanied by Bess and her college roommate, Elizabeth Watkins. In an unusual fit of largesse, Lomax had offered to take his other children as well, but Shirley and Alan had family or business matters which prevented their going and Johnny could get away for only a few weeks in the summer; he would join the travelers in the later stages of their journey.

Bess, just turned seventeen, had completed her freshman year at the University of Texas the previous spring with a record somewhat less distinguished than her father expected, and Deanie—Miss Terrill—persuaded Lomax to let his daughter drop out of college for a year. Bess had come with them to Washington in the fall and lent a valuable hand to her father, Alan, and Ruth Crawford Seeger in the preparation of *Our Singing Country,* which Macmillan hoped to bring out the following year.

The sea crossing to Europe was a horror for everyone but Lomax. Two days out, Bess reported that they had a "'good sea running,' which means that the ship wallows sideways and then bucks forward with a little shimmy in the middle." She, Elizabeth, and Miss Terrill were desperately seasick and took to their beds, but Lomax boasted that he "never turned a hair." Said Bess from her bunk, between heaves, "Father violates every rule of landsman etiquette, eats prodigiously, never steps on deck, and feels marvelous, damn it."[27]

They landed at Cherbourg five days later in a storm of sleet and snow. Paris was also wintery and bleak, and they all came down with colds. After a miserable week there, they decided to go to the Riviera and took the train to Marseilles, then on to Nice. Lomax at least found the prices invigorating. He boasted to Shirley that their luxurious room at St.-Jean-Cap-Ferrat cost less than he paid at the Lubbock Hotel. But porters and cab drivers expected a tip for each piece of luggage, and "this means war with my economic heritage." Ever the provincial Texas country boy, he complained also of the problems of dealing with foreigners who spoke a language "we can only vaguely guess at."[28] Bess said, "He never got over the feeling that if he just spoke slowly and loudly enough, any fool would be able to understand English—and he would bellow at the top of his voice, V-E-R-R-R-Y S-L-O-W-LY."[29]

He and Miss Terrill visited the casino at Monte Carlo, and Lomax told Shirley that as soon as Miss Terrill learned some of the rules, she was going to play for both of them. There is no report of winnings or losses, but surely windows rattled in Baptist churches all over Texas. The girls bicycled, went to the movies, and flirted with French soldiers at a carnival in Nice. Not entirely comfortable out of the traces, Lomax seemed apologetic that he was not working. All he had done, he told Shirley only half humorously, was wait on three females who had their charming moments but traveled with twelve pieces of luggage that he had to look after.[30]

The girls quietly hatched a plan to return alone to Paris, ostensibly to improve their French. Elizabeth, who was paying her own way, was concerned about expenses, and her mother had written her about a Paris pension for students, where room and board cost only a dollar a day and the woman who owned it gave instruction in French to Americans. Miss Terrill, as a Latin scholar, was anxious to see Italy—which young radical Bess detested for its fascism—and when the elder Lomaxes decided to go to Rome, the foursome "broke peaceably," as Bess put it, and went their different ways.[31] In the next two months, while the girls lived cheaply in Paris and grew fluent in French, Lomax and Miss Terrill traveled to Rome, visited Sicily, saw Florence and Milan, passed through the Tyrol on their way north, and rejoined the girls in Zurich in early May. By this time a pattern had developed—even when they were traveling to the same places together, Lomax and Miss Terrill stayed in hotels while the girls found beds in youth hostels and joined their elders only for meals. "I was at the disagreeable stage of adolescence," Bess admitted later, "and Father sometimes wasn't too agreeable either, so we tended to skirt each other."[32]

Exhausted from almost six years of uninterrupted labor and stress, Lomax was also beginning to feel his age. More and more he was having intimations of mortality, intensified by the passing of old friends like Harry Benedict, who had died suddenly, in the traces, the previous May. Miss Terrill reported that Lomax enjoyed seeing ancient Roman temples and Pompeii, but he was at best a lethargic tourist, moody and morose, more interested in eating and sleeping than anything else. He was also consoling himself more than usual with fruits of the vine. To Spivacke he spoke of "a recently developed inertia" resulting from two month's consumption of French and Italian cognac and recently intensified by "the rare and unparalleled vintage of hilly Sicily."[33]

For a man who spent his life examining and preserving cultural byways, he showed curiously little interest in what was going on around him—at a time of immense historical significance, with Europe drawing daily nearer to World War II. Bess said later that his behavior on the trip reminded her of Mark Twain in such books as *Following the Equator* and *Innocents Abroad;* he was interested in antiquities and amused by the people, but oblivious to contemporary events.[34] Uncharacteristically, he kept no account of their travels, wrote few letters, and afterward rarely ever mentioned the trip. He was an indifferent sightseer, he told Spivacke in April. "Museums and the like are beginning to pall on me."[35] But he slept well and his appetite flourished. After trips to several spas in the Tyrol, where he "took the waters," his spirits began to revive.

By the time they reached Innsbruck in early May, he was showing signs of his old form. Fretting over the progress of half a dozen projects back home, he fired off a long letter, full of orders, instructions, complaints, and questions, to Alan—who was now the first full-time salaried employee of the Archive of Folk Song, with the title of "Assistant in Charge"(that is, the Music Division assistant who was in charge of the Archive). Alan did his best to comply, assuring his father that everything was under control. But he too was struck by the latter's lack of interest in his surroundings and urged him to send more news about his travels, complaining that his father wrote home about Austria, Switzerland, and other enchanted lands as impassively as though they were "just other corn-fed counties in the Midwest."[36]

Bess and Elizabeth rejoined Lomax and Miss Terrill in Zurich, and the four of them reached Vienna less than two months after Hitler's *Anschluss,* the Nazi occupation of Austria. The streets were filled with soldiers and

Brown Shirts, there were swastikas everywhere, even on baby carriages, and hung from buildings all over the city were huge paintings of Hitler wearing white armor astride a black horse. Bess wrote lively, colorful letters to Alan (she and Elizabeth thought the Hitler painting absurd and stood in the street laughing at it endlessly),[37] but if any of the political turmoil made an impression on Lomax or Miss Terrill, there is no evidence.

From Vienna they took a river steamer down the Danube to Budapest, where life was even bleaker than in Austria. After three days they returned to Vienna and again separated, the girls off to Prague while Lomax and Miss Terrill journeyed by train to Amsterdam to meet Johnny, arriving from the States. Bess and Elizabeth reached Prague late at night and took a cab to the address of their hotel, only to find it transformed into an office building housing the Nazi Youth headquarters. Two handsome young Nazis undertook to show them about the city. Said Bess later, with considerable understatement, "We were very much the innocent Americans arriving in Europe at a period of enormous crisis—and innocent of what was happening all around us. It seems to me to be quite mad, when I look back on it now."[38]

Meanwhile, Lomax and Miss Terrill toured the Alps, with robust Johnny flexing his muscles and hiking ahead of them. Then they went to Scandinavia. From Stalheim, Norway, in June, Lomax reported to Alan that Johnny "climbs mountains and dives into ice cold waterfalls."[39] In early July they sailed to England, landing at Newcastle and then traveling on to Scotland.

While taking a stroll after high tea one day in Edinburgh, they were joined by a band of small boys who offered to be their guides. When the boys learned that the visitors were from Texas, their eyes lit up. In the shadow of the Castle, Lomax told them cowboy stories and, as they departed, said lightly, in his hospitable-Texan manner, "Come to Texas." When the smallest of the lot said he would, Lomax told him he would have a pony waiting for him when arrived. "When you get to the Red River, just call my name and I'll come get you with the pony." He and Miss Terrill had gone only a few yards toward their hotel when the little boy came running back. "Please, sir, when I come to Texas, what name shall I say?" Lomax gave him his card. Six years later, in 1944, writing about the episode for the *Southwest Review,* he reflected, "I hope the war spares him for his pony ride in Texas."[40] It was the only experience of his European trip that he ever wrote about.

Within a few weeks the tour began to wind down. Johnny returned to the States. Lomax and Miss Terrill went to London, where they were joined by Bess and Elizabeth. Elizabeth left the group in London and sailed for home by herself. The three Lomaxes traveled to Italy and sailed from Trieste aboard the Italian liner *Vulcania* on August 22, arriving in New York on September 5, just in time for Bess to enroll at Bryn Mawr that fall.

Back in Texas, Lomax and Miss Terrill moved into a vacation home that she owned at Port Aransas, on San Jose Island off the Gulf coast. Dubbed "Fiddler Crab Retreat," it was an airy, comfortable little beach cottage built on pilings at the water's edge. Initially Lomax reported that his seven months abroad had quite restored his health—"I seem to have more physical reserve than for ten years"[41]—but while fishing one day, he slipped trying to land a large sheephead and badly skinned his leg. The wound became infected, and the sulfanilamide prescribed by the doctor made him nauseous. After several days in the hospital, he was confined to bed at home. Inactivity always depressed him, and for weeks he was in poor spirits, complaining to Spivacke that he felt neglected by the Library of Congress and telling Johnny morosely that he was thinking of following Ambrose Bierce's example of going to Mexico and disappearing. His only purpose in life, he said, was never to become a burden to his children.[42] He told Alan that he was realizing he had only a few years to live and, lamenting his failures, touchingly urged his son "to achieve in some such way as I have dreamed for myself." He had started too late, he said, pointing out that he was twenty-eight before he ever got to a college worthy of the name. He had also been held back by his brother's debt and the care of his mother and sister—and perhaps even more by his own iron character, lacking from boyhood the resilience of youth and (he told Alan) "sober to somberness before my term."[43]

Then, after he'd suffered physically and spiritually for nearly a month, Miss Terrill cooked him a delicious rare steak, and he reported that "the eating thereof has given me a fresh lease on life."[44] Spivacke sent earnest assurances that he found working with the Lomaxes a delightful experience, and promised that the Music Department would do its best to get him a recording machine for another field trip in early 1939.[45] With his leg on the mend, this news sent Lomax back to his desk, scribbling off letters to arrange recording dates and working out the details of an ambitious three-month, 6,500-mile trip that would take him and Miss Terrill through eight states.

· · · · ·

By the late 1930s, Lomax had acquired a national reputation as an authority on folksong, his lack of academic credentials notwithstanding. Selections from his work appeared in many textbooks and anthologies, and so many schoolchildren wrote to him asking for information about him and his ballad collecting that he had to instruct Miss Terrill to stop sending out copies of a biographical sketch he'd prepared for newspapers and instead tell students to read his books and consult his entry in *Who's Who.*[46] There was a steady flow of correspondence with the band of literary and semiliterary lights who considered themselves keepers of the flame of the Old West, such as E. A. Brininstool, Charles Badger Clark, Curley Fletcher, Owen Wister, and Charley Marshall of radio's "Death Valley Days." Vying for his attention as well were a large number of lady folklorists, female aesthetes, and garden-club matrons. In addition to his many acquaintances in the higher circles of education, journalism, and politics, over the years Lomax had rubbed shoulders with such well known Americans as Carl Sandburg, Amy Lowell, William Rose Benét, Lowell Thomas, Will Rogers, and Irvin S. Cobb. Further verification of his growing stature came in the fall of 1938 when the British Broadcasting Corporation asked him to serve as consultant and commentator for a thirteen-week series of radio programs on American music, with records supplied from the Archive of American Folk Song.

But all that counted for little when he found himself back in Texas, now aged beyond his allotted three score years and ten, farther than ever from power within the Archive, engaged in a struggle with his publisher over page limits on his forthcoming book, and feeling that his children were growing ever more distant from him. As he recovered from his leg wound in the early days of 1939, his major efforts were directed toward convincing Spivacke to send him a recording machine and authorize the field trip he was planning.

This turned into a protracted struggle, magnified by the tenuous nature of Lomax's relationship with the Archive. Still "Honorary Consultant and Curator," he continued to enjoy the prestige and imprimatur of the Library of Congress for his own work, and Alan's appointment as nominal head of the Archive had ostensibly strengthened his position. In fact, Lomax was ambivalent about the arrangement—he was eager to promote Alan's advancement and willing to benefit from it, but at the same time extremely cautious for fear he might do something that seemed improper or jeopardize Alan's standing with Library officials.[47] Later, when rumors of such impropriety surfaced, he felt compelled to go on record "that never at any time did I recommend Alan Lomax for an appointment in the Library, to Mr. Putnam or to any one else,"[48] but the circumstances of Alan's employment were not further revealed, and the rumors persisted.

Spivacke took a genial attitude toward it all, frequently reassuring Lomax that he was delighted to be working with the Lomaxes, father and son—but remained vague about future recording trips.[49] Lomax, increasingly impatient, threatened to buy a machine himself, in which case, he said, he would feel no obligation to share the records with the Archive.[50] Spivacke finally got around to asking him for a detailed itinerary and proposed budget; then, after Lomax had complied but heard nothing for several days, he wrote Spivacke again in an unusually humble tone. The chief must feel free to tell him what to do, he said; despite appearances, he did not have "an overplus of ego" or think he knew it all, and he was always willing to admit his mistakes. "You can speak your mind to me," he said. "*I'll welcome any suggestions.*"[51] When that failed to budge Spivacke, he wrote again, practically begging for a machine and gave a solemn promise that he would keep strictly to whatever budget Spivacke would allow. (Four months later, after the trip, it turned out that he had spent $267.80 more than authorized. Spivacke quietly approved payment of the overage.)[52]

All this was compounded by Lomax's growing sensitivity to criticism that anyone who held his high connection with the Music Division of the Library of Congress ought to have formal training in music. Still smarting from his rejection by the AFS on similar grounds, he had this very much on his mind as he went about trying to convince Spivacke to authorize another field expedition for 1939. He discussed the matter at length with Alan, pointing out that he had done his best to prepare Spivacke for the criticism he would get from those who blamed him for keeping an amateur like Lomax on the job.[53] To Spivacke he acknowledged "the reasonableness of this point of view" but countered that his lack of technical training was more than offset by his expertise in other areas. Let him offer the evidence of his worth, he urged—evidence that could be presented to Librarian Putnam, "should he again, for any reason, become disturbed about me."[54] At long last, on March 17, Spivacke recommended to Putnam that the trip be approved. Three days later he wired Lomax that the recording machine was being shipped.

Simultaneously, Lomax had been carrying on a running battle with Macmillan over the length of the yet-untitled new book (he was still referring to it as "Ballads #2"). There was also the problem of just who—or how many—would have the responsibility of finishing the manuscript. In the fall of 1937, prior to leaving for Europe, Lomax, Bess, and Miss Terrill had done a great deal of preparation, selecting songs, duplicating and transcribing recordings, and making notes. While they were abroad, Alan notified his father that he was now ready to lend his hand with the book. Ruth Crawford Seeger was asked to do the musical annotation, under a vague financial arrangement that would cause trouble later.

After returning from Europe, Lomax had asked Macmillan to enlarge the book to include new material, but the publishers insisted that they must stay within the limit of four hundred pages specified in the contract.[55] Whereupon Lomax defiantly told Alan to go ahead and put together all the songs that he and Mrs. Seeger felt should go into the book. "I'll fix Macmillan," he said.[56] He was staking a great deal on this book, anxious to avoid the errors in selection and musical notation that critics felt had marred *American Ballads and Folk Songs.* The most offensive of these criticisms, in Lomax's view, came from the imperious George Herzog, who had botched the Leadbelly book, and from Herbert Halpert, a folklorist with the Federal Theatre Project and an ally of the academics who were Lomax's persistent foes. Lomax told Alan that he—Alan—would soon be so firmly entrenched at the Library that their critics couldn't touch him, not even "the uppity Mr. Halpert." In any event, he said, the blame for the condition of *American Ballads and Folk Songs* was all his, but with the help of Mrs. Seeger they could redeem the book's reputation in a new edition, and together with the second volume, it would find a lofty and permanent place in folksong scholarship ("despite the criticisms of Halpert, Herzog and Co., we'll make it hard to supplant"). Halpert's criticism of the Lomaxes, he said, "won't get him no folksongs."[57]

Lomax had no sooner told Alan and Mrs. Seeger to go ahead with the book on their own than he reversed his field and wrote Alan to drop it entirely—he was coming to Washington to finish the job. But when that trip was repeatedly postponed while he awaited approval from Spivacke, he went on issuing orders and directions from faraway. For a brief time even Oliver Strunk was drawn into the project, apparently by the Music Division as a consultant for the musical notation. Strunk suggested changes in music already typeset, and Macmillan warned that each change would cost $2.50. Lomax threw up his hands when he saw that incorporating Strunk's recommendations would cost over $500. "Strunk . . . does not and never will understand Negro music," he told Alan. They would simply discard most of Strunk's suggestions, he said, but he wanted the serious errors corrected at any cost.[58]

Impressed by Mrs. Seeger's work in redoing Strunk's meddling, he suggested that she be credited as "Music Editor" and perhaps even write the principal introduction, if she would write as simply and lively as she did in her letters. For the introductory matter which he and Alan were to prepare, he proposed fresh accounts of their collecting adventures, rather than the "dry-as-dust, often futile and pointless, stories of the Columbia school of folklorists." No one read that academic stuff, anyway, he said; why, the *Journal of American Folklore* probably had fewer than two hundred subscribers.[59]

The matter of space limitations remained a concern. Earlier he had threatened—perhaps only to Alan—that he would cancel his contract with Macmillan and find another publisher if they didn't give him carte blanche on the size of the book. Having failed to persuade his editor, James Putnam, and still bent on having his way, he resolved to go over Putnam's head to Macmillan vice-president H. S. Latham and present him with a manuscript "so grand that he won't dare cut it down." If necessary, he'd even take it to the firm's president, George Brett.[60] Some months would pass before he realized that he was fighting a losing battle and that a lot of hard work would have to be redone, and undone. Meanwhile, on March 21 he sent off a layout for the book to Macmillan, with great confidence that it would be in print by May. Ten days later, he and Miss Terrill left on the first leg of a new recording expedition.

CHAPTER TWENTY-FIVE

Home on the Range
1939–41

"John Lomax had an almost uncanny sense of where to look and where to stop," Miss Terrill wrote in her account of their travels. "We'd be driving along, come to some crossroad—he'd say, 'Let's go up that road a piece'—and often we'd find an old lady singing at her work, maybe get some new churn-song, or a new version of some hymn, or some old English ballad. Or maybe it was a Negro in the field gee-hawing his team with hollers. John Lomax would stop him and talk, and if he found the man knew interesting songs or interesting versions, or if the 'old woman up at the house' knew some old songs, we'd proceed with an hour or two of recording." She recalled that schoolhouses were a favorite objective, especially if children were playing in the yard at recess. "After a few minutes' chat the Ballad Hunter would have the suspicious teacher reassured, and we'd set up the machine to catch their game-songs, which was a great adventure for the children, especially if it prolonged their recess."[1]

Armed with the nearly new Presto recording machine sent by the Library of Congress, Lomax and Miss Terrill spent some six weeks in April and May of 1939 traveling around South Texas, calling on song sources from his past travels and locating new ones. With the help of Sister Joan of Arc in San Antonio they arranged to record a sacred drama, *The Good Thief,* presented by a group of "Mexican Texans," as Miss Terrill carefully described them.

Lomax had learned of a young man named Frank Goodwyn, a distant cousin of J. Frank Dobie, who had grown up on the King Ranch and later developed an interest in folklore as a student at Texas College of Arts and Industries at Kingsville. From his father, one-time foreman of the King

Ranch, Goodwyn had absorbed cowboy lore, and he could sing many songs current among the vaqueros, accompanying himself on guitar. Some of the tales and songs he collected had appeared in publications of the Texas Folklore Society. When Lomax and Miss Terrill found him, he was teaching school at La Gloria, a small community of Mexicans and Mennonites near Falfurrias. Goodwyn and his wife lived in what had once been a tourist cabin; he took the Lomaxes there to get his guitar and demonstrate a few songs. Years later, Goodwyn recalled the incident: "You know, John was full of bull, he was really heavy with it that day. He bragged a lot about how he was going to make me famous." Lomax sat on a bed as Goodwyn played, and after a song or two, "he really got carried away; he liked what I was doing and said he was going to take me to New York and this-that-and-the-other, it was going to be the greatest thing that ever hit the country." Suddenly, in the midst of Lomax's spiel, the bed collapsed and threw him to the floor.[2] Goodwyn suppressed a laugh; he had few illusions about becoming famous on the strength of his folk material. But the Lomaxes came away with recordings of several songs and folktales, and Goodwyn agreed to act as guide and interpreter whenever Lomax returned to the area.

Following his nose through the Texas countryside, Lomax found odds and ends here and there, but most of the rural schools had closed for the summer and pickings were slim. There were also problems with the new recording machine. After repairs at Texas A&M, they drove to the State Penitentiary at Huntsville for four days of recording, then to prison farms in Arkansas and Mississippi. By May 26 they had arrived back at in Livingston, Alabama, where the indefatigable Mrs. Tartt had again rallied large numbers of local songsters, including the two old favorites, Dock Reed and Vera Hall. In less than a week the Lomaxes filled twenty discs, most of it new material. Two days of recording at the Florida State Penitentiary produced similar results.

At a prison road camp in Anderson County, South Carolina, near Clemson, Lomax encountered more than a hundred convicts chained together at the ankle, resting from their labors in a large tent. When a few of them agreed to sing for him, the whole group had to move out of the tent, shuffling along on the chain that bound them, and stand in the summer sun. Lomax had long defended penitentiary officials from what he considered to be unfair charges of mistreating black convicts and more than once had asserted publicly that he had never seen two prisoners chained together. Now that he had evidence to the contrary, he wrote to South

Carolina governor Burnet Maybank, saying that he had never seen anything which seemed "so unnecessarily inhuman" and asked that the governor correct the situation. Establishing his credentials, Lomax pointed out that although he was a Texan and for many years associated with the University of Texas, his father came from South Carolina and his mother from Alabama. "By inheritance I hold dear the righteous ideals of a Southern man."[3]

Lomax and Miss Terrill reached Washington on June 14. They had traveled 6,502 miles and brought with them 142 disks to be added to the Archive. In his annual report to the Librarian, Alan pronounced them "musically and acoustically . . . one of the best groups of records accessioned."[4]

• • • • •

Lomax's primary reason for going east that summer was to work on what he was shortly referring to as "the interminable book," which had originally been scheduled for publication in May. It was still a long way from completion, and James Putnam at Macmillan, by now accustomed to Lomax's tardiness, offered another six-month extension on the deadline. The Lomaxes rented a furnished house in Hyattsville, Maryland, and Lomax began commuting daily to the Archive, where he selected and duplicated records from field expeditions, got copies to Ruth Crawford Seeger for musical notation, and conferred with Alan about notes and commentary for the book.

He had hardly established a routine when it was interrupted by a return of the inflammation of the leg that had been a major source of his physical anguish back in 1931. He was hospitalized for several days, then his doctor "tired of my wailings and sent me back to Miss Terrill," as he told Johnny.[5] Confined to bed with his leg elevated, he doggedly tried to get back to work on the book, but there was still another interruption when Edward Weeks, editor of the *Atlantic Monthly,* called and asked him to write a profile of the late Will Hogg. It was a prestigious assignment and, given Lomax's deep affection for Hogg, one that he could scarcely turn down. Alan and Ruth Seeger went on with work on the book, but without Lomax the project lacked a rudder.

Alan by now was also busy with an important new undertaking at the Archive of Folk Song. The national radio networks had largely ignored the Archive, but after the British Broadcasting Corporation programs the previous year, using Archive materials and Lomax as consultant and commentator, Spivacke was able to convince ("shame" is the word he used)

CBS to schedule twenty-four folk music segments for its popular American School of the Air broadcasts during the 1939–40 season.[6] Alan was assigned to do the programming and act as narrator, host, and occasional performer.

It was a long, hot summer for Lomax, hobbled by his bad leg and struggling with projects he couldn't finish. Spivacke was too busy to spend time with him, and Lomax took offense, erroneously deciding that Spivacke, like Strunk, had turned against him. About the only note of cheer was a healthy royalty statement from Macmillan for nearly seven hundred dollars. *Cowboy Songs,* just out in a new, enlarged edition, accounted for two-thirds of the total, but *Songs of the Cattle Trail and Cow Camp,* in print after twenty years, sold a respectable 128 copies. *Negro Folk Songs as Sung by Leadbelly* was still more than a hundred dollars short of paying back the advance.

• • • • •

By mid-August, Lomax had all he could stand of Washington. He and Miss Terrill drove up to New York to conduct business and attend the World's Fair, then left for Texas by way of Canada. From New York to Quebec he was pursued by wires and letters from RCA Victor representatives, trying to arrange a deal to record Frank Goodwyn singing cowboy songs. But they were reluctant to make an offer—"shy as country maidens," Lomax said sarcastically—and Lomax, adhering to the first law of deal-making, wouldn't tell them what his price was.[7] The dickering went on for days, but nothing came of it.

A more serious hitch developed when Alan reached his father with word that CBS wanted Lomax to guarantee the copyrights to the material they would use for the American School of the Air broadcasts—that is, he was asked to indemnify the company against any future legal action regarding rights and permissions. In the interests of furthering Alan's career, he'd already taken a blow to the pocketbook by allowing CBS free use of the material, and well aware of past events that showed him on shaky ground when it came to provenance, he balked, refusing to "guarantee Columbia against some fake reuben suing them for misuse of material." He would formally agree to waive his rights for one broadcast and say that he earnestly *believed* the material to be the property of the Lomaxes, but he would not *guarantee* anything to anyone. He preferred that CBS simply take Alan's word; they might dock his salary if someone sued, but otherwise Alan and Mrs. Seeger had nothing to lose. They could not be imprisoned for debt, he said, but as for himself, all his meager savings would be wiped out by a judgment against him.[8]

The trip through eastern Canada and down through the Midwest was a sort of second honeymoon for Lomax and Miss Terrill. Their first stop in Texas was with the Mansells in Lubbock, where Bess and Johnny had come to visit. Then it was on to Dallas; by early October they had moved into the newly refurbished House in the Woods at 7456 San Benito Way, and Lomax notified Spivacke that that would be his permanent address from now on.[9]

Being back in familiar surroundings did not improve his disposition. After Alan's first CBS broadcast in October, his father complained that his performance was "ragged," "stilted," and "unnatural." In an effort at damage control, Miss Terrill slipped in a note telling Alan that despite these remarks his father was "proud as a peacock" over the series.[10] Nevertheless, Lomax remained a persistent critic of the broadcasts. He particularly objected to professional black singers, such as the Golden Gate Quartet, performing the tame old chestnuts like "Swing Low, Sweet Chariot" that most whites identified as Negro spirituals. The group had "zip and precision," he said, but their songs were a travesty—"superfine, joggling, tin-panny jazz" rather than "the sweep and power and grandeur of genuine Negro singing." He couldn't understand how Alan could have heard the likes of Dock Reed and Vera Hall and still use such "phony" groups. Maybe Alan's New York sophisticates wanted that sort of showy stuff, he said, but only because they hadn't heard the real thing.[11]

Leadbelly had resurfaced in New York, and Alan used him on the program as often as he could, much to Lomax's dismay. Listening in, Lomax found the black troubadour's voice a sad echo of its former majesty and his performance redeemed only by his skill with the guitar. Lomax was even less impressed with Woody Guthrie, whom he referred to as "The Oklahoma Dust Bowl man . . . an absolute zero on any program at any time."[12] Months after the series began he was still complaining that Leadbelly had lost all his appeal and Woody Guthrie probably never had any. Thanks to Alan's training, the Golden Gate Quartet was "tolerable," he said, but their spirituals had less religious energy than he could get by beating on a tin pan.[13]

His other aggravation was "the interminable book." Having left Washington in August with assurances from Alan and Ruth Seeger that they were in the last stages of completing it, he had gradually withdrawn from the nuts-and-bolts preparation and assumed the role of general consultant. But he'd scarcely reached Texas in the fall when his editor notified him that the manuscript Alan and Mrs. Seeger had turned in would run 712 pages in print. Macmillan refused to consider more than the four hundred pages specified by their contract, citing the uncertain economy and possible U.S. involvement any day in the war now raging in Europe. Lomax was faced with the task of reducing the manuscript by almost 50 percent, either on his own or in awkward collaboration with the two people off in Washington who knew most about it.

No longer confident that he could "fix Macmillan" in the dispute over the book's length, Lomax ceased his threats of finding another publisher, telling Alan they were lucky that Macmillan was even willing to consider such a book, with war looming and business in turmoil.[14] Initially he decided he'd have the manuscript sent to him and do the editing himself. Then he abruptly changed course, realizing they would save time if copy were not sent back and forth to Texas, and wrote Alan lengthy instructions for making the cuts.[15] He had no sooner done that than he notified Macmillan that Alan and Mrs. Seeger were to have final authority, and Alan would act as his spokesman for any changes, with instructions to keep Mrs. Seeger happy by allowing her to approve every detail (a move he would later regret).[16] Still, he couldn't leave the project alone and kept nagging Alan about getting the final copy to Macmillan. Yet when Alan asked if his father could supply additional source material for some songs, he drew back again, saying it was useless: "One of my many mistakes has been my indifference to [song] origins"[17]—a point that his critics roundly affirmed. Macmillan optimistically scheduled *Our Singing Country* for publication in the spring of 1940, six months away. Almost two years would elapse before it finally appeared.

Still further disappointment was Edward Weeks's response to his profile of Will Hogg. The *Atlantic* editor wrote a long letter outlining shortcomings in the manuscript.[18] Lomax had shown mostly the public side of Hogg, and Weeks wanted details of his "off duty" life, a physical description, and more information about Hogg's financial wheeling and dealing, all of which Lomax had obscured for fear of offending Hogg's family. Lomax went back to his sources, and Mike Hogg, Will's brother, generously arranged for him to meet with humorist Irvin S. Cobb, a longtime intimate of the family.[19] Lomax struggled through numerous revisions of the article; when the manuscript was finally accepted for the May issue, he referred to it as "my poor emasculated story of Will Hogg."[20] After it appeared in print, however, he was widely applauded, and dozens wrote to compliment him—even Hogg's sister, the icy and elegant Miss Ima, who considered herself the keeper of the flame.

But as Christmas 1939 approached, Lomax grew increasingly morose, telling Alan that every letter might be his last one ("No one knows but that awful Judge, away up somewhere above").[21] He set about trying to arrange for all his children to spend the holidays with him and Miss Terrill in Dallas, saying he had a strong feeling that if they weren't together this Christmas, it wouldn't happen again "this side of Jordan." He was especially anxious for Alan to come—their relations had become increasingly strained over financial matters and Alan's politics—and Lomax tried every inducement he could think of, promising among other things good weather, the biggest turkey in Dallas County, country sausage, Texas pecans, chocolate cake, and a visit to the Callaways, who were like foster parents to Alan.[22] But Alan kept stalling and in the end did not come, although he'd arranged to broadcast his January 2 radio program from San Antonio. He had even gotten Bess an extended holiday from Bryn Mawr so she could sing with him, a plan he knew his father opposed. That may have had something to do with his staying away from Dallas on Christmas Day. In any event, Lomax suffered a bleak holiday and tried his best to conceal the hurt.[23]

• • • • •

Lomax spent the early days of the New Year coping with a miserable winter in Texas, mending fences with Spivacke, and dispiritedly planning another recording trip for 1940. Spivacke had offered a belated apology for what he referred to as his "unsociable attitude last summer," and Lomax promptly wrote back, telling him to forget it. Alan, he said, would attest that his father was "thin-skinned and a grumbler . . . [and] sensitive about my ignorance of technical music," adding that Strunk's behavior in a similar situation made him unreasonably nervous in the presence of Library officials.[24] But he was still feeling put upon, ambivalent about Spivacke, and unsure of just where he stood with the Archive. He told Alan to read Spivacke carefully and if it turned out that the chief was less than enthusiastic about Lomax's proposed field trip, he would give it up. He wasn't begging favors from anyone, he said emphatically, and most of all, "I . . . decline to be a burden to anybody."[25]

Entering his seventy-third year, he was increasingly preoccupied by thoughts of death. He had begun to understand, he told Alan, how a man felt when he said he had no reason to live. "Such a state of mind will, I hope, make it easier to pass on."[26] On a more worldly plane, he was depressed again about money—earlier he had told Alan that he seemed to have lost his canniness as a financier—and hoped he wouldn't have to ask for a government pension or become a burden on his children. Miss Terrill spent too much money, he complained, on her church, organizations, clubs, and "poor kinnery."[27] He'd had to sell some securities to keep Bess in school; Alan owed him money, despite Lomax's every effort to give him a lucrative share of their joint ventures; and the outlook was further clouded by threats of war and the domestic political scene. "With Hitler and Co. on the move," he wrote Alan, the future looked dim, especially with the Democrats proclaiming that "one man only can save us."[28] That man, of course, was Franklin Roosevelt. When war news that summer and Roosevelt's nomination for a third term sent Lomax's Republic National stock tumbling nearly ten points, he was in real pain. "To hell with Roosevelt is my war cry!" he blurted out to Johnny.[29] Despite the much-needed financial boost he'd gotten from the WPA, he'd never been a firm supporter of the New Deal; now it was open season on FDR, whose bid for a third term Lomax and others saw as an arrogant attempt to establish himself as dictator-for-life. To Lomax, it was all the fault of gutless, opportunistic politicians and governmental officials who were too weak to oppose the president. In the wake of the Democratic convention in Chicago, he wrote to Alan of his outrage—along with thousands of other Texans, he said—over the "disgusting exhibition of the hypocritical and subservient crowd" at the convention—"the low water mark of democracy."[30]

The increasing world turmoil worried some members of the family for other reasons. War fears renewed national concerns about loyalty and patriotism, and Shirley was afraid Alan might be among those targeted as radicals by the House Un-American Activities Committee, chaired by the reactionary Texas representative, Martin Dies.[31] Lomax fussed over an even greater threat to family harmony: the inevitable growing apart as the children married, busied themselves with their own families, and returned less and less frequently to the old home. He'd undergone a painful period of adjustment on moving into the House in the Woods again, which called up old memories. He kept hearing the ghostly sounds of his children at play, and complained that his longing for them and his loneliness was at times almost unbearable. His greatest trial was witnessing "the inevitable disintegration . . . of the Lomax family."[32]

· · · · ·

One other project he had been delaying he could no longer ignore. Back in 1935, while in New York with Leadbelly, he had signed a contract with Macmillan for a book of memoirs. Originally, the manuscript was due in May 1937; otherwise the advance Macmillan had paid him would be charged against the royalties of his other books. He had asked for and gotten three extensions on the deadline. In October 1939, with the expectation that *Our Singing Country* would be out the following spring, Macmillan agreed to a fourth and supposedly final deadline of June 31, 1940. But in May there was a another extension to September and that too came and went with no sign of a manuscript.[33]

He had at least begun to try. Pressure from James Putnam sent him into his files, and he complained to Johnny of the great mass of material he had saved over the years and had to sort through.[34] He set Johnny to work polishing the narrative of their cross-country lecture tour in 1932 and asked his other children to write down their reminiscences of various events. Coincidentally, he began writing to old friends in his past—Kittredge, Barrett Wendell Jr., Orville Bullington, and C. S. Potts—as well as others he had not heard from in years, renewing acquaintances, mending (or trying to mend) old wounds, dredging up half-forgotten names and events that brought a flood of memories. Some were harsh, some comforting. Filled with an impulse to make amends before it was too late, remembering or imagining slights he'd given and received, he wrote apologies for things few of his correspondents remembered. An old classmate, Adrian Pool, now a U.S. customs collector, replied, "I am absolutely astounded at the contents of [your] letter. You said that [long ago] you were rude to me. If you were, I was too dumb to detect it." Pool added that he respected Lomax above most others. "I have always felt that you were probably the University's most useful alumni, outside of Bill Hogg, and I have gotten a great kick out of your experiences with the negro you took out of jail and tried to teach to sing."[35]

Not all of these efforts to relive the past had so mellow an outcome. Lomax wrote to Tom Connally, returning a letter Connally had written him on the eve of departure into the army in World War I. Connally's 1917 letter had been filled with endearments, recounting their long friendship and telling Lomax, "You have always been a sort of big brother and I love you very much." Now Lomax accused Connally of shifting loyalties, of neglecting him, and, in a snit over Roosevelt's renomination, attacked his old friend for supporting the man Lomax considered a dictator (Connally had been a delegate at the convention). Connally replied calmly, "You have not lost the intimate friendship which you say you have lost," and patiently explained the Texas delegation's strategy at the convention. To Lomax's charge that Connally had failed to be "the one brave man" who would challenge Roosevelt's bid for a third term, Connally responded, "The 'Charge of the Light Brigade' gave Tennyson a gallant and magnificent subject for his poetical genius, but it was pretty hard on the Brigade."[36] His feelings, he assured Lomax, were no different than those he had expressed in his 1917 letter, but Lomax never replied. It was sorry repayment to the man who had befriended the Lomax family for years, gotten Johnny his job with the RFC, rescued Lomax's fat from the Library of Congress fire, and paved the way for his employment with the WPA.

Halfheartedly Lomax pursued the possibility of another recording trip on behalf of the Archive. Spivacke was less interested in his proposals for song collecting than in getting him to Washington to clean up paperwork in the Archive. Spivacke finally proposed a summer trip, but Lomax declined, angrily telling Alan that "Not for the Library, not for any man or any institution" would he subject Miss Terrill to the heat and discomforts of a recording trip through the Deep South in July.[37] After weeks of discussion, the trip was postponed until September, while Spivacke juggled funds from a Carnegie endowment to cover Lomax's expenses in Washington.[38]

In the meantime, at the urging of J. Frank Dobie, Lomax had renewed his membership in the Texas Folklore Society and in April was elected president. Although the organization maintained a substantial membership, it was perennially low on funds to support its many activities, especially publication of the "annual book," which had become an institution since its first edition in 1916, when Lomax convinced Stith Thompson to edit and publish a collection of the year's best Texas folklore scholarship. For many years, Dobie had been a mainstay of the TFS, serving as secretary-treasurer since 1922, editing the annual publication, and trying to cope with money problems. By the late 1930s, however, he was busy with his own books and casting about for someone to share the load—ideally, someone who could help secure long-term support from outside sources. Lomax, with his national reputation and ties to the Dallas financial world, seemed a likely prospect, and he was willing if not eager to get back in the traces. The honor of being elected president wasn't lost on him, either. That would show those louts in the American Folklore Society that he still counted for something among his own. Shortly after his election, Johnny scribbled a note to his siblings, "Father is taking a new interest in life due to Presidency of Texas Folk-Lore Society."[39]

But helping Dobie round up wealthy patrons for the Texas Folklore Society was hardly a full-time job, and Lomax needed more than that to take his mind off his troubles. His relations with Alan were at an all-time low, exacerbated by what he perceived to be Alan's carelessness with money and his bad influence on Bess's political leanings (they were both "hopelessly involved in the slimy toils of Communism," from which he was unable to save them, he told Johnny melodramatically).[40] Bess had not helped matters by getting herself on academic probation at Bryn Mawr that spring for excessive absences, Alan's pleas to the dean notwithstanding. Added to Lomax's trials were books he couldn't get finished, uneasy relations with Spivacke, and increasingly bad news from Europe, where the Battle of Britain was underway that summer. He had moments of contentment but was constantly fighting depression. From the House in the Woods he wrote Johnny that he was more tranquil there than anywhere else, but the newspapers and radio reports upset him and left him feeling as depressed and defeated as whenever he had to confront Bess and Alan's "foolish devotion to Communism."[41] He worked haphazardly at his memoirs, played golf, went fishing at Port Aransas, and made short trips around the state with Johnny, who had finally left the RFC after nine years and gone into business as a contractor of building stone in Houston.

In January, Macmillan notified Lomax that they had a "complete and satisfactory" manuscript of *Our Singing Country,* but three months later it became clear that Mrs. Seeger had not turned in all the musical notations and Alan was still working on what became the "Music Preface."[42] Lomax could get nothing out of either of his collaborators. Alan was accustomed to ignoring his father's proclamations, and for some time Lomax had been complaining that Mrs. Seeger, despite her many virtues, did not answer his letters.[43] Now he fretted that "her disposition to refine the rose may run into a heavy expense"; she had been known to play a record as many as a hundred times to be sure she had transcribed it correctly.[44] Not only was this time-consuming, it tended to wear out priceless master copies that could not be replaced. Finally, in July, after several scolding letters from Lomax, she wrote him at length, offering excuses for her delay and explaining their problems getting the music ready.[45]

The crisis with Alan continued to mount, complicated by their almost identical temperaments—political outlook excepted—and by Alan's growing tendency to ignore his father, failing to respond to repeated requests for news from the Archive and only infrequently answering Lomax's weekly, sometimes daily, letters. In Alan, Lomax had invested all his hope for his own thwarted dreams and ambitions, and Alan's waywardness was almost more than he could bear. He would repeatedly swear he would never write Alan again, and then promptly break the vow. Alan's formidable place in his life—and one explanation for their odd behavior to each other—is revealed in a desperate, soul-shaking letter Lomax was finally driven to write that summer. He had utterly no reason to communicate with his younger son, he said, except that long ago, before Alan was even born, "the core and centre of my being was set in time to a Conglomerate known as You."[46]

About this time Lomax developed a terrible rash and was in such discomfort that he gave up work on his memoirs and everything else. His affliction was aggravated by the hottest and driest Texas summer in many years; after a few weeks he and Miss Terrill fled to the cool mountains of northern New Mexico. From Eagle Nest, in the Sangre de Cristo Range near Taos, he wrote Alan, "I have been in Hell and couldn't reach the water." He had amassed enough material for his memoirs to make three books, he said, but feared he lacked the ability to cull and focus it—he seemed to have no power of imagination, and worried that his prose was stiff with academic jargon and clichés. If he could only shape the material before him into simple, forceful English, he said, the book would make Alan proud to be his son. But he couldn't do it, "and what I write is chatter and a waste of words."[47]

· · · · ·

His mood was not improved when he sent a few early pages to James Putnam, and Putnam replied that he feared the book was going to turn out to be purely anecdotal, which was not what they wanted. Macmillan agreed to postpone delivery of the manuscript one last time, to April 1, 1941, but they were deducting half of his advance from current royalties, and the other half would be collected if he failed to meet that deadline.[48]

That distressing news was compounded by another flare-up of his ailment, which he described to Alan as "pyro-tiedoulaureaux of the male organs."[49] Feeling plagued from all sides, he showed little enthusiasm for the upcoming field trip. His outlook was so low that Bess, who was planning to accompany him and Miss Terrill on the early stages of the journey, wrote quietly to Alan to ask what she should do in case she had to take command. Her father and Miss Terrill weren't to know; they were both "pretty touchous" and tired. Alan replied with a store of practical advice for attending properly to the fieldwork.[50]

They left Dallas on September 14 and traveled around central and southern Texas for a week or so. From Houston Bess departed for Bryn Mawr. With Lomax's spirits somewhat revived, he and Miss Terrill headed east, into Louisiana and Mississippi. As always, trouble developed with the recording machine, and the Library prepared to ship them another one, but after a few weeks, Lomax notified Alan that Miss Terrill had turned into an excellent recording engineer and by careful attention to the machine had solved their problems.[51] By this time they had arrived in Livingston, Alabama, and Mrs. Tartt kept them supplied with singers for over a week of steady recording that resulted in fifty records and "some priceless stuff," as Lomax reported to Alan. No one, he said, was as good as Mrs. Tartt in finding such valuable sources.[52]

They spent two days in the Atlanta area, then turned north through South Carolina. From Columbia, Lomax reported that "we two are just about worked out." When they reached Washington on November 12, they brought with them 145 records containing 755 items for the Archive, as well as 84 photographic negatives documenting the performances they had recorded.[53] In three months they had traveled six thousand miles through eight states.

There was plenty of work for them in the Archive, cataloging and arranging the results of several recent field trips, but Lomax was distracted by another overriding concern: *Our Singing Country* was still hanging fire, and the major culprit appeared to be Mrs. Seeger. For months he'd been asking her to send him all the material that had been deleted so that he could review it for possible use in his memoirs. It turned out that she'd acted with good intentions, but a series of miscommunications had delayed the material. When he finally heard from her, he was too busy in the field—and too miffed—to reply. Meanwhile, Mrs. Seeger asked Macmillan for still more proofs of the book, which she again went over with excruciating care, instituting further changes in the original copy. In October she wrote Lomax a long explanation, with more detailed excuses for her delay.[54] The process dragged on.

By the time he reached Washington, Lomax was in high dudgeon. Fueling his anger was the fact that he had to keep silent; long ago he had turned the job over to Alan and Mrs. Seeger and repeatedly told them he had withdrawn from the project. He knew that Mrs. Seeger was not solely to blame for the delays; Alan too was dragging his feet. Matters reached a crisis when he overheard Mrs. Seeger in the Archive asking that copies be made of five or six records so she could take them home to determine the accuracy of a single footnote. Lomax fired off a stern letter to James Putnam at Macmillan, directing him to tell Alan and Mrs. Seeger that the time had definitely come to finish *Our Singing Country.* If the last proofs weren't wrenched from Mrs. Seeger's grasp, "I think she will come down with nervous prostration."[55] Five more months passed before the publisher could report that the final pages of the manuscript were being set into type and the book was scheduled for publication in midsummer. It did not appear until November 1941, over four years from its inception.

Lomax and Miss Terrill took rooms at the Carroll Arms Hotel at First and C Streets in Washington and settled down for three months of diligent work in the Archives, to finish their field notes, copy records, and bring the files up to date. In these early weeks of 1941, he also selected records and served as commentator for a series of radio transcriptions entitled "The Ballad Hunter," produced by the Library's Radio Research Project and syndicated to stations across the country.

· · · · ·

By mid-March he and Miss Terrill were back in the House in the Woods in Dallas. He continued to hold the title of "Honorary Consultant and Curator" of the Archive of American Folk Song, but his work for that institution was largely behind him. Increasingly, his attention would turn to affairs in Texas.

CHAPTER TWENTY-SIX

Pass around Your Bottle

1937–45

In the late 1930s, Lomax had become acquainted with a young Texan named John Henry Faulk, whose father was a lawyer in Austin. Faulk had been in classes with Alan at the University of Texas and had introduced the Lomaxes to the Gant family, whose songs eventually occupied many discs in the Archive of American Folk Song. Faulk's interest in folksong collecting was further intensified when he came under the influence of J. Frank Dobie, who had established a national reputation with his books and magazine articles on southwestern lore. Following World War II, with the support of Alan Lomax, Faulk went to New York and became a radio personality on the CBS network. Then, at the height of the McCarthy era in the mid-1950s, he was the victim of a right-wing smear group called AWARE, which claimed that he was part of some nebulous "Communist conspiracy" in the entertainment world. Having lost his job with CBS as a result, Faulk waged a protracted lawsuit against AWARE and eventually won a judgment of three and a half million dollars, only to discover that the backers of the organization were bankrupt.[1] Practically penniless from the long legal battle, he returned to Texas and, in the ensuing years until his death in 1990 at age seventy-six, acquired considerable notoriety as a champion of individual rights, a popular dinner speaker, and an entertainer, appearing as a regular on *Hee Haw* for several seasons. He played bit parts in nearly every Hollywood movie filmed in Texas—including the role of Gov. Pat Neff in *Leadbelly,* Gordon Parks's 1976 screen biography of the black songster. From many perspectives and for many reasons, Faulk was well qualified to assess John Lomax.

"Lomax was such a dear old soul," Faulk said. "You would delight in his stories and accounts of people. But of course he was also very pompous, very self-righteous . . . and, my god, he hated Roosevelt, hated the whole New Deal. He was very conservative in his politics." Lomax also regarded himself as the father and chief potentate of all folklore collecting in Texas, although Faulk acknowledged that he was "the best I ever met at doing it." Lomax, he said, had an almost mystic ability to find singers and get what he wanted, and he "was tireless in his energies."[2]

Faulk's earliest encounter with Lomax came in the fall of 1941, when Lomax appeared in Austin on a self-appointed mission to "straighten out" Faulk's mentor, Frank Dobie. Dobie was writing a popular weekly column for several Texas newspapers in addition to teaching at the University of Texas. He had been invited to speak at the San Jacinto Monument on San Jacinto Day, Texas's annual commemoration of the battle on April 21, 1836, when Sam Houston's tattered band of Texians routed Santa Anna's army and established the Republic of Texas. As Dobie was about to speak, he was preempted by the unexpected arrival of Gov. W. Lee "Pappy" O'Daniel and his entourage. O'Daniel, a populist demagogue who fancied himself another Huey Long, took the podium to announce, on this great and momentous patriotic occasion, his choice of an appointee to serve the unexpired term of U.S. Senator Morris Sheppard, who had died in office two weeks earlier. The appointee was none other than Sam Houston's last remaining son, Andrew Jackson Houston, who was eighty-seven, senile, and bedridden. As Dobie saw all too clearly, the appointment of Houston was simply a ploy by O'Daniel to fill the office with someone who would be incapable of running for reelection the following year, when Sheppard's term expired. That would leave the race wide open for O'Daniel, who could not succeed himself as governor but who, as the state's most prominent Democratic politician, was a shoo-in for nomination as senator.[3] It was said that many Texans would vote for O'Daniel just to get him out of the state by sending him off to Washington.

Dobie, who hated Pappy O'Daniel anyway, was furious over the San Jacinto incident. It was bad enough that the bumptious governor had shouldered Dobie aside on the platform to announce Houston's appointment, but he proceeded to commit an even worse offense—he had the gall to lead the San Jacinto crowd in singing "Beautiful Texas," a maudlin bit of homespun balladry that he himself had composed for his hillbilly band. Dobie got revenge in his newspaper column, savaging O'Daniel's political opportunism and trashing the trite sentiments of "Beautiful Texas" with an acidic parody that ended in "Oh beautiful Texas—oh buzzard puke and puppy vomit."[4]

It was Lomax's turn to be outraged. He was no admirer of Pappy O'Daniel, but insults in the name of Beautiful Texas were another matter entirely. Besides, there were certain things one simply didn't say in print, and puppy vomit and buzzard puke were two of them. Lomax made a special trip to Austin for the express purpose of upbraiding Dobie. "You're disgracing yourself, and you're disgracing Texas," he stormed. "You'll ruin your reputation writing trash like this. Those words don't appear in family newspapers." Dobie only laughed, perhaps sensing that he and Lomax acted from the same motive, each defending his own deeply rooted notion of "Texas" (Dobie's column was in fact entitled "My Texas").

Defused by Dobie's cheerful response, Lomax soon returned to good humor. "Dobie was very fond of Mr. Lomax, as I was," said Faulk. "Mr. Lomax's idiosyncrasies and his posturing became the source of just endless anecdotes for us." For many years, from the late 1930s into the 1950s, there were weekend gatherings at Dobie's place outside Austin or at Walter Prescott Webb's Friday Mountain Ranch, where Dobie, Webb, Bedichek, and various young turks—John Henry Faulk, Mody Boatright, Henry Nash Smith, and others—met to cook steaks over an open fire, sip whiskey, and tell stories. The Lomax-O'Daniel-buzzard-puke episode was a recurring favorite.

"We'd spend half our time each time we got together, talking, telling Lomax stories about Mr. John A. because he was a character of the first water," said Faulk. "Arbitrary, huffy, a great pouter if you hurt his feelings." Lomax was most frequently offended when, as he held forth on some exotic tale from his collecting adventures, his listener's attention would wander, or merely appear to. Instantly he would turn stone silent and refuse to continue.

After Lomax's death, Dobie lamented that few of the Lomax anecdotes had been written down. "I was thinking what a pity it will be," he wrote to Bedichek, "if we do not sometime for our own delectation set down the warty realities, along with the hearty and not-warty other realities about Lomax."[5] So far as is known, that was never done, but it seems fitting that Lomax was the subject of a substantial body of narrative, both rollicking and solemn, that remained largely in what folklorists call "the oral tradition," himself the central character in stories told over and over and passed around among his colleagues and contemporaries. Faulk may have been the last of the line to know and appreciate at first hand both the warty and nonwarty realities of John Lomax.

The wartiest reality was his racial attitude. Faulk was asked why anyone who thought as Lomax did about race would collect black folklore. "Because Lomax was unquestionably a genius," he said. "He was a man of a magnificent mind [but] he never put . . . two and two together. He never questioned the system. . . . He would just say, 'These [crimes against blacks] are the aberrations of lawless people.' But he would never approve an injustice, an overinjustice to a black. . . . And Lomax, I don't think, ever felt that this system would change or could change."[6]

As he aged, Lomax's racial attitudes only hardened, and he resorted to more and more convoluted arguments to defend them. Yet in these complex episodes his dreary prejudices were often tangled with noble motives and the old humanism, however shaky and patriarchal, that had first sent him out to live and work among blacks. When Sterling Brown, a black poet and professor at Howard University, charged that the death of Bessie Smith, "Empress of the Blues," was the result of her having been turned away from a white hospital in Mississippi after being injured in a car accident, Lomax was indignant. He took it upon himself to look into the matter, and eventually obtained a statement from the governor of Mississippi, Paul B. Johnson, who asserted that a thorough investigation had determined that the story was "without foundation in fact."[7]

Conveying this information to Alan with some satisfaction, Lomax admitted that there were doubtless similar instances of injustice which Brown could cite, "perpetrated or condoned by representative people of the South." Yet he could not resist a further verbal assault on Brown, who had worked with him on the WPA Writers' Project as national editor of Negro affairs. From this experience, Lomax had concluded that Brown was an idealist whose notions of blacks focused not on what they were but what Brown wanted them to be. Moreover, Brown had little immediate experience with the black masses and really didn't know what he was talking about, as demonstrated by his promulgating the Bessie Smith story, "an outrageous slander on the Southern white man." In the end, said Lomax, one's actions could only be guided by truth: "No permanent reform can be born on a lie."[8] He had arrived on firm moral ground, expressing a truism, however self-serving, with which no one could disagree.

Lomax was also concerned that the attitudes of educated blacks were affecting Alan's fieldwork. These corrupting influences included men like Brown and the officials of Fisk University, where Alan went to record the university quartet. Lomax cautioned him to guard against the attitudes of such "'advanced' Negroes," who would allow their race to be presented only as they wanted it to appear. Efforts to revise history or distort social conditions were doomed, he told Alan, whose job it was "to record what you find, regardless of its import."[9] These were noble sentiments, but they did not express principles that Lomax himself had always maintained, as when he had moved field-workers inside for better recording conditions and, in effect, taught singers the chants he thought they ought to interject in their songs.

In the same letter, he encouraged Alan to read William Alexander Percy's *Lanterns on the Levee* if he wished to know "how a bourgeois Southerner (I am so branded in your mind by Miss Barnicle) feels." Percy lived in Greenville, Mississippi, only a stone's throw from Lomax's birthplace in Holmes County, and his views on race, which some have considered advanced for their time, were rooted in the same soil: blacks were lovable but childlike beings, always in danger of reverting to their primitive ways and coming to harm unless cared for and kept in line by white folks, by which Percy mostly meant the gentry—modern-day cavaliers dwindled down to small-town lawyers and doctors and judges and landowners, the patrician inheritors of the Southern Way of Life. Percy expressed his racial views more eloquently—some might say more democratically—than Lomax, but their attitudes were essentially the same. Perhaps most compelling to Lomax was Percy's fierce notion that efforts to change the system or reform old ways would only doom them all. As one who also felt himself beset by liberals and do-gooders (and, like Percy, seemed to sense from time to time that he was in a sinking boat), Lomax could fully appreciate that "Mr. Percy faces the truth unflinchingly."[10]

• • • • •

Feeling increasingly distanced from the Library of Congress, Lomax turned his energies to the Texas Folklore Society, and as president he was notably successful at putting new life in that organization. When the society met in San Antonio on May 2, 1941, at the end of Lomax's first year at the helm, the treasurer reported membership up and $1311.06 in the till—by far the highest balance on record. For the first time in years, there was enough money to underwrite the society's yearly anthology before it was published.[11]

Lomax had personally scored an even greater coup. Discussing financial matters with Stanley Marcus of Neiman Marcus, he hit upon the idea of having the defunct Book Club of Texas (which Marcus had founded, with Lomax's support, in 1929) transfer its assets of $122.51 in cash and an inventory of books worth over a thousand dollars to the society, with the understanding that the membership would undertake to sell the books at a profit and with the proceeds continue the Book Club's tradition of publishing fine books on regional subjects.[12] Although this project did not last, it resulted in the prestigious five-volume Range Life Series and helped fill the society's coffers through the early 1940s. As a reward for his leadership, Lomax was unanimously reelected to a second term as president, although he told Dobie he was afraid "my feeble bolt is shot." Dobie gave him the reassurance he needed, and Lomax again bent his shoulder to the wheel, mounting fund drives and exhorting the ranks to round up new members.[13]

By midsummer he was spry enough to attend the Western Folklore Conference in Denver, where in two days (July 21 and 22) he delivered three talks, "Reminiscences of a Folklorist from Texas," "Gathering Folk Songs," and "The Folk Song Archive, Library of Congress," the latter accompanied by representative recordings. "The musicians of Denver liked the records, the public was apathetic," he reported to Alan.[14] Then he was off to attend the Cheyenne Frontier Days celebration with his host, University of Denver folklorist Duncan Emrich (who later succeeded B. A. Botkin at the Archive of American Folk Song and thus inherited Alan's old job).

That fall, from his refuge in Texas, Lomax waged a war by correspondence with Alan, Burl Ives, and Columbia Records. Ives had recorded an album of folk songs for Columbia, and Lomax discovered that several of them came (apparently through Alan) from the still-unpublished *Our Singing Country.* He also heard Ives on the radio claiming credit for finding "The Midnight Special" and others taken from the Lomax books.[15] Lomax had earlier cautioned Alan that they should allow no use of their copyrighted material except for cash in advance or a contract with reliable firms.[16] While Ives might feel he could take advantage of his friendship with Alan, there was nothing to explain "why he should feel justified in dealing so ungenerously with me." Ives's defense was that he had told the recording company to check with CBS Radio about sources, and it was all their fault. After some deliberation, Columbia Records informed Alan that they felt the songs were in public domain, but they would try to do "the right thing." Alan, who had rarely been privy to his father's publishing arrangements, had little idea what the right thing was, and he was anxious not to disturb his carefully cultivated relationship with both Columbia Records and CBS. He began to have second thoughts. Reflecting on the fact that the songs in *Our Singing Country* were all taken from public domain material in the Library of Congress, he told his father that it would be very difficult to make a case for his claim in court.[17]

Tension between Alan and his father went up another notch when CBS Radio paid Lomax the nominal sum of $425 for one-year broadcast rights to any of his material. Alan protested that his father was highly inconsistent in complaining about some minor infraction on the part of Ives while giving rights to CBS for practically nothing. Lomax erupted. All of Alan's courses in philosophy and mathematics, he roared, had obviously done nothing to develop his understanding of logic. It was "reductio ad absurdum" to argue that because CBS had gotten the best of him—a proposition he didn't accept anyway—Ives and Columbia Records should go scot-free.

Lomax's position on proprietary rights was cogent if not entirely defensible. He admitted that he and Alan had only limited reprint rights to the songs in their books but insisted that because they had found them and published them first, he was within those rights wherever he could "wangle . . . a fee for the re-use of our finds."[18] Amid the scramble of folklore publishing and in the rough-and-tumble world of field recording (no less than in Tin Pan Alley) it was every man for himself, and there were many others who practiced the same thing. The idea was to guard one's work carefully, assume the stance of ownership, and create a climate in which would-be users—performers, anthologists, publishers, record companies, radio networks—would pay for permission to avoid trouble. Fees were whatever the traffic would bear, and fierce noises were made in the direction of anyone who violated the system. Lomax had, after all, invested his own time, money, and expertise, and he felt entitled to recover whatever he could. But his nebulous and never-quite-formalized relationship with the Library of Congress complicated matters and created a hazy ethical dilemma that was never resolved. Even Alan saw it; sorting his way through the Burl Ives affair, he told his father that, in trying to exact payment from Ives, his position as curator of an archive of public domain folk music "becomes at this point rather hard to justify."[19]

• • • • •

In the fall of 1941, John Henry Faulk and his wife, Hally Wood, came to visit the Lomaxes in Dallas. Faulk, who had a Rosenwald Fellowship that year to collect Negro folk religion in Texas, was there to lecture, in Lomax's view, "to some social reform outfit." Lomax lectured Faulk in turn, telling him his job was in the river bottoms with the black folk, not among the high-minded living-room-liberals. But the Faulks stayed for the weekend, and the two men got on warmly; it was a curious but compelling fact of Lomax's nature that he did not let ideology stand in the way of lasting friendship with those he admired for their character and integrity. "I have never met a more likable and agreeable pair than John and his wife," Lomax said of the Faulks, despite his disagreements with their political views.[20] On several occasions, he upbraided Alan for liking only those who agreed with his point of view: that wasn't something Alan had inherited from his father, said Lomax, citing his own friendships with men like Roy Bedichek and Carl Sandburg, whom he loved and admired and could find no fault with, although they were men "whose ideas in nearly every field run counter to mine."[21]

All year Lomax had been trying to arrange another field trip that would include a return visit to Mrs. Tartt in Alabama. Aware that she was in dire financial straits, he suggested to Spivacke that the Library supply her with a recording machine, which Lomax would deliver, and pay her a modest sum to collect on her own for a few months. Spivacke and Alan dragged their feet all through the summer, as Lomax fumed. His opinion of those who ran the Music Division, he muttered stormily, "would make a finely-grained sifter out of an asbestos curtain."[22] When the arrangement was finally authorized in October, Mrs. Tartt's work with the WPA had ended and she and her husband were subsisting on her last check, but she told Lomax that it would be a waste to pay her for song collecting at that time of year, when weather conditions would make it difficult to get the sort of material he wanted. She couldn't take money for a job badly done, she said, and declined the offer.[23]

In the meantime, *Our Singing Country* had at last been published, after countless problems with the manuscript, several threatened lawsuits over copyrights, and Lomax's ongoing tussle with Alan and Ruth Crawford Seeger. In April the final installment—Alan's introduction—was at last edited and set into type. By this time everyone's patience was exhausted. Their copy editor at Macmillan, Susan Prink, notified Lomax sternly that should there be any further questions about the text, "I am going to send them on to you rather than to Alan for I do not want further changes in the book."[24]

In the last stages of the book's production, Macmillan learned that the Edward B. Marks Music Corporation was about to sue over the use of "Alla en El Rancho Grande" in *American Ballads and Folk Songs*. This set off a panic wave of inquiries, depositions, and investigations; fearful that more suits would evolve from the new book about to be published, Macmillan sent Lomax back to his files and extracted solemn assurances that all was well.[25] Then, at the last minute, Macmillan wired him that, because of increased manufacturing costs, they would have to raise the retail price of *Our Singing Country* from five to six dollars unless he was willing to accept a reduced royalty. He grudgingly agreed, knowing that at a time when the average book price was less than $2.00, they would have difficulty selling *Our Singing Country* even at five dollars.[26]

The final product proved worthy of the pains and predicaments it had caused. Although *Our Singing Country* has fewer than half the pages of *American Ballads and Folk Songs,* it contains more than two-thirds as many songs, accompanied by Ruth Crawford Seeger's meticulous tablature and her detailed "Music Preface," which not only complements the volume as a treasury of American musical culture but offers common-sense advice for its use as a songbook. For scholars, it is the first Lomax collection to make a consistent effort at citing sources, analogues, and textual variants. Annotations follow a consistent format, free of the earlier volume's hodgepodge of headnotes, footnotes, epigrams, and typographical oddities. More importantly, the selection of songs is richer, fresher, and more varied, offering many obscure gems rather than a preponderance of familiar chestnuts. Both scholars and musicians today consider *Our Singing Country* the Lomaxes' best book.

Unhappily, it appeared just as the country was girding for war—less than a month before Pearl Harbor—and the wave of depression-born interest in folksong had already begun to subside. Reviewers for the most part were friendly but unenthusiastic. Louise Pound seemed merely relieved that the Lomaxes had published songs previously available to scholars only at the Library of Congress, but she allowed that the book sustained the Lomax reputation.[27] The *New York Times* review, mostly a catalog of song titles in the book, concluded that it and the preceding volume "combine to express America and the American spirit more fully and faithfully than any other art form."[28] Wilbert Snow complained that many of the songs were of doubtful value and of interest only to scholars.[29] But out across the country, the book attracted favorable attention in such papers as the *Springfield (Massachusetts) Republican,* the *El Paso Herald-Post,* and the *Lexington (Kentucky) Herald Leader.* The latter ran a lengthy, thoughtful review by A. B. Guthrie Jr. about this "satisfying, illuminating book, . . . one that students and historians will want to have and that the casual reader will enjoy."[30] The highest accolade came from Lewis Gannett in the *New York Herald Tribune:* "The poetry is superb. . . . The musical notation is impeccable. . . . A profoundly exciting book that cuts deep into America and into music."[31]

Lomax perhaps took greatest pride in the book's introduction by Archibald MacLeish, newly appointed Librarian of Congress, who praised *Our Singing Country* as "a body of words and music which tells more about the American people than all the miles of their quadruple-lane express highways and all the acres of their bill-board-plastered cities."[32] MacLeish had only recently succeeded the much-revered Herbert Putnam as Librarian, and he took the opportunity afforded by the introduction to strew petals in many directions, praising the "brilliant" Putnam, crediting the Lomaxes with creating the Archive of American Folk Song (no mention of poor discarded Robert Gordon), and smoothly stroking the Carnegie Corporation for its generous financial support. His introduction was as much a promotion piece for himself and the Library as it was an imprimatur for the book, but Lomax saw it as another stage of Arrival, proof that he had indeed reached tall cotton. The handsome, urbane MacLeish—famous poet, Ivy Leaguer, socialite, confidant of the president—embodied much that had held Lomax in thrall for years, and as soon as he saw MacLeish's introduction on its way to the printer, he wrote the librarian to say how it had moved him. Then it was MacLeish's turn to bow, remarking that he was "deeply touched" by Lomax's letter.[33] "Please come to see me the next time you are in Washington," he wrote. Whenever Lomax did, MacLeish was "in conference."

In the wake of the publication of *Our Singing Country* came another contretemps with Mrs. Seeger, which threatened to permanently rupture their relationship. Inspired by the initial reception of the book, she had written cordially to Lomax with plans for more joint projects.[34] But when she received Macmillan's bill for the music corrections for *Our Singing Country,* amounting to slightly more than fifty dollars, she visibly stiffened, pointing out that (a) the printer's errors had outnumbered her corrections ten to one, (b) she had patiently and with great effort corrected all those errors, and (c) Macmillan had hired a proofreader for Lomax's text but none for the music, requiring her to do that work, repeatedly, without compensation. Could she assume, she asked icily, that he and Alan were being asked to pay for their corrections to the text, "which, as I recall, were substantial"?[35]

As it happened, Macmillan had canceled Lomax's charges for text changes as a favor for his having agreed to the reduced royalty rate (a reduction which Mrs. Seeger, without being consulted, had to accept as well). Lomax had offered, more or less pro forma, to pay the musical charges if she wouldn't or couldn't pay them, but that had escaped her attention. Moreover, James Putnam further connived to keep her in the dark regarding the financial arrangements, alerting Lomax to the problem but leaving him to handle it as he saw fit.[36] When Mrs. Seeger inadvertently discovered what was going on, she accused Lomax of "join[ing] Mr. Putnam in a virtual conspiracy against my interests."[37] The indignation level at Lomax's end rose instantly. He would not respond to her offensive letter, he told Alan, nor to any other communication from her, ever. He pointed out that he had already advanced her $330 against her eventual royalties and had nothing to do with Macmillan's decision to cancel the text charges. Moreover, he said, on several occasions while they were working on the book (once during one of their heated quarrels over the delay), Mrs. Seeger had indicated a willingness to pay for the changes, and he had merely given her the opportunity. Along with the bill he sent a polite note ("unbelievable but true," he said), and all he had gotten in return was "a blast." He would settle the bill with Macmillan and have done with Mrs. Seeger. "People who are suspicious of other people's integrity will probably prove to be unpleasant partners," he warned Alan.[38]

Alan did his best to mediate. He suggested to his father that the correction charges be divided according to the royalty split, two-thirds to the Lomaxes and one-third to Mrs. Seeger. But Lomax, irked that his honor had been questioned, sent Macmillan a check for the entire bill, telling Alan that ought to end all the wrangling over charges for the music corrections.[39] In this case pride meant more to him than his pocketbook.

Time passed, and after a year or two, Mrs. Seeger was again writing cheery notes to "Dear John Lomax and Deanie," asking him to recommend her son Mike for the congressional pages' school and proposing new book projects for Lomax-Seeger collaboration.[40] (Sidney Robertson Cowell said that the Seegers were always broke and saw Lomax as "their financial savior, through the books," adding, "but that wasn't going to make them any money if John could avoid it. He thought he'd invented books on [folksong] collecting.")[41]

Still smarting from the bureaucratic tangle that had forestalled a recording expedition with Mrs. Tartt, Lomax finally got authorization from Spivacke for another trip in late November. Accompanied by Miss Terrill, he drove to the Oscar Callaway ranch near Comanche, where Callaway and some of his neighbors performed cattle calls and told cowboy stories. But the collecting work there was interrupted by a failure in the rural electrical system—"the W.P.A. New Deal power," sneered Lomax, who could never resist a jibe at the Roosevelt administration—and they drove on to Austin, where John Henry Faulk supplied them with batteries and a converter.

In their hotel room, they gathered with Faulk, Frank Goodwyn, and J. Frank Dobie to record some of Dobie's ranching stories. Lomax had taken to carrying a pint of whiskey with him and having a tipple now and then when Miss Terrill wasn't looking. "Worst thing about it," said Faulk affectionately, "was that afterwards he'd get this very pious look on his bleary old face."[42] The polite fiction between Lomax and Miss Terrill was that her Baptist scruples forbade his drinking, but in fact she quietly tolerated it in moderation. In the presence of others, Lomax made a great show of stashing his bottle somewhere in the room and whipping it out whenever she turned her back. According to Frank Goodwyn, this explained the extraneous noises on Dobie's recording of "Sancho, the Pet Steer," which they made that afternoon in the Lomaxes' hotel room. While Dobie recited, Lomax stationed himself around the corner, out of Miss Terrill's sight, and sneaked a snort or two. Then he sensed that she was moving in his direction and began desperately trying to hide his flask under the mattress, but kept striking the metal rail of the bed, making a series of muffled clangs that were picked up by the microphone.[43]

Leaving Miss Terrill with friends in San Antonio, Lomax and Goodwyn drove south into Goodwyn's home territory near the King Ranch. At San Perlita, Goodwyn introduced Lomax to José Gómez, a vaquero who played the guitar and sang "versos" from a vast repertoire, "endless ballads about outlaw bulls, wild men, and wilder women," as Lomax put it. Sipping beers between songs, Gómez sang on and on. Whenever he paused, Lomax supplied another beer, remarking that Gómez's voice got sweeter with each drink, and the singer would begin again. After many hours the recorder's battery began to run down. Through Goodwyn, who was acting as interpreter, Lomax asked if Gómez knew enough more songs to make it worthwhile for him to buy a new battery. Gómez responded indignantly that there weren't enough batteries in the county to record all the songs he knew, so a new battery was obtained, and the recording went on late into the night. Lomax reported that they used up fourteen bottles of beer, two sets of batteries, and all but four of the fifty record blanks he had with him. It was one of the high points of his recording experience, he told Alan.[44]

All that expense for alcohol and electricity may have been wearing on Lomax the next day, when, after recording a quartet in Falfurrias from morning until late afternoon, he rewarded them each with a dime. That was not particularly unusual (Sidney Robertson Cowell reported that he once kept a dozen black prisoners recording all night, then left eighty cents with the warden to buy them cigarettes), but Goodwyn was appalled and decided this would be his last trip with Lomax. That notion was confirmed later when they went to record another vaquero at a general store in Sarita. The owner of the store was a blind poet named Margil López, respectfully known as Don Margil, whose verses were admired by everyone in the area. Unable to read or write because of his blindness, López was eager to have his work recorded, but when Goodwyn introduced him to Lomax, Lomax said abruptly, "No, I don't want your poems. I want cowboy folksongs." Said Goodwyn, "the atmosphere just froze. Everybody in the place clammed up. The cowboy singer who was there to record kept silent, refused to sing. And he had at least one very fine song. Lomax never got it. All Lomax had to do was record maybe one of López's poems, make the old man happy, and everything would have been all right. But he didn't do it."[45] As Lomax aged, that element of his character which made him arbitrary and high-handed came increasingly to the surface; his interest in the lives and personalities of his sources and his easy manner of dealing with them seemed to slip away with the years.

His tactlessness and penchant for contention extended even to family matters, sometimes with unintentionally humorous consequences. On this same trip in South Texas with Frank Goodwyn, they drove to Corpus Christi to visit Shirley, who had moved there to be near her husband, now a Navy doctor in training. Goodwyn drove to the address Lomax gave him, but when Lomax went to the door and asked for Shirley Mansell, the woman who answered politely assured him that no Shirley Mansell lived there. "She certainly does," Lomax stormed. "I've got it written down right here, and I don't make mistakes." The lady of the house, instead of slamming the door, grew only more polite, gently suggesting that he might be confused. She invited him in, and offered to check the telephone book for him. When the phone book revealed that Shirley's correct address was three blocks down the street, Lomax not only failed to apologize but upbraided the woman for not being personally acquainted with his daughter, "a very fine girl, a beauty when she was at the University of Texas, married to a fine, upstanding doctor, and you ought to know her." Within moments Goodwyn and Lomax were at the correct address and being warmly greeted by Shirley, who thanked Goodwyn for bringing her father to see her. Whereupon Lomax turned on her harshly: "I don't know why you say you're glad to see me. You aren't. You never answer my letters." With a weary sigh, Shirley said, "No, Father, we're not going to start all that again," but Lomax only picked up speed, ranting about serpent's teeth and thankless children and accusing his daughter of being faithless, ungrateful, lazy, and a burden to his old age—the same daughter he had just praised to the lady down the street as a paragon of virtue. Shirley quickly had enough. "Father, I'm not going to put up with this," she said. "If you keep on, I'll have to ask you to leave." He was on his feet in an instant and out the door, leaving the embarrassed Goodwyn behind to extract himself and follow along.[46]

Bess suffered the consequences of a similar visit. After graduation from Bryn Mawr, she had gone to New York and joined a group of young folk musicians to form the now-legendary Almanac Singers, booking occasional radio broadcasts, performing in clubs and union halls, and recording for John Hammond's small Keynote label. By early 1942 the Almanac Singers were attracting considerable attention in the entertainment world, but they were still struggling to establish themselves. To make ends meet, they rented a rickety old townhouse on Sixth Avenue in Greenwich Village and settled in as a sort of informal commune. Bess and Pete Seeger platonically shared a room in the attic, their beds chastely separated by a curtain (it was Seeger's idea; Bess admitted later that she'd had a crush on him at the time). Woody Guthrie lived on the second floor; Leadbelly was back in town and dropped by from time to time to join in late-night sessions of picking and singing. Every Sunday afternoon the group hosted regular hootenannies that sometimes doubled as rent parties and attracted a steady stream of musicians, artists, journalists, and assorted hangers-on.

Word reached Lomax that his younger daughter was living in some horrible den of iniquity. He immediately ordered Miss Terrill to pack his bag and caught the next train north. Only moments before his arrival, Bess learned he was coming, rushed to the attic room, packed her things, and decamped to the apartment of a girlfriend around the corner. Pete Seeger answered Lomax's knock and found him on the stoop, fuming and red-faced. "Where," he boomed, "is my daughter?" Seeger anxiously tendered him the address around the corner and the old man stalked off down the street.[47] He later reported that Bess's living arrangement was satisfactory, but Miss Terrill told Shirley she was afraid Bess's companions "are not very high-class."[48] A year or so later, Bess married Baldwin "Butch" Hawes, the brother of Peter Hawes, who had been briefly associated with the Almanac Singers. Butch Hawes, a struggling young photographer and commercial artist, was the scion of an old southern family; when Lomax learned that one of his prospective son-in-law's ancestors was George Washington Cable, he erupted in a fury, declaring that "no daughter of mine will marry a relative of that degenerate." Perplexed that her father should hold such an opinion of one of the South's more genteel, if minor, men of letters, Bess only later discovered that Lomax had confused George Washington Cable with James Branch Cabell, author of *Jurgen,* the mildly daring novel which had set polite society atwitter in the 1920s.[49]

Lomax stormily declined to meet Leadbelly while in New York, and he created a mild scene during a rehearsal in the CBS studios when he overheard Woody Guthrie "indulging in low gutter oaths, without excuse or apology," while talking to Bess.[50] "The Oklahoma Dust Bowl man" got an earful of Lomax's own brand of invective and a lesson in southern gentility, but he laughed it off. Typically, Lomax later worried that his outburst had offended Bess, but by this time his foibles were well known and no one seemed to pay it much mind.

As he grew older, his truculence was aggravated by any number of things. For several months in the spring of 1942 he suffered a recurrence of his old eye trouble, claiming to Alan that he was blind in one eye much of the time. He was sure, too, that he'd had at least one mild heart attack, and references to his imminent death were part of nearly every letter he wrote. He had "spells," probably caused by high blood pressure, and one night when illness kept Miss Terrill up into the small hours tending to him, he told her, "This business of dying certainly is messy." She assured him he wasn't dying. "No," he said, "not this time. But it won't be long." Letters to old friends grew increasingly melancholy; his life had been a failure, he said, and he had nothing to live for.[51]

Still, he kept working—or trying to. Spivacke (and Alan) continued to stonewall his appeals for new recording trips, but he plugged away at his memoirs and made an occasional lecture appearance. He needed the lectures, he said, to pay bills, "to keep the wolf from the door or [avoid] begging my children for bread"—but a few weeks later told Alan that he had a poor stomach for lectures and wouldn't resort to it "until hunger begins to press."[52] There was little demand anyway, he felt, and no one appreciated his accomplishments; in Texas not a single music teacher or member of the cultural establishment had ever shown the least interest in his work. "To hell with them if I can exist without them, say I."[53]

Ignored as he may have been in Texas, the war brought a renewed interest in his work nationally, among educational agencies and publishers of anthologies, who wanted "American songs"—those which lent themselves to patriotic propaganda. Few days passed without requests for permission to use selections from the Lomax books. Nonprofit groups were patriotically given free rights; the numerous commercial operations paid modest fees of ten to twenty dollars per song.

But the onset of war also brought tire and gas rationing, which severely jeopardized the one thing he wanted most—more field recording trips. Lomax without his car was almost as bad off as a cowboy without a horse. His efforts to get tires went all the way to Luther Evans, who was now MacLeish's chief assistant at the Library (and would succeed him as librarian in 1945). Evans worked through channels, eventually going as high as the Office of Price Administration, and the necessary ration coupons finally came.[54] But even that didn't budge Spivacke.

After numerous attempts to get budgets approved for new recording trips, Lomax undertook to pay his own way, with only vague assurance from Spivacke that he would ever be reimbursed. Then he spent months filing expense accounts and cursing the pinko government bureaucracy that held up his checks. In frustration he aimed a tirade at Alan, telling him to deliver a bitter message to Spivacke: when Stalin and the American communists took over the country after the war, he hoped that their first order of business would be to line up "the entire fiscal department" of the Library, with Spivacke in the front rank, "and shoot 'em for rank inefficiency."[55] Rational thinking hadn't entirely deserted him, however; the message was to be delivered only *after* he'd gotten his delinquent reimbursement. Later he learned from Spivacke that the delays were mostly the result of Alan's desultory handling of bureaucratic paperwork.[56]

In spite of all obstacles, Lomax and Miss Terrill traveled three thousand miles with a recording machine in 1942 and added some ninety records to the Archive collection. These trips were mostly around Texas, but on occasion they ranged as far as Oklahoma and Arkansas. Each time he went out, it was "my last trip" or "the swan song of my ballad collecting career."[57] The scope of his travels diminished in the ensuing years, but he went right on pestering Spivacke for new authorizations and asking for the use of a recording machine. Only months before his death five years later, he was imploring Duncan Emrich, who had succeeded Botkin at the Archive, to send him a machine so he could record a square dance festival in Dallas.[58] The machine was never sent.

· · · · ·

Another tempest erupted in March 1942, when Elie Siegmeister, founder of the American Ballad Singers, brought his troupe from New York to Dallas to present their program of "Native American Music" at Southern Methodist University. Lomax, as the Grand Old Man of American Folk Song, appointed himself to attend and offer his welcome, despite the fact that Siegmeister had earned his wrath by publishing in *A Treasury of American Song* (1941) two pieces from *American Ballads and Folk Songs* without the credit Lomax felt was his due. He went to the performance at SMU with the intention of going backstage afterward to greet Siegmeister, but, as he told Alan, when it was over, "wild horses could not have pulled me into the wings."[59] He stormed out of the auditorium in a huff.

The program had been all too slick, sterile, and commercial for his tastes, in his view the work of some Broadway hack ignorant of the true merits of folksong and contemptuous of those who understood it. But what was worse, he said, Siegmeister had baldly lifted material from the Lomax books. It surely did not help that Siegmeister was well known as a political activist on the Left and had been associated with the New School of Social Research in the late 1930s.

Lomax, fired to righteous indignation and warming to his purplest prose, concluded that Siegmeister was "the royal-Bengal prize shit-ass of the universe," a nincompoop who had nothing but nerve. In the face of such villainy, he said, "I retire into the innocuous oblivion where I belong, being only a humble devotee of the beautiful and true—and despising a liar."[60] Self-pity aside, this expressed the hurt feelings of a good man, aging and ignored, who felt himself badly used. One kind mention of his name from the stage that evening would have averted it all.

Siegmeister later requested and got (for a fee) permission to use Lomax songs in his books, but the Dallas episode festered and grew. After Siegmeister's *Work and Sing,* a children's songbook, appeared in 1944, Lomax wrote what Siegmeister termed "a bitter, accusing" letter, charging that he had again invaded the Lomax domain and failed to give proper credit for numerous songs. Siegmeister's lengthy response was one of controlled indignation; he pointed out that he had placed Lomax's work prominently in the bibliography, and the book itself contained more references to Lomax than to anyone else in the field. The songs in question, he told Lomax, had all been widely printed and sung in various forms; "I was not aware that you were the first to have heard all of them, if such be the case, as you state. If I had been aware of this, there would be no reason not to give you credit." In any event, Lomax's letter was "in extremely bad taste" and his "implication of bad faith . . . regrettable and unjustified." It was too bad, Siegmeister said, that "some collectors of folk music are pervaded by a feeling of mistrust and suspicion, rather than by the good fellowship of the folk singers, who create the music in the first place"[61]—a not-so-subtle reminder that, whatever the merits of Lomax's complaint, he was not the true source of the material he was so anxious to claim as a proprietary right. If Lomax responded, there is no record. It seems more likely that he simply dismissed the whole affair, as he usually did whenever his hand had been called.

Still another contretemps was set in motion shortly after the Siegmeister concert, when the Texas Folklore Society convened in Denton for its 1942 meeting. Lomax, as outgoing president, was in charge of the proceedings. For the occasion he had invited down from the Panhandle town of Dalhart his feisty old cowboy acquaintance, Jess Morris, one of the sources for "Goodbye, Old Paint" many years earlier. Morris's original recording of the song, sung as he accompanied himself on the fiddle, was of poor sound quality, and Lomax wanted a better one. Or, as Morris put it later, Lomax "bellyached" about the first record, and suggested that if Morris had a "snort or two of Scotch," he could do a better job. To persuade Morris to meet him in Denton and go back to Dallas to record, Lomax resorted to his standard tactics, offering, in addition to Scotch, heavy praise for the old fellow's talents and assuring him that great fame would come his way. Although he couldn't pay Morris for the trip, he invited him to stay with the Lomaxes and promised that he would get lots of publicity whenever Lomax was being interviewed about his collecting work.

Wary but eager for fame, Morris came to Denton, attended the folklore meeting, and then rode to Dallas with Lomax, Miss Terrill, and R. R. ("Railroad") Smith, an old schoolmate of Lomax's from University of Texas days. Upon reaching the House in the Woods, Miss Terrill retired, and Lomax declared, "Well, boys, the cook has taken a lay off, so I'll take you two boys to town and get your dinner." They stopped along the way so Lomax and Morris could each arm himself with a pint of whiskey, then went on to a cafeteria. There Lomax adroitly maneuvered to lay the check off on Morris, who was "chagrined and mortified," having assumed he was the guest. "Lomax is nothing but an old imposter and bald-headed ingrate!" Morris complained to the secretary of the Texas Folklore Society. The situation did not improve as the evening wore on. When they got back to the House in the Woods, Morris announced he was ready to go home and asked when the first train to Dalhart was. Lomax, he reported, commenced "that line of 'bull,' about me being an honored guest, and that I was doing a wonderful work, and that the Gov. would be proud & ect."[62]

The worst was yet to come. In 1945, when Donald Day profiled Lomax for *Reader's Digest*,[63] Morris rushed to get his copy and anxiously scanned the pages of America's most widely circulated magazine for notice of himself as the source of one of its popular cowboy songs. He looked in vain. Observing that Lomax had complained, in Day's article, about losing his health, Morris said scathingly that the old man not only lost his health but his memory as well. Lomax had assured him, he said, that he would share in all the publicity Lomax got, but now the collector had elected to give all the honor to "his ellustrous son Allan, and the erstwhile corn field negro guitar picker and ex Convict, 'Lead-Belly.'"[64]

Apparently Morris never took his complaint directly to Lomax. But he was probably behind a letter to Lomax from the secretary of the XIT Cowboy's Association (of which Morris was a member), gently chiding the Ballad Hunter for omitting Morris's name from the *Reader's Digest* article. Lomax bristled. Pointing out that he hadn't written the piece, he took offense at the implication that he had mistreated Jess Morris or anyone else. "As the cowboys would say, 'I do not operate that way.'"[65]

• • • • •

These skirmishes with Siegmeister and Morris were merely a prelude to a much bigger and more prolonged squabble, the last in a long line of bitter conflicts for Lomax. It involved the University of Texas, taking him back, figuratively at least, to the scene of his most stinging defeat, at the hands of Farmer Jim Ferguson. This time he would be on the winning side. Unfortunately, it was the wrong side.

CHAPTER TWENTY-SEVEN

Look down That Lonesome Road

1939–47

In the summer of 1932, when a road-weary John Lomax had traveled through Pennsylvania headed for New York, peddling his lecture wares as he went along, one of the places where he spoke was Bucknell University. While there, he and John Jr. were invited to dinner by Bucknell's president, Dr. Homer P. Rainey, a native Texan and rising star in the field of education. Lomax was much impressed by Rainey, and the two of them got on famously. Seven years later, in April 1939, Lomax wrote to his fellow Texan: "For several weeks I have had in mind to tell you how pleased I am that you decided to come back to Texas as President of our University."[1] He made a special effort to attend Rainey's inauguration in Austin in December and extended his felicitations once more.

Within a year Lomax was one of Homer Rainey's most implacable enemies.

Rainey came to the University of Texas with an exemplary record. Beyond the fact that he was a Texan—perhaps the most important qualification to Lone-Star-gazers like Lomax—he had, as one writer observed, "all the credentials of that local ideal, 'a good old boy.'"[2] Born poor, he had worked his way through college and excelled as both scholar and athlete; by the time he was twenty-one he had been ordained as a Baptist minister and played professional baseball briefly. After military service in World War I, he earned a Ph.D. at the University of Chicago and launched an impressive career as scholar, educator, and university administrator. He left Bucknell in 1935 to become director of the American Youth Commission, a Washington-based adjunct of the privately operated American Council on

Education, where he gained a national reputation as a man of skill and vision.

Among those impressed by Rainey's talents was J. R. Parten, wealthy Texas oilman and New Deal Democrat who had been appointed chairman of the board of regents of the University of Texas during the moderately liberal administration of Gov. James Allred (1935–39). For nearly two years, since the death of H. Y. Benedict in 1937, the University had been searching without success to find someone to fill Benedict's presidential shoes. Parten felt that Rainey had what it took; he urged him to apply for the job and recommended him to the regents. Later, Roosevelt haters in Texas would spread the word that Mrs. Roosevelt had gotten Rainey hired, that she had "sold" Parten on him and infiltrated him into Texas to spread her nefarious, do-gooder socialist schemes.

By the time Rainey arrived at the University, the governorship of Texas had passed from Allred to W. Lee 'Pappy' O'Daniel, a reactionary of the first rank. Like Jim Ferguson, O'Daniel scorned higher education and what he considered its effete intellectualism, but he was much slicker than Farmer Jim and knew better than to take on the University single-handedly. Instead, through conservative allies in business and industry around the state, he set about to take control of the board of regents. Parten, in later testimony before an investigating committee of the Texas Senate, recalled how, in mid-1940, he had learned of a meeting of business executives and lawyers, together with O'Daniel and a group of cronies, "whose declared purpose was to influence educational board appointments of men who could be counted upon to eliminate from the teaching staffs in higher education of Texas all radical elements in the faculties."[3]

As Lomax's earlier experiences at the University of Texas demonstrated, the campus always seemed to be erupting in one firestorm or another. But it was hardly the sort of place that nurtured radical elements. Since the time of Jim Ferguson, most campus controversies had been minor, brief, and confined to internal squabbles. In between were long periods of relative calm. Scattered among the faculty was a modest quota of liberals and freethinkers, but the halls of knowledge were still safe in the hands the University's old guard, many of whom, like W. J. Battle and E. C. Barker, had been friends and colleagues of Lomax in the long ago.

In the preceding forty years, the University had truly come to life only under the administrations of two presidents, R. E. Vinson (1916–23), who stood up to Ferguson, and H. Y. Benedict (1927–37), a man of great character and considerable skill who quietly guided the school through the depression. In spite of its many pretensions to being "a university of the first class," as decreed by the state constitution, the University of Texas had ambled along into modern times on pretty much the same footing as other colleges in the South and Southwest, no better than the best, rarely as bad as the worst. The most damning criticism lay in the direction of J. Frank Dobie's scalding remark that the University's chief purpose was "to make useful technicians for Humble Oil."[4] It was a most unlikely setting for what became one of the more notorious knock-down-drag-outs in the modern history of higher education in the United States.

As president of the University, Rainey's problems began almost as soon as he took office. In November 1939, when he had been there scarcely five months, Lomax heard from Alonzo Wasson, his old friend on the *Dallas News,* that "Rainey is virtually on probation as respects a majority of the Regents."[5] As Lomax saw it, Rainey had "dived into the maelstrom of the University" and "I don't think he will ever come up."[6]

The first storm broke in the spring of 1942, when a group of right-wing Texas business interests sponsored a rally in Dallas to protest Roosevelt's Fair Labor Standards Act. With their fierce notions about independence and self-reliance, Texans—even the most oppressed of working-class Texans—had never taken kindly to labor unions, and the promoters of the rally had persuaded the public that among the other noxious edicts of the act was a provision that prohibited employees in defense industries from working more than forty hours a week. Texas boys were fighting and dying overseas, went the popular litany, while the guns they needed were being delayed by oppressive government regulations and featherbedding workers.

The rally was advertised as an open forum, and four economics instructors from the University of Texas asked for time on the platform to point out the truth of the matter: no one was prohibited from working more than forty hours a week; the Fair Labor Standards Act merely required that employers pay time-and-a-half to any employee who worked *beyond* forty hours a week. The four instructors were politely ignored, their request to speak refused, as Lomax later explained it, on the grounds that the rally was being broadcast and had to adhere to a fixed schedule because of radio time.[7] Frustrated, the four faculty members took a written statement to the *Dallas News,* protesting that the rally had been rigged, as indeed it had, in favor of speakers who were known to be antilabor. Later, back in Austin, they repeated these charges to a local newspaperman.

Several prominent Texans, including John Lomax, took offense at what they considered the insulting tone of the instructors' statements. The University's board of regents—which included the attorney and lobbyist for the business interests of the rally's chief organizer—demanded that the outspoken faculty members apologize. They declined, and when contract time came around in June, they were not reemployed, despite their department's recommendations and the strong support of President Rainey, who viewed the affair as a serious threat to academic freedom.

Lomax vigorously defended the board's action; in his view the men were fired not because they wanted to speak but because of their "outrageous attack on Texas citizens." To him, this offense was compounded by the fact that the faculty members were not natives of the state but nobodies who had nothing to recommend them except their connection with the University. The very idea of outsiders coming to a local meeting, demanding a hearing, and then insulting everyone when they failed to get it—any community in Texas would resent such a thing. Besides, the offenders were only lowly instructors. If a group of professors had opposed the meeting, he said, the organizers would probably have found some way to accommodate them.[8] He apparently overlooked the fact that the regents, in a separate case, were at that very time pressuring Rainey to fire several distinguished full professors for what the board considered "unsound economic views," among which was advocating public ownership of public utilities. As a young man coming up, Lomax had known his place and kept to it (or been kept to it). He saw no reason why these upstarts shouldn't do the same.

The rising conflict between Rainey and the regents was intensified by rumors and behind-the-scenes manipulations among a clique of aging alumni that included, in addition to Lomax, his old friend from the *Dallas News*, Alonzo Wasson, Professors Barker and Battle, Ed Crane, E. E. Witt, and John Lang Sinclair. Soon the self-appointed council of old turks had a direct line into the board of regents, in the person of Orville Bullington, erstwhile Republican candidate for governor and longtime Lomax mainstay, a militant, stiff-necked conservative who was appointed to the board by Pappy O'Daniel in 1941. It was Bullington who led the charge to fire the economics instructors.

By bizarre chance, the anti-Rainey board of regents included still another persona out of Lomax's past, one with the same Dark Ages mentality as Bullington (but with no affinity for Lomax). This was H. J. Lutcher Stark, whose notoriously philistine attitudes had once provoked Lomax mightily—and sent him packing from the University of Texas back in 1925. Now they were fellow enemies of Homer Rainey and righteous protectors of the University. In this instance, however, Lomax and Stark kept a wary distance between them, allied only by their mutual opposition to Rainey. But Lomax, if he ever thought about it, must have reflected on the irony of having once been the persecuted victim of Stark, a man he had denounced as an enemy of enlightenment and whom he now joined in a similar witch-hunt. But there were other schisms among the anti-Rainey forces; even Barker occasionally defected from the hard liners like Lomax and Bullington, telling another member of the group that he did not "attach much importance to Lomax's opinion because I think his judgments are not always well balanced."[9]

Although Lomax sided with O'Daniel's supporters on the issue of the Fair Labor Standards Act and the firing of the economics instructors, he clearly regarded the governor as the biggest vulgarian of all. As O'Daniel's campaign for the U.S. Senate neared its successful climax in the summer of 1942, Lomax glumly predicted that Pappy would win, and the reasons he gave offer insight into both his own brand of cobbled-together populism and the complicated nature of Texas politics. O'Daniel's victory was assured, he said, because Pappy had the support of old-age pensioners, the ignorant masses, fans of hillbilly and gospel music, "nearly all the Germans," and everyone who opposed the New Deal, which included the wealthy who were financing O'Daniel's campaign.[10]

Whether O'Daniel had the support of Germans—meaning Texans of German ancestry—is a moot point (it seems more likely to have been merely a wartime slur), but Lomax was right on most other counts. His reasoning, however, demonstrates his complex nature. One would expect him to have had some sympathy for the old-age pensioners, since he considered himself a man of uncertain means and worried constantly that he would become financially dependent on his children in his old age. But the pensioners were "'Gimme' cases" looking for a handout, while he was proud and self-sufficient. Singling out the music audience among O'Daniel supporters shows his unfortunate bias against rural musicians who made records or sang on the radio, which rendered them "hillbillies" rather than "folk," but it's odd that he faulted the O'Daniel camp for opposing the New Deal, since he and O'Daniel were both virulent Roosevelt haters. Clearly his concern here was O'Daniel's rich backers, behind which was the hazy specter of Wall Street Interests, Jews, out-of-state do-gooders, and pampered effetes of the leisure class—all foreign to Lomax's sense of what was right and proper.

In any event, he told John Jr., fuming, that this was an unbeatable combination and O'Daniel would surely win; thus Texas, "the mother of fighting men," would send to the U.S. Senate "a sycophantic ignoramus [and] consummate hypocrite, an egotistic paranoid" who was bent on leading a populist revolution in the style of Huey Long.[11] In another letter he lumped many of his *bêtes noires* together, telling Johnny that it was a sad world where there was such overwhelming support for people like O'Daniel, Frances Perkins (secretary of labor), Eleanor Roosevelt, and John L. Lewis, president of the United Mine Workers. "Square your chin and fight 'em," he said.[12]

• • • • •

Lomax and Bullington had been corresponding for some time, carrying on a mutually grumpy dialogue in which they complained to each other about Roosevelt's third term, labor unions, and the general sorry state of things. As tension grew on the University of Texas campus with the widening rift between Rainey and the regents, it became increasing clear to Lomax and Bullington that one of their enemies was J. Frank Dobie, whose weekly newspaper column syndicated around the state had become a rallying point for the small and rather timid pro-Rainey faction. Thus Dobie emerged as a serious thorn in the side of the Establishment. "As you well know," Bullington complained to Lomax, "our mutual friend, Frank Dobie, has been writing a lot of political articles attacking the Junior Senator [O'Daniel], the Governor [Coke Stevenson], Lieutenant Governor [John Lee Smith, whom Dobie called "a homemade fascist"] and others who are opposed to the New Deal and labor racketeers who are now looting this country." Of even greater concern to Bullington, as a University regent, was Dobie's position on the faculty; the board was getting complaints, and the University's image was bound to be tarnished. Although Bullington felt that it would set a dangerous precedent for the board to interfere with Dobie, after pondering the school regulation which permitted professors to speak on public issues, he decided that "This is one rule I might want to change, and even nullify."[13] Later he declared that the board could fire Dobie if it so desired, but that would only play into Dobie's hands—the man clearly wanted to be a martyr, and Bullington had no intention of allowing that to happen. Prof. E. C. Barker tended to agree. "There are two assumptions to make about Dobie," said Barker. "One is that he is too important to be fired. The other is that he is too insignificant."[14]

After a particularly scathing Dobie column in the spring of 1943, Lomax was livid. He reprimanded Dobie for disgracing the University and "stirring up class feeling." Dobie replied calmly; after praising an excerpt from Lomax's autobiography-in-progress that had appeared in the *Southwest Review,* he pointed out that he was not stirring up class feeling but only calling attention to it. "It is coming more and more to the point where a man has to go right or go left," he added. "There is no middle road left." Dobie's own political and cultural attitudes had changed considerably during the 1930s, from the days when he condoned segregation, suspected Catholicism, and tried the patience of Roy Bedichek (who it seems had always been a liberal, despite the same rural Texas upbringing). Dobie told Lomax that while he used to worship the past and be afraid of change, he found it a great joy to be no longer bound to the past. But he was tired of contention: "Friend John Lomax, I am not going to argue. Believe it or not, I am coming to where I can state a point of view . . . without feeling combative." Soon Dobie was removed from the fray, at least temporarily; Cambridge University had invited him to England for a year, and he felt that it was his patriotic duty to go. "I had far rather go out into the brush and write about the bears, the coyotes, the trail drivers, and other paisanos," he told Lomax, "but I can't withdraw to the far away and long ago now. While young men are fighting to the death, I can't keep from taking some part in the war of ideas."[15]

Dobie was right when he said there was no middle ground left in the war between Rainey and the regents. On the establishment side, even Barker realized that the source of the problem was that the regents didn't trust Rainey, and he didn't trust them.[16] There was no basis for a compromise. The battle lines had become rigidly drawn, and each side saw the other as the serpent who had invaded the garden. Conservatives were genuinely concerned that Rainey and his flunkies would bring down civilization as they knew it, while the Raineyites viewed with horror and dismay the board's high-handed encroachment on the University, which threatened the principles of free thought and discourse. Each camp felt it was a beleaguered minority, and each was confident that sooner or later popular opinion would come to the rescue—or if defeat came first, history would surely vindicate them. Men like Dobie, no less than Lomax and Bullington, were inclined to deal in absolutes, to reduce the issues to black and white and entertain no compromise. In truth, there was more than a little obstinacy and self-righteousness on both sides. The simple difference was that Rainey and his followers, whatever their occasional peccadillos, were right. That did not mean they would prevail.

• • • • •

The dust had not settled from the firing of the economics instructors when another donnybrook erupted. In the fall of 1942 the reading list of a University English course included *The Big Money*, part of the widely praised *U.S.A.* trilogy by John Dos Passos, which the *Saturday Review of Literature* had ranked among the five best novels of the day. But the masses of unlettered, Bible-bred Texans had little tolerance for books that reigning intellectuals found stimulating and thought-provoking. *The Big Money* depicted all sorts of seamy carryings-on between men and women, many of whom were not married, or not married to each other, and it said bad things about Big Business, which, as most Texans knew, was what had made this country great. Anyway, the book was "hard to read," what with all those typographical shenanigans and Joycean streams-of-consciousness that dazzled the intellectuals. Several protests had been lodged by parents and old-line professors (notably Barker, who was outraged to learn that his sophomore son had been assigned the book). The English department had already decided to remove it from the reading list at the end of the semester when word of the controversy reached the board of regents.

Faculty who taught the course were called before the regents and subjected to a minor inquisition, during which each teacher was vigorously grilled about his place of birth (non-Texans were immediately suspect), family and educational background, marital status, and whether or not he knew who had placed *The Big Money* on the reading list. All that could be learned was that the book had been chosen by group action. When no individual could be singled out, the regents wisely hesitated to fire the whole department. But to show their authority, and ignoring the fact that the department had already decided to drop the book at semester's end, they ordered it banned immediately, less than two weeks before final exams. Several regents had not bothered to read the book before voting to remove it.

When Orville Bullington finally got around to reading *The Big Money*, he wrote Lomax that while he was "no 'Miss Nancy,'" he realized he had not known that such books were being published, not to mention required as reading matter for sophomore girls in the University of Texas. "In addition to being filthy and vulgar, and downright indecent, this book also attempts to exalt and glorify Sacco and Vanzetti and the whole Communistic ideology."[17]

Lomax agreed. Noting that while *U.S.A.* contained passages that were forceful and sometimes brilliant, he thought it was otherwise beyond redemption; he had never read such "foul, sluttish, putrid obscenity." Worse, it was full of thinly disguised Communist propaganda and repeatedly showed vile contempt for the flag, the church, and the nation's most sacred institutions.[18] The majority of ordinary Texans felt the same way, and public opinion stood foursquare behind the regents as they moved in on the University, crowding Rainey and his small band of liberals to the wall.

Yet as Lomax saw the situation, it was the regents who were oppressed. Nothing but unanimous approval and support of their authority would do. He was perturbed by what he felt was the persecution of the board by various churches and organizations. He proposed printing up a pamphlet composed of excerpts from the most salacious passages of *U.S.A.* and sending a copy to each Rainey supporter, suggesting in a cover letter that Rainey's "implied defense" of the book amounted to an endorsement of it as a textbook for school children.[19] In fact, Rainey had spoken neither for nor against the book but merely noted that it was considered a major literary work and defended the faculty's right to choose its own texts.

Rainey had more to worry about than textbooks. Over the next eighteen months he and the regents were locked in combat over one issue after another—tenure and promotion, administration of the medical school at Galveston, suspected "Communism" and immorality on the campus, "outside agitators," and charges that Rainey wanted to admit black students to the staunchly all-white University. ("There is not the slightest danger of any negro attending the University of Texas as long as the present Board are on the throne," said the imperial Bullington.)[20]

Congressman Martin Dies, another of Texas's contributions to political demagoguery, was called in to investigate charges that there were "1,000 Communists" at the University. Even Dies had to admit that he couldn't find one. University Vice-President J. Alton Burdine said it amounted to "about a dozen pinkish students with Utopian dreams." The eminent historian Walter Prescott Webb eloquently defended the University's right to teach all theories of government, while J. Frank Dobie pointed out the absurdity of fearing a Communist takeover: "All the Communists [in Texas] together couldn't elect a county commissioner in the whole damn state. A great deal of talk of isms is based not on distrust of Communism but in distrust of Democracy."[21] Bullington repeatedly alluded to "a nest of homosexuals" at the University—supposedly created by Rainey's indulgence and the evil influence of *U.S.A.*—but finally had to admit that an all-out investigation directed by Col. Homer Garrison, respected director of the Texas Department of Public Safety, had turned up only one person on campus who would admit to deviant sexual behavior. (A second suspect resigned from the faculty rather than submit to the regents' inquisition.) As for the board's effort to protect Texas womanhood from the horrors of *U.S.A.*, its only female member, Mrs. I. D. Fairchild of Lufkin, said, "I felt guilty because I didn't get excited about it." Some of the book was pointless, she said, but it wasn't nearly so bad as the self-appointed critics claimed. She agreed with Rainey that the real issue was the board's authoritarian handling of the matter and its arbitrary infringement of free discourse.[22] Or, as Bedi put it to the otherwise progressive Webb, who had been only lukewarm to Rainey, "The whole point is not the virtue of Rainey but the evil purpose of the gang that has captured the university. . . . Rainey's virtue (you may say it is his sole virtue) is that he sees the point and has enough courage to fight the issue out—and that's enough virtue for me."[23]

Until matters reached a full impasse, Bullington exercised as much forbearance toward Rainey as he could muster. "The trouble is," he told Lomax, "we have a little boy running the mill, and I have about decided he is not going to grow up." Like a distraught parent dealing with unruly offspring, he saw the faculty as "a bunch of children." Bullington decided it was his duty to take Rainey aside and counsel him in the ways of the world; he invited the president out to his palatial ranch, where he intended to "carry him up on a high mountain and show him the glory of the world, and get him out of his complex."[24] Rainey's "complex," of course, was his habit of not trying to see things the board's way.

Unfortunately, there was a small obstacle to entertaining Rainey at the ranch—there was no cook. The country was in the midst of war, and all of Bullington's house servants had been drafted or gone into defense work; his most frequent complaint to Lomax, other than University affairs, was the difficulty of getting good help these days.[25] In any event, Rainey never came to the mountain—whether because he declined or because of the manpower shortage is not known. Instead, he and his "complex" went on antagonizing the board.

Lomax, off in Dallas, *hors de combat* because of his health and distance from the firing line in Austin, kept himself busy rallying the troops, comforting the wounded, and passing ammunition. He wrote encouraging letters to various regents,[26] praising their "patient, even indulgent attitude" toward the obstreperous faculty, and he sent the president of the board a long account of everything negative he knew about Rainey, dating back to the time when they first met in 1932. To Bullington, Lomax suggested that the regents needed a spy in Austin—an "Ambassador Extraordinary and

Minister Plenipotentiary"—to keep them informed about what Rainey and the faculty were up to. Bullington promptly found such an agent—the University comptroller, C. D. Simmons, who was already in place and eager to ingratiate himself with the regents. At the same time, Lomax warned Bullington about a fifth columnist on the other side—Dobie's "young satellite," John Henry Faulk.[27] After checking up on Faulk, Bullington told Lomax: "He is like a lot of these young radicals on the negro problem that are trying to use the Southern attitude on the race problem as being against the war effort." In a telling slip of the pen, he wrote, "Patriotism, as you know, is the last refuge of every Southerner," then marked through the last word and corrected it to "Scoundrel," adding, "Of course stooges like these young radicals do not know any better. They think they are the elect of the Almighty, and [think] when the droolings of Roosevelt's lips fall on them, they are actually under the drippings of the sanctuary."[28]

. . . . .

By the fall of 1944, Rainey had come to realize that he could no longer function under the present state of affairs. On October 12, he called the faculty together and presented a list of sixteen instances in which the board of regents had violated academic freedom, arbitrarily meddled with the running of the University, or otherwise acted improperly. The faculty responded with a standing ovation and afterward gave him a unanimous vote of confidence.

Three weeks later, the regents met in Houston in closed session—"of course we can not afford to indulge in a public debate with the President or any other member of the staff," Bullington had fumed.[29] After a late-night meeting on November 1, they declared an emergency and announced that they had voted six to two for Rainey's dismissal. As acting president they appointed an Old Steady Tiger from the biology department, Dr. Theophilus Shickle Painter, who immediately assured the faculty that he had taken the job only on an interim basis, to bring peace, and would under no circumstances accept permanent appointment. Viewing this as the best of a bad deal, the faculty reluctantly went along.

The illusion of peace was shattered two days later by a highly unusual event on campus. Twenty years before mass student demonstrations became fashionable, or even possible in Texas, eight thousand normally docile and conformable students of the University gathered in a huge rally and moved to strike all classes until Rainey was reinstated. Forming ranks, they marched on the capitol in a slow, solemn parade through the center of Austin, accompanied by muffled drums and the wailing moan of trombones from the Longhorn band. "Academic Freedom Is Dead" proclaimed a banner draped across a flower-strewn coffin. Outside the governor's mansion, the marchers sang "The Eyes of Texas Are upon You"—which must have struck pain in the heart of the man who wrote it, John Lang Sinclair, Lomax's old ally and a fervent opponent of Rainey. The protesting students found surprising support among townspeople; the parade was declared a legitimate funeral procession, and city police cleared streets and detoured public transportation. Students weren't the only ones who felt that the regents had brought nationwide shame to the University and made a mockery of the motto inscribed above the main entrance of the University tower: "You shall know the truth and the truth shall make you free." (Bullington had publicly declared, "We have heard too much of the University's motto. . . . Our real motto should be the inscription on our state crest, 'Discipline is the foundation of the state.'")[30]

Rainey and his supporters had no more chance of prevailing than Lomax had had when he went up against Farmer Jim Ferguson or Lutcher Stark. After a week, the students returned to classes under protest and, despite a campaign to take their case to the public and rally support for Rainey by mail and telegram, the movement faded. The regents had behind them all the power and much of the statewide popular sentiment; they needed only to hold their ground, keep silent, and wait for the crisis to pass. A committee of state senators convened to investigate the matter, but while an impartial observer could only conclude that the testimony of witnesses offered clear evidence of the board's villainy—much of it from the mouths of various regents themselves—no action was taken by the legislature.

The controversy drew national attention. Stories critical of the regents and sympathetic to Rainey's ideals appeared in *Time, The New Republic,* and other magazines, as well as in student publications around the country. Bernard De Voto in *Harper's Magazine* attacked the forces of reaction asserting that "the University of Texas can no longer seek the truth, discover the truth, or teach the truth. It has been taken over by a dictatorship."[31] When the American Association of University Professors sought to intervene and the Southern Association of Colleges and Secondary Schools threatened to withdraw the University's accreditation, the board responded that these groups were outside agitators and had no business telling Texans what to do. Bullington, true to form, told his fellow regents that he felt "we had better remain ignorant and free rather than to be educated and have the State of Texas subordinated in educational matters to the Federal Government."[32] His demons, it seemed, were all somehow operatives of the New Deal, and his mindset was such that he thought the AAUP was the "American Association of University Publicity Agents." To the senate investigating committee, he said, "No out of state bunch is going to dictate to the Board of Regents—the A.A.U.P. or the American College Publicity Association or anybody else. We've listened to them with all the courtesy they're entitled to, and then we go ahead and do our duty."[33] This variation on the Old Western Code which required that accused horse thieves be given a fair trial and then hung only reflected popular sentiment, characterized by the headline of a *Fort Worth Star-Telegram* editorial about the Rainey affair: "Texas Can Run Its Own Business."[34]

· · · · ·

Three months after Rainey was forced out, Bullington complained to Lomax that "the faculty morons are still raving about academic freedom."[35] He supported some general policy statement from the board "to re-assure the faculty that we, like Lincoln, have malice toward none and charity for all." But he had no sooner asserted that the regents weren't going to mount a purge against the remaining Raineyites when he quoted Robert E. Lee's remark that "the sublimest word in the English language was 'duty'" and said it was the duty of the faculty to repudiate Rainey's "slanders against the University." Furthermore, if they didn't recant, "then may God in his infinite compassion have mercy for them for I am afraid the Board will not."[36] It was characteristic of Bullington that he would see the conflict in terms of the Civil War, an event nearly a hundred years in the past, and, in quoting Lincoln, identify himself with the Yankee victors, whom he despised.

By this time the old guard had gained a new champion, in the form of J. Evetts Haley, scion of a West Texas ranching family and a popular historian of the Old West. Despite an M.A. in history from the University of Texas and his position on the faculty of West Texas State Teachers College at Canyon, Haley was if anything more reactionary and virulent than Bullington. To him academic freedom, so called, was nothing more than a treacherous smokescreen to hide all sorts of subversive evils (his infamous phrase, "the dangerous and unctuous cloak of academic freedom," struck terror in the hearts of campus liberals around the state for years to come). A right-wing version of Frank Dobie, Haley was a literary freebooter and gadfly with a dim view of intellectuals, more interested in ranging among the common folk and writing popular books about them than playing the academic game. He now proposed a series of stories for state newspapers "tracing the University racket," and wanted to enlist Lomax to provide his slant on a variety of subjects affecting the Rainey controversy.

Lomax was flattered by Haley's attention, but first there were some matters that had to be straightened out. In 1943, Haley had published a generally laudatory biography of George Littlefield, whom Lomax had never forgiven for his role in the Ferguson affair, and Lomax felt obliged to take Haley to task for that. Haley not only declined to defend himself but said that as far as he was concerned, Ferguson had probably been right to attack the "over-grown, crazy nature of the 'higher educational' system."[37] The difference in their positions, it seems, was that Lomax had only lately come to realize that the University was out of hand; Haley had known it all along. Lomax couldn't bear a kind word about Ferguson or Littlefield, but he had to admit that Haley was right about one thing: whether or not the University was overgrown and crazy in 1917, it certainly was now. Satisfied that he and Haley were on the same wavelength, he was willing to proceed.

• • • • •

With Painter in place as acting president of the University, the search for Rainey's permanent replacement got underway. Lomax and his cadre of elders stepped up their behind-the-scenes activity. John Lang Sinclair voiced their common concern in a letter to Lomax: "I hope the Regents have learned their lesson, and that they will choose for the next president someone who is a business man or a student, not a propagandist, and above all, not an 'educator.'"[38] Edgar Witt concurred: "I am not so strong for too much scholarship." Witt, former lieutenant governor of Texas and a Roosevelt appointee to the American Mexican Claims Commission, recommended a Texas lawyer who had served in Washington on the legal staff of Henry Wallace's Department of Agriculture. In Witt's view, his candidate's greatest strength was that he "does not have a very scholarly background from the academic point of view." (Lest anyone infer from the man's association with Henry Wallace that he was "too 'New Dealish,'" Witt assured Lomax that was not true; he was foremost a lawyer—trained at the University, of course—and an administrator, rather than an academic.) Witt, who was not known for temperance, went on flailing at Rainey long after the man was gone from the University.[39]

Meanwhile, Barker, for his part, thought Painter was "making an extraordinarily good president, and a courageous one."[40] And well he might think so. Painter had told Bullington that he consulted closely with Barker on most University decisions.[41] In July, Bullington gave the University $2,500 to "start a library of Texas History named in honor of Dr. E. C. Barker."[42]

Barker's praise for Painter was a harbinger of what happened next. On the heels of a statement by Barker and his coterie that academic freedom was safe at the University, the regents declared the presidential search over and done. Painter had proved to be a faithful hireling, and the regents decided he was minding the store so well that they would let him stay on permanently. Painter quickly accepted, despite his earlier declaration to the faculty that he was not a candidate for president and absolutely would not accept the job if it was offered to him. Said Dobie, in retrospect, "His mission was to draw salary and act as waterboy for the regents."[43]

The already demoralized faculty protested, but only weakly. Walter Prescott Webb, who had eventually supported Rainey but kept a low profile in the controversy, convened a small band of professors to draw up a resolution expressing their regret that Painter had "broken faith and violated his pledge" to the faculty, but in the end they waved the white flag—"Despite this regret we will give our support to all measures conducive to the success and progress of the institution we serve."[44] This scarcely satisfied University rooters like Ed Crane and John Lomax, who objected to such tepid approval of Painter. Responding to harsh criticism from Crane, Webb pointed out that the administration of nearly all the state's colleges and universities was in the hands of scientists and technicians: "Nowhere in Texas does any person trained in the humanities or in the social sciences—in human relationships—have a look-in."[45]

Many other faculty members remained bitter over what they considered to be Painter's act of betrayal. That produced equally acidic outbursts from the conservative opposition. Referring to the faculty dissidents, Ed Crane sniffed, "Alleged students, as they purport to be, of history, it would seem that they would not condemn Painter for changing his mind since civilization today is in its last analysis an epitome of man's change in his concepts for the various phases of life."[46] To men like Roy Bedichek, this was only specious rationalization, as he told Webb: "To say in defense of your charge of broken faith that any man has a right to change his mind is merely to repudiate all pledges by putting them in a class with the dyspeptic who changes his mind from fried to boiled eggs for breakfast. Thus the most solemn compacts become false as dicers' oaths." Old Dr. Battle, once a victim of the same sort of demagoguery that toppled Rainey, now solemnly proclaimed Painter "an honorable man," and Bedichek saw the unwitting irony. "I was surprised at Battle's reiteration of the term 'honorable man,'" he wrote Webb, "as it was a mistake in connotation which no literary man should have made. Says he, 'Dr. Painter is an honorable man' and repeats, and every literate person in his audience (and there were many) completed the sentence under his breath, 'So are they all, all honorable men.'"[47]

• • • • •

An old antagonist of the conservative faction was removed from the battle line in the fall of 1947 when J. Frank Dobie ran afoul of a regents' rule concerning faculty leaves, and his connection with the University was severed.[48] Lomax had concluded long before that Dobie's usefulness to the University had ended. "It's a damn shame," he told Haley, "that such a lovable person should write himself down as so unbelievably silly."[49] Although Dobie still remained as friendly as ever, Lomax backed away from their once-warm relationship, only firing off salvos accusing Dobie of trying to tear down the University. Ed Crane, to his credit, sought to make peace, even going so far on one occasion to tell Lomax that he now suspected there were strong grounds for "Dobie's fulminations"—namely, matters which the board of regents had deliberately concealed from the public.[50] He pointed out Dobie's forbearance in the face of Lomax's harsh outbursts and urged him to meet Dobie halfway: "he may re-act like Saul did in attempting to answer your gentle but searching question—'Why, Dobie, doest thou persecute the University?'"[51] Barker offered similar counsel, although it was qualified by his huffy notion that Dobie still hadn't shown enough penitence for his part in the Rainey fight.[52]

Lomax gave in and wrote to Dobie, trying his best to let bygones be bygones. Still, there was a strident air to his letter, and Dobie, in an otherwise pleasant and newsy reply, said, "I am not going to argue or discuss the University with you. . . . The University will go on. Life will go on."[53] Lomax had said something similar to Bullington, who more or less agreed, in his own fashion: "You are correct—the University will go on despite all the subversive elements that undertake to wreck it."[54] They were all tiring of the fray.

• • • • •

In July 1945, the Southern Association of Colleges and Secondary Schools placed the University of Texas on probation, citing an "unhealthy" intellectual climate there. Orville Bullington spoke again for the powers-that-be: "You will be glad to know," he told Lomax, in the voice of a man who knows he is wrong but can't admit it, "that the action of the Southern Association did not cause me to lose one wink of sleep. . . . I do not give a damn about what they think or what action they take, nor will I pay any attention to their demands."[55]

The following year, after extensive investigation, the AAUP censored the University administration, citing "attempts by a politically dominant group to impose its social and educational views on the University."[56] The response from the Texas establishment was much the same as it had always been: who cares? The University remained in the grip of know-nothingism well into the next decade, a seed ground for the wretched excesses of McCarthyism in the fifties.

CHAPTER TWENTY-EIGHT

• • • • •

When the Work's All Done This Fall

1942–48

Throughout the Rainey affair, Lomax had suffered poor health, which contributed to his fits of temper and general crankiness. In the fall of 1942 he was hospitalized briefly with hypertension and digestive troubles and spent several weeks that winter recuperating at home in the attentive care of Miss Terrill. By spring he was up and around but still unable to return to his normal routine. He puttered in his garden, read the papers, listened to the radio, and, as he told Johnny, continued to "swear at the News . . . especially Harry Hopkins and Eleanor." He was still bothered by what he considered to be Alan's distorted ideas about social issues, but took heart in supporting the American war effort and railing against communism and the Axis powers.[1] With considerable effort, he had dieted off fifteen pounds but soon gained it back. To a newspaper feature writer who asked for a physical description, Miss Terrill replied, "John Lomax weighs usually 180 pounds, is about 5 feet 10." Discussing a Lomax book on the radio, Professor John T. Frederick of Northwestern University had referred to him as "a pudgy little man," and Lomax, pretending to be upset, demanded that Frederick apologize for "pudgy." Replied Frederick cordially, "That adjective was unfortunate," but Miss Terrill said it was "little" that didn't fit him.[2]

By summer, with his health improving and the Rainey affair in full swing, Lomax longed for the company of kindred spirits. Roy Bedichek traveled about the state frequently as director of the University Interscholastic League, and Lomax urged him to stop by the House in the Woods for a visit. Bedi declined, on the grounds that he didn't want to endure Lomax's tirades against Roosevelt and the New Deal. Then Lomax learned that Dr. W. J. Battle, who was involved with him against Rainey and shared his animosity to Roosevelt, wanted to pay a visit. Battle was getting on in years and disliked driving, so it was arranged that Bedichek would bring him to Dallas, leave him with Lomax overnight, and return the next day to have lunch and drive Battle back to Austin—all predicated on Lomax's solemn promise that he would not mention President Roosevelt in Bedi's presence. Lomax and Battle had a fine visit, Bedi returned as planned, and the three old friends had a convivial lunch together at the House in the Woods. Afterward, saying their good-byes, they walked out to Bedi's car, parked in the long circular drive that led to the street. Battle's suitcase was stowed in the car, they all shook hands, and Lomax followed Bedichek around to the driver's side as he got in behind the wheel. Then, as Bedi started the motor and eased off down the drive, he saw Lomax begin to follow alongside, moving into a trot and shouting at the top of his voice, "God damn Roosevelt! God damn Roosevelt! God damn Roosevelt!" all the way to the street.[3] From Lomax's point of view, when Bedi got in the car to leave he was technically no longer a guest.

Although he was feeling better, health problems and his involvement in the Rainey feud delayed work on his autobiography. He missed another deadline that summer, but by December was back at work on the manuscript again. Macmillan had grown accustomed to his excuses and missed deadlines, but H. S. Latham still hoped to have the book out by spring of 1944. It was another doomed hope.

Keeping to a schedule wasn't Lomax's only problem with the book. When James Putnam finally got a large part of the manuscript in July 1944, he found it episodic, impersonal, and lacking in particulars. Because Lomax had failed to supply key dates, the chronology was confusing, and the chapters he had prevailed upon John Jr. and Alan to put together further blurred the focus. Lively and well written as these chapters were, they didn't fit the tone or pattern of the book Lomax was trying to write, and Putnam rejected them. "It's *your* book," Putnam told him, and urged that he provide more detail for the years from 1910 and 1932,[4] a period between *Cowboy Songs* and *American Ballads and Folk Songs* that held little interest for Lomax. This gap was never more than sparsely filled. Lomax seemed more interested in corresponding with famous people who would offer testimonials to the importance of his work—Admiral Richard E. Byrd, for instance, who gave him permission to say that "Home on the Range" was

Bryd's favorite song and a source of inspiration during his lonely vigil at the South Pole.[5] Newspapers reported that "Home on the Range" was also the president's favorite song, but Lomax, Roosevelt-hater that he was, would not stoop to confirm that story. He did not hesitate, however, to include it in the book.

Trying to recover the past and confirm an identity for his autobiography, Lomax wrote not only to famous people for testimonials but to dozens of old friends and acquaintances who might provide him with their perspective on events that had transpired years before. Lawton Walton of Sturgis and Walton, his first publisher, was dead; Lomax located his partner, Lyman Sturgis, but Sturgis died after their initial exchange of letters. At last he got what he wanted when Sturgis's brother, Edward, wrote him, generously saying that although he was never connected with Lyman's publishing business, "I am not exaggerating when I say that the advent of 'Cowboy Songs' was perhaps the cause of greatest excitement to all of us. It was something *new* and different. At any rate the name of 'Lomax' meant much to us at that time . . . and continued to mean much."[6]

In other instances, Lomax's many letters to people in his long ago past were meant either to vindicate himself or simply nurse old grudges. He asked various people for their versions of the Great A&M Strike, Winston's presidency at the University of Texas, Ferguson's Big Bear Fight, and other traumatic events which still gnawed at him in old age. At times these forays into the past seemed obsessive, as if he thought he could rewrite his life by straightening out the bends and bobbles that lay behind him. Often the fences he sought to mend were never broken, or had been repaired long ago. Typical was a letter from Lloyd Gregory, a staff member of the *Daily Texan* when Lomax left the University in 1925 and now managing editor of the *Houston Post.* "My Old Friend," wrote Gregory, "the little unpleasantness we once had long ago was forgotten by me. I can't forget you helped me with a job, when I desperately needed every dollar I could earn."[7]

Weatherford College earned Lomax's wrath when it solicited donations from graduates. He angrily declined in a three-page letter detailing a minor incident there, fifty years earlier, that had embarrassed him.[8] Miss Terrill's "kinnery," whom Lomax never much liked, were another source of irritation. When several in-laws came to stay though the Christmas holidays in 1944, he complained that they talked endlessly about themselves, while he took refuge, cussing under his breath, in his study in the back of the house. Once they were gone, it would be his job to help Miss Terrill recover. "Not a damn one of them," he said, "is worth the smallest tip of her littlest finger."[9]

There was a plenitude of other grievances. Lomax renewed his quarrel with Elie Siegmeister, kept up running attacks on Raineyites, complained loudly to the Dallas city council about the stairs at the train station, and angrily demanded that his name be taken off the mailing list of the Southern Conference for Human Welfare, whose executive secretary wondered if he was the same Lomax who was once secretary of alumni at the University of Texas: "If you are the same Lomax, I find it difficult to associate your bitter letter with the warm human spirit I used to know."[10] His growing cantankerousness surprised and disappointed many who had known a more genial John Lomax. Among these was the editor of the *Scroll,* official publication of Phi Delta Theta, who solicited an article from him, as one of the organization's more distinguished members. Lomax replied with a scalding blast at all fraternities, declared they ought to be exterminated, and severed himself entirely from Phi Delta Theta. His letter, the editor responded, "came as a distinct surprise" but if that was the way he felt about Phi Delta Theta, they would see that his name was removed from the fraternity roll.[11]

Even Lomax's old allies began to have trouble dealing with his moods and outbursts. Matters finally grew so grim that Edgar Witt, not known as a ray of sunshine himself, took it on himself to upbraid Lomax. "I dread my own old age . . . if I am to sour like you seem to have," he wrote, adding sarcastically, "Of course the world and life has [*sic*] done so little for you—only provided two charming wives, a wonderful family, none of whom was taken or injured by the 2 World Wars that saddened at least ⅓ or ½ of the families of the U.S., wonderful personal success financially & otherwise—& many, many devoted friends." Lomax's "don't give a damn" attitude toward those friends, said Witt, was an outright insult.[12] Unfortunately, this came too late to have much effect.

Working with his autobiography raised anew the question of where he would leave his papers. Earlier it had been assumed that they would go to either the Library of Congress or the University of Texas. Now the Rainey affair had alienated him from the University, and although his disaffection with the Library of Congress was never marked by any similar dramatic eruption, for some time he'd grumbled about the way the Archive of American Folk Song had treated him, delaying his expense checks and ignoring his plans for more field trips. Sifting through his papers for *Adventures of a Ballad Hunter* brought back old memories of earlier victories, and Harvard resurfaced as a contender for the Lomax archives. When he'd threatened to send everything there a few years earlier, Alan was running the Archive and complained that it would be an embarrassment to him personally if his father deposited his folklore materials anywhere but in the Library of Congress. Such an act would be seen as a repudiation of the very institution—the Archive of American Folk Song—which Lomax had created, and while Harvard had certainly supported him in the beginning, the Library of Congress, said Alan, had done far more to make his work known and establish his reputation.[13]

Now the present head of the Archive, Duncan Emrich, told him much the same thing. "I am from Harvard as you were," he wrote. "And next to the Library of Congress, there is no other place comparable." But the American people identified Lomax with the Library of Congress, said Emrich: "You have grown from a Harvard graduate student and Sheldon scholar, grown from Harvard, to become a great national figure."[14] In the end, such flattery only partially succeeded, perhaps because Lomax saw that there was more than a little self-interest in it, on the part of both Alan and Emrich. He was dissuaded from trying to remove material he'd already deposited in the Archive and ship it to Harvard (which he knew would have been difficult, if not impossible, anyway), but he firmly decided that nothing else of his would go to Washington. Eventually, with the passing of time—which dimmed his memories of the Rainey affair—and through the determined efforts of the persistent and charming University of Texas Archivist, Winnie Allen, Lomax warmed once more to the institution of his first affection, and his papers went to the special collection of Texas history there, named for one of his old friends, Eugene Barker, and endowed by another, Orville Bullington.

• • • • •

In the summer of 1944, Lomax was invited to appear as the expert on folklore at the Southwest Writers' Conference to be held in Corpus Christi under the auspices of a local writers' club. Unsure that his health would stand the strain, he responded playfully to the invitation with a list of demands he was sure the sponsoring group couldn't meet. He asked for round-trip railroad fare from Dallas for him and Miss Terrill, a first-class hotel suite, expenses for an additional week for them both at the plush Tarpon Inn at nearby Port Aransas, three days of charter fishing, and finally "one full quart of A-1 Rye Whiskey for my personal use."[15] To his surprise, the ladies in charge promptly agreed. Other writers on the program were Dr. John Erskine (described by Miss Terrill as "the big shot"), Dr. W. S. Campbell of the University of Oklahoma, who published historical fiction and biography under the pen name Stanley Vestal, and Miss Leigh Peck, author of children's books.

As Lomax knew, local writers' soirees such as this were fraught with peril, but the Corpus Christi gathering was well organized, and everything went smoothly. "John Avery knocked 'em in the aisles," Miss Terrill reported happily. At Port Aransas, she read, walked on the beach, and ate her fill of the Tarpon Inn's famous seafood cuisine while Lomax went fishing on the boat of his favorite skipper, crusty old Captain George "Florida" Roberts. He and Roberts brought back nearly four hundred pounds of mackerel and kingfish, partook of Lomax's A-1 rye, and relived high adventures from the old days when they had fished the Gulf together.[16]

Briefly rejuvenated, Lomax accepted an invitation that fall to travel to Los Angeles and present "The Gang Songs of the Negro" at the newly organized Musicians' Congress, meeting at UCLA in mid-September. The prestigious panel on which he appeared included Dr. George Pullen Jackson, Dr. Sigurd Hustvedt of UCLA, and Earl Robinson from Metro-Goldwyn-Mayer studios. Alan was invited but couldn't get leave from the army. Leadbelly, however, was on the West Coast futilely pursuing a movie career and accepted an invitation to perform. Lomax pointedly avoided him.

Back in Texas, despite his declining health and fallout from the Rainey fight, Lomax stayed busy, reviewing folklore books, dabbling in other quasi-literary chores, and keeping up a steady stream of correspondence to far-flung places. By mail he argued with Carl Sandburg about labor unions, complained to Gov. Coke Stevenson about poor economy in state government, and exchanged conservative ideology with Barrett Wendell Jr. after a long hiatus in their relationship.[17]

He and Wendell were especially upset by a recent ruling of the Supreme Court in the case of *Smith v. Allright,* which declared unconstitutional the Texas Democratic party's primary elections because they excluded blacks. Declaring the Supreme Court's action "a basic fundamental mistake," Wendell said, "My mother was always opposed to women suffrage not because she didn't want intelligent women to vote but because she felt [suffrage] would double the ignorant vote and, in general, this has been true."[18] The clear implication was that enfranchised blacks, like women, would "double the ignorant vote."

Lomax's political philosophy was spelled out once more in a letter to Prof. Wilbert Snow of Wesleyan University in Middletown, Connecticut. He was, he said, one of those Texans who had decided that the New Deal was the foe of democracy; Roosevelt and his supporters had created the notion of "a superman"—Roosevelt himself—who alone could save the nation by telling everyone what to do and what to think. That would lead to autocracy, said Lomax, and "I can't go along with that idea."[19] As election day loomed in the fall of 1944, with the war reaching a climax and the nation clearly disposed to give Roosevelt an unheard-of fourth term in office, Lomax withdrew in a silent rage. "I guess old Lomax is sulking in his tent," Dobie wrote to Bedichek from England.[20]

Lomax's incidental labors that summer included a review of Botkin's *Treasury of American Folklore* for the *Saturday Review*. Although he used the piece subtly to settle a few old scores, he genuinely liked Botkin's book and said so. Botkin, who had succeeded Alan as assistant in charge of the Archive, immediately wrote to thank him, but when Lomax saw in that a glimmer of hope that he might be recalled for another field recording trip or to perform other services for the Archive, Botkin coolly avoided the issue; his response was little more than a polite inquiry about the progress of Lomax's autobiography. Lomax pouted. He sent Botkin's letter to Alan, indicating that he wasn't going to answer it. "A typical Washington-ian flying-Jenny-get-you-nowhere letter," he said, adding that Alan should give up any notion he might have of returning to the Archive after the war, because Botkin was the darling of the bureaucracy.[21]

As early as 1943 Lomax had declared that his fieldwork for the Archive was finished, but he kept in touch with Spivacke, Ed Waters, Luther Evans, and others at the Library, indicating from time to time that he would be willing to make another recording trip if the chance came along, although he knew that all collecting activities had been suspended for the duration of the war.[22] When normal operations resumed in the fall of 1945, he again volunteered his services, although that may have been merely a gesture, from force of habit. His health was precarious, and other projects were occupying his time. Luther Evans, now Librarian of Congress, replied that he was delighted to know that Lomax was willing to continue recording for the Library, but neither he nor Lomax seemed to have any specific plan in mind, and nothing ever came of their correspondence.[23] When Lomax wanted to record cowboy singer Dick Devall the following year, the Archive had no recorder available, and Spivacke instructed him to use the facilities of a commercial studio in Dallas.[24] Those were the last records Lomax made for the Archive.

• • • • •

Hard work and keeping busy were lifetime habits with Lomax. Now nearing eighty and in poor health, he nevertheless found plenty to do. He wanted desperately to finish his autobiography, but going back over his life so disturbed him that he welcomed interruptions, as when Stith Thompson asked him to contribute to an anthology of regional folklore. In late 1944 Lomax began compiling "Forty Best Ballads," a list which Stanley Marcus proposed to have privately printed. That project kept growing until it became "The Ninety-Nine Best Ballads," and Thomas Y. Crowell Co. contracted to publish it. Lomax later changed his mind about the publisher but died before the book was in final form. It was eventually published—with 111 songs—by Duell, Sloan, and Pearce as *Folk Song U.S.A.*

For the "Best Ballads" book Lomax once again needed the services of someone to make musical notations for piano and voice. He and Arthur Wang at Crowell discussed several prospective "composers," and Lomax finally agreed to leave the choice to the publisher. But when Crowell hired Mrs. William Woods for the job and notified Lomax that her $500 fee would be charged against his royalties, he balked and decided to hire someone on his own.[25] Ruth Crawford Seeger, it turned out, was available—and considerably cheaper. Lomax offered her five dollars per song (and knowing her tendency to procrastinate, raised the figure to six dollars if she could finish the job in thirty days).[26] At this point the book was still "The Forty-Four Best Ballads," which meant that the musical notations would cost him at most $264. Mrs. Seeger readily agreed. But the situation required some fancy footwork: not only had the job already been offered to Mrs. Woods, Lomax now became concerned that Mrs. Seeger would find out that he had maneuvered her into underbidding it. To be sure that his hands were clean in case the plan backfired, he suggested to Crowell that the publisher handle further transactions with Mrs. Seeger. He had no commitment to her, he assured Wang, and would even go along with Mrs. Woods—so long as Crowell paid half the cost (which Wang had finally offered to do).[27] Just how Mrs. Woods was disposed of is not known, but Wang decided it would be best that they hire Mrs. Seeger because the Lomaxes had collaborated with her before and knew her work.[28] As more ballads were added, Charles Seeger's talents were drawn on as well, and Alan began to assume most of his father's share of the work. Eventually Lomax offered, and the Seegers accepted, a more equitable financial arrangement which made the Seegers one-third partners in the project.[29]

For Stith Thompson's projected anthology of regional folklore, Lomax was asked to write on the subject of the cattle range and Thompson sent him a sheet of suggestions on how to go about it. He wanted a more personal account of cowboys than had surfaced in *Cowboy Songs,* and he hoped Lomax would include contemporary material. "The period has come to be looked on nostalgically, and Hollywood has become interested," he wrote. "Perhaps a word about Will Rogers, Bob Burns, and Will James belongs here."[30] Thompson's inclusion of Bob Burns is an interesting grace note on popular culture and an insight into the perceptions of an academic folklorist of the day: Burns, a hillbilly humorist from Arkansas, popular on network radio as "The Arkansas Traveler," was about as far removed from cowboys and cattle trails as one could imagine, but—as evidenced by the evolution of "hillbilly" music into "country-western" during this period—in the mid-1940s any sort of rural folksiness tended to be equated with the image of the Old West. Will James was only marginally more authentic as a westerner, born Joseph Ernest Nephali Dufault in Quebec and in his teens before leaving eastern Canada for the American West with his sketchbook, pistol, and faulty command of English.[31]

Lomax had urged Thompson to call on some black scholar for the sections on Negro folklife, but Thompson replied that even if he knew a Negro competent to do the work, he would still hesitate because the material had to be treated with more objectivity than any black could have.[32] At the suggestion of anthropologist Melville Herskovits, Thompson enlisted Prof. Richard Waterman of Northwestern University for these sections. In the end, ironically, Waterman drew on so much of Lomax's material on blacks that he had to apply for permissions, holding up publication of the book, and he eventually wound up paying Lomax a substantial fee for the songs that were used.[33]

· · · · ·

The appearance of Donald Day's profile of Lomax in the October 1945 issue of *Reader's Digest* propelled the ballad collector briefly into the national spotlight and created an unexpected flood of attention. In reference to Lomax's present circumstances, the article mentioned only that "Today, in his 70's, John Lomax sits in a neat cottage above White Rock Lake near Dallas, writing his *Adventures of a Ballad Hunter.*"[34] That brought a swarm of letters addressed simply to "John Lomax, Near White Rock Lake, Dallas, Texas," many of them, as he said, from the usual "cranks and plain damn fools" enlisting his help to get their songs published or promote some zany scheme. Amateur composers, figuring they were as much "folk" as anybody else, swamped him with their output, songs whose titles reflected the influence of the recent global disturbance: "Old Glory Will Ever Wave," "A Love Nest, a Victory Garden, and You," and "Please Protect My Little Boy." A lady in Tampa, Florida, offered him her original lyrics to "Minuet with

Lafayette—A True Story" and "The Lord's Prayer (Words to Ad Lib Chorus)," which she was certain he would want to record immediately. Lomax patiently suggested that, while he was not interested in composed songs, there was surely a place in Tampa where she could get her songs recorded.[35] Many letters came from servicemen in veterans' hospitals or waiting at disembarkation centers to be discharged. One, who planned to go into evangelistic song work after his release from the army, thought it would be an interesting sideline to record local singers as he traveled from church to church, and he wrote to ask for advice. Lomax said that was an excellent idea, and told the young man to stay away from cities and record only singers—especially old-fashioned ones—in small towns and rural areas. Most of all, "Don't record singers who have had any musical education—whites or blacks."[36]

Not all of the mail came from kooks and amateurs. Within ten days after the *Reader's Digest* article appeared, the Library of Congress had received four thousand letters requesting the catalog of Lomax recordings in the Archive, and eventually the number of inquiries—according to Lomax—had reached 30,000. "Did [the Library] rejoice?" he asked rhetorically. "Far from it." All they did, he said, was complain that they had to hire more secretaries to answer the mail.[37]

Even more impressively, the Lomax story had attracted the attention of Hollywood. Russell Holman, Paramount Studios' eastern production manager, wrote Lomax on October 19 that Paramount was "extremely enthusiastic" about the possibility of a film depicting his colorful adventures. But Holman also injected a note of caution, pointing out that Lomax's still-unfinished autobiography, portions of which Macmillan had shown him, lacked dramatic shape and in order to film it the studio might have to "take a few liberties about the actual facts in the lives of yourself and your son." He offered a 120-day option for $1,000, during which time a producer and writer would attempt an adaptation. If it was successful and the option exercised, Paramount would pay an additional $6,500.[38]

Lomax of course fancied himself a horse trader; he had spent his life cutting deals, and although many of them had been less than successful, he instinctively played his cards close to his vest. Everything Holman proposed was fine, he replied—except the money. To justify a higher figure, he cited the recent flood of mail to the Library of Congress and the public's "immense interest in folk songs." He also called Holman's attention to the thousands of miles he had traveled, the money he had spent, the hardships he had been subjected to, the indifference and hostility he had endured from prospective sources, and his failure to gain popular recognition for his work.[39] In light of all that, he told Holman, he was sure Paramount would make him a more liberal offer.

Holman simply tossed the ball back to Lomax by asking him to name his minimum price, hinting also that if the deal went through, Lomax and Alan might be hired as consultants. After conferring with Alan, Lomax said he would take $2,500 for the option and an additional $22,500 if it were exercised. For this amount, Paramount could have the rights to everything Lomax had done, both published and unpublished; "the hair goes with the hide," he said, invoking an old cattleman's phrase which may have amused or only confused Holman.[40]

Paramount accepted the offer, and Lomax immediately announced to friends and acquaintances that he had sold his autobiography to Hollywood for "$25,000" (the film was never made, and all he ever got out of it was $2,500 for the option). Old stock-and-bond trader Barrett Wendell Jr. urged him to keep dealing: "You might be able to get more than $25,000 if you were to say that your hearing was a little bad and that you weren't sure you heard had heard the figure correctly." Start listening at fifty thousand, he advised.[41] Said Orville Bullington, "I am certainly delighted to hear you got $25,000 out of those movie kikes in California."[42] There was a brief rumor, which reached a few papers in Texas, that Lomax's role in the movie would be played by Bing Crosby, a story perhaps inspired by Lomax, or perhaps merely by the fact that Crosby was Paramount's leading musical star at the time.[43] Wags joked that Alan would be played by Shirley Temple—or Rin-Tin-Tin.

Purists in the folklore community were alarmed to behold the ogre of commercialization again pounding at the gates. Aroused by rumors of Bing Crosby as Lomax, the formidable Helen Hartness Flanders, doyenne of Vermont folklorists, wrote to Alan, "I simply cannot think that such folk-musicians as you and your father are known to be would betray the gullible public by the unauthentic."[44] Neither of the Lomaxes was much troubled by such sentiments.

Paramount would not pay for the option until a final manuscript of *Adventures of a Ballad Hunter* was submitted. That provided the long-suffering James Putnam with what he needed to light a fire under Lomax and get him to finish the book, which had been dragging on for nearly a decade. Countless deadlines had come and gone, and although the pages piled up, Lomax seemed no nearer to a publishable manuscript than ever. As it turned out, Putnam did much of the final work on the book himself, organizing and editing material that Lomax gave him, supplying necessary transitions, straightening out Lomax's often confused chronology, even writing certain passages that he felt ought to be included. His changes and suggestions were submitted for approval, but in most cases Lomax automatically accepted them, without comment. Putnam suggested so many changes that Lomax began to refer to him, jokingly but with some validity, as "my co-author."[45]

By January 1946, Putnam was still having trouble finding a structural pattern among the plethora of anecdotal material Lomax had supplied him, but he got together a manuscript which satisfied the movie people, and in early February Lomax got his check for the option.[46] Putnam hoped to have *Adventures of a Ballad Hunter* on Macmillan's fall publication list, but there were still problems with it, and he went on struggling to organize what he had while eliciting from Lomax yet another, final chapter that everyone at Macmillan deemed necessary. "To my mind this [last chapter] should be one which ties the whole book up and gives it a unity which, at the moment, it still lacks," he told Lomax. "Since the main thread of the book is autobiographical I think that this last chapter should be a very personal one. . . . The chapter should end, it seems to me, on an evaluation by you of what your life has meant to you, particularly in relation to your work as a ballad collector."[47]

What Lomax came up with again missed the mark, and Putnam had to reject it, along with new material the author had added to earlier chapters. This included a fuller account of the Leadbelly episode, mostly extracts of letters Lomax had written at the time, which he apparently slipped into the book with the notion that this material would vindicate him of charges that he'd mismanaged or exploited the black singer. Unfortunately, these passages also revealed Lomax's insecurity and often convoluted reasoning in racial matters, and Putnam thought their inclusion "unwise." He advised eliminating everything but a brief allusion to the Leadbelly affair: "I am certain that [including the whole story] would backfire and might well let you in for a libel suit."[48] Putnam felt so strongly about this matter that he took it to Alan, who was of course sympathetic to Leadbelly and instantly agreed. But Putnam had already said the magic words to Lomax when he mentioned a possible libel suit. The offending passages were straightaway excised.

Putnam finally had to write a draft of the last chapter to demonstrate what he wanted, and from that Lomax came up with an acceptable conclusion. As late as June, Putnam was still hoping that the book could be published during the fall, but that was not to be. It appeared in February 1947, twelve years after Lomax signed the contract.

Although *Adventures of a Ballad Hunter* wound up as something less than a full and accurate account of Lomax's life and career, it was given a warm reception by readers and reviewers. Edward Weeks, long a Lomax booster, wrote in the *Atlantic,* "His is the saltiest, singingest autobiography of our time; its character and color, its dialect and melody come straight from the heart of our people."[49] Similarly, Lloyd Lewis applauded the book in the *Chicago Sun* and Lewis Gannett in the daily edition of the *New York Herald Tribune.* Horace Reynolds, who had written enthusiastically about other Lomax books, praised *Adventures of a Ballad Hunter* in the *New York Times Book Review* for its sincerity: "These people really existed, said and did and sung these things. If anybody ever did, John Lomax really heard America singing."[50]

Discouraging words were rarely heard—Bedichek told Dobie privately that he thought Macmillan had done a "flimsy, shoddy job" in editing and printing the book[51]—but several reviews revealed how superficially their authors had read it, looking only for sunshine and smiles. "As one reads he knows the author, John Lomax, has led a happy life, doing what he likes to do," wrote Carl Carmer in the *New York Herald Tribune Weekly Book Review.*[52] Well, yes and no. It is true that Lomax had sought to show the positive side of most events and deliberately omitted or foreshortened his darker moments, but no careful reader could fail to note the grinding poverty of his early years; his hard struggle to educate himself and "be somebody"; the anguish of his several defeats at the hands of powerful antagonists (notably Jim Ferguson); the many obstacles he had faced, and sometimes succumbed to, in the field; and the cold and uncaring public, as he saw it, which had so often ignored the fruits of his work. Yet a reviewer for the *San Francisco Chronicle* spoke of "how [Lomax] found enthusiasm in many places, genuine support and specific help in others, people everywhere who were eager to contribute to his researches."[53] Ultimately, no one paid much attention to the cobbled-up quality of the book, with its loosely connected anecdotes, chapters that zoom across vast stretches of time in a single bound, and the often impersonal tone of its author (in spite of all of James Putnam's efforts to get him to write with more warmth and feeling). Nor did any reviewer feel obliged to complain that it was printed on cheap paper with a shabby cover and no index. On the whole, it was probably fortunate that no one took a very careful look at the book. Lomax was growing old; his victories, like his days, were numbered. In one way or another, he had earned the praise which *Adventures of a Ballad Hunter* brought him, and it gave him bright moments in an otherwise sour and brooding old age. One of the brightest came when the Texas Institute of Letters honored *Adventures of a Ballad Hunter* as the "Best Texas Book of the Year," with an award of $1,000.

Lomax was busy with some philanthropy of his own, although it was carried out quietly, behind the scenes, and against the grain of his public image as a grumpy old tightwad. For some years, usually at Christmas, he had sent small gifts of money and clothing to various of his song sources, including Henry Truvillion, Vera Hall and Dock Reed, and any number of black convicts still behind bars.

He had also given help to Ruby Pickens Tartt, sending her modest sums of money from time to time in the polite guise of "reimbursements." More importantly, he convinced Donald Day to publish some of her stories in the *Southwest Review,* for which she was paid fifty dollars, and selections of these later appeared in several anthologies. Largely as a result of Lomax's efforts, Tartt's "Alabama Sketches" was included in Martha Foley's *Best American Short Stories 1945*.[54] That year, the Tartts lost most of their possessions in a tornado which destroyed their home and sent Mrs. Tartt to the hospital with a broken arm and sprained shoulder. Without their knowledge, Lomax contributed to her medical expenses. Later, after the Tartts found a small duplex to rent, he quietly arranged for the purchase of a new stove and refrigerator for them, no mean feat in those early postwar days, when supplies were still severely limited.

Another beneficiary of Lomax's generosity was Mike Stephens, the black "hired man" who had worked around the House in the Woods in the late 1930s and early 1940s. Although visitors sometimes accused Lomax of speaking harshly to Stephens and treating him in a patronizing fashion, the two men developed a lasting friendship (Stephens and his wife, Emma, named their son John Alan in honor of the two Lomaxes). During the war Mike and Emma Stephens had moved to Washington state to find work in the defense industry, but wrote frequently to Lomax and Miss Terrill. Long after their departure from Dallas, Lomax, as he was going through his papers and putting his affairs in order during the last year of his life, instructed his bank to deliver to Stephens a savings bond worth $1,150.00 at maturity.[55]

• • • • •

Despite declining health, Lomax remained active. In the summer of 1946, he was one of several prominent panelists at a seminar of the Folklore Institute of America, hosted by Indiana University, and in October he was invited to a literary festival at Coker College in South Carolina, where he lectured on cowboy songs. He and Miss Terrill took advantage of these outings to tour the breadth of the country, traveling all the way from New York to San Francisco and back to Texas that summer and fall.

Once *Adventures of a Ballad Hunter* had appeared, John Jr. decided that his father ought to write a history of the University of Texas and bought him a newfangled wire recorder from Sears, Roebuck so that he could dictate "the unvarnished truth." (Lomax got a 10 percent discount on the machine "because of my position in the Folk Song world" but complained that the discount wasn't 20 percent.)[56] Publication would probably cause an uproar, Johnny said, but if necessary it could be postponed "until 1960 or 1980 when all the actors on the stage have departed." This only reminded Lomax that he would be among the departed; he grumbled a few desultory notes into the machine, but the project never really got underway. Earlier, E. C. Barker, trying to cheer him in a moment of gloom, had written extoling the many contributions Lomax had made as secretary of the Texas Exes Association, adding, "If the history of the University is ever written, the author will be writing about you, whether he knows it or not."[57] That knowledge may have also contributed to Lomax's lack of interest in the University history project; having only recently struggled through his autobiography, he had had his fill, for the time being, of writing about himself.

He was left with little to do but putter in his garden and fret. "Daily I fight bugs that eat my peas and beans and cabbage," he had written to Johnny, but he couldn't work. Whenever he tried, he said, he began to worry and fret and gave it up to read or listen to the radio and "think of my blunders."[58] He was again filled with remorse, pondering old quarrels, missed opportunities, dreams that had failed. Old friends were dead or dying—Harry Benedict, Bates McFarland, Reed Smith, Richard Kimball, several of them much younger than he was. He himself soon would be gone and forgotten, he was sure, unmourned by a world that had never really understood him or what he was trying to do. He talked of selling all he owned and moving to Mexico, among strangers, where living was cheap and he would never have to ask anyone—especially not his thoughtless children or the hated government of his native land—to look after him. He couldn't even take solace in food or drink; his doctor had put him on a rigid diet and ordered, "Limit yourself to two ounces of whiskey a day."[59] But he'd always had trouble following doctor's orders.

In the summer of 1947, he reluctantly agreed to spend some time with Shirley and her children at the Mansells' summer cottage in the mountains near Walsenburg, Colorado, while Miss Terrill went to New York for a convention of her Delta Kappa Gamma sorority. John Jr., his wife Margaret, and their toddler son came along on the trip to Colorado, and while they were all there, various Mansell in-laws visited from time to time.

Lomax was miserable almost from the beginning, suffering from the high altitude, a toothache which kept him from sleeping, and a seeming horde of small children. Moreover, Shirley ordered him about, he complained, and had no patience "with a sick old man." He wanted to leave, but there was no transportation; his car had been left in Texas for repairs, and whenever visitors to the camp departed, their cars were always full. His weight and high blood pressure affected his legs and rendered him increasingly immobile. He had difficulty walking, he wrote Miss Terrill, so he stayed indoors, played solitaire, and reflected on "the vanity of life."[60]

He read *Tom Sawyer* to his grandchildren, tried to stay out of the way, and even commiserated with Shirley despite the way she treated him. "She has no patience with my foibles and weaknesses," he complained, but acknowledged that she didn't have it easy, trying to cope with a crowd of company in the small cottage and deal with his infirmities. Even John Jr. was sometimes short with him, and Lomax vowed that he would never place himself in the hands of his children so long as he could maintain a home of his own.[61] Miss Terrill offered to return as soon as her convention was over, but he told her to "go on Gamma-Gammering to your heart's content."[62] He would bear up somehow; occasional trips down the mountain to Walsenburg gave him respite from the altitude and restored his vigor for a time.

After two weeks, the ordeal was finally over. Lomax traveled back to Lubbock with Shirley and her children and caught a bus there for Wichita Falls, where he had left his car. For months, Miss Terrill had been talking up a trip to the Caribbean, but Lomax had scheduled a few lectures around Dallas for the fall and early winter. When that was done, he assured her, they would go off for a long, restful vacation in the sun.[63]

For some time an old friend, Charles Cason, an insurance agent and businessman in Greenville, Mississippi, had been trying to arrange a celebration for Lomax in the state where he was born. Cason originally hoped that the event could be timed to coincide with Lomax's eightieth birthday in September. But Lomax procrastinated. His health was poor and he was tippling again; several times he had absentmindedly wandered away from home without telling Miss Terrill, setting off anxious searches that usually located him, safe but confused, at some neighbor's place.

His eightieth birthday was observed quietly at home with a small group of family and close friends. The event did not go unnoticed, however; some two hundred other friends made a point of writing to express their affection and appreciation. Among these were Carl Sandburg, Luther Evans, Herbert Putnam, Carl Van Doren, Sam Rayburn, Texas governor Beauford Jester—and Dock Reed, Lomax's favorite singer in Livingston, Alabama. Reed had dictated his letter to Mrs. Tartt, who typed it and sent it along, to be bound into a volume with the tributes from other well-wishers and presented to Lomax. "Tell Mr. Lomax," he had said, "he's a mighty nice man, and he's the best white friend I ever had."

Cason persisted in his efforts to get Lomax to Mississippi. When Lomax's health seemed somewhat improved in November, he told Cason he would come after Christmas if Alan, who was now working for Decca Records in New York, could also be induced to appear. It turned out that Alan would be doing fieldwork in the South during January, and when he expressed an interest in recording a Negro church service in Mississippi, Cason quickly agreed to make the arrangements if Alan would appear on stage with his father to sing and talk about folksongs. It was finally settled that the two Lomaxes would arrive in Greenville on January 23, give a public lecture and song performance the next morning at the high school auditorium, and appear as guests of honor that evening at a gala dinner at the Hotel Greenville. Two hundred and fifty guests were expected, including Paul Flowers, book editor and columnist of the *Memphis Commercial Appeal;* Hodding Carter, Pulitzer-Prize-winning publisher of Greenville's *Delta Democrat Times;* the mayor and city officials of Greenville; and, ultimately, the governor of Mississippi.

Cason's enthusiasm for the affair grew by leaps and bounds. He had already gotten the Greenville Travelers Club, a businessman's group of which he was a member, to underwrite the event and act as official sponsor; now he churned out a steady stream of newspaper publicity, arranged an additional round of receptions, scheduled a broadcast by the local radio station, and saw to it that displays were set up in book and music stores. Two weeks before the scheduled date, he persuaded the mayor of Greenville to proclaim Saturday, January 24, as "John Lomax Day," solemnly assuring Hizzoner that it would commemorate Lomax's eightieth birthday ("This birthday anniversary idea is good publicity," he told Lomax, "it's my story, and I'm going to stick to it. You can celebrate such an occasion any time, either before or after.")[64] There was the further implication that Lomax was returning to the place of his birth, although Goodman was actually some sixty miles away. That was close enough for a man who generally claimed that he was a Texan, anyway.

The weather had been harsh that January, and Lomax insisted that Miss Terrill, who was recovering from the flu, not accompany him to Mississippi. A terrible ice storm struck just the day before he boarded the train in Dallas, spreading across the South and Southwest, extending as far away as the West Texas plains. But Lomax was undeterred, despite his uncertain health and the necessity of traveling alone. Not many honors had come his way in recent years, and what lay ahead of him in Greenville would help to assuage the feelings of neglect and misunderstanding he'd long suffered. In any case, he was accustomed to voyaging about under all sorts of inclement conditions; now he set forth buoyantly, anticipating the acclaim and attention about to be given him.

A delegation of hardy Greenvillians braved the elements to meet him at the station. Alan, whom Lomax had not seen for more than a year, was waiting for him at their hotel, and father and son shared a warm reunion. With a small group of well-wishers and representatives of the local press, they adjourned to Lomax's room at the Hotel Greenville for an informal press conference and come-all-ye. Lomax was in high spirits as people moved in and out of the room, talking, telling stories, and sharing a drink or two. He was the center of attention, pulling out stories and songs from the ages, practicing his old magic as tale-teller and raconteur. He launched into a bit of gentle bawdy, singing, "Big Leg Rose," laughing heartily through the end: "The only thing I ever done wrong, stayed in Mississippi one day too long." As he finished singing, he slumped suddenly to the floor, unconscious.[65]

He was taken to King's Daughters Hospital, where the cause was diagnosed as a severe heart attack. Notified by telephone, Miss Terrill caught a night plane to Memphis, where she was met by members of the Travelers Club and brought to Greenville, 150 miles away, arriving in the early dawn of Saturday morning. Despite weather conditions, John Jr. came from Houston that afternoon, but heavily iced roads out on the Texas plains kept Shirley stranded at home in Lubbock. Bess, off in faraway Boston and expecting her second baby, was also kept away by the weather. Lomax remained in a coma through the weekend. Alan, John Jr., and Miss Terrill were at his bedside when he died, without regaining consciousness, shortly after 7:00 Monday evening, January 26. As he lay dying, "John Lomax Day" had come and gone. Again, for one last time, he had missed the cheering crowds.

. . . . .

Soon after Lomax's death, Miss Terrill wrote to Ruby Pickens Tartt to tell her the sad news. Mrs. Tartt immediately thought of Dock Reed, who had formed a strong feeling for "Mr. Lomac," as he called him. Reed had told Mrs. Tartt that "Mr. Lomac" was the best man he ever knew.[66]

Headed toward Reed's farm on foot to give him the news, Mrs. Tartt saw Reed coming toward her in his wagon. When he stopped and got down, she told him of Lomax's death, and they stood together in the road and wept. "We can't hep it," Reed said. "I feels like a fatherless child. Mr. Lomac done gone to glory, and us here. What I'm going to do? He was such a friend, such a good man. I'm going to miss him bad."

After a few days Reed appeared at the county library in Livingston where Mrs. Tartt worked. He had tried to write Miss Terrill, he said, but he could not. "I had to wait and get myself pacified." But he was still too upset to write, and he wanted Mrs. Tartt to do it for him. "I can't say no more now, Miss Ruby. I've got to get pacified somehow."

After Reed had gone, Mrs. Tartt thought to take from a shelf the inscribed copy of *Adventures of a Ballad Hunter* which Lomax had sent her. It reminded her of their fruitful collaboration and the many warm and moving experiences they'd had during their song collecting efforts. More particularly, it reminded her of Lomax's great affection for Dock Reed, which Lomax had written of in his autobiography. The next day she left the library in the care of her husband, put her copy of *Adventures of a Ballad Hunter* in a sack, and set out in her old car for Reed's farm. When she arrived, he was at the woodpile, chopping wood. "I've brought you a message from Mr. Lomax," she said.

To Reed's look of puzzlement, she offered the last pages of the book. There, after praising Reed's exceptional songs and singing, Lomax tells of his own perseverance against great odds, ending his life story with lines from a spiritual Reed had sung for him. As Mrs. Tartt read the words, Reed closed his eyes and began to sway, humming the mournful tune, increasing in volume and anguish until he broke into full voice:

Cryin, "Holy Lord,"
Cryin, "Holy Lord,"
Cryin' "Holy my Lord,"
Cryin, "Holy!"

Weep like a willow, moan like a dove,
You can't get to Heaven 'thout you go by love.

As the last deep notes sounded away, he stood motionless, spent. "I'm pacified, Miss Ruby. Glory, glory."

Notes

The major source for this work has been the extensive archive of Lomax papers and related items at the Center for American History (which now includes the former Barker Texas History Center) at the University of Texas, Austin. Unless otherwise indicated, letters and documents cited in the notes may be found in that depository; in a few instances where there might be confusion about the location, I have specifically indicated this source with the abbreviation "CAH." Originally it was my intention to include the relevant CAH file box number or numbers in all citations, as I have done for materials archived at Harvard University's Houghton Library and the American Folklife Center files at the Library of Congress. However, after I had completed my research at the Center for American History and while the manuscript was in its final stages, the Lomax collection there was entirely recatalogued; many items were distributed into files with new headings, and all file boxes were given various new numbers, often in a different series. Consequently, it was highly impractical, if not impossible, to ascertain the new file numbers.

Not infrequently, letters and documents in the Lomax collections are undated or misdated. For example, Lomax habitually failed to recognize the beginning of a new year for weeks after its advent, often retaining the old year well into February or March. Some of his correspondents were equally desultory. This creates no end of labyrinths and merry chases for the researcher, but in many instances internal evidence reveals the correct chronology. A further complication is that, in some cases, missing dates have been casually supplied by a later hand, probably that of John Lomax Jr. or Miss Terrill, whose apparent practice it was to simply apply the postmark date found on envelopes attached to or in the proximity of undated letters. (All envelopes have since been removed from the files.) Where other evidence clearly corrects an erroneous date or supplies a missing one, I have placed the correction in brackets, e.g., May [9], 1902; when a likely but not certain date is suggested, I have indicated it as probable (e.g., prob. Oct. 14, 1914); any date, original or by a later hand, which is suspect but not contradicted by clear evidence is in quotation marks (e.g., "Jan. 12"). Citations bearing the shelf marks bMS Am 1907.1 (753), (807), (1104), and (1653a); bMS Lowell 19.1 (747) and (789); bMS Am 1787 (230); and HUG 4481.10; and HUG 4486.12 are by permission of the Houghton Library, Harvard University.

Abbreviations

AAFS.Hist.	"Archive of American Folksong: A History, 1928–1938"
AB&FS	*American Ballads and Folk Songs*
ABH	*Adventures of a Ballad Hunter*
AFC.JAL	John A. Lomax Collection, American Folklife Center, Library of Congress
AFC.LC	Archive of Folk Culture, American Folklife Center, Library of Congress
AFC.LoFam	Lomax Family Papers, American Folklife Center, Library of Congress
AL	Alan Lomax
BB	Bess Brown; later BBL = Bess Brown Lomax
BL	Bess Lomax; later BLH = Bess Lomax Hawes
BW	Barrett Wendell
BW Jr.	Barrett Wendell Jr.
CAH	Center for American History, University of Texas
CE	Carl Engel
EC	Ed Crane
ECB	Eugene C. Barker
GLK	George Lyman Kittredge
HS	Harold Spivacke
HU	Harvard University Archives, Houghton Library, Harvard University
JAL	John A. Lomax
JAL Jr.	John A. Lomax Jr.
JP	James Putnam
LB	Huddie Ledbetter ("Leadbelly")
LC	Lon Cooper
NFSLB	*Negro Folk Songs as Sung by Leadbelly*
OB	Orville Bullington
OS	Oliver Strunk
RCS	Ruth Crawford Seeger
RT	Ruby Terrill; later RTL = Ruby Terrill Lomax
SFL	Susan Frances Lomax
SG	Shirley Green
SL	Shirley Lomax; later SLM = Shirley Lomax Mansell; later SLD = Shirley Lomax Duggan
TFS	Archives of the Texas Folklore Society

Prologue

1. Fehrenbach, *Lone Star,* p. 223.

Chapter 1: Texian Boys

1. Fehrenbach, *Lone Star,* p. 408.
2. Joseph Lomax, *Genealogical and Historical Sketches,* p. 144.
3. Quoted in JAL, *ABH,* p. 2.
4. Joseph Lomax, *Genealogical and Historical Sketches,* p. 144.
5. JAL to BB, Dec. 14, 1903.
6. Joseph Lomax, *Genealogical and Historical Sketches,* p. 146.
7. JAL to BB, Dec. 14, 1903.
8. Susan Frances Lomax, "A Trip to Texas," p. 254. (Originally written in 1914 at the request of her son John and edited by him for publication some thirty years later.)
9. Ibid., p. 255.
10. "In the 1870s and 80s, [its] geographical features made Bosque County a nexus of socio-economic frontiers, and gave it a heightened, if not unique, sense of cultural contrasts" (McNutt, "Beyond Regionalism," pp. 19–22). The geographic center of the state is in fact less than ninety miles southwest of Meridian—scarcely a hop, skip, and jump in an area the size of Texas.
11. Ford, *Rip Ford's Texas,* p. 445.
12. Hogan, *Texas Republic,* p. 22; Fehrenbach, *Lone Star,* p. 683.
13. JAL, "Of Books and People."
14. Ibid.
15. JAL to SG, Aug. 22, 1898.
16. JAL to AL, Apr. 22, 1942, AFC.LoFam.
17. JAL, *ABH,* pp. 4, 5.
18. JAL, "Of Books and People."
19. Ramsdell, *Reconstruction in Texas,* p. 312; Fehrenbach, *Lone Star,* pp. 433–34.
20. Nichols, *Ed Nichols Rode a Horse,* pp. 56–67.
21. JAL to SG, Apr. 9, 1900.
22. JAL, *ABH,* p. 6.
23. Ibid., pp. 13–14.
24. Ibid, pp. 12–13. In old age, recalling how as a child he would "show off" at Sunday school by reciting a hundred verses from the Bible, he remarked, "I cannot say that any of the excellent advice contained in these passages has had any marked influence on my life" (JAL, "Of Books and People").
25. JAL, *ABH,* pp. 12ff.
26. JAL, "Of Books and People."
27. Ibid.; cf. JAL, *ABH,* p. 21.
28. JAL, *ABH,* p. 19, is only one of dozens of occurrences, in both letters and published works.

29. Ibid., p. 4.

30. Ibid., pp. 19, 15. His renderings of these events—and the words of the songs—are a bit too precise, however faithful they may be to the actual circumstance, suggesting "emotions recollected in tranquility." Similarly, when he writes of cowboys "yodeling" to their cattle, the term can be understood only in a loose, generally descriptive sense. When Lomax's autobiography appeared in 1947, J. Frank Dobie wrote to their mutual friend, Roy Bedicheck: "I meant to jump [Lomax] about his yodeling cowboys away back there 65 years ago or more. I feel sure that at that time there was no yodeling among people of the soil anywhere in America" (Dugger, *Three Men in Texas,* p. 263). Ultimately, this may depend on what one means by "yodel," a term which has been used variously and appears to lack a single, "scientific" definition. Both Alan Lomax and Bess Lomax Hawes have remarked that their father's yodel was not the typical sound associated with Swiss warblers but something of a low, crooning moan with falsetto. In a 1941 letter to the *Cattleman,* Lomax refers not to "yodels" but to "calls, shouts, or hollers" used by working cowboys (JAL to Ted Moses, Nov. 19, 1941, AFC.JAL). Lomax's story that he began to write down cowboy songs while he was still a small boy (*ABH,* p. 20) has also been questioned; see Chap. 4.

31. Note by Lomax on the back of a letter to him from Mary Nancy Graham, Jan. 16, 1942, AFC.JAL.

Chapter 2: Hard Times in the Country

1. JAL to BB, Jan. 1, 1904.

2. JAL, *ABH,* p. 12. McNutt comments, however, on the discomforting fact that Lomax's love for Nat did not preclude his insistence, according to the mores of the time, that Nat address him and his brother as "Mr. John" and "Mr. Richard"—"nor did he see anything unusual about a nine-year-old boy teaching a nearly grown man his letters" ("Beyond Regionalism," p. 30).

3. JAL to BB, Jan. 1, 1904.

4. JAL to BB, Jan. 31, 1904.

5. JAL, *ABH,* p. 22.

6. Ibid.

7. JAL to JAL Jr., Sept. 25, 1936.

8. Houston [Ross], "Early Years of John Lomax," p. 33; *Catalogue of the Officers and Members of Granbury College,* p. 24 (cited below as *Catalogue*).

9. JAL, *ABH,* p. 25.

10. Although Lomax wrote (*ABH,* p. 25) that "English literature, history and civics were not taught in Granbury College," the 1886 catalog lists "history of English and American literature," English, Roman, and Greek history, and government (*Catalogue,* pp. 15–17). Lomax's own report card belies what he wrote in his autobiography; for the spring 1888 term he was awarded a "99" in "History." It

seems clear, however, that the emphasis was on mathematics and the sciences rather than the arts and humanities.

11. *Catalogue,* pp. 15–17.
12. JAL, *ABH,* p. 28.
13. *Catalogue,* pp. 21–22.
14. JAL, *ABH,* p. 25.
15. Ibid., p. 24.
16. Houston [Ross], "Early Years of John Lomax," pp. 39–40.
17. JAL, *ABH,* p. 25.
18. JAL to SG, Nov. 10, 1904.
19. One story has it that Lomax taught on one floor of the three-story building, his brother Jesse on another, as a result of which students referred to the brothers as "Low-Max" and "Hi-Max." See Prude, "Contribution of John Avery Lomax to American Folklore," p. 18. As McNutt notes ("Beyond Regionalism," p. 51), "No other source confirms this anecdote." Prude's work is little more than a superficial biographical account which does not address Lomax's "contribution to American folklore."
20. JAL, *ABH,* p. 26.
21. *Catalogue,* p. 11; Lomax (*ABH,* p. 25) says, "Again no library, no laboratories worthy of the name."
22. JAL, *ABH,* p. 25.
23. Ibid., p. 26.
24. Henry G. Howard to JAL, July 16, 1947. See also Jim McCall to JAL, Feb. 26, 1947; Mrs. W. W. McCrary to JAL, Aug. 30, 1947; Fred Cotton to JAL, June 24, 1947.
25. *Eastman Business College Catalogue, 1886,* pp. 4, 6, 10–11; quoted in Griffen and Griffen, *Natives and Newcomers,* p. 32. Harvey Eastman, a cousin of George Eastman, inventor of the Kodak camera and roll film, was a tireless proponent of the gospel of success. At various times he owned similar schools in Oswego, New York, and St. Louis, all founded on the principles of his uncle, George Eastman's father, who is credited with having begun, in 1842, the nation's first training school using actual business transactions in its course of study. See Ackerman, *George Eastman.*
26. E. Keister to JAL, Feb. 20, 1920.
27. JAL, *ABH,* p. 26.
28. Ibid.
29. Lomax Papers, CAH. Houston [Ross] ("Early Years of John Lomax," pp. 44–45), without citing a source, reports that "He paid several visits to Miss Mary Carter in the nearby town of Witt," but there is no further evidence of romantic interests during this time.
30. Quoted in Niven, *Carl Sandburg,* p. 56.
31. Ferguson, *Organizing to Beat the Devil,* pp. 305–6.
32. JAL, *ABH,* p. 27.

33. Ibid.

34. Fehrenbach, *Lone Star,* pp. 611, 615.

35. JAL to SG, Apr. 27, 1902.

36. Houston [Ross], "Early Years of John Lomax," p. 49; McNutt, "Beyond Regionalism," pp. 45–46.

37. JAL to BB, Oct. 25, 1903. Earlier, to another friend, Lomax also spoke in grim detail of his distress over the feeling that he had "misrepresented" and "falsified" himself in signing Richard's note. Worst of all was his fear that the family name, which "had come to me from an honest man, should be dishonored."

Chapter 3: The Highly Educated Man

1. JAL to SG, Apr. 27, 1902.

2. JAL, *ABH,* pp. 27–28.

3. Ibid., p. 28.

4. JAL to RTL, [prob.] Nov. 22, 1936. He overlooked the fact that he had taught accounting there during summer terms after returning from A&M and also in the teens conducted various U.T. extension courses.

5. *Texas Constitution of 1876,* sect. 10, art. 7.

6. JAL to Bess Lomax [Hawes], Sept. 20, 1936, AFC.LoFam.

7. *Alcalde,* Apr. 28, 1897, p. 3.

8. *Texas University* (later *University of Texas Magazine*), 11, no. 8 (May 1896): 68–69.

9. Humphrey, *Austin,* p. 82.

10. Ibid., pp. 149–50.

11. JAL, *ABH,* pp. 29–30.

12. Ibid., p. 30.

13. Ibid., p. 29.

14. JAL, "William Lawrence Chittenden," *Texas University* 11, no. 4 (Jan. 1896): 112–16.

15. Ibid., p. 115.

16. See *Texas University* 11, no. 8 (May 1896): 302; and 12, no. 4 (Jan. 1897): 145.

17. Ibid., 12, no. 1 (Oct. 1896): 30.

18. See JAL to SG, Aug. 7, 1898.

19. Recently the title has been changed to *Texas Alcalde.*

20. Connally, *My Name Is Tom Connally,* p. 30.

21. "A Damaging Confession," *Alcalde,* Apr. 28, 1897, p. 3; and "Below the Belt," *Alcalde,* Apr. 21, 1897, p. 3.

22. *Alcalde,* Jan. 13, 1897, p. 7, and Feb. 3, 1897, p. 5.

23. Ibid., Mar. 3, 1897, p. 6, and Apr. 21, 1897, p. 3.

24. JAL, *ABH,* p. 31.

25. Switzer, "To Whom It May Concern," May 1, 1897.

26. *Alcalde,* June 2, 1897, p. 4.

Chapter 4: Come All You Fair and Tender Ladies

1. JAL, *ABH,* p. 31. There is evidence that the stipend was only fifty dollars a month. See LC to JAL, June 11, 1898. By 1901, Lomax's annual salary had increased to $1500, plus $600 at his disposal for hiring help to manage B. Hall.
2. Darden, "Grace Hall and the University in the Late Nineties," p. 611.
3. LC to JAL, Dec. 3, 1897.
4. Rhodes Baker to JAL, Oct. 16, 1898; JAL to SG, June 2, 1899. For "J. Amorous Lomax," see *Cactus,* 1901, p. 142.
5. Houston [Ross], "Early Years of John Lomax," p. 3.
6. *Austin Statesman,* Feb. 20, 1903.
7. JAL to SG, July 16, 1899.
8. Taylor, "Lomax-Wooldridge Scrap," p. 438.
9. Ibid.
10. LC to JAL, June [11], 1898. Connally, although rejected by the Rough Riders, rose to the rank of sergeant-major in the regular army before the war ended late that summer and he returned to the University. In the meantime, Lomax had handled Connally's business affairs and settled his debts in Austin. Connally to JAL, Aug. 18, 1940.
11. JAL to SG, Apr. 13, 1899.
12. JAL to SG, Aug. 5, 1898; SG to JAL, Aug. 7, 1898.
13. JAL to SG, Aug. 22, 1898.
14. JAL to SG, Sept. [13], 1898.
15. SG to JAL, Sept. 21, 1898.
16. SG to JAL, Sept. 29, 1898.
17. SG to JAL, Sept. 21, 1898.
18. SG to JAL, Feb. 4, 1899.
19. JAL to SG, Oct. 15, 1898.
20. JAL to SG, Oct. 19, 1898.
21. JAL to SG, Oct. 15, 1898.
22. JAL to SG, undated.
23. JAL to SG, Sept. 3, 1898.
24. For the early poems, see *Cactus,* 1897, p. 186; *Cactus,* 1898, p. 160; and *University of Texas Magazine,* Jan. 1898, p. 138; Mar. 1898, pp. 192–93; Feb. 1899, p. 172; Apr. 1898, p. 246; and Dec. 1899, p. 64.
25. The story of the "little manuscript roll of cowboy songs" was first related in Lomax's introduction to *American Ballads and Folk Songs* (1934), in which the trunk he carried off to the University of Texas was also said to contain "my pistol and other implements of personal warfare" (p. xi). For the most commonly known and quoted version of the story, see *ABH,* p. 32.
26. *University of Texas Magazine,* Jan. 1898, p. 126.
27. JAL to SG, Aug. 22, 1898.
28. SG to JAL, Dec. 20, 1898.

29. "A Story," Oct. 16, 1906, in Lomax School Papers.
30. A. C. Green to JAL, Jan. 3, 1899.
31. SG to JAL, Jan. 5, 1899.
32. SG to JAL, Jan. 19, 1899.
33. JAL to SG, Mar. 18, 1899.
34. SG to JAL, Oct. 19, 1898.
35. JAL to SG, Apr. 6, 1899.
36. SG to JAL, June [1], 1899.
37. SG to JAL, Aug. 10, 1899.
38. SG to JAL, Aug. 22, 1899.
39. JAL to SG, June 2, 1899.
40. JAL to SG, May 4, 1899.
41. JAL to SG, July 13 and 16, 1899.
42. JAL to SG, Aug. 1, 1899.

Chapter 5: Trouble, Trouble

1. JAL to BB, Feb. 3, 1904.
2. JAL to SG, Feb. 3, 1899.
3. JAL to SG, undated (prob. fall 1899).
4. Dozens of such letters are found among Lomax's business correspondence (CAH) for the period.
5. Fehrenbach, *Lone Star,* p. 633.
6. JAL, "Will Hogg, Texan," *Atlantic,* May 1940, p. 663.
7. JAL to SG, undated (prob. fall 1899).
8. JAL to SG, undated (prob. fall 1899).
9. JAL to SG, undated (prob. fall 1899).
10. *Texan,* Jan. 10, 1901, p. 3.
11. For various accounts of the lively B. Hall episode in Lomax's life, see *Texan,* Jan. 8 and Feb. 4, 1901, and Feb. 12, 1902; *University [of Texas] Record* 2, no. 2 (June 1901): 169, and 4, no. 3 (July 1902): 326–27, 376; L. G. Bugbee to JAL, Sept. 17, 1901, and JAL to Bugbee, Nov. 12, 1901, and unidentified, undated fragment, CAH (probably written by Lomax for the Bugbee memorial). Lomax's participation in the plan apparently ended in the spring of 1902, when he moved into the Phi Delta Theta house off campus at 2006 University Avenue.
12. W. L. Prather to JAL, July 1, 1901.
13. See Anderson, "Putting the Experience of the World at the Nation's Command," pp. 121, 141.
14. JAL to SG, undated [ca. 1901].
15. JAL to SG, undated; Steger to JAL, Feb. 25, 1909.
16. JAL to SG, June 2, 1899.
17. JAL to SG, Feb. 13, 1900.

18. JAL to SG, June 26 and July 31, 1901.

19. A. S. Burleson to JAL, Dec. 17, 1901.

20. JAL to SG, undated (prob. Dec. 1901).

21. SG to JAL, Sept 22, 1901; "Letters of Judge James B. Clark," *Alcalde* 2, no. 2 (Dec. 1913): 129. See also *San Antonio Express,* Aug. 13, 1901, and *Dallas Morning News,* Aug. 13, 1901.

22. J. T. Lomax to JAL, July 9, 1901.

23. Alice's letter is undated but is clearly of this period. Further evidence of her hasty marriage is in JAL to BB, Feb. 1, 1904.

24. SG to JAL, Aug. 26, 1901.

25. SG to JAL, undated.

26. JAL to SG, May 13, 1899. For other authors he was reading, see JAL to BB, Aug. 24, 1902.

27. SG to JAL, Oct. 27, 1902; JAL to SG, Nov. 2, 1902.

28. JAL to SG, Nov. 2, 1902. See also JAL to BB, Oct. 19, 1902.

29. JAL to SG, Nov. 8, 1901.

30. SG to JAL, Sept. 7, 1901.

31. JAL to SG, Nov. 8, 1901.

32. See, for example, JAL to AL, Feb. 15, 1940, and Oct. 9, 1941, AFC.

33. JAL to SG, Feb. 17, 1902.

34. SG to JAL, Feb. 14, 1902. For "Shadows," see *Cactus,* 1901, pp. 201–4.

35. JAL, "Legislature and the University," p. 364.

36. JAL to BB, July 22, 1902.

37. JAL to SG, Feb. 17, Mar. [9], and June 6, 1902.

38. SG to JAL, Mar. 12, 1902.

39. JAL to SG, June 7, 1902.

40. JAL to SG, June 15, 1902; SG to JAL, June 8, 1902. Cf. SG to JAL, July 7, 1902, re Bess Brown: "There's another of the girls I would have picked out for you!"

41. JAL to SG, June 16, 1902.

42. JAL to BB, June 22, 1902.

43. See Robert Lomax to JAL, July 28, 1901; and, especially, David S. Switzer to JAL, Dec. 24, 1901; Switzer asserts his confidence that "you will be successful in the management of the Agricultural and Mechanical College at Bryan, if you accept the position of President."

44. JAL to SG, Aug. 1, 1902.

45. JAL to SG, Aug. 6 and 9, 1902; SG to JAL, Aug. 10, 1902.

46. JAL to SG, Aug. 22 and 28, 1902.

47. JAL to SG, Sept. 7 and Oct. 6, 1902.

48. SG to JAL, Sept. 15, Oct. 10, 18, and 27, and Nov. 9, 1902.

49. SG to JAL, Oct. 27, 1902.

50. SG to JAL, Jan. 21, 1903.

51. JAL to SG, Nov. 9, 1902.

52. JAL to BB, Feb. 24, 1903.

53. Tennyson, *In Memoriam,* ll. 325–28. Note her changes of pronoun form; the original has "*thou mayest* roam," "*My* blessing," and "guards *thee* home."

There is some question concerning the circumstances and the sequence of events through which Lomax received these lines. The page on which Shirley Green copied out the stanza is dated Sept. 6, 1902, and below another hand has written, "Found Nov. 23rd 1903 by E. E. Madera of Tarthon's S.S. Crew, Shore Harbor, N.J." Across the envelope enclosing it, Lomax wrote, "Sent to me six months after Shirley Green's death." Yet in a letter to Bess Brown on Mar. 29, 1903, only a little more than a month after Shirley's death, he alludes to the incident and to the poetry he has received, "which she threw off the Comal last summer into the Atlantic Ocean."

Chapter 6: Married Me a Wife

1. *University [of Texas] Record* 5, no. 2 (Aug. 1903): 207. His resignation was never recognized in the minutes of any meeting of the board. Although changes in faculty and administration were customarily published in the official *Record,* the only notice he got there did not appear until nine months later, as a brief line in "Alumni Notes": "John A. Lomax, B.A., '97, for several years Registrar of the University, is now instructor in English at the A. & M. College" (*University Record* 5, no. 3 [Mar. 1904]: 302).

2. David F. Houston to JAL, June 27, 1903.

3. JAL to BB, Oct. 19, 1902; JAL to SG, Oct. 19, 1902.

4. JAL to BB, Jan. 25, 1903.

5. JAL to BB, Feb. 4 and Mar. 1, 1903.

6. JAL to SG, July 31, 1901; see also JAL to SG, Aug. 26, 1901.

7. JAL to BB, Mar. 29, 1903.

8. JAL to BB, Aug. 7 and 14, 1903.

9. JAL to BB, Aug. 16, 1903.

10. JAL to BB, July 30, 1903.

11. BB to JAL, Aug. 8, 1903.

12. JAL to BB, Sept. 3 and 5, 1903.

13. JAL to BB, Sept. 3, 1903.

14. "John A. Lomax, Utility Man," *Alcalde* 2, no. 7 (May 1914): 770.

15. Unidentified, undated clipping in CAH.

16. JAL to BB, Oct. 7, 1903.

17. In his first report to the board of directors after going to A&M as president in 1902, David Houston noted that "the serious work of the College had been hampered by large numbers of immature students sent out to college for domestic convenience and not for technical training" (Ousley, "History of the Agricultural and Mechanical College of Texas," p. 63).

18. JAL to BB, Oct. 4, 1903.
19. JAL to BB, Nov. 4, 1903.
20. JAL to BB, Oct. 22, 1903.
21. James B. Clark to JAL, Aug. 21, 1903.
22. Harry Peyton Steger to JAL, July 29, 1903. See also Steger to JAL, Oct. 26, 1903.
23. BB to JAL, Oct. 23, 1903.
24. JAL to BB, Oct. 26, 1903.
25. JAL to BB, Oct. 24, 1903.
26. J. M. Brown to JAL, Jan. 14, 1904.
27. BB to JAL, Nov. 22, 1903. The emphasis is hers.
28. JAL to BB, Dec. 1, 1903. "Tar-baby ain't sayin' nuthin', en Brer Fox, he lay low" (Joel Chandler Harris, *Uncle Remus and His Friends* [1892]).
29. JAL to BB, Feb. 3, 1904.
30. JAL to BB, Dec. 3, 1903.
31. JAL to BB, Jan. 14, 1904.
32. JAL to BB, Dec. 3 and 5, 1903, and Jan. 14, 1904. See also JAL to M. M. Coleman, Oct. 27, 1917.
33. JAL to BB, undated (prob. early 1906). Morgan Callaway appears to have been universally disliked. J. Frank Dobie said of him, "Dr. Callaway thought everybody ought to have somebody to look up to and he was that somebody" (Dugger, *Three Men in Texas,* p. 178). Walter Prescott Webb disparagingly referred to "the dead English department—the Callaway School" (Furman, *Walter Prescott Webb,* p. 39).
34. BB to JAL, Dec. 6, 1906.
35. JAL to BB, Feb. 7, 1904.
36. JAL to BB, Mar. 29, 1904.
37. JAL to BB, Jan. 15, 1904.
38. JAL to BB, Feb. 14, 1904.
39. JAL to BB, Jan. 15, 1904; BB to JAL, Jan. 19, 1904.
40. Quoted by RTL in "Adventures with the Ballad Hunter," p. 5.
41. BB to JAL, Feb. 15, 1904.
42. BB to JAL, Mar. 10, 1904, and BB to JAL, undated but of this period.
43. JAL to BB, Dec. 12, 1903.
44. BB to JAL, Apr. 5, 1904. Her emphasis.
45. JAL to BB, Apr. 22, 1904.
46. JAL to BB, Apr. 25, 1904.
47. See, in particular, BB to JAL, Jan. 5, 1904, and JAL to BB, Jan. 6, 1904.
48. BB to JAL, Apr. 10, 1904.
49. BB to JAL, Feb. 15, 1904.
50. Her daughter Bess Lomax Hawes recalled that "she was enormously

stoical . . . her message was very much that you were supposed to put up with things . . . she herself did not cry" (interview, Washington, D.C., Aug. 2, 1989).

51. JAL to BB, May 18, 1904.

52. JAL to BB, May 30, 1904. Quoted by McNutt, "Beyond Regionalism," p. 68.

53. E. P. R. Duval to JAL, May 22, 1904.

Chapter 7: The Boston Come All-Ye

1. Throughout the fall and early winter of 1904, when Bess was with her parents in Austin, she and John were exchanging letters almost daily. Details and quoted passages in this and the next several paragraphs are taken from various letters written between Sept. 19 and Dec. 8, in CAH.

2. JAL to BBL, Feb. 21, 1905.

3. Will Brown to JAL, Feb. 12, 1904.

4. BB to JAL, Feb. 15, 1904.

5. JAL to AL, Apr. 2, 1942, AFC.LoFam.

6. JAL to BBL, July 24, 190[5].

7. JAL to BBL, Nov. [20], 1905.

8. BBL to JAL, May 5, 1906.

9. JAL to BBL, May 6, 1906.

10. Mezes to Prof. J. H. Wright, Harvard, Feb. 8, 1906.

11. JAL to BBL, undated.

12. JAL to BBL, June [9], 1906. Quoted by McNutt, "Beyond Regionalism," p. 69.

13. GLK, Introduction to Child's *English and Scottish Popular Ballads,* p. xxv.

14. Quoted in Brown, *Dean Briggs,* p. 301.

15. In addition to all his other duties, at that time Briggs was also serving as president of Radcliffe, but the standing of Harvard's "affiliate" school for woman was such that the job was considered only "part-time."

16. Brown, *Dean Briggs,* p. 90.

17. Of work done for Wendell there exist only two loose pages of his introduction to "Some Ballads of West Texas," of that done for Kittredge, nothing—and Lomax was Kittredge's student not only in "Shakespere" but also in "Beowulf" the following spring. The partial introduction to "Some Ballads of West Texas" for Wendell appears to have survived only because Lomax later submitted the paper to Briggs also.

18. Brown, *Dean Briggs,* p. 75.

19. Briggs's comment is written on Lomax's essay, untitled but beginning "Coming to Harvard Form [*sic;* uncorrected by Briggs] Texas," dated Dec. 6, 1906, among Lomax's school papers. Other Harvard papers referred to in the following pages of this chapter are in the same file.

20. Lomax School Papers. Quoted by McNutt, "Beyond Regionalism," pp. 73–74.

Chapter 8: The Highly Educated Man, Part 2

1. H. N. McCracken, quoted in Hyder, *George Lyman Kittredge,* p. 125.
2. Brown, *Dean Briggs,* p. 61.
3. JAL, *ABH,* p. 33.
4. Ibid.
5. Lon Tinkle in his biography of J. Frank Dobie (*American Original,* p. 103) tells the story of Lomax burning his roll of cowboy songs after being discouraged by Callaway, then adds, without citing a source: "Nevertheless, when the faculty had a distinguished visitor interested in the region, Lomax was summoned to sing his songs. Immediately aware of their significance, George Lyman Kittredge later arranged that Lomax come to Harvard on a scholarship." This improbable incident is unreported elsewhere—even by Lomax—and appears to have been Tinkle's version of hearsay accounts.
6. Not the following February, as Lomax has it in his autobiography (*ABH,* pp. 33–34). JAL to BBL, Dec. 23, 1906, verifies the actual date.
7. Just when Lomax actually began collecting folk music may always be a mystery. His story of carrying a roll of cowboy songs with him to the University of Texas and burning them in the wake of Professor Morgan Callaway's scorn has been widely discounted. An editor's letter (discussed in the following chapter) once seemed to indicate collecting activity as early as 1902, but that letter has been shown to be misdated and clearly belongs to a later time. After his first work began to appear in print, Lomax offered various accounts which suggest that his collecting interests developed during his early years at A&M. All of these, however, are ex post facto; what is lacking is a single shred of external evidence which dates prior to October 1906. There is one small, indirect hint that he was looking for cowboy songs in the summer of 1906. In November, after the search was clearly on, one of his former students at A&M wrote to apologize that he had "totally neglected to get those songs for you last summer. I got out on the ranch and forgot all about it" (W. Bogel to JAL, Nov. 21, 1906).
8. JAL to BBL, Dec. 23, 1906. Quoted by McNutt, "Beyond Regionalism," p. 77.
9. "On an impulse, in the renowned manner of the great Harvard man George Lyman Kittredge, I held out both my arms and marched across [the intersection at Harvard Yard], heedless of whether traffic was moving or not, assuming that it was the motorists' responsibility to look out for me" (Ved Mehta, "Personal History," *New Yorker,* Dec. 19, 1988, p. 42).
10. "I don't say my beard is better or worse than Shaw's, but it is different" (Hyder, *George Lyman Kittredge,* p. 185).
11. Occasionally Kittredge assigned as secondary reading his own Tercentenary Lecture, *Shakespere.* Concerned that students might resent the royalty he would get from this arrangement, he implied that he would refund the amount of the royalty to any student who came to him personally—which few were likely to do. "The royalty on a copy of this book is not enough to buy me a cigar," he said. "Of

course it might buy the kind of cigar you smoke, but not the kind I smoke" (Hyder, *George Lyman Kittredge,* p. 61).

12. GLK to unidentified correspondent, HU.HUG 4486.12.

13. Lewis Nichols, *New York Times Magazine,* Apr. 19, 1936, p. 10; quoted in Hyder, *George Lyman Kittredge,* p. 53.

14. Hyder, *George Lyman Kittredge,* p. 59.

15. See various letters of Wendell, Kittredge, and Lomax, Jan. 3, 1907; Mar. 23, 1907; May 20, 1907 (all CAH); and BW to GLK, May 27, 1907, in Kittredge Papers, HU.HUG 4486.12.

16. JAL to BBL, Dec. 22, 1906.

17. JAL to BBL, Dec. 30, 1906.

18. David F. Houston to JAL, Jan. 8, 1907. See also Houston to JAL, Feb. 16, 1907.

19. BBL to JAL, Apr. 6, 1907, and JAL to BBL, Apr. 8, 1907.

20. For the complete letter, see JAL, *ABH,* pp. 34–35. Several original copies are found in various places among the papers at Austin and Harvard.

21. Morgan Callaway to BW, May 17, 1907, CAH; JAL to BBL, May 8, 1907.

22. JAL to BBL, Apr. 18, 1907, and various undated letters, clearly of this period.

23. JAL to BBL, May 4, 1907; BBL to JAL, May 9, 1907.

24. Herbert Putnam to JAL, Apr. 2, 1935, AFC.JAL.

25. JAL to BBL, undated; BBL to JAL, May 18, 1907. Kittredge apparently gave encouragement to the black dialect study, telling Lomax that "the field is untouched, promising" (see JAL to BBL, May 24, 1907), but as Bess had suggested, the plan was overly ambitious, and it was soon discarded.

26. JAL to Russell Holman, Oct. 30, 1945.

27. JAL, *ABH,* p. 35; JAL to BBL, May 6, 1907, and BBL to JAL, May 22, 1907.

28. JAL to BBL, May 4, 1907, and undated.

29. In 1923, Lomax told his friend Ed Crane that his illness at Harvard was caused when a blood vessel erupted in his brain "from the foolish results of overstudy" (JAL to Crane, May 21, 1923). It seems likely that he was simply suffering from a general nervous collapse, or "neurasthenia." Tom Lutz in *American Nervousness, 1903* points out that "neurasthenia" or "American nervousness" was a term widely invoked in those days to explain almost every disorder affecting those engaged in "brain-work." Theodore Roosevelt was a notable sufferer of neurasthenia.

30. JAL, "Dean Briggs," ms in AFC.JAL. Published in *Harvard Alumni Bulletin,* Apr. 24, 1942, unpaged.

31. Ibid.

32. Ibid.

33. GLK to unknown recipient (possibly Lomax), June 11, 1907, among Lomax's academic records at Harvard. On July 24, 1907, the Harvard Graduate School wrote to Lomax to inform him that the faculty had voted to recommend him for the A.M. degree despite the fact that his health "obliged you to go away and leave

your record incomplete." The letter (CAH) indicates that this was a rare action, evidence of the quality of his work and the high regard which the faculty held for him. His illness is referred to as "a nervous collapse."

34. BBL to JAL, May 25, 1907.

35. JAL to BW, July 3, 1907, HU.bMS Am 1907.1 (753). Lomax's knowledge of Texas geography was normally excellent, but in this letter he suffered a serious and mysterious lapse, locating Wichita Falls "in the Texas Panhandle." Wichita Falls is in north central Texas, at least a hundred miles south and east of any area that might properly be considered any part of the Panhandle.

36. JAL to BW, July 27, 1907, HU.bMS Am 1907.1 (753).

37. BBL to JAL, Aug. 12, 1907.

38. BW to JAL, Aug. 2, 1907, CAH; JAL to BW, Aug. 6 and 25, 1907, HU.bMS Am 1907.1 (807). Wendell identified the source of the second fifty dollars only as "a friend interested in folklore." Later Evert Wendell was the source of yet another fifty dollars "from a stranger."

39. JAL to BW, Aug. 6, 1907, HU.bMS Am 1907.1 (807).

40. C. P. Fountain to JAL, Aug. 8, [1907].

41. JAL to BBL, undated but clearly Aug. 1907.

42. JAL to BBL, undated and Aug. 13, 1907. Quoted by McNutt, "Beyond Regionalism," p. 80.

43. JAL to BBL, Sept. 9 and Aug. 27, 1907.

44. BBL to JAL, Sept. 13, 1907.

Chapter 9: John Was A-Writin'

1. "Statement by John A. Lomax," Oct. 20, 1942, History File, University of Texas Ex-Students' Association.

2. F. N. Robinson to David F. Houston, July 28, 1907.

3. GLK to JAL, Jan. 9, 1908. See also BW to GLK, Oct. 7, 1907, HU.HUG 4486.12; BW to JAL, Nov. 12 and 18, 1907; JAL to BW, Jan. 9 and 14, 1908, HU.bMS Am 1907.1 (807); and drafts of Lomax's proposal, dated Nov. 16, 1907, and Jan. 10, 1908.

4. JAL to Trustees of the Carnegie Foundation, Jan. 14, 1908. Lomax's salary for 1907–8 is indicated in Bess Lomax's household records.

5. Lomax's immediate superior at A&M, C. P. Fountain, had also written a pithy letter of support—"[Lomax's] social qualities are of just the kind to enlist the sympathetic help of the ignorant negro, the rough cowboy, and the accomplished gentlemen"—that was unaccountably discarded, possibly because Fountain's position was not lofty enough (Fountain to Carnegie Trustees, Jan. 15, 1908).

6. William Loeb Jr. to JAL, Nov. 22, 1907.

7. GLK to Trustees of the Carnegie Foundation, Jan. 21, 1908.

8. Robert S. Woodward to JAL, Feb. 4, 1908.

9. "Are you not acquainted with Weir Mitchell? I believe he has Woodward's ear, and perhaps he could be a good channel through which to pour our information" (GLK to BW, Feb. 15, 1908, HU.bMS Am 1907.1 [753]). BW to GLK, Feb. 15, 1908, HU.HUG 4486.12, and Oct. 27, 1908, HU.HUG 4481.10, indicate that BW followed his suggestions.

10. *Statement by Members of the House of Representatives* (n.p., n.d.), p. 9.

11. His salary by this time was actually slightly over $1700, as recorded in Bess's household journal. In many other places, Lomax left the impression that $1300 per year (his starting salary) was the most he ever earned at A&M.

12. The exact structure of Lomax's "The Great A. & M. Strike" (CAH) is difficult to reconstruct from the extant pages, which appear to be from two or three different drafts. It is clear, however, that he never reached a conclusion, nor, more importantly, was he ever able to focus on the motives which drove him to attempt the piece. For a student's version of the event, see Casey, *History of the A. & M. College Trouble 1908.* A more objective account is contained in Ousley, "History of the Agricultural and Mechanical College of Texas," pp. 68–69. Lomax's account (or various accounts) in draft pages differs considerably from the testimony he gave to the board of inquiry which investigated the incident shortly after the "strike" was resolved. A summary of his testimony is in Casey, pp. 183–84.

13. "The Twenty Thousand Club" in Casey, *History of the A. & M. College Trouble 1908,* appendix 2, n.p.

14. Casey, *History of the A. & M. College Trouble 1908,* appendix 17, n.p.

15. *Dallas News,* Feb. 11, 12, 13, and 14, 1908. Lomax's hand, however invisible, is seen in references to the cadets as "the flower of young, sturdy Texas manhood" and frequent reminders that "no rowdyism or boisterous conduct was attempted during the trouble, and the boys have won unstinted praise by their action in this respect." His relentless efforts to see the strikers as paragons of manly virtue who were merely suffering from momentary confusion sadly reminds one of Ronald Reagan's judgment of John Hinckley: "He was a mixed-up young man from a fine family" (Ronald Reagan, *An American Life* [New York: Simon and Schuster, 1990], p. 263).

16. Ousley, "History of the Agricultural and Mechanical College of Texas," p. 68.

17. Among the latter was a note from crusty Ambrose Bierce, sojourning in Washington, who said he could be of no help, "having given no attention to the matter" (Bierce to JAL, Dec. 13, 1907).

18. JAL to BBL, July 14, 1908.

19. BBL to JAL, Mar. 9, 1908.

20. JAL to BBL and BBL to JAL, both June 23, 1908.

21. BBL to JAL, Sept. 22, 1908.

22. JAL to BBL, July 16, 1909.

23. JAL to BW, Jan. 14, 1909, HU.bMS Am 1907.1 (807).

24. BW to GLK, Oct. 27 and Nov. 18, 1908, HU.HUG 4481.10.

25. BW to JAL, Jan. 23, 1909; see also Elihu Root to BW, Jan. 26, 1909, CAH; R. S. Woodward to Theodore Roosevelt, Jan. 25, 1909; Roosevelt to BW, Jan. 26, 1909.

26. Woodward to Roosevelt, Jan. 25, 1909.

27. BW to JAL, Jan. 28, 1909. Woodward's grounds for the rejection appeared to be in direct contradiction to a circular issued by the institution, explaining the kinds of projects it funded, including "small projects, which may be carried out by individual experts for a limited period of time." Lomax seized on that passage and, despite the present rejection, continued to feel that the Carnegie was his first best hope.

28. JAL to BW, Feb. 1, 1909, HU.bMS Am 1907.1 (807).

29. Steger to JAL, Feb. 25, 1909.

30. Sturgis and Walton to JAL, Mar. 8, 1909.

31. BW to JAL, Aug. 4, 1909; GLK to JAL, July 17, 1909.

32. JAL to BW, Apr. 28, 1909, HU.bMS Am 1907.1 (807).

33. BBL to JAL, undated, and JAL to BBL, undated.

34. JAL to BBL, July 13, 1909.

35. JAL to BBL, June 25, 1909.

36. JAL to BBL, Aug. 3, 1909.

37. JAL to BW, Sept. 25, 1909, HU.bMS Am 1907.1 (807).

38. BW to JAL, Nov. 5 and 20, 1909. Copies of his letters to Lowell and Briggs, dated June 11 and Aug. 29, 1909, respectively, are in the same file at CAH.

39. BW to JAL, Sept. 16, 1909; Charles Read Nutter to JAL, Sept. 22, 190[9], and Sept. 27, 1909. Taken at a glance, the first letter of Nutter to Lomax, dated "September 22, 1902," would appear to suggest collecting activity by Lomax much earlier than any other evidence indicates. However, the contents show the date to be in error; the letter is unmistakably a part of the sequence of correspondence that took place between Nutter and Lomax in September, 1909, a conclusion further borne out by other letters (e.g., JAL to BW, Sept. 25, 1909, HU.bMS Am 1907.1 (807), and BW to JAL, Nov. 5, 1909. The ultimate proof is that Nutter was an instructor at Harvard in 1902 and did not leave to join Appleton until sometime after June 1, 1908.

40. JAL to Board of Directors of the A&M College, Nov. 23, 1909.

41. Briggs to Robert Milner, Nov. 20, 1909; Robinson to Milner, Nov. 10, 1909; GLK to Milner, Nov. 20, 1909.

42. GLK to Robert Milner, Nov. 20, 1909.

43. BW to JAL, Nov. 11, 1909.

44. Quoted by Briggs to JAL, Jan. 21, 1910.

45. JAL, "Beginnings of the Texas Folk-Lore Society," p. 17.

46. In light of Kittredge's remark to Lomax about founding a "branch" of the American Folklore Society in Texas, it is worth noting that while the organizations were quite separate, in the beginning the Texas group enjoyed a fairly close

alliance with its presumed parent, offering joint membership and coordinating its meetings with the national organization. Sometime in the teens, however, the Texans began to sever their connections with the AFS, apparently at the instigation of J. Frank Dobie, who, according to Lomax, "early acquired a prejudice against the American Folklore Society." Lomax regretted the separation: "In my judgment this relation or lack of relation has been unfortunate" (JAL, "Beginnings of the Texas Folklore Society," p. 18.) For an account of Dobie's role, see Stone, "J. Frank Dobie and the American Folklore Society," pp. 47–66.

47. JAL to BW, Mar. 25, 1910, HU.bMS Am 1907.1 (807). Quoted by Abernathy, *Texas Folklore Society,* p. 8.

48. BW to JAL, Nov. 11, 1909.

49. Kittredge accepted the communal theory "only in modified form." For an extended discussion, see Hyder, *George Lyman Kittredge,* pp. 103–5.

50. BW to JAL, Nov. 11, 1909.

51. There is some evidence that Lomax's Cornell paper, or part of it, was published in essentially its original form in the *Fort Worth Star Telegram* (date unknown). It rather clearly formed the core of two articles, both entitled "Cowboy Songs of the Mexican Border" and essentially identical, published in *Texas Magazine* 3, no. 15 (Mar. 1911): 27–37, and *Sewanee Review* 19, no. 1 (Jan. 1911): 1ff. See JAL to BBL, July 26, 1910.

52. JAL, *ABH,* p. 82.

53. BBL to JAL, Jan. 2, 1910. In *ABH,* pp. 82–85, and elsewhere, Lomax repeatedly misdates the Cornell meeting of the MLA as occurring in 1911. That the year was 1909 is clearly shown by his correspondence of the time and by records of the MLA itself; moreover, in 1911 the organization met in Chicago, not at Cornell.

54. JAL to BBL, Dec. 30, 1909.

55. Raymond Weeks to JAL, Jan. 24, 1943. In a note to his son John Jr. on the back of Weeks's letter, Lomax wrote that Weeks "is one of the 'high ups'" who first encouraged him to pursue the ballad work. Weeks also referred to the Cornell event as being in 1911, but simply because he was following Lomax, who had told him that was when it occurred.

56. "The Modern Language Association," *Nation,* Jan. 6, 1910, p. 9.

57. JAL, *ABH,* p. 84.

Chapter 10: Git Along, Little Dogies

1. Sidney E. Mezes to JAL, May 17, 1910.
2. *Alcalde* 11, no. 8 (Mar. 1924): 749.
3. JAL, *ABH,* pp. 40–41.
4. JAL to BBL, June 17, 1910.
5. *Alcalde* 2, no. 7 (May 1914): 771.
6. JAL to BW, Feb. 19, 1910, HU.bMS Am 1907.1 (807).

7. JAL to BBL, June 17 and 19, 1910.

8. JAL to BW, May 10, 1910, HU.bMS Am 1907.1 (807).

9. JAL to BBL, July 18, 1910. He retained "Cowboy Songs of the Mexican Border" for the two extracts—practically identical—which he published some months later in *Texas Magazine* and *Sewanee Review.*

10. H. Mewhinney, "There Is at Least One Full Man," p. 19.

11. JAL to BBL, July 30, Aug. 1, 2, and 9, 1910.

12. JAL to BBL, Aug. 5 and 7, 1910.

13. JAL to BBL, Aug. 13, 1910.

14. JAL to BBL, Aug. 16, 1910.

15. JAL, *ABH,* p. 65.

16. L. B. R. Briggs to JAL, Jan. 21, 1910.

17. JAL, *ABH,* pp. 46–47.

18. JAL to BW, May 10, 1910, HU.bMS Am 1907.1 (807).

19. JAL to BBL, Aug. 28, 1910.

20. Ibid. Quoted by McNutt, "Beyond Regionalism," p. 6.

21. JAL to BBL, Sept. 3 and 7, 1910.

22. JAL, *ABH,* p. 77; JAL, "Field Experiences with Recording Machines," p. 58; "Report to Professor Reed Smith," typescript (CAH), undated but ca. 1937, p. 2. See Wilgus, *Anglo-American Folksong Scholarship since 1898,* p. 79: "John A. Lomax was not . . . the first to publish a collection of native American folksongs printed with the music." Wilgus does not specify just who takes that honor, but the list surely includes William Frances Allen, Charles Pickard Ware, and Lucy McKim Garrison, compilers of *Slave Songs of the United States* (1867), as well as William Wells Newell, *Games and Songs of American Children* (1883). N. Howard "Jack" Thorp's *Songs of the Cowboys* (1908), privately published by the author, was the first collection of cowboy songs, but it does not contain music. It does, however, contain nineteen of the songs Lomax published two years later and claimed were "never before in print." Much later Lomax would assert, privately and without much foundation, that Thorpe's book was "largely cribbed from mine," along with "a lot of so-called songs" which Thorpe claimed to have written himself (JAL to J. W. Jones, Nov. 26, 1923). If anyone did any cribbing, it was probably Lomax himself. J. Frank Dobie humorously said, "Lomax took generously from [Thorp's] collection without any tedious explanation," noting also that when the Lomaxes revised and enlarged *Cowboy Songs* in 1938, Thorp's work was duly acknowledged ("John A. Lomax," p. 67). For an incisive account of Lomax's methods, see West, "Jack Thorp and John Lomax: Oral or Written Transmission?"

23. McNutt, "Beyond Regionalism," p. 128.

24. Many years later, in an unguarded moment, Lomax casually told a colleague that most of the material in *Cowboy Songs* came from a single notebook given him by a ranch foreman (telephone interview with Sidney Robertson Cowell, Shady, N.Y., July 30, 1990). While this clearly does not seem to have been the

case, the very fact that he would have made such a statement supports other evidence that his collection process was less extensive than it is generally understood to have been.

25. JAL, "Cowboy Songs of the Mexican Border," *Texas Magazine,* p. 28; *Sewanee Review,* p. 2.

26. Ibid.

27. JAL to BW, Sept. 25, 1909, HU.bMS Am 1907.1 (807). Just when he began using the phonograph to preserve the tunes is yet to be determined; there are many ex post facto references to it in later years, but the earliest contemporaneous evidence is here, in September 1909. Two years earlier, however, in the summer of 1907, Wendell had suggested the use of the phonograph to him, and Lomax indicated that he was planning to obtain one, having also corresponded about the matter with Charles Lummis in California, who at that time was using such a machine to record Native American songs and chants in the Southwest (JAL to BW, Aug. 25, 1907, HU.bMS Am 1907.1 [807]). See also Fiske and Lummis, *Charles F. Lummis,* p. 123. Lummis printed some of his results in the magazine he was editing, *Out West,* which was in all likelihood one of Lomax's sources. (For a concise account of the extravagant exploits of Lummis, see Roberts, "Tough Little Guy," pp. 116–26. Roberts does not mention Lummis's use of the phonograph.) In 1937, Lomax wrote that "During vacations and week-ends of the years from 1907 to 1910 I traveled through Texas and the West, hunting for folk songs and recording them on an Edison phonograph" ("Field Experiences with Recording Machines," p. 57).

28. JAL to BW, Feb. 1, 1909, HU.bMS Am 1907.1 (807). Kittredge's ultimate definition, as interpreted by Lomax: "A ballad, then, is a story in song, written no one knows when, no one knows where, no one knows by whom, and perhaps, some may think, no one knows 'for why.'" Lomax was quick to point out that by this definition, America "has none [i.e., no ballads] at all" (JAL, "Some Types of American Folk-Song," p. 1). For Kittredge's full view of the subject, see his introduction to the Student's Cambridge Edition of *The English and Scottish Popular Ballads;* also Hyder, *George Lyman Kittredge,* p. 102.

29. JAL, *ABH,* pp. 46–47. Lomax later asserted that "practically every song" in the book was anonymous (JAL to Homer E. Woodbridge, Jan. 11, 1924), although in his introduction ("Collector's Note") to *Cowboy Songs,* he had indicated that "in a few instances" he had been able to "discover" the author.

30. JAL to John I. White, Nov. 10, 1924.

31. JAL, *Cowboy Songs,* p. xxiii.

32. JAL, *ABH,* p. 62.

33. JAL to M. Clifford Harrison, Oct. 26, 1920; JAL to John I. White, Nov. 10, 1924. At the time White was a student at the University of Maryland, but Lomax mistook him for a professor. White does not mention this exchange in his fine

book, *Git Along, Little Dogies,* although he discusses Lomax's work frequently and, in general, favorably.

34. Lawton Walton to JAL, Nov. 11, 1909, and Charles Read Nutter to JAL, Nov. 12, 1909. JAL to BW, Sept. 12, 1909, HU.bMS Am 1907.1 (807), indicates that Doubleday had also asked to see the manuscript. There is no record of Doubleday's involvement beyond Steger's letter to JAL of Feb. 25, 1909, and the lines which Lomax scribbled across a letter of Nutter's (Sept. 22, 190[9]) relating to the book: "Appleton turned it down. Also Doubleday Page & Co."

35. Charles Read Nutter to JAL, Jan. 1, 19[10]. The letter is dated "1909," but that is, once again, an error on Nutter's part, as other evidence clearly indicates. Appleton's formal rejection did not come until Jan. 25, by which time Lomax had already signed a contract for publication with Sturgis and Walton.

36. JAL, *ABH,* p. 77; Walton to JAL, Dec. 3, 1909.

37. JAL to BBL, Jan. 2, 1910. Typically, Lomax never stopped bargaining; unhappy with the 10 percent royalty but unable to drive it up, he soon demanded fifteen author's copies instead of the usual six, and finally said he would settle for ten if Sturgis and Walton would supply him additional copies at half the retail price rather than the standard author's discount of 25 percent. At this juncture, Lawton Walton wearily agreed (Walton to JAL, Jan. 27, 1910). In later years, Lomax's income from buying wholesale copies and retailing them by mail, in direct competition with his publisher, would amount to twice and sometimes three times the sum paid to him in royalties.

38. JAL to Edith (Greenough) Wendell, Jan. 16, 1910, HU.bMS Am 1907.1 (1653a).

39. JAL, *ABH,* p. 80.

40. In a promotional flyer for *Cowboy Songs,* Lomax quoted the *St. Louis Post-Dispatch* ("This book puts the cowboy into Literature as Frederick Remington put him into Art"), but a search of the newspaper's files from Oct. 1910 to May 1911 has failed to reveal the review. According to Lomax's flyer, other positive reviews appeared in the *Houston Post* and the *Los Angeles Times.* For other American reviews, see *New York Times,* Feb. 26, 1911, p. 105; *Independent,* Apr. 20, 1911, p. 850; *Dial,* Apr. 1, 1911, p. 261; *Bookman,* Feb. 1911, p. 636. For an account of the English reviews, see JAL to BW, Apr. 24, 1912, HU.bMS Am 1901.1 (807), which contains clippings.

41. JAL, *ABH,* p. 77. For 1911, Sturgis and Walton paid Lomax 10 percent (fifteen cents per copy) on the sale of 807 copies, for a total of $121.05 (statement in CAH). That sum, of course, does not include income which Lomax may have gotten for copies he sold, but those sales were probably inconsequential; he did not get actively into peddling his books by mail for another two or three years. As late as 1932, *Cowboy Songs* paid him $193.55, a figure worth at least ten times that amount today. Lomax's salary in 1910 was $2300 per year (roughly $32,000 today).

He had been making $1800 at A&M and got a raise of a little over $40 a month when he went back to the University of Texas.

42. J. Frank Dobie called Lomax "a landmark in preserving and popularizing the folksongs of the United States" ("John A. Lomax," p. 3).

Chapter 11: Man on the Flying Trapeze

1. JAL, *ABH,* p. 82.
2. JAL to Benjamin Wyche, Aug. 9, 1912.
3. Ibid.
4. Vivid evidence of the exhausting workload in Lomax's office may be seen in a letter to him from his secretary, Ethel Barron, May 1, 1911, written while he was lecturing out of state. Lomax once characterized his position as that of "traveling errand boy for President Mezes" (JAL, "Governor Ferguson and the University of Texas," p. 14).
5. *Alcalde* 5, no. 8 (Aug. 1917): 739–40. Many stories attest to his reputation for generosity; typical is that of Lynn Landrum, later a prominent Texas newspaperman, recalling his struggles as a student at the University: "Got some money one year as editor of the *Texan.* Received $5.00 anonymously and don't know the donor to this day. Suspect John Lomax, but he would never confess" (Taylor, *Fifty Years on Forty Acres,* p. 145).
6. McNutt, "Beyond Regionalism," pp. 136–37.
7. JAL, *ABH,* p. 41.
8. JAL to President D. H. Hill of North Carolina A. & M., Mar. 14, 1911.
9. JAL to Reed, Feb. 13, 1911.
10. Phelps to JAL, Mar. 17, 1911.
11. JAL to GLK, Apr. 11, 1911.
12. For an account of the tour, with names of the institutions involved, see *University Record,* July 8, 1911, pp. 62–63.
13. JAL to John L. Senior, Oct. 18, 1911.
14. JAL to Phelps, Mar. 3, 1911; Phelps to JAL, Mar. 17, 1911; JAL to Phelps, June 20, 1911; Phelps to JAL, June 26, 1911. JAL to William Strunk Jr., Cornell, Mar. 11, 1911, indicates that Lomax arranged for a similar tableau of urban cowboys to accompany him there.
15. JAL to Steger, July 17, 1911.
16. JAL to BBL, undated but almost certainly early 1908. Another letter, also undated but clearly June 20, 1909, reports that Fountain had taken a party of men to his plantation on the Brazos river, where "we saw his plantation negroes celebrate the Juneteenth" and were fed a dinner that consisted "solely of bread, barbecue meat, and pickles." See also manuscript fragment, "Some Types of American Folk-Song" (probably 1913) and undated, untitled manuscript (probably 1911–12), both in CAH.

17. JAL to BW, Feb. 19, 1910, HU.bMS Am 1907 (807).

18. The American Folklore Society's "1912" meeting actually took place on Jan. 1, 1913, in Cleveland (the week following the MLA meeting in Philadelphia on Dec. 26–28). The Society's "1913" meeting was in New York on Dec. 31, 1913.

19. JAL to Mrs. Dave Coolidge, June 18, 1912. See also JAL to Harry Steger, June 11, 1912; JAL to Clayton Gilbert, July 19, 1912; JAL to R. W. G. Vail, June 18, 1913; JAL to S. P. Martin, Oct. 15, 1913.

20. "The most important object [of a recent faculty meeting] . . . was that of making every member of the Faculty understand that we had before us a problem, and that the problem was a Jew problem and not something else" (A. Lawrence Lowell, President of Harvard, to GLK, June 3, 1922, HU.HUG 4486.12).

21. [D. A. Frank], "The Negro Question Always with Us," *Alcalde* 11, no. 3 (May 1923): 112. Frank, a close friend and former schoolmate of Lomax, was nominally editor-in-chief of the *Alcalde* at this time and from all indications was the author of this unsigned piece. Lomax certainly saw it in proof; it is possible but improbable that he wrote it. The style is not his, and although he surely agreed with its substance, the piece is harsher and more blunt than anything he ever committed to print.

22. JAL to Homer E. Woodbridge, Jan. 11, 1924.

23. JAL to Mrs. C. S. Prosser, May 15, 1913.

24. Ed B. Patrick to JAL, [June] 7, 1912; JAL to Patrick, June 14, 1912.

25. JAL, "Stories of an African Prince," p. 1.

26. Ibid., p. 3.

27. JAL to J. Wesslay Hoffman, Dec. 18, 1911.

28. JAL to unidentified correspondent, Jan. 25, 1912.

29. Ajayi to JAL, Dec. 22, 1911.

30. Hoffman to JAL, Dec. 20, 1911.

31. JAL to Hoffman, Dec. 21, 1911.

32. Ajayi to JAL, June 10, 1912; JAL to Ajayi, June 12, 1912.

33. JAL to BBL, Mar. 9, 1912.

34. JAL to BBL, Mar. 14, 1912.

35. Ibid.

36. JAL to BBL, Mar. 16, 1912.

37. JAL to BBL, Mar. 24, 1912, and undated of this period.

38. JAL to BBL, Mar. 24, 1912.

39. Ibid.

40. JAL to BBL, Mar. 26, 1912.

41. JAL to BBL, Mar. 30, 1912.

42. JAL to Steger, July 11, 1912.

43. "The Letters of Harry Steger," *Alcalde* 3, no. 7 (May 1915): 660; "O. Henry's Guide," *Alcalde* 20 (Oct. 1931): 16. My description of Lomax's visit to Steger is based on the account of Christopher Morley (as reprinted in *Alcalde*), who was

probably the last to see him alive.

44. JAL to BBL, Jan. 3, 1913.
45. JAL to BBL, Jan. 7, 1913.
46. JAL to BBL, Jan. 3, 1913.
47. JAL to BBL, Jan. 7 and 17, 1913.
48. JAL to Richard O. Jones, Mar. 22, 1922.
49. A. Lawrence Lowell to GLK, Dec. 3, 1912, HU.HUG.4486.12.
50. *Alcalde* 1, no. 2 (May 1913): 160.
51. JAL to GLK, Nov. 17, 1913, HU.HUG 4486.12.
52. JAL to BBL, Dec. 31, 1913; JAL to W. G. Howard, Oct. 13, 1915.
53. JAL to BBL, Dec. 31, 1913, and Jan. 17, 1914.
54. JAL to BBL, Jan. 13 and 15, 1914.
55. JAL to BBL, Dec. 31, 1913.
56. JAL to Arthur Page, Feb. 23, 1914.
57. JAL to BBL, Jan. 17, 1914.
58. JAL to RTL, Dec. 20, 1934.
59. JAL to Homer Woodbridge, Jan. 11, 1924.
60. Robert Kerlin to JAL, Nov. 16, 1915.
61. JAL to Prof. Joseph B. Thoburn, Jan. 5, 1915.
62. "Lecture reading" is from JAL to Franklin Cooper, Feb. 6, 1914; the description is from JAL to A. B. Frey, Nov. 5, 1914.
63. JAL to BBL, Jan. 2 and 3, 1915.

Chapter 12: Long Summer Day

1. JAL to BBL, undated but probably mid-1907, following his return from Harvard.
2. See, for instance, Lewis Winston to JAL, Sept. 5, 1899, and JAL to BB, Mar. 10, 1904, and Feb. 13, 1905 (misdated 1904).
3. JAL to SL, July 19, 1910.
4. SL to JAL, Oct. 27, 1913; JAL Jr. to JAL, May 19, 1915.
5. JAL to W. M. Wood, Jan. 20, 1912, and Ramsey's Nursery, Jan. 29, 1912.
6. Houston [Ross], "Early Years of John Lomax," pp. 20–21.
7. Household ledger, Lomax Financial Papers, CAH.
8. Lomax Financial Papers. This figure includes 50 copies sold in England, on which the royalty was only $.03. The 348 domestic copies earned 15 percent royalty on the publisher's net price of $1.00, a total of $52.20.
9. JAL to J. E. Crites, Oct. 13, 1911.
10. BLH, interview, Washington, D.C., Aug. 2, 1989.
11. See, for example, BBL to JAL, [Sept.] 17, 1912 (misdated Oct.), Jan. 5 and 10, 1914.
12. BBL to JAL, Jan. 5, 1914, and two others undated but clearly of the same period.

13. SLD, interview, Lubbock, Tex., June 27, 1988. Given the condition of Texas public schools and the absence of mandatory attendance laws in those days, educating children at home was not an unusual arrangement. Although the Lomax children were taught by their mother much of the time, they did attend the public schools at certain periods. See BBL to JAL, undated but of this period, in which Bess says that she had decided to leave Shirley in school for the remainder of the present year, but "shall probably keep her out next year."

14. See JAL to BBL, Feb. 7, 1904, and Jan. 8, 1913; JAL to J. A. Brown, Jan. 23, 1912.

15. SLD, interview, Lubbock, Tex., June 27, 1988.

16. BBL to JAL, undated.

17. BBL to JAL, Jan. 19, 1916.

18. JAL to Luther A. Lawthon, Jan. 28, 1915.

19. See JAL to BW, Oct. 14 and 26, Nov. 13, and Dec. 23, 1915, HU.bMS Am 1907.1 (807). Unaccountably, Wendell's letters to Lomax regarding this matter are missing from the Lomax papers at the University of Texas.

20. JAL to BBL, undated, prob. Dec. 30 and 31, 1915.

21. JAL to BBL, Jan. 4, 1916.

22. JAL to BBL, Jan. 2, 1916.

23. JAL to BBL, Jan. 4 and Jan. 8, 1916.

24. JAL to BBL, prob. Jan. 14, 1916.

25. JAL to BBL, undated but clearly of this period, and JAL to BBL, Jan. 21, 1916.

26. JAL to BBL, Jan. 21, 1916.

27. Ibid.

28. BBL to JAL, Jan. 4, 1916. Presumably "the Negro book" was the study of black dialect which he had discussed with Dean Briggs a decade earlier, but if he had done anything more than the sketchiest preliminary work on it at this stage, there is little evidence.

29. BBL to JAL, Jan. 25, 1916.

30. BBL to JAL, Jan. 13, 1916.

31. Miscellaneous papers and documents relating to the Curtis contest, CAH.

32. SLD, interview, Lubbock, Tex., June 27, 1988.

33. JAL to BBL, Jan. 22, 1916.

34. JAL to BBL, Jan. 25, 1916.

35. JAL to W. F. McCaleb, July 30, 1912.

36. Oscar Callaway to JAL, May 1, 1910 (with postscript by his wife, Stella Couch Callaway).

37. See, for example, William Pierson to JAL, Oct. 16, 1911; JAL to Pierson, Oct. 20, 1911; and JAL to E. M. Baker, Nov. 28, 1913.

38. JAL and Benedict, *Book of Texas*, p. 373.

39. *Reasons for Supporting the Educational Amendment to Sections 49 and 52 of Article 3 of the Constitution*, pp. 5–7, passim.

40. See Lee to JAL, Dec. 11, 1912.

41. See, for example, JAL to Wasson, Feb. 6 and Mar. 18, 1913.
42. JAL to Prof. B. M. Davis, June 15, 1913; JAL to Prof. Boynton, June 21, 1913.

Chapter 13: Hell in Texas

1. JAL, "Governor Ferguson and the University of Texas," pp. 11, 12.
2. JAL, *ABH,* p. 85.
3. Testimony of Will C. Hogg in the case of *John Lomax vs. G. S. McReynolds, et al,* pp. 174–75. See "His Own Words," p. 715.
4. Quoted in Tinkle, *American Original,* pp. 63–64.
5. Fehrenbach, *Lone Star,* pp. 636–37; Nalle, *Fergusons of Texas,* p. 79.
6. *Dictionary of American Biography,* supplement 3.
7. Taylor, *Fifty Years on Forty Acres,* p. 106.
8. JAL, "Governor Ferguson and the University of Texas," p. 15.
9. Testimony of Dr. A. W. Fly in the case of *John Lomax vs. G. S. McReynolds, et al,* pp. 221, 234, 240–41. See also "His Own Words," pp. 718–20.
10. Testimony of Regent George W. Littlefield in the case of *John Lomax vs. G. S. McReynolds, et al,* pp. 182, 184, 197. See also "His Own Words," p. 716.
11. Testimony of Dr. R. E. Vinson in the case of *John Lomax vs. G. S. McReynolds, et al,* pp. 57–59. See also "His Own Words," p. 713.
12. Diaries of Mrs. Barrett Wendell, HU.bMS 1907.1 (1104).
13. JAL and Benedict, *Book of Texas,* facing p. 441. For other references to Ferguson, see pp. 336, 376, and 438.
14. JAL and Benedict, *Book of Texas,* pp. 441, 116, 331.
15. Note in Lomax's hand at the bottom of a letter to him from R. W. Steen, Apr. 13, 1942, AFC.JAL.
16. JAL and Benedict, *Book of Texas,* p. 170.
17. McNutt, "Beyond Regionalism," p. 138.
18. Ferguson to Vinson, Sept. 9, 1916; "His Own Words," pp. 697–98.
19. Ferguson to Dr. M. Faber, Sept. 11, 1916; "His Own Words," p. 700.
20. "Professors at the University 'Objectionable' to the Governor," p. 727.
21. "His Own Words," p. 741.
22. Mezes to JAL, June 19, 1916.
23. Testimony of Dr. A. W. Fly in the case of *John Lomax vs. G. S. McReynolds, et al,* p. 239. See also "His Own Words," pp. 718–20.
24. Bedichek to JAL, Dec. 21, 1916.
25. Bedichek to JAL, Apr. 25, 1917.
26. JAL, "Governor Ferguson and the University of Texas," p. 15.
27. See, for instance, JAL to BW, Oct. 16, 1916, HU.bMS Am 1907.1 (807).
28. Phelps to JAL, Oct. 17, 1916.
29. A typical blurb in the *Alcalde* (5, no. 3 [Feb. 1917]): "John Avery Lomax is in the East, but not for the purpose of selling Cowboy Ballads [*sic*]. Mr. Lomax is

taking his vacation now, for it is easier for him to get away at this time of year than any other. (It should be understood that while we have an editorial board, J. A. L. does about 99 44/100 per cent of the work)."

30. JAL to BBL, Dec. 30, 1916.
31. JAL to BBL, Dec. 27 and 30, 1916.
32. JAL to BBL, Dec. 27, 1916; BBL to JAL, Jan. 1 and 2, 1917.
33. BBL to JAL, Jan. 19, 1917.
34. JAL to BBL, Dec. 27 and 29, 1916.
35. JAL to BBL, Dec. 27, 1916, and Jan. 10 [1917] (misdated 1916).
36. JAL to BBL, Dec. 27, 1916.
37. JAL to BBL, Dec. 29 and 30, 1916, Jan. 6 and 12, 1917.
38. Telleen to JAL, Feb. 23, 1917.
39. JAL to BBL, Jan. 12, 1917.
40. BBL to JAL, undated but clearly of this period.
41. BBL to JAL, Jan. 17, 1917.
42. JAL to BBL, Jan. 6, 1917. See also Mezes to JAL, Feb. 27, 1917.
43. BBL to JAL, Jan. 1, 1917.
44. BBL to JAL, Jan. 25, 1917.
45. Frank to Henry Bercowich, Mar. 24, 1917.
46. [Illegible], U.S. Attorney, Northern District of Texas, to JAL, Apr. 10, 1917; T. B. Gregory, Office of the Attorney General, to JAL, Apr. 13, 1917.
47. Frank to JAL, Apr. 14, 1917.
48. Bedichek to JAL, Apr. 25, 1917.
49. Connally to JAL, Apr. 19, 1917.
50. Bedichek to JAL, Apr. 25, 1917.
51. Theodore Roosevelt to JAL, Apr. 14, 1917.
52. Bedichek to JAL, Apr. 25, 1917.
53. Potts to JAL, July 10, 1917.
54. Houston to Wilson, Aug. 26, 1917.
55. Mezes to JAL, May 16, 1917; Phelps to JAL, Aug. 23, 1917.
56. JAL, "Governor Ferguson and the University of Texas," pp. 19–20.
57. Nalle, *Fergusons of Texas*, p. 118.
58. JAL, "Governor Ferguson and the University of Texas," p. 20.
59. Ibid., p. 16. In 1940 Lomax in a letter to E. C. Barker again insisted that he had been out of town when the suit was filed, suggesting, in a circuitous fashion, that someone had forged his signature to the petition which instituted the lawsuit (JAL to Barker, Jan. 22, 1940, Barker Papers, CAH). Among indications that Lomax was actively involved in the lawsuit is a letter dated Sept. 24, 1917, from him to his old friend and Harvard classmate, Alex Weisberg, one of six lawyers who argued his—the plaintiff's—case; in this letter Lomax expresses his gratitude to "my lawyers" for their performance against Ferguson and says he hopes that he will some day have "some real profitable business" for them. See also Leonard

Doughty to JAL, June 4, 1917.

60. JAL to Weisberg, Sept. 24, 1917.

61. "His Own Words," p. 704.

62. For Lomax's full account of the incident, see JAL, "Governor Ferguson and the University of Texas," pp. 22–23.

63. Testimony of Regent George W. Littlefield in the case of *John Lomax vs. G. S. McReynolds, et al*, pp. 208–9. See also "His Own Words," p. 717.

64. JAL to Vinson, Jan. 5, 1940.

65. Vinson to JAL, July 16, 1917.

66. JAL, "Governor Ferguson and the University of Texas," p. 14.

67. JAL to B. H. Powell, July 16, 1917. See also JAL to John Brady, Sept. 17, 1917.

Chapter 14: Good-bye Old Paint

1. JAL to Briggs, July 14, 1917, HU.bMS Am 1907.1 (753).

2. BW Jr. to JAL, Jan. 22, 1917; Charles Schweppe to JAL, Jan. 30, 1917; wire BW Jr. to JAL, Feb. 7, 1917; Charles Schweppe to JAL, Feb. 10, 16, and 23, 1917.

3. Schweppe to JAL, June 20, 1917.

4. In *ABH,* Lomax recorded his children laughing that his salary was "as much as the Governor of Texas gets," but in fact Ferguson was paid only $4,000 per year.

5. JAL to Brady, Sept. 17, 1917.

6. JAL to Frank Ewart, Oct. 27, 1917.

7. JAL to BW, Sept. 1, 1917, HU.bMS Am 1907.1 (807).

8. JAL, *ABH,* p. 85.

9. Interview with SLD, Lubbock, Tex., June 27, 1988.

10. Quoted in Emmett Dedmon, *Fabulous Chicago* (New York: Random House, 1953), pp. 191–92.

11. JAL to Benedict, Nov. 8, 1917.

12. JAL to Leslie Waggener Jr., Sept. 27, 1917.

13. Architectural historian Carl Condit, quoted in Harold M. Mayer and Richard C. Wade, *Chicago: Growth of a Metropolis* (Chicago: University of Chicago Press, 1969), p. 32.

14. JAL to Richard Inglis, Dec. 21, 1917.

15. BBL to JAL, undated but prob. Feb., 1918.

16. Vinson to JAL, Sept. 15, 1917.

17. JAL to Vinson, Sept. 18, 1917.

18. *San Antonio Express,* Sunday, Sept. 3, 1917, p. 28.

19. Potts to JAL, Sept. 17, 1917.

20. Miller to JAL, Sept. 24, 1917.

21. J. W. Calhoun to JAL, Sept. 18, 1917.

22. Quoted in JAL, *ABH,* p. 99.

23. Hogg to JAL, Dec. 28, 1917.

24. JAL, "Bond Selling in 1918," pp. 125–36.

25. Ibid., p. 130.

26. JAL, *ABH,* p. 86.

27. No copy of his paper survived, and the abstract of proceedings does not reveal who the "poetic interpreters" were, only that, in Lomax's words, they "have recently written of [western] life, taking for their hero the cowboy. If cowboys are not quite as here represented, they ought to be" (*Proceedings of the Annual Meeting of the Modern Language Association, 1917,* p. lviii).

28. JAL, *ABH,* p. 87.

29. Lewis to JAL, June 5, 1940. Lomax quotes this letter at length in *ABH,* pp. 87–91.

30. Ibid.

31. Ibid. Niven in *Carl Sandburg,* pp. 443–44, relates a similar story about Sandburg singing "Buffalo Skinners" to Sinclair Lewis ("Sandburg had gotten the song from Texas folklorist John Lomax"). Lloyd Lewis observed that none of them knew what "doughies" were until Lomax came along, and Lomax himself spent considerable energy over the years trying to ascertain the origins of the word—and promulgate its correct pronunciation. Ultimately he paid lip service to Jack Thorp's notion that it derived from the Spanish *dogal,* or halter, used to tie off a suckling calf from its mother and eventually applied to the calf itself. But personally he preferred the opinion of "ranchers in the Southwest," who maintained that it came from "dough-bellied," the cowboy's colorful phrase for an orphaned calf, which has "nothing in its guts but dough" and thus is a "little dough-guts," shortened to "doughies" and misspelled as "dogies" by greenhorns and scholars. A simpler explanation might be that cowboys jokingly (but quite naturally) identified orphaned calves with stray dogs, pronounced "doags" in the South (from which so many of the waddies came) and diminutized into "doagies" or "dogies." In any event, as Lomax insisted, it is not pronounced "doggies." See also JAL to Carl Engel, Nov. 15, 1933, AFC.JAL.

32. White, *Git Along, Little Dogies,* p. 200. Lomax's original title for the book was in fact *Poetry of the Cattle Trail and Cow Camp.* He changed it while the book was in press (Macmillan to JAL, July 12, 1919).

33. Various undated letters of this period, in CAH.

34. JAL to Pedigo, Jan. 16 and Mar. 11, 1918; Pedigo to JAL, undated.

35. JAL to BBL, Feb. 14 and 20, 1918.

36. JAL to Barker, May 20, 1918, Barker Papers, CAH.

37. *Alcalde* 11 (Mar. 1924): 750.

38. Hamilton to JAL, July 24, 1918.

39. BW Jr. to JAL ("Personal and Confidential"), Dec. 30, 1918.

40. JAL to BBL, Nov. 8 and 9, 1918.

41. JAL to BBL, Nov. 9, 1918.

42. Benedict et al. to JAL, May 20, 191[8]. This letter is dated 1919 but clearly in error; Lomax had already returned to Texas by early March 1919.

43. JAL to BBL, Feb. 2, 1919, and undated.

44. JAL to BW Jr., Jan. 20, 1919; BW Jr. to JAL, Jan. 22, 1919; JAL to Hamilton, Jan. 21, 1919.

45. JAL, *ABH,* p. 98.

46. JAL to J. W. Bass, Jan. 16, 1923.

47. JAL to H. P. Duncan, Dec. 5, 1919.

Chapter 15: More Hell in Texas

1. JAL to BBL, undated.

2. The name of the organization until Dec. 1914 was officially "The Alumni Association of the University of Texas." That month, with little or no fanfare, it became "The Ex-Students' Association of the University of Texas." To almost everyone it was, and remains, simply "The Texas Exes."

3. Hamilton to JAL, Jan. 17, 1919.

4. Publication of *Alcalde* was suspended between May 1918 and February 1919. The thin February and March 1919 issues resumed, with no break in volume or number sequence, under the aegis of Bedichek as "Acting Managing Editor"; the March edition carried a notice that Lomax would be "in the saddle by the next issue, as soon as he gets the carpet down in the sitting room and the gate mended on the chicken yard fence."

5. JAL, *ABH,* p. 99.

6. JAL to Rom J. Rhone, Judge James O. Wilson, Pierce B. Ward, Nov. 18, 1919; JAL to Claude Chesteen and Rev. Richard Oxford and others, Nov. 24, 1919.

7. See, for example, JAL to R. M. Kelly, Dec. 5, 1919.

8. JAL to Dr. J. E. Butler, Oct. 2, 1919.

9. JAL, *Songs of the Cattle Trail and Cow Camp,* pp. ix-xi.

10. Barnes, "Cowboy and His Songs," p. 14.

11. Carlson, "Cowboy Ballads at Our Own Fireside," *Reader's Digest,* Dec. 1931, p. 176. Carlson was "formerly instructor of English at the University of Illinois, now living in Kansas."

12. *New York Times Book Review,* Mar. 28, 1920, p. 140.

13. JAL to Hogg, Feb. 27, 1920.

14. JAL to Torbert, Feb. 12, 1920. It is clear that by "world negro," Lomax meant "worldly negro"—his interest was essentially in black secular music.

15. The MLA had postponed its normal December meeting in 1919 until the following March because of coal shortages and travel restrictions in the aftermath of the war.

16. BBL to JAL, Mar. 24, 1920.

17. RTL, "Adventures with the Ballad Hunter," p. 2.

18. *Alcalde* 9, no. 3 (Aug. 1921): 703–6.

19. JAL to Sandburg, Oct. 23 and 25, 1920.

20. See, for example, Sandburg to JAL, Mar. 27, 1922.

21. Sandburg to JAL, Mar. 31, 1924: "I can see your book filtering its way; it won't be really known and reaching its real audience till about ten years from now; it is a 'goddammed mule' they have to live with and learn how to handle."

22. JAL to Pedigo, Jan. 29, 1929.

23. One of their deals involved a $12,000 loan to the owner of an oil exploration company at a rate of interest several points above what banks were charging, and the borrower was required to put up collateral that could be sold for a minimum of $15,000 and (Bullington gleefully told Lomax) "probably as high as $22,500.00" (OB to JAL, June 23, 1924).

24. Tax records and other financial papers.

25. Macmillan Co. to JAL, May 8, 1922; Fox to JAL, Nov. 28, 1922.

26. JAL to Briggs, June 20, 1921.

27. JAL to "Dear Crutt," Nov. 1, 1923, with response on back.

28. JAL to [Ms.] F. Jennie Hoover, Oct. 21, 1920.

29. JAL to Amy Lowell, Oct. 5, 1921, HU.bMS Lowell 19.1 (747); Lowell to JAL, Oct. 17, 1921, HU.bMS Lowell 19.1 (789); JAL to Lowell, "Abt Oct 12, 1921," HU.bMS Lowell 19.1 (747); Lowell to JAL, Nov. 3, 1921, HU.bMS Lowell 19.1 (747); JAL to Lowell, Jan. 2, 192[2] (misdated 1921), HU.bMS Lowell 19.1 (747).

30. Mezes to JAL, Nov. 25, 1921.

31. JAL to Mrs. Florence Bell, Jan. 17, 1924.

32. JAL to R. B. Creager, Apr. 22, 1922.

33. W. K. Ewing to JAL, June 4, 1920.

34. JAL to Creager, June 17, 1922. McCauley had been one of Lomax's sources for *Cowboy Songs,* having supplied "The Buffalo Skinners" for the first edition. Shortly afterward McCauley wrote an autobiography, *A Stove-Up Cowboy's Story,* and sent the manuscript to Lomax. It was not published, however, until 1943, fourteen years after McCauley's death. See Al Lowman, "Beautifully Printed and Expressive of Texas: Carl Hertzog and the Texas Folklore Society," *Corners of Texas* (Denton: University of North Texas Press, 1993), pp. 73–74.

35. Richard Lomax to JAL, May 31, 1923; JAL to Lon Smith, Sept. 15, 1923.

36. BW Jr. to JAL, May 24, 1924; JAL to Connally et al., May 29, 1924.

37. *Alcalde* 9, no. 8 (Mar. 1922): 1199.

38. *Outlook,* Sept. 13, 1922, pp. 49–50; JAL to *Outlook,* Sept. 18, 1922; JAL to Robert M. Field, Nov. 23, 1922.

39. JAL to Crozier, Oct. 3, 1921.

40. SLD, interview, Lubbock, Tex., May 15, 1989.

41. EC to T. W. Davidson, May 12, 1923; *Dallas Morning News,* May 26, 1923.

42. *Dallas Morning News,* May 26, 1923.

43. JAL to Adrian Pool, June 2, 1940.

44. *Alcalde,* Feb. 1933, p. 101.

45. JAL to EC, Aug. 24, 1923.

46. *Daily Texan,* May 26, 1923, p. 1.

47. JAL to EC, May 21 and 22, 1923.
48. JAL to EC, May 21, 1923.
49. EC to OB, June 1, 1923.
50. EC to L. Theo Bellmont, Nov. 5, 1923.
51. *Alcalde* 11, no. 1 (Apr. 1923): 32.
52. JAL to EC, June 8, 1923.
53. JAL to Hester Joynes Means, Apr. 23, 1924.
54. EC to JAL, May 16, 1924.
55. *Alcalde* 11, no. 4 (Nov. 1923): 356, and 11, no. 2 (May 1923): 112.
56. Section 4, article 1: "No religious test shall ever be required as a qualification to any office or public trust in this state; nor shall anyone be excluded from holding office on account of his religious sentiment, provided he acknowledge the existence of a Supreme Being."
57. M. W. Terrel to JAL, Nov. 20, 1920.
58. EC to O. O. Touchstone, May 16, 1924.
59. OB to JAL, June 6, 1924.
60. *Alcalde* 12, no. 6 (Jan. 1925): 513.
61. *Alcalde* 12, no. 7 (Feb. 1925): 584.
62. JAL, *ABH,* p. 101.

Chapter 16: Fare Thee Well, Babe

1. Wineburgh, *Texas Banker,* pp. 25–27.
2. JAL, *ABH,* p. 103.
3. Ibid., p. 101.
4. *Alcalde* 13, no. 2 (May 1925): 795.
5. Ibid., p. 834; 13, no. 3 (July 1925), 877–78.
6. *Alcalde* 13, no. 3 (July 1925): 879.
7. JAL to Mrs. Bird T. Baldwin, Jan. 28, 1922.
8. Fehrenbach, *Lone Star,* p. 711.
9. JAL, *ABH,* p. 102.
10. Ibid.
11. Ibid., p. 103.
12. Ibid. Young Waggener, only twenty-four, was shot by a close friend, Latimer Murfee, as they were practicing quick draws with a pistol. A grand jury exonerated Murfee and called the incident "a most deplorable but unavoidable accident" (*Dallas Morning News,* July 11, 1928, p. 1).
13. JAL to Elizabeth Baker, Jan. 30, 1925; see also JAL to Louise Pound, Jan. 23, 1925.
14. JAL to Dobie, Dec. 29, 1924.
15. JAL to John B. Jones, Apr. 25, 1929.
16. R. L. Holliday to JAL, Aug. 26, 1930; JAL to Holliday, Aug. 28, 1930.

17. SLD, interview, Lubbock, Tex., June 27, 1988.
18. JAL Jr. to BBL, July 24, 1925.
19. JAL Jr. to JAL, Oct. 5, 1928.
20. JAL to Elizabeth Darley, Feb. 14, 1931.
21. Ibid.
22. JAL to JAL Jr., May 11, 1931.
23. JAL to JAL Jr., May 18, 1931.
24. JAL to JAL Jr., Sept. 23, 1931.
25. JAL to Mezes, Nov. 29, 1930.
26. Unidentified (prob. John E. Owens) to Sage, Dec. 16, 1931.
27. Owens to JAL, Jan. 11, 1935.
28. Fred F. Florence to JAL, Jan. 27, 1939.
29. Pedigo to JAL, Jan. 19, 1929; JAL to Pedigo, Jan. 21 and 29, 1929.
30. Anna Brown to JAL, Feb. 28, 1924.
31. JAL to JAL Jr., Oct. 16, 1931.
32. BLH, interview, Washington, D.C., Aug. 2, 1989.
33. JAL Jr., "Twenty-Five Thousand Miles in Nancy Ford," p. 1.
34. *Dallas Morning News,* Jan. 2, 1932, p. 3. A decade later, when Johnny was compiling "Twenty-Five Miles in Nancy Ford," his usually reliable memory faltered and he misremembered the football game as a contest between "a bunch of Southwest football stars" and "a squad from the Big Ten Conference."

Chapter 17: Johnny, Won't You Ramble?

1. Lomax's 1932 lecture tour is documented in detail by a lively and humorous journal, known as "The Log," which John Jr. kept, complete with occasional drawings, for most of the trip. (He turned it over near the end to Alan, whose account is less lively and more impersonal.) On at least three occasions, John Jr. attempted to summarize the Log and put it into narrative form, ostensibly to be included as a chapter in Lomax's autobiography (for a variety of extraneous reasons, it was discarded). There are references among the correspondence to a version done in February 1939, another in May 1940, and finally, "Twenty-Five Thousand Miles in Nancy Ford" (cited hereafter simply as "Nancy Ford"), a twenty-five-page manuscript written during the summer of 1943 and the only one of the three which survives. Occasionally the chronology of John Jr.'s later narrative account differs from that of the Log; I have drawn on both accounts but for the most part have followed the chronology of the Log for its fidelity to the actual sequence of events, while also attempting to compress the story, avoid the dulling repetitions of their zigzag itinerary, and retain the flavor of both "Nancy Ford" and the Log.
2. "Nancy Ford," p. 3.
3. Ibid., p. 5.

4. Log, Apr. 20.

5. "Nancy Ford," p. 9.

6. JAL, *ABH,* p. 107.

7. Ibid., p. 110. A letter from K. King, Macmillan, to Lomax indicates that Lomax did not receive the "agreement covering the publication of your book of American ballads," until July 27. The advance check is reported to Johnny in a letter of Aug. 24.

8. "Nancy Ford," p. 12.

9. Connally to JAL, Jan. 26, 1932. The RFC had been established that month to provide emergency funds to banks and other financial institutions to enable them to make loans to farmers, businessmen, and industrial concerns. This involved, among other things, audits of participating institutions; John Jr. was eventually employed to work with one of the auditing crews.

10. Log, June 9.

11. Anderson, "Putting the Experience of the World at the Nation's Command," p. 120.

12. JAL to HS, Mar. 6, 1941, included in Draft Annual Reports, 1941–74, AFC.LC.

13. Log, June 10.

14. "Nancy Ford," p. 11.

15. This entry in the log is dated May 24, suggesting that Lomax and John Jr. had gone through Cambridge prior to reaching New York. Both the log and "Nancy Ford" confirm that the three of them did not depart for the West from Harvard until June 16.

16. The "Ohio Bull Incident" became a family classic, and Lomax later took a happier attitude toward it. In 1939, when he asked Johnny to write an account of the trip, ostensibly to be included in *Adventures of a Ballad Hunter,* he admonished his son to make the most of the comic elements in the bull story and "pour it on your father! He needs it and can take it" (JAL to JAL Jr., Jan. 17, 1939, AFC.LoFam). My account of the story is compiled from the log, from "Nancy Ford," and from a letter which John Jr. wrote to Bess and the Mansells on July 16, 1932.

17. JAL Jr. to BBL, Apr. 30, 1931.

18. "Nancy Ford," p. 17.

19. Ibid., pp. 21–22; interview with SLD, Lubbock, Tex., July 27, 1988.

20. Log, Aug. 17; "Nancy Ford," p. 25.

21. Log, Aug. 20. An Aug. 24 letter from Lomax in Lubbock to Johnny indicates that "Alan and Nancy Ford and I rolled in here Sunday morning," which would have been Aug. 21. The log is probably more reliable.

22. JAL Jr., Introduction to *Cow Camps and Cattle Herds,* p. ix.

23. JAL to JAL Jr., Aug. 24, 1932.

Chapter 18: Hallelujah, Bum Again

1. DeWitt Neighbors, M.D., to JAL, Oct. 10, 1932.

2. L. H. Titterton, NBC, to H. S. Latham, Oct. 18, 1932; JAL to "Fellow-Citizen" (form letter), Oct. 20, 1932; C. P. Kelly, Thomas A. Edison, Inc., to J. R. de la Torre Bueno Jr., Macmillan, Oct. 22, 1932.

3. JAL Jr. to JAL, Sept. 10, 1932.

4. JAL Jr. to JAL, Dec. 2, 1932.

5. Ibid. Gordon's offer of "a shake-down bed in his house" was particularly magnanimous in light of the fact that his "house" was actually a small, crowded apartment in the home of a Washington couple who had befriended him, his wife, and his daughter. The host couple were the parents of young John I. White, who acquired an early interest in folksong, sang on radio for some ten years as "The Lonesome Cowboy" over WEAF and WOR in New York, and later became a serious collector and authority on folk music (Kodish, *Good Friends and Bad Enemies,* p. 176; White, *Git Along, Little Dogies,* pp. 1–15, 201, passim).

6. My account of Gordon is drawn from Debra Kodish's excellent biography of Gordon, *Good Friends and Bad Enemies,* from "Archive of American Folksong: A History, 1928–1938" (AAFS.Hist), and from Bartis, "History of the Archive of Folk Song."

7. As a graduate student and assistant to several professors, including Kittredge and Greenough, Gordon was the bane of Fred Robinson's existence as chairman of the English Department. Robinson to Barrett Wendell: "I want to talk with you . . . about Gordon. He is hopelessly behind again in English A, & Greenough and I am [*sic*] worried about him" (Robinson to BW, Feb. 5, 1916). In September that year Robinson wrote again to BW: "For English 28 the best fitted of our instructors seems to be Robert Gordon, if only he can be trusted to do the work. Greenough's experience with him . . . has been most discouraging, but my impression is that you have found him faithful and efficient in 41" (Barrett Wendell Papers, HU.bMS Am 1907.1 [807]).

8. CE to Gordon, Sept. 16, 1927, AFC.LC, cited by Kodish, *Good Friends and Bad Enemies,* p. 157.

9. Kodish, *Good Friends and Bad Enemies,* p. 160. At the time, the donor (or donors) who put up the money to back Gordon were something of a mystery. Although various names later turned up in Music Division reports—John Barton Payne, Andrew Mellon, Mrs. Adolph Miller, and Mrs. J. Brooks Parker—the initial money came essentially from the Carnegie Corporation, directly from its head, Frederick W. Keppel, to his close friend Herbert Putnam, the Librarian of Congress. Keppel and Putnam purposely underplayed the corporation's role in the hope of encouraging private gifts ("Carnegie Corporation Project: Harold Spivacke," pp. 2–3).

10. "Carnegie Corporation Project: Harold Spivacke," p. 3. Bartis ("History of the Archive of Folk Song," p. 39) is less willing to attribute Gordon's dismissal to his personality and lack of productivity, emphasizing instead budgetary considerations and quite correctly crediting Gordon with "constructing the foundation and conceptual models upon which the Archive was built and continues to stand" (p. 35). Yet Kodish (*Good Friends and Bad Enemies*, p. 191) states flatly, "Engel and Putnam had seen no products, no tangible results, from their folksong project," and her more detailed account shows the extent to which Gordon's erratic behavior and work habits caused problems with his colleagues at the Library—problems they were anxious to be rid of.

11. "I've been canny enough to keep title to *all* my original records and documents. The Library has copies, but does not in any way control the originals" (Gordon to Joanna Colcord, Jan. 10, 1932, quoted by Kodish, *Good Friends and Bad Enemies*, p. 192).

12. Ibid.

13. JAL, *ABH*, p. 110. See also C. P. Kelly to J. R. de la Torre Bueno Jr., Oct. 22, 1932; American Council of Learned Societies to JAL, Mar. 27, 1933; CE to Herbert Putnam, Apr. 29, 1933, AFC.LC; Nat Shilkret to JAL, May 29, 1933.

14. Okeh's "field expedition" to Atlanta in June 1923 was apparently the first to use such equipment. Of course, Edison's original cylinder phonograph could record and play back instantaneously, and for some forty years anthropologists, folklorists, and others—including Lomax—had used such machines in the field. Small, compact models were available, and the spring-driven motor eliminated the need for batteries or for generated current in remote areas. But reproduction quality was often poor, and the cylinders were fragile, impermanent, and difficult to store. See Brady, "The Box That Got the Flourishes."

15. JAL to CE, May 24, 1933, AFC.JAL.

16. JAL to Dan Williams, May 23, 1933.

17. JAL to "My Friends," May 1, 1933.

18. JAL to CE, May 24, 1933, AFC.JAL.

19. BLH, interview, Washington, D.C., Aug. 2, 1989.

20. Dobie, "John A. Lomax," p. 9.

21. JAL to CE, May 30, 1933; CE to JAL, June 3, 1933, AFC.JAL.

22. C. E. Hallenborg, Dictaphone Corp., to JAL, June 6, 1933. In almost every account afterward, Lomax persisted in calling it an "Edison" machine, and, in at least one instance, an "Edison dictaphone," but he had his terminology mixed; it was definitely a Dictaphone, and there was no corporate connection between the two companies.

23. JAL to RT, June 29, 1933.

24. JAL to RT, July 1, 1933.

25. Ibid.

26. Ibid.

27. JAL to RT, July 4, 1933.

28. JAL, *ABH,* p. 112.

29. JAL to RT, July 4, 1933. See AAFS. Hist., "Report of the Honorary Consultant and Curator" for 1934: "Folk songs and folk literature flourish, grow—are created, propagated, transformed—in the eddies of human society, particularly [prisons] where there is isolation and homogeniety of thought and experience. These communities of Negro men and women, shut out from the clamor of the world, thrown back almost entirely on their own resources for entertainment, lonely, few with any background of reading, naturally resort to song. . . . And through this singing, more new songs are bred and old ones are polished and lengthened."

AAFS.Hist., "Report of the Honorary Consultant and Curator" for 1935: "During the months of September, October, November, and December, we recorded songs in the States of Arkansas, Alabama, Georgia, South Carolina, and North Carolina—principally from Negro convicts in the penitentiaries of those five States. . . . The ballad singing and guitar-picking Negro sings when he is happy; he also sings when he is miserable. Enough of these people get into serious trouble to make any large group of black convicts a repository of folk songs."

30. JAL to RT, July 7, 1933.

31. JAL to CE, undated [prob. July 7, 1933], AFC.JAL.

32. JAL to RT, July 7 and 21, 1933; JAL, *ABH,* p. 120. In *AB&FS,* Lomax spells the name "Trevelyan"; it is "Truvillion" in *ABH* and in letters.

33. JAL to RT, July 11, 1933; JAL, *ABH,* pp. 119–20.

34. JAL, *ABH,* p. 121.

35. JAL to RT, July 21, 1933. In Lomax's letter to Miss Terrill of this date, he did not identify the "one man, who knew many songs," but years later, when he was excerpting the letter for inclusion in his autobiography, he inserted the name (see JAL, *ABH,* p. 121), leaving no doubt as to the singer's identity. Otherwise, Leadbelly is scarcely mentioned in *Adventures of a Ballad Hunter;* curiously missing entirely is any account of their travels together and Leadbelly's brief but electrifying appearances in New York and environs in early 1935, under Lomax's management. Apparently this was omitted at the insistence of Lomax's editor at Macmillan, James Putnam, who told Lomax, "I am certain that it [i.e., the Leadbelly story as Lomax had written it for the book] would backfire and might well let you in for a libel suit" (JP to JAL, Apr. 25, 1946).

36. JAL, *ABH,* p. 121.

37. Walter Garwick to JAL, June 28, 1934; JAL wire to CE, July 12, 1933, AFC.JAL.

38. JAL to CE, July 19, 1933, AFC.JAL.

39. JAL to RT, July 23, 1933.

40. AL to RT, July 28, 1933, quoted in JAL, *ABH,* p. 122.

41. JAL to CE, undated, AFC.JAL.

42. AL to RT, July 28, 1933, quoted in JAL, *ABH,* p. 123. See also JAL to RT, Aug. 2, 1933.

43. AL to RT, Feb. 27, 1934. There is an indication that this earlier episode occurred in Shreveport, date undetermined.

44. AL to RT, July 28, 1933, quoted in JAL, *ABH,* p. 122. Two days later, on July 30 (presumably following a medical diagnosis), Alan wrote to CE that his father was suffering with "a rather bad attack of malarial fever" (AFC.JAL).

45. JAL to RT, Aug. 5, 1933, quoted in JAL, *ABH,* p. 123.

46. Ibid.

47. JAL to RT, Aug. 7, 1933, quoted in JAL, *ABH,* p. 124.

48. JAL to RT, Aug. 10, 1933, quoted in JAL, *ABH,* p. 125.

49. Ibid.

50. Ibid., quoted, with changes and omissions, in JAL, *ABH,* p. 126.

51. JAL to RT, Aug. 17, 1933.

52. JAL to RT, Aug. 22, 1933; JAL, *ABH,* p. 126.

53. Ibid.; JAL, *ABH,* pp. 126–27.

54. Extracts in the preceding two paragraphs, in the order quoted, are from JAL to RT, June 29, 1933, July 23, 1933, Oct. 7, 1933, Aug. 5, 1933; RT to JAL, Sept. 14 and Aug. 25, 1933; JAL to RT, Sept. 4, 1933.

55. AAFS.Hist., 1933; Bartis, "History of the Archive of Folk Song," p. 49. A summary account of Lomax's 1933 expedition is contained in his "'Sinful Songs' of the Southern Negro."

56. JAL to RT, Aug. 24, 1933.

57. JAL to RT, Sept. 4, 1933.

58. *Texas Digest,* Feb. 15, 1941, pp. 16–17.

59. CE to the Librarian [of Congress], Sept. 11, 1933, AFC.JAL. Bartis, "History of the Archive of Folk Song," p. 50, suggests that Lomax accepted the position "with some reluctance," but he bases that on what Lomax wrote later, when he was concerned with refuting charges that he had used the Archive for personal benefit.

60. The Librarian to JAL, Sept. 13, 1933, AFC.JAL.

61. JP to JAL, Apr. 7, 15, and 20, 1933. The evidence indicates that Macmillan was as eager as Lomax to keep the two projects from clashing, and there is nothing to suggest that Macmillan responded to whatever Lomax had to say about the Gordon book.

62. Gordon to CE, Jan. 14, 1927, AFC.LC, quoted by Kodish, *Good Friends and Bad Enemies,* p. 156.

63. JAL to HS, Jan. 28, 1940, AFC.LC.

64. Charles Seeger, "Reminiscences of an American Musicologist," p. 243.

65. JAL, *ABH,* p. 127.

66. JAL to RT, Oct. 9 and Oct. 7, 1933; JAL to CE, Oct. 12, 1933, AFC.JAL.

67. JAL, *ABH,* pp. 128–29.

68. JAL to RT, Oct. 7, 1933.

Chapter 19: Wedlock

1. RT to JAL, Oct. 14, 1933. John Henry Faulk said that the Lomax-Terrill romance "shook Austin" but "not in an unpleasant way; they just thought it quaint, weird . . . that old Lomax would marry Miss Terrill, a very proper lady" (interview, Austin, Tex., Mar. 10, 1988).

2. JAL to RT, Oct. 17 and Oct. 18, 1933.

3. RT to JAL, Oct. 23, 1933.

4. JAL to RT, Nov. 19, 1933.

5. Ibid.

6. Briggs to JAL Jr., Nov. 10, 1933.

7. JAL to RT, Nov. 10, 1933.

8. Ibid.

9. JAL to RT, Nov. 15, 1933.

10. JAL to RT, Nov. 17, 1933

11. JAL and AL, *AB&FS*, p. xxix; J. R. Schultz to JAL, June 20, 1941, AFC.LoFam.

12. JAL to RT, Nov. 21, 1933.

13. JAL to RT, Nov. 27 and Nov. 28, 1933.

14. JAL to RT, Dec. 24, 1933.

15. RT to JAL, Dec. 19 and 23, 1933.

16. JAL Jr. to JAL, Nov. 15, 1933. See also AL to JAL, undated but ca. Sept. 1934.

17. JAL to JAL Jr., Jan. 3, 1934.

18. AL to JAL Jr., Jan. 3, 1934.

19. The funding brouhaha is detailed in the following: JAL, *ABH*, pp. 131–33; Dr. Frederick Keppel, Carnegie Corp., to Herbert Putnam, Dec. 21, 1933; JAL to CE, Dec. 23 and 31, 1933; CE to JAL, Jan. 5, 1934; JAL to CE, Jan. 9, 1934; Herbert Putnam to JAL, Jan. 12, 1934; JAL to CE, Jan. 26, 1934 (all AFC.LoFam); Stevens to JAL, Jan. 2, 8, and 11, 1934; Herbert Putnam to JAL, Jan. 6 and 25, 1934; JAL to Herbert Putnam, Jan. 26, 1934; Stevens to JAL, Jan. 29, 1934 (all CAH). Copies of some letters are in both AFC.LoFam and CAH.

20. Stevens to JAL, Jan. 8 and Jan. 11, 1934; JAL to Herbert Putnam, Jan. 25, 1934.

21. JAL to Stevens, Jan. 26, 1934.

22. JAL to HS, Mar. 6, 1941; Draft Annual Reports, 1941–74, AFC.LC.

23. Edward Waters, interview, Washington, D.C., Aug. 14, 1989.

24. Ethel Matthews Casey to JAL, Feb. 13, 1934.

25. JAL to JAL Jr., July 9, 1934.

26. "Miss Terrill" quickly became "Deanie" to the children, a name Alan gave her to avoid any embarrassment over whether they should call her "Mother." Bess and her friends thought it clever and daring to refer among themselves to Miss Terrill as "Miss Terror" until they realized that she knew and was mildly amused by it. It was probably derived as much from Leadbelly's mispronunciation of "Ter-

rill" as by Deanie's moral earnestness, real or perceived. To Lomax she was never anything but "Miss Terrill"; she found both amusing and troubling his habit, long after they were married, of registering them at hotels as "Mr. and Mrs. John A. Lomax," then turning to her and saying, loudly and quite seriously, "Come along, Miss Terrill." If she ever addressed him as anything but "Mr. Lomax," no one else heard it (interview with SLD, Lubbock, Tex., May 15, 1989). See also RTL, "Adventures with the Ballad Hunter," p. 4.

27. JAL Jr. to RT, Feb. 18, 1934; RT to JAL, Feb. 21, 1934.

28. RTL, "Adventures with the Ballad Hunter," p. 1.

29. RT to JAL, Jan. 26, 1934.

30. JAL to RT, Jan. 21, 1934.

31. My account of Lomax's excursion into southwest Texas in February 1934 is constructed from details in "Diary of John A. Lomax, 1934" (hereafter "Diary") in CAH and typed extracts transcribed from letters to RT (possibly prepared for an early draft of *ABH*), dated Feb. 7, 8, and 10, 1934, in CAH.

32. JAL to CE, Feb. 13, 1934, AFC.JAL.

33. Frank Goodwyn, interview, Washington, D.C., June 15, 1990. Almost three months after Lomax tried to enlist Engel's help, Robert Kleberg finally responded to his requests, indicating that Kleberg would cooperate and providing the names of possible informants (Robert Kleberg to JAL, May 24, 1934). By this time, however, Lomax was on his way to Louisiana. In the late 1930s he tried again to record on the King Ranch, but without success, according to Goodwyn, who accompanied him on those trips.

34. RT reported this in a letter to JAL Jr., Feb. 25, 1934.

35. JAL to RT, Mar. 2, 1934.

36. AL to RT, Feb. 24, 1934.

37. JAL to RT, Feb. 28, 1934.

38. "Diary," Apr. 6, 1934.

39. JAL to RT, Mar. 4, 1934.

40. Typescript pages, untitled, undated, and otherwise unidentified, containing Alan's account of the car theft (possibly prepared for an early draft of *ABH*), in CAH.

41. JAL to JAL Jr., Mar. 30, 1934. To CE, May 17, 1934, JAL said the loss relating to the theft of the car was $350 (AFC.JAL).

42. JAL to CE, Apr. 3, 1934, AFC.JAL.

43. "Diary," Apr. 17, 1934. Simmons's note, dated Apr. 5, 1934, is also in CAH.

44. "Diary," Apr. 17, 1934. See also JAL to JAL Jr., Apr. 12, 1934.

45. "Diary," Apr. 17, 1934.

46. "Charming and vivacious" is in the minutes of the meeting, kept by Dobie as secretary; "nothing duller" is reported by John Henry Faulk in McNutt, "John Henry Faulk: An Interview," p. 113.

47. Susan Prink, Macmillan, to JAL, Feb. 21 and Apr. 24, 1934.

48. Boner's detailed analysis of the machine, dated May 14, 1934, was mailed by JAL to CE on May 19, 1934 (AFC.JAL).

49. JAL to CE, May 17, 1934, AFC.JAL.

50. CE to JAL, May 23, 1934, AFC.JAL.

51. AAFS.Hist., "Report of the Honorary Consultant and Curator," 1934.

52. Garwick to JAL, Nov. 3, 1934. Garwick's rebuttal of Boner is dated June 28, 1934. Refereeing the dispute over the recording machine is a difficult task. Boner was clearly an expert, and his evaluation of the technology is hard to refute; at the same time, Garwick made a detailed and at times convincing defense, supplying empirical evidence from his own field recording experiences to show that quality results were possible. According to sound engineers at the Archive, recordings made on the much-maligned Garwick machine compare favorably in quality with other field-made recordings of the era. No doubt some of the problems which the Lomaxes encountered were due in the beginning to their almost total lack of experience with such equipment, although Alan apparently learned fast and in time could do as well as anyone else to coax the machine to operate properly. The situation is further clouded by certain circumstances of the business relationship between Garwick and Lomax; originally Lomax had hoped to make money on the side by acting as a sales agent for Garwick, demonstrating the machine from place to place and taking orders for production models from schools, clubs, and other such organizations where he lectured. This may help to explain why he was willing to struggle on with Garwick, in the hope of eventual financial return, although he could hardly have hoped to drum up sales with the faulty prototype. On the other hand, he constantly stalled payments to Garwick for the recording supplies, whether from oversight or deliberately, as a means of expressing his displeasure with the situation. Garwick patiently bore the arrears, unwilling to upset so important a client as the Library of Congress.

53. For accounts of McIlhenny and Avery Island, see James Conaway, "On Avery Island, Tabasco Sauce Is the Spice of Life," *Smithsonian,* May 1984, pp. 72–82, and "Salt and Pepper Flavor This Island," *Southern Living,* Mar. 1989, pp. 34–35.

54. JAL to RT, June 17, 1934.

55. In his annual report to the Library of Congress for 1934, Lomax said they were in Louisiana six weeks, but the earliest they could have been there was June 5, and they were back in Houston by July 6. As to the number of recordings, Lomax's report indicated only that he and Alan recorded "eighty-nine records, or approximately 400 songs" for the year.

56. JAL to RT, June 19, 24, 25, 26, and 29, 1934.

57. JAL to Carnegie Corp., Jan. 18, 1935.

58. JAL to CE, June 7, 1934, AFC.JAL.

59. CE to Herbert Putnam, June 11, 1934, AFC.JAL. His emphasis.

60. Herbert Putnam to CE, June 13, 1934, AFC.JAL.

61. CE to JAL, June 18, 1934, AFC.JAL.

62. Interview with Jon Newsom, Library of Congress, Washington, D.C., June 19, 1990.

63. JAL to Oliver Strunk, July 19, 1934, AFC.JAL.

64. Loose typescript page in CAH. In *ABH,* pp. 129–30, Lomax places the edited version of this incident within the context of events of 1933 and sets it "in the office of Oliver Strunk, Chief of the Music Division" but he was clearly confused. Strunk did not become chief of the division until July 1934.

65. OS to JAL, July 12, 1934.

66. JAL, *ABH,* pp. 61–64. See also JAL, "Half-Million Dollar Song," pp. 1ff. The Arizona claimants lost their suit when it was discovered that "Home on the Range" had been published in a Kansas newspaper in 1873, the work of a "writing doctor" named Brewster Higley. The case illustrates the difficulty of distinguishing between "folk songs" and "composed songs"; "Home on the Range" was a bit of both. Fortunately for the defendants in the lawsuit—and for John Lomax—it was old enough to be in public domain. The story of "Home on the Range" is told by Croy in *Corn Country,* pp. 164–80.

67. Susan Prink to JAL, July 17, 1934.

68. Interview with SLD, Lubbock, Texas, May 15, 1989.

69. JAL to the Oscar Callaways, June 23, 1934.

Chapter 20: Prison Moan

1. "Lomax Arrives with Lead Belly, Negro Minstrel," *New York Herald Tribune,* Jan. 3, 1935. Evidence indicates that July 1, 1934, was the "drizzling rainy Sunday" on which Leadbelly was recorded. In any event, it seems highly unlikely that Lomax took the record to the governor on a weekend (although one must allow, of course, that Lomax was merely speaking impressionistically).

2. *Life,* Apr. 16, 1937, p. 33.

3. As recently as 1991, the legend was perpetuated in an Associated Press news story that observed, "Lomax helped arrange for Leadbelly's release." See, for instance, David Germain, "Blues Revival Rekindles Interest in 'King of the 12-String,'" *Albany (N.Y.) Times Union,* July 31, 1991, p. C7. The story also appeared in newspapers in Texas, Pennsylvania, Arizona, and Nebraska. (I am grateful to Sean Killeen for calling this to my attention.)

4. Curiously, the original of Himes's letter to Lomax, dated Feb. 15, 1935, together with Leadbelly's prison record, is among the papers of Mary Elizabeth Barnicle Cadle at Radcliffe.

5. Warden L. A. Jones to Irving Halpern, Chief Probation Officer, Court of General Sessions, New York, May 13, 1939, in Huddie Ledbetter's prison file. Copies of these files were generously made available to me by Becky Schroeder, of Columbia, Mo., who obtained them in the 1960s. Excerpts and Jones's letter to Hal-

pern are printed in Vivian Mium, "'Leadbelly'—Hard Facts Not So Hard," *Second Line,* Mar.-Apr. 1959, pp. 1–2, 18–21, a copy of which was provided to me by Kip Lornell.

6. JAL and AL, *NSFLB,* p. 33. Strictly speaking, Lomax's use of the term "pardon" was incorrect; Himes's letter to JAL, dated Feb. 15, 1935, states unequivocally that "Huddie Ledbetter was not pardoned in Louisiana, but was released by operation of the 'good-time' laws. . . . Disposition of his case was not affected in any manner by the commutation of the minimum sentence."

7. JAL to OS, Oct. 1, 1934, AFC.JAL.

8. LB to JAL, Aug. 10, 1934. The draft of Lomax's wire in reply is undated, but it was probably sent during the third week in September.

9. In *NFSLB* (p. 29), Lomax gave the date of their meeting as Sept. 16, but his wire to Leadbelly and letters to Miss Terrill clearly show that it was Sept. 24. There seems to be no reason for the error beyond Lomax's normal confusion with dates and places.

10. JAL and AL, *NFSLB,* p. 29.

11. JAL to RTL, Sept. 23 and 24, 1934.

12. JAL to RTL, Sept. 26, 27, 28, and Oct. 2, 1934.

13. JAL to RTL, Oct. 2, 1934. An account of the Arkansas episode is in *ABH,* pp. 145–49.

14. JAL to RTL, Oct. 18, 1934.

15. JAL to RTL, Oct. 20, 1934.

16. JAL to RTL, Oct. 27 and 28, 1934.

17. JAL to RTL, Nov. 21, 1934. (Dated by a later hand.)

18. *Books,* Oct. 28, 1934, p. 9. To Lomax, the collection was composed of songs which "we may by courtesy call ballads" (JAL and AL, *AB&FS,* p. xxvi).

19. Mark Van Doren, review of *AB&FS, Nation,* Oct. 31, 1934, p. 514.

20. Dorothy Scarborough, review of *AB&FS, New York Times Book Review,* Nov. 11, 1934, p. 2.

21. Review of *AB&FS, Christian Science Monitor,* Oct. 23, 1934, p. 16.

22. JAL to RT, Oct. 9, 1933.

23. "Train wrecks have been the subject of widely popular American songs. But neither Jack Hinton, Casey Jones, Joseph Michel, or Charley Snyder—all of them 'good engineers'—come to greater grief than does Mr. Lomax when his musical notation leaves the rails" (CE, "Views and Reviews," p. 110). Engel concluded: "Of villainy . . . there is a great deal in Mr. Lomax's volume. But there is also a considerable amount of charm, of picturesque humor, and of sensitive beauty" (p. 112).

24. See Ed Waters to JAL, Feb. 22, 1944, and Jan. 29, 1945. Waters admitted that "many of the songs and shouts and hollers that [Gresham] tried to take from records are extraordinarily difficult. Only the most expert person in the world can do justice to unusual or exotic Negro airs." A further complication in attempting

to make new annotations for later editions was that Gresham had worn out many of the original discs. It might be said that Lomax, as always, was looking for cheap help when he hired Gresham, and he got what he paid for.

25. H. S. Latham, Macmillan, wires to JAL, Nov. 8, 10, and 17, 1934; JAL, wire to Latham, Nov. 17, 1934.

26. Fletcher to JAL, Nov. 28 and Dec. 8, 1934; JAL to AL, Jan. 9, 1939, AFC.LoFam.

27. John Jacob Niles to Macaulay and Co., Dec. 6, 1934, copy in Lomax papers.

28. Macmillan to JAL, Dec. 12, 1934; a draft of Lomax's response, penciled at the bottom, is undated but was probably sent several days later (he added "Sorry for the delay").

29. Macmillan to JAL, Dec. 19, 1934.

30. JAL to RTL, Jan. 3, 1934.

31. Bedichek to JAL, Aug. 13, 1934.

32. AL to JAL, undated.

33. Sandburg to JAL, Sept. 29, 1934.

34. Reed Smith to JAL, Dec. 13, 1934.

35. George L. Selby, Acting Principal Keeper, New Jersey State Prison, to JAL, Dec. 5, 1934.

36. JAL to RTL, Dec. [11], 1934.

37. JAL to RTL, prob. Dec. 12 or 13, 1934.

38. JAL, *ABH,* pp. 152–56 passim.

39. JAL to RTL, Dec. 20, 1934.

40. JAL to RTL, Dec. 26, 1934.

41. Tom B. Blocker to JAL, Dec. 6, 1934.

42. L. E. Widen to JAL, Nov. 8, 1934.

43. JAL to RTL, Dec. 27, 1934.

44. Townsend Scudder III to JAL, Oct. 31, 1934.

45. *Proceedings of the Annual Meeting of the Modern Language Association, 1934,* pp. 1324–25.

46. Untitled ledger sheets in the Lomax papers, CAH. Lomax kept detailed accounts of transactions relating to Leadbelly from the time they arrived in Philadelphia. To RTL on Dec. 29 he rounded off the "take" from the hat collection to "47.50," substantially in agreement with the figure recorded in the ledger. Initially, all money from the hat collections went to Leadbelly, but the ledger sheets indicate that after about the middle of January, there was a three-way split between Leadbelly, Lomax, and Alan.

47. JAL, *ABH,* p. ix.

48. JAL to RTL, Dec. 29, 1934.

49. JAL to RTL, Dec. 30, 1934.

50. JAL to RTL, Dec. 29 and 30, 1934. The Bryn Mawr appearance is not well documented because it took place during the Christmas holidays; students were

away and the school paper was not being published. In *NFSLB,* Lomax indicates that the event took place on the evening of the same day (Saturday) that he gave his paper at MLA, but considerable evidence confirms that it was on Sunday, Dec. 30.

51. Leadbelly's hat collections were not frowned upon by all elements of culture and refinement. Writing to Lomax to arrange their appearance at the Booksellers League Dinner, Margaret Conklin, Macmillan editor and an enlightened liberal of the day, pointed out that there would be as many as 125 people in attendance and observed that "Leadbelly should be able to make quite a little with such a group when he passes his hat" (Conklin to JAL, Jan. 11, 1935). My account of the Janice Reed Lit affair is constructed from her original invitation to JAL, Dec. 19, 1934; JAL to RTL, Dec. 29 and 30, 1934; and Lit to JAL, Jan. 1, 1935, on which he has underlined her remark about the hat collection and written, "This finishes her!" Her later inquiry, dated Jan. 8, 1935, and torn apart, is also in CAH.

Chapter 21: Yankee Doodle

1. JAL and AL, *NFSLB,* p. 35.
2. Ibid., p. 10.
3. *New York Herald Tribune,* Jan. 3, 1935; *Time,* Jan. 14, 1935, p. 30; *Brooklyn Daily Eagle,* Jan. 17, 1935.
4. JAL to RTL, Jan. 3, 1935. As for Lomax's use of what has now become an epithet, one is reminded that the context was more than half a century ago; moreover, as he himself carefully pointed out in print, it was a word that Leadbelly habitually used in reference to himself and other blacks.
5. JAL and AL, *NFSLB,* p. 48.
6. Barnicle to JAL, Sept. 15, 1933; see also Barnicle to JAL, Nov. 15, 1934.
7. Barnicle to JAL, Nov. 15, 1934. The birthdate of Mary Elizabeth Barnicle, who died in 1979, is unknown. It has been given variously as "ca. 1898" and "the late 1890's" (*Tennessee Folklore Society Bulletin* 52, no. 2 [Summer 1986]: 1, 34). The index to her papers at the Schlesinger Library at Radcliffe states that she was born "in about 1891," placing her in her mid-forties in 1934. Thus Lomax's estimate of "about fifty" seems reasonably accurate; in a letter dated Sept. 16, 1935, Zora Neale Hurston also refers to Barnicle as "a fifty year old woman."
8. *New Yorker,* Jan. 19, 1935, p. 40.
9. JAL to RTL, Jan. 3 and Jan. 15, 1935.
10. Joseph Utay to JAL, July 8, 1935.
11. JAL to RTL, "Jan. 14" [prob. Jan. 12], 1935.
12. JAL to RTL, Jan. 6, 1935.
13. Ibid.
14. JAL to RTL, Jan. 15, 1935.
15. *New York Herald Tribune,* Jan. 14, 1935, p. 30.

16. JAL to RTL, Jan. 13, 1935.

17. Ibid.

18. JAL to RTL, Jan. 14 and 19, 1935. "Leadbelly at this moment is the most famous Nigger in the world and I am the most notorious white man." JAL to RTL, "Thursday" [prob. Jan. 20, 1935].

19. "Gay Lead Belly in Cinnamon Suit Weds Martha on 45th Birthday," *New York Herald Tribune*, Jan. 21, 1935, p. 30. The lyrics reported in this contemporaneous account differ slightly from those printed two years later by Lomax in *NFSLB*, p. 51.

20. JAL to RTL, "Jan. 13" [prob. Jan. 11], 1935.

21. JAL to RTL, Jan. 8, 1935.

22. JAL to RTL, Jan. 15, 1935.

23. JAL to RTL, Jan. 23, 1935.

24. JAL to RTL, Dec. 20, 1934; Jan. 5 and 15, Feb. 13, 1935.

25. JAL to RTL, Oct. 15, 1934.

26. Houston [Ross], "Early Years of John Lomax," p. 20.

27. See, for example, JAL to RTL, undated [prob. Jan. 25, 1935].

28. See JAL to RTL, Jan. 26 and 27, 1935, as well as an undated letter, prob. Jan. 31: "Alan's script set to a more fetching tune will likely prevail." Examination of scattered pages of the script in the Lomax papers suggests that Lomax provided details (especially for the Marshall meeting, where Alan was absent), Alan drafted the script, possibly in several versions, and then minimal editing was done by the *March of Time* director (perhaps Jack Glenn).

29. JAL to RTL, Feb. 4, 1935.

30. Fielding, *March of Time, 1935–1951*, pp. 69–74.

31. AAFS.Hist., "Report of the Honorary Consultant and Curator," 1934.

32. RTL, "Adventures with the Ballad Hunter," p. 10.

33. Charles Seeger to JAL, Feb. 17, 1944, AFC.JAL.

34. JAL to RTL, undated [prob. Jan. 31, 1935].

35. AL to JAL Jr., Mar. 5, 1935.

36. JAL to RTL, Jan. 26, 1935.

37. JAL to RTL, Mar. 17, 1935.

38. Katy Thompson De Porte, interview with Kip Lornell, Delmar, N.Y., Dec. 20, 1989. (While Mrs. De Porte's account differs somewhat from that of Lomax, who indicated that Martha had already reached Albany with Alan, I believe her version to be more credible. Among the evidence is an entry in Lomax's account book indicating money given to Martha for her bus fare to Albany. I am grateful to Kip Lornell for making available a transcript of his interview with Mrs. De Porte and to Mrs. De Porte for permission to use portions of it.)

39. Ibid.

40. JAL to RTL, "Mar. 24" [prob. Mar. 14 or 15], 1935. See also the *Harvard Crimson*, Mar. 13, 1935, which confuses John and Alan Lomax and contains other errors of fact.

41. JAL to RTL, undated [prob. Mar. 25], Mar. 5 and 7, 1935.
42. JAL to RTL, undated [prob. Mar. 24], and Mar. 17, 1935.
43. JAL to RTL, Feb. 11, 1935.
44. "Entertain Your Crowd," *New Masses,* Nov. 20, 1934, p. 19.
45. "Southerner's Prejudice," *New Masses,* Dec. 11, 1934, pp. 21–22.
46. "Lawrence Gellert's Reply," *New Masses,* Dec. 11, 1934, p. 22.
47. Katy Thompson De Porte, interview with Kip Lornell, Delmar, N.Y., Dec. 20, 1989.
48. JAL to RTL, prob. Mar. 27, 1935; Kimball to JAL, Mar. 16, 1935; JAL, *ABH,* pp. 151–52.
49. JAL to Carnegie Corporation, Jan. 26, 1935. In addition to plans for a complete bibliography of commercially recorded folk music and consolidating all existing folksong collections within the Library of Congress, he proposed to outfit a trailer to serve as sleeping quarters and recording lab, which he would take to Negro, Cajun, and Mexican communities all over the country for extensive recording sessions.
50. JAL to RTL, undated [prob. Mar. 22, 1935].
51. JAL to RTL, undated [prob. Apr. 1, 1935].
52. Herzog to JAL, Feb. 27 and Mar. 6, 1935.
53. JAL to JAL Jr., July 9, 1934.

Chapter 22: Rambled the Country Early and Late

1. BLH, interview, Washington, D.C., Aug. 2, 1989.
2. Ibid.; SLD, interview, Lubbock, Tex., June 27, 1988; AL to JAL Jr., Mar. 5, 1935.
3. See, for example, JAL to RTL, "Jan. 14" [prob. Jan. 12], 1935.
4. JAL to RTL, Jan. 21, 1935.
5. JAL to RTL, Jan. 13, 1935.
6. RTL to JAL, Jan. 24, 1936.
7. W. G. Johnson to JAL, Jan. 24, 1936.
8. Wire JAL to Sheriff T. R. Hughes, Apr. 5, 1935; wire Hughes to JAL, Apr. 8, 193[5] (misdated 1939).
9. JAL to EC, Sept. 5, 1935.
10. A. E. Satherley to AL, May 5, 1935.
11. JAL to AL, July 23, 1940, AFC.LoFam.
12. E. S. Pearce to JAL, May 8, 1935; George P. Brett Jr. to JAL, May 13, 1935.
13. LB to JAL, May 22, 1935.
14. Joseph Utay to JAL, June 11, 1935, with Lomax's note to Alan scribbled at the top. See also Utay to JAL, June 19, 1935.
15. Utay to JAL, July 8, 1935.
16. Leadbelly's "contract," in the form of a letter to JAL, dated Jan. 5, 1935, while in typescript, had blank spaces where key terms were to be entered—the length of the agreement and the percentage which Lomax would receive from Leadbelly's

earnings. These blanks were filled in—perhaps later, as any attorney would argue—in Lomax's hand.

17. Brett to JAL, July 23, 1935.

18. Brett to JAL, Aug. 6, 1935.

19. Crane pointed out that the deal would cost Lomax only $167.67, because Leadbelly gave up his right to one-third of the second $250 which Macmillan was to pay upon delivery of the manuscript. See JAL to Crane, Aug. 29, Sept. 5 and 9, 1935; Crane to JAL, Sept. 7 and 12, 1935; and Brett to JAL, July 23, Aug. 6, and Sept. 7, 1935.

20. LB to JAL, Dec. 18 and 23, 1935.

21. Brett to JAL, May 19, 1937.

22. Barnicle to JAL, Oct. 1, 1935.

23. Hurston to JAL, July 15, 1935.

24. Barnicle to JAL, July 15, 1935.

25. Hemenway, *Zora Neale Hurston,* p. 212.

26. Barnicle to JAL, July 15, 1935.

27. Hurston to JAL, Aug. 30, 1935.

28. Hurston to JAL, Sept. 16, 1935.

29. Barnicle to JAL, Oct. 1, 1935.

30. JAL to RTL, Mar. 16, 1935.

31. RTL to JAL, Oct. 3, 1935.

32. JAL to RTL, prob. Mar. 27, 1935.

33. Lomax treasured the phrase so much that he used it in dedicating *Our Singing Country* to Will Hogg.

34. JAL to AL, July 23, 1940, AFC.LoFam.

35. Herzog to JAL, June 16, 1935; Waters to JAL, Apr. 10, 1935.

36. JAL to RTL, "Jan. 10" [prob. Jan. 31], 1935; JAL to Carnegie Corp., Jan. 26, 1935.

37. Hight to JAL, May 19, 1935; JAL to RTL, [prob. July 3], 1935. See also "Old Ranch Spirit Rules Stamford Cowboy Reunion/Governor Allred, Will Rogers, and John Lomax Are among Guests," *Dallas Morning News,* July 4, 1935, p. 1.

38. JAL to RTL, undated [prob. Oct. 19, 1935].

39. JP to JAL, Oct. 29, 1935.

40. JAL to JAL Jr., Sept. 27, 1935.

41. Pleading that "Barnicle and I are broke," Conklin dunned Lomax for payment above what he had already made for cleaning and utilities, complaining that the occupants had used excessive electricity and left the place a mess (RTL to JAL, June 9, 1936).

42. Conklin to JAL, Mar. 21 and May 10, 1935.

43. JAL to RTL, prob. Jan. 4, 1936.

44. JAL to RTL, Feb. 13, 1936.

45. JAL to RTL, undated.

46. JAL, *ABH,* pp. 289–93.

47. JAL to RTL, Jan. 24, 1936.
48. JAL to RTL, Jan. 5, 1936.
49. JAL to RTL, prob. Mar. 7, 1936.
50. JAL to RTL, Nov. 27, 1936.
51. James Baker to JAL, Dec. 24, 1935.
52. In fact, Iron Head couldn't have stolen the car, for he never learned to drive, despite Lomax's comical efforts to teach him. "Folk Song Seeker's 'Big House' Loan Nearly Returned by Police," *Fort Worth Star-Telegram,* Apr. 8, 1936. See also JAL, *ABH,* p. 176.
53. JAL to RTL, prob. Apr. 8, 1936.
54. JAL to JAL Jr., Apr. 10, 1936.
55. JAL to JAL Jr., prob. Apr. 10, 1936.
56. JAL to JAL Jr., Apr. 14, 1936.
57. RTL to JAL, Apr. 17, 1936.
58. JAL to RTL, Apr. 16, 1936.
59. JAL to RTL, prob. Mar. 14, 1936.
60. RTL to JAL, May 6, 1936.
61. JAL to RTL, May 15, 1936.
62. JAL to RTL, May 10, 1936.
63. JAL to RTL, May 17, 1936.
64. JAL, *ABH,* p. 176.
65. JAL to RTL, May 19, 1936.
66. JAL to RTL, May 22, 1936. See also JAL, *ABH,* pp. 176–77.
67. He supposedly held on to Lomax's arm and prayed silently as they drove along (JAL, *ABH,* p. 176). At the time, Lomax reported merely that in New York, Iron Head gave him so many directions—"more . . . than my entire family"—that he had to make him shut up (JAL to RTL, May 26, 1936).
68. JAL to RTL, May 26, 1936.
69. JAL to RTL, May 29, 1936.
70. JAL to RTL, May 26, 1936.
71. JAL to RTL, May 23, 1936.
72. JAL, *ABH,* p. 177.
73. JAL to RTL, June 4, 1936.
74. JAL to RTL, June 1, 1936.
75. JAL, *ABH,* p. 175. In 1941, a chastened Iron Head told Lomax, "Crime don't pay. I'm walking the straight road now and won't turn back" (JAL to AL, Oct. 9, 1941, AFC.LoFam).

Chapter 23: White House Blues

1. OS to JAL, July 12, 1934; "indifference" is from a loose typescript page in CAH, apparently part of an early draft of *ABH.*
2. OS to JAL, Oct. 1, 1934.

3. JAL to Robert W. Lester, Carnegie, Nov. 26, 1935, with attached memo; OS to Herbert Putnam, Nov. 29, 1935, AFC.JAL (copy in CAH).

4. Herbert Putnam to JAL, Apr. 2, 1935, AFC.JAL.

5. JAL to JAL Jr., May 4, 1936.

6. JAL to RTL, May 23, 1936.

7. JAL to RTL, prob. June 29, 1936.

8. JAL to RTL, June 2, 1936.

9. JAL to RTL, May 23 and June 3, 1936.

10. JAL to RTL, June 3, 1936.

11. JAL to RTL, June 5, 1936. Lomax mistakenly refers to the Librarian as "Evans" but it was clearly Putnam. Luther Evans was at that time the head of the Historical Records Survey of the WPA and did not become Librarian of Congress until 1945.

12. JAL to RTL, June 5, 1936.

13. JAL to RTL, June 12, 1936.

14. Mangione, *Dream and the Deal,* p. 265.

15. As Mangione points out (ibid., p. 47) the Historical Records Survey was originally part of the Federal Writers' Project but early in 1936 had become an independent unit. Their functions were interrelated, however, and the two operations continued to work closely together. From the beginning, it was probably understood that they would share Lomax—Alsberg was present when Evans offered him the job—but the salary and his initial assignments came from the Historical Records Survey. Later, his time was almost entirely taken up by the Federal Writers' Project.

16. JAL to RTL, June 12, 1936; RTL to JAL, June 14, 1936.

17. JAL to RTL, June 12, 1936 (second letter of that date; "Later").

18. Mangione, *Dream and the Deal,* pp. 71–72.

19. JAL to RTL, prob. June 26, 1936.

20. Quoted in Mangione, *Dream and the Deal,* p. 263.

21. Ibid., p. 266.

22. Ibid., p. 268.

23. JAL to RTL, prob. June 26, 1936.

24. JAL to Alsberg, undated (prob. fall 1936 or early 1937), AFC.Jal. The same episode, somewhat sanitized, appears in JAL, *ABH,* pp. 149–51.

25. JAL to Allred, Oct. 29, 1936. Lomax probably did not help his cause by addressing the letter to "James *L.* Allred," when any Texas schoolchild could have told him that the governor's middle initial was V.

26. JAL to RTL, prob. June 29, 1936.

27. JAL to RTL, June 12, 1936.

28. Henry Cowell described Seeger: "He is personally a bundle of contradictions; but where a majority of people are self-contradictory without suspecting themselves of it, he knows it of himself and is satisfied! All his vagaries are quite

self-conscious. He is outstandingly (and to many people obnoxiously) intellectual, but with a leaning toward sentimental outpouring. Here again he sees the tendency in himself plainly, but instead of frowning on it as a thing to be hidden, he takes prankish delight in it" (quoted in Pescatello, *Charles Seeger,* p. 281).

29. Charles Seeger, "Reminiscences of an American Musicologist," pp. 242–43. For other biographical accounts of Seeger, see Reuss, "Folk Music and Social Conscience"; Green, "Resettlement Administration Song Sheet"; Dunaway, *How Can I Keep from Singing,* pp. 26–50 passim.

30. Sidney Robertson Cowell, telephone interview, Shady, N.Y., July 30, 1990.

31. Dunaway, *How Can I Keep from Singing,* p. 26; Pescatello, *Charles Seeger,* p. 9.

32. Sidney Robertson Cowell, telephone interview, Shady, N.Y., July 30, 1990.

33. JAL to RTL, June 9, 1936.

34. Sidney Robertson Cowell, telephone interview, Shady, N.Y., July 30, 1990.

35. JAL to RTL, June 2, 1936.

36. JAL to RTL, prob. June 18, 1936.

37. JAL to RTL, June 11, 1936. Among his other accomplishments, Otto Praeger had been in charge of establishing the U.S. Air Mail Service, which made its maiden flight in 1918.

38. "Carnegie Corporation Project: Harold Spivacke," p. 9.

39. My account of Spivacke's recording trip with Lomax is compiled from JAL, *ABH,* pp. 156–59; "Carnegie Corporation Project: Harold Spivacke," p. 9; and JAL to RTL, June 18, 1936.

40. Sidney Robertson Cowell, telephone interview, Shady, N.Y., July 30, 1990; Seeger to JAL, Feb. 17, 1944.

41. JAL to RTL, prob. July 14, 1936.

42. JAL to RTL, prob. July 14, 17, and 21, 1936.

43. AAFS.Hist., "Report of the Honorary Consultant and Curator," 1936 and 1937.

44. Quoted by JAL in a letter to SLM, July 8, 1936.

45. JAL to BL, Sept. 20, 1936.

46. "Carnegie Corporation Project: Harold Spivacke," p. 7.

47. JAL to RTL, Sept. 14, prob. Sept. 17, Sept. 24, prob. Sept. 25, and prob. Sept. 29, 1936.

48. JAL to RTL, Oct. 4, 1936.

49. JAL to JAL Jr., Sept. 25, 1936.

50. JAL to Clarence Weller, M.D., Oct. 6, 1936. Weller's reply is written on the back.

51. JAL to RTL, Oct. 13, 1936.

52. JAL to RTL, Oct. 26, 1936.

53. Herbert Putnam to Dr. H. T. Parlin, Sept. 26, 1936, AFC.LoFam.

54. JAL to RTL, Nov. 11, 1936.

55. JAL to AL, June 8, 1938, AFC.LoFam.

56. JAL to RTL, Nov. [10], 1936. Misdated Nov. 3 by a later hand.

57. JAL to RTL, Nov. 15, 1936.

58. JP to JAL, July 15, 1936, and wire, July 23, 1936. Alan Lomax blamed Herzog for the title change. It was, he said, part of a compromise "imposed to satisfy Herzog's academic fears" (Herzog doubted the folk authenticity of much of Leadbelly's material). In any event, the title change, said Alan, "helped kill the book." Wolfe and Lornell, *Life and Legend of Leadbelly,* p. 195.

59. JAL to RTL, prob. Nov. 22, 1936.

60. Quoted as a "full-page review" in the *New York Times* in Wolfe and Lornell, *Life and Legend of Leadbelly,* p. 196. Examination of the *New York Times Index* and a search through editions of 1935, 1936, and 1937 has failed to disclose this review. It probably appeared in another metropolitan paper. A review of *NFSLB* by R. Emmet Kennedy appeared in the *New York Times Book Review* on Dec. 29, 1935.

61. Harry Hansen, *New York World Telegram,* Nov. 25, 1936.

62. *Saturday Review of Literature,* Dec. 5, 1936.

63. Undated, unidentified fragment in CAH, possibly part of an early draft for *ABH.* For a review typical of those critical of Herzog's musical notation, see "The 'King of the Twelve-String Guitar Players,'" *New York Times Book Review,* Dec. 29, 1935.

64. The "unearned balance" was $152.83, or, as Lomax explained to Alan, they owed that amount to Macmillan; subtracting it from the $166.66 which was their share of the advance left them with the grand total of $13.83 for all their work on the book, from which Leadbelly had gotten $333.33. In 1938 *Negro Folk Songs as Sung by Leadbelly* sold a pitiful ninety-eight copies, taking the unearned balance down to $119.86. See undated note on the back of royalty statement dated May 1, 1937, and royalty statement dated July 29, 1938. The advance was for $500, but paid in two installments. The first installment of $250 was divided two-thirds ($166.66) to the Lomaxes, one-third ($83.33) to Leadbelly. In effect, all of the second installment went to Leadbelly when Lomax later paid him $250.00 for rights to the book.

65. JAL to RTL, Nov. 27, 1936.

66. JAL to RTL, Nov. 17, 1936.

67. Edward N. Waters, interview, Washington, D.C., Aug. 14, 1989.

68. JAL to RTL, prob. Nov. 22, 1936.

69. Stith Thompson, "John Avery Lomax (1867–1948)," *Journal of American Folklore* 61, no. 241 (1948): 305. Quoted in Bartis, "History of the Archive of Folk Song," p. 112. There is further evidence that Lomax was better received by the MLA than he would admit. When he renewed his dues for 1942, Percy Long, the organization's secretary, wrote him: "Next year in Washington we shall have an Old Guard dinner. You would be a capital decorative feature for that occasion" (Long to JAL, Dec. 9, 1941).

70. RTL to JAL, two letters dated Nov. 24, 1936.

71. JAL to RTL, Nov. 25 and 27, 1936.
72. RTL to JAL, prob. Dec. 16, 1936.

Chapter 24: Ten Thousand Miles from Home

1. AAFS.Hist., "Report of the Honorary Consultant and Curator," 1936, 1937.
2. Bartis, "History of the Archive of Folk Song," p. 69.
3. RTL, "Adventures with the Ballad Hunter," pp. 1 and 5.
4. JAL to RTL, Apr. 20, 1937.
5. JAL to RTL, Apr. 19, 1937.
6. JAL to RTL, prob. Apr. 18, 1937.
7. JAL to HS, Aug. 7, 1937, AFC.JAL.
8. Brown and Owens, *Toting the Lead Row,* p. 14.
9. Lomax spelled it "Doc" Reed; I believe Mrs. Tartt's and Miss Terrill's "Dock" to be more reliable.
10. Brown and Owens, *Toting the Lead Row,* pp. 18–19.
11. AAFS.Hist., "Report of the Honorary Consultant and Curator," 1937.
12. Jon Newsom, interview, Washington, D.C., June 19, 1990.
13. Ibid.
14. JAL to HS, Aug. 7, 1937, AFC.JAL.
15. "Carnegie Corporation Project: Harold Spivacke," passim.
16. JAL to HS, Aug. 7, 1937, AFC.JAL.
17. JAL to JAL Jr., Jan. 26, 1937.
18. JAL to JAL Jr., June 13, 1937.
19. JAL to HS, Aug. 7, 1937, AFC.JAL.
20. See AL to JAL, May 26, 1937, AFC.LoFam.
21. "Proceedings of the Forty-Ninth Annual Meeting of the American Folklore Society," *Journal of American Folklore* 51 (1938), 103. See also Mangione, *Dream and the Deal,* p. 276.
22. JAL, "Songs We Sing and Tales We Tell," p. 19 (a laudatory review of Botkin's *Treasury of American Folklore,* in which Lomax recounts the 1937 AFS meeting).
23. "Proceedings of the Fiftieth Annual Meeting of the American Folklore Society," *Journal of American Folklore* 52 (1939), 209.
24. Preece to JAL, Dec. 17, 1936; JAL to Preece, Dec. 23, 1936.
25. JAL to JAL Jr., Jan. 26, 1937.
26. This figure did not include the Leadbelly book, which as late as 1942 still had a negative balance of $73.82 (JP to AL, Feb. 6, 1942, AFC.LoFam). Royalties from *Negro Songs as Sung by Leadbelly* would never equal the advance Macmillan had paid.
27. BL to AL, "Friday" (Feb. 11, 1938), AFC.LoFam.
28. JAL to SLM, Feb. 24 and Mar. 7, 1938, AFC.JAL.
29. BLH, interview, Washington, D.C., Aug. 2, 1989.

30. JAL to SLM, Mar. 7, 1938, AFC.JAL.

31. BL to AL, Mar. 7 and 23, 1938, AFC.LoFam.

32. BLH, interview, Washington, D.C., Aug. 2, 1989.

33. JAL to HS, Apr. 12, 1938, AFC.JAL.

34. BLH, interview, Washington, D.C., Aug. 2, 1989. Ironically, part of his original plan for the European trip was "to arrange syndicated letters that ought to sell for real money" (JAL to JAL Jr., June 11, 1937). There is no evidence that he ever attempted to make such an arrangement.

35. JAL to HS, Apr. 12, 1938, AFC.JAL.

36. JAL to AL, May 10, 1938, AFC.JAL; AL to JAL, May 26, 1938, AFC.LoFam.

37. BL to AL, May 11, 1938, AFC.LoFam; see also BL to AL, June 24, 1938, and various undated letters, AFC.LoFam.

38. BLH, interview, Washington, D.C., Aug. 2, 1989.

39. JAL to AL, June 29, 1938, AFC.LoFam.

40. JAL, "Call Me at Red River," p. 224.

41. JAL to AL, Oct. 31, 1938, AFC.LoFam.

42. JAL to HS, Dec. 13, 1938, AFC.JAL; JAL to JAL Jr., Nov. 25, 1938.

43. JAL to AL, Oct. 31, 1938, AFC.LoFam.

44. JAL to AL, Dec, 19, 1938, AFC.LoFam.

45. HS to JAL, Dec. 19, 1938, AFC.JAL.

46. JAL to RTL, prob. Dec. 5, 1936.

47. See esp. JAL to AL, Dec. 15, 1937, AFC.LoFam.

48. JAL to HS, Mar. 6, 1941, AFC.JAL. Quoted by Bartis, "History of the Archive of Folk Song," p. 67.

49. HS to JAL, Dec. 19, 1939, AFC.JAL.

50. JAL to HS, Jan. 15, 1939, AFC.JAL.

51. JAL to HS, Feb. 7, 1939, AFC.JAL.

52. JAL to HS, Mar. 12, 1939, AFC.JAL; HS to the Librarian, June 27, 1939, AFC.LC.

53. JAL to AL, Mar. 12, 1939, AFC.LoFam.

54. JAL to HS, Mar. 11, 1939, AFC.JAL.

55. JP to JAL, Jan. 12, 1939, AFC.LoFam. As finally published after much wrangling, the book ran 416 pages.

56. JAL to AL, Jan. 15, 1939, AFC.LoFam.

57. JAL to AL, Feb. 2, 1939, AFC.LoFam.

58. JAL to AL, undated but clearly of this period, AFC.LoFam.

59. JAL to AL, Mar. 21, 1939, AFC.LoFam.

60. Ibid.

Chapter 25: Home on the Range

1. RTL, "Adventures with the Ballad Hunter," p. 7.

2. Frank Goodwyn, interview, Washington, D.C., June 15, 1990.

3. JAL to Maybank, June 30, [1939] (misdated 1941 by another hand).

4. AAFS.Hist., "Report of the Honorary Consultant and Curator," 1939. My account of the trip is compiled from various letters and the report filed by Miss Terrill (copy in CAH).

5. JAL to JAL Jr., July 14, 1939.

6. "Carnegie Corporation Project: Harold Spivacke," p. 9.

7. JAL to AL, dated only "Sunday" (prob. Aug. 20, 1939), AFC.LoFam.

8. JAL to AL, Aug. 26 and 28, 1939, AFC.LoFam.

9. JAL to HS, Oct. 10, 1939, AFC.JAL.

10. JAL to AL, Oct. 2, 1939 (note from RTL on back of last page), AFC.LoFam.

11. JAL to AL, Feb. 15, 1940, AFC.LoFam.

12. JAL to AL, Apr. 25, 1940, AFC.LoFam.

13. JAL to AL, May 4, 1940, AFC.LoFam.

14. Undated fragment, prob. to AL and dated by internal evidence Oct. 1939, AFC.LoFam.

15. JAL to AL, Oct. 24, 1939, AFC.LoFam.

16. JAL to AL, Nov. 10, 1939, AFC.LoFam.

17. JAL to AL, Nov. 12 and 18, 1939, AFC.LoFam.

18. Weeks to JAL, Sept. 12, 1939.

19. Cobb to JAL, Oct. 16, 1939; Mike Hogg to JAL, Nov. 29, 1939.

20. JAL to AL, Mar. 16, 1940, AFC.LoFam.

21. JAL to AL, Nov. 27, 1939, AFC.LoFam.

22. JAL to AL, Dec. 6, 1939, AFC.LoFam.

23. JAL to AL, Nov. 10, 1939; AL to Dean Manning, Bryn Mawr, Dec. 9, 1939, JAL to JAL Jr., Jan. 2, 1940, all AFC.LoFam; RTL to AL, Dec. 13, 1939.

24. HS to JAL, Jan. 16, 1940; JAL to HS, Jan. 17, 1940, AFS.JAL.

25. JAL to AL, Feb. 13, 1940, AFC.LoFam.

26. JAL to AL, Jan. 12, 1940, AFC.LoFam.

27. JAL to AL, Mar. 26 and Oct. 17, 1939, AFC.LoFam.

28. JAL to AL, Mar. 18, 1940, AFC.LoFam.

29. JAL to JAL Jr., July 17, 1940.

30. JAL to AL, July 29, 1940, AFC.LoFam.

31. SLM to JAL, undated.

32. JAL to AL, June 12, 1940, AFC.LoFam.

33. JP to JAL, Oct. 18, 1939, Apr. 4 and May 1, 1940.

34. JAL to JAL Jr., May 15, 1940.

35. Pool to JAL, May 28, 1940.

36. Connally to JAL, Aug. 18, 1940.

37. JAL to AL, May 44, 1940, AFC.LoFam.

38. HS to the Librarian, July 5, 1940, AFC.JAL.

39. Written at the top of a letter from his father dated Aug. 7, 1940, AFC.LoFam.

40. JAL to JAL Jr., Feb. 28, 1940.

41. JAL to JAL Jr., June 1, 1940.

42. JAL to AL, Jan. 28, 1940, AFC.LoFam.; JP to JAL, Apr. 4, 1940.

43. JAL to AL, Mar. 22, 1939, AFC.LoFam.

44. JAL to AL, June 1, 1940, AFC.LoFam.; *ABH,* p. 296. According to Dunaway, *How Can I Keep from Singing,* p. 48, Ruth Crawford Seeger "transcribed with a maniacal precision."

45. RCS to JAL, July 30, 1940.

46. JAL to AL, Aug. 2, 1940, AFC.LoFam.

47. JAL to AL, Aug. 22, 1940, AFC.LoFam.

48. JP to JAL, Aug. 8, 1940, and Sept. 30, 1940.

49. JAL to AL, Sept. 1, 1940, AFC.LoFam.

50. BL to AL, undated; AL to BL, Sept. 10, 1940, AFC.LoFam.

51. JAL to AL, Oct. 28, 1940, AFC.LoFam.

52. JAL to AL, Nov. 8, 1940, AFC.LoFam.

53. JAL to HS, Dec. 19, 1940, AFC.JAL; RTL to HS, Feb. 7, 1941. Mileage and itinerary are compiled from the undated report of RTL in CAH.

54. RCS to JAL, Oct. 7, 1940.

55. JAL to JP, Nov. 19, 1940.

Chapter 26: Pass around Your Bottle

1. For Faulk's account of these events, see his *Fear on Trial.*

2. Faulk's remarks about Lomax were made to me in an interview in Austin on Mar. 10, 1988, and to James McNutt in the interview published in *Folklife Annual 1987* (pp. 106–29). There is considerable overlap between the two; with the generous permission of Dr. McNutt, I have in places combined comments from both interviews and edited Faulk's remarks in the interest of brevity.

3. As it happened, Andrew Jackson Houston died three months after taking office; a special election was held, and O'Daniel won over a large field of candidates, including young Congressman Lyndon Johnson.

4. *Dallas Morning News,* Sept. 7, 1941, p. 12.

5. Dobie to Bedichek, Feb. 15, 1948, in Owens, *Three Friends,* p. 184.

6. McNutt, "John Henry Faulk: An Interview," p. 126.

7. Johnson to JAL, undated. The letter has been postdated "1937," probably by Miss Terrill and probably because that was the year of Bessie Smith's death. There is good reason to believe that Johnson's letter was written ca. Oct. 1941. At that time, on receiving a copy of the letter from his father, Alan said "it looks like you won the argument," but added that, based on the evidence, it was still not clear whether Bessie Smith had been turned away from a white hospital before being admitted to a Negro one (AL to JAL, Oct. 17, 1941, AFC.LoFam). See also JAL to B. A. Botkin, Aug. 4, 1943; Luther Evans to Botkin, Sept. 10, 1943; and Botkin to JAL, Sept. 29, 1943, all AFC.JAL. Evidence brought to light years later tends to sup-

port Lomax's contention that Bessie Smith's death was not the result of her having been refused admission to a white hospital. See Chris Albertson, *Bessie* (New York: Stein and Day, 1972), pp. 215–26.

8. JAL to AL, Oct. 10, 1941, AFC.LoFam. See also JAL to AL, Oct. 11, 1941, AFC.LoFam.

9. JAL to AL, Oct. 9, 1941, AFC.LoFam.

10. Ibid.

11. Abernathy, *Texas Folklore Society,* p. 263.

12. Stanley Marcus to JAL, Apr. 18, 1941.

13. JAL to Dobie, Sept. 22, 1941; Dobie to JAL, Oct. 1, 1941, TFS.

14. JAL to AL, Aug. 31, 1941, AFC.LoFam.

15. JAL to AL, Sept. 29, 1941, AFC.LoFam.

16. JAL to AL, May 15, 1940, AFC.LoFam.

17. AL to JAL, Nov. 13, 1941, AFC.LoFam.

18. JAL to AL, Dec. 4, 1941, AFC.LoFam.

19. AL to JAL, Nov. 13, 1941, AFC.LoFam. The Burl Ives controversy is further detailed in AL to JAL, Sept. 16, 1941; JAL to AL, Oct. 16, 1941; JAL to AL, Nov. 9, 1941; JAL to AL, Nov. 18, 1941; and AL to JAL, Nov. 19, 1941, all in AFC.LoFam.

20. JAL to AL, Oct. 16, 1941, AFC.LoFam.

21. JAL to AL, Dec. 15, 1938, AFC.LoFam.

22. JAL to AL, Oct. 16, 1941, AFC.LoFam.

23. Tartt to JAL, Nov. 3, 1941. So concerned was Lomax over Mrs. Tartt's finances that he offered, uncharacteristically, to pay all her traveling expenses for the projected trip (JAL to AL, Oct. 28, 1941, AFC.LoFam).

24. Prink to JAL, Apr. 1, 1941.

25. George Brett to JAL and AL, Apr. 8, 1941. The case of "Alla en el Rancho Grande" was settled amicably. The Lomaxes got it from Dobie, who had innocently published it as a "traditional" song in a Texas Folklore Society publication. Dobie, Macmillan, and Lomax all disowned it and denied evil intent, Marks asked for and got a modest reprint fee, and a credit line was inserted in the next edition.

26. JP to JAL, Oct. 30, 1941; draft reply JAL to JP, on back, n.d.; JP to JAL, Oct. 31, 1941, AFC.LoFam.

27. Louise Pound, *Saturday Review,* Jan. 3, 1942, p. 10.

28. *New York Times Book Review,* Dec. 28, 1941, p. 4.

29. Wilbert Snow, *Books,* Dec. 11, 1941, p. 7.

30. A. B. Guthrie Jr., *Lexington Herald Leader,* Dec. 28, 1941.

31. Lewis Gannett, *New York Herald Tribune,* Dec. 28, 1941.

32. Archibald MacLeish, Introduction to JAL, *Our Singing Country,* p. vii.

33. MacLeish to JAL, Oct. 31, 1941, AFC.LoFam.

34. RCS to JAL, Dec. 11, 1941.

35. RCS to JAL, Mar. 6, 1942.

36. JP to JAL, Jan. 28, 1942.

37. RCS to JAL, Mar. 22, 1942.

38. JAL to AL, Mar. 25, 1942, and Apr. 28, 1942, AFC.LoFam.

39. JAL to AL, Apr. 28, AFC.LoFam.

40. RCS to JAL, Nov. 13, 1943, and Nov. 21, 1944.

41. Sidney Robertson Cowell, telephone interview, Shady, N.Y., July 30, 1990. For details of the "vague financial arrangement," see RCS to JAL, Aug. 18, 1937.

42. John Henry Faulk, interview, Austin, Tex., Mar. 10, 1988.

43. Frank Goodwyn, interview, Washington, D.C., June 15, 1990.

44. JAL to AL, Dec. 3, 1941, AFC.LoFam.; Frank Goodwyn, interview, Washington, D.C., June 15, 1990.

45. Frank Goodwyn, interview, Washington, D.C., June 15, 1990.

46. Ibid.; John Henry Faulk, interview, Austin, Tex., Mar. 10, 1988.

47. Pete Seeger, interview, Beacon, N.Y., Aug. 6, 1992.

48. RTL to SLM, Feb. 3, 1942.

49. BLH, interview, Washington, D.C., Aug. 2, 1989.

50. JAL to AL, June 6, 1942, AFC.LoFam.

51. RTL to BL, May 19, 1942, AFC.LoFam.; RTL to SLM, Oct. 20, 1942.

52. JAL to AL, Feb. 6, 1942, and Mar. 17, 1942, AFC.LoFam.

53. JAL to AL, Mar. 17, 1942, AFC.LoFam.

54. Evans to Tire Rationing Board, Dallas, Feb. 17, 1942; Evans to Leon Henderson, OPA, Mar. 4, 1942.

55. JAL to AL, June 3, 1942, AFC.LoFam.

56. HS to JAL, Jan. 21, 1943.

57. JAL to AL, Mar. 6 and June 13, 1942, AFC.LoFam.

58. Emrich to JAL, Mar. 28, 1947, AFC.LoFam. Lomax's recording trip in the late summer and early fall of 1942 was probably his last formal expedition, but there was never a clear conclusion to his relationship with the Archive of American Folk Song. Bartis ("History of the Archive of Folk Song," p. 125) indicates that "with Alan's resignation [in October 1942], John Lomax's Honorary Curatorship passed as well," but Lomax was still using the title publicly as late as 1945. Miss Terrill later asserted that he was "Honorary Curator [of the Archive] at the time of his death" ("Adventures with the Ballad Hunter," p. 5). Clearly, no one at the Library of Congress ever felt it necessary to withdraw a largely honorific title which, after all, had been loosely bestowed in the beginning.

59. JAL to AL, Mar. 19, 1942, AFC.LoFam.

60. Ibid.

61. Siegmeister to JAL, Sept. 22, 1944.

62. Morris to Marcelle Lively Hamer, Oct. 14, 1945, TFS.

63. Day's *Reader's Digest* article was a condensation of a longer one which had been published in *Saturday Review,* Sept. 22, 1945, pp. 5–7. Another condensation appeared in the *Kansas City Times,* Oct. 5, 1945, p. 18.

64. Morris to Hamer, Oct. 14, 1945, TFS.

65. W. A. Askew, Secretary, XIT Cowboy's Association, to JAL, Oct. 6, 1945; JAL to Askew, Oct. 17, 1945.

Chapter 27: Look down That Lonesome Road

1. JAL to Rainey, Apr. 14, 1939.

2. Tinkle, *American Original*, p. 175.

3. "Educational Crisis," p. 9.

4. Quoted by EC in a letter to JAL, Apr. 9, 1947.

5. Wasson to JAL, Nov. 10, 1939. At the same time, Wasson predicted that the war in Europe would be over in four months, or certainly in time to forestall Roosevelt's bid for a fourth term. This was the man Lomax cited as "having the keenest mind I have ever known on the *Dallas News*" (JAL to OB, Nov. 22, 1944).

6. JAL to AL, May 21, 1940, AFC.LoFam.

7. JAL to (Ms.) Hal March, May 30, 1945.

8. Ibid.

9. ECB to Harbert Davenport, Sept. 7, 1943, Barker Papers. Quoted by Pool, *Eugene Barker, Historian*, p. 200.

10. JAL to JAL Jr., Aug. 18, 1942.

11. Ibid.

12. JAL to JAL Jr., May 11, 1942, AFC.LoFam.

13. OB to JAL, Mar. 31, 1943.

14. OB to JAL, Aug. 5, 1943; ECB to JAL, Mar. 3, 1945.

15. Dobie to JAL, Apr. 14, 1943.

16. ECB to JAL, Oct. 6, 1944.

17. OB to JAL, Jan. 25, 1943. To his credit, Bullington distinguished between "*permitting* someone to read a book and *requiring* them to do so," but in the same breath he asserted the board's right to prescribe textbooks and tell professors how to conduct their classes (OB to Sam Atcheson, *Dallas News*, Jan. 25, 1943).

18. JAL to OB, Nov. 22, 1944.

19. Ibid.

20. OB to JAL, Jan. 7, 1944.

21. "Educational Crisis," p. 2; see also McNutt, "John Henry Faulk: An Interview," p. 129.

22. "Educational Crisis," p. 5.

23. Bedichek to Webb, Mar. 13, 1945, in Owens, *Three Friends*, p. 74.

24. OB to JAL, Aug. 5, 1943.

25. See also OB to JAL, June 25, 1945.

26. See JAL to John H. Bickett Jr., Sept. 21, 1943, and JAL to D. K. Woodward Jr. Dec. 28, 1944.

27. JAL to OB, Apr. 9 and 15, 1944; OB to JAL, Apr. 13 and 24, 1944.

28. OB to JAL, Apr. 24, 1944.

29. OB to JAL, Sept. 12, 1944.

30. Quoted in (Ms.) Hal March to JAL, June 21, 1945.

31. De Voto, "The Easy Chair," *Harper's,* Aug. 1945, p. 137. Quoted in Goodwyn, *Lone-Star Land,* p. 301. See also *Time,* Nov. 13, 1944, p. 54, and Dec. 2, 1946, p. 70; *New Republic,* Nov. 13, 1944, p. 615, and Dec. 4, 1944, p. 740; *Nation,* July 20, 1946, p. 68; *Colliers,* Jan. 6, 1945, p. 18; *Newsweek,* Nov. 13, 1944, p. 24, Aug. 6, 1945, p. 78, and Sept. 10, 1945, p. 14; *American Mercury,* Oct. 1945, p. 505.

32. OB to JAL, Mar. 17, 1944.

33. "Educational Crisis," p. 5.

34. *Fort Worth Star-Telegram,* Oct. 6, 1943.

35. OB to JAL, Jan. 31, 1945.

36. OB to JAL, Feb. 13, 1945.

37. Haley to JAL, Jan. 8, 1944.

38. Sinclair to JAL, Mar. 9, 1945.

39. See Witt to JAL, Feb. 27, 1945. More than a year after the firing, Roy Bedichek wrote to Frank Dobie, "Edgar Witt was by a week or two ago, drinking and talking very loud. He is obsessed with the Rainey controversy and becomes apoplectic upon mention of *Big Money.* His rage knoweth no bounds. It has been a curious thing that indignation over the 'obscenity' of that book has been in direct proportion to the general looseness and nastiness of the lives of the person who feel the indignation" (Bedichek to Dobie, Dec. 8, 1945, in Owens, *Three Friends,* p. 171).

40. ECB to JAL, May 10, 1945.

41. OB to JAL, Jan. 31, 1945.

42. Unidentified newspaper clipping in CAH. The Bullington-endowed library eventually became the Barker Texas History Center, now a part of the prestigious Center for American History at the University of Texas.

43. Tinkle, *American Original,* p. 202.

44. The text of Webb's resolution appears in Owens, *Three Friends,* pp. 78–79.

45. Webb to EC, Oct. 17, 1947.

46. EC to Robert L. Holliday, June 4, 1945, Lomax Papers.

47. Bedichek to Webb, May 30, 1946, in Owens, *Three Friends,* p. 77.

48. Although "the firing of Dobie" became part of the liberals' litany of shame against the University, even his strongest partisans ultimately conceded that there was no direct evidence that the regents had been "out to get Dobie." It was true, of course, that few of them mourned his departure. See Boatright, "A Mustang in the Groves of Academe," in Dugger, *Three Men in Texas,* pp. 199–200.

49. JAL to Haley, Jan. 1, 1945, Haley Papers.

50. EC to JAL, Apr. 9, 1947.

51. EC to JAL, May 27, 1947.

52. ECB to JAL, June 2, 1947.
53. Dobie to JAL, June 3.
54. OB to JAL, Feb. 8, 1947.
55. OB to JAL, Sept. 2, 1945.
56. Goodwyn, *Lone-Star land,* p. 303.

Chapter 28: When the Work's All Done This Fall

1. JAL to JAL Jr., May 22, 1943. See also JAL to JAL Jr., Apr. 24, 1943.
2. RTL to Carol Hovious, Apr. 12, 1946; Frederick to JAL, Feb. 13, 1942.
3. SLD, interview, Lubbock, Tex., June 27, 1988. J. Frank Dobie's version of this event is in "John Lomax," pp. 10–11.
4. JP to JAL, July 14 and Nov. 20, 1944; JAL to JP, Nov. 25, 1944.
5. Byrd to JAL, Feb. 10, 1944.
6. Edward Sturgis to JAL, Oct. 20, 1944.
7. Lloyd Gregory to JAL, Nov. 22, 1945.
8. JAL to Weatherford College ("Dear Sir"), June 21, 1944.
9. JAL to JAL Jr., Dec. 29, 1944.
10. James A. Dombrowski to JAL, Oct. 20, 1945.
11. J. H. Wilterding to JAL, May 15, 1947.
12. Witt to JAL, Dec. 6, 1947.
13. AL to JAL, June 16, 1942.
14. Emrich to JAL, Nov. 8, 1945. (Only an unsigned carbon exists in this file, but internal evidence clearly indicates that it is from Emrich.) Lomax was still saying that all his papers were "destined ultimately to go to the Harvard Library" (JAL to Russell Holman, Oct. 30, 1945).
15. JAL to JAL Jr., Mar. 18, 1944, on the back of Mrs. Lyle McCaleb to JAL, Mar. 15, 1944.
16. RTL to Tartt, July 4, 1944.
17. See, for example, JAL to Sandburg, Aug. 11, 1945; JAL to Stevenson, Oct. 23, 1942; and various letters from Wendell to JAL, 1941–47.
18. BW Jr. to JAL, Apr. 17, 1944.
19. JAL to Snow, Sept. 18, 1944.
20. Dobie to Bedichek, Sept. 20, 1944, in Owens, *Three Friends,* p. 160.
21. See JAL, "Songs We Sing and Tales We Tell," pp. 18–19; Botkin to JAL, June 30, 1944; Botkin to JAL, Nov. 14, 1944, with JAL's note to AL on back.
22. HS to JAL, Jan. 21, 1943, and Mar. 3, 1944.
23. Evans to JAL, Dec. 19, 1945.
24. HS to JAL, Oct. 29 and Dec. 5, 1946.
25. JAL to Thomas Y. Crowell, Nov. 1, 1945.
26. RCS to JAL, Oct. 18, 1945.

27. JAL to Crowell, Nov. 1, 1945.
28. Arthur Wang to JAL, Nov. 15, 1945.
29. Charles and Ruth Seeger to JAL, Aug. 20, 1946.
30. Thompson to JAL, Jan. 13, 1945.
31. See Turner, "Artist Whose Cowboys Were Based Mostly on Himself," pp. 168–78.
32. Thompson to JAL, July 24, 1945.
33. Thompson to JAL, July 24, 1945, Jan. 9 and Feb. 5, 1946.
34. Day, "John Lomax and His Ten Thousand Songs," p. 71. (A condensation of an earlier piece that had appeared in *Saturday Review* [Sept. 22, 1945], pp. 5–7.)
35. JAL to Leulle O'Neal Mitchell, Nov. 14, 1945.
36. JAL to E. C. Knippers, Oct. 17, 1945.
37. JAL to Horace Reynolds, Dec. 18, 1947, HU.bMS Am 1787 (230).
38. Russell Holman to JAL, Oct. 19, 1945.
39. JAL to Holman, Oct. 23, 1945.
40. Holman to JAL, Oct. 26, 1945; JAL to Holman, Oct. 30 and Nov. 14, 1945; Holman wire to JAL, Nov. 19, 1945; J. S. Polk, Paramount, to JAL, Jan. 18, 1946.
41. BW Jr. to JAL, Nov. 17, 1945.
42. OB to JAL, Nov. 28, 1945.
43. *Dallas Morning News,* Mar. 25, 1946; *Daily Texan* (University of Texas), Apr. 4, 1946.
44. Flanders to AL, May 10, 1946.
45. JAL to JP, Nov 25, 1944.
46. J. S. Polk, Paramount, to JAL, Feb. 1, 1946.
47. JP to JAL, Mar. 21, 1946.
48. JP to JAL, Apr. 25, 1946.
49. Edward Weeks, *Atlantic,* Apr. 1947, p. 146.
50. Horace Reynolds, *New York Times Book Review,* Mar. 2, 1947, p. 7.
51. Bedichek to Dobie, May 8, 1947, in Owens, *Three Friends,* p. 237.
52. Carl Carmer, *New York Herald Tribune Weekly Book Review,* Mar. 9, 1947, p. 1.
53. J. H. Jackson, *San Francisco Chronicle,* Feb. 20, 1947, p. 16.
54. JAL to Foley, July 4, 1945; Tartt to JAL, June 29, 1945.
55. Republic National Bank to Mike Stephens, June 25, 1947.
56. JAL Jr. to JAL, Nov. 5, 1945; JAL to JAL Jr., Oct. 21, 1947.
57. ECB to JAL, Apr. 10, 1944.
58. JAL to JAL Jr., Apr. 28, 1943.
59. Alex Terrell, M.D., to JAL, Feb. 3, 1947.
60. JAL to RTL, Aug. 11, 1947.
61. JAL to RTL, Aug. 11 and 12, 1947.
62. RTL to JAL, Aug. 9, 1947; JAL to RTL, Aug. 12, 1947.
63. JAL to RTL, Aug. 12, 1947.
64. Cason to JAL, Jan. 14, 1948.

65. Hodding Carter, "John Lomax, Famed Ballad Hunter, Dies," *Delta Democrat-Times* (Greenville, Miss.), Jan. 27, 1948. See also "Ballad Hunter John Lomax Dies," *White Rocker* (Dallas, Tex.), Jan. 29, 1948 (clippings in CAH). The song Lomax sang is entitled simply "Rosie" in *AB&FS* (pp. 62–65).

66. The story of Dock Reed's response to Lomax's death appears, in much greater length, in Brown and Owens, *Toting the Lead Row,* pp. 46–52.

Sources

Manuscripts and Archives

Archive of Folk Culture, American Folklife Center, Library of Congress
John A. Lomax Papers
Lomax Family Papers
Draft Annual Reports, 1941–74
Center for American History, University of Texas
E. C. Barker Papers
Lomax Family Papers
Texas Folklore Society Archives
Edwin Seymour Nichols Papers
Houghton Library, Harvard University
Le Baron Russell Briggs Papers
George Lyman Kittredge Papers
Amy Lowell Papers
Barrett Wendell Papers
Diaries of Mrs. Barrett Wendell
Schlesinger Library, Radcliffe College
Mary Elizabeth Barnicle Cadle Papers

Interviews and Oral Histories

"Carnegie Corporation Project: Harold Spivacke." Carnegie Corporation of New York. Oral History. Oral History Research Office, Columbia University, 1969. Transcript in the Music Division of the Library of Congress.

Cowell, Sidney Robertson. Shady, N.Y., July 30, 1990.

De Porte, Katy Thompson (interviewed by Kip Lornell). Delmar, N.Y., Dec. 20, 1989.

Duggan, Shirley Lomax. Lubbock, Tex., June 27, 1988, and May 15, 1989.

Faulk, John Henry. Austin, Tex., June 8, 1987, and Mar. 10, 1988.

Goodwyn, Frank. Washington, D.C., June 15, 1990.

Hawes, Bess Lomax. Washington, D.C., Aug. 2, 1989, and Feb. 19, 1992.
Newsom, Jon. Washington, D.C., June 19, 1990.
Seeger, Charles. "Reminiscences of an American Musicologist." UCLA Oral History Program, 1972.
Seeger, Pete. Beacon, N.Y., August 6, 1992.
Waters, Mr. and Mrs. Edward N. Washington, D.C., Aug. 14, 1989.

General Sources

Abernethy, Francis E. *The Texas Folklore Society, 1909–1943*. Vol. 1. Denton: University of North Texas Press, 1993.
———, ed. *Corners of Texas*. Denton: University of North Texas Press, 1993.
Ackerman, Carl W. *George Eastman*. Boston: Houghton Mifflin Co., 1930. Reprint. Clifton, N.J.: Augustus M. Kellog, 1973.
Adams, Henry H. *Harry Hopkins*. New York: G. P. Putnam's Sons, 1977.
Anderson, Gillian B. "Putting the Experience of the World at the Nation's Command: Music at the Library of Congress, 1800–1917." *Journal of the American Musicological Society* 42, no. 1 (1989): 108–49.
"Archive of American Folksong: A History, 1928–1938." Washington, D.C.: Library of Congress Project, Works Projects Administration, 1940.
Barnes, Will C. "The Cowboy and His Songs." *Saturday Evening Post*, June 27, 1925, pp. 14, 122–28
Bartis, Peter Thomas. "A History of the Archive of Folk Song at the Library of Congress: The First Fifty Years." Ph.D. diss., University of Pennsylvania, 1982.
Bluestein, Gene. *The Voice of the Folk: Folklore and American Literary Theory*. Amherst: University of Massachusetts Press, 1972.
Brady, Erika. "The Box That Got the Flourishes: The Cylinder Phonograph in Early Ethnographic Fieldwork." Ph.D. diss., Indiana University, 1985.
Brown, Rollo Walter. *Dean Briggs*. New York: Harper & Brothers, 1926.
———. "'Kitty' of Harvard." *Atlantic Monthly* 182, no. 4 (1948): 65–69.
Brown, Virginia Pounds, and Laurella Owens. *Toting the Lead Row: Ruby Pickens Tartt, Alabama Folklorist*. University: University of Alabama Press, 1981.
Carlson, Avis D. "Cowboy Ballads at Our Own Fireside." *Better Homes and Gardens*, Nov. 1931; reprinted in *Reader's Digest*, Dec. 1931, pp. 175–77.
Casey, Paul D. *The History of the A. & M. College Trouble 1908*. Waco, Tex.: J. S. Hill & Co., 1908.
Catalogue of the Officers and Members of Granbury College. Fort Worth, 1886.
Connally, Tom, as told to Alfred Steinberg. *My Name Is Tom Connally*. New York: Thomas Y. Crowell Co., 1954.
Croy, Homer. *Corn Country*. New York: Duell, Sloan & Pearce, 1947.
Darden, Mary Lou Prather. "Grace Hall and the University in the Late Nineties." *Alcalde* 7, no. 7 (Feb. 1920): 611–17.

Day, Donald. "John Lomax and His Ten Thousand Songs." *Reader's Digest,* Oct. 1945, pp. 68–71. Reprinted from *Saturday Review of Literature,* Sept. 22, 1945, pp. 5–7.

Dobie, J. Frank. "John Lomax." In *Sunny Slopes of Long Ago.* Edited by Wilson M. Hudson and Allen Maxwell. Dallas: Southern Methodist Press, 1966.

Dugger, Ronnie, ed. *Three Men in Texas: Bedichek, Webb, and Dobie.* Austin: University of Texas Press, 1967.

Dunaway, David King. *How Can I Keep from Singing: Peter Seeger.* New York: McGraw-Hill Book Co., 1981.

Engel, Carl. "Views and Reviews." *Musical Quarterly* 21 (1935): 107–12.

"An Educational Crisis: Summary of Testimony before a [Texas] Senate Committee Investigating the University of Texas Controversy." Nov. 1944. Lomax Papers, CAH.

Faulk, John Henry. *Fear on Trial.* New York: Simon & Schuster, 1964. Rev. ed., reprint. Austin: University of Texas Press, 1983.

Fehrenback, T. R. *Lone Star: A History of Texas and the Texans.* New York: Macmillan Co., 1968.

Ferguson, Charles W. *Organizing to Beat the Devil.* Garden City, N.Y.: Doubleday & Co., 1971.

Fielding, Raymond. *The March of Time, 1935–51.* New York: Oxford University Press, 1963.

Fiske, Turbese Lummis, and Keith Lummis. *Charles F. Lummis: The Man and His West.* Norman: University of Oklahoma Press, 1975.

Ford, John Salmon. *Rip Ford's Texas.* Edited, with an introduction and commentary, by Stephen B. Oates. Austin: University of Texas Press, 1963.

Frantz, Joe B., and Julian Ernest Choate, Jr. *American Cowboy: The Myth and the Reality.* Norman: University of Oklahoma Press, 1955.

Furman, Necah Stewart. *Walter Prescott Webb: His Life and Impact.* Albuquerque: University of New Mexico Press, 1976.

Goodwyn, Frank. *Lone-Star Land: Twentieth-Century Texas in Perspective.* New York: Alfred A. Knopf, 1955.

Green, Archie. "A Resettlement Administration Song Sheet." *John Edwards Memorial Foundation Quarterly* 11, pt. 2, no. 38 (Summer 1975): 80–84.

Griffen, Clyde, and Sally Griffen. *Natives and Newcomers: The Ordering of Opportunity in Mid-Nineteenth-Century Poughkeepsie.* Cambridge, Mass.: Harvard University Press, 1978.

Hand, Wayland D. *Eyes on Texas: Fifty Years of Folklore in the Southwest.* Austin: Texas Folkore Society, 1967.

Hemenway, Robert. *Zora Neale Hurston: A Literary Biography.* Urbana: University of Illinois Press, 1977.

"His Own Words to Discover His Motives," *Alcalde* 5, no. 8 (Aug. 1917): 697–721.

Hogan, William Ransom. *The Texas Republic: A Social and Economic History.* Norman: University of Oklahoma Press, 1949. Reprint. Austin: University of Texas Press, 1969.

Houston [Ross], Maude. "The Early Years of John A. Lomax." Master's thesis, University of Texas, 1953.

Humphrey, David C. *Austin: An Illustrated History.* Northridge, Calif.: Windsor Publications, 1985.

Hyder, Clyde Kenneth. *George Lyman Kittredge: Teacher and Scholar.* Lawrence: Univerity of Kansas Press, 1962.

Kittredge, George Lyman. Introduction to *Child's English and Scottish Ballads.* Boston: Houghton Mifflin Co., 1882–98.

Kodish, Debora. *Good Friends and Bad Enemies: Robert W. Gordon and the Study of American Folksong.* Urbana: University of Illinois Press, 1986.

Lomax, John A. *Adventures of a Ballad Hunter.* New York: Macmillan, 1947.

———. "Amy Lowell at Baylor." *Southwest Review* 32 (1947): 133–34.

———. "Beginnings of the Texas Folk-Lore Society." In *When the Woods Were Burnt,* edited by Mody Boatright. Austin: University of Texas Press, 1946.

———. "Bond Selling in 1918." *Southwest Review* 28 (1943): 125–36.

———. "Call Me at Red River." *Southwest Review* 30 (1945): 224.

———. *Cowboy Songs.* New York: Sturgis and Walton, 1910.

———. "Cowboy Songs of the Mexican Border." *Sewanee Review* 19, no. 1 (Jan. 1911): 1–18.

———. "Cowboy Songs of the Mexican Border." *Texas Magazine* 3, no. 5 (Mar. 1911): 27–37.

———. "Dean Briggs." *Harvard Alumni Bulletin* 44 (1942): 39–41.

———. "Field Experiences with Recording Machines." *Southern Folklore Quarterly* 1 (1937): 57–60.

———. "Governor Ferguson and the University of Texas." *Southwest Review* 28 (1942): 11–29.

———. "Half-Million Dollar Song: Origin of 'Home on the Range,'" *Southwest Review* 3 (1945): 1–8.

———. "The Legislature and the University." *University Record* 3, no. 4 (Dec. 1901): 360–66.

———. "Of Books and People: John A. Lomax Tells of the Reading That Influenced Him in His Early Life; A Tribute to the Newspapers." *Dallas Times-Herald,* Aug. 19, 1945.

———. "Self-Pity in Negro Folk-Songs." *Nation,* Aug. 9, 1917, pp. 141–45.

———. "'Sinful Songs' of the Southern Negro." *Musical Quarterly* 20 (1934): 177–87.

———. "Some Types of American Folk-Song." *Journal of American Folklore* 28 (1915): 1–17.

———. *Songs of the Cattle Trail and Cow Camp.* New York: Macmillan, 1919.

———. "Songs We Sing and Tales We Tell." *Saturday Review,* July 1, 1944, p. 19.

———. "Stories of an African Prince." *Journal of American Folklore* 26 (1913): 1–12.

———. *Will Hogg, Texan.* Reprinted from *Atlantic Monthly,* 1940. Austin: University of Texas Press, 1956.

———. "William Lawrence Chittenden—Poet Ranchman." *Texas University Magazine* 11, no. 4 (Jan. 1896): 112–16.

Lomax, John A., and H. Y. Benedict. *The Book of Texas.* Garden City, N.Y.: Doubleday, 1916.

Lomax, John A., and Alan Lomax. *American Folk Songs and Ballads.* New York: Macmillan, 1934.

———. *Folk Song U.S.A.* New York: Duell, Sloan and Pearce, 1947.

———. *Negro Folk Songs as Sung by Lead Belly.* New York: Macmillan 1936.

———. *Our Singing Country.* New York: Macmillan, 1941.

Lomax, John A., Jr. Introduction to *Cow Camps and Cattle Herds.* Austin: Encino Press, 1967.

———. "Twenty-Five Thousand Miles In Nancy Ford." Manuscript in Lomax Family Papers, CAH.

[Lomax, John A., Jr., and Alan Lomax.] "The Log." Manuscript journal of Lomax's 1932 lecture and collecting trip, CAH.

Lomax, Joseph. *Genealogical and Historical Sketches of the Lomax Family.* Grand Rapids, Mich.: Rookus Publishing House, 1894.

Lomax, Ruby Terrill. "Adventures with the Ballad Hunter." Draft manuscript, with revisions, of a talk given before the Dallas Philological Society, Dec. 1950, CAH.

Lomax, Susan Frances. "A Trip to Texas." Edited by John A. Lomax. *Southwestern Historical Quarterly* 48, no. 2 (Oct. 1944): 254–61.

Lutz, Tom. *American Nervousness, 1903.* Ithaca: Cornell University Press, 1991.

Mangione, Jerre. *The Dream and the Deal: The Federal Writers' Project, 1935–1943.* Philadelphia: University of Pennsylvania Press, 1983.

McNutt, James Charles. "Beyond Regionalism: Texas Folklorists and the Emergence of a Post-Regional Consciousness." Ph.D. diss., University of Texas, 1982.

———. "John Henry Faulk: An Interview." In *Folklife Annual 1987,* edited by Alan Jabbour and James Hardin. Washington, D.C.: Library of Congress, 1988.

Mewhinney, H. "There Is at Least One Full Man." In *Three Men in Texas,* edited by Ronnie Dugger. Austin: University of Texas Press, 1967. Pp. 19–20.

Nalle, Ouida Ferguson. *The Fergusons of Texas.* San Antonio: Naylor Co., 1946.

Nichols, Edwin Seymour, as told to Ruby Nichols Cutbirth. *Ed Nichols Rode a Horse.* Dallas: University Press, 1943.

Niven, Penelope. *Carl Sandburg: A Biography.* New York: Charles Scribner's Sons, 1991.

Ousley, Clarence. "History of the Agricultural and Mechanical College of Texas." *Bulletin of the Agricultural and Mechanical College of Texas* 6, no. 8 (Dec. 1935).

Owens, William A. *Three Friends: Roy Bedichek, Frank Dobie, Walter Prescott Webb.* Austin: University of Texas Press, 1967.

Percy, William Alexander. *Lanterns on the Levee.* New York: Alfred A. Knopf, 1941.

Pescatello, Ann M. *Charles Seeger: A Life in American Music.* Pittsburgh: University of Pittsburgh Press, 1992.

Pool, William C. *Eugene Barker, Historian.* Austin: Texas Historical Association, 1971.

"Professors at the University 'Objectionable to the Governor." *Alcalde* 5, no. 8 (Aug. 1917): 722–49.

Prude, Kate. "The Contributions of John Avery Lomax to American Folklore." Master's thesis, Hardin-Simmons University, 1950.

Ramsdell, Charles William. *Reconstruction in Texas.* New York: Columbia University Press, 1910. Reprint. Austin: University of Texas Press, 1970.

Reasons for Supporting the Educational Amendment to Sections 49 and 52 of Article 3 of the [Texas] Constitution. Austin: Conference for Education in Texas, n.d.

Reuss, Richard. "Folk Music and Social Conscience: The Musical Odyssey of Charles Seeger." *Western Folklore* 38 (1979): 221–38.

Roberts, David. "A Tough Little Guy Became the Original Southwest Booster." *Smithsonian,* May 1990, pp. 116–26.

Stone, Paul. "J. Frank Dobie and the American Folklore Society." In *Corners of Texas,* edited by Francis E. Abernethy. Denton: University of North Texas Press, 1993. Pp. 47–66.

Taylor, T. U. *Fifty Years on Forty Acres.* Austin: Alec Book Co., 1938.

———. "Lomax-Woodridge Scrap." *Alcalde* 2, no. 5 (Mar. 1914): 437–38.

Thorp, N. Howard. *Songs of the Cowboys.* Estancia, N.M.: News Print Shop, 1908.

Tinkle, Lon. *An American Original: The Life of J. Frank Dobie.* Boston: Little, Brown Co., 1978.

Turner, Frederick. "The Artist Whose Cowboys Were Based Mostly on Himself." *Smithsonian,* Feb. 1988, pp. 168–78.

Webb, Walter Prescott. *The Great Plains.* Boston: Ginn & Co., 1931.

West, John O. "Jack Thorp and John Lomax: Oral or Written Transmission?" *Western Folklore* 26 (1967): 113–18.

White, John I. *Git Along, Little Dogies: Songs and Songmakers of the American West.* Urbana: University of Illinois Press, 1975.

Wilgus, D. K. *Anglo-American Folksong Scholarship since 1898.* New Brunswick, N.J.: Rutgers University Press, 1959.

Wineburgh, H. Harold. *The Texas Banker: The Life and Times of Fred Ferrel Florence.* Dallas: Privately printed, 1981.

Wolfe, Charles, and Kip Lornell. *The Life and Legend of Leadbelly.* New York: HarperCollins, 1992.

Acknowledgments

This book was first suggested by Erika Brady, who was then on the staff of the American Folklife Center at the Library of Congress. I was so taken with her enthusiasm for the Lomax saga that, after having persuaded her to marry me, I went off to look at the great store of Lomax letters and other documents at the Center for American History at the University of Texas. The collection there proved to be so vast and engrossing that it kept me occupied, off and on, for nearly six years. Over that time, Dr. Don Carleton, director of the Center, gave me able assistance and sage advice, while his staff helped answer my many odd and often bizarre questions, located elusive materials, and otherwise made numerous contributions to my work. I am especially indebted to Ralph Elder and John Wheat, whose expertise in all things Texan proved invaluable. Others at the Center who deserve special thanks are Trudy Croes, Bill Richter, and Steve Stein.

From the beginning, Bess Lomax Hawes and Shirley Lomax Duggan gave their support and encouragment to the project, providing rare material and valuable insights regarding their father's life and career. Another member of the family without whom this book could not have been done was John Lomax III, who enthusiastically urged me on and allowed me to quote from copyrighted materials originating with his father and grandfather. Obviously, Alan Lomax is an invaluable source for information about his father, but he regretfully declined to participate because of the press of other matters; I am grateful to him, however, for supplying his photograph and helpful advice.

Joe Hickerson and the late Gerald Parsons guided me patiently through the archives of the American Folklife Center, Library of Congress; others there who rendered valuable assistance were Jennifer Cutting, Catherine Kerst, Judith Gray, and Greg Jenkins. In the Music Division of the Library, Gillian Anderson, Jon Newsom, and Betty Auman were extremely helpful.

Thanks also to the jovial Sam Brylawski, of the Library's Motion Picture, Broadcasting, and Recording Services Division.

I am equally indebted to a number of other archivists, libraries, and organizations: Leslie A. Morris, Curator of Manuscripts, and Melanie Wisner at Harvard's Houghton Library; Mike Raines and Sarah Polirer at the Pusey Library, Harvard; Caroline Rittenhouse, College Archivist at Bryn Mawr; and Wendy Thomas, Public Service Librarian at the Schlesinger Library, Radcliffe. At the Country Music Foundation in Nashville, Bob Pinson and Ronnie Pugh performed their usual yeoman service. Permission from Maurice C. Greenbaum and Frank M. Parker, Trustees of the Sandburg Family Trust, to quote from the letters of Carl Sandburg is gratefully acknowledged.

Francis E. Abernethy, secretary-editor of the Texas Folklore Society, provided important information about that organization and encouraged me by publishing an early version of the first chapter in *Corners of Texas*, the TFS annual for 1993. Suzanne S. Holland of *Harvard Magazine* and Jim Swift of *Waterways* supplied key details at critical points.

If for no other reason, my long labor on John Lomax was justified by the circumstance that it led me to a close acquaintance with the late John Henry Faulk, who had long been a hero of mine. Faulk was a rare and infinite human being, with a gently acid wit and a mind as wondrous as any I've known. He became a source of insight and inspiration for my work in its early stages, and if he had lived, this might have been a far better book.

Special thanks also to others who knew John Lomax and told me about him: Katy De Porte, Frank Goodwyn, Sidney Robertson Cowell, Pete Seeger, and John Langenegger. James McNutt, whose fine dissertation, "Beyond Regionalism," broke much of the research ground for me, was generous with his advice and his knowledge of the subject. Good friends Charles Wolfe and Kip Lornell provided not only moral support but materials relating to Leadbelly that I could not have obtained elsewhere. Becky Schroeder gave me access to her research on Leadbelly's prison records and much encouragement. Several of the missing biographical links relating to Shirley Green were provided by C. D. Pennybacker and Mrs. J. F. Neel, of Palestine, Texas.

My daughter, Kelly Porterfield, who was strategically located in Austin, did a lot of legwork and found answers for all sorts of oddball questions that must have seemed only remotely related to John Lomax (e.g., "How high is Mt. Bonnell?"). My colleagues Linda Burns, Katherine Parrish, Pauline Fox, Henry Sessoms, and Peter Hilty cheerfully dealt with similarly strange queries. From time to time other research assistance and valuable support was supplied by Mary Renaud, along with Amy Surman, Joy Mier, Ginger McCloud, and Lynn David. At the University of Illinois Press, Patricia Hollahan copyedited the manuscript with great skill and precision, thereby saving me from any number of infelicities. I am grateful for the opportunity to thank them all.

Thanks also to Laura Gilliam, Jeff Todd Titon, Gary Hammond, Judith Tick, Betty Black, Sheila Caskey, Martin Jones, and Betty Curry.

Sylvia Grider and Roger D. Abrahams read the manuscript and offered wise counsel. I'm sorry that time and other circumstances did not permit me to make even further, better use of their perceptive and very relevant comments. Portions of my work were supported by grants from the Research Funding Committee of Southeast Missouri State University and a travel grant from the National Endowment for the Humanities.

I'm no less indebted to my wise and furry research assistants, Bubba and Kittredge, who kept me company through the long hours, solemnly approved of all I did, and served nobly as feline paperweights.

And finally, again, Erika.

Index

Items in quotations and not otherwise identified are song titles.

NOLAN PORTERFIELD is the author of five books, including the novel, *A Way of Knowing,* and a biography of "the Father of Country Music," *Jimmie Rodgers: The Life and Times of America's Blue Yodeler,* which won the ASCAP-Deems Taylor Award. His short stories and articles have appeared in numerous anthologies and national magazines. He and his wife, the folklorist Erika Brady, live near Bowling Green, Kentucky.

Books in the Series Folklore and Society

George Magoon and the Down East Game War: History, Folklore, and the Law *Edward D. Ives*

Diversities of Gifts: Field Studies in Southern Religion *Edited by Ruel W. Tyson, Jr., James L. Peacock, and Daniel W. Patterson*

Days from a Dream Almanac *Dennis Tedlock*

Nowhere in America: The Big Rock Candy Mountain and Other Comic Utopias *Hal Rammel*

The Lost World of the Craft Printer *Maggie Holtzberg-Call*

Listening to Old Voices: Folklore in the Lives of Nine Elderly People *Patrick B. Mullen*

Wobblies, Pile Butts, and Other Heroes: Laborlore Explorations *Archie Green*

Transforming Tradition: Folk Music Revivals Examined *Edited by Neil V. Rosenberg*

Morning Dew and Roses: Nuance, Metaphor, and Meaning in Folksongs *Barre Toelken*

The World Observed: Reflections on the Fieldwork Process *Edited by Bruce Jackson and Edward D. Ives*

Steppin' on the Blues: The Visible Rhythms of African American Dance *Jacqui Malone*

Last Cavalier: The Life and Times of John A. Lomax, 1867-1948 *Nolan Porterfield*